Third Edition

THE WRITE STUFF

Thinking Through Essays

IDEAS

ANALYSIS

POINT OF VIEW

SUPPORT

PURPOSE

5M
ASSUMPTIONS
BIASES

CONCLUSIONS

PEARSON

Boston   Columbus   Indianapolis   New York   San Francisco   Upper Saddle River
Amsterdam   Cape Town   Dubai   London   Madrid   Milan   Munich   Paris   Montreal   Toronto
Delhi   Mexico City   Sao Paulo   Sydney   Hong Kong   Seoul   Singapore   Taipei   Tokyo

MARCIE SIMS

Executive Editor: Matt Wright
Editorial Assistant: Laura Marenghi
Head of Marketing: Roxanne McCarley
Senior Development Editor: Gillian Cook
Development Editor: Karen Fein
Senior Supplements Editor: Donna Campion
Executive Digital Producer: Stefanie A. Snajder
Digital Editor: Sara Gordus
Digital Content Specialist: Erin Jenkins
Production Manager: Ellen MacElree

Project Coordination, Text Design, and Electronic Page Makeup: Laserwords
Cover Design Manager: John Callahan
Cover Designer: Kay Petronio
Cover Images: ©89studio/Shutterstock, ©Bukhavets Mikhail/Shutterstock
Senior Manufacturing Buyer: Roy L. Pickering Jr.
Printer/Binder: R. R. Donnelley & Sons at Crawfordsville
Cover Printer: Lehigh-Phoenix Color/Hagerstown

Credits and acknowledgments borrowed from other sources, and reproduced, with permission, in this textbook, appear on page 677.

Library of Congress Cataloging-in-Publication Data

Sims, Marcie.
   The Write Stuff : Thinking Through Essays / Marcie Sims, Green River Community College.
— Third edition.
      pages cm
   Includes index.
   ISBN 0-321-89988-1
  1. English language—Rhetoric—Study and teaching (Higher)   2. Critical thinking—Study
and teaching (Higher)   3. College readers.   4. Academic writing—Study and teaching
(Higher)   I. Title.
   PE1408.S533 2014
   808' .0420711—dc23
                                                                    2013045161

10 9 8 7 6 5 4 3 2 1—DOC—16 15 14 13

www.pearsonhighered.com

Student Edition ISBN-13: 978-0-321-89988-0
Student Edition ISBN-10: 0-321-89988-1
A la Carte Edition ISBN-13: 978-0-321-89991-0
A la Carte Edition ISBN-10: 0-321-89991-1

The author and Pearson-Prentice Hall sincerely thank the following instructors who reviewed the manuscript, helping the author refine and improve upon instructional content. We are most grateful for their comments.

Amarillo College: Ann Hamblin; Bergen Community College: Michael Bodek, Elizabeth Marsh, and Anne Marie Prendergast; Broward Community College: Patrick Ellingham; City College: Aileen Gum; Community College of Philadelphia: Gina Masucci-MacKenzie; Dalton State College: Kelli Keener and Mary Nielsen; Daytona State College: Susan Gronet; DeVry University, Columbus: Nancy Meyer; Eastfield College: Anastasia Lankford; Georgia Perimeter College: Kenneth McNamara and Carissa Morris; Glendale Community College: David Nelson; Grand Rapids Community College: Julie Spahn; Green River Community College: Callae Frazier, Hank Galmish, Erin Gilbert, and Kirsten Higgins; Harford Community College: Jonas Prida; Heald College: Emily Brienza-Larson; Hudson County Community College: Harvery Rubinstein; Illinois Valley Community College: Emily Lesman; Inver Hills Community College: Wanda Synstelien; Ivy Technical Community College: Sharon Bone and Gwen Eldridge; Kingswood College: Leslie Brian (also Houston Community College) and Mandy Kallus; Kishwaukee College: Tina Hultgren; Macon College: Mary Mears; Miami Dade College: Jessica Carroll, Billy Jones, and Maria Villar Smith; Miramar College: Kevin Degnan; Mission College: Audry Lynch; Modesto Junior College: Dimitri Keriotis; Mt. San Antonio College: Peter Francev; Northeast Iowa Community College: Christine Ross; Northeastern Illinois University: Elaine Pierce Chakonas; Northern Virginia Community College: Shonette Grant and Debbie Naquin; Oklahoma City Community College: Carlotta Hill; Olive Harvey College: Barbara Brown and Andrew Cutcher; Pierce College: Kristin Brunnemer; Pittsburgh Technical Institute: Carrie Harrison; Pueblo Community College: Luis Nazario; San Antonio College: Lennie Irvin; Santa Monica College: Gina Ladinsky; Seminole Community College: Chrishawn Speller; Seminole State College: Karen Feldman; Shelton State Community College: Janice Filer; Sinclair Community College: Karen Fleming; Southern State Community College: J. Kevin Bruce; Southwest Tennessee Community College: Tina Bodenheimer; Sussex Community College: Janet Cutshall; Tallahassee Community College: Sue Hightower, Patrick McMahon, and Sharisse Turner; Temple College: Elaine Herrick; Tidewater Community College: Joseph Antinarella; University of Maryland: Jeffrey Simon; University of Texas: Marshalla Hutson (Permian Basin) and Dixie Shaw-Tillmon (San Antonio); Vance-Granville Community College: Linda Barnes and Wendy-Jean Frandsen; Virginia College Online: Dunia Ritchey; West Hills Community College: Neomi Daniels; West Virginia Wesleyan College: Paula McGrew; and Western Wyoming Community College: Jennifer Sorenson and Sharon Taylor.

Brief Contents

PART I   **CRITICAL THINKING SKILLS** 1

Introduction to Part I 1

  1   Critical Thinking in Reading and Writing 2

  2   Critical Thinking and Reading Techniques 22

  3   Paraphrase, Summary, and Analysis 44

PART II   **WRITING EXPOSITORY PARAGRAPHS AND ESSAYS** 58

Introduction to Part II 58

  4   Writing Expository Paragraphs 59

  5   The Building Blocks of Essays 82

  6   The Process of Drafting an Essay 103

PART III   **WRITING AND CRITICAL THINKING IN THE MODES** 142

Introduction to Part III 142

  7   Narration and Description 145

  8   Process 175

  9   Classification 197

  10   Definition 221

  11   Example and Illustration 241

  12   Cause and Effect 263

  13   Comparison and Contrast 287

  14   Argument and Persuasion 308

  15   Timed In-Class Essays and Essay Exams 335

PART IV   **USING SOURCES** 345

Introduction to Part IV 345

16   Using Sources with Integrity 346

17   Writing Essays about Visuals 384

18   Writing Essays about Readings 402

PART V   **SENTENCE CONSTRUCTIONS AND COMMON SENTENCE ERRORS** 463

Introduction to Part V 463

19   Sentence Parts 464

20   Sentence Variety 501

21   Correcting Major Sentence Errors 515

PART VI   **HANDBOOK OF GRAMMAR, MECHANICS, AND STYLE** 534

Introduction to Part VI 534

22   Comma, Semicolon, and Colon 535

23   Other Punctuation 558

24   Correcting Common Shift and Construction Errors 582

25   Spelling and Mechanics 607

26   Tone, Style, and Word Choice 649

27   Vocabulary in Context 665

Detailed Contents

To the Instructor   xii

Preface to the Student   xix

PART 1   CRITICAL THINKING SKILLS   1

Introduction to Part I   1

1   Critical Thinking in Reading and Writing   2

Critical Thinking   3

Defining Critical Thinking   3

Using Critical Thinking   4

Critical Thinking Toolbox   5

Critical Thinking Tools   6

Critical Thinking Checklist   10

Critical Thinking Checklist   10

Critical Thinking in Action   11

Reading: Texting: Blessing or Curse? Matthew Zellmer   11

Reading: Business School Makes PowerPoint a Prerequisite, Justin Pope   13

Glossary of Critical Thinking Terms   15

Dive Deeper into Your Thinking Process   20

Learning Objectives Review   21

2   Critical Thinking and Reading Techniques   22

Critical Thinking and Reading   23

Active Reading   23

Six Steps for Active Reading   23

Example of the Six Steps in Action   28

Reading: "Yo Quiero Made in USA," Nick Miroff   28

Highlight and Annotate as You Read   33

Codes You Can Use   34

The T-Ked Method for Marking Textbooks and Articles   34

Example of Using T-KED, Highlighting, and Codes as You Read   36

Use the Critical Thinking Checklist   37

Critical Thinking Checklist   37

Reading: How to Mark a Book, Mortimer J. Adler   38

Learning Objectives Review   43

3   Paraphrase, Summary, and Analysis   44

How Paraphrase, Summary, and Critical Analysis Differ   45

Paraphrase   46

Six Steps for Paraphrasing Material   47

Sample Paraphrase   48

Checklist for a Good Paraphrase   49

Summary   50

Eight Steps for Writing a Summary   50

Sample Summary   51

Checklist for a Good Summary   52

Combining Summary and Critical Analysis   53

Steps 9 and 10 for Writing Critical Analysis   54

Sample Critical Analysis   54

Learning Objectives Review   56

PART II   WRITING EXPOSITORY PARAGRAPHS AND ESSAYS   58

Introduction to Part II   58

4   Writing Expository Paragraphs   59

Writing Expository Paragraphs   60

The Topic Sentence   61

Support and Analysis   64

Providing Support: The Ice Cream Sandwich Technique   65

The Concluding Sentence   69

Paragraph Structures   70

Model Paragraph   70

Classic Paragraph Structure   71

Topic Sentence at the End of the Paragraph   72

Topic Sentence in the Middle of the Paragraph   73

Self- and Peer Assessment   75

Paragraph Checklist: Self-Assessment Version   75

Paragraph Checklist: Peer-Assessment Version   76

Paragraph to Essay: Pattern Similarities   78

Learning Objectives Review   80

5   The Building Blocks of Essays   82

Expository Essays   83

The Building Blocks of an Expository Essay   83

Essay Title   84

Introductory Paragraph(s)   84

Thesis Statement   86

Body Paragraphs   88

Concluding Paragraph   96

Putting It All Together   97

Basic Essay Structure: A Quick Review   97

Student Essay   98

Checklist for the Building Blocks   101

Learning Objectives Review   102

6   The Process of Drafting an Essay   103

Essay Writing in Five Stages   104

Stage One: Prewrite to Generate Ideas   104

Thinking and Talking   105

Freewriting   105

Mapping   106

Brainstorming   106

Clustering   107

Journaling   107

Outlining   107

Narrowing a Subject to a Topic   108

Establish Subject, Purpose, and Audience   111

Stage Two: Organize Your Ideas   116

Create a Thesis Statement   116

Outlines: Perfecting Your Essay's Order of Development   117

Outline Critique Checklist   119

Stage Three: Write a First Draft   120

Stage Four: Revise and Edit Your Draft   121

Revision   121

Revision Checklist   122

Stage Five: Proofread   124

Check Spelling   124

Check Word Usage, Word Choices, Tone, and Style   125

Check for Sentence-Level Errors   125

Self- and Peer Assessment of Writing   126

Revision Checklist   126

A Sample Essay: Modeling the Process   126

Learning Objectives Review   140

PART III   WRITING AND CRITICAL THINKING IN THE MODES   142

Introduction to Part III   142

Choosing the Right Approach   143

To Mode or Not to Mode?   144

Thinking Critically about Modes and Media   144

7 Narration and Description 145

Narrative and Descriptive Essays 146

Critical Thinking and Narration and Description 146

Before Writing a Narrative and Descriptive Essay 147

Writing a Narrative and Descriptive Essay 149

Organizational Pattern for a Narrative and Descriptive Essay 150

Basic Structure for a Narrative and Descriptive Essay 150

Structuring a Narrative and Descriptive Essay 151

Narrative and Descriptive Essay Critique Form 162

Complementary Modes for Narrative Essays 163

Student Essay 164

Professional Narrative Essay: Half a Day, *Naguib Mahfouz* 166

Critical Thinking Checklist 170

Learning Objectives Review 173

8 Process 175

Process Essays 176

Critical Thinking and Process Mode 176

Before Writing a Process Essay 176

Writing a Process Essay 178

Organizational Pattern for a Process Essay 178

Basic Structure for a Process Essay 179

Structuring a Process Essay 180

Process Essay Critique Form 185

Complementary Modes for Process Essays 186

Student Essay 187

Professional Process Essay: Making the Pitch in Print Advertising, *Courtland L. Bovée, John V. Thill, George P. Dovel, and Marian Burk Wood* 189

Critical Thinking Checklist 194

Learning Objectives Review 196

9 Classification 197

Classification Essays 198

Critical Thinking and Classification 198

Before Writing a Classification Essay 200

Writing a Classification Essay 201

Organizational Pattern for Classification Essays 201

Basic Structure for a Classification Essay 203

Structuring a Classification Essay 203

Classification Essay Critique Form 209

Complementary Modes for Classification Essays 210

Student Essay 210

Professional Classification Essay: Race in America, *George Henderson* 213

Critical Thinking Checklist 218

Learning Objectives Review 220

10 Definition 221

Definition Essays 222

Critical Thinking and Definition 222

Before Writing a Definition Essay 223

Writing a Definition Essay 224

Organizational Pattern for a Definition Essay 226

Basic Structure for a Definition Essay 226

Structuring a Definition Essay 227

Definition Essay Critique Form 232

Complementary Modes for Definition Essays 233

Student Essay 233

Professional Definition Essay: Cyberbullying: A Growing Problem, *Science Daily* 236

Critical Thinking Checklist 238

Learning Objectives Review 240

11 Example and Illustration **241**

Example and Illustration Essays 242

Critical Thinking and Example and Illustration 242

Before Writing an Example and Illustration Essay 243

Writing an Example and Illustration Essay 244

Organizational Pattern for an Example Essay 244

Basic Structure for an Example and Illustration Essay 245

Structuring an Example and Illustration Essay 245

Example and Illustration Essay Critique Form 250

Complementary Modes for Example and Illustration Essays 251

Student Essay 251

Professional Example and Illustration Essay: Learning to Read and Write, *Frederick Douglass* 254

Critical Thinking Checklist 259

Learning Objectives Review 261

12 Cause and Effect **263**

Cause-and-Effect Essays 264

Critical Thinking and Cause and Effect 264

Before Writing a Cause-and-Effect Essay 265

Writing a Cause-and-Effect Essay 267

Organization Pattern for Cause-and-Effect Essays 268

Basic Structure for a Cause-and-Effect Essay 269

Structuring a Cause-and-Effect Essay 269

Cause-and-Effect Essay Critique Form 274

Complementary Modes for Cause-and-Effect Essays 275

Student Essay 276

Professional Cause-and-Effect Essay: The Columbine Syndrome: Boys and the Fear of Violence, *William S. Pollack* 278

Critical Thinking Checklist 283

Learning Objectives Review 285

13 Comparison and Contrast **287**

Comparison and Contrast Essays 288

Critical Thinking and Comparison and Contrast 288

Before Writing a Comparison/Contrast Essay 289

Writing a Comparison/Contrast Essay 290

Organizational Pattern for a Comparison/Contrast Essay 290

Basic Structure for a Comparison/Contrast Essay 293

Structuring a Comparison/Contrast Essay 293

Comparison/Contrast Essay Critique Form 298

Complementary Modes for Comparison/Contrast Essays 299

Student Essay 299

Professional Comparison and Contrast Essay: American Space, Chinese Place, *Yi-Fu Tuan* 302

Critical Thinking Checklist 304

Learning Objectives Review 306

14 Argument and Persuasion **308**

Argument and Persuasion Essays 309

Critical Thinking and Argument 309

Logical Fallacies 310

Before Writing an Argument Essay 312

Writing an Argument Essay 313

Organizational Pattern for an Argument Essay 314

Basic Structure for an Argument Essay 315

Structuring an Argument Essay 315

Argument Essay Critique Form 321

Complementary Modes for Argument Essays 322

Student Essay 323

Professional Argument Essay: Can You Be Educated from a Distance? *James Barszcz* 327

Critical Thinking Checklist 330

Learning Objectives Review 333

15 Timed In-Class Essays and Essay Exams **335**

Strategies for Taking Essay Exams or Writing Timed Essays 336

Critical Thinking and Timed Essays 336

Before the Essay Exam or Timed Essay 336

Study and Prepare in Advance 336

During the Essay Exam or Timed Essay 337

Common Terms Used in Writing Prompts 338

Practice Timed In-Class Essays and Essay Exams 340

Learning Objectives Review 343

PART IV USING SOURCES 345

Introduction to Part IV 345

16 Using Sources with Integrity **346**

Writing a Documented Paper 347

Ten Steps for Writing a Documented Paper 347

Types of Sources 349

Finding, Evaluating, and Integrating Sources 350

Finding Sources 350

Evaluating Potential Sources 353

Integrating Sources into Your Paper 355

Plagiarism 358

How to Avoid Plagiarism 358

Using Modern Language Association (MLA) Format 360

Formatting Your Paper 360

In-Text Citations 361

Compiling a Works Cited List 365

MLA-Style Student Paper 371

Using American Psychological Association (APA) Format 375

In-Text Citations 375

References List 376

Learning Objectives Review 382

17 Writing Essays about Visuals **384**

Visual Communication and Critical Thinking 385

Similarities Between Analyzing Text and Visuals 386

Read Visuals Actively 387

Visual Detective Checklist 387

Analyzing Various Types of Visuals 389

Political Cartoons 389

Photographs 391

Advertisements 393

Campaign Ads 394

Video and Film 395

Learning Objectives Review 400

18 Writing Essays about Readings **402**

Writing about Readings 403

Interpret and Infer Meaning 403

Structure of an Analysis Essay 404

Introductory Paragraph 404

Body Paragraphs 404

Concluding Paragraph 406

Student Essay 406

Analytical Essay Critique Form 409

Reading Selections for Analysis 410

Gotta Dance, *Jackson Jodie Daviss* 410

What Adolescents Miss When We Let Them Grow Up in Cyberspace, *Brent Staples* 416

One Man's Kids, *Daniel R. Meier* 421

The Discus Thrower, *Richard Selzer* 425

The Mystery of Mickey Mouse, *John Updike* 430

Thread, *Stuart Dybek* 438

Mute in an English Only World, *Chang Rae Lee*   444

On Being a Cripple, *Nancy Mairs*   449

Learning Objectives Review   462

 PART V   SENTENCE CONSTRUCTIONS AND COMMON SENTENCE ERRORS   463

Introduction to Part V   463

19 Sentence Parts   464

The Building Blocks of Sentences   465

Subjects and Predicates (Verbs)   465

Subjects: Who or What It's All About   466

Predicates (Also Known as Verbs): Action Words   470

Inside the Predicate: Objects   481

Phrases   482

Noun Phrases   482

Prepositions and Prepositional Phrases   483

Participles and Participial Phrases   487

Adjectives and Adjective Phrases   488

Adverbs and Adverb Phrases   490

Articles and Other Noun Determiners   491

Conjunctions   493

Coordinating Conjunctions   494

Subordinating Conjunctions   495

Conjunctive Adverbs   496

Learning Objectives Review   500

20 Sentence Variety   501

Coordination and Subordination   502

Coordination   502

Subordination   502

Sentence Types and Purposes   505

Sentence Structures   506

Sentence Variety   509

Before and After Revising for Sentence Variety   510

Learning Objectives Review   514

21 Correcting Major Sentence Errors   515

Fragments   516

Identifying Sentence Fragments   517

Correcting Sentence Fragments   519

Run-Ons and Comma Splices   525

Run-On Sentences   525

Comma Splices   525

Learning Objectives Review   533

PART VI   HANDBOOK OF GRAMMAR, MECHANICS, AND STYLE   534

Introduction to Part VI   534

22 Comma, Semicolon, and Colon   535

Comma   536

Five Comma Rules   536

Semicolon   547

Colon   551

Learning Objectives Review   557

23 Other Punctuation   558

End Punctuation   559

Period   559

Question Mark   560

Exclamation Point   561

Apostrophe   562

Apostrophe and Contractions   562

Apostrophe and Possession   564

Apostrophe and Plurals   566

Apostrophe and Missing Letters or Numbers   567

Quotation Marks   568

Punctuation and Quotation Marks   571

Parentheses   573

Hyphen   574

Dash   576

Slash   577

Ellipsis   578

Brackets   579

Learning Objectives Review   581

24 Correcting Common Shift and Construction Errors   **582**

Construction and Shift Errors   583

Subject-Verb Agreement   583

Subject-Verb Agreement Errors   584

Pronoun-Antecedent Agreement   587

Pronoun-Antecedent Agreement Errors   587

Pronoun Reference   589

Pronoun Reference Errors   589

Point-of-View Shifts   592

Indefinite Pronouns   593

Faulty Parallelism   595

Dangling and Misplaced Modifiers   597

Dangling Modifiers   597

Misplaced Modifiers   598

Passive Voice Construction   600

Learning Objectives Review   605

25 Spelling and Mechanics   **607**

Ten Tips to Improve Your Spelling   608

Spelling Tip 1: Use a Dictionary   608

Spelling Tip 2: Check for Correct Pronunciation   608

Spelling Tip 3: Do Not Confuse Homophones   608

Spelling Tip 4: Use Rules for Making Words Plural   609

Spelling Tip 5: Distinguish Between *ei* and *ie*   609

Spelling Tip 6: Learn the Rules for Adding Suffixes and Prefixes   610

Spelling Tip 7: Keep a List of Your Errors   611

Spelling Tip 8: Be Familiar with Commonly Misspelled Words   611

Spelling Tip 9: Be Aware of Common Letter Groupings   611

Spelling Tip 10: Use Spell-Check   611

The Rewards and Dangers of Spell-Check   612

The Rewards   612

The Dangers   612

Commonly Confused Words   614

Tips for Using a Dictionary   630

Anatomy of a Dictionary Entry   630

Tips for Using a Thesaurus   632

Anatomy of a Thesaurus Entry   632

Spelling Checklist   635

Capitalization   635

Capitalization Basics   636

Numbers   640

Abbreviations   642

Learning Objectives Review   647

26 Tone, Style, and Word Choice   **649**

Thinking Critically about Tone and Style   650

Emailing, Texting, and Audience   650

Formal Style and Tone versus Academese   651

Word Choice   653

Slang   654

Jargon   655

Dialect   655

Foreign Words   655

Clichés   656

Avoiding Sexist Language   659

Use Gender-Specific Terms Only When Appropriate   659

Don't Assume an Occupation Is Exclusively Male or Female   660

Use Parallel Terms for Men and Women   661

Learning Objectives Review   664

27 Vocabulary in Context   **665**

Vocabulary Building   666

Five Tips for Building Your Vocabulary   666

Pronunciation   669

Critical Thinking and Context Clues   671

Using Context Clues   672

Learning Objectives Review   676

Credits   677

Index   678

To the Instructor

The Write Stuff: Thinking Through Essays, Third Edition, is an all-in-one writing text designed for upper developmental and beginning-level college composition courses. *The Write Stuff* provides all the information students need to build their analytical reading and writing skills, as well as the information and practice they need for doing so using correct grammar and an appropriate style. Most beginning composition texts do not provide the basic instruction and exercises needed while at the same time developing more difficult-to-grasp skills: interpretation and analysis. This text not only provides students with the basic tools for writing well-organized and developed essays that are grammatically and mechanically correct, but it also teaches students the critical thinking skills they need to interpret and analyze information and express their ideas clearly and logically in writing. Critical thinking provides the theme that integrates the instruction throughout the text.

Students in developmental and entry-level composition courses need detailed instruction on how to write paragraphs and essays; how to spot and correct their spelling, usage, and sentence-level errors; and how to include quotes correctly from other writers. They also need instruction on how to interpret what they read, how to go deeper into the topics they've chosen to write about, how to choose the best approach for communicating their ideas to their target audience, and how to pull all of these aspects together into a meaningful purpose for writing. *The Write Stuff* encourages students to think critically during all stages of reading and writing and helps them to move beyond defending the obvious in their understanding of others' ideas as well as their own.

The tone and level of *The Write Stuff* speaks to students who are on the cusp of college-level reading and writing. The user-friendly tips and exercises help students develop the tools they need to succeed in reading and writing, and the critical thinking focus throughout the book helps them move past rote learning and summary into true interpretation and analysis of what they are reading or what they are writing about.

CRITICAL THINKING IN *THE WRITE STUFF*

Critical thinking, the unifying theme of *The Write Stuff*, is defined in Chapter 1, which also includes clear explanations of the meaning and function of specific critical thinking terms and tools that are used throughout the book. These terms include *purpose, ideas, support, assumptions and biases, conclusions, point of view,* and *analysis.*

Critical thinking terms may be unfamiliar to many students and seem abstract and hard to grasp. In order to make explicit the connection between these terms and their application to writing essays that clearly articulate and support ideas and arguments, the concept of a critical thinking toolbox is used. Each of the terms listed above is linked to a specific tool icon. The idea is to provide students with visual cues that identify critical thinking tools they can use whenever they embark on a writing or reading assignment. For example, blueprints are used to represent purpose, and beams to represent the main ideas expressed in topic sentences to support a thesis. Nails are used to represent the support (examples, details, facts) a writer uses to underpin ideas, while a magnifying glass represents the importance of looking closely at and analyzing the elements of an argument, an essay, or even an individual sentence.

These icons are used consistently throughout the text to make explicit to students the connection between the critical thinking tools they have learned about in Part I of this book and their application to real-world writing. The icons work not only on a visual identification level, alerting students that a specific tool is being used, but on a subliminal level, so that students begin automatically to connect the icons with important critical thinking concepts. As they progress through the text, students will become increasingly familiar with these critical thinking concepts and tools and develop confidence in using them in their writing assignments.

NEW TO THIS EDITION

- **Deeper MyWritingLab integration** is new to this edition. Many activities and writing prompts from the print text along with new chapter assessments designed specifically for *The Write Stuff* can be completed right in MyWritingLab. When students see the MyWritingLab logo in the print text, they have the option of completing the activity or writing prompt online at MyWritingLab. Chapter assessments will flow to your instructor Gradebook in MyWritingLab, reducing grading time and allowing you to focus attention on those students who may need extra help and practice.

    - All Thinking Critically chapter opening activities, Essay Assignments, and end-of-chapter Grammar review exercises can be completed right in the MyWritingLab book-specific module. There are also chapter assessment quizzes for each and every chapter in *The Write Stuff*, Third Edition.

- A **redesigned part structure** with 27 chapters instead of the second edition's 32 makes the entire book more flexible and easier to use overall.

- New **part introductions** help students truly see why various aspects of writing are important and allows them to examine their own grasp of the content.

- **Half of the essay topics are new**, including media, technology, and social issues.
- A new section on **multimodal writing** places a unique emphasis on real world writing.
- **One third of the professional reading selections are new**, including essays by John Updike, Chang Rae Lee, and Stuart Dybek as well as Mortimer Adler's classic "How to Mark a Book."
- Remodeled chapters on **thinking critically and writing about visuals and stories** allow for better consumption of the material and makes the material more accessible overall.
- A new section on thinking critically about how to use **multimedia in writing** is included in Part 3 and introduces students to this critical piece of college-level writing.
- Includes a **streamlined chapter on evaluating and citing sources**, with continued coverage of MLA style and the addition of APA style.
- Students learn better when they have a clear understanding of what they are expected to master. Therefore, **Learning Objectives** at the beginning of each chapter give students an overview of what they will accomplish by working through each page in the chapter. To provide further guidance, each objective is keyed to the appropriate section of that chapter.

CONTENT

The Write Stuff focuses on upper developmental writing, reading, and analysis skills, and it works well for both developmental and entry-level composition classes. It includes the following features:

- **Critical thinking skills defined and applied** with critical thinking pointers, prompts, and exercises throughout the text
- **Critical reading and analysis techniques** for reading college-level assignments, including visual aids
- **Applying Critical Thinking boxes** that either briefly define the critical thinking tools relevant to specific sections of these chapters and explain in concrete terms how students can apply them, or demonstrate practical applications of these tools
- **Critical thinking icons** that keep the terminology and tools discussed in Part I fresh in students' minds, integrating them into the ongoing instruction, and showing them to have practical use in all aspects of essay writing
- Clearly defined and attainable chapter learning objectives

- A review of the basics for writing paragraphs
- Thorough coverage of the basics for writing essays
- An overview on combining modes and separate chapters on each of the modes, including argument
- Professional reading selections, with writing prompts, for analysis
- Annotated student essays that provide achievable models for student writers
- A chapter that shows students how to find, evaluate, summarize, analyze, and cite sources, and how to use MLA and APA documentation style
- A section on sentence construction and common sentence construction errors with ample practice exercises
- A handbook that provides information and helpful tips on correct use of grammar, spelling, vocabulary, and style, plus plentiful sentence- and paragraph-length exercises
- A chapter on writing about visuals
- Detailed strategies for writing about readings

ORGANIZATION

Part I introduces students to the concept of critical thinking, defines important terms, and outlines critical thinking skills and how they apply to reading and writing.

In Part II, students are given a review of how to write expository paragraphs and essays. They learn about paragraph and essay structure and how to generate ideas, clarify their purpose for writing, assess their audience, and customize their approach to a topic. They are introduced to the essay writing process, shown how to organize and provide details and support for their essay's purpose, and learn about the importance of order, unity, and coherence.

In Part III, students learn about various modes, or essay types, including narration and description, process, classification, definition, example and illustration, cause and effect, comparison and contrast, and argument and persuasion, as well as how to combine them. Each chapter contains critical thinking pointers, specific instruction on how to write in a particular mode, an annotated student essay that provides a realistic and level-appropriate model, an annotated professional sample of the mode with exercises, and tips for possible mode combinations depending on an essay's purpose and assignment. This part ends with a chapter that provides tips on how to write timed essays and take essay exams.

In Part IV of *The Write Stuff*, students learn how to write from sources including readings, articles, literature, and visuals, as well as how to summarize, paraphrase, and analyze other writers' work. They learn how to find sources to support their own ideas (research), how to evaluate these sources, and how to cite them correctly in their own writing (MLA and APA citation format). Students learn how to write about visual forms of communication, including photos, film, TV, cartoons, and advertisements. Moreover, they get detailed advice for writing about readings and a selection of readings for analysis with comprehension and critical thinking questions and writing prompts. All of the reading selections have exercises and writing prompts that emphasize critical thinking and encourage deeper understanding and analysis by students.

Part V provides a review of sentence parts and common sentence construction errors and contains tips and exercises for avoiding sentence fragments, run-ons, and comma splices.

Part VI, a grammar handbook, covers the following topics and provides a wealth of sentence- and paragraph-level exercises for each:

- Punctuation
- Common shift and construction errors (with tips for spotting and fixing them)
- Spelling, usage, and mechanics
- Tone, style, and diction
- ELL tips
- Tips for building vocabulary and using context clues to figure out unfamiliar words

Hopefully, you and your students will find that this text provides *the right stuff* to help them develop critical thinking abilities and learn how to apply them in every aspect of writing and reading.

ACKNOWLEDGMENTS

I am grateful to all of my students, colleagues, friends, and family who have supported me in the process of writing *The Write Stuff: Thinking Through Essays*.

First, I would like to thank my editors, Matthew Wright, Karen Fein, and Gillian Cook, for their support, vision, and encouragement throughout the development of this text. Kudos to Karen Berry and all the staff at Laserwords for their careful attention to and formatting of *The Write Stuff*.

Thanks also to all the editorial assistants, design staff, marketing support, and representatives at Pearson.

I am also grateful to all my colleagues who helped review chapters or preliminary editions (their names are on the copyright page) and those who adopted *The Write Stuff*. Thanks also to my colleagues at Green River Community College for their support and encouragement as I wrote this text.

Another thanks to the artists and photographers who let me feature their beautiful visuals in this text: I am especially indebted to Tom Shugrue, Hannah Shugrue, Wayne Buck, Tommy Corey, Annie Musselman, Cindy Small, Julie Moore, Hank and Richard Galmish, and the other artists featured in the book.

Furthermore, I am extremely grateful to my students, past and present, who have inspired me in the classroom and who inspired me to begin writing textbooks in the first place. Thank you also to those students who have given me permission to use their work and to those who provided their feedback on this text and its exercises. *The Write Stuff* would not be if not for you.

Finally, I want to thank my family for their patience and support as I worked on this text. Special thanks to my sons, Marcus and Thomas. Thanks also to my mother, Delores Sims, and to my brothers and sister and their families: Nick, Charlie, Dolly, Diana, Jerith, Mathew, Krysta, and Ashley Sims. Thanks also to Tom and Hannah Shugrue; Douglas Cole; Sharon Thornton and Fumitaka Matsuoka; Doug and Nancy Cole; Halvor and Ilona Cole; Traci Cole and David and Rachel Haygood; Katharine deBaun; Sandy Johanson; Jaeney Hoene; Jennifer Whetham; Suzanne Paola and Bruce and Jin Beasley; Hank Galmish; Julie Moore; Brad Johnson; Jim and Linda Wood; Neal Vasishth; Richard, Cara, and Josh Berman; Jeb, Darci, Levi, and Jaspar Wyman; and all of my extended family across the country. I dedicate this edition to my brother, Dominic (Nick) Sims.

SUPPLEMENTS AND ADDITIONAL RESOURCES

Book-Specific Ancillary Material

Annotated Instructor's Edition for The Write Stuff: Thinking Through Essays, 3/e
ISBN 0321899938

The Annotated Instructor's Edition for *The Write Stuff* includes all the answers to the exercises and activities.

Instructor's Resource Manual for The Write Stuff: Thinking Through Essays, 3/e
ISBN 0321899946

The Instructor's Manual offers additional material to help instructors meet their course objectives. The manual also contains a unique section on teaching critical thinking in the writing classroom and offers teaching tips and activities to foster critical thinking.

Additional Instructor Resources

The Pearson Writing Package

Pearson is pleased to offer a variety of support materials to help make teaching writing easier for teachers and to help students excel in their coursework. Many of our student supplements are available free or at a greatly reduced price when packaged with *The Write Stuff,* Third Edition. Visit www .pearsonhighereducation.com, contact your local Pearson sales representative, or review a detailed listing of the full supplements package in the *Instructor's Resource Manual.*

MYWRITINGLAB

MyWritingLab™   What makes MyWritingLab so effective?

- Diagnostic Testing: MyWritingLab's diagnostic test comprehensively assesses students' skills in grammar. Students can be given an individualized learning path based on the diagnostic's results, identifying the areas where they most need help.

- Progressive Learning: The heart of MyWritingLab is the progressive learning that takes place as students complete the Recall, Apply, and Write exercises within each topic. Students move from literal comprehension (Recall) to critical understanding (Apply) to the ability to demonstrate a skill in their own writing (Write).

     This progression of critical thinking, not available in any other online resource, enables students to truly master the skills and concepts they need to become successful writers.

- Online Gradebook: MyWritingLab captures student work results in the Online Gradebook. Students can monitor their progress and see updated scoring results on the exercises in the course. Instructors can run various reports to monitor student progress and overall success, see which topics their students have mastered, access other detailed reports, such as class summaries that track the development and progress of their entire class, and display useful details on individual student progress.

- eText: *The Write Stuff* e-text is accessed through MyWritingLab. Students now have the e-text at their fingertips while completing the various exercises and activities within MyWritingLab.

Preface to the Student

USE THIS TEXT AS A RESOURCE

The Write Stuff is a tool, so remember to use it in a way that best serves your purpose. You don't need to read the chapters in sequence, though it does help to read Part I first. Read them in the order assigned by your instructor, and use the index to look up what you need help with and to answer questions that arise as you study.

Critical thinking practice is woven throughout *The Write Stuff*. You will learn about the basic components of critical thinking in Chapter 1. In Chapters 2 and 3, you'll learn how to apply critical thinking skills to reading. Then, in the chapters on writing essays, the chapters on reading and analysis skills, and in the readings chapter, you will find critical thinking questions and writing prompts to hone your analysis skills.

The critical writing and reading skills you learn here will help you do better in courses you will take throughout your college career (not just in English or writing classes).

ORGANIZATION

The Write Stuff provides the basic skills you'll need for successful college writing, reading, and critical thinking—skills you will continue to use after college, in your career, and beyond. Throughout the text, you will find helpful Learning Objectives and Learning Objective Reviews, Applying Critical Thinking boxes, tips, and icons to help you apply critical thinking skills in your reading and writing.

Part I of *The Write Stuff* provides an overview of critical thinking skills, including a definition of critical thinking and of the specific tools and terms you can use to apply critical thinking to reading and to your own writing. It also provides step-by-step instruction in how to think critically and read analytically.

Part II reviews paragraph writing, introduces the writing process, and guides you step by step through the process of writing expository essays.

Part III introduces different modes or types of essays and discusses how to choose which mode for what purpose and when to use a combination of two or more modes. It provides the tools you need to write a clear argument and to read and evaluate the arguments of others.

In Part IV, you will learn how to evaluate and use outside sources in your writing and be introduced to both MLA (Modern Language Association) and APA (American Psychological Association) formats for documenting sources correctly and avoiding plagiarism. Part IV also describes how to critically analyze visuals, and provides a selection of professional and student sample readings for analysis, critical thinking, and writing tasks. Part V focuses on sentence construction and common sentence errors, and Part VI features a grammar, mechanics, and style handbook that explains the most common grammar and usage, tone, and style errors with exercises for practice. This part of the text also has a chapter on how to build your vocabulary and how to figure out words you don't know from their context in a reading. This all-in-one textbook provides what you'll need to succeed in your college writing and reading tasks.

PART I CRITICAL THINKING SKILLS

CONTENTS

1 Critical Thinking in Reading and Writing

2 Critical Thinking and Reading Techniques

3 Paraphrase, Summary, and Analysis

INTRODUCTION TO PART I

The construction of the brick arch, stone walls, and roof beams in this photograph required a plan, tools, and a process. Similarly, the first section of this textbook provides advice and tools for thinking, reading, and writing critically. Both reading and writing require active engagement on your part. The tools introduced in this part turn your reading and writing into that active process: one in which you think about each step and take action based on informed decisions. These three chapters are the foundation for the rest of the book and will help you become a better thinker, reader, and writer. Throughout this book, you are asked to apply terms and techniques from these three introductory chapters.

Ultimately, the skills you learn in Part I will prepare you to write critical analysis paragraphs and essays about readings, which is what most college-level writing is. You need these skills to do well in every stage of your writing process and for reading others' writing. You need to have a set of tools to help you think about your own ideas as well as the ideas of others. Part IV circles back to this skill in more detail, with Chapter 18, "Writing About Readings." On that note, be sure that when you are writing about others' work that you use the skills from Part I to be a good critical reader and to write accurately and analytically about what you have read, and then be sure to cite any sources you have used, taking Chapter 16, "Using Sources with Integrity," as your guide.

LEARNING OBJECTIVES

In this chapter, you will learn about

1 Critical thinking and why it is important.

2 Critical thinking tools you can use to write well.

Thinking Critically MyWritingLab™

Photo Shoot
Hannah Shugrue

Think: Think about the photo above with the following questions in mind.

1. Whose point of view is this picture taken from? How do you know?

2. How is a layer effect created in this picture, and what intrigues you when you look at this image?

Write: Using specific examples and details, write a short description of what you see in this photo.

_____

_____

_____

_____

_____

_____

_____

_____

CRITICAL THINKING

❶ Critical thinking and why it is important.

Critical thinking is a term you will hear quite a bit in college because it refers to the kind of thinking you'll be asked to do in your courses and later in your career. You'll be happy to know that you are already a critical thinker! You engage your critical thinking skills every day. Whenever you make a decision, solve a problem, or prioritize tasks, you are using critical thinking. For instance, when you choose your classes each term, you have to think carefully about your schedule: What classes are open this term? Which classes count toward your degree or certificate? How many classes can you take in one term and still be successful? Which classes are most important for you to take first? Making these decisions, weighing the choices, and prioritizing all involve critical thinking. Even on a day-to-day basis, you engage your critical thinking skills. When you shop for groceries, when you decide which bills you should pay first on a limited budget, when you work out problems and arguments between you and your friends or you and your coworkers, you are thinking critically.

This chapter defines critical thinking in terms of performing college tasks. The skills involved in thinking critically are essential to effective reading and writing; good thinking and good writing go hand in hand. This chapter provides you with tools and tips designed to help you read and write analytically (to read looking for answers to questions and to draw some conclusions about your topic) and to evaluate your own reading and writing processes.

Defining Critical Thinking

Critical thinking is not a new concept. The evaluation of one's own thinking has been around since human history began. Critical thinking was an essential part of ancient cultures, including the Egyptian (3150 BCE), Sumerian (2900 BCE), and Babylonian (2300 BCE) cultures, and later was an integral skill and focus for the ancient Greek philosophers. Socrates (469–399 BCE) is known for teaching his students how to analyze their critical thinking processes. In fact, the word *critical* comes from the Greek word *kritikos*, meaning "to question" or "to analyze."

Various experts define critical thinking differently, but it always involves actively thinking through and evaluating all the steps in your own thinking or the thinking of others. Many teachers and experts emphasize the importance of critical thinking in college courses. Richard Paul is one of today's most well-known scholars of critical thinking skills. According to Paul, critical thinking is a "mode of thinking—about any subject, content, or problem—in which the thinker improves the quality of his or her thinking by skillfully taking charge" of each step in the process of thinking and the conclusions reached as a result of that thinking (Foundation for Critical Thinking, www.criticalthinking.org).

Using Critical Thinking

The key point is that you must be aware of your own thoughts and how they affect your conclusions. There are different skills and tools you can use to understand and evaluate the writings of others and to discover the strengths and weaknesses in their reasoning or arguments. As you learn these critical thinking skills, your own thinking and writing abilities will improve. Always use a step-by-step process to think about each part of an argument or idea. Once you get hooked on the power that comes from using your critical thinking skills, you may not be able to stop—you will find yourself using them all the time: while reading the newspaper, listening to the radio, reading a novel, or even watching a movie. Thinking critically may seem awkward at first, but, once you have some practice, it will come as naturally as feeling or breathing.

Think, Feel, Breathe
Cindy Small

Think of each step in the critical thinking process as a domino in a long line of dominoes set up to fall in a certain pattern and to end in a specific place. Knock over one domino, and it will knock over the next.

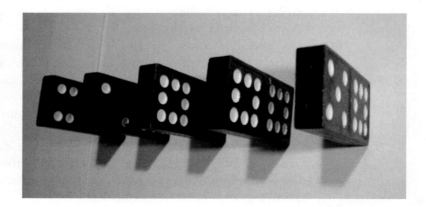

CRITICAL THINKING TOOLBOX

Icons	Critical Thinking Terms	Definitions	Writing Terms
PURPOSE (Blueprints/plans)	Purpose	What you want to say about your topic: the point(s) you are making. The purpose is the plan or blueprint for what you want to say in your essay.	Thesis statement
IDEAS (Support/beams)	Ideas	The foundation for your argument: Ideas develop your purpose. They form the structure of your overall sentences (beams), develop your thesis (plans), and hold up your conclusion.	Topic sentences
SUPPORT (Nails)	Support	Examples, details, and evidence illustrate the ideas you use to support your purpose. They provide support (nails) for the ideas (beams) that support your purpose.	Major and minor details
ASSUMPTIONS BIASES (Tape measure)	Assumptions and Biases	Assumptions (information you take for granted) and biases (personal beliefs you have about particular topics) can be helpful tools, or they can discredit your ideas if they are not valid. Always evaluate them and measure their accuracy when making an argument.	
CONCLUSIONS (Finished house)	Conclusions	The results of your argument or purpose. The result of carefully building your argument (using plans, beams, and nails) is a well-thought-out conclusion (house).	Conclusion
POINT OF VIEW (Camera)	Point of View	How you see the subject you are discussing.	
ANALYSIS (Magnifying glass)	Analysis	Breaking down an idea, closely examining the meaning of each individual part (as if under a magnifying glass), and evaluating how the parts relate to the whole. Look at the overall meaning and the connections between the parts.	

But if one domino is out of place, it will keep all the others that follow it from falling correctly. In the same way, one error in your reasoning can throw off your whole chain of thinking and interrupt the flow and logic of your ideas. So line up each step in your critical thinking process carefully: Weigh each piece of evidence you provide, evaluate your reasons and conclusions, and make sure every point you make is valid. Otherwise, your chain of thought and evidence will be thrown off, and your end result will be derailed. You want your dominoes to fall into place properly, one idea sparking the next: a perfect process.

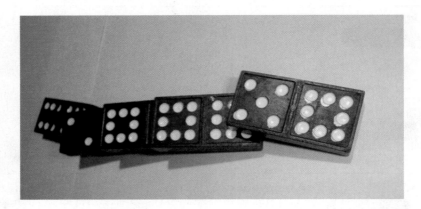

CRITICAL THINKING TOOLS

❷ Critical thinking tools you can use to write well.

The critical thinking tools—terms and elements of argument—on page 5 are used throughout this textbook to help you evaluate your thinking, reading, and writing processes; to explore your ideas, arguments, and conclusions; and to analyze the arguments and writing decisions of other writers. The icons (pictures) that accompany these key critical thinking tools will alert you to when they are being used in the text and remind you when to use them yourself as you read selections and practice your writing skills.

These critical thinking terms are essential to the critical thinking process, and they are also the tools of argument. *Most college writing contains some level of argument:* You always have a purpose, your argument or set of arguments, to present to your readers.

Read the following more detailed explanations of each of these terms, and consider the questions related to them that you should ask yourself as you read and write in order to think more critically and analyze more thoroughly.

1. **Purpose.** When you write, your purpose—the point(s) you want to make—should be clear and consistent from the beginning to the end of your essay or paragraph. Everything you include should develop that purpose. Your purpose is the argument(s) about the essay's topic that you present to your readers.

When you read, ask yourself:

- What is the author's purpose for writing?
- What argument(s) is the author presenting?
- What *direct or implied questions* is he or she addressing?

When you write, ask yourself:

- What is my purpose in this writing assignment?
- What is my argument for this topic?
- What conclusion(s) have I reached related to it?
- How will I argue this conclusion or these conclusions?

2. **Ideas and Information.** You develop your purpose using your own ideas, personal knowledge, and information you have gained from other sources (if allowed by your instructor). Your ideas and background information are the roots of the tree that support your trunk—your purpose—they bolster it. Later, you develop these individual ideas using examples, concepts, details, and commentary.

When you read, ask yourself:

- What ideas does the author include to support his or her purpose?
- What background information does he or she provide?

When you write, ask yourself:

- What ideas do I want to include to support my purpose, the arguments I am making related to my subject?
- What background or personal information can I use to develop the purpose?

3. **Support.** You need to provide evidence to support your purpose, ideas, and conclusions on a subject. You can draw on your personal experiences or those of others, use facts and statistics you have researched if your instructor allows it, provide examples and specific details, or supply information provided by your instructor to support your reasoning. Always evaluate information provided by others. Include commentary to explain the examples and details you use.

When you read, ask yourself:

- What evidence or examples is the author using to support his or her reasoning?
- Are the examples and support believable and clearly explained?
- Do they adequately support the author's purpose?

When you write, ask yourself:

- What evidence and examples can I provide to back my ideas?
- Are the evidence, examples, and commentary I provide credible and clearly explained?
- Do they support my purpose?

Cross Reference
See Chapter 14, pp. 310–311, "Argument and Persuasion," for a list of common logical errors, or fallacies, that writers often make.

4. **Assumptions and Biases.** Be sure that the assumptions you or another author make about a topic or idea are not flawed or based on misinformation. Check for any errors in ideas resulting from an unfounded bias in your thinking process or that of another. Any mistakes in the concepts or ideas that your reasoning is based on can cause problems in your argument. Thus, although assumptions and biases are helpful tools, they can sabotage your arguments if they are unfounded; examine them carefully.

When you read, ask yourself:

- Is there an error in the idea the author is explaining?
- Does the author include assumptions or biases that are flawed or unfair?

When you write, ask yourself:

- Is there an error in the idea I'm explaining?
- Are the assumptions I made or the biases I brought to my topic based on false information?

5. **Conclusions, Implications, and Consequences.** A *conclusion* is the final point in your argument, the place you reach after discussing the ideas that support your purpose, your argument. *Consequences* are the results of a point you have argued. *Implications* are more subtle: They are the possible results of an argument that you have inferred (or an author has implied). Be sure to look at all the possible consequences of your argument. For example, if you argue that your school's music program should be canceled and the money should be used to add more parking spaces on campus, be sure to address all the implications and consequences of canceling the music program. You need to be aware that you are implying that having more parking spaces is more important to your school than having a music program. The consequences could be a loss in the artistic identity of your school, a decrease in the number of applications from students who want to focus on music, and so on.

When you read, ask yourself:

- What are the implications of the author's ideas in this reading?
- Are the consequences of his or her arguments acceptable?

When you write, ask yourself:

- What are the implications of my ideas in this paper?
- Are the consequences of my ideas acceptable and clearly thought out?

Back to the domino idea again: Think of the concluding argument in your writing not as the last domino in the chain but one near the end. The consequences of your argument are the last few dominoes that follow that one. They might not be directly stated in your paper: You'll have to imagine those last dominoes falling and what they mean. For instance, will canceling the music program lead to a decrease in enrollment and hurt the overall budget at the school and the quality of the education provided?

6. **Point of View.** Your point of view is your perspective on a topic. Be sure to check the assumptions your point of view is based on and whether your point of view is unreasonably biased.

When you read, ask yourself:

- What point of view does the author have on his or her topic?
- Did he or she consider other points of view that might be relevant?
- Is the point of view one-sided or biased?

When you write, ask yourself:

- What is my point of view on the topic?
- Have I considered other points of view that might be relevant?
- Is my point of view too biased for my intended audience?

7. **Analysis.** Analysis involves breaking down an idea and working out the meaning of the individual parts and how they relate to the whole. It is an in-depth look at every detail of an idea or argument, like using a magnifying glass to carefully examine something up close. When you analyze, use your own opinions and commentary to examine the subject. Then, supply evidence (examples, details, and conclusions you reach and how you reached them) to support your opinions.

When you read, ask yourself:

- What is the author saying?
- Does the author develop his or her ideas well using specific concepts, support, and analysis?

When you write, ask yourself:

- What am I saying, and how can I explain it? What are my ideas and opinions on this subject?
- Do I develop all the ideas well using specific concepts, support, and analysis?

Using the critical thinking tools for reading and writing will help you focus on the basic parts of your written arguments. With practice, these skills will become an automatic and natural part of your reading and writing processes.

Critical Thinking Checklist

The critical thinking skills defined in this chapter can help you get into the habit of analyzing and evaluating the ideas and techniques you and other writers use to present arguments. Throughout this book, you will see critical thinking questions based on the concepts covered here. Be sure to use the general Critical Thinking Checklist below to evaluate your critical thinking process or the process of another writer.

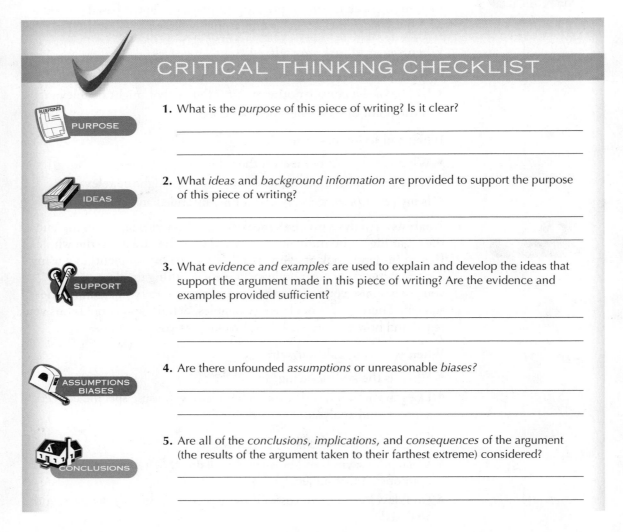

CRITICAL THINKING CHECKLIST

PURPOSE

1. What is the *purpose* of this piece of writing? Is it clear?

_____

_____

IDEAS

2. What *ideas* and *background information* are provided to support the purpose of this piece of writing?

_____

_____

SUPPORT

3. What *evidence and examples* are used to explain and develop the ideas that support the argument made in this piece of writing? Are the evidence and examples provided sufficient?

_____

_____

ASSUMPTIONS BIASES

4. Are there unfounded *assumptions* or unreasonable *biases?*

_____

_____

CONCLUSIONS

5. Are all of the *conclusions, implications,* and *consequences* of the argument (the results of the argument taken to their farthest extreme) considered?

_____

_____

6. Is the *point of view* clear and consistent, and have other points of view been considered?

_____

_____

7. Using these critical thinking tools, *analyze* the overall structure of this essay and the strength of the author's argument, ideas, and support. Was the author successful in accomplishing the purpose? Why, or why not?

_____

_____

Critical Thinking in Action

In order for these tools to become second nature, you need to practice using them in your own writing and when you read. Practice using them on the following reading.

ACTIVITY 1-1 **Using the Critical Thinking Checklist**

Directions, Part 1: *Review the critical thinking terms on pages 6–9 and read the article "Texting: Blessing or Curse?" Then answer the seven questions in the Critical Thinking Checklist above.*

PROFESSIONAL ESSAY

Texting: Blessing or Curse?

Matthew Zellmer

Journal-Sentinel Online, March 10, 2009

1 Sports fans do it from their seats. Millions do it to help choose the next "American Idol." President Barack Obama even used it to give supporters the scoop on his choice for a running mate. Indeed, text messaging is everywhere, and it's here to stay. It's equal parts communication tool and cultural phenomenon. Depending on whom you ask, texting might be the greatest innovation since the Internet. But its ubiquitousness is hardly met with universal love.

2   The criticisms are many. Among them: Texting is expensive, it distracts us from daily work, it feeds our destructive need for instant gratification, it encourages short attention spans and, lastly, it's making us dumb.

3   Full disclosure: Since I have a disability that limits motor functioning, I find texting tedious and use it only in crowded, noisy environments when absolutely necessary. But I typically have dismissed most of the above objections as overblown, given all the worse bad habits one can name. But the recent arrest of a 14-year-old Wauwatosa East High School student made me reconsider.

4   According to a *Journal-Sentinel* report, the student disobeyed a teacher's order to stop texting and denied she had a phone, forcing the school's resource officer to search the room. A police officer discovered the phone in the student's pants while the student laughed. School officials suspended the student for a week, and she was cited twice for trespassing on school grounds.

5   School officials were quick to say the arrest was for the girl's behavior toward the teacher and police officer, not the act of texting. However, while classroom disruption takes many forms, texting was the means in this case. As someone too old to have texted in high school, I sought counsel from some teacher friends. I already knew that cell phones aren't allowed in classrooms, so I wondered how often students smuggle them in.

6   Predictably, my friends told me phones frequently are confiscated. One said his school district requires parents to pick up their child's phone in person after it has been taken away and that a second violation results in the school keeping the phone for the remainder of the academic year. Unfortunately, the prevalence of texting may pose an even more substantive problem for educators: an erosion of students' writing skills.

7   The consensus among the teachers I spoke with was that the texting culture of abbreviation and brevity makes for poorer quality work and worsens grades, especially in the first weeks of school before correct grammar and proper mechanics can be instilled. These problems usually are overcome easily but not without "whining and disregard for directions," according to one. Allegedly "complete" assignments are sometimes three sentences. One suggestion has been to require writing in all subjects, including math.

8   This seems like a worthy idea, as kids must be taught the importance of writing skills in the professional world. Parents and educators are uniquely qualified to do so by any reasonable method necessary. Except, of course, text messaging.

Part 2: *What effect did knowing that you would have to answer critical thinking questions afterward have on the way you read the article?*

_____
_____
_____
_____
_____
_____
_____
_____
_____
_____
_____
_____
_____
_____
_____
_____
_____

ACTIVITY 1-2 Checking Your Critical Thinking Skills

Directions, Part 1: _Read the article below, and draw icons from the Critical Thinking Toolbox in the margin next to the places where the writer uses those tools. Don't worry about your drawing skills._

PROFESSIONAL ESSAY

Business School Makes PowerPoint a Prerequisite

Justin Pope
Seattle Times Online, July 31, 2007

1   Chicago business-school administrator Rose Martinelli says PowerPoint presentations permit potential students to demonstrate creativity that might not come through in traditional applications. At business meetings the world over, PowerPoint-style presentations are often met with yawns and glazed eyes.

2   But at one of the world's top business schools, such slide shows are now an entrance requirement. In a first, the University of Chicago will begin requiring prospective students to submit four pages of PowerPoint-like slides with their applications this fall.

3   The new requirement is partly an acknowledgment that Microsoft's PowerPoint, along with similar but lesser-known programs, has become a ubiquitous tool in the business world. But Chicago says so-called "slideware," if used correctly, also can let students show off a creative side that might not reveal itself in test scores, recommendations and even essays.

4   By adding PowerPoint to its application, Chicago thinks it might attract more students who have the kind of cleverness that can really pay off in business, and fewer of the technocrat types who sometimes give the program a bad name. "We wanted to have a free-form space for students to be able to say what they think is important, not always having the school run that dialogue," said Rose Martinelli, associate dean for student recruitment and admissions.

5   Online applications are already the norm, and it's not uncommon for colleges to let students submit extra materials such as artwork. Undergraduate and graduate applications also are beginning to ask for more creative and open-ended essays. Partly that's to better identify the students with a creative spark. Partly it's to fend off the boredom of reading thousands of grinding, repetitive responses to "Why is University X right for you?" But asking for four electronic slides appears to be a new idea.

6   Chicago's new requirement may provoke groans from some quarters. It could be called corporate America's final surrender to a technology that, in the name of promoting the flow of information, often gums it up by encouraging bureaucratic jargon and making colorful but useless graphics just a little too easy to produce.

7   Nonetheless, PowerPoint has become the lingua franca of business meetings worldwide. Its 500 million copies are used (or misused) in 30 million presentations per day, Microsoft has estimated.

8   Technology isn't a hurdle for most University of Chicago applicants, but "other schools might have to think about that," said Nicole Chestang, chief client officer for the Graduate Management Admission Council, a worldwide group of management programs that oversees the GMAT entrance exam.

9   It's also business schools that traditionally have the most boring essays, focusing on workplace accomplishments rather than passions or unusual talents, which are increasingly interested in creativity. Michael Avidan, a second-year Chicago MBA student, predicts some applicants will be turned off by the requirement but says it's an opportunity for clever students whose test scores and other application materials might not stand out to shine.

Part 2: *Write a few sentences about what effect looking for these specific critical thinking tools had on the way you read and understood this article.*

_____

_____

_____

_____

_____

Part 3: *On a separate sheet of paper, answer the seven Critical Thinking Checklist questions for this article.*

Glossary of Critical Thinking Terms

Here is a glossary of critical thinking terms to help you with your reading and writing. Some of these terms have already been covered in the chapter, and some of them are new but will also help you use your critical thinking skills.

ANALYSIS   Analysis involves breaking down an idea and working out the meaning of the individual parts and how they relate to the whole. For example, if you were asked to analyze a paragraph or a poem, you would go through each line or sentence and figure out what each individual part is saying; then you would look at the connections between the parts and the overall meaning.

ARGUMENT   In most college writing, you must make some type of argument(s) and present a conclusion about a topic using reason and evidence to convince your readers of your point. Your purpose, then, is to promote the argument(s) you are making. Arguments in writing can be casual and entertaining (such as arguing for the best place in town to go on a first date), or they can be more formal and structured (such as arguing for the need for a new science building on your campus). Either way, you are arguing to persuade readers to accept your conclusions and your point of view on the subject.

ASSUMPTION   An assumption is a belief or claim that you take for granted or that a society, a culture, or an author takes for granted without providing or asking for evidence or proof to support the idea. Almost everything you believe and do is based on assumptions; for instance, you assume the sun will rise each morning and set each evening. Some, however, are more individual assumptions that you take for granted but that not everyone would agree with. It is important to learn to separate the assumptions that have a basis in fact from ones that don't. When reading, look carefully for the author's assumptions, the ideas they take for granted, and consider whether these are based on undeniable truths.

BIAS   Bias is a particular viewpoint that you or an author has about an idea or a topic. All ideas or opinions reflect a bias. Sometimes you (or an author) are conscious of the biases in your ideas, and sometimes you are not. Having biases is not necessarily a bad thing (it is inevitable), but when one's biases are founded on misinformation or unrealistic assumptions, they can get in the way of good critical thinking.

CONCLUSION   A conclusion is the end result of an argument. It is the main point you make in your paper and should be the logical result of the reasons you provide to support your argument. When you evaluate an author's argument, you are looking for his or her conclusion about the chosen topic and how well it has been developed using reasons, examples, and details as support.

EVALUATION   Evaluation is looking at the strength of your reasoning, support, and conclusions (or those of another writer) to determine how well those ideas are developed and explained. In both reading and writing, evaluate the arguments you or the author put forth and how well they are supported by examples, reasons, and details. Also, consider the counterarguments—what people who argue for a different conclusion might say to refute your conclusion on the issue—and evaluate how well those arguments are constructed.

IMPLY   To imply means "to hint that something is so, to say it indirectly." For instance, if your aunt visits you and says, "My, aren't you looking *filled out* these days!" she may be implying, or hinting, that you need to go on a diet.

INFERENCE   To infer involves reading between the lines to figure out what someone means based on clues in what they say or write. For instance, in the example above, your aunt has *implied* that you are getting fat, and you, in receiving those clues from her language, have *inferred* her meaning.

INTERPRETATION   Interpretation involves decoding an idea so you understand its meaning. When you interpret an author's idea, you decode it using your own words. You need to interpret and understand an author's ideas before you can analyze their meanings and evaluate them.

OPINION   Your opinion is what you (or another writer) believe about an idea, question, or topic. To express an opinion requires that you think about an idea or question and come to your own conclusions about it. An opinion is based on weighing information and deciding where you stand on a question.

POINT OF VIEW   Point of view in critical thinking refers to the perspective you are coming from in your reasoning and writing (or the perspective of the author). Be aware of your own point of view and the biases, assumptions, and opinions that make up that point of view, and be prepared to think of potential points of view that differ from yours (or from the views of the author).

PURPOSE   Purpose refers to the reason you are writing a piece: It is what you are arguing for, your conclusions on the topic. What have you (or the author) set out to explain or prove to your readers? Sometimes the purpose of your writing is directly stated, as in a thesis statement, and sometimes it is implied by the arguments and reasons you provide throughout your writing.

SYNTHESIS   Synthesis involves pulling together your ideas, and sometimes the ideas of others, in order to make or support an argument. Often, in writing, synthesis involves combining ideas from several authors that connect on a particular subject or argument to give a bigger picture.

ACTIVITY 1-3   Critical Thinking Review and Practice

Directions: *Answer the following questions.*

1. Reread the definition for critical thinking on page 3. Then write a definition of critical thinking using your own words.

   _____

   _____

   _____

   _____

2. List three assumptions you had about college before you began. Then write a line or two about whether each assumption ended up being valid (true) or invalid (not true or unfounded).

   Assumption 1: _____

   _____

   _____

   True or unfounded: _____

   Assumption 2: _____

   _____

   _____

   True or unfounded: _____

Assumption 3: _____

_____

_____

True or unfounded: _____

3. List two benefits you predict you will gain from learning and applying the critical thinking tools and terms explained in this chapter.

1. _____

_____

_____

2. _____

_____

_____

MyWritingLab™　　**ACTIVITY 1-4**　**Critical Thinking Terms and Tools**

Directions: *Answer the following true/false, multiple-choice, and matching questions to test your understanding of the terms and concepts discussed in this chapter.*

1. T/F _____ Critical thinking is a new concept from the last ten years or so.

2. T/F _____ We engage critical thinking skills in college and also in our day-to-day life.

3. T/F _____ It is always a bad idea to have a *bias* in your ideas or views about a subject.

4. T/F _____ An assumption that you have as the foundation of your thinking can be an accurate assumption or a false assumption.

5. T/F _____ *Inference* means the ability to read between the lines and figure out what an author means using clues from the text.

6. T/F _____ *Synthesis* means adding supporting examples.

7. _____ Which of the following critical thinking terms **best** matches the term *thesis statement*?

   a. Bias

   b. Support

   c. Purpose

   d. Point of view

Matching Terms to Definitions: *Draw the tool icon (for example, beams, nails, and so on) for each term on the line provided next to it. Then, draw a line from each term to its definition.*

_____ **8.** Analysis

a. Looking at the individual parts closely to assess the whole purpose or argument

_____ **9.** Bias

b. The end result of an argument

_____ **10.** Support

c. A belief or claim one takes for granted without providing or asking for evidence or proof to support the idea

_____ **11.** Ideas

d. The perspective you (or the author) are coming from in your reasoning and writing

_____ **12.** Conclusion

e. A particular viewpoint that you (or an author) have about an idea or a topic

_____ **13.** Purpose

f. Personal knowledge and information (specific roots of the tree that form your purpose)

_____ **14.** Point of view

g. The reason you are writing a piece in the first place; what you (or the author) set out to explain or prove to readers

_____ **15.** Assumption

h. Personal experiences or those of others, facts and statistics you have researched, examples and specific details to develop your purpose

Dive Deeper into Your Thinking Process

Be sure to refer to the critical thinking terms and tools provided in this chapter, whenever necessary, as you work through different sections of this text. You will see these tools and terms used in different places throughout the book (watch for the icons), and you will need to use some or all of them in the writing assignments, reading selection activities, and grammar exercises. Also, critical thinking skills are essential to developing good arguments in paragraphs and essays. Finally, you'll need to engage critical thinking skills to evaluate the writing of others: classmates, professional authors you read for class, and any sources you consult. As with any new language, the language of critical thinking gets easier with familiarity and practice. Training yourself to use critical thinking skills is challenging, but using these skills will significantly improve your reading and writing abilities, and it may become a treasured, lifelong habit.

Learning Objectives Review

❶ Critical thinking and why it is important.

What is critical thinking, and why is it important? (See pp. 3–6.)

Critical thinking is actively thinking through and evaluating all the steps in your thinking process or the thinking process of others. It is essential for good analytical reading and clear, fair-minded analytical writing. You can use critical thinking skills to understand and evaluate the writings of others and to discover the strengths and weaknesses in their arguments. You can also use them to examine your own thinking, your biases and assumptions, and the strength and logic of the reasons you provide for an argument.

❷ Critical thinking tools you can use to write well.

What critical thinking terms are included in the Critical Thinking Toolbox, what do they mean, and how do you use them? (See pp. 6–20.)

The **critical thinking terms** discussed in this chapter are *purpose* (your reason for writing), *ideas* (the personal knowledge, and outside information or research used to develop your purpose), *support* (facts, statistics, examples, and research used to support your reasoning), *assumptions and biases* (information taken for granted or personal beliefs about a topic that may create errors in your ideas or those of others when reading and writing), *conclusions* (the results of your argument), *point of view* (the way you see an issue), and *analysis* (breaking an idea into its individual parts to see how they relate and contribute to overall meaning). Use these tools to help you evaluate your thinking, reading, and writing processes; to explore your ideas, arguments, and conclusions; and to analyze the arguments and writing techniques of others.

In this chapter, you will learn how to

1 Apply critical thinking to reading.

2 Read actively and create a dialogue with the text.

3 Use six steps for active reading.

4 Highlight and annotate as you read.

5 Use the T-KED method for annotation.

Pain
Tommy Corey

Thinking Critically **MyWritingLab™**

Think: Good reading skills and good critical thinking skills go hand-in-hand. We need to "read" an image as carefully as we read text. Sometimes words are even combined with images to create a message, as in the picture above.

Write: Have you ever read something, and then not remembered or absorbed anything that you read? What do you think you can do to retain information as you read?

_____

_____

_____

_____

_____

_____

_____

_____

_____

CRITICAL THINKING AND READING

1 Apply critical thinking to reading.

Critical thinking can take you beyond basic comprehension of what you read. If you get into the habit of asking critical thinking questions as you read a selection, you will be able to understand it better and reach deeper analytical conclusions. Not only will you be able to assess the arguments an author is making in a story or essay, you will also be able to recognize the writing techniques used and the ideas on which the author is building arguments and conclusions. You can also check to see if the author makes any errors in the introduction or conclusion. In addition, as you read, you can make connections to your own experience and what you know about the world to help you think more deeply about the author's ideas and arguments and how he or she develops them.

ACTIVE READING

2 Read actively and create a dialogue with the text.

To become a better reader, you must read actively instead of passively. Active reading habits will help you read critically and analyze thoughtfully as you read. The difference between *passive* and *active* reading is like the difference between *hearing* and *listening*. You can hear what someone says without listening to the words, and you can read words passively without understanding what they mean. Good listening takes concentration, and so does active reading. Active reading involves communication between you and the text: It's a dialogue, not a monologue.

Once you develop a system for reading actively that works for you, use it regularly. Many of the readings you'll be assigned in college require you to think critically and analyze the ideas and arguments, the techniques, and the reasoning of the author. Try out the following active reading systems to see which one works best for you, or combine and customize these techniques into a system of your own. As with developing any new habit, it takes commitment, but the time you spend will result in a more thorough understanding of what you read and an increased ability to remember what you have learned. Also, if you make connections among the reading assignment, your own experience, and the world around you, such as social rules or current events, your understanding of the reading and your retention of what you read will improve.

SIX STEPS FOR ACTIVE READING

3 Use six steps for active reading.

Use the following six steps to turn reading into an active engagement between you and the text instead of a passive process that leaves you bored or keeps you from understanding and remembering what you read. First, buy a notebook for your Reader's Log. For each textbook chapter, article, or essay

APPLYING CRITICAL THINKING

PURPOSE   IDEAS   SUPPORT   ASSUMPTIONS BIASES   CONCLUSIONS   POINT OF VIEW   ANALYSIS

Here are some questions you can ask as you read in order to think critically about what an author is saying.

1. What is the author's **purpose** or **goal** in this reading selection? What does he or she set out to explain, argue, or prove?

2. What are the **implied** or **stated** questions being addressed in this reading selection?

3. What **ideas** and **support** (evidence, data, experience, or facts) does the author use to develop a purpose or goal for the reading? Is the support adequate? Convincing?

4. Does the author present alternative **points of view** when needed?

5. What **assumptions** does the author make in this reading selection? (Assumptions are ideas or reasons the author takes for granted and upon which he or she bases judgments or develops his or her reasoning.) Are the assumptions valid?

6. What are the **implications** or **consequences** of the author's reasoning and/or ideas and arguments (direct or implied) in this selection? What **conclusions** does the author reach?

Cross Reference

The entire Staples essay appears in Chapter 18, pp. 416–418.

you read, follow the six steps below, and record them in your Reader's Log. Start each entry in your log with the date, title of the chapter or article, and the page numbers of the reading. The entries in the sample student log that follow are based on the essay "What Adolescents Miss When We Let Them Grow Up in Cyberspace," by Brent Staples.

> **Reading Log**
>
> **Date:** 10-8-13
>
> **Reading:** "What Adolescents Miss When We Let Them Grow Up in Cyberspace," by Brent Staples, pages 416–418.

Step One: Preview the Reading

Previewing what's coming in a chapter or article helps increase your retention as you read—it's like glancing at a whole picture before you study its individual parts.

Preview the entire selection before you read it, as follows:

1. Read the chapter or article title and any subtitles.
2. Read the introduction or the first paragraph.
3. Read the first sentence of each paragraph. In textbooks, this is often the topic sentence and will tell you the main point of the paragraph.
4. Look for text that is in boldface or italic font, underlined, or presented in a bulleted or numbered format. Key words that are defined in the text are often in boldface, and authors use italics or underlining to emphasize important information.
5. Look at any photographs, graphs, charts, diagrams, or other visual aids, as these are included to provide additional information that supports and illustrates the text.
6. Read the summary at the end of the chapter or article (if there is no summary, then read the last paragraph).

Step Two: What Do You Already Know about the Topic?

After you have previewed the reading, *ask yourself what you already know about the topic.* Chances are you have heard or read some things about it before reading the piece. What can you tap into in your memory or knowledge that will help you better understand this new reading? If you don't know anything about the specific topic, what do you know about related topics, subtopics, or ideas within the article? For instance, if the article is about how to fly fish successfully, but you've never fly fished, have you ever fished with a rod at all? Have you seen someone fish with a rod on TV? What do you know about fishing in general? Even a little bit of background helps you feel more comfortable and better retain new information, so take a moment to scan your knowledge about the topic itself or information related to the topic.

Reading Log

Date: 10-8-13

Reading: "What Adolescents Miss When We Let Them Grow Up in Cyberspace," by Brent Staples, pages 416–418.

Prior knowledge/background: I know that spending too much time on the Internet has affected a lot of my friends and that it can interfere with in-person social interactions.

Step Three: Create Questions to Begin Your Dialogue with the Text

Questions keep you active and engaged in your reading as you look for answers. Turn the title and subheadings into questions before you read, and then look for answers to them as you read the whole selection. This active method will help you build a more detailed picture of the reading. Write the questions that you create from the title and subtitles in your Reading Log and leave space beneath your questions to fill in your answers after you read (Step Four).

Then, create a few questions of your own based on your preview of the chapter or article (for example, What is osmosis? Why do volcanoes erupt? How does the American jury system work?) and write them in your log.

Reading Log

Date: 10-8-13

Prior knowledge/background: I know that spending too much time on the Internet has affected a lot of my friends and that it can interfere with in-person social interactions.

Questions made from title and subtitles and/or topic ideas:

1. What do adolescents miss?
2. What does the author mean by "cyberspace"?
3. How has the Internet changed adolescents' social habits?
4. Does the article also cover the positive effects of the Internet?

Step Four: Read in Blocks

Either read from one subtitle to the next, or if there are no subtitles, read one or two paragraphs at a time, and then, after each section, complete Step Five.

▶ **NOTE**   Reading in blocks instead of straight through a chapter without stopping keeps you focused and careful. It helps prevent the "I just read the whole chapter or article, and I have no idea what I read" syndrome.

Step Five: Write in Your Reader's Log

Write the following in your Reader's Log for each block of text you read:

1. **A two- to three-sentence summary of the main ideas from each section** (or one- or two-paragraph block) as you finish it.
2. **The answers to the questions from Step Three** as you discover them—or amend your questions if you find your questions were off track.
3. **Any vocabulary words** from each block that you don't know. If you can't figure out their meanings by the end of the block, then look them up in a dictionary after finishing the block (not understanding a key word or term can sabotage your understanding of that section).

When you are sure you have understood the section you have read, place a check mark at the end of it, and move on to the next one.

Reading Log

Summary of Section 2, paragraphs 4–8: This section explains the kinds of things teens and other people are doing in cyberspace, such as checking and writing email, spending time in chatrooms and on social networking sites, and shopping online. It also discusses what effects all this added time online has on couples, families, and especially on teens—isolating them more from others.

What do adolescents miss?

According to Staples, they miss out on needed real-life social experience and genuine connections with others.

How has the Internet changed adolescents' social habits?

In addition to being more isolated and not learning in-person social skills and lessons, adolescents also often create false identities or alternate versions of themselves, which has a negative effect on their self-esteem and social skills.

Vocabulary: I didn't know the word "hermetic"—so I looked it up; it is an adjective that means like a hermit—isolated.

Step Six: Review and Answer the Questions You Created in Step Three

When you've finished reading the article or essay and writing your summary statements, answers, and new vocabulary for each block of the text, go back and read (review) them all.

Next, using your Reader's Log, review all the questions and your answers from Step Three without looking at the chapter or article or your notes from Step Five. If you can't remember the answers easily without looking, or if you are unsure of your answers, then review your Step Five notes and, if necessary, the relevant sections of the reading selection.

▶ FINAL NOTE   If you follow all these steps, you will engage in active reading. Also, you will have notes to review for class discussions, tests, or writing assignments. At first, using the Six Steps for Active Reading will take longer than passively reading a chapter or article. However, with practice, you will be able to go through these steps quickly, sometimes doing Steps One, Two, and Six completely in your head as you get into the habit of reading as a dialogue. Finally, this process can actually *save you time* by preventing you from having to reread whole chapters or articles because you didn't understand or retain the information.

Example of the Six Steps in Action

Read through the excerpt below from an article from the *Seattle Times* about increasing interest in American goods in Mexico, and see how the Six Steps worked for one student.

Reading Log

Step One: I have previewed the entire article and read the title, introduction, first sentence of each paragraph, and the last paragraph.

Step Two: I already know that there are some U.S. goods and U.S.-based stores in Mexico.

PROFESSIONAL ESSAY

Step Three, Question 1:
Why does Mexico want U.S. products?

"Yo Quiero Made in USA"

Nick Miroff

Seattle Times, September 11, 2012

1   When the governor of Colorado came to Mexico on a trade mission earlier this year to see the sights, "one of the most amazing" was a Costco.

2   "It was as big, clean and modern as any in America," recalled John Hickenlooper, a Democrat, who found the aisles filled with shoppers bearing "nothing but positive feelings toward the United States."

3   Especially toward U.S. stuff.

4   The Costco was stocked with products stamped "Made in USA," including some of the $755 million in goods that Colorado exports to Mexico each year: marbled slabs of steak from Greeley, cans of pinto beans from Holyoke, and sacks of russet potatoes out of Monte Vista.   ✓

Step Three, Question 2:
What types of U.S. products are sent to Mexico?

5   Trade between the United States and Mexico is surging, up 17 percent in 2011 to a record $461 billion, as Mexico vies with China to become America's second-largest trading partner after Canada. China and the United States did $502 billion in trade last year.

6   The growing middle class that is fast becoming Mexico's majority is buying more U.S. goods than ever while turning Mexico into a more democratic, dynamic and prosperous American ally.

7   "We are obsessed with China when we ought to seriously focus, for our own benefit, on our neighbor Mexico," said Robert Pastor, a professor of international relations at American University and author of "The North American Idea."

8   While news about headless torsos, drug barons and illegal immigration dominate the headlines, and much of the Obama administration's agenda south of the border has focused on law enforcement, economists say another story is one of roaring trade.   ✓

9   "Not only is Mexico doing better, macro-economically speaking, than the false stereotypes would have us think, Mexico is actually doing better than the United States," said Richard Fisher, president of the Federal Reserve Bank of Dallas, who applauds Mexico for controlling inflation, balancing budgets and managing debt.

10   Fisher grew up in Mexico City in the 1950s and remembers a Mexico that "was our soft underbelly, a country of tremendous poverty and horribly bad governments."

11   Now Fisher and his peers praise Mexico for pouring billions of pesos into infrastructure, including ports, railroads, refineries and highways.

12   In the same breath, investors worry about everything Mexico still needs to do: enforce the rule of law, reduce poverty, bust wasteful telephone and media monopolies, open the national oil industry to foreign investment and curb its endemic corruption, the kind that exposed Wal-Mart to allegations the company paid $24 million in bribes to speed permits for construction.

13   In the World Bank's 2012 annual report "Doing Business," which measures benchmarks like enforcing contracts, paying taxes and protecting investors, Mexico finished a middling 53rd among 183 countries, an embarrassment for the pro-business government of outgoing President Felipe Calderón. But the trend lines are up. "The better off Mexico is, the better off we are," Fisher said. "And all these Walmarts, Sam's Clubs and Costcos are for the emerging middle class."

14   Trade with the United States has increased sixfold since the North American Free Trade Agreement (NAFTA) went into effect in 1994, according to Bank of Mexico and U.S. Commerce Department data. The trade agreement eliminated tariffs for goods and made it easier to invest across the border.

15   In the United States, NAFTA is still often used as a pejorative shorthand for outsourced jobs, particularly in Rust Belt states where manufacturers have closed plants and moved south. The torrid expansion of auto manufacturing in Mexico, for instance, is viewed by some industry experts as a potential long-term threat to much touted U.S. job growth in the sector.

16   But NAFTA today generates far less controversy in Mexico. The last large protests, by farmers angry about cheap corn imports from Canada and the United States, occurred in 2008.   ✓

Step Three, Question 3: What is NAFTA?

Step Three, Question 4: Is the U.S. responding to the demand?

Step Four: I went through the article and read in blocks (see check marks).

Reading Log

Step Five, Summary: This section of the article discusses Mexican consumers' positive attitude toward American-made goods and the growing middle class's desire for U.S. products. Also, the article discusses the prestige that comes with American-made products and the growing presence of American stores and goods and the overall increase in trade with Mexico.

Answers, Question 1: The middle class in Mexico is growing and has spending power, and there is a prestige associated with buying American products.

Question 2: Clothes, food, household items . . . anything that would be sold at Costoc, Walmart, etc.

Question 3: NAFTA stands for the North American Free Trade Agreement, which went into effect in 1994. The trade agreement eliminated tariffs for goods and made it easier to invest across the border.

Question 4: Yes, the trade has increased "sixfold" and more and more American stores and products are going to Mexico.

Vocabulary words: vies, macro-economically, infrastructure

Step Six: My answers to the questions were accurate, so I will review them. Vocabulary words mean (1) vies: competes for, (2) macro-economic: the larger world of money/spending, (3) infrastructure: the underlying base or foundation for an organization.

ACTIVITY 2-1 Six Steps Practice

Directions, Part 1: *Apply the Six Steps method to the next excerpt from the article. Write your questions in the margin of the reading; place check marks after each section after you have read and understood it; and write the answers to your questions, your summary, and any unfamiliar vocabulary words in your Reader's Log or on a separate sheet of paper.*

PROFESSIONAL ESSAY

"Yo Quiero Made in USA" (*continued*)

17   During Mexico's presidential campaign this year, none of the candidates—not even leftist challenger Andrés Manuel López Obrador—campaigned against NAFTA or threatened to revoke it. The winner, President-elect Enrique Peña Nieto, said he wants to expand it.

18   And there is little wonder why. Mexican exports to the United States have soared from $42 billion in 1993 to $263 billion in 2011, according to the U.S. Commerce Department. Almost 80 percent of Mexico's exports go to the U.S. market, led by crude oil, fruits, vegetables, televisions, cellphones, computers and passenger vehicles.

19   "Before NAFTA, we had a slight trade deficit with the United States," said Daniel Chiquiar, a Bank of Mexico statistician. "Now we have a huge trade surplus."

20   U.S. businesses exported about $198 billion in merchandise in 2011, a 10-year high. . . . U.S. exports have also multiplied, especially as the consumption tastes of the growing Mexican middle class increasingly resemble those of U.S. shoppers.

21   "Mexico and the United States are no longer competitors, where one country wins and the other loses. They are partners," said Christopher Wilson, of the Mexico Institute in Washington, who is author of the report "Working Together." "The Mexican and U.S. economies are now as deeply integrated as any on Earth."

22   In a Costco store in the suburbs of Mexico City, shoppers browse shelves loaded with pallets of Kirkland vitamins, value packs of Nature Valley granola bars and sacks of Cape Cod kettlecooked potato chips.

23   From 2009 to 2011, 825 new discounters and more than 3,000 convenience stores opened for business in Mexico. The biggest growth came in modern retail chains, filled with U.S. products, which are challenging, for better or worse, the traditional mom-and-pop stores doling out soda, eggs and tortillas.

24   Mexico bought $198 billion worth of U.S. goods last year, up from $41 billion in 1993. This makes Mexico the No. 2 destination for American merchandise after Canada.

25   The United States sold more stuff to Mexico than to Brazil, India, Japan and Britain combined.

26   At Costco, even the walls in the butcher aisle boast the "USDA Premium" and "USDA Choice" labels, in English.

27   Sales were up 12 percent last year at the Issaquah-based company's 32 stores in Mexico, according to Iqigo Astier, the executive in charge of purchasing for Costco's Mexico operations.

28   "Costco members here in Mexico are middle class, even upper middle class," he said. "As our economy grows, consumers are looking for quality products, and Costco is consistent in quality."

29   Some 6 million jobs in the United States depend on trade with Mexico, according to the consulting group Trade Partnership Worldwide, which generated the total for the Mexican government in 2008.

30   More than 70 percent of the chickens Texas ships beyond its borders go to Mexico; New Jersey sends $1 billion in pharmaceuticals; Iowa exports $121 million in pork, Montana $59 million in copper and molybdenum.

31   In Mexico's Costco stores, staples like tortilla chips and chipotle salsa are trucked in from factories in California and Texas that produce for both sides of the border.

32   With 32 million people of Mexican descent living in the United States and extensive travel—and shopping—up north, Mexico's middle class has come to equate American-made products with higher quality, even if the products cost slightly more.

33   "The Mexican consumer is less focused on price, and more focused on freshness," said Sonia Denham, a senior sales manager for California organic-produce giant Earthbound Farms, which supplies Costco stores in Mexico and the United States.

34   "A salad produced or labeled in the U.S. is a more prestigious item," said Denham, who explained that the "USDA Organic label" is sought out by the discerning Mexican salad eater.

35   More and more, Mexican and U.S. companies work together. Researchers say that an imported product from Mexico sold in the United States actually is 40 percent "Made in USA" because of the sharing of parts and labor between neighbors. That same import from China to the United States is only 4 percent "Made in USA."

36   U.S. companies have been steadily increasing their investments in Mexico and have poured $145 billion into 18,000 companies since 2000. Their Mexican counterparts have not been idle.

37   Products selling under the brands Sara Lee, Thomas' English Muffins, Borden Milk, Weight Watchers Yogurt and Ready-Mix Cement are actually wholly owned by Mexican companies.

38   This year, the Obama administration is expanding its "Select USA" initiative to Mexico, hoping to bring Mexican business leaders north for a visit, to tempt them to invest in America and place a bet north of the border.

Part 2: *Write a few sentences describing the effect using the Six Steps for Active Reading had on the way you read the selection and on your understanding of it.*

_____

_____

_____

_____

ACTIVITY 2-2   **More Six Steps Practice**

Directions: *Pick an article or essay from Chapter 18, from outside of class, or from a chapter in a textbook from one of your other classes, and apply the Six Steps method. Explain below what effect this process had on the way you read the chapter, article, or essay, and your understanding of its content.*

_____

_____

_____

_____

HIGHLIGHT AND ANNOTATE AS YOU READ

4 Highlight and annotate as you read.

Annotate readings by using **highlighting**, underlining, codes, or other methods to mark up the text. Highlighting and underlining are ways to separate the main ideas from the rest of the sentences in a reading. Highlight or underline the thesis, topic sentences, and major ideas for each section. You can also use a highlighter to mark words you don't know and then define them in the margins.

Also, write notes to yourself in the margins as you read. You can use the margins to:

1. Write what you already know about the subject or any insights that you gain as you read
2. Number subpoints or examples supporting the main idea of a paragraph or of the entire reading

3. Write definitions of unfamiliar vocabulary words you've marked

4. Write questions you think of as you read

5. Make comments about illustrations

6. Make comments about an author's biases or assumptions

7. Add codes (see some suggestions below)

8. Make any other notes that will aid your understanding when you review later

Codes You Can Use

You can create your own list of symbols and codes to use as you annotate a reading. Here are a few common symbols or codes:

?	Use a question mark when you don't understand a term or a concept. It will remind you to later reread that part of the text to increase your understanding.
□	Draw boxes around key words—you can write the definitions for those words in the margins.
O	Or draw circles around key terms, and write the definitions in the margins.
1, 2	Use numbers to indicate listed points that are not already numbered, or use numbers to mark the examples given for each main idea.
☆, *, ☺	Use symbols such as stars, asterisks, or smiley faces to indicate important points or sections you particularly enjoyed.

THE T-KED METHOD FOR MARKING TEXTBOOKS AND ARTICLES

❺ Use the T-KED method for annotation.

The **T-KED method** is a system designed to help you mark your text as you read. It gives you codes you can use, in addition to highlighting and regular symbols. It works best for nonfiction articles, textbook chapters, or essays. The process involves marking the **thesis (T)** or main point of the article or essay, the **key ideas (K)** in each body paragraph, the **examples (E)** that provide major support for those key ideas, and the minor **details (D)** that support those examples. Marking these elements as you read increases your comprehension and your ability to distinguish main ideas and arguments from supporting examples and details.

T = Thesis

The **thesis** is the main idea, argument, or point of an article or essay. It is the stated purpose of a piece. A thesis can be one sentence, or it can be a few sentences, depending on the length and complexity of the reading. Usually, the thesis is located in the first or second paragraph of an article or essay, but sometimes it is stated at the end.

On rare occasions, the thesis is never stated and is only implied by a series of arguments and examples. In an essay with an implied thesis, the author doesn't directly state his or her final conclusion or argument in the introduction, though the author sometimes expresses it fairly clearly in the conclusion. Instead, the author provides hints through the examples and details given about the subject throughout the essay that lead you to come to the desired conclusion on your own. If you find that an article's thesis is implied instead of directly stated, write a sentence of your own that explains what the main idea or argument of the reading is *after* you have read all the information and examples (as clues).

Try this: After reading the first two paragraphs of an article or essay, **circle** the one to three sentences that you think state the main argument. **Mark a T** in the left margin next to the sentences you have circled as the thesis statement.

▶ **NOTE**   As you read the article or essay, you may find you were wrong about the thesis statement and will have to circle the correct one. Or, if the thesis is implied, you will have to write it yourself.

K = Key Idea

For each paragraph of an article or essay, **underline** the one- to two-sentence key idea for that paragraph. **Mark a K** in the left margin next to each underlined key idea. The **key idea** is the *topic sentence* for the paragraph.

▶ **TIP**   Read the entire paragraph before you underline the key idea. Often the key idea or topic sentence for a paragraph is the first or second sentence of the paragraph, but sometimes it's in the middle or even at the end of the paragraph.

E = Examples

In each paragraph, **put an E** over each sentence or part of a sentence that provides a **major supporting detail** or **major example to support** the key idea or topic sentence of that paragraph.

D = Details

In each paragraph, **put a D** over any **minor detail that supports** a major detail or example used to support the paragraph's key idea or topic sentence.

PURPOSE

T (again!)

Double-check your T (thesis) to make sure it still works as the main idea of the article or essay. If not, circle the real thesis, or write out the implied thesis of the article.

▶ **TIP** What was the essay or article trying to explain or show through implied ideas or prove though evidence? The answer to that question is the thesis.

Example of Using T-KED, Highlighting, and Codes as You Read

Note the codes, highlighting, and T-KED notations in blue in the following excerpt from "How to Mark a Book," by Mortimer Adler, an essayist who wrote a famous essay about marking a book in 1940. Its advice still stands today.

▶ **NOTE** The entire essay appears on pages 38–42.

K
E   If you're a die-hard anti-book-marker, you may object that the margins, the space between the lines, and the end-papers don't give you room enough. All right. How about using a scratch pad slightly smaller than the page-size of the
D   book—so that the edges of the sheets won't protrude? Make your index, outlines and even your notes on the pad, and then insert these sheets permanently inside the front and back covers of the book.

K
*   Or, you may say that this business of marking books is going to slow up your reading. It probably will. That's one of the reasons for doing it. Most of us have been taken in by the notion that speed of reading is a measure of our intelligence. There is no such thing as the right speed for intelligent reading. Some
E   things should be read quickly and effortlessly and some should be read slowly and even laboriously. The sign of intelligence in reading is the ability to read
E   different things differently according to their worth. In the case of good books, the point is not to see how many of them you can get through, but rather
D   how many can get through you—how many you can make your own. A few friends are better than a thousand acquaintances. If this be your aim, as it should be, you will not be impatient if it takes more time and effort to read a
☺   great book than it does a newspaper.

*K   You may have one final objection to marking books. You can't lend them to your friends because nobody else can read them without being distracted
E   by your notes. Furthermore, you won't want to lend them because a marked
D   copy is kind of an intellectual diary, and lending it is almost like giving your
☺   mind away.

ACTIVITY 2-3 | T-KED Practice

Directions: *Pick a chapter from this text, an article from outside of class, or a chapter from a textbook from one of your other classes, and read and apply the T-KED method to it. Then explain what effect this process had on the way you read the chapter or article and your understanding of the chapter or article.*

_____

_____

_____

Use the Critical Thinking Checklist

Remember to apply the questions from the Critical Thinking Checklist to every reading you study for a class. To make sure you are reading with a critical mind, weave these questions into your active reading process after you have completed the Six Steps for Active Reading or the T-KED Method.

CRITICAL THINKING CHECKLIST

1. What is the *purpose* of this piece of writing? Is it clear?

_____

_____

2. What *ideas* and *background information* are provided to support the purpose of this piece of writing?

_____

_____

3. What *evidence* and *examples* are used to explain and develop the ideas that support the argument made in the piece of writing? Are the evidence and examples provided sufficient?

_____

_____

Continued ▶

4. Are there unfounded *assumptions* or unreasonable *biases*?

_____

_____

5. Are all of the *conclusions*, *implications*, and *consequences* of the arguments (the results of the arguments taken to their farthest extreme) considered?

_____

_____

6. Is the *point of view* clear and consistent, and have other points of view been considered?

_____

_____

7. Using these critical thinking tools, *analyze* the overall structure of this essay and the strength of the author's arguments, ideas, and support. Was he or she successful in accomplishing the purpose? Why, or why not?

_____

_____

Mastery Test: Reading

Directions: *Choose either the Six Steps for Active Reading or the T-KED approach and annotate the following reading. Then answer the questions in the Critical Thinking Checklist above.*

PROFESSIONAL READING

How to Mark a Book

By Mortimer J. Adler, Ph.D.

1   You know you have to read "between the lines" to get the most out of anything. I want to persuade you to do something equally important in the course of your reading. I want to persuade you to write between the lines. Unless you do, you are not likely to do the most efficient kind of reading.

2   I contend, quite bluntly, that marking up a book is not an act of mutilation but of love. You shouldn't mark up a book which isn't yours.

3   Librarians (or your friends) who lend you books expect you to keep them clean, and you should. If you decide that I am right about the usefulness of marking books, you will have to buy them. Most of the world's great books are available today, in reprint editions.

4   There are two ways in which one can own a book. The first is the property right you establish by paying for it, just as you pay for clothes and furniture. But this act of purchase is only the prelude to possession. Full ownership comes only when you have made it a part of yourself, and the best way to make yourself a part of it is by writing in it. An illustration may make the point clear. You buy a beefsteak and transfer it from the butcher's icebox to your own. But you do not own the beefsteak in the most important sense until you consume it and get it into your bloodstream. I am arguing that books, too, must be absorbed in your bloodstream to do you any good.

5   Confusion about what it means to "own" a book leads people to a false reverence for paper, binding, and type—a respect for the physical thing—the craft of the printer rather than the genius of the author. They forget that it is possible for a man to acquire the idea, to possess the beauty, which a great book contains, without staking his claim by pasting his bookplate inside the cover. Having a fine library doesn't prove that its owner has a mind enriched by books; it proves nothing more than that he, his father, or his wife, was rich enough to buy them.

6   There are three kinds of book owners. The first has all the standard sets and best sellers—unread, untouched. (This deluded individual owns woodpulp and ink, not books.) The second has a great many books—a few of them read through, most of them dipped into, but all of them as clean and shiny as the day they were bought. (This person would probably like to make books his own, but is restrained by a false respect for their physical appearance.) The third has a few books or many—every one of them dog-eared and dilapidated, shaken and loosened by continual use, marked and scribbled in from front to back. (This man owns books.)

7   Is it false respect, you may ask, to preserve intact and unblemished a beautifully printed book, an elegantly bound edition? Of course not. I'd no more scribble all over a first edition of 'Paradise Lost' than I'd give my baby a set of crayons and an original Rembrandt. I wouldn't mark up a painting or a statue. Its soul, so to speak, is inseparable from its body. And the beauty of a rare edition or of a richly manufactured volume is like that of a painting or a statue.

8   But the soul of a book "can" be separate from its body. A book is more like the score of a piece of music than it is like a painting. No great musician confuses a symphony with the printed sheets of music. Arturo Toscanini reveres Brahms, but Toscanini's score of the G minor Symphony is so thoroughly marked up that no one but the maestro himself can read it. The reason why a great conductor makes notations on his musical scores—marks them up again and again each time he returns to study them—is the reason why you should mark your books. If your respect for magnificent binding or typography gets in the way, buy yourself a cheap edition and pay your respects to the author.

9   Why is marking up a book indispensable to reading? First, it keeps you awake. (And I don't mean merely conscious; I mean awake.) In the second place, reading, if it is active, is thinking, and thinking tends to express itself in words, spoken or written. The marked book is usually the thought-through book. Finally, writing helps you remember the thoughts you had, or the thoughts the author expressed. Let me develop these three points.

10   If reading is to accomplish anything more than passing time, it must be active. You can't let your eyes glide across the lines of a book and come up with an understanding of what you have read. Now an ordinary piece of light fiction, like, say, "Gone With the Wind," doesn't require the most active kind of reading. The books you read for pleasure can be read in a state of relaxation, and nothing is lost. But a great book, rich in ideas and beauty, a book that raises and tries to answer great fundamental questions, demands the most active reading of which you are capable. You don't absorb the ideas of John Dewey the way you absorb the crooning of Mr. Vallee. You have to reach for them. That you cannot do while you're asleep.

11   If, when you've finished reading a book, the pages are filled with your notes, you know that you read actively. The most famous "active" reader of great books I know is President Hutchins, of the University of Chicago. He also has the hardest schedule of business activities of any man I know. He invariably reads with a pencil, and sometimes, when he picks up a book and pencil in the evening, he finds himself, instead of making intelligent notes, drawing what he calls 'caviar factories' on the margins. When that happens, he puts the book down. He knows he's too tired to read, and he's just wasting time.

12   But, you may ask, why is writing necessary? Well, the physical act of writing, with your own hand, brings words and sentences more sharply before your mind and preserves them better in your memory. To set down your reaction to important words and sentences you have read, and the questions they have raised in your mind, is to preserve those reactions and sharpen those questions.

13   Even if you wrote on a scratch pad, and threw the paper away when you had finished writing, your grasp of the book would be surer. But you don't have to throw the paper away. The margins (top and bottom, as well as side), the end-papers, the very space between the lines, are all available. They aren't sacred. And, best of all, your marks and notes become an integral part of the book and stay there forever. You can pick up the book the following week or year, and there are all your points of agreement, disagreement, doubt, and inquiry. It's like resuming an interrupted conversation with the advantage of being able to pick up where you left off.

14   And that is exactly what reading a book should be: a conversation between you and the author. Presumably he knows more about the subject than you do; naturally, you'll have the proper humility as you approach him. But don't let anybody tell you that a reader is supposed to be solely on the receiving end. Understanding is a two-way operation; learning doesn't consist

in being an empty receptacle. The learner has to question himself and question the teacher. He even has to argue with the teacher, once he understands what the teacher is saying. And marking a book is literally an expression of differences, or agreements of opinion, with the author. There are all kinds of devices for marking a book intelligently and fruitfully. Here's the way I do it:

- **Underlining [or highlighting]:** of major points, of important or forceful statements.
- **Vertical lines at the margin:** to emphasize a statement already underlined.
- **Star, asterisk, or other doo-dad at the margin:** to be used sparingly, to emphasize the ten or twenty most important statements in the book. (You may want to fold the bottom corner of each page on which you use such marks. It won't hurt the sturdy paper on which most modern books are printed, and you will be able to take the book off the shelf at any time and, by opening it at the folded-corner page, refresh your recollection of the book.)
- **Numbers in the margin:** to indicate the sequence of points the author makes in developing a single argument.
- **Numbers of other pages in the margin:** to indicate where else in the book the author made points relevant to the point marked; to tie up the ideas in a book, which, though they may be separated by many pages, belong together.
- **Circling [or highlighting] of key words or phrases.**
- **Writing in the margin, or at the top or bottom of the page, for the sake of:** recording questions (and perhaps answers) which a passage raised in your mind; reducing a complicated discussion to a simple statement; recording the sequence of major points right through the books. I use the end-papers at the back of the book to make a personal index of the author's points in the order of their appearance.

15   The front end-papers are to me the most important. Some people reserve them for a fancy bookplate. I reserve them for fancy thinking. After I have finished reading the book and making my personal index on the back end-papers, I turn to the front and try to outline the book, not page by page or point by point (I've already done that at the back), but as an integrated structure, with a basic unity and an order of parts. This outline is, to me, the measure of my understanding of the work.

16   If you're a die-hard anti-book-marker, you may object that the margins, the space between the lines, and the end-papers don't give you room enough. All right. How about using a scratch pad slightly smaller than the page-size of the book—so that the edges of the sheets won't protrude? Make your index, outlines and even your notes on the pad, and then insert these sheets permanently inside the front and back covers of the book.

17   Or, you may say that this business of marking books is going to slow up your reading. It probably will. That's one of the reasons for doing it. Most of us have been taken in by the notion that speed of reading is a measure of our intelligence. There is no such thing as the right speed for intelligent reading. Some things should be read quickly and effortlessly and some should be read slowly and even laboriously. The sign of intelligence in reading is the ability to read different things differently according to their worth. In the case of good books, the point is not to see how many of them you can get through, but rather how many can get through you—how many you can make your own. A few friends are better than a thousand acquaintances. If this be your aim, as it should be, you will not be impatient if it takes more time and effort to read a great book than it does a newspaper.

18   You may have one final objection to marking books. You can't lend them to your friends because nobody else can read them without being distracted by your notes. Furthermore, you won't want to lend them because a marked copy is kind of an intellectual diary, and lending it is almost like giving your mind away.

19   If your friend wishes to read your *Plutarch's Lives*, *Shakespeare*, or *The Federalist Papers*, tell him gently but firmly, to buy a copy. You will lend him your car or your coat—but your books are as much a part of you as your head or your heart.

Learning Objectives Review

MyWritingLab™   Complete the chapter assessment questions at mywritinglab.com

❶ Apply critical thinking to reading.

Why is it useful to apply critical thinking skills to reading? (See p. 23.)

It is **useful to apply critical thinking skills** to reading because it increases your overall understanding of the author's purpose, and you can come to deeper analytical conclusions about the reading, its arguments, and the author's techniques.

❷ Read actively and create a dialogue with the text.

What does it mean to read actively? (See p. 23.)

To **read actively means to** create a dialogue with a text as you read, asking and answering questions about the material, which helps you understand and remember it.

❸ Use six steps for active reading.

What are the six steps for active reading? (See pp. 23–33.)

The **six steps for active reading** are (1) preview the material, (2) think about what you already know about the topic, (3) create questions from titles and headings, (4) read in blocks, (5) write in your reader's log, and (6) review your summaries and answer your questions.

❹ Highlight and annotate as you read.

Why are highlighting and annotating useful? (See pp. 33–34.)

Annotate readings by using **highlighting**, underlining, codes, or other methods to mark up the text. Highlighting and underlining are ways to separate the main ideas from the rest of the sentences in a reading. Highlight or underline the thesis, topic sentences, and major ideas for each section. Highlight words you do not know and write their definitions in the margins.

❺ Use the T-KED method for annotation.

What is the T-KED method, and why is it useful? (See pp. 34–42.)

The **T-KED method** involves marking key elements in a selection as you read (T = thesis, K = key ideas, E = examples, and D = details), which increases your understanding of the content and your ability to identify the thesis and distinguishes main ideas from supporting examples and details.

LEARNING OBJECTIVES

In this chapter, you will learn how to

1 Distinguish between paraphrase or summary and critical analysis.

2 Paraphrase accurately.

3 Summarize accurately.

4 Combine summary and critical analysis.

Tommy Corey

Thinking Critically MyWritingLab™

Think: Study the photograph.

Write: Briefly describe, or summarize, the scene and the main action.

_____

_____

_____

_____

_____

_____

_____

_____

_____

_____

_____

_____

HOW PARAPHRASE, SUMMARY, AND CRITICAL ANALYSIS DIFFER

❶ Distinguish between paraphrase or summary and critical analysis.

Both paraphrase and summary are tools for concisely conveying the main points made by an author. Once you fully understand an author's ideas, you will be able to explain them and his or her use of support using your own words. It takes careful reading and good summary and paraphrase skills to accurately represent an author's ideas and to keep your own biases and opinions separate—until it is time for a critical analysis.

Many of your teachers will ask you to **summarize** a reading—to briefly state, in your own words, the main points the author has made—and you'll need to know this skill to master many writing tasks in the workplace, such as taking the minutes of a meeting or summarizing the points of a presentation before critiquing it. The purpose of a **paraphrase** is to accurately recount someone else's ideas, usually just a few sentences or a paragraph, in your own words, either to support a point you are making or to show you have fully understood the original passage.

- **Paraphrase** involves rephrasing, in your own words, just a couple of sentences of another author's work. Think of paraphrasing as translating what the author is saying, in detail, in order to get a closer look.

- **Summary** focuses on stating an author's main ideas using your own words but not in the same level of detail as a paraphrase. Therefore, though a paraphrase may be the same length or close to the same length as the original, a summary is a condensed overview of the main ideas and support of a longer work, so it is much shorter than the original reading.

You should not include your own opinions or commentary in a summary or paraphrase, but you *must* include them in a critical analysis. Whereas summary and paraphrase deal with the *what* of the content, critical analysis concerns *how* that content is delivered.

- **Critical analysis** involves adding your opinion about and **interpretation** of (explanation of what you think the author is saying) an author's ideas. The focus is *analysis*—evaluation of the ideas or arguments of the author by breaking the ideas down and evaluating their effectiveness. You may even add a *critique* of the author's writing techniques and overall style, evaluating the individual parts as well as the overall success of the presentation of the ideas and arguments. Some assignments will require you to combine summary (and/or paraphrase) with critical analysis.

APPLYING CRITICAL THINKING

PURPOSE   IDEAS   SUPPORT   ASSUMPTIONS BIASES   CONCLUSIONS   POINT OF VIEW   ANALYSIS

When writing about readings, whether you are paraphrasing, summarizing, making a critical analysis, or combining all three, you must think about certain elements of the reading.

Summary/Paraphrase	Critical Analysis
What is the author's **purpose**?	Has the author accomplished the intended **purpose**? How? Why or why not?
What are the main **ideas** in the reading?	Are the author's **ideas** clear?
What are the major examples providing **support** in the reading?	Do the examples develop the purpose well? Why or why not? Is there enough **support**, and is the support valid?
What are the author's **assumptions and biases** in the piece?	Are any of the author's **assumptions and biases** unfounded? How so? What effect did they have on your reading?
What are the author's **conclusions**?	Are the author's **conclusions** sound? Are they well supported? Why or why not?
What **point of view** is the author coming from?	How does **point of view** affect his or her purpose or support?

PARAPHRASE

 Paraphrase accurately.

A **paraphrase** involves using one's own words to *rephrase* a sentence or two (rarely much more than that) of an original piece of writing. A paraphrase should be about the same length and contain about the same amount of detail as the original sentence(s) you are paraphrasing. Paraphrasing is like doing a phrase-by-phrase translation of an author's words into your own words. Make sure that you change both the word choice and the sentence structure of a paraphrase so you are not plagiarizing, and give the original author credit.

If you paraphrase more than a few sentences, you are coming dangerously close to plagiarizing the author's writing. In most cases, when you are writing a description of someone's else's work, you will summarize the main ideas in a general way and only paraphrase (rephrase) the sentences that need to be given in detail—again, using only your own words, not the original author's. It is essential to be objective in your paraphrasing of an author's ideas. Do not add your own biases, opinions, or personal reactions to the material. *A paraphrase is much more detailed than a summary* because you are literally rephrasing a sentence or two with the same level of detail; thus, your paraphrase may end up being the same length or longer than the original piece of writing.

Six Steps for Paraphrasing Material

Here are six steps for writing a complete and accurate paraphrase.

Step One: **Read the sentences you want to paraphrase carefully before writing anything** (if it is a section from a longer piece, be sure to read the whole piece before paraphrasing the passage to be sure you understand the context). Use the T-KED (Thesis, Key Ideas, Examples, and Details) reading system or one of the Six Steps for Active Reading from Chapter 2 to gain a thorough understanding of the work. You must understand an author's main and supporting points before you can paraphrase them.

Step Two: **In your first sentence, give the author's full name and the name of the work you are paraphrasing.** If it is a story, essay, or article, put the title in quotation marks; if it is a book or play, underline or italicize the title, depending on your instructor's preference.

Step Three: **Paraphrase the sentence(s).** You may combine two or more sentences into one concise, paraphrased sentence of your own. However, use the same level of detail in your paraphrase as was used in the original reading.

Step Four: **Write the paraphrase *using your own words*,** not the words of the author (no direct quotations). Also, be sure to use your own sentence structures and style—they should not be too similar to the original.

▶ **TIP** In order to avoid writing the paraphrase in the same words or style as the original author, try not looking at the original and writing a sentence or two paraphrasing the sentences you have just read. Look at the text again and make sure you included all of the author's main ideas and details. It also helps to explain the author's ideas and support to a friend, using your own words, before you write a paraphrase.

Step Five: **Stay objective; do not offer your opinion in the paraphrase.** Add no interpretation and do not agree or disagree. Read over your paraphrase to check for accuracy. Did you present the author's main ideas and details without adding your own bias or opinion?

Step Six: **Include a page citation or publication information where needed.** Even paraphrased references need citations; otherwise you are guilty of plagiarism (stealing someone else's work).

Cross Reference
You can read the Updike essay in its entirety in Chapter 18, pp. 430–435.

Sample Paraphrase

Below is a paragraph from "The Mystery of Mickey Mouse" by John Updike followed by a paraphrase of the opening sentences. Read the paragraph carefully and then read the paraphrase. Note that in the paraphrase the author's name and the article's title are mentioned in the first sentence, and the author's points have been restated using different words.

Original Paragraph

But other popular phantoms, like Felix the Cat, have faded, where Mickey has settled into the national collective consciousness. The television program revived him for my children's generation, and the theme parks make him live for my grandchildren's. Yet survival cannot be imposed through weight of publicity; Mickey's persistence springs from something unhyped, something timeless in the image that has allowed it to pass in status from a fad to an icon.

Paraphrase of Opening Sentences

In John Updike's essay, "The Mystery of Mickey Mouse," he explains that while other popular cartoon character contemporaries of Mickey's are practically forgotten, Mickey has stayed a constant in the American pysche. He says that the 1950s TV show *The Mickey Mouse Club* helped to establish Mickey's appeal with his children's generation, and the theme parks (such as Disneyland) have done so for his grandchildren's generation. However, Updike points out that promotion alone cannot account for Mickey's unfaltering popularity: It is Mickey's spirit, not the publicity, that makes him a lasting hero and not a passing craze (Updike 2).

Use this checklist to ensure that you have accurately paraphrased the original sentence(s).

CHECKLIST FOR A GOOD PARAPHRASE

1. Check to make sure that you paraphrased the ideas in the original sentence(s) in the same order they were presented.

2. Check to make sure the paraphrase includes all of the main ideas and main examples for support from the original sentence(s).

3. Check to make sure that the paraphrase is in your own words and that there are no significant phrases from the original (no direct quotes, not even partial quotes).

4. Check to make sure that the paraphrase is accurate in its restatement of the original material and that you have not added any reaction to or opinion about the material (the restatement is objective).

5. Make sure you have included the author's name and the title of the original piece at the beginning of your paraphrase and included a citation of the source at the end.

Cross Reference

See Chapter 2, the Six Steps for Active Reading (pp. 23–28) or T-KED Method (pp. 34–36) to make sure you thoroughly understand the passage you want to paraphrase.

ACTIVITY 3-1 **Paraphrasing**

Directions: *Pick a reading from another text or from Chapter 18 (or your instructor might assign a passage) and write a paraphrase of one to three sentences from it, following the Six Steps for Paraphrasing Material above.*

_____

_____

_____

Then, explain below what effect writing your paraphrase had on your overall understanding of the ideas contained in the reading.

_____

_____

_____

_____

SUMMARY

 Summarize accurately.

A **summary** is an objective, condensed description of the main ideas of a piece of writing, using your own words. As a rule of thumb, a summary is about one quarter or less of the original reading's length. A summary should not include direct quotations. Be objective in your summary of the author's ideas; add no bias, opinion, or personal reaction to the material.

Here are eight steps for writing a complete and effective summary. *Be sure to read all eight steps before you begin because some of these steps overlap.*

Eight Steps for Writing a Summary

Step One: **Read the entire work at least twice before you write your summary**. Be sure to gain a thorough understanding of the work before you try to summarize it.

Step Two: **Be brief**. A summary is a condensed form of the work's main ideas. Usually a summary uses about one paragraph for each two to three pages of original text.

Step Three: **Write the summary in your own words**. Do not use direct quotations in a summary. Be sure to give page citations and/or publication information after the summarized text if your summary is part of a longer paper.

▶ **TIP**   To avoid writing a summary using the same words or style as the original author, reread one section of the work at a time (a couple of paragraphs to a page or so), and then, while not looking at the original work, write a few lines of summary for the section you read. Then, look at the text again, and ensure your summary includes all of the author's main ideas from that section. It may also help to explain the author's main ideas to a friend first.

Step Four: **Stay objective**. Do not offer your opinion. Add no interpretation and do not agree or disagree with the author. Read over your summary to check for accuracy. Did you present the author's main ideas without adding your own bias or opinion?

Step Five: **Provide the author's full name and the title of the work in the first sentence**. The titles of stories, essays, articles, and poems should be in quotation marks, and book or play titles should be italicized or underlined. Also, provide a general statement about the topic of the selection.

Step Six: **State the author's main idea—the author's overall thesis— using your own words**. You can identify the thesis by answering the question, "What is the main message of this work?"

▶ **NOTE** This step can be combined with Step Five above. However, your restatement of the author's thesis should be in the first or second sentence of your summary.

Step Seven: **Divide summaries longer than 200 words into two or more paragraphs**. Use a natural break or change of main idea to decide where paragraph breaks should occur; if you break your summary into two or more paragraphs, add transitional words, phrases, or sentences as needed.

Step Eight: **Evaluate, revise, and edit the summary**. Go back and reread the work to double-check your summary for accuracy. Check to make sure you covered all the main ideas or arguments and all the main subtopics, and that you haven't included any minor supporting details that are not needed. Check to make sure you consistently used your own words and that you did not offer any judgment or opinion in the summary. Finally, check for grammar errors, spelling errors, overall sentence variety, and needed transitions so your summary has a nice flow and doesn't sound choppy.

▶ **TIP** Try putting your summary away for a day or two. Then come back to it and *read it aloud*. Listen to make sure that it flows smoothly and captures the author's main ideas in a clear and accurate way.

▶ **NOTE** Some instructors will assign a summary that *begins* with pure summary and then adds the element of critical analysis *after* you've summarized the reading. Most assignments that require analyzing a reading usually include some amount of summary and then critical analysis.

Cross Reference
See p. 53, Combining Summary and Critical Analysis, for further information.

Sample Summary

Here is a sample summary of John Updike's essay "The Mystery of Mickey Mouse." Read the entire selection carefully before reading this summary. Then note how the summary keeps the same order of ideas as the article, provides the major ideas and the examples used to support those ideas, remains objective in its presentation of the concepts, and uses transitions to flow smoothly from one idea to the next.

John Updike's essay "The Mystery of Mickey Mouse" examines the enduring appeal of the cartoon character Mickey Mouse. Updike traces Mickey's history and tries to figure out what it is that makes Mickey a reflection of America and an international icon. Updike starts the essay with a description of Mickey's beginnings, both in how he was drawn and how he behaved. He also explores the evolution of Mickey's look or design and of his character as time passed. Next, Updike shows the growth in Mickey's popularity and explains how Mickey came to represent a certain part of the American character and the common person. Updike ties some of Mickey's popularity to the issue of race, arguing that Mickey, like America, has black blood and soul. Furthermore, he explains how Mickey's early films, particularly *Steamboat Willie* and *Fantasia*, helped establish him as a nice guy and increased his popularity worldwide. Updike provides examples of Mickey's global popularity as a testament to his iconic image. Finally, Updike explains how Mickey fulfills the criteria for a good as well as an enduring icon and a simple and memorable representation of the American character.

Use this checklist to ensure that you have accurately summarized a reading.

CHECKLIST FOR A GOOD SUMMARY

Check to make sure that:

1. You summarized the ideas in the original work in the same order they were presented.

2. The summary includes all of the main ideas and supporting examples from the passage.

3. The summary is in your own words and there are no significant phrases from the original passage (no direct quotes or even partial quotes).

4. The summary accurately condenses the original material's ideas, and you have not added any reaction to or opinion of the material (the summary is objective).

5. You have included the author's name and the name of the original article and included a citation at the end of your summary.

Cross Reference
See Chapter 2, the Six Steps for Active Reading (pp. 23–28) or T-KED Method (pp. 34–36) to make sure you thoroughly understand the passage you want to summarize.

ACTIVITY 3-2   Summarizing

Directions: *Pick a reading from another text or from Chapter 18 (or your instructor might assign a reading) and, on a separate sheet of paper, summarize it, following the Eight Steps for Writing a Summary. Then, on the lines provided, explain what effect summarizing had on your understanding of the reading.*

_____

_____

_____

_____

_____

_____

COMBINING SUMMARY AND CRITICAL ANALYSIS

4 Combine summary and critical analysis.

Now that you have mastered summarizing an original work using your own words, you are ready to analyze the meaning or significance of the selection's messages and arguments and the effectiveness of those arguments and of the overall work. A *summary* explains *what* the author is saying; an *analysis* looks carefully at each part of what an author says and explains *what he or she means* (*interprets*); and a *critical analysis* includes analysis plus a detailed critique of the effectiveness of an author's work, based on his or her style and writing techniques. A critique looks at both the strengths and weaknesses of an author's ideas and the techniques he or she uses to present them. Check your assignment or ask your instructor if you are unsure whether you should add a critical analysis to your summary.

APPLYING CRITICAL THINKING

| BLUEPRINTS PURPOSE | IDEAS | SUPPORT | ASSUMPTIONS BIASES | CONCLUSIONS | POINT OF VIEW | ANALYSIS |

Summary versus Analysis: Know Your Purpose

Summary and analysis are two very different skills. In a *summary*, you restate briefly and objectively what an author says in an article, essay, or other piece of writing using your own words without adding interpretation, commentary, or opinions on the material. *Analysis* involves using your critical thinking skills to *interpret* the important ideas in a piece of writing, to break down and look closely at the author's ideas and arguments and how effective they are, and sometimes to critique the techniques an author uses to present his or her ideas. Some assignments only require you to summarize assigned material, while others will ask you to add analysis and interpretation of the messages in the assigned reading.

To analyze a work correctly, you need to include some summary of the original ideas and arguments in an unbiased way. You should interpret the direct and implied messages and critique the author's techniques and style choices; you can even add your own opinion about how well the author has proved his or her intended arguments and ideas.

You learned how to write an unbiased summary of an article, textbook chapter, or story earlier in this chapter using the Eight Steps for Writing a Summary (pp. 50–51). To add critical analysis to your summary, use these two additional steps.

Steps 9 and 10 for Writing Critical Analysis

Step Nine: **Interpret and analyze.** First, *interpret* what the author is saying. You need to go beyond just a summary or paraphrase and add an explanation of the main arguments and claims the author is making, both direct and implied ideas. Analyze the author's overall purpose and arguments by breaking the original work into smaller sections; review one piece at a time and examine each individual idea or claim and how effective it is. Ask yourself, "What are the author's main arguments, claims, or messages? What are the direct messages or points made, and what indirect messages are implied? What are the author's biases, and what assumptions does he or she make that might not be accurate?"

Step Ten: **Critique the style, language, and writing techniques used by the author to make his or her point.** Use specific examples from the text to illustrate your assessment or to demonstrate the writing or style choices the author has made. Also use examples to show what effect those writing or style choices have on the reader and on the delivery of the message(s) in the writing. Ask yourself, "Are there any weaknesses in the author's claims and ideas? What are the strengths? What effects do his or her style and language choices have? Are the writing choices effective for communicating his or her ideas? Do any of the writing techniques get in the way of or weaken his or her ideas?"

Sample Critical Analysis

Here is a paragraph that uses Steps 9 and 10 to add critical analysis to the end of the summary of Updike's essay on pages 51–52.

Updike's essay pays tribute to a favorite childhood cartoon character and includes personal connections and examples that draw the reader in. However, Updike also traces the history of Mickey Mouse and provides facts and details about his development as a character and the growth and endurance of his popularity. In this essay, Updike uses Mickey as a way to look at American values and popular culture. He also explores what causes a character to transition from just a fad to an enduring icon and argues that Mickey successfully fulfills that role. Updike's exploration of the mystery of Mickey's popularity is successful: Readers are able to see the evolution of Mickey as a character and as an icon and understand what Mickey represents for America itself. Moreover, Updike's casual style and familiar voice strengthen his essay.

ACTIVITY 3-3   Summary and Critical Analysis

Directions: *Choose a reading from Chapter 18 or another class and write two paragraphs about it that include both a summary of the main ideas and specific critical analysis of them (the Eight Steps plus Steps Nine and Ten—summary plus critical analysis). After you've finished, describe below what effect the process of summarizing and analyzing this reading had on your overall comprehension of the author's ideas.*

_____

_____

_____

_____

_____

ACTIVITY 3-4   Adding Analysis

Directions: *Review the summary you wrote for Activity 3-2, and add Steps Nine and Ten to make it a summary with critical analysis. After you finish, describe below how your thinking process differed from when you were writing pure summary. How did you have to think differently in order to add analysis?*

_____

_____

_____

_____

Learning Objectives Review

MyWritingLab™ **Complete the chapter assessment questions at mywritinglab.com**

❶ Distinguish between paraphrase or summary and critical analysis.

What are the differences between a paraphrase or summary and critical analysis? (See pp. 45–46.)

Paraphrase and **summary** are tools for concisely conveying an author's main points. A critical **analysis** looks more carefully at the effectiveness of an author's ideas and arguments and how he or she presented them.

❷ Paraphrase accurately.

What is a paraphrase, and how do you write one? (See pp. 46–49.)

A **paraphrase** is a *restatement* in your own words of a sentence or two from a piece of writing. It should be about the same length and contain about the same amount of detail as the original. You can write an accurate paraphrase and avoid plagiarism by (1) carefully reading the material you want to paraphrase, (2) including the author's full name and the title of the work in the first sentence, (3) rephrasing the material using your own words, (4) not offering your opinion, and (5) including an in-text citation when needed.

❸ Summarize accurately.

What is a summary, and how do you write an accurate one? (See pp. 50–53.)

A **summary** is an objective, condensed statement (usually a quarter the length of the original) of the main points of an original work written in your own words. It should include the author's *main ideas* and support for them in the order they appear in the original; it should not include any direct quotations. To write an accurate summary and avoid plagiarism, you should (1) read the entire work at least twice before you start; (2) be concise; (3) use your own words; (4) avoid offering your opinion; (5) note the topic of the selection, the author's name, and the title of the work in the first sentence; (6) state the author's main idea (the thesis) and support using your own words; (7) divide summaries longer than 200 words into two or more paragraphs; and (8) evaluate, revise, and edit the summary as needed.

4 Combine summary and critical analysis.

How can you combine summary and critical analysis, and why would you do so? (See pp. 53–55.)

A **summary** explains *what* the author is saying; a critical **analysis** looks more carefully at the effectiveness of the author's ideas and arguments and how he or she presented them. Some assignments require you to use a synthesis of both skills. Begin by first summarizing an author's main ideas, and then interpret the direct and implied ideas, analyze the effectiveness of each part of the work, and critique the author's techniques and overall effectiveness.

PART II WRITING EXPOSITORY PARAGRAPHS AND ESSAYS

CONTENTS

4 **Writing Expository Paragraphs**

5 **The Building Blocks of Essays**

6 **The Process of Drafting an Essay**

Beach Art

INTRODUCTION TO PART II

Part II of this text focuses on how to write expository paragraphs and essays (writing that has a purpose or lesson to impart). Throughout the three chapters in this section, you will learn how to write well-organized and well-supported paragraphs and essays with a clear purpose that is developed with unity and coherence. You will be asked to use the critical thinking skills you learned in Part I to create more thoughtful and engaging paragraphs and essays.

These chapters are the foundation for paragraph and essay writing, with all the basics you will need to know to draft college-level paragraphs and essays. Part II will prepare you for Part III, in which you will learn about specific types, or modes, of writing and how you can use, combine, or customize them depending on your subject, purpose, and audience. Finally, once you have mastered the tools, tips, and techniques covered in Part II, you will be ready to create final drafts by polishing your sentences, which is explained in Parts V and VI.

LEARNING OBJECTIVES

In this chapter, you will learn how to

1 Define the elements of an expository paragraph.

2 Draft an effective topic sentence.

3 Support your topic sentence with examples, details, and analysis.

4 Draft an effective concluding sentence.

5 Identify various paragraph structures.

6 Use self- and peer-assessment techniques.

7 Identify the similarities between paragraphs and essays.

Thinking Critically MyWritingLab™

Think: When you first looked at this picture, were you immediately aware of what it was you were seeing?

Write: Look at the individual parts of the picture—first the people in the foreground, then the stage and background—and write a brief description of what you see. What kind of event do you think is happening? What evidence leads you to that guess?

_____

_____

_____

_____

_____

_____

_____

_____

WRITING EXPOSITORY PARAGRAPHS

① Define the elements of an expository paragraph.

Just like the parts of the photograph on the previous page, the sentences of a paragraph should not appear randomly, or your readers will be disoriented and have difficulty understanding your point. To communicate effectively, put your paragraph's ideas in order. A well-ordered paragraph includes a statement of purpose; examples, details, and analysis that support and develop the purpose statement; and a conclusion that reiterates the purpose and wraps up the topic.

The Paragraph Format

> **Topic sentence (topic + purpose)**
> **Support (examples and details)**
> **Analysis and interpretation**
> **Concluding sentence**

The word *expository* is derived from a Latin term meaning "to explain." So, an **expository paragraph** always has a purpose or message that it tries to explain. Even if you are writing an essay that describes something you witnessed, you usually have a critical point you want to make about that experience, something you want to convey to your readers. Many expository paragraphs contain an **argument**, a point the writer presents to readers, that needs evidence and support to back it up.

Because, in your expository paragraphs, you are attempting to persuade readers to agree with your conclusions or your opinion about your topic, you need to develop those paragraphs with evidence to support your arguments. The **evidence** you use can be personal experiences, the experiences of others, research, facts, statistics, or quotes from assigned readings. You also need to evaluate the strength of your arguments and ideas and the way you've organized your ideas and supporting details.

Paragraphs can be stand-alone units of writing, or they can be building blocks in an essay. For shorter writing assignments about a specific topic, a paragraph is a helpful writing tool for organizing and developing your ideas. Paragraphs can be customized, depending on the purpose of your assignment, your topic, and your audience—essays can be customized as well.

However, all paragraph types share the same basic elements:

- A topic sentence
- Support statements, examples, and details
- Opinion and analysis
- Transitions to maintain the flow from sentence to sentence
- A concluding sentence

APPLYING CRITICAL THINKING

PURPOSE IDEAS SUPPORT ASSUMPTIONS BIASES CONCLUSIONS POINT OF VIEW ANALYSIS

Use critical thinking to determine your **purpose** for writing a paragraph, the **argument** you want to make, the **support** you will provide, and the **conclusion** you will reach. To write an effective paragraph, you will need to consider the following:

- What is your **point of view**? What do you think or believe about the topic?
- What are your **assumptions** or **biases**? What do you take for granted about the topic? Is your point of view based on correct information?
- What is your **analysis** of the topic? Have you broken the topic down so that you understand it? Have you examined your argument to make sure it is clear and based on solid evidence?

THE TOPIC SENTENCE

2 Draft an effective topic sentence.

Before you begin your paragraph, you need to narrow down your topic so it has a specific focus, and you need to be clear about the point you want to make about the topic. Then you can create a good topic sentence to set up your paragraph.

Topic → Narrowed topic with specific focus → Topic sentence with clear point

IDEAS

The **topic sentence** is the *controlling idea* or *main idea* of a paragraph: It establishes the paragraph's topic and purpose. Ask yourself, "What point do I want to make about this topic? What opinion do I want to present about this topic?" Your topic sentence should be more than just a fact or detail: It should be a conclusion you've reached related to the topic. Your topic sentence should state your opinion about your topic, and the goal of your paragraph should be to convince your readers of the truth or validity of your opinion by supporting it with examples and details that prove your point.

PURPOSE

A strong topic sentence will have an *analytical point*, not just a fact or detail. It is the blueprint for that paragraph's purpose. Therefore, the topic sentence states not only your topic for that paragraph but the opinion, argument, or analytical point you plan to make about that topic, as shown in this example:

> To begin with, due to a growth in student enrollment, we have more students than we have parking spaces, and this imbalance has caused many problems.

The information that there are more students than parking spots would be just a detail or fact, but as soon as the writer adds her opinion about this imbalance and its effects, she presents an idea that she will demonstrate throughout the paragraph with support and analysis.

Assess your topic sentence. Is it an idea or opinion and not just a fact or detail? You also need the scope of your topic sentence to be right for the length of a typical paragraph, not too broad or too narrow.

A topic sentence is **too broad** if it is too generalized or too large in scope to develop and support in one paragraph. A topic sentence is **too narrow** if it is just a fact or detail and not an opinion that can be supported and developed. For instance, if your topic is tennis, you need to think of something you want to say about the sport. If you begin with a topic sentence that is too broad, such as "Tennis is a popular sport," it will be hard to make a specific point in the space of one paragraph. To narrow the broad topic, ask yourself specific questions about the topic such as "What aspect of tennis are you going to address? How popular is it as a spectator sport? How many people like to play tennis as a leisure activity? How many young people start playing tennis in high school and college?"

Make sure your topic sentence isn't too narrow or limited either. You don't want just to state a fact or detail, such as "One common stroke in tennis is the forehand," because then there is nothing else for you to discuss in the paragraph. Try to come up with a focus and an opinion that needs to be developed through examples and details. For example, "Tennis is a sport that requires both physical and mental training."

Topic Sentence Revision

Too Broad: Tennis is a popular sport.

Too Narrow: One common stroke in tennis is the forehand.

Just Right: Tennis is a sport that requires both physical and mental training.

Too Broad: Weather is important.

Too Narrow: Storms usually bring rain.

Just Right: Assessing weather conditions is an important factor in safe driving.

Too Broad: There are lots of choices of what to drink in the morning.

Too Narrow: Coffee is a breakfast beverage.

Just Right: People have different favorite morning drinks, including coffee, tea, and juice.

ACTIVITY 4-1   Creating a Good Topic Sentence

Directions: *Mark the following topic sentences as TB (too broad), TN (too narrow), or TS (good topic sentence). If a topic sentence is too broad or too narrow, rewrite it on the line provided so that it makes a specific point you can support in the space of a paragraph.*

_TB_   **Topic Sentence:** TV is entertaining.

Cartoon Network is a network dedicated to entertaining children and adults alike by showing cartoons 24 hours a day.

_____   **1.** Music adds to the quality of life.

_____   **2.** A crucial staple in Italian food is pasta.

_____   **3.** Soccer and football have a few similarities.

_____   **4.** Snowboarding is a popular sport.

_____   **5.** Fireworks are used to mark many celebratory occasions in America.

_____   **6.** One popular breed of dog is the Labrador.

_____   **7.** There are many popular breeds of dog in America.

_____ **8.** Jogging is a good overall workout.

_____

_____

_____ **9.** There are a few steps one should take before changing an exercise routine.

_____

_____

_____ **10.** A marathon's course is a little over 26 miles long.

_____

_____

SUPPORT AND ANALYSIS

❸ Support your topic sentence with examples, details, and analysis.

You need to provide support and analysis to develop the idea reflected in your paragraph's topic sentence. You can use your own knowledge about and personal experience with your subject to provide support, as well as examples from other people (if you use quotes or factual information, be sure to identify your sources).

Examples are most convincing when you include specific minor details about them that further demonstrate your point. After you provide examples and details, explain what purpose they serve in developing your topic. *Analyze* their significance in proving the point you made in your topic sentence.

Support → Examples → Details → Comments/Analysis

For instance, if you state that tennis strokes are some of the most important elements of the game, you want to give some examples of the different types of strokes and some details that explain what they are and how they work. In the following excerpt, look for examples of the kinds of strokes a player needs to learn (serve, volley, backhand, and lobs), details about the serve, and then analysis of what the player must do to master these skills.

> The most important physical skills tennis players must learn are the serve, the volley, forehand and backhand strokes, and the lob. The serve, for example, has several components such as the toss, form, speed, and technique. Therefore, tennis players must work on their technical skills in order to improve their game. Moreover, in addition

> to the physical demands of tennis, players must work on their mental game to become great at the sport. Much of tennis is psychological.

Finally, you need to use transitional words or phrases between one example and the next to keep your paragraph flowing smoothly. Note how the sentences in the excerpt build on each other to provide support (examples and details) and analysis and how transitional words such as *also, for example,* and *moreover* help the reader move from one point to the next smoothly.

You can support your topic idea with strong examples and details as in the following example about campus parking problems, which shows how to use examples, details, and analysis to support a topic sentence.

How to Provide Support for a Topic Sentence:

Sample Topic Sentence

> Parking at our campus is a problem that must be fixed.

Examples: Give two to four specific examples to support your topic sentence.

> Over the past 40 years, since the existing parking structures were first built, our campus enrollment has nearly doubled.

Details: Give a concrete detail or two to support each of your examples.

> According to our campus's *New Student Handbook*, our school has over 10,000 students; however, it has only 5,000 parking spaces.

Analysis: After you have given examples and details to support your topic sentence, be sure to *interpret the significance* of your examples and details with an analytical statement. Don't assume that the facts will speak for themselves: Most readers need and want commentary from you that explains the significance of the details and examples you've provided and their relevance to your argument.

> When we look at the numbers, we can see that the growth of our campus has created the current parking crisis: The number of parking spaces simply has not kept up with the population growth.

Providing Support: The Ice Cream Sandwich Technique

Be sure to provide meaningful support for your ideas. The Ice Cream Sandwich Technique helps you to remember all the elements of good support.

ANALYSIS

An ice cream sandwich has two chocolate cookies that surround an ice cream filling. Think of the facts, examples, or details you include in your paragraphs as the ice cream filling. You need to surround that filling with two cookies to hold it together. The top cookie is your topic sentence, which introduces the point you want to make in the paragraph, and the bottom cookie is your concluding sentence, which frames your examples with interpretation and analysis.

The Analytical Ice Cream Sandwich

Top cookie: Topic sentence (controlling idea of paragraph)

Ice cream filling: Facts, examples, or details (support to develop the topic sentence)

Bottom cookie: Concluding sentence (interpretation and analysis of the examples and details and how they support the topic sentence)

Ice Cream Sandwich Example

Top cookie: The parking problem has gotten worse due to the growth of the student population.

Ice cream filling: Over the last five years, the student population has grown by over 3,000 students.

Bottom cookie: This large increase has put an unmanageable burden on existing parking lots and parking staff.

ACTIVITY 4-2   **Ice Cream Sandwich Practice**

Directions: *Choose one of the topic sentences you revised in Activity 4-1 and create a full ice cream sandwich to support that topic sentence.*

Top cookie: _____

_____

Ice cream filling (example/detail): _____

_____

Bottom cookie (concluding sentence—interpretation and analysis): _____

_____

_____

ACTIVITY 4-3   **Providing Support: Examples, Details, and Comments/Analysis**

Directions: *Provide a specific example to illustrate each of the topic sentences below. Then, provide at least one detail about the example and one comment analyzing the significance of the example and detail.*

Topic Sentence: Severe weather can cause many problems with traffic.

Specific example/s: *For instance, extremely cold temperatures after a lot of rain can cause particularly dangerous road conditions.*

Concrete detail/s: *One of the most dangerous effects of cold temperatures after rain is the buildup of black ice on roads.*

> **Comment** analyzing the significance of the example and detail provided to support the topic sentence:
>
> *Ice on roads, particularly hard-to-see black ice, causes some of the worst conditions for drivers and leads to many car accidents because drivers lose control of their vehicles.*

1. One can find many useful items at a typical yard sale.

   Specific example/s: _____

   _____

   Concrete detail/s: _____

   _____

   Comment analyzing the significance of the example and detail provided to support the topic sentence:

   _____

   _____

2. Texting while driving is a bad idea for several reasons.

   Specific example/s: _____

   _____

   Concrete detail/s: _____

   _____

   Comment analyzing the significance of the example and detail provided to support the topic sentence:

   _____

   _____

3. College students tend to have certain types of part-time jobs.

   Specific example/s: _____

   _____

   Concrete detail/s: _____

   _____

   Comment analyzing the significance of the example and detail provided to support the topic sentence:

   _____

   _____

4. Some hobbies can help reduce stress.

   Specific example/s: _____

   _____

   Concrete detail/s: _____

   _____

   Comment analyzing the significance of the example and detail provided to support the topic sentence:

   _____

   _____

5. A few incentives would encourage more people to carpool.

   Specific example/s: _____

   _____

   Concrete detail/s: _____

   _____

   Comment analyzing the significance of the example and detail provided to support the topic sentence:

   _____

   _____

THE CONCLUDING SENTENCE

4 Draft an effective concluding sentence.

A paragraph ends with a **concluding sentence** that re-emphasizes the topic sentence's focus and *purpose*. Be careful not to just restate your topic sentence. Instead, end with a closing thought related to your topic sentence but with an idea for further development of the topic. Be careful not to introduce a completely new argument or purpose in your concluding sentence that changes the focus of your original topic sentence. Sometimes, the concluding sentence in a paragraph can serve as a transition to the next paragraph if you are writing several paragraphs or an entire essay. In the case of the tennis paragraph, a good concluding sentence might be, "Indeed, tennis is a sport that requires players to have both physical and mental discipline in order to be at the top of their game." For the parking problem example, you could use the following concluding sentence: "As you can see, the current parking situation on our campus has gotten out of hand."

ACTIVITY 4-4   Creating a Good Concluding Sentence

Directions: *For each of the five topic sentences in Activity 4-3, create a concluding sentence that connects to the topic sentence; highlights the examples, details, and comments you added; and leaves the reader with an ending thought.*

> **Topic sentence:** Severe weather can cause many problems with traffic.
>
> **Concluding sentence:**   *As you can see, bad weather has disastrous effects on the roads and, consequently, also on drivers, who face dangerous conditions and slower traffic.*

1. _____

_____

2. _____

_____

3. _____

_____

4. _____

_____

5. _____

_____

PARAGRAPH STRUCTURES

5 Identify various paragraph structures.

Once you've practiced the ice cream sandwich technique and feel confident about using it, you can experiment with different paragraph structures to add interest and variety to your essay.

Model Paragraph

Here is the full paragraph about playing tennis, which follows classic paragraph form. It has been annotated to show all the elements of an effective paragraph: topic sentence, support (examples, details, and analysis), and concluding sentence. Transitions are highlighted in blue.

Topic sentence
Supporting example
Specific detail
Supporting example

Specific detail

Supporting example

Supporting example

Supporting example
Supporting example
Specific detail
Concluding sentence

Tennis is a sport that requires dedication. To begin with, tennis requires a player to be in good shape. Tennis demands speed and agility. For instance, a player must be able to run from the baseline to the net very quickly. He or she must also learn important physical skills such as the serve, the volley, forehand and backhand strokes, and the lob. The serve, for example, has several components such as the toss, form, speed, and technique. Therefore, tennis players must work on technical skills to improve their games. Moreover, in addition to the physical demands of tennis, players must work on their mental game to become great at the sport. Much of tennis is psychological. If a player loses mental focus during a match, his or her strokes and techniques begin to fall apart. For example, if a player loses mental focus while serving, the toss may not be done correctly. Then it's easy for the player to begin double faulting (missing two serves in a row and losing a point). Indeed, *tennis is a sport that requires the players to have discipline and dedication in order to be at the top of their game.*

Classic Paragraph Structure

The classic paragraph form—another way of looking at the ice cream sandwich—is often shown as an inverted triangle: The topic sentence comes first (or at the top); examples, details, and analysis are in the middle; and the concluding sentence comes at the end (or at the bottom). In most cases, you should use this pattern when writing a single paragraph or a couple of paragraphs. It is also the most common pattern for body paragraphs within essays.

Sample Paragraph

Topic sentence

Supporting example

Supporting example

Reality TV is really more about escaping reality than capturing it. The whole point of reality TV is to be capture real life on screen. However, most people watch reality TV to escape from the reality and predictability of their own lives. My friends tell me they watch reality TV to "chill," to get away from the day-to-day activities of their normal lives. The "real" people in reality TV shows are put into artificial situations and are supposed to act normally. But who could act normally in such extreme conditions? One reality show, for instance, focuses on people surviving for a month on a remote island, living off their wits

Specific detail

and the land. Some of the contestants resort to eating bugs, strange plants, and anything that will help them get the nutrition they need. But with camera crews filming every move, how could the people on the show ever be real or natural? Maybe they could ask the camera crew for a sandwich! Other reality shows feature artificial living situations where extremely diverse personalities are forced to live together. For instance, a show might feature a German sports star forced to live with a rapper from New York City. Again, with the cameras rolling, no one acts as he or she would in normal life. So why do people watch these unrealistic reality shows? *They watch them because they provide a brief escape from their very real lives and so they can indulge in a false reality.*

Supporting example

Concluding sentence

However, there are a couple of variations in the placement of the topic sentence that are available as alternatives to the classic pattern.

Topic Sentence at the End of the Paragraph

In this structure, the paragraph starts out with general information or a personal story to introduce the purpose; then it builds to the controlling idea (topic sentence). The topic sentence, then, serves as the concluding sentence as well. This variation on the typical pattern is best represented by the triangle below.

Sample Paragraph: Variation One

Supporting example

There are many different types of toys on the market today. There are many action figures that let children use their imagination to role play. For instance, superhero figures still spark the imagination. Spiderman is an example of an action figure that many children use to "save the day." Also, many puzzle games and strategy board games are popular and help children build their math and logic skills. For example, the classic game Battleship is available in peg form and electronic form: Both forms help children improve prediction and math skills. Another popular type of toy is one that lets children construct shapes and objects. For instance, Legos are more popular than ever. They even have Star Wars–based Legos that allow children to play out Star Wars

Supporting example
Specific detail
Supporting example

Specific detail

Specific detail

Topic sentence

stories. Legos also help children refine their analytical and hand–eye coordination skills. *Overall, there are many toys on today's market that help enhance children's imagination and physical and intellectual skills.*

Topic Sentence in the Middle of the Paragraph

In this structure, the paragraph begins with a more generalized and elaborate setup for the main purpose. Then, in the middle, the topic sentence states the paragraph's controlling idea or purpose. Finally, the paragraph moves into broader examples and analysis again. There may or may not be a specific concluding sentence in this pattern. This variation is best represented by a diamond shape.

Sample Paragraph: Variation Two

Supporting example
Supporting example
Specific detail
Supporting example

Topic sentence

Supporting example
Specific detail

There are many different types of toys on the market today. There are many action figures that let children use their imagination to role play. For instance, superhero figures still spark the imagination. Spiderman is an example of an action figure that many children use to "save the day." Also, many puzzle games and strategy board games are popular and help children build their math and logic skills. For example, the classic game Battleship is available in peg form and electronic form: Both forms help children improve prediction and math skills. *In fact, there are many toys on today's market that help enhance children's imagination and physical and intellectual skills.* Another popular type of toy is one that lets children construct shapes and objects. For instance, Legos are more popular than ever. They even have Star Wars–based Legos that allow children to play out Star Wars stories. Legos also help children refine their analytical and hand–eye coordination skills.

APPLYING CRITICAL THINKING

PURPOSE   IDEAS   SUPPORT   ASSUMPTIONS BIASES   CONCLUSIONS   POINT OF VIEW   ANALYSIS

Check the parts of your paragraph to ensure you have developed your **purpose** and provided enough **ideas**, **support**, and **analysis**. Here are some tips you can use to write effective paragraphs.

Tip One: Avoid awkward announcements. Don't announce what you are going to write about: Just say it.

> **Announcement:** In this paragraph I will show that shopping can be an addiction.
>
> **Revised:** Shopping can be an addiction.

Tip Two: Delete *It seems*, *I think*, or *I feel* statements in paragraphs. They weaken your voice and argument.

> ***I think* statement:** I think credit card companies should be monitored more closely.
>
> **Revised:** Credit card companies should be monitored more closely.

Tip Three: Avoid the common pitfalls of introducing new ideas or contradicting yourself in the conclusion: the "shoot yourself in the foot" effect.

> **"Shot in the foot" conclusion:** Another addiction that's worse though is food addiction.
>
> **Revised conclusion sentence:** Shopping can, in fact, be a serious addiction with negative consequences.

Tip Four: Choose the appropriate paragraph length based on your topic and purpose. The number of sentences in a body paragraph varies, depending on the topic sentence and its scope. The length of a paragraph is also affected by how many supporting examples and details are needed to develop the purpose. On average, most body paragraphs range from 4 to 15 sentences. Decide carefully how much support and how many examples your purpose and topic will need.

Tip Five: Check that you have provided enough support, using examples and details, and that you have framed your examples with analysis and interpretation when needed.

Tip Six: Make sure you provide transitions to keep your sentences flowing smoothly from one to the next.

SELF- AND PEER ASSESSMENT

6 Use self- and peer-assessment techniques.

Self-assessment and peer assessment of drafts let you evaluate the effectiveness of your writing by going through it, step by step, and looking at the separate elements that contribute to the success of your paragraph. Think of these elements *before* you begin an actual draft, and use the following self-assessment checklist to make sure you have addressed them well. Then have your peers (classmates, friends, or even tutors) use the peer-assessment checklist to critique your paragraph. Remember to use your critical thinking tools also to assess the writing of others.

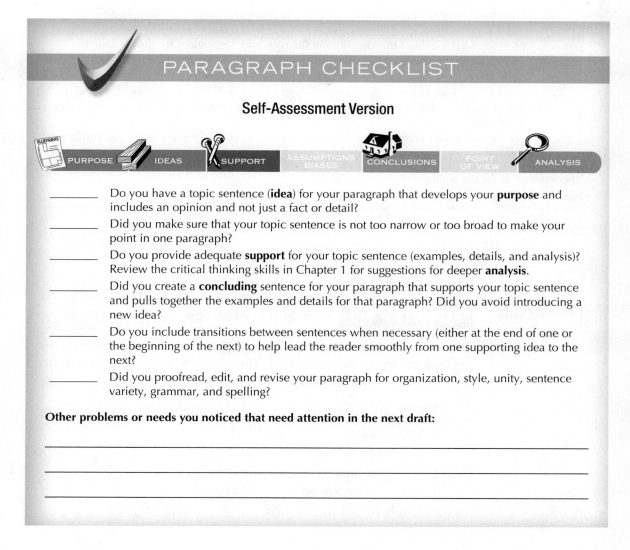

PARAGRAPH CHECKLIST

Self-Assessment Version

PURPOSE · IDEAS · SUPPORT · ASSUMPTIONS BIASES · CONCLUSIONS · POINT OF VIEW · ANALYSIS

_____ Do you have a topic sentence (**idea**) for your paragraph that develops your **purpose** and includes an opinion and not just a fact or detail?

_____ Did you make sure that your topic sentence is not too narrow or too broad to make your point in one paragraph?

_____ Do you provide adequate **support** for your topic sentence (examples, details, and analysis)? Review the critical thinking skills in Chapter 1 for suggestions for deeper **analysis**.

_____ Did you create a **concluding** sentence for your paragraph that supports your topic sentence and pulls together the examples and details for that paragraph? Did you avoid introducing a new idea?

_____ Do you include transitions between sentences when necessary (either at the end of one or the beginning of the next) to help lead the reader smoothly from one supporting idea to the next?

_____ Did you proofread, edit, and revise your paragraph for organization, style, unity, sentence variety, grammar, and spelling?

Other problems or needs you noticed that need attention in the next draft:

_____

_____

_____

PARAGRAPH CHECKLIST

Peer-Assessment Version

| BLUEPRINTS PURPOSE | IDEAS | SUPPORT | ASSUMPTIONS BIASES | CONCLUSIONS | POINT OF VIEW | ANALYSIS |

_____ Does the writer have a topic sentence (**idea**) for the paragraph that develops the **purpose** and includes an opinion and not just a fact or detail?

_____ Is the topic sentence too narrow or too broad to make the point in one paragraph?

_____ Did the author provide adequate **support** for the topic sentence (examples, details, and analysis)? Review the critical thinking skills in Chapter 1 for suggestions for deeper **analysis**.

_____ Did the author create a **concluding** sentence that supports the topic sentence and pulls together the examples and details for that paragraph? Did the author avoid introducing a new idea?

_____ Did the author include transitions between sentences when necessary (either at the end of one or the beginning of the next) to help lead the reader smoothly from one supporting idea to the next?

_____ List suggestions for improvement in organization, style, unity, sentence variety, grammar, and spelling.

Other comments for the author:

_____

_____

_____

MyWritingLab™   **ACTIVITY 4-5** **Paragraph Practice**

Directions: *Choose one of the following topics and narrow it down to a focused topic you can write a paragraph about. Then, using the steps outlined below, create a paragraph, one element at a time.*

Topics

- Smartphones
- Learning a new language
- Exploring future job/career interests
- Your favorite teacher
- Family traditions

Step One: Choose one of the topics above, and write a list of **three to five possible focused topics** on the subject.

Topic: _____

Focused topics: _____

_____

Step Two: Create a **topic sentence** that is neither too broad nor too narrow and includes an opinion about the topic.

_____

_____

Step Three: Provide a **supporting example and a detail** to illustrate that example.

Supporting example (one or two sentences):

_____

_____

Detail to illustrate and develop the example (one or two sentences):

_____

_____

Step Four: Provide a **second supporting example and detail**. Be sure to include a **transitional word or phrase** to move smoothly from the first example to this one.

Transitional word or phrase and supporting example (one or two sentences):

_____

Detail to illustrate and develop the example (one or two sentences):

_____

_____

Step Five: Provide a **concluding sentence** that pulls your ideas together and/or leaves the reader with a further thought on the topic. Remember to avoid introducing a completely new opinion or idea.

_____

_____

Step Six: **Review and revise** what you have written. Read the entire paragraph to see if you need to fix the language or add transitions to make your writing flow smoothly from one point to the next. You should now have a solid draft of a complete paragraph.

MyWritingLab™ | ACTIVITY 4-6 | **More Paragraph Practice**

Directions: *Choose one of the topics below to write a paragraph about. Be sure to include the essential elements of a paragraph, and choose the best paragraph structure (see pages 70–74) for your narrowed topic. Be sure to have a clear topic sentence, specific examples and details to illustrate your points, transitions when needed, and a concluding sentence.*

Topics

- The first day of college
- Managing your finances
- Learning to drive
- Reading a book versus watching a movie
- The scariest moment of my life

Paragraph: _____

_____

_____

_____

_____

_____

_____

_____

PARAGRAPH TO ESSAY: PATTERN SIMILARITIES

 Identify the similarities between paragraphs and essays.

It is necessary to understand the structure of a paragraph in order to understand how to write essays. The major components of a paragraph are also present in an essay. Both feature a statement of purpose, both include examples, details, and analysis to support and develop the purpose statement, and both include a conclusion that reiterates the purpose and wraps up the topic.

As you can see in the following chart, both the paragraph and the essay begin with an introduction that presents the topic and purpose. They both include supporting examples and details as well as analysis and interpretation of those examples and details. Both use transitions between major points to maintain flow and coherence, and, finally, both end with a conclusion that reiterates the statement of purpose and provides a closing remark or idea for further thought.

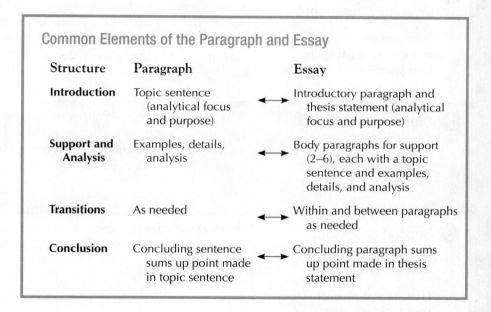

Common Elements of the Paragraph and Essay

Structure	Paragraph		Essay
Introduction	Topic sentence (analytical focus and purpose)	←→	Introductory paragraph and thesis statement (analytical focus and purpose)
Support and Analysis	Examples, details, analysis	←→	Body paragraphs for support (2–6), each with a topic sentence and examples, details, and analysis
Transitions	As needed	←→	Within and between paragraphs as needed
Conclusion	Concluding sentence sums up point made in topic sentence	←→	Concluding paragraph sums up point made in thesis statement

Learning Objectives Review

MyWritingLab™   Complete the chapter assessment questions at mywritinglab.com

❶ Define the elements of an expository paragraph.

What are the elements of an expository paragraph? (See pp. 60–61.)

An expository paragraph has the following elements: a topic sentence, supporting examples and details and commentary/analysis/opinion, a concluding sentence that refers back to the topic sentence, and transitions to maintain the flow from sentence to sentence.

❷ Draft an effective topic sentence.

What makes a good topic sentence? (See pp. 61–64.)

The topic sentence is your main idea or purpose for your paragraph: It states a point, an analytical idea, or an argument. It should be clear without being too broad or too narrow.

❸ Support your topic sentence with examples, details, and analysis.

How do you support your topic sentence? (See pp. 64–69.)

Support includes examples, details, analysis, and commentary to develop the purpose of your topic sentence.

❹ Draft an effective concluding sentence.

How do you draft an effective concluding sentence? (See pp. 69–70.)

A paragraph ends with a **concluding sentence** that re-emphasizes the purpose of the topic sentence without just restating the topic sentence. A concluding sentence expresses a closing thought related to the topic sentence but with an idea for further development of the topic. Be careful not to introduce a completely new argument or purpose in your concluding sentence that changes the focus of your original topic sentence.

5 Identify various paragraph structures.

What are some paragraph structures to choose from? (See pp. 70–74.)

You can use the most common and clear **paragraph struc-ture**, which is to start with your topic sentence, follow with support, and then end with a concluding sentence. Or you can place the topic sentence in the middle or end of your sentence.

6 Use self- and peer-assessment techniques.

What is self- and peer assess-ment, and why is it helpful? (See pp. 75–78.)

Self- and peer assessment means that you, and, later, a peer, use a checklist to review a draft of your paragraph step-by-step and evaluate the separate elements to ensure a well-thought-out and organized presentation of your purpose.

7 Identify the similarities between paragraphs and essays.

What are the similarities between paragraphs and essays? (See pp. 78–79.)

Both the paragraph and the essay begin with an intro-duction that presents the topic and purpose; include supporting examples and details as well as analysis and interpretation of those examples and details; use transitions between major points to maintain flow and coherence; and end with a conclusion that reiterates the statement of purpose and provides a closing remark or idea for further thought.

LEARNING OBJECTIVES

In this chapter, you will learn how to

1 Explain what an expository essay is.

2 Define the building blocks of an essay.

3 Draft thesis statements with purpose.

4 Use transitions to achieve unity and coherence.

Thinking Critically   MyWritingLab™

Think: Look at the picture. What are these men doing? What clues do you have?

Write: Write a brief description of the mood of this picture using concrete details to explain your view.

_____

_____

_____

_____

_____

_____

_____

_____

_____

_____

_____

EXPOSITORY ESSAYS

1 Explain what an expository essay is.

Writing an essay requires having a clear purpose; providing support in the form of examples, details, and comments; and arranging the essay parts in an effective order so that you can clearly communicate your point to your intended audience. An **expository essay** (expository = to explain a purpose) has a specific format that allows you to focus on your topic and the point you want to make about it. Like an expository paragraph, it has a clear statement of purpose (thesis statement); is developed using examples, details, and analysis; has a strong conclusion; uses an organized pattern to convey information; and includes clear transitions to maintain the flow of ideas from sentence to sentence and paragraph to paragraph.

First, you need to know the audience for your essay and your subject, then you need to narrow that subject to a manageable topic.

The **subject** is the general topic you are writing about, which you need to focus into a manageable topic for the length of your essay.

The **purpose** is what you want to explain or prove related to that topic, so your **thesis** is a statement of purpose of your overall goal.

Your **audience** is the intended reader(s) of your essay—who you are addressing—so you'll need to customize both your tone (casual, informal, or more formal and academic) and the amount and types of information you include, depending on the intended audience.

An expository essay includes an **introductory paragraph** (or paragraphs, depending on the length and style of the essay); **body paragraphs**, which develop the thesis statement (purpose); and a **concluding paragraph**, which restates the purpose and adds closing remarks.

The number of paragraphs in an essay varies, depending on the scope of your topic and the goal(s) of your thesis statement. Most essays have at least four paragraphs, but an essay can have as many paragraphs as it needs. Let your topic, your goals, and your instructor's guidelines about the assignment determine the length and number of paragraphs. Do not rely on a formula with a set number of paragraphs that might limit your ideas and the goals for your essay.

Writing any type of essay, whether you are using a specific mode or combination of modes, calls for some building blocks of organization: the basic essay format.

THE BUILDING BLOCKS OF AN EXPOSITORY ESSAY

2 Define the building blocks of an essay.

The basic building blocks of an essay include the title, the introduction and thesis, the body paragraphs, and the conclusion. Once you can identify these basic building blocks in essays, you can use them to write your own essays.

Essay Title

The title for your essay is the key to introducing your topic and drawing in your reader. Aim for titles that are clear, yet interesting. You can start with a working title before you begin writing your essay, or you may not come up with a title until you have finished your first draft. Either way, the title plays an important part in making your reader interested in your essay.

> Pesky Parking Problems at Our Campus

Title Format

Your title should be centered and single-spaced. Do not use a larger font than the one for the body of your paper. Do not use bold type, underlining, or quotation marks (unless you have a quotation within your title). If you have a title with a subtitle, use a colon between the two parts.

> Too Many Students, Not Enough Spaces: The Parking Problem
> at Our Campus

ACTIVITY 5-1   Creating Catchy Titles

Directions: *For each of these statements of purpose for an essay, come up with a working title that would help draw the interest of your audience.*

1. Going to college and working part time is difficult.

   Working title: _____

2. Using the Internet for research is tricky.

   Working title: _____

3. Regular exercise can help with weight, mood, and sleep.

   Working title: _____

Introductory Paragraph(s)

The purpose of your introduction is to draw in your reader, establish your topic, and explain the purpose you want to develop—the argument or take on the subject you want to communicate. Your introduction establishes the style and tone of your essay and the kind of language and voice you will use. To create a successful introduction, include the following elements:

Opening Line(s)/Attention-Grabber

Your essay's first sentence or two should intrigue your readers and introduce the subject of your paper. Here are some techniques for accomplishing this goal:

1. **Begin with a rhetorical question:**

   When was the last time you spent over 20 minutes trying to find on-campus parking?

   ▶ **NOTE**   Usually, it is best to avoid the second-person ("you") point of view in an essay because it is too informal for most essay topics and purposes, but opening an essay with a rhetorical question is a widely used exception.

2. **Begin with a declaration:**

   Campus parking has gotten out of hand.

3. **Begin with a definition, a statistic, or a quotation:**   Define a key term, present a powerful statistic related to your topic, or use an intriguing quotation to hook your readers.

   There is one parking spot for every ten students at our campus.

   ▶ **NOTE**   If you use a definition, statistic, or quotation, you must give credit to its source or you could be accused of plagiarism.

4. **Begin with a poignant detail or example:**

   Most students at our campus wait at least 20 minutes for a parking space if they arrive between the hours of 9:00 AM and noon.

   ▶ **NOTE**   If it is a detail you learned through research, you'll have to cite your source.

5. **Begin with a creative scenario or anecdote:**

   Imagine your first day at a new college. You pull into the main parking lot 15 minutes before your first class is scheduled to begin. However, as soon as you enter, you see at least 20 cars circling the very full lot.

Again, be cautious about using the second-person point of view—"you"—in your essay. Most essays should be in third person (*he, she, they, people,* etc.), but first person (*I/me, we/us*) might be used for a personal example; second person should only be used for rhetorical questions or attention grabbers such as the examples shown above.

▶ **NOTE**   Avoid using a generalized dramatic statement for your opening line. For instance, "All people feel the need to drive their own cars." You may be wrong, and this statement is too broad. Also, avoid formulaic introductory sentences such as "In today's society" or "Throughout history . . ." or "According to the dictionary . . . ." Your teacher has probably seen these formulaic openers hundreds of times, and they either lose their power or are too exaggerated to be credible.

General Background on the Topic

Provide some general information about your topic and begin narrowing down to your focused thesis statement. Sometimes you need to provide background information about the problem or subject for your audience and give a brief history of the issue to give context for the point you want to make. For instance, if you were writing about the parking problem at your campus for an audience from your campus only, you may need just a little background, more of a reminder really, about the parking problem. However, if your audience is the general public, including many readers who don't attend your campus, you would have to give specific details and background on the growth and severity of the parking issue at your campus.

Thesis Statement

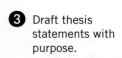
3 Draft thesis statements with purpose.

A good thesis statement establishes the narrowed scope of your topic, provides at least one controlling idea or analytical purpose the essay will develop, and gives a basic "map" to let your readers know how you will structure and develop your ideas.

You want to write a thesis statement that explains exactly the purpose for your essay. A good thesis statement has a message to convey: It makes a claim. A thesis always includes your opinion, not just facts or details. Your thesis statement is the conclusion you've come to about your topic; therefore, *it is what you want your readers to understand about your topic.*

For essays that are one to four pages long, most thesis statements will be one sentence. Here is a thesis statement that includes the answers to the questions mentioned in the Applying Critical Thinking box on page 87:

[*What?*] Our campus has a serious parking problem [*How?*] because we have far more students than parking spots, [*So what?*] so our college needs to build a second parking lot.

APPLYING CRITICAL THINKING

| PURPOSE | IDEAS | SUPPORT | ASSUMPTIONS BIASES | CONCLUSIONS | POINT OF VIEW | ANALYSIS |

Ask yourself these critical thinking questions to create a strong thesis statement:

1. *What* is the **purpose** of my essay?

2. *How* will I develop it?

3. *So what* do I want to explain or prove to my readers through this essay?

Asking and answering these questions forces you to create a specific and well-developed thesis statement that addresses *what* the purpose of your essay is, *how* the essay will be developed (plan of development or essay map), and *so what* (the point you want to prove).

Remember, though, that your thesis statement should not be a question or a series of questions; it should be your *answers* to the questions you want to address on the topic. Also, avoid awkward announcements such as "In this essay, I will attempt to show you that parking is a serious problem at our campus." Instead, simply state your point: "Parking is a serious problem at our campus." In fact, throughout your essay, don't begin statements with phrases such as *I believe*, *I feel*, or *I think* because they imply that the essay will contain only your opinions, not facts or evidence. You can use "I" in expository essays, but use it only when you are giving a personal experience as a supporting detail. For instance, "I once drove around the parking lot for over 30 minutes." Also, it is best to avoid indecisive statements in essays such as "It seems that . . ." because such language weakens your argument by making you seem unsure.

Finally, your thesis needs to be narrow enough to be developed thoroughly in the essay, but it cannot be too broad to be covered in sufficient detail in the projected length of your essay.

ACTIVITY 5-2 Thesis Practice

Directions: *Create a thesis statement that is neither too broad nor too narrow and that provides an opinion and purpose to pull together the three supporting points listed for each of the following thesis statements.*

> **Thesis:** _Small-breed dogs share many characteristics with their larger-breed counterparts._
>
> a. Chihuahuas may be tiny, but they tend to form packs like bigger dogs.
> b. Miniature greyhounds are fast, like their larger-version breed.
> c. Toy poodles, like the standard poodle, are dogs with strict rules for breeding.

1. **Thesis:** _____

   a. Jazz music makes people feel relaxed.
   b. Rock 'n roll music creates a festive mood.
   c. Classical music is intellectually stimulating and calming.

2. **Thesis:** _____

   a. Hybrid cars get better gas mileage.
   b. Technology for hybrid cars is improving.
   c. Hybrid cars are better for air quality.

3. **Thesis:** _____

   a. Ceramics is one type of art class offered at my college.
   b. Students can take many levels of photography classes at my college.
   c. Drawing classes are offered every semester at my college.

---

4 Use transitions to achieve unity and coherence.

IDEAS

SUPPORT

ANALYSIS

Body Paragraphs

The function of body paragraphs is to develop the purpose and arguments presented in your introduction and thesis statement. Each body paragraph has a topic sentence based on a subtopic or idea derived from the thesis that it develops and supports with examples, details, and analysis. The purpose of the body of your paper is to provide the evidence to back up the arguments in your thesis. The number of sentences in a body paragraph varies, depending on the topic sentence and its scope; most body paragraphs range from 4 to 15 sentences in length. The number of body paragraphs in an essay varies based on the topic, your purpose, your plan for development or essay map, and the tasks and length requirements of your writing assignment.

Be sure that your body paragraphs provide the basic elements needed for a stand-alone paragraph:

Cross Reference
See Chapter 4, pp. 61–64, The Topic Sentence, and pp. 70–74, Paragraph Structures.

- **A Topic Sentence:** The controlling idea for that body paragraph based on the overall thesis. Create your topic sentences to develop aspects of your essay's overall thesis and purpose.
- **Development:** Elaboration on your purpose, ideas, and analysis
- **Support:** Ample examples and evidence for and analysis of your ideas
- **Unity:** Each sentence helps to support the topic sentence.
- **Coherence:** The sentences and ideas flow smoothly from one to the next with a logical order and appropriate transitions between sentences, if needed, and between body paragraphs.
- **A Concluding Sentence:** The concluding sentence in a body paragraph sums up and relates back to the topic sentence and may also serve as a transition to the next body paragraph.

ACTIVITY 5-3 Creating Topic Sentences from Your Essay Thesis

Directions: *Create three topic sentences for each of the thesis statements provided below.*

> **Thesis:** Traveling to foreign countries calls for an open mind and a sense of adventure.
>
> **Topic sentence 1:** *To begin with, you may have to learn the basics of another language and be willing to sound silly trying it out.*
>
> **Topic sentence 2:** *Also, you may be exposed to new and unusual foods as you travel.*
>
> **Topic sentence 3:** *You may experience differences in customs and behaviors that require an open mind and a good sense of humor.*

1. **Thesis:** Electronic books, or ebooks, are more popular now for many reasons.

   Topic sentence 1: _____

   _____

Topic sentence 2: _____

_____

Topic sentence 3: _____

_____

2. **Thesis:** Strong math skills help in most careers and in day-to-day tasks.

   Topic sentence 1: _____

   _____

   Topic sentence 2: _____

   _____

   Topic sentence 3: _____

   _____

3. **Thesis:** Technology has created many new and intriguing career opportunities.

   Topic sentence 1: _____

   _____

   Topic sentence 2: _____

   _____

   Topic sentence 3: _____

   _____

Cross Reference
See Chapter 4, pp. 64–69, Support and Analysis, for help to create well-developed and well-supported paragraphs.

After you have created topic sentences customized to your thesis statement, it's time to write your body paragraphs.

Unity and the Art of Achieving Coherence with Transitions

Good writing flows smoothly from one point to the next with nothing out of place. When writing an essay, it is important to maintain both **unity** (every detail belongs) and **coherence** (a smooth flow from one point to the next). Transitional words, phrases, or sentences provide the bridges that help the text flow smoothly from sentence to sentence or paragraph to paragraph. They are the mortar that holds the building blocks together.

Unity

Unity means that each sentence you've included in your essay helps develop the point you have set out to make. In order to achieve unity, each paragraph must support and develop your essay's thesis statement. Also, within the paragraphs, each sentence must develop or support the topic sentence or controlling idea of that paragraph. For example, which sentence in this paragraph does not belong?

(1) Italian food is comfort food. (2) To begin with, most Italian food is loaded with carbohydrates, which are fundamental for that feeling of comfort from food. (3) Pasta, a main staple in Italian food, is full of carbohydrates and is satisfying and delicious. (4) Spaghetti, for instance, is one of the most famous Italian pasta dishes. (5) Moreover, lasagna is a delicious pasta dish, and it satisfies the cheese lover, too. (6) Enchiladas, though a Mexican dish, are a great comfort dish, too. (7) Also, ravioli, one of my favorite Italian specialties, is an excellent comfort food choice. Indeed, most pasta dishes confirm the belief that Italian food equals comfort food.

Did you spot the sentence that didn't belong in this paragraph? The sentence that does not support the topic sentence (and interferes with the unity of this paragraph) is sentence number 6. Enchiladas are a Mexican dish, and, therefore, this sentence does not support the idea that Italian food is comfort food. Not all unity errors will be this easy to spot. Sometimes, you will find you have changed direction or switched focus in a very subtle way while writing your first draft.

ACTIVITY 5-4 Test for Unity

Directions: *Read the paragraph and underline the two sentences that do not belong (that do not directly support and develop the topic sentence). Then explain briefly, on the lines provided, why they don't belong in this paragraph.*

(1) Taking classes online gives students who work full time or are stay-at-home parents the opportunity to complete their educational goals. (2) Before distance learning and online class offerings, students had no choice but to physically attend college classes or try to find limited, old-fashioned correspondence courses. (3) With the arrival of the Internet age, students with limited schedules or children at home have more opportunities to attend college. (4) For instance, students who work full time can sign up for an online class and "attend" the course on their own schedule. (5) Employers, too, will be happy because

workers schedules can be more flexible. (6) Moreover, online classes give at-home parents more chances to take college courses without worrying about expensive daycare. (7) Stay-at-home moms and dads can take the college courses they need while still being home with their children. (8) Some fathers even choose to be the main at-home parent. (9) The Internet and distance-learning opportunities have made scheduling classes much easier for students who work or who are parents.

Sentences that don't belong: _____

Explain why: _____

_____

To check your own writing for unity, go through your entire first draft to make sure that each sentence belongs in each particular paragraph and in the essay as a whole. To help you accomplish this task, ask yourself the following questions:

1. Does every sentence in each paragraph support or develop the topic sentence?
2. Does each paragraph in my essay support my thesis?
3. Does every sentence in this draft develop my thesis statement?

If you answer no to any of these questions, go back to your essay and revise or delete the sentences and/or paragraphs that don't directly support your thesis or topic sentences.

Coherence and Transitions

Coherence means that every sentence in each paragraph and each paragraph in an essay flows smoothly from one point to the next. Coherence relates to the order of development you choose for your paragraph or essay and involves the use of transitions between key sentences and between paragraphs in an essay. **Transitions** are words, phrases, or sometimes even complete sentences that help move the reader smoothly from one point to the next. They point readers in the direction you want them to take. Transitions are necessary both *within* paragraphs and *between* them. When a transitional word, phrase, or sentence is used to connect one paragraph to the next, the transition can come at the end of the previous paragraph or at the beginning of the next, whichever works best for your purpose and organization.

Here is a list of transitional words or phrases categorized by type for use in paragraphs and essays:

TRANSITIONS TO . . .

Introduce Another Point

again	but also	in addition	nor
also	equally important	last	plus the fact
and	finally	lastly	second
and then	first	likewise	then too
another	further	moreover	third
besides	furthermore	next	too

Show Contrast or a Change in Idea

although	even though	instead	on the other side
anyhow	for all that	nevertheless	otherwise
at the same time	however	notwithstanding	regardless
but	in any event	on the contrary	still
despite this	in contrast	on the other hand	yet

Show a Comparison

in like manner	in the same way	likewise	similarly

Show Summary or Repetition

as has been noted	in closing	in other words	on the whole
as I have said	in conclusion	in short	to conclude
in brief	in essence	in summary	to sum up

Illustrate or Give Examples/Specifics

a few include	essentially	in particular	the following
an example	for example	let us consider	specifically
especially	for instance	the case of	you can see this in

Continued ▶

TRANSITIONS TO . . .

Strengthen a Point

basically	indeed	truly	without a doubt
essentially	irrefutably	undeniably	without question

Show Result or Cause/Effect Relationships

accordingly	consequently	since	therefore
as a result	for this reason	so	thereupon
because	hence	then	thus

Explain a Purpose

all things considered	for this reason	to accomplish	with this in mind
for this purpose	in order to	to this end	with this objective

Locate a Place (Usually Prepositions)

above	beside	inside	outside
across	between	nearer	over
adjacent to	beyond	nearly	there
below	farther	next to	through
beneath	here	opposite	under

Show Time

after	before	in the meantime	not long after
afterward	between	later	soon
at last	first	meanwhile	then
at length	immediately	next	while

Show Amount

a great deal	less than	most	smaller
few	many	over	some
greater	more than	several	under

ACTIVITY 5-5 Provide Transitions

Directions: *Choose transitions from the tables above, or use a transition of your own, to fill in the blanks below and help this paragraph flow more smoothly.*

Advertisements often convey messages that negatively affect women's self-esteem. _____, advertisements in magazines often depict women as extremely thin. _____, the message is women must be thin to be beautiful. _____, television commercials often depict women in the home using some form of cleaning product. _____, one commercial has a woman dancing romantically with her mop in a perfectly clean kitchen. _____, the message to men and women is that women should do the cleaning. _____, they should enjoy the cleaning. _____, many magazine and television ads push cosmetics and hair products and feature glamorous, heavily made-up women. _____, women feel pressured to buy these products in order to be as glamorous as the women in these ads. These forms of advertising, _____, convey messages to women that can hurt their self-worth and self-perception.

ACTIVITY 5-6 Improving Coherence

Directions: *Read the following list of sentences about starting an on-campus club. Next, arrange the list of sentences into the most logical order, and then create a paragraph with those sentences using transitional words and phrases when needed to help the flow.*

1. Create officer positions with clear job descriptions.
2. Find a faculty advisor.
3. Find out if other students are interested in starting up the club with you.
4. Write a mission statement and/or definition of vision for your club.
5. Create and post fliers to recruit more members.

6. Plan activities for the year.

7. Have an election to choose officers for your club after you have created the descriptions of duties.

8. Find a meeting time that works for all members, and set a regular time.

_____

_____

_____

_____

_____

_____

The Concluding Sentence in Each Body Paragraph

The concluding sentence sums up the purpose and main idea of a body paragraph. It pulls all your ideas and purpose from that paragraph together in a finished product. In a complete essay, the concluding sentence of a body paragraph may also include a transition to your next body paragraph, although usually the transition appears at the beginning of the next paragraph.

> As you can see, the current parking situation has gotten out of hand at our campus.

Sometimes the concluding sentence in a body paragraph serves both as a close for one paragraph or idea and an introduction to the next example, idea, or concept you want to discuss.

Concluding Paragraph

The concluding paragraph sums up the main purpose of your essay, re-emphasizing your thesis (without repeating it word for word) and providing an overall sense of conclusion. Most successful concluding paragraphs are at least three sentences long, but they can be several sentences longer, depending on the scope of the thesis and the assignment. Regardless, they should be succinct and end with a "ta-da!"—an overall sense of wrapping up and reiterating your essay's purpose. Simply re-emphasize your thesis, add a few general comments related to your topic, and avoid introducing a new idea.

▶ NOTE   Be sure to avoid the common pitfall of introducing a new idea or contradicting yourself in the conclusion: the "shoot yourself in the foot" effect.

> As you can see, the parking problem at our campus is bad, but the lack of class offerings at night is an even worse problem.

By introducing a whole new idea, this ending belittles the importance of the chosen topic.

Putting It All Together

Once you are familiar with how to use the building blocks of an essay and the transitions that help ideas flow smoothly, you are ready to create well-organized and well-developed essays. After you have written a complete draft of an essay, use the Checklist for the Building Blocks on page 101 to make sure you have included all the necessary building blocks while maintaining unity and coherence.

BASIC ESSAY STRUCTURE: A QUICK REVIEW

INTRODUCTORY PARAGRAPH

Opening Line/Attention Grabber: Designed to draw in your readers

General Background for the Topic: The setup

Thesis Statement (or Statement of Purpose): Your thesis statement expresses the purpose of your essay. It outlines what you plan to explain to your readers about your subject; it's the conclusion you've reached about the topic.

Ask yourself these questions to create a strong thesis statement:

- *What* am I writing about?
- *How* will I demonstrate my purpose? What is my plan of development?
- *So what* is the main conclusion I've reached about my topic? What do I want my readers to know?

BODY PARAGRAPHS

Topic Sentence: Main idea for the paragraph and develops the thesis

Support: Backs up your topic sentence idea with evidence, facts, or opinions (1–3 support statements per body paragraph)

■ **Examples:** One or two examples to illustrate each idea

■ **Details:** One or more details to illustrate and explain each example

■ **Analysis/Commentary:** Analysis and commentary on the importance of the supporting examples and details and how they illustrate the topic sentence

■ **Concluding Sentence:** Sums up the main idea of the topic sentence, provides ideas for further thought, or serves as a transition to the next paragraph

Include these elements in each body paragraph in your essay. You should use transitions at the end of one body paragraph or at the beginning of the next to make your essay flow smoothly.

CONCLUDING PARAGRAPH

Re-emphasizes your essay's thesis without restating it: Reminds your reader of your thesis and sums up your main points

■ Sums up your analytical conclusions

■ Ends with closing ideas for further thought

▸ **NOTE**   Do not introduce any contradictory ideas in the concluding paragraph (ideas that go against your previous opinions or purpose).

Student Essay

Here is a sample draft essay modeling the building blocks put together.

Grant 1

Lina Lopez

English 100

Argument Essay

November 20, 2013

Pesky Parking Problems at Our Campus

Most students at our campus wait at least 20 minutes for

a parking space if they arrive between the hours of 8:00 AM and

Grant 2

noon. Searching for a parking spot creates stress before one even gets to class and is not a good way to start a productive day of learning. Overall, our campus has a serious parking problem because we have far more students than parking spots, so our college needs to build a second parking lot.

To begin with, due to a growth in student enrollment, we have more students than we have parking spaces, and this imbalance has caused many problems. Over the past 40 years, since the existing parking structures were first built, our campus enrollment has nearly doubled. According to our campus's *New Student Handbook*, we have over 10,000 students; however, we have only 5,000 parking spaces. Therefore, when we look at the numbers, we can see that the growth of our campus has created the current parking crisis: The number of parking spaces simply has not kept up with the population growth. This large increase in the number of students has put an unmanageable burden on existing parking lots and parking staff.

The parking problem at our campus is also increasing student stress and dissatisfaction. When one enters the campus parking lot in the morning, one commonly sees students driving around the lots or lining up and waiting for someone to return to his or her vehicle. Often, students are late for class, even if they have arrived on campus 30 minutes before class starts. Some teachers are understanding, but many do not tolerate tardiness, even though they know about the parking situation. The parking issue is therefore increasing student dissatisfaction with our college. The stress and inconvenience of the lack of parking has caused students to feel unhappy with the college as a whole.

The parking issue seeps into the overall satisfaction rating of the college. In surveys, students almost always cite the parking issue as one of their main concerns. The college estimates that as much as five percent of the students who start college every fall switch to another campus due to dissatisfaction with some aspect of our campus. Parking has to be among the top of those issues. Not enough has been done about the problem, and, if the college doesn't act soon, it will soon begin to lose more students over the issue.

Therefore, the college needs to build a second parking lot at our campus. Carpooling and alternative forms of transportation have not been enough to resolve the problem of too many students and not enough spaces. Many students cannot carpool due to work and daycare schedules. Even though it will cost money, a new parking lot is the only way to get the balance right. Unfortunately, because the state does not fund parking lots, the college must either increase students' tuition slightly or charge students a limited-time parking fee to cover the costs of the new lot. Many students will not like paying more, but the benefits will outweigh the minor increase in fees. For example, the college could implement a $10 a quarter parking fee for five years to cover the costs. Being able to drive to campus and find a parking spot right away will relieve a lot of stress and make the small monetary sacrifice worthwhile.

Our campus parking problem has gotten out of hand, and it must be solved by adding more parking spaces. The student population has continually increased, and, therefore, the problem has gotten progressively worse. The only way to solve the issue is

Grant 4

to build another parking lot, and the satisfaction and relief that will come from the resolution of our parking issues will make the situation better for students and staff alike.

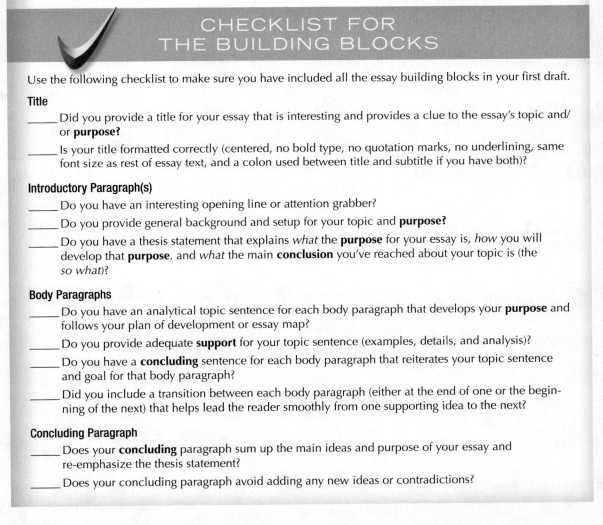

CHECKLIST FOR THE BUILDING BLOCKS

Use the following checklist to make sure you have included all the essay building blocks in your first draft.

Title

_____ Did you provide a title for your essay that is interesting and provides a clue to the essay's topic and/ or **purpose?**

_____ Is your title formatted correctly (centered, no bold type, no quotation marks, no underlining, same font size as rest of essay text, and a colon used between title and subtitle if you have both)?

Introductory Paragraph(s)

_____ Do you have an interesting opening line or attention grabber?

_____ Do you provide general background and setup for your topic and **purpose?**

_____ Do you have a thesis statement that explains *what* the **purpose** for your essay is, *how* you will develop that **purpose**, and *what* the main **conclusion** you've reached about your topic is (the *so what*)?

Body Paragraphs

_____ Do you have an analytical topic sentence for each body paragraph that develops your **purpose** and follows your plan of development or essay map?

_____ Do you provide adequate **support** for your topic sentence (examples, details, and analysis)?

_____ Do you have a **concluding** sentence for each body paragraph that reiterates your topic sentence and goal for that body paragraph?

_____ Did you include a transition between each body paragraph (either at the end of one or the beginning of the next) that helps lead the reader smoothly from one supporting idea to the next?

Concluding Paragraph

_____ Does your **concluding** paragraph sum up the main ideas and purpose of your essay and re-emphasize the thesis statement?

_____ Does your concluding paragraph avoid adding any new ideas or contradictions?

Learning Objectives Review

MyWritingLab™   Complete the chapter assessment questions at mywritinglab.com

❶ Explain what an expository essay is. **What is an expository essay? (See p. 83.)**	**An expository essay is** an essay with a specific purpose or point to make that must be developed using examples, details, and analysis.
❷ Define the building blocks of an essay. **What are the building blocks of an essay? (See pp. 83–86.)**	The **building blocks** of an essay are the title, the introductory paragraph, the thesis statement, the body paragraphs, and the concluding paragraph.
❸ Draft thesis statements with purpose. **How do you write thesis statements with a purpose? (See pp. 86–88.)**	A good **thesis statement** establishes the narrowed scope of your topic, provides at least one controlling idea or analytical purpose the essay will develop, and gives a basic "map" to let your readers know how you will structure and develop your ideas.
❹ Use transitions to achieve unity and coherence. **What do unity and coherence mean, and what are transitions? (See pp. 88–96.)**	**Unity** means that each sentence you've included in your essay helps develop the point you have set out to make. **Coherence** means that every sentence in each paragraph and each paragraph in an essay flows smoothly from one point to the next. Coherence relates to the order of development you choose for your paragraph or essay and involves the use of transitions between key sentences and between paragraphs in an essay. **Transitions** are words, phrases, or sometimes even complete sentences that help move the reader smoothly from one point to the next.

LEARNING OBJECTIVES

In this chapter, you will learn how to

1 Define the five stages of the essay-writing process.

2 Prewrite to establish your subject, purpose, and audience.

3 Create a thesis statement and rough outline.

4 Write a first draft.

5 Revise your essay.

6 Proofread your essay.

Thinking Critically · MyWritingLab™

Think: Think about the steps involved in making a folded paper fortuneteller like this.

Write:

1. What habits do you have when you sit down to do any kind of writing?

_____

_____

_____

_____

2. Of those habits, which are most effective for you and why, and which are not and why?

_____

_____

_____

_____

ESSAY WRITING IN FIVE STAGES

① Define the five stages of the essay-writing process.

Can you imagine building a house without first coming up with a plan and then, after the structure is erected, not finishing the house with paint and furnishings? Yet many students write a first draft without prewriting or planning and then hand it in without revising or editing. Writing a strong expository essay is a process that requires critical thinking and developing your ideas in stages. If you become aware of your process and tune it, it will become easier with practice to write essays that are well organized and fully developed and successfully present your arguments.

Basically, the writing process includes five major stages:

1. **Stage One: Prewriting.** Generate ideas and establish your paper's purpose.

2. **Stage Two: Organizing.** Organize your ideas and develop a plan or outline for presenting your purpose and ideas.

3. **Stage Three: Drafting.** Create a first draft of your essay based on your plan from Stage Two; develop support for your essay's purpose.

4. **Stage Four: Revising.** Reassess your draft for content, development, organization, and support (examples and details).

5. **Stage Five: Editing.** Check for sentence-level effectiveness, style, diction, grammar, and spelling errors. Edit your draft and ask your peers to as well.

Remember that you can for the most part change the order of these stages—this process is a tool—and decide what works best for you in each writing task. In fact, over time, most writers figure out what writing process works best for them and which steps of the writing process they can switch, modify, or even skip completely. You may modify the process differently from assignment to assignment; however, until you have developed a writing process that works for you and produces fully developed, well-organized, well-written essays, try this traditional approach to the stages of the writing process. The key is to analyze what works and to think critically about your ideas and how best to develop them in your essay.

STAGE ONE: PREWRITE TO GENERATE IDEAS

② Prewrite to establish your subject, purpose, and audience.

To begin, you must figure out your assignment and decide on your subject, purpose, and audience. Using these three elements, you will develop a more specific topic, thesis, plan for development, and appropriate tone and style for your essay.

APPLYING CRITICAL THINKING

PURPOSE IDEAS SUPPORT ASSUMPTIONS BIASES CONCLUSIONS POINT OF VIEW ANALYSIS

Use your critical thinking skills throughout the writing process. As you go through these stages, be sure to keep in mind your **purpose**, the information (**ideas**, **support**) you will need to develop that purpose, the implications of your ideas and arguments, the **assumptions** you make, the **point of view** you are expressing, and the audience you are writing for.

You can use several techniques to generate ideas, narrow your topic, determine your purpose, and organize your ideas, including thinking about your topic, freewriting, mapping, brainstorming, clustering, journaling, and outlining. Everyone's writing process is different; try these techniques, and figure out which ones work best for you. Some people prefer to do their prewriting on paper using a pen or pencil, and some prefer to use their computer to type brainstormed lists or rough outlines. Others like to use the columns function of their word processing program to create categories and brainstorm within these separate categories. Discover what works for you.

Thinking and Talking

As soon as you get your assignment or choose your topic, begin thinking about it. Some prewriting happens in your head before you even put pen to paper. Talk it out with a classmate or friend if you can. Ask yourself, "What do I want to accomplish in this paper?" "What do I have to say about this subject?" "What aspect of this subject am I most interested in, and how do I want to narrow it down to a manageable topic?" "What are some questions or issues related to this subject I can address?"

Freewriting

Freewriting is a popular technique for generating ideas and narrowing your topic. When you **freewrite**, you just put pen to paper and let the ideas flow without worrying about spelling, grammar, or "dumb" ideas. As you freewrite, don't judge your work; you can sort out the good material from the bad later.

I know I want to write about adopting an unwanted pet instead of buying one at the pet store . . . let me see . . . I have lots of reasons why I feel this way . . . hmmm, some of them include all the unwanted animals that get put down or go without companionship, oh yeah, also, the money for adopting pets goes into spaying and neutering cats and dogs so there are not even more unwanted pets created

Mapping

Mapping is a way to literally map out your essay plan and the structure of your essay. You can map using boxes and arrows, a flowchart, or whatever works best for your style.

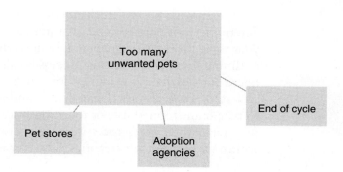

▶ **TIP**   Computer software designed for generating ideas and mapping is available on most college campuses.

Brainstorming

Brainstorming is a free-flowing, free-association list of words or ideas that you write to get the ideas flowing. As in freewriting, you need to turn off your inner editor and just jot down as many ideas and details or even associations related to your subject or assigned writing prompt as you can.

Unwanted pets, pets for profits, unspayed or neutered pets, animals put to sleep, dogs, cats, rabbits, hamsters, rats, mice, ferrets, adoption agencies, pet stores, choosing to get pets from rescue centers over pet stores, ending the cycle

Clustering

Clustering is another way to represent your ideas visually. You can circle your main subject and then draw lines to further circles around connected ideas or subtopics. Each subtopic should have its own cluster of connected circles.

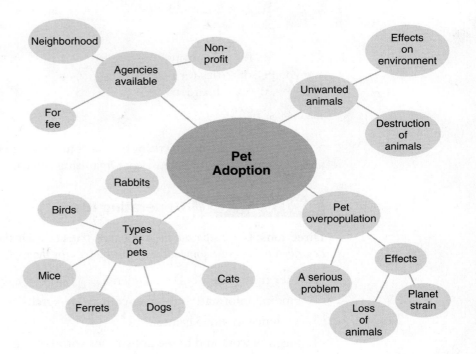

Journaling

Journaling involves writing your thoughts down in a journal. Some instructors will require you to keep a writer's journal to jot down ideas and record the steps in your writing process. You can also start a journal on your own to write down ideas as you think of them—that way, your thoughts can be collected in one place even though they may come to you in bits and pieces over the course of a few days.

Outlining

Outlining involves writing a list of main topics and subtopics using a formal, numbered structure. See Stage Two on pages 128–129 for a sample detailed outline and information about how to structure a full outline. During prewriting, you might create a very skeletal, brief outline containing just the main ideas and a few key supporting ideas; probably you wouldn't have all the details worked out yet as you would in a complete outline. A prewriting outline might look something like this:

> I. Snowboarding
>   A. Costs
>   B. Best Locations
> II. Skiing
>   A. Costs
>   B. Best Locations
> III. Personalities for Both Sports
>   A. Snowboarders
>   B. Skiers

As you can see, this prewriting outline is just a way to brainstorm main ideas and categories. During Stage Two: Organizing you can create a full outline.

ACTIVITY 6-1 Generating Ideas

Directions: *On a separate sheet of paper, practice using the prewriting techniques described to generate some ideas and subtopics for the topics provided.*

1. Your tips for new college students
2. Finding information for your courses (research)
3. Violence in video games
4. Juggling work and home obligations with college
5. Buying used items online, pros and cons

Narrowing a Subject to a Topic

After you have generated some ideas, use critical thinking to figure out a good topic that is narrow enough for the scope of your essay's purpose. For instance, if you begin with a broad subject such as "parks in our city," then you need to figure out what aspects of parks (size, location, amenities) or what kind of parks (theme parks, recreational parks, green zones) you want to focus on before you come up with exactly what you want to say (purpose). If your subject is too broad (the scope is too big), you won't be able to cover the nuances of the topic in depth, and your essay will stay too general and superficial instead of delving deeper into the topic. For instance, the topic "baseball" is too broad: Can you imagine trying to cover everything about this game in one essay? You could narrow this broad topic down to the idea of free agents in baseball.

However, if your topic is too narrow, the issue or question will not be big enough to address in your essay, so make sure your proposed topic is not a detail or fact that doesn't need development. For instance, if your topic was "A baseball is a specific kind of ball used in the game," you would have great difficulty coming up with enough description and support for a full essay.

APPLYING CRITICAL THINKING

| PURPOSE | IDEAS | SUPPORT | ASSUMPTIONS BIASES | CONCLUSIONS | POINT OF VIEW | ANALYSIS |

Ways to Narrow a Broad Subject to a Manageable Topic

Here are a few techniques that can help you move from a broad subject to a narrowed topic. They include brainstorming, which is a way to get your ideas flowing, and asking questions that help you **analyze** the subject—break it down into its different parts. The more you think about a broad subject and analyze what it is about, the better you will be able to narrow it down to a workable topic.

The subject of *volunteering* is used here to demonstrate how you can narrow a subject to a topic that would work well for a focused expository essay.

Broad Subject: Volunteering

1. Brainstorm a list of issues related to, ideas about, or types of volunteering.

   Volunteering: community service, Girl Scouts, tutoring, cleanup in neighborhood, school aide, hospitals, nursing homes, types of volunteering, benefits of volunteering

2. Ask yourself why you thought of this topic in the first place—why is it interesting or important to you?

   School aides: I am sad and surprised that local schoolteachers are not getting the support they need to help our children learn.

3. Generate a question or several questions related to the topic you chose.

   How can I get teachers at my son's school the help they need to provide successful classroom experiences? How can I get more people in our community to volunteer their time in our schools?

4. Start with a problem related to the topic.

   My son's third-grade class doesn't go on field trips or have arts-and-crafts time because of the student-to-teacher ratio: There is only one teacher for 30 students.

5. Start with a point or purpose in mind.

   I want to convince the other parents from my PTA that we need parents to get involved in the classrooms and take a more active role in helping our teachers.

ACTIVITY 6-2 Narrowing Your Topic

Directions: *The following subjects are too broad to develop into successful thesis statements. Use one or more of the techniques given to create two more focused subtopics for each broad topic listed.*

> **Topic:** Television
>
> Subtopic 1: *The unrealistic side of reality TV*
>
> Subtopic 2: *Television as an addiction*

1. **Topic:** Studying in another country

   Subtopic 1: _____

   Subtopic 2: _____

2. **Topic:** The Olympic Games

   Subtopic 1: _____

   Subtopic 2: _____

3. **Topic:** Successful study habits

   Subtopic 1: _____

   Subtopic 2: _____

4. **Topic:** YouTube

   Subtopic 1: _____

   Subtopic 2: _____

5. **Topic:** Texting

   Subtopic 1: _____

   Subtopic 2: _____

Establish Subject, Purpose, and Audience

Once you have determined the *subject* you will write about (based on an assignment or your own choice), you must narrow your subject to a manageable topic, come up with a *purpose* for writing about it, and adjust your approach and overall tone to suit your intended *audience*.

Use the flowchart below to help you move from *subject, purpose*, and *audience* to *topic, thesis*, and *tone* and/or *approach*.

Subject, Purpose, and Audience

Subject	**Purpose**	**Audience**
A broad subject that you chose or was assigned to you.	What do you want to *explain* or *prove* about your topic?	Who is your target audience? Instructor? Classmates? Other?
For example: "Music"	What point do you want to make?	Is your essay appropriate for your target audience?
	For example: I want to argue that lipsyncing should never be allowed at live concerts.	

▼ ▼ ▼

Topic	**Thesis**	**Tone/approach**
A narrowed aspect of your subject, for example, "Lipsyncing at Concerts"	**What** are you arguing? **How** will you develop that argument? **So what?** What is the significance of your conclusion or argument?	Modify your tone and your approach based on your audience.
	For example: Lipsyncing at concerts should not be allowed, and there should be serious fines if it happens.	For example: My classmates and instructor are my target audience, so I will use a semiformal approach.

Purpose and Approach

Sometimes, just narrowing your topic will lead you to your essay's purpose, and you'll be able to create a thesis statement effortlessly. Otherwise, once you have narrowed your subject to a manageable topic, the next step is to come up with your essay's purpose (what you want to explain or prove to your readers about your topic) and how you will approach it. To create a more analytical thesis, consider the questions in the Applying Critical Thinking box.

APPLYING CRITICAL THINKING

PURPOSE | IDEAS | SUPPORT | ASSUMPTIONS BIASES | CONCLUSIONS | POINT OF VIEW | ANALYSIS

Critical thinking will help you develop a **purpose** or **blueprint** for constructing your essay. Your purpose should be clear and consistent from the beginning to the end of your essay. Everything you include should develop that purpose. Knowing what you want to say will help you write a clear, precise thesis statement. Ask yourself these questions to determine your purpose for writing:

1. What is my **point of view** (**perspective**)? What do I think or believe about this topic? What do I want to explain or prove to my reader?

2. What questions do I want to address (or problem I need to solve) in my essay, and how will I develop my **ideas**?

3. What **assumptions** or **biases** do I have about the topic? What ideas do I take for granted? Is my point of view based on correct information?

4. What **evidence (support)** can I use to back up my ideas and purpose (e.g., personal experience, facts, outside evidence or research)?

5. Have I **analyzed** the topic and broken down all its parts? Do I have a clear **point** or **argument** to make about the topic?

ACTIVITY 6-3   Identifying Your Purpose and Approach to a Topic

Directions: *Choose one of the narrowed topics you came up with in Activity 6-2. Answer the following questions to develop a sense of what your purpose would be for writing about the topic and how you would approach it.*

1. Based on the narrowed idea you chose from Activity 6-2, what would be your purpose or goal if you wrote an essay on this topic?

   _____

   _____

   _____

2. What *questions* would you attempt to address in the essay?

   _____

   _____

   _____

3. Is there a *problem* (or problems) you would attempt to solve or address in the essay? If so, what is it?

   _____

   _____

   _____

4. What *evidence* (support) could you use to back your ideas and purpose (e.g., personal experience, facts, outside evidence or research)?

   _____

   _____

   _____

5. What is your point of view (perspective) about the topic, and what assumptions or biases do you already have related to the subject?

   _____

   _____

   _____

Assessing Your Audience

Another key question to ask yourself before writing your essay draft is, "Who am I writing this essay for?"

Who is going to be reading your essay, and how will you adjust your writing to speak best to that target audience? If you are writing about how to register for classes successfully, then your target audience is probably your professor and other students in college. If you are writing about getting a degree in nursing and the prerequisite classes needed, then your target audience is a more narrow group of students. Thinking about who you are writing for will make your writing more focused and will help you make good choices as you write.

Determine your target audience so you can write your essay using the correct approach and tone.

Types of Audience

General—all types of people

Academic—college students and faculty

Specialized—specific to a certain field or background, such as nursing students or the instructor for a class you are taking

Based on your target audience, assess how much background information on the topic you will have to provide, what level of vocabulary you will use (and how many specialized terms you'll need to define), what approach and tone (more serious/formal, casual/playful, or somewhere in between) would work best, and how much evidence you'll need to provide to persuade your readers.

ACTIVITY 6-4   **Adjusting Your Approach for an Intended Audience**

Topic: *Increasing violence on college campuses*
   Audience 1: Other college students
   Audience 2: Parents of college students
   Audience 3: State legislators

Directions: *How would you need to adjust your tone, approach, amount of background information, and even purpose for these three different audiences?*

_____

_____

_____

_____

_____

_____

After you have determined the target audience for your essay, choose an appropriate tone and choose sentence structures and vocabulary that match it.

ACTIVITY 6-5 Finding the Right Tone

Directions: *For each of the topics given, determine a suitable audience. Then explain the type of tone you would use (formal or informal) and briefly explain why.*

> **Topic:** Lack of hospitals in our state
>
> Potential target audience: *The state legislature (senators)*
>
> Best tone choice and reason: *Formal because I would be making a formal proposal to lawmakers and need to be taken seriously*

1. **Topic:** Online dating

   Potential target audience: _____

   Best tone choice and reason: _____

   _____

2. **Topic:** How to study for a midterm

   Potential target audience: _____

   Best tone choice and reason: _____

   _____

3. **Topic:** Tips for downloading songs onto a smartphone

   Potential target audience: _____

   Best tone choice and reason: _____

   _____

4. **Topic:** Studying abroad: pros and cons

   Potential target audience: _____

   Best tone choice and reason: _____

   _____

5. **Topic:** Safety dos and don'ts while driving

   Potential target audience: _____

   Best tone choice and reason: _____

   _____

STAGE TWO: ORGANIZE YOUR IDEAS

3 Create a thesis statement and rough outline.

Next, you need to create a basic plan for your essay and generate examples and details to support your topic. Take the ideas you've generated in the prewriting stage and fine-tune and organize them to develop them further. To help organize your ideas, try these suggestions:

1. **Think about your purpose.** Ask yourself, "What do I want to explain about my topic or prove with this essay?" "Am I arguing for a certain point of view?"

2. **Create questions about the topic.** Generate more ideas by prewriting on your subject and use these ideas to come up with some questions that you could address or answer in your essay.

3. **Delete ideas.** Delete any ideas or subtopics you generated that don't fit your topic or seem off topic or tangential.

4. **Add ideas.** As you review your prewriting, add new ideas or subtopics that didn't occur to you before.

5. **Re-brainstorm.** Brainstorm more ideas, now that your focus is more manageable. You need to create more supporting ideas now.

6. **Re-freewrite.** Freewrite again now that your ideas are more focused so you can generate specific details for your ideas.

Create a Thesis Statement

Cross Reference
See Chapter 5, pp. 86–88, Thesis Statement.

Once you have a topic, know your purpose, have identified your audience, and know what you want to say about your topic, you are ready to craft your statement of purpose—your **thesis**. A thesis statement should be a complete sentence that narrows the topic and expresses your opinion about that topic. It is what you want to explain or prove about your topic: the argument(s) you put forth. Make sure your thesis statement is broad enough that it can be developed but not so broad that it can't be developed well in a short essay.

ACTIVITY 6-6   Writing Your Thesis Statement

Directions: *Choose two of the topics from Activity 6-5 for which you assessed an audience, and write a one-sentence thesis statement in a tone that is appropriate for that audience.*

1. Thesis: _____

_____

_____

2. Thesis: _____

_____

_____

Outlines: Perfecting Your Essay's Order of Development

Now that you have generated ideas for support and have crafted a thesis statement, you are ready to create a fully developed outline of your ideas and subtopics to see how they could be put together in a first draft. An outline helps you to order your thoughts: It creates a plan for your essay's development. It's like a table of contents for each component of your essay. Outlines allow you to order your main ideas and supporting examples and details in the most logical way and, therefore, most effectively develop your essay's purpose.

Some writers create a rough outline of their papers before they've written a draft. However, even if you didn't *start* with an outline, it is a powerful tool to use *after you have written your first draft* to check and revise the organization and structure of ideas. Here is an example of a rough outline on the subject of the advantages and disadvantages of getting a pet from a pet store or a shelter:

Example Rough Outline

Topic: Adopting pets versus buying in a pet store

I. Disadvantages of pet stores
   A. For profit—therefore do not always have the best interests of pets in mind
   B. Encourage the creation of more pets for profit
   C. Favor pedigreed breeds over mixed-breed pets
II. Advantages of adoption
   A. Spaying and neutering are guaranteed
   B. Saves the lives of unwanted animals
   C. Discourages creating pets for profit
   D. Helps stop the cycle of unwanted pets

Guidelines for Structuring a Complete Outline

An outline has a consistent format, with the main ideas placed closest to the far left margin. Then the subpoints, examples, and details used to develop those main ideas are indented; the farther right your ideas are placed, the more specific or detailed is the support they provide.

If you have four main sections to develop in your essay, you'll have four main ideas. Then you can add as many subpoints, examples, and details as needed for each section to fully develop those ideas. Here are some guidelines for writing an outline:

1. **Thesis Statement:** Write your thesis statement at the top of the outline, but do not include the general introduction that will come before your thesis statement in your essay.

2. **Main Ideas:** List the main ideas (concepts for each **topic sentence**) that will be developed in the body paragraphs of your essay and label them using Roman numerals (I, II, III, and so on). Use a short phrase, not a complete sentence, to explain each main idea. Think of these phrases as titles for each paragraph of your paper. The main ideas are formatted in the left margin.

3. **Subpoints:** List the **subpoints** you will use to support the main idea/topic sentence of each paragraph using capital letters (A, B, C, and so on). Use short phrases to represent each subpoint. These subpoints are formatted one tab right from the left margin.

▶ **NOTE**   You must have at least two subpoints: If you have an A then you must have at least a B. If you have only one subpoint, then combine it with the main idea or develop a second subpoint.

4. **Support:** List supporting examples and details below each subpoint. The next level of detail is labeled with numbers (1, 2, 3, and so on). If you have details to illustrate these examples, they are labeled with lowercase letters (a, b, c, and so on). If you have yet another level of details to develop those, label them with numbers followed by a single parenthesis [1), 2), 3), and so on]. Each level of detail will also progressively tab right.

▶ **NOTE**   You must have at least two of each supporting level of information, so if you have a "1" you need at least a "2"; if you have an "a" detail under "1" then you also need a "b." If you do not have a second detail at the same level, create one or wrap the single detail into the previous example.

5. **Conclusion:** Provide a brief statement of conclusion at the end of your outline.

▶ **NOTE**   Check on campus for software that automatically creates outlines in the correct format. These tools and programs make your task easier and ensure that your format is correct.

APPLYING CRITICAL THINKING

As you design your outline, ask yourself the following questions.

1. What is the main point or **conclusion** I've made about my topic? What **purpose** do I want to convey to my readers?

2. What are the main **ideas** and **support** I will use in my paper, and in what order do I want to present them? Which evidence and examples are main examples, and which are supporting details?

3. Do I have any claims that may need more support to convince my readers of my point?

4. How will I order my main body paragraphs and my reasons for support? What is the best order of development to successfully argue my conclusions and present my evidence?

5. Are there any parts that need to be deleted, expanded upon, or rearranged? **Analyze** to see.

Finally, use the Outline Critique Checklist below to review your outline or have it peer reviewed.

OUTLINE CRITIQUE CHECKLIST

1. Does the outline start with a thesis statement? _____

2. Is the thesis statement an idea or opinion that can be developed through examples and details? Is there a clear message or point being made? _____

3. Did the author use the correct outline format (see above for outline format rules)? _____

4. Are the subtopics/sections/categories clear and explained with a short phrase? _____

5. Are the categories and subpoints detailed enough to be clear but not overly detailed? _____

6. If there is a "1" or an "A" in a category or subpoint, is it followed by at least one more point ("2" or "B")? _____

7. If secondary sources are included in the outline, can you tell how they will be used as support? _____

Comments and suggestions for revision:

_____

_____

_____

_____

_____

_____

ACTIVITY 6-7 **Creating a Rough Outline**

Directions: *Choose one of the topics you did prewriting for in the earlier activities, and generate a working thesis. Then on a separate sheet of paper, write a rough outline for an essay based on your thesis using the numbered list above.*

_____

_____

STAGE THREE: WRITE A FIRST DRAFT

 4 Write a first draft.

Time to dive in! Use your prewriting and organizing stages to create a first draft of your essay. While writing your first full draft, don't worry about spelling and grammar: You will only lose your train of thought and become derailed from the points you are making. Instead, check grammar and spelling later in the editing stage. You'll have plenty of time to check the technical stuff later: for now, create, let go, and write!

You can start by drafting a general introduction that narrows your topic, ending that first paragraph with your draft thesis statement. Then, draft your topic sentences and write your draft body paragraphs with support for those topic sentences: come up with support that will illustrate and explain your purpose. Can you provide any personal examples that would help illustrate your ideas? Are there examples from your community or your culture that would support your ideas? Should you provide some data and facts to support your ideas? (Before conducting and using research, be sure to check with your instructor to see if outside research is allowed.) Then, write a draft of your concluding paragraph that begins with a restatement of your purpose using different phrasing from your original thesis. Overall, try to structure your essay using a strong introductory paragraph and thesis statement; body paragraphs with clear topic sentences, support, and details; and a conclusion that ties everything back together. Use the ideas and details you generated in Stages 1 and 2 to support your ideas.

ACTIVITY 6-8 Developing Support for Your Topic

Directions: *Using the same narrowed topic you chose for Activity 6-2, provide some examples you could use for support.*

1. Example 1: _____

   _____

2. Example 2: _____

   _____

3. Example 3: _____

   _____

ACTIVITY 6-9 Write a First Draft

Directions: *Use the ideas you generated from prewriting, your rough outline, and your answers to Activity 6-8 to write a rough draft of your essay (375–500 words) and give it a title.*

STAGE FOUR: REVISE AND EDIT YOUR DRAFT

5 Revise your essay.

Revision has several steps. Here's your chance to take that first draft you created and polish it into a strong, well-organized, well-supported final product.

Revision

Although revision is the most crucial stage of the writing process, it is the one that students skip more than any other. Few writers are such naturals that they crank out perfect first drafts. Most writers need several drafts to accomplish a well-designed, well-written, and well-supported essay. Many students mistake revising for proofreading. In revision, you focus on improving organization, style, and content, whereas in proofreading (Stage Five), you focus on fixing grammar and spelling errors.

Edit for Organization and Style

Essay writing is recursive (a process of going back and reworking what you have written): Revision is the key to excellence in content and delivery. Think critically about the use of order, unity, coherence, and sentence variety in your draft. During revision, check the order of your paragraphs and the details within them; move things that need to be moved, and delete things that don't belong. Make sure your paragraphs have enough support from examples and details to develop their topic sentences. Check that each paragraph develops the thesis of your paper and each sentence in each paragraph develops the topic sentence. Ensure your essay flows smoothly by adding appropriate transitional words or phrases where needed, and check to make sure that you have varied your sentence lengths and sentence types.

Use the following checklist to make sure you revise all the elements of your essay:

REVISION CHECKLIST

_____ Restructure paragraph order, if needed.
_____ Delete unnecessary words, sentences, ideas, or details.
_____ Add more support (examples and details) to fully develop your topic sentences.
_____ Add transitions between paragraphs and between sentences where needed (see pp. 93–94 for potential transitional phrases).
_____ Check for sentence variety.

ACTIVITY 6-10 Revision

Directions: *On a separate sheet of paper, revise your essay draft using the Revision Checklist in Stage Four.*

Edit for Content

Fine-tune your thesis and topic sentences. Make sure that your thesis statement is analytical, with a clear opinion or argument that you want to explain or prove. Check to make sure that your topic sentences are also ideas and not just facts or details, and make sure that they support and develop your thesis statement.

Then, provide support—add more examples, details, and analysis. Be sure that each body paragraph has at least two statements of support for the idea set out in the topic sentence. Include examples and corresponding details to illustrate your point and analyze the examples and details to demonstrate your essay's purpose.

ACTIVITY 6-11   **Providing Supporting Examples**

Directions: *Come up with at least one new example to support each of the topic sentences in your essay draft.*

Supporting example for topic sentence 1: _____

_____

Supporting example for topic sentence 2: _____

_____

Supporting example for topic sentence 3: _____

_____

Supporting example for topic sentence 4: _____

_____

ACTIVITY 6-12   **Supporting Details**

Directions: *Come up with two supporting details or facts to further define, illustrate, or explain the examples you created in Activity 6-11.*

1. Detail 1: _____

Detail 2: _____

2. Detail 1: _____

Detail 2: _____

3. Detail 1: _____

Detail 2: _____

4. Detail 1: _____

Detail 2: _____

ACTIVITY 6-13 **Creating Ice Cream Sandwiches for Your Examples**

Directions: *Choose a topic sentence from your essay draft, and use it to create an "ice cream sandwich."*

Top cookie: Your original topic sentence. _____

_____

Ice cream filling: Provide at least one supporting example and one detail to illustrate that example.

Example(s): _____

_____

Supporting detail(s): _____

_____

Bottom cookie: Provide a sentence that interprets the importance of the examples and details and what they illustrate.

_____

_____

STAGE FIVE: PROOFREAD

❻ Proofread your essay.

After you have revised for style and content, you need to proofread your essay for grammar and spelling errors. Many students delay writing their first draft and then run out of time to proofread and edit their final draft. Try to turn in professional-quality work; don't let minor errors and typos sabotage the thought behind your ideas, arguments, and support. It helps if you can put your final draft aside for a day before you complete this stage; waiting a day helps you spot simple errors and typos that are difficult for you to see immediately after you finish your paper (because you just wrote the sentences and know what they are *supposed* to say). Also, be sure to have your textbook and a dictionary handy as you go through your essay. Remember: When in doubt, look it up.

Check Spelling

Use a dictionary or spell-check to check the spelling of any words you are unsure about, and also check for words that you might have used incorrectly.

▶ **NOTE** Don't just blindly trust spell-check: It is a tool, and it can give you the wrong word. For example, if you wanted to say "I *definitely* will study the next time I take a test," but spell-check thought you wanted to write, "I *defiantly* will study the next time I take a test," then the spell-check substitution changes your meaning from "certainly" to "with attitude or against someone."

ACTIVITY 6-14 Check Spelling

Cross Reference
See also Chapter 25, pp. 614–628, Commonly Confused Words, to see if you have made mistakes in word choice.

Directions: *Use a dictionary or spell-check to double-check your spelling. When in doubt, look it up.*

Check Word Usage, Word Choices, Tone, and Style

Use a thesaurus to find synonyms (words that mean the same thing) to avoid overusing particular words. Check for slang, biased language, clichés, and inappropriate tone or changes in tone.

ACTIVITY 6-15 Check Usage and Tone

Directions: *Go through your essay draft and make sure you have used a consistent and appropriate tone throughout. Also, check word choices and revise any inappropriate dialect, slang, or clichés.*

Cross Reference
See Chapter 21, pp. 516–524, Fragments, and pp. 525–532, Run-Ons and Comma Splices, and Chapters 22–26 for guidance on grammar, mechanics, and style.

Check for Sentence-Level Errors

1. Check especially for fragments, run-ons, and comma splices.
2. Check for incorrect comma use, point of view shifts, pronoun agreement, subject–verb agreement, pronoun reference errors, semicolon and colon use, apostrophe use, faulty parallelism, dangling or misplaced modifiers, and unnecessary passive voice constructions.

ACTIVITY 6-16 Grammar Review and Final Revision

Directions: *Go through your essay and check for the common sentence-level grammar errors summarized above. Correct any errors you find. Then use the Revision Checklist on page 126 to evaluate the basic elements of your essay.*

Self and Peer Assessment of Writing

Using a checklist and reviewing your own work—or having someone else review it—helps you evaluate the effectiveness of your writing. Go through your essay, and look at the separate elements that contribute to its success and the success of your purpose or argument. If you know your instructor's criteria for grading essays *before* you begin an actual draft, be sure to focus on those elements as you write it; then you can assess your essay to see if you addressed those elements well. Finally, you can have your peers (classmates, friends, or tutors) critique your essay using the checklist below.

REVISION CHECKLIST

_____ Check for a clear and interesting title in correct format.

_____ Check for an interesting introductory paragraph that sets up your purpose and leads into your thesis.

_____ Check for purpose and a clear thesis statement.

_____ Check that you have used appropriate vocabulary, tone, and approach for your target audience.

_____ Check to make sure that you have organized your paper logically, with clear topic sentences in the body paragraphs and transitions.

_____ Check to make sure you have maintained unity—all sentences and paragraphs help develop your purpose and thesis.

_____ Check to make sure you have included enough support in your essay to develop your purpose. Do you need more examples and details?

_____ Check to make sure that your sentence structure and your vocabulary choices are varied and interesting.

_____ Check for a strong concluding paragraph that sums up the analytical conclusion (purpose) established in your thesis.

_____ Check for complete sentences (eliminate fragments, run-ons, or comma splices).

_____ Check for correct punctuation throughout the paper (commas, semicolons, colons, other punctuation marks).

_____ Check for mechanics (spelling, capitalization, underlining, italics, abbreviations, numbering) using the grammar section of this text and a dictionary.

A Sample Essay: Modeling the Process

It helps sometimes to see another student go through a draft and revise an essay in stages. As the student who wrote the model essay creates various drafts of her paper on the following pages, look at the annotated changes in the drafts.

Stage One: Prewriting

PURPOSE

I've been assigned to write something about the city I live in. Hmmm. I live in Seattle; there's so much to say about it. Maybe I'll begin with a brainstormed list to narrow my topic. I'll remember to let everything just flow here and write down everything that comes to mind without any judgment or editing at this point.

Let's see . . .

Topic: Seattle

I'll just brainstorm a list of what comes to mind on this topic:

Rain, trees, Space Needle, Mt. Rainier, ferries, coffee, music, grunge, restaurants, people, diversity, fish, the aquarium, the Waterfront, down-town, Woodland Park Zoo, University of Washington, community colleges, rhododendrons, parks, beaches, Alki, Golden Gardens, flannel, tourists . . .

OK, OK, I'll stop here. I already have plenty of topic ideas.

I'll pick Seattle's downtown Waterfront as my narrowed topic, and next, I'll do a cluster to generate ideas for an essay on this topic:

Narrowed Topic: Seattle's Downtown Waterfront

Stage Two: Organizing

OK, next, I'll develop the categories/subtopics I've developed in the cluster above. First, I'll create an outline for my paper.

Thesis: Seattle's Waterfront is an ideal place to spend a full day in the city because it provides everything one could want for a perfect Seattle experience.

I. Seattle's Waterfront: Restaurants
   A. Affordable restaurants
      1. McDonald's
         a. extra-value meals
         b. several meals under $5
      2. fish and chips shop
         a. full meal under $5
         b. outdoor seats/no tipping
   B. Fancy/higher budget restaurants
      1. Red Robin
         a. medium- to higher-priced items
         b. good comfort food
      2. Elliot Bay Fishhouse
         a. higher-priced seafood entrees
         b. full view
      3. Ivar's Restaurant
         a. higher-priced seafood items
         b. full view

II. Waterfront Shopping
   A. Ye Olde Curiosity Shoppe
      1. gags
         a. magic tricks
         b. gag/joke gifts
      2. artwork
         a. carvings
         b. Native American paintings
   B. Street vendors
      1. T-shirts
      2. Seattle mementos

III. Activities and Entertainment
   A. Seattle Aquarium
      1. sea animals
      2. gift shop

      B. Street performers
          1. musicians
          2. comedians
          3. jugglers
      C. Summer concerts
  IV. People watching
      A. Tourists
          1. U.S. tourists
          2. International tourists
      B. Local artists and musicians

Conclusion: The waterfront offers the best of all possible spots to squeeze in a full day of activities.

Here are some questions you can ask as you develop your outline to ensure you have thought critically about what you want to say and how you want to say it: What are the main points I want to make in my essay? What examples and details can I include for each major point? What order do I want to use for my main points? Is that the most effective order for my purpose?

▶ NOTE   Here the student could go back and brainstorm again for each subcategory to develop additional examples and ideas.

Stage Three: Drafting

OK, let me see, my *audience* is my classmates and my instructor. My *subject* is narrowed to the *topic* of Seattle's downtown Waterfront. What is my *purpose*? What do I want to explain, show, or prove about Seattle's Waterfront?

Looking at my *categories* and my rough outline, I can see that I will be focusing on what to do and see on the waterfront. So maybe my working thesis or statement of purpose will be something like: *There are many things to do on Seattle's Waterfront.*

OK, here goes my first draft . . .

First Draft

Seattle's Waterfront

There are so many things to do in the Seattle area. One of my favorite places to go in Seattle is its downtown waterfront. I always take visiting relatives there too. I like the variety of choices I have when I go there. Seattle's Waterfront offers many things to see and do.

First, there are lots of good restaurants on Seattle's Waterfront. If you don't have a lot of money and want a casual experience, try good old McDonald's. Also, there is a hotdog stand that is open all year. There are lots of places that sell fish and chips to go for not very much money. If you want to go fancier, then there's a great range, there's a Red Robin with a medium priced menu that offers anything from hamburgers to salads. If you want to go even fancier, try one of the many nice Seafood restaurants along the piers. For instance, Elliott Bay Fish house or Ivar's.

There is great shopping at the waterfront. If you want a great spot for souveneers or little trinkets, go to Ye Olde Curiousity Shoppe. It's also a very entertaining place and kind of a tourist attraction all on its own. You can buy anything from candy, shells and "Seattle" pens and cups to strange stuff that will amaze your friends—even gag gifts. If you want a nicer gift, there are many clothes and gift shops that offer nicer gifts, there are also art galleries that sell to the public.

There is also the aquarium, with all kinds of fish and sea animals. There is the Cinemax/Omni theater that shows movies. There is also an arcade with all kinds of games and prizes, and even a carousel. There are lots of street performers too, musicians, comedians, jugglers, etc. You can take a ferry ride or a boat cruise from the pier.

There are lots of people at Seattle's Waterfront. There are tourists from all over the United States and even all over the world. But not only the tourists come to the waterfront, locals like it too. You can see whole families out for some fun on the pier or in the arcade. You can see couples strolling along the walkway after a romantic dinner for two. You can also see local musicians and street vendors trying to make some money.

So, next time you go to downtown Seattle, be sure to visit it's waterfront. There is so much to do including great restaurants, shopping, activities and people to see.

Stage Four: Revision

1. Reorganize for unity, coherence, and sentence variety.

I need to check whether every sentence or example in my body paragraphs belongs there—are they in the right spots? Does anything need to be deleted? Do I need transitions? Do my sentences have variety? I'll work on making these changes in the next draft.

2. Fine-tune thesis and topic sentences.

OK, I can see that both my thesis and my topic sentences could be improved.

Thesis—*Let me use* what, how, *and* so what *questions.*

> **What is the purpose of my essay?** *Seattle's Waterfront offers many things to see and do (my existing thesis works perfectly as a "what").*

> **How will I develop it?** *The waterfront has a great variety of restaurants, shopping, activities, and types of people. (I used my categories to create a plan of development, a map for how I will develop my thesis.)*

So what is the main point I want to prove? Therefore, the water-front is an ideal place to spend a full day in Seattle because it provides everything one could want for a perfect Seattle experience.

Topic Sentences: OK, when I look at my topic sentences, I see that they are a bit broad and don't offer any real point or main idea. They should be more of an opinion than just a fact or detail. Let me try to rewrite each topic sentence so it has more of an analytical message and a bit more focus.

Topic Sentence 1: First, there are lots of good restaurants on Seattle's Waterfront.
Revision: To begin with, Seattle's Waterfront offers a variety of restaurants to suit any palate and any budget.

Topic Sentence 2: There is great shopping at the waterfront.
Revision: Also, there are several great shopping opportunities on the Waterfront, from kitsch to classy.

Topic Sentence 3: There is also the aquarium, with all kinds of fish and sea animals. (This is not really a topic sentence, since it is not the main idea for my paragraph; it's an example with details to support an idea for things to do. I'll change it.)
Revision: The Waterfront is a great place to go for activities and entertainment.

Topic Sentence 4: Finally, there are lots of people at Seattle's Waterfront.
Revision: Finally, Seattle's Waterfront provides the best people watching in the city.

3. Add more support, examples, and details.

In this draft, I'm going to add my new thesis statement and topic sentences and see where I can provide more supporting examples and details.

Second Draft

Changes made by the student in the second draft—including reorganization for unity, coherence, and sentence variety; a new thesis; and new topic sentences—have been underlined and annotated. Transitions are highlighted in blue.

Seattle's Waterfront

There are so many things to do in the Seattle area. For instance, one of my favorite places to go in Seattle is its downtown Waterfront. I always take visiting relatives there too since I like the variety of choices I have when I go there. No matter what you want, Seattle's Waterfront offers many things to see and do. The waterfront has a great variety of restaurants, shopping, activities, and types of people. *Therefore,the waterfront is an ideal place to spend a full day in Seattle as it provides anything you could want in a perfect Seattle experience.*

To begin with, Seattle's Waterfront offers a variety of restaurants to suit any palate and any budget. If you don't have a lot of money and want a casual experience, try good old McDonald's. McDonald's offers many full-meal options for under five dollars. For instance, you can get a Big Mac, fries, and a Coke for less than five dollars. Also, there is a hotdog stand that is open all year and has great dogs and Polish sausages for under three dollars, and there are lots of places that sell fish and chips to go for not very much money. Ivar's is the most famous place to get fish and chips to go. You can get a full order of fish and chips for six dollars or less. If you want to go fancier, then there's a great range, there's a Red Robin with a medium priced menu that offers anything from hamburgers to salads. Most burgers there, along with unlimited French fries, cost less than eight dollars. They also have a full range of desserts and the best two-dollar shake in town. If you want to go even fancier, try one of the many nice seafood restaurants along the piers. For instance, Elliott Bay Fishhouse, which has fresh salmon and other grilled fish entrées, ranging from thirteen to twenty dollars and has a fancier atmosphere with candles and white tablecloths or Ivar's, the indoor restaurant which serves the full entrée and salad plates for about

Thesis statement

TS

Supporting example
Supporting detail
Supporting example

Supporting example
Supporting detail

Supporting example
Supporting detail

Supporting example

Supporting detail

Supporting example

Concluding sentence

the same range. Both of these restaurants are a more romantic atmosphere with higher-priced and more elaborate menus. The Waterfront has any type of dining experience you could want.

TS   Also, there are several great shopping opportunities on the Waterfront, from kitsch to classy. If you want a great spot for souvenirs or little trinkets, go to Ye Olde Curiosity Shoppe. It's also a very entertaining place and kind of a tourist attraction all

Supporting example

on its own. In this shop, you can buy anything from candy, shells and "Seattle" pens and cups to strange stuff that will amaze

Supporting detail

your friends—even gag gifts. For instance, you can get soap that turns your friends' hands black when they use it and disappearing ink. If you want a nicer gift, there are many clothes and gift shops that offer nicer gifts, for instance, there are art shops with

Supporting example

beautiful Native American carvings and paintings there are also art galleries that sell to the public, most of these feature local art-

Concluding paragraph

ists and include paintings, carvings, and glassworks. It's a place where you can find anything.

TS   Moreover, the Waterfront is a great place to go for activities and entertainment. There is the aquarium, with all kinds of fish

Supporting example

and sea animals. You can see seals and otters, and you can touch live sea urchins in a touching tank. There is also the Cinemax/

Supporting example

Omni theater that shows movies, an arcade with all kinds of

Supporting detail

games and prizes, and even a carousel. The carousel is a refurbished, old-fashioned carousel with elaborately painted and decorated horses. There are lots of street performers too, musicians, comedians, jugglers, etc. Furthermore, you can take a ferry ride or a boat cruise from the pier. Some of these cruises include dinner

Supporting example

and dancing as you cruise the Puget Sound. There are even formal Summer Concerts at the Pier concerts that feature famous R&B

Supporting detail

and rock artists such as BB King and the Indigo Girls. As you can

Concluding sentence

see, there are lots of entertaining attractions on the waterfront.

TS   Finally, Seattle's Waterfront provides the best people watching in the city. There are tourists from all over the United States
and even all over the world. On any given day in the summer,
you can see tourists from the Midwest, from Japan, China, Africa,
India, and many other countries from around the world. But not
only the tourists come to the Waterfront, locals like it too. You can
see whole families out for some fun on the pier or in the arcade;
also, you can see couples strolling along the walkway after a
romantic dinner for two. You can also see local musicians and
street vendors trying to make some money. Some musicians play
solo, usually with a guitar or a drum, and some musicians include
complete bands, with a singer and sometimes even a whole sound
system. All types of people like the waterfront.

So, next time you go to downtown Seattle, be sure to visit
it's waterfront. There is so much to do including eating at great
restaurants, shopping, doing activities and watching people.

Supporting example

Supporting example

Concluding sentence
Concluding paragraph

Stage Five: Editing

1. Check spelling.

I'm a pretty good speller. But I've been burned by spell-check before. I'll just double-check the words I'm not one hundred percent sure of with a dictionary.

2. Check word usage, word choices, tone, and style.

I see that I have repeated some words a lot and that some of the words are slang terms. The tone is also too informal. I'll check a thesaurus for synonyms I can use. I used the second person ("you") too much in my essay, so I'll change the point of view to third person. I have quite a few "There are" or "There is" statements or "is" and "has" verbs, so I'll try and make them into more active verb constructions. Also, I think now that the title is too broad, so I'll add a subtitle.

3. Check for sentence-level errors.

Now I'll go through the whole paper checking for each of the common errors listed in the Revision Checklist.

Final Draft

All of the changes in this final version have been underlined and annotated.

Allegria 1

Debra Allegria

Professor Edelstein

English 095

23 May 2010

Seattle's Waterfront: <u>Fun and Adventure for All</u>

<u>The Seattle</u> area is full of great things to do. <u>For instance,</u> one of my favorite places to go in Seattle is its downtown waterfront. I always take visiting relatives there, too, since I like the variety of choices I have when I go there. <u>In fact,</u> Seattle's waterfront in particular offers many things to see and to do. The waterfront <u>offers</u> a great variety of restaurants, *shopping*, activities, and types of people. *Therefore, the <u>waterfront</u> is an ideal place to spend a full day in Seattle as it provides anything one could want in a perfect Seattle experience.*

To begin with, Seattle's waterfront offers a variety of restaurants to suit any palate and any budget. If <u>a person does not</u> have a great deal of money to spend and <u>wants</u> a casual experience, <u>he or she</u> can go to <u>reliable</u> McDonald's on the <u>waterfront.</u> McDonald's offers many full-meal options for under five dollars. For instance, <u>a shopper</u> can get a Big Mac, fries, and a Coke for less than five dollars. <u>Also, the waterfront boasts</u> a famous hot-dog stand that is open all year and has great dogs and Polish sausages for under three dollars. <u>Moreover,</u> several places

Thesis statement

Topic sentence

Allegria 2

along the waterfront sell fish and chips to go for not very much money. Ivar's is the most famous place to get fish and chips to go. A hungry visitor can get a full order of fish and chips for six dollars or less.

If a person wants to go to a fancy restaurant on the waterfront, then there's a great range. Red Robin features a medium-priced range menu that offers anything from hamburgers to salads. Most burgers there, along with unlimited French fries, cost less than eight dollars. Red Robin also offers a full range of desserts and the best two-dollar shake in town. If one wants to go even fancier, he or she can try one of the many nice seafood restaurants along the pier. For instance, Elliott Bay Fishhouse has fresh salmon and other grilled fish entrées, ranging from thirteen to twenty dollars, and has a nicer atmosphere with candles and white tablecloths. Also, Ivar's provides an indoor restaurant that serves full entrée and salad plates for about the same range. Both of these restaurants boast a more romantic atmosphere and feature higher-priced and more elaborate menu options. Indeed, Seattle's waterfront has any type of dining experience one could want.

Also, Seattle's waterfront offers great shopping opportunities with all kinds of merchandise, from kitsch to classy. If a visitor wants a great spot for souvenirs or little trinkets, he or she can go to Ye Olde Curiosity Shoppe, a very entertaining place and kind of a tourist attraction all on its own. In this shop, one can buy anything from candy, shells, and "Seattle" pens and cups to strange stuff that will amaze one's friends—even gag gifts. For instance, one can get soap that turns friends' hands black when they use it and infamous disappearing ink. If a shopper desires a nicer gift, many clothes and gift shops offer nicer gifts; for

[New paragraph started]

Topic sentence

Concluding sentence

Topic sentence

Allegria 3

instance, the waterfront sports art shops with beautiful Native American carvings and paintings and art galleries that sell to the public; most of these feature local artists and include paintings, carvings, and glassworks. Truly, the waterfront is a place where experienced shoppers can find anything.

Moreover, the waterfront is a great place to go for activities and entertainment. In the Seattle Aquarium, with all kinds of fish and sea animals, guests can see seals and otters and can touch live sea urchins in an open tank. Also, the Cinemax/Omni Theater shows movies and features an arcade with all kinds of games and prizes, and even a carousel. The carousel is a refurbished, old-fashioned merry-go-round with elaborately painted and decorated horses. Street performers frequent the waterfront too: musicians, comedians, jugglers, etc. Furthermore, one can take a ferry ride or a boat cruise from the pier. Some of these cruises include dinner and dancing as they cruise the Puget Sound. Finally, the summer weather brings Summer Concerts at the Pier, which feature famous R&B and rock artists such as BB King and the Indigo Girls. As you can see, several entertaining attractions exist on the waterfront.

Finally, Seattle's waterfront provides the best people watching in the city. Tourists from all over the United States and even all over the world visit the waterfront. On any given day in the summer, one can see tourists from the Midwest and from Japan, China, Africa, India, and many other countries from around the world. However, not only the tourists come to the waterfront; locals like it, too. Whole families come out for some fun on the pier or in the arcade; also, couples regularly stroll along the walkway

Concluding sentence

Topic sentence

Concluding sentence

Topic sentence

Allegria 4

after a romantic dinner for two. <u>Moreover,</u> local musicians and street vendors are prominent on the waterfront. Some musicians play solo, usually a guitar or a drum, and some musicians have complete bands, including a singer and sometimes even a whole sound system. All types of people like the waterfront, <u>making it the best spot to be seen and do some people watching.</u>

Concluding sentence

Restatement of thesis

<u>As you can see,</u> Seattle's waterfront offers the best of all possible spots to squeeze in a full day of activities. No other spot can offer so much in one place, including a wealth of great restaurants, shopping, activities, and people to see.

Each person will have a different experience using the process, which can also differ from assignment to assignment, but following these steps will help you write an effective essay and ensure that your final draft contains all the elements of a good essay.

ACTIVITY 6-17 More Practice Writing an Essay

Directions: *Choose from the following broad topics, or choose one of your own, to practice the five stages to writing an essay.*

Topic choices:

1. Political Campaign Ads

2. Identity Theft

3. Cyberbullying

4. The Pros and Cons of Mail-in Voting Ballots

5. Working Out at a Gym

   Topic of your own: _____

Learning Objectives Review

MyWritingLab™ Complete the chapter assessment questions at mywritinglab.com

❶ Define the five stages of the essay-writing process.

How can you break down essay writing into five stages? (See p. 104.)

The five stages in planning and drafting an essay are: (1) generating ideas and purpose; (2) developing a plan for presenting your purpose and ideas; (3) creating a first draft based on your plan and the pattern(s) of organization you have chosen and developing support for your essay's purpose; (4) reassessing the draft for content, development, organization, and support (examples and details); and (5) checking for sentence-level effectiveness, style, diction, grammar, and spelling errors.

❷ Prewrite to establish your subject, purpose, and audience.

Why should you prewrite to determine your subject, purpose, and audience? (See pp. 104–115.)

Prewriting helps you to generate ideas and answer the following questions: What is my **subject** and how do I narrow it to a topic? What is my **purpose** for writing this essay? What am I trying to explain or prove? And who is my target **audience**, and how do I modify my approach and tone for that audience?

❸ Create a thesis statement and rough outline.

What are some ways to organize your ideas after generating them? (See pp. 116–120.)

Based on the ideas generated in prewriting, you can **create a thesis statement and rough outline** to figure out the main ideas versus the supporting ideas and to create a specific plan for developing the essay and structuring it in the most effective way.

❹ Write a first draft.

How do you create a first draft? (See pp. 120–121.)

To **draft** your essay, use the ideas you generated and the outline you created. Just dive in!

5 Revise your essay.

How do you revise an essay? (See pp. 121–124.)

Revise for organization, style, and content. Think critically about your essay's order, unity, coherence, and sentence variety, and fine-tune your thesis statement and topic sentences. Also, provide additional support, and check word choice, tone, and style.

6 Proofread your essay.

How do you proofread an essay? (See pp. 124–126.)

Proofread your essay by checking for grammatical errors and spelling mistakes.

PART III WRITING AND CRITICAL THINKING IN THE MODES

CONTENTS

7 Narration and Description

8 Process

9 Classification

10 Definition

11 Example and Illustration

12 Cause and Effect

13 Comparison and Contrast

14 Argument and Persuasion

15 Timed In-Class Essays and Essay Exams

Wayne Buck

INTRODUCTION TO PART III

The dancer in this picture is strong and flexible. Knowledge of the modes will give you strength and flexibility as a writer. Essay modes are types of essay patterns or structures designed to address specific purposes. You can use different modes to write about the same topic: It all depends on your purpose and your intended audience. For example, if you were writing about the last presidential election, you could choose one specific mode or combine two or more modes based on your audience, purpose, and intended arguments about the subject: Are you comparing and contrasting two candidates? Are you arguing for one candidate? Are you defining the process of the election? Some essays will benefit from the use of a specific mode or pattern, while others will benefit from a combination of several different modes, and some will do better with a customized structure based on your purpose and audience.

Whether you choose to use a single mode, a combination of modes, or a different structure altogether will be based on several key factors:

1. Your instructor's assignment or specific request for a mode essay
2. The purpose of your essay and the most efficient way to structure it
3. Your intended audience and the best combination of modes to illustrate and develop your intended purpose

Carefully assess your topic, purpose, and audience to make the best choice.

CHOOSING THE RIGHT APPROACH

All essays should have an expository purpose, a point they wish to explain. You have a choice in how you structure your essay, and there are specialized modes you can use or combine to do this. First figure out your essay's topic (Chapter 6) and purpose (Chapter 1), then choose the best way to organize and develop that purpose. Although each mode explained in the chapters in Part III has a specialized purpose and format, they can all be used to make an argument or analytical point. Below are nine traditional essay modes:

Narration	Tells a story using concrete details and description
Description	Paints a picture with words through vivid details
Process	Describes a series of steps
Classification	Categorizes people, things, or concepts; sometimes called "classification and division"
Definition	Defines an item or a concept
Example and illustration	Provides examples in order to illustrate an idea or set of ideas
Cause and effect	Relates reasons and results
Comparison and contrast	Draws out and explores similarities and differences between or among subjects
Argument or persuasion	Reasons in favor of a particular viewpoint or change in the status quo

Some essay assignments call for one of the above modes, and some require a combination. Many times your essay will have a dominant mode, such as argument, and will rely on other modes for support, such as narration, example, and comparison and contrast. As you saw in Chapter 5, all the essay modes follow a simple template for developing a purpose:

1. They begin with a paragraph that introduces the topic and presents the purpose of the essay in an analytical thesis statement.

2. They develop the thesis statement with body paragraphs using clear topic sentences and supporting examples and details.

3. They end with a concluding paragraph that restates or sums up the main purpose and sometimes comments on it.

TO MODE OR NOT TO MODE?

The field of composition is changing dramatically with the onset of the Digital Revolution; today, myriad forms of information and text that go beyond just words are available to us to use to communicate with others. One of the questions that students (and teachers) of composition are asking is, "Do we still need to learn (or teach) essay modes?" Some people worry that if students learn formulas their writing will become formulaic—but learning modes gives you structures and patterns you can use as a type of essay writing toolbox. If you learn the essay modes and how to use them, then you can combine or customize them as needed or reject them for a new approach. Even Picasso had to learn to paint traditionally before he could experiment!

THINKING CRITICALLY ABOUT MODES AND MEDIA

Digital technology and the wealth of multimedia resources available on the Internet have helped expand the boundaries of composition. Once you have the basic modes down, you can start to think critically about incorporating multimedia into your compositions. Your generation of composition students has more options than any before to use a variety of media to best communicate your ideas and arguments. Some colleges offer composition classes that focus specifically on multimedia writing, sometimes called digital or multimodal writing. Not only in composition courses but also in courses such as sociology, history, psychology, and the hard sciences, professors are asking students to create multimedia compositions.

For example, you might create an argument essay and enhance the text with video, audio, animation, still images, graphics, hyperlinks, or interactive Internet sites that get your readers involved in the project. A photograph or chart may serve as an example in your definition of a subject; a hyperlink may lead your readers to a more thorough definition; a short video may illustrate a process you've described—the possibilities are endless. Just remember to acknowledge any sources you have used in your compositions, whether they be print, electronic, visual, or any other media (see Chapter 16 for how to cite sources).

LEARNING OBJECTIVES

In this chapter, you will learn how to

1 Describe the narrative and descriptive mode.

2 Apply critical thinking skills to writing narrative and descriptive essays.

3 Prepare to write a narrative and descriptive essay by asking critical thinking questions.

4 Structure a narrative and descriptive essay.

5 Use modes that complement narrative and descriptive essays.

Wayne Buck

Thinking Critically MyWritingLab™

Think: Study the photograph.

Write: Write a brief story explaining what is going on in the picture. Use your imagination, and include as many specific details about the situation and the subjects as you can.

1. What did you focus on when you wrote the story?

_____

_____

_____

_____

2. What effect did looking at a concrete (actual) image have on the way you wrote your story and the details you included?

_____

_____

_____

_____

NARRATIVE AND DESCRIPTIVE ESSAYS

❶ Describe the narrative and descriptive mode.

In a **narrative and descriptive essay,** you recount an event, story, or series of events in order to explain some insight or truth gained from an experience. For good description in your narration, use concrete details, vivid descriptive words, and as many of the senses as possible—sight, sound, touch, smell, and taste.

Narration means to tell a story or describe an event, and an expository (purpose to explain) narrative and descriptive essay should include an analytical purpose: You should have a point or lesson to impart to the reader through telling a story or recounting an event and framing it with analysis of what you learned through the experience. For example, you might write about your first days in a new country and what you learned about yourself or human nature during that time. When people read your essay, they can learn through your experience as well.

CRITICAL THINKING AND NARRATION AND DESCRIPTION

❷ Apply critical thinking skills to writing narrative and descriptive essays.

It is the *inclusion of a lesson* that distinguishes the expository narrative and descriptive essay from a summary narration and description of events. This analytical purpose is stated in the first paragraph of the essay in the *thesis* (or *purpose*) *statement*. This lesson or message is then restated in the conclusion. In between, concrete descriptions and vivid details create the story in the reader's mind. If you are describing something, be specific. If you say "The dessert was delicious," the reader probably wouldn't picture a thing, but if you described that dessert in detail, using sensory language, he or she will likely picture it or imagine it with you. For example, "The hot fudge cake was oozing with dark brown warm chocolate sauce that was melting the bright layer of vanilla ice cream, and it smelled like a mug of fresh hot chocolate with whipped cream" is much more appealing and creates a visual and sensory image.

Because analytical, narrative, and descriptive essays have a lesson to impart to readers, they require more thought than an essay that merely recounts an event. You must use your critical thinking skills to figure out what you want to say about the event, how you want to say it, how you'll organize your ideas, and how you'll weave in analysis and commentary about the event.

When you recall the event(s) and describe what happened and what resulted from the actions that took place, be careful not to assume that because one event happened first, it must be the cause of the event that followed it. For example, if you say that you were in a car accident because you didn't wear your favorite socks that day, well, that's not necessarily true. That kind of

APPLYING CRITICAL THINKING

PURPOSE   IDEAS   SUPPORT   ASSUMPTIONS BIASES   CONCLUSIONS   POINT OF VIEW   ANALYSIS

In order to determine your **purpose** for writing—the message you want to convey in your narrative and descriptive essay—use the following questions to help you clarify what you learned from the experience you are writing about:

1. What is my **analysis** of the story? What have I learned or what do I want my readers to learn from the story I am telling? What point do I want to make through telling this story?

2. What is my plan for how to structure my narrative to impart my message? How will I convey that message in my essay?

3. What **ideas** will I include? What **support** (facts, examples, evidence) can I include to illustrate and explain the point of my narrative?

4. How can I include as many descriptive details as possible to illustrate the event? What sensory details should I include in this story?

thinking is called a **post-hoc fallacy** (*post hoc* is a Latin phrase that means "after this"). It is an unsupported claim that something is the result of something else. But, if you say you were in a car accident because you were texting while driving, now that cause-and-effect series of events makes much more sense. You can avoid post-hoc fallacies by providing evidence to support the connection between two events.

BEFORE WRITING A NARRATIVE AND DESCRIPTIVE ESSAY

❸ Prepare to write a narrative and descriptive essay by asking critical thinking questions.

Before you begin to write a narrative and descriptive essay, ask yourself these questions:

1. Who is my audience, and what is my purpose?

2. What do I want my readers to learn or understand after reading about the event I experienced or witnessed, how will I set up the introduction to the story, and how can I put my lesson into a clear thesis statement?

3. How can I recreate the event vividly in my readers' minds? What examples and details should I use to recreate the story? How can I include as many sensory details as possible in my descriptions of the settings and characters in my story?

4. How should I organize my paragraphs after my introduction and thesis, and how can I move smoothly from one event or detail to the next?

   ▶ NOTE   Creating an outline will make answering this question much easier.

5. What's the best way to conclude my essay?

Answering these questions will help you generate an expository thesis statement, help you decide which examples and details to include for support, and give you a general idea of how to organize and conclude your essay so you can create an outline and your first draft.

ACTIVITY 7-1   Outlining a Specific Event

Directions: *Think of an event you witnessed or a specific happy or sad event in your own life. Then answer the following questions about that event.*

1. What happened? (Describe briefly in one paragraph.)

   _____

   _____

   _____

   _____

   _____

2. What did you learn about yourself and/or others during that time, and why?

   _____

   _____

   _____

3. What would you want your readers to understand after reading about the event?

   _____

   _____

   _____

4. What specific details and examples could you use to recreate the event and vividly tell the story?

_____

_____

_____

5. What critical thinking tools could you use to plan, support, organize, and develop the purpose of the narration?

_____

_____

_____

WRITING A NARRATIVE AND DESCRIPTIVE ESSAY

4 Structure a narrative and descriptive essay.

A narrative and descriptive essay usually begins with an introduction that briefly describes an event or time and then presents the analytical thesis showing what you learned from that event. Then, the body paragraphs describe the event, or series of events, in chronological order (the order in which the actions occurred).

The *point of view* in narrative essays is usually *first person*. Therefore, it is perfectly appropriate to use the word "I" throughout a narrative essay. For example:

> When I was 12 years old, I learned a valuable lesson about the dangers of playing with fire. It all started when my brother and I found a lighter in our backyard.

Moreover, in the body paragraphs, you should develop your narrative and descriptive essay using vivid *descriptive details*. Include specific details about the setting and detailed descriptions of the people and their actions. Choose words that conjure up vivid images, not vague descriptors such as "beautiful." Use as many sensory details (sight, sound, touch, taste, smell) as possible in your descriptions.

> **Vague descriptors:** The cake was *beautiful* and looked *delicious*.
>
> **Revised:** The wedding cake was three layers high and snowy white, covered with fluffy whipped cream and delicate pastel pink roses made of butter cream frosting.

Another important and effective technique you can use in a narration and description essay is to include dialogue. Use real dialogue, as far as you can remember it from the event, to make the scene(s) come alive on paper. Using actual dialogue in a narration and descriptive essay is a great way to provide supporting details in the body paragraphs. For information on how to use dialogue correctly, see pages 159–161 later in this chapter.

Organizational Pattern for a Narrative and Descriptive Essay

Your essay needs unity (all details support the thesis), coherence (a smooth flow from one sentence to the next and one paragraph to the next), and a well-chosen order pattern (such as time order or order of importance); these elements should all come together to make your essay organized and easy to follow. Consider what order pattern will work best for your subject, purpose, and audience. Then, make sure your essay has unity and coherence throughout. Narration essays typically use time order (sometimes called chronological order), so the writer can describe events in the order that they happened, creating a descriptive story that the readers can follow.

> **Narration time order example:** I learned a very important lesson yesterday about my ability to forgive others. The morning began as usual, but after a few hours, a series of events changed my day from anything but usual.
>
>   First, when I went out to the parking lot to get my car, I realized it was missing . . .

Therefore, a narrative and descriptive essay has a fairly simple order. The chart below provides a brief overview of the structure of a narrative and descriptive essay.

BASIC STRUCTURE FOR A NARRATIVE AND DESCRIPTIVE ESSAY

See the sample essay on pages 164–166.

INTRODUCTORY PARAGRAPH

Sets up background for the event or story.

Thesis statement: what you are trying to explain, show, prove, or argue; what you learned from the experience.

IDEAS

BODY PARAGRAPHS (Two to five, depending on assignment and purpose)

Develop the narrative of the event using time order.

Use transitions within and between paragraphs to emphasize time changes and/or significant turns in the narrative.

Provide concrete details and description.

SUPPORT

Use as many sensory details as possible in the description.

Add dialogue when appropriate.

ANALYSIS

Add commentary and analysis about the details and descriptions to help develop the expository purpose/thesis statement.

Explain what you were thinking and feeling as the events took place.

CONCLUDING PARAGRAPH

CONCLUSIONS

Sums up and re-emphasizes the thesis: the lesson learned and message of the story you've told in your narrative essay.

Structuring a Narrative and Descriptive Essay

Many events stand out in people's memories as pivotal points in their lives. Topics around which you could structure a narrative essay include: the birth of a child; the happiest day of your life; an accident; a tragedy; an embarrassing event; your first day on a job; the death of a loved one; the saddest day of your life; a surprise; a celebration; a proud moment; your first day at college. You also need to create a title for your essay that reflects the topic and your purpose: for example, A Lesson from My Grandmother.

Topic

Cross Reference
For more on prewriting techniques, see Chapter 6, pp. 104–115, Stage One: Prewrite to Generate Ideas.

If your instructor has assigned a narrative/descriptive topic, be sure to read the assignment carefully to determine its requirements and how to best create your thesis and analytical purpose. If you are choosing your own topic, prewrite about possible events using such techniques as brainstorming or clustering.

Focus on what happened and what you learned from this event.

Thesis Statements

PURPOSE

The thesis statement in a narrative and descriptive essay should contain the lesson learned from the event. Engage your critical thinking skills to figure out why the event or story you've chosen to write about stood out to you.

What can readers learn from your experience? If you have been assigned a specific narrative and descriptive essay task, be sure to include key words from the assignment to fulfill the assignment's purpose. If you are generating your own topic and purpose, prewriting will help you to come up with ideas, details, and a purpose for telling a story about this event. For instance, if you decided to write about the death of someone you loved, you'd need to explain how you felt and what you learned about yourself, about the nature of life, and so on. Use your critical thinking and analysis skills to explain the significance of the event.

The easiest way to generate a meaningful thesis statement for your narrative and descriptive essay is to begin with the story that is your topic, come up with a point you want to convey to your readers about it, and then directly state the conclusion you've reached or the lesson you've learned. Here are some examples of this process:

Topic = My vacation to Italy

A point I want to convey = How I learned to be flexible and open-minded

Thesis: Last year, during my vacation in Italy, I learned to not expect everything to be the same as it is in my country and that I need to be open-minded, flexible, and respectful when I travel to other countries.

Topic = Trying out for the football team

A point I want to convey = How it felt when I didn't get picked and dealing with that

Thesis: When I tried out for the football team this fall and didn't get picked, I learned a lesson about humility and carrying on.

Topic = The birth of my child

A point I want to convey = Changing priorities

Thesis: The day my daughter was born, my priorities changed completely.

ACTIVITY 7-2   Creating Thesis Statements

Directions: *For each of the following narrative topics, create a one-sentence thesis statement. Make sure the thesis statement has a clear message or lesson to convey about what you learned from the experience.*

1. **Topic:** My earliest memory

   A point I want to convey = _____

   Thesis statement: _____

   _____

2. **Topic:** My first experience with death or illness

   A point I want to convey = _____

   Thesis statement: _____

   _____

3. **Topic:** The happiest day of my life

   A point I want to convey = _____

   Thesis statement: _____

   _____

4. **Topic:** The first time I [choose an event such as "drove a car"]

   A point I want to convey = _____

   Thesis statement: _____

   _____

5. **Topic:** The most embarrassing thing that ever happened to me

   A point I want to convey = _____

   Thesis statement: _____

   _____

Cross Reference
See Chapter 6,
pp. 104–115, Stage One:
Prewrite to Generate
Ideas.

Creating a Rough Outline

Once you have determined your topic and your thesis statement, you are ready to create a rough outline to determine your essay's structure and organizational plan. Use prewriting techniques such as brainstorming or clustering to generate supporting examples and concrete details. Then create a rough outline using this template:

Rough Outline Template for a Narrative and Descriptive Essay

    I. Introductory Paragraph
       A. Brief, general description of the event you will narrate
       B. Thesis Statement: What lesson you want to impart to your
          readers that you learned from this experience

II. Body Paragraphs: Two to four body paragraphs that tell what happened/narrate the event in time order
   A. Include concrete description and sensory details to paint an image in the reader's mind
   B. Include descriptions of people present during the event and some actual dialogue that occurred
   C. Include commentary about what you were thinking or feeling as the event transpired
III. Concluding Paragraph
   A. Restate in a new way the lesson you learned
   B. Add some general closing comments without introducing any new ideas

Introductory Paragraph

Begin your narrative and descriptive essay with a general introduction to draw the reader in and set up the event you will be recounting. You may need to provide some background information to put the event and its importance in context to what was going on in your life or the world at the time. End the introductory paragraph with your thesis statement.

Body Paragraphs

Body paragraphs in a narrative and descriptive essay develop details and description to recount an event vividly and support the purpose. Topic sentences in body paragraphs support the thesis statement. Topic sentences in narrative and descriptive essays often introduce the next step in a sequence of events using time order and transitions. Sometimes, though, a topic sentence in a narrative and descriptive essay can explain what you were feeling or thinking as the event was taking place. For instance, for the thesis about traveling in Italy, in addition to topic sentences that use time order and transitions to introduce the next step in a sequence of events, you could create topic sentences that analyze each point of the trip and what you learned about yourself or others. For example:

Thesis: Last year, during my vacation in Italy, I learned to not expect everything to be the same as it is in my country and that I need to be open-minded, flexible, and respectful when I travel to other countries.

Time and event topic sentence for the same thesis: In the morning, I encountered a situation that made me rethink my previous beliefs.

Analytical statement topic sentence for this thesis: First, I learned that I need to be open-minded when traveling outside my own country.

When you recount an event in time order, be sure to include transitional words and phrases to move the reader from one point in time to another. Here are some common transitions used to convey time order (for other transitions commonly used with narration, see pages 93–94):

TRANSITIONS TO . . .

Show Time

after	before	in the meantime	not long after
afterward	between	later	soon
at last	first	meanwhile	then
at length	immediately	next	while

After we returned from the hospital, I went straight to bed.
Next, my husband went to pick up the kids.
Later, we showed them their new baby brother.

ACTIVITY 7-3 Creating Topic Sentences

Directions: *Choose one of the thesis statements you developed in Activity 7-2 and write two possible topic sentences that could introduce two body paragraphs to support that thesis.*

Thesis statement: _____

_____

Topic sentence 1:

_____

_____

Topic sentence 2:

_____

_____

ACTIVITY 7-4   Providing Examples and Details

Directions: *Now, using the two topic sentences you created in Activity 7-3, provide a specific example and a supporting detail for that example.*

Example for topic sentence 1:

_____

_____

Supporting detail to demonstrate/develop the example:

_____

_____

Example for topic sentence 2:

_____

_____

Supporting detail to demonstrate/develop the example:

_____

_____

Vivid, Concrete Description   Specific, or concrete, details provide **support** in a narrative/descriptive essay and create realistic images in your readers' minds that let them experience the event with you as you describe it. This ultimately helps them identify with you and learn the lesson you want to share. Use the following tips to write clear, vivid descriptions:

1. Choose words that conjure vivid images, not vague descriptors such as "pretty" or "nice," which are subjective terms and do not evoke a particular image.

> **Vague descriptors:** She had a pretty face and nice hair.
>
> **Revised:** Her face was oval and pleasantly rosy, and her hair was sleek and golden.

2. Use words related to the senses (sight, hearing, touch, taste, and smell) when you describe a person, place, or thing to create a picture in your reader's mind. For instance, when describing a room, include visual

details (light streaming through the window), sounds (wind in the trees outside), taste (if possible—e.g., the sweet-tart taste of a strawberry ice cream cone), smells (of clean laundry), touch (the texture of a blanket), and the overall atmospheric feel.

3. Use similes (comparisons of one thing to another that begin with the words "like" or "as") or metaphors (comparisons in which one thing is described as being another thing). For instance, you can use a simile to help someone get a better image of your grandmother's hands:

My grandmother's hands were *as rough as a lizard's skin.*

Or you can use a metaphor to describe your grandmother's hands:

Her hands were *gentle spiders* playing with the edge of the quilt.

Be careful, though, not to resort to clichés in your description such as "He looked like a Greek god." Such phrases do not create vivid images because they are overused.

ACTIVITY 7-5 Generic to Specific

Directions: *Translate the abstract descriptive words bolded in each following sentence into concrete, specific descriptions of the thing or person in the sentence.*

Example: It was a **big** house.

The house was <u>three stories high</u> and had a <u>three-car garage</u>, a <u>wraparound porch</u>, and a <u>one-acre lawn</u>.

1. She is a **beautiful** woman.

_____

_____

2. The movie's action scene was **awesome**.

_____

_____

3. Her dress was **indescribable**.

_____

_____

4. The crowd was **unbelievable**.

_____

_____

5. The party was **fantastic**.

_____

_____

ACTIVITY 7-6   Describe a Monster

Directions: *This activity requires you to work with a partner. This classic description exercise is a fun way to practice using specific and concrete description and also a great way to increase your awareness of your reader's need to visualize what you are describing.*

Step One: On a sheet of paper, draw a monster. Be creative, and enjoy yourself. Don't let anyone see your monster drawing; turn it over on your desk when you are done.

Step Two: Now, on a separate sheet of paper, write a one-paragraph description of your monster using specific, concrete descriptive words.

Step Three: Exchange your written description with your partner. Keep your monster drawing upside down so that your partner doesn't see it.

Step Four: Read your partner's written description of his or her monster. Then, on a separate sheet of paper, draw the monster based on the description given.

Step Five: Compare the original drawings to the ones created based on the written descriptions.

Step Six: Answer the following questions.

1. Did the later drawings look close to the originals? (Ignore differences in drawing talent; focus on the basic features such as number of eyes, legs, overall shape, and so on.)

_____

_____

2. What problems arose from details missing in the description?

_____

_____

3. What would you do differently now if you were asked to rewrite your description of your monster?

_____

_____

_____

_____

Use Dialogue Including dialogue in a narrative and descriptive essay helps make the people in your story come to life and helps make the story you are telling more vivid and real. You should only use dialogue in the body paragraphs as you are describing and narrating the series of events and people's actions. Here are some tips for how to correctly include dialogue in a narrative and descriptive essay.

Tips for Correct Use of Dialogue in Narrative/Descriptive Essays

1. **Use tags and quotation marks.** When you use dialogue, you need a tag to indicate who is speaking and quotation marks around the words they are saying.

> **Tag:** Bob said,
> **Quotation Marks:** "I have to leave this party early."
> **Used Together:** Bob said, "I have to leave this party early."

Tag placement can also come in the middle or at the end of the dialogue:

> "Today," **Bob said,** "is the first day of the rest of my life."
> "Today is the first day of the rest of my life," **Bob said.**

2. **Use correct punctuation.** Start sentences of dialogue within quotation marks with a capital letter.

> Andrea sighed, "Yes, I know it's time to leave."

Punctuation goes inside the quotation marks (except when using in-text citation in documented papers).

> "The key point," Dominic said, "is to listen first."

3. **Begin a new paragraph every time you switch speakers in dialogue.**

> Mary asked Bob, "Will you change jobs, too?"
> "Yes," Bob responded, "I will."
> "And how will you afford the rent until you get settled?" Mary asked sharply, unable to mask her concern.
> "I'll just figure it out as I go along," Bob responded, shaking his head and smiling at Mary's worried frown.

4. **Weave descriptions of the characters and their actions into blocks of dialogue.** When you use blocks of dialogue in your essay, weave in descriptions of the characters and their movements or actions as they speak. Create a "movie" of the scene by including details of what people are saying and what they are doing as they say it. Again, the key to good narrative writing is concrete description. Look again at the dialogue exchange between Mary and Bob in tip 3 for an example of how to weave description into dialogue.

5. **Use varied and specific verbs in your dialogue tags.** Try not to just use "said" over and over, for instance. Choose the most specific verb for the emotion of the person and what was being said (e.g., she yelled, she sobbed, she questioned, she blurted).

6. **Don't let the dialogue take over.** Use dialogue as a supporting detail in your essay, not as the main vehicle for imparting your story and your story's message. Be sure to *frame your dialogue with analysis*, the realizations you came to and what you were feeling and thinking as the words were said during the incident—always re-emphasize your *analytical purpose*.

> She screamed, "No, I refuse to leave. I can't. I won't!"
> Until that moment, I hadn't realized how hard it was for her to leave the house in which she had spent her entire life.

ACTIVITY 7-7 Writing Dialogue

Directions:

1. *On a separate sheet of paper, write a short dialogue, with each person speaking at least twice. You can use an actual dialogue that occurred between you and someone else (as clearly as you can remember it), or you can make up a dialogue between two fictional characters.*

2. *Be sure to include tags, start a new paragraph whenever you switch speakers, and include some physical motion or description of the characters as they speak. Review the tips on using dialogue for help.*

Concluding Paragraph

The concluding paragraph for a narrative and descriptive essay is basic: Restate the thesis statement, focusing on the purpose for recounting the event. Be sure not to use the same sentence you used in your introductory paragraph, though. Explain what you learned from the experience, and reiterate the purpose required by the specific assignment (if there is one). Then, end your paragraph with some general concluding comments about the event or what you learned and how those lessons still affect you now.

ACTIVITY 7-8 Writing a Conclusion

Directions: *Using the thesis, topic sentences, and examples you chose for Activities 7-2, 7-3, and 7-4, write a three- to five-sentence conclusion for the topic as if you had written the entire essay.*

_____

_____

_____

_____

_____

ACTIVITY 7-9 Creating Your Outline and First Draft

Cross Reference
See Chapters 21–25, pp. 515–648, for help with the Editing section of the critique form.

Directions: *Choose a topic from one of the activities you already completed in this chapter, from the assignment choices at the end of this chapter, or from a topic assigned by your instructor and create a rough outline using the template on pages 153–154 of this chapter. Then, using your rough outline, write a first draft of your essay. After you have finished, use the critique form below to check for the basics in your essay draft.*

NARRATIVE AND DESCRIPTIVE ESSAY CRITIQUE FORM

PURPOSE   IDEAS   SUPPORT   ASSUMPTIONS BIASES   CONCLUSIONS   POINT OF VIEW   ANALYSIS

Overall

	Done well	Needs work

1. Does the essay tell a story using description that has a clear **purpose** (lesson(s) learned from the experience)?

2. Does the essay use time order in the body paragraphs?

3. Are the paragraphs organized clearly and logically and are they a good length—3–15 sentences?

Introduction

4. Is the title interesting and in the instructor's required format?

5. Is there a general introduction that gives the background for the story (the situation that led up to the events described)?

6. Is there a clear thesis statement that explains the message of the story being told—the lesson learned or expository purpose?

Body

7. Do the **ideas** in the body paragraphs develop the story logically and flow smoothly?

8. Are transitions used between and, when needed, within the paragraphs?

9. Do the body paragraphs include **support** and descriptive details that enhance the story?

10. Does the writer use as many sensory details as possible to describe what happened and how it made the writer feel?

11. Does the body of the paper include some dialogue to bring the action to life?

12. Is **analysis** woven throughout the body paragraphs to emphasize the significance of the story and develop the lesson(s) learned from the event? Are critical thinking tools such as ideas, **point of view, assumptions and biases,** and analysis used?

Conclusion

13. Does the **concluding** paragraph sum up the story with an analytical frame that re-emphasizes the introductory paragraph and thesis, without adding new ideas?

Editing

14. Circle the following errors you think you see in this draft: spelling errors, fragments, run-ons/comma splices, errors in commas and semicolon/colon use, pronoun disagreement, pronoun reference errors, errors in parallelism, apostrophe use, verb use/tense, and passive voice construction.

15. Other types of grammar or sentence-level errors:

_____

Comments (For example: What works well in this draft? What needs to be added? Did you, or will your readers, feel drawn into the story? Why or why not?):

_____

_____

COMPLEMENTARY MODES FOR NARRATIVE ESSAYS

5 Use modes that complement narrative and descriptive essays.

When writing a narrative and descriptive essay, of course, the dominant modes will be narration and description; however, you can create a more powerful message by weaving in sentences or paragraphs in other modes. For example:

- **Illustration and example:** Most good narrative essays include specific illustrations and examples to develop the purpose of the writing. These modes overlap quite a bit: the difference is that, in narration, the examples are used to develop a story, and, in example essays, you might not have any story, just examples to support a point of view.
- **Process:** Process focuses on describing a series of steps to accomplish a task and can be used in narration to describe a particular sequence of events in minute detail.
- **Cause and effect:** You can describe an event in detail and employ cause-and-effect analysis to look at the consequences of the actions that take place.
- **Comparison/contrast:** One way to narrate or describe an event or an item or person is to compare or contrast the event or person with another event or person.
- **Argument:** All analytical essays have some level of argument in them. Your reason for narrating an event in detail in expository writing (a purpose to explain) is to persuade your readers to learn a particular lesson or feel a particular way: You are combining argument techniques with your narration.

Student Essay

The dominant mode used in this student's paper is narration and description. Look for other modes used in this essay, such as illustration and example, and cause-and-effect analysis.

Grant 1

Jamie Grant

Professor Nolan

English 100

20 April 2013

Learning Through Loss

A few years ago, my beloved grandmother, Belle, died after a sudden and severe illness. At first I was devastated by the loss.
Thesis statement
However, after a while, I found that I could honor her life by living my life based on her example of keeping our family connected and being generous, and by appreciating my life and my family while I can because life is short and therefore precious.

Topic sentence
My grandmother was beautiful to me both inside and out. She was a tiny woman who was somewhat hunched over, her back round from osteoporosis. Her face was lined, and the backs of her hands were spotted and shiny, the skin fragile and paper-like. Her hair was a stunning silver and soft and wispy. She was also the best and wisest person I've ever known. Through her life
Concluding sentence
and my times with her, she taught me the importance of family and the importance of giving to others.

Topic sentence
Our family has always been close, and my grandmother was the matriarch who kept our family connected and whose life was a model for all of us. She actively invited all of her grandchildren, including me and my brother, to visit regularly. My brother and I would spend long summers at my grandmother's lake property. She made sure that my parents sent us to visit, and

she invited our cousins who we rarely saw over for visits while we were there; she believed that connecting with family is a vital and active process. She told us regularly that nothing is more important than family.

Concluding sentence

Topic sentence

Furthermore, my grandmother gave to her community. She volunteered for the local Red Cross, and she helped with the local food bank every week. Once, when I was eight years old and visiting her, I went with her to help give out food to the needy. I asked her, "Why do you do this every week, Grandma, even when you are tired?"

"It's important to give back to your community, to do something selfless for the good of others without expecting something in return," she said. She then winked at me as she passed her rough fingers through her silver hair.

Concluding sentence

"Oh," I said, knitting my brow in concentration. Even though I was young, I remember thinking about how wise and generous she was. Now that I'm older and she is gone, I appreciate her true wisdom and admirable character even more.

A week prior to her death, my brother and I visited her at the lake property and had a special time as usual. I didn't know it then, but that would be the last time I saw her. She became severely ill a few days later and was taken to the hospital. On September 21, 2005, at five a.m., we got a call from her doctor who told us she had passed away. We were all shocked and heartbroken. Though she was ill, we never thought she would pass away that soon. I had never experienced death before, and I didn't really know what to do. I was sad and grieving at first, but I began to understand that my grandmother had had a full life, and that she could live on in our thoughts and in our actions.

Topic sentence

I could become the kind of charitable person she was. I could help keep our family close in her absence. In addition, I began to understand that life is short and that I need to cherish my family and my life now, like my grandmother did.

Restatement of thesis

    The death of my grandmother taught me to appreciate my life and my loved ones and to live a life that gives to others. Though she is gone and I'm sad for the loss of her physical presence, I keep her in my heart and thoughts, and I use her model of love of family and giving to others to be a better person in my life.

This student's draft has a good basic narrative structure and organization and a strong message or lesson learned. This draft also includes some dialogue. The next draft would need more descriptive details and concrete images of the grandmother and the setting. Also, the essay would be stronger with more examples, sentence variety, and changes in style and vocabulary.

ACTIVITY 7-10   Thinking Critically about the Student Essay

Directions: *Identify the features and details characteristic of the narrative/descriptive mode in the student essay. Mark them on the essay. Then, reread the essay, and make a list of specific revisions you would make to correct any problems with content, organization, transitions, and style.*

PROFESSIONAL NARRATIVE ESSAY

Half a Day

Naguib Mahfouz

Translated by Denys Johnson-Davies

Naguib Mahfouz was born in Cairo, Egypt, in 1911, and he died in 2006. He wrote stories, novels, and articles about life in the Middle East. He won the Nobel Prize for Literature in 1988.

1

Thesis

I proceeded alongside my father, clutching his right hand, running to keep up with the long strides he was taking. All my clothes were new: the black shoes, the green school uniform, and the red tarboosh. My delight in my new clothes, however, was not altogether unmarred, for this was no feast day but the day on which I was to be cast into school for the first time.

2

Narration in time order

My mother stood at the window watching our progress, and I would turn toward her from time to time, as though appealing for help. We walked along a street lined with gardens; on both sides were extensive fields planted with crops, prickly pears, henna trees, and a few date palms.

3

Use of dialogue

"Why school?" I challenged my father openly. "I shall never do anything to annoy you."

4

"I'm not punishing you," he said, laughing. "School's not a punishment. It's the factory that makes useful men out of boys. Don't you want to be like your father and brothers?"

5

Metaphor and example

I was not convinced. I did not believe there was really any good to be had in tearing me away from the intimacy of my home and throwing me into this building that stood at the end of the road like some huge, high-walled fortress, exceedingly stern and grim.

6

When we arrived at the gate we could see the courtyard, vast and crammed full of boys and girls. "Go in by yourself," said my father, "and join them. Put a smile on your face and be a good example to others."

7

I hesitated and clung to his hand, but he gently pushed me from him. "Be a man," he said. "Today you truly begin life. You will find me waiting for you when it's time to leave."

8

I took a few steps, then stopped and looked but saw nothing. Then the faces of boys and girls came into view. I did not know a single one of them, and none of them knew me. I felt I was a stranger who had lost his way. But glances of curiosity were directed toward me, and one boy approached and asked, "Who brought you?"

9

"My father," I whispered.

10

"My father's dead," he said quite simply.

11

Examples and details

I did not know what to say. The gate was closed, letting out a pitiable screech. Some of the children burst into tears. The bell rang. A lady came along, followed by a group of men. The men began sorting us into ranks. We were formed into an intricate pattern in the great courtyard surrounded on three sides by high buildings of several floors; from each floor we were overlooked by a long balcony roofed in wood.

12

"This is your new home," said the woman. "Here too there are mothers and fathers. Here there is everything that is enjoyable and beneficial to knowledge and religion. Dry your tears and face life joyfully."

13

We submitted to the facts and this submission brought a sort of contentment. Living beings were drawn to other living beings, and from the first moments my heart made friends with such boys as were to be my friends and fell in love with such girls as I was to be in love with, so that it seemed my misgivings had had no basis. I had never imagined school would have this rich variety. We played all sorts of different games: swings, the vaulting horse, ball games. In the music room we chanted our first songs. We also had our first introduction to language. We saw a globe of the Earth, which revolved and showed the various continents and countries. We started learning the numbers. The story of the Creator of the universe was read to us, we were told of His present world and of His Hereafter, and we heard examples of what He said. We ate delicious food, took a little nap, and woke up to go on with friendship and love, play and learning.

Examples and commentary

14　As our path revealed itself to us, however, we did not find it as totally sweet and unclouded as we had presumed. Dust-laden winds and unexpected accidents came about suddenly, so we had to be watchful, at the ready, and very patient. It was not all a matter of playing and fooling around. Rivalries could bring about pain and hatred or give rise to fighting. And while the

Comparison/contrast

lady would sometimes smile, she would often scowl and scold. Even more frequently she would resort to physical punishment.

15　In addition, the time for changing one's mind was over and gone and there was no question of ever returning to the paradise of home. Nothing lay ahead of us but exertion, struggle, and perseverance. Those who were able took advantage of the opportunities for success and happiness that presented themselves amid the worries.

16　The bell rang announcing the passing of the day and the end of work. The throngs of children rushed toward the gate, which was opened again. I bade farewell to friends and sweethearts and passed through the gate. I peered around but found no trace of my father, who had promised to be there. I stepped aside to wait. When I had waited for a long time without avail, I decided to return home on my own. After I had taken a few steps, a middle-aged man passed by, and I realized at once that I knew him. He came toward me, smiling, and shook me by the hand, saying, "It's a long time since we last met—how are you?"

17　With a nod of my head, I agreed with him and in turn asked, "And you, how are you?"

18　"As you can see, not all that good, the Almighty be praised!"

19　Again he shook me by the hand and went off. I proceeded a few steps, then came to a startled halt. Good Lord! Where was the street lined with gardens? Where had it disappeared to? When did all these vehicles invade it? And when did all these hordes of humanity come to rest upon its surface? How did these hills of refuse come to cover its sides? And where were the fields that bordered it? High buildings had taken over, the street surged with children, and disturbing noises shook the air. At various points stood conjurers showing off their tricks and making snakes appear from baskets. There was a band announcing the opening of a circus, with clowns and weight lifters walking in front. A line of trucks carrying central security troops crawled majestically by.

The siren of a fire engine shrieked, and it was not clear how the vehicle would cleave its way to reach the blazing fire. A battle raged between a taxi driver and his passenger, while the passenger's wife called out for help and no one answered. Good God! I was in a daze. My head spun. I almost went crazy. How could all this have happened in half a day, between early morning and sunset? I would find the answer at home with my father. But where was my home? I could see only tall buildings and hordes of people. I hastened on to the crossroads between the gardens and Abu Khoda. I had to cross Abu Khoda to reach my house, but the stream of cars would not let up. The fire engine's siren was shrieking at full pitch as it moved at a snail's pace, and I said to myself, "Let the fire take its pleasure in what it consumes." Extremely irritated, I wondered when I would be able to cross. I stood there a long time, until the young lad employed at the ironing shop on the corner came up to me. He stretched out his arm and said gallantly, "Grandpa, let me take you across."

Message/lesson

MyWritingLab™   **Reading Reflection Questions**

1. What are the direct or indirect (implied) messages in this story?

   _____

   _____

   _____

2. How is the title of this narrative, "Half a Day," important to the overall story and message? (Note that the phrase appears again in the last paragraph of the story.)

   _____

   _____

3. How does Mahfouz's use of concrete examples, details, and metaphors contribute to the story? Give a specific example in your answer. What effect does the inclusion of these details have on you as a reader?

   _____

   _____

   _____

MyWritingLab™   **Objective Questions**

4. T/F_____The entire narration actually does take place in just half a day.

5. T/F_____His neighborhood has changed immensely in the course of his lifetime.

6. T/F_____Comparing his school to a "high-walled fortress" at the beginning shows his apprehension about starting school.

7. How does dialogue contribute to the narrative? Provide one example and explain why it stood out for you.

_____

_____

MyWritingLab™   ### Checking Vocabulary

Define the following in your own words, or provide a dictionary definition if you don't know the word.

8. unmarred (paragraph 1): _____

9. pitiable (paragraph 11): _____

10. submission (paragraph 13): _____

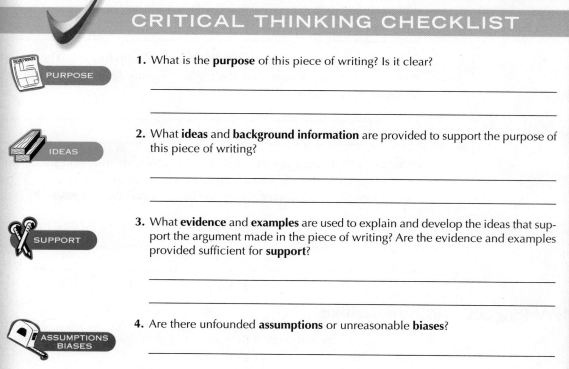

CRITICAL THINKING CHECKLIST

PURPOSE

1. What is the **purpose** of this piece of writing? Is it clear?

_____

_____

IDEAS

2. What **ideas** and **background information** are provided to support the purpose of this piece of writing?

_____

_____

SUPPORT

3. What **evidence** and **examples** are used to explain and develop the ideas that support the argument made in the piece of writing? Are the evidence and examples provided sufficient for **support**?

_____

_____

ASSUMPTIONS BIASES

4. Are there unfounded **assumptions** or unreasonable **biases**?

_____

_____

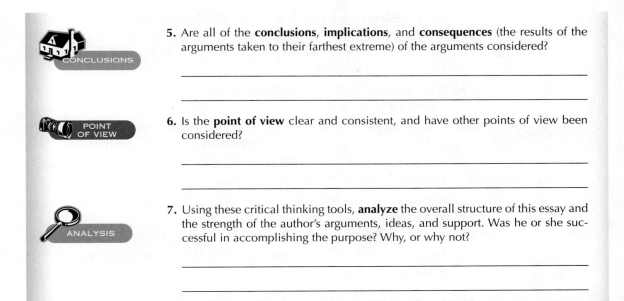

5. Are all of the **conclusions**, **implications**, and **consequences** (the results of the arguments taken to their farthest extreme) of the arguments considered?

_____

_____

6. Is the **point of view** clear and consistent, and have other points of view been considered?

_____

_____

7. Using these critical thinking tools, **analyze** the overall structure of this essay and the strength of the author's arguments, ideas, and support. Was he or she successful in accomplishing the purpose? Why, or why not?

_____

_____

MyWritingLab™   Essay Assignments

1. Write an essay using the thesis statement, topic sentences, supporting examples, and concluding paragraph you wrote in the activities in this chapter.

2. Write an analytical essay about an incident that happened to you (or that you witnessed) that had a significant impact on you. Describe what happened using specific details and explain the impact. What lesson did you learn that day (about yourself, others, your culture, or something else)?

   a. The organization for this essay requires a general introduction that explains the incident briefly and includes a thesis statement, which tells exactly what lesson(s) you learned from the experience.

   b. The body paragraphs should use time order to tell what happened. Be sure to include some dialogue to make the event come alive for your readers; follow the tips for using dialogue correctly given earlier in this chapter.

   c. When describing the incident, include specific details and use as many sensory details as possible (sight, sound, touch, smell, taste).

   d. In the conclusion, sum up the lesson(s) you learned and how you feel now about the incident.

After you finish your first draft of this essay, use the narrative and descriptive essay critique form from this chapter to check for the basics. You can also have a classmate or friend examine your draft using the checklist. Then review your essay.

3. Write a narrative/descriptive essay about your first day of college or first day on a job.

4. Write a narrative/descriptive essay about a world event you learned about on the news that affected you emotionally or intellectually.

5. Write a narrative/descriptive essay about an event that taught you something about yourself that you hadn't realized before.

6. Write a narrative/descriptive essay about an occurrence that resulted in your losing trust in someone.

7. Write a narrative/descriptive essay about a complex or difficult situation that you or a close family member went through and how you or that person got through it.

Multimodal Writing Assignment

Choose any of the essay assignments above, and then add some visuals (drawings, photographs, icons) to illustrate the event. Then create a PowerPoint presentation of three to five slides that explores the series of events in time order and what you learned at each point. Finally, post a summary and analysis of your essay on your classroom blog or discussion board site for your classmates to read and comment upon.

Learning Objectives Review

My WritingLab™ **Complete the chapter assessment questions at mywritinglab.com**

1 Describe the narrative and descriptive mode. **What distinguishes the narrative and descriptive mode from other modes? (See p. 146.)**	**Narrative and descriptive mode** recounts an event, story, or series of events, using concrete details and vivid descriptive words from as many of the five senses as possible.	
2 Apply critical thinking skills to writing narrative and descriptive essays. **What do you want to achieve by thinking critically about writing a narration/description essay? (See pp. 146–147.)**	**Thinking critically** helps you identify what you have learned, decide what message you want to convey, and determine what details to include and how to organize them.	
3 Prepare to write a narrative and descriptive essay by asking critical thinking questions. **What questions will help you plan a narrative/descriptive essay? (See pp. 147–149.)**	**Ask the following questions**: (1) What did I learn from the experience? (2) What do I want my readers to learn or understand after reading about the event I experienced or witnessed? (3) How can I recreate the event vividly in my readers' minds using examples and details? (4) How should I organize my sentences and paragraphs, and how can I move smoothly from one event or detail to the next? (5) How might I conclude my essay?	
4 Structure a narrative and descriptive essay. **How do you structure a narrative and descriptive essay? (See pp. 149–163.)**	You **structure a narrative/descriptive essay** by crafting a thesis statement in the introductory paragraph about a story that makes a point (lesson learned), organizing the essay in chronological order, developing your topic sentences using specific sensory details, and using real dialogue to add details and develop your purpose.	

❺ Use modes that complement narrative and descriptive essays.

What modes complement a narrative/descriptive essay? (See pp. 163–172.)

Modes that work well within a narrative/descriptive structure include example and illustration, process, cause and effect, comparison and contrast, and argument.

LEARNING OBJECTIVES

In this chapter, you will learn how to

1 Describe the process mode.

2 Apply critical thinking skills to writing process essays.

3 Prepare to write a process essay by asking critical thinking questions.

4 Structure a process essay.

5 Use modes that complement process essays.

Making a Sauce

Thinking Critically MyWritingLab™

Think: Study the photograph.

Write: Describe the process that is demonstrated in this image.

_____

_____

_____

1. If you had to write a short essay describing a process that you perform routinely at home or at work, how would you organize the essay?

_____

_____

_____

2. What are some reasons for writing a description of a specific process? Provide an example.

_____

_____

_____

PROCESS ESSAYS

1 Describe the process mode.

Essays that explain how things work (e.g., a combustion engine or the digestive system) or how to do something (bake a cake, get legislation through Congress, find a job) are written in the process mode. This mode is very common in business, in science and math classes, or wherever tasks are part of a process. It is even used to analyze a process to see how efficient it is or to demonstrate a better alternative (for example, a process essay could explain how a traditional combustion engine works, how this type of engine contributes to pollution, and how a hybrid engine works and decreases pollution).

CRITICAL THINKING AND PROCESS MODE

2 Apply critical thinking skills to writing process essays.

Be sure to make the **purpose** of your process essay clear: to simply describe a process so someone else can repeat it; to inform; to critique; or to propose an alternative process after describing the status quo (the way things are now). Think carefully about the best way to describe the process and demonstrate the purpose for your essay: What do you want your readers to learn about this process besides how to do it? How can you best structure the essay to achieve your goal, and what details will you include? As you describe a process, you will need to **analyze** the steps and the best way to clearly explain the procedure.

Be careful not to present a conclusion without providing the evidence and reasoning that led to that conclusion. This error can be caused by logical fallacies, such as **hasty generalization**, which means you assume that all similar things are exactly alike, or **post-hoc fallacy**, thinking that because one event happened first it must be the cause of the event that followed it. It is easy to commit a post-hoc fallacy in a process essay if you are not thinking carefully about whether one step actually leads to the next. You should not make a cause-and-effect analysis without providing evidence to support the connection between two events.

BEFORE WRITING A PROCESS ESSAY

3 Prepare to write a process essay by asking critical thinking questions.

Before you begin to write a process essay, ask yourself these questions:

1. What process am I describing?
2. What specific steps, examples, and details should I use to describe the process?
3. How should I organize my paragraphs after my introduction and thesis statement, and how can I move smoothly from one step or detail to the next?

4. What is my purpose for writing this process description (to describe how something works, to tell someone how to accomplish a task, to critique a process and provide a better alternative, other)?

5. Who is my intended audience, and how much do they already know about my topic?

Answering these questions will help you generate an expository thesis statement, help you determine what examples to use, and give you a general idea of how to organize your essay.

ACTIVITY 8-1 Steps in a Process

Directions: *Briefly describe the major steps in each of the following common processes. Then come up with a purpose for writing about such a process (what you would want your readers to understand or learn through your description of the process).*

1. Brushing teeth properly: _____

_____

_____

Purpose: _____

_____

2. Making a sandwich: _____

_____

_____

Purpose: _____

_____

3. Registering for classes: _____

_____

_____

Purpose: _____

_____

4. Grocery shopping: _____

_____

_____

Purpose: _____

_____

5. Reading a textbook chapter: _____

_____

_____

Purpose: _____

_____

WRITING A PROCESS ESSAY

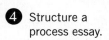

In a process essay, the steps of a process are usually described in chronological order, one step at a time, in the order they happen. For example, if you were telling your readers how to make a bed, you might describe it like this:

> To make your bed in the best possible way, start by putting one corner of the fitted sheet tightly over the top left corner of your mattress. Next, put the other top corner of the fitted sheet over the top right corner of your mattress. Carefully pull the bottom two corners of the sheet to the bottom of your bed, and do the same process with the bottom two corners of your mattress. Next, get your flat sheet ready . . .

A process essay can also be organized by the order of importance of the individual steps if the process doesn't require a particular sequence of steps. For example, if you were describing the process of applying for a job, you might choose order of importance to list the paragraphs on how to present yourself during an interview, how to best prepare your resumé and application letter, how to determine which companies to apply to, and so on.

Therefore, if you are not just writing a recipe or a how-to description, you will need to decide what the *expository purpose* or message is for writing a process description (for example, to evaluate a process, to teach or instruct, or to propose an alternative process). Always include *descriptive details* that explain and illustrate each step. Then make sure that your essay's conclusion reiterates the purpose of your process description or analysis.

Organizational Pattern for a Process Essay

Be sure to describe the steps in **chronological order** (time order—one step at a time) or order of importance. **Order of importance** is a perfect organizational order to use when you want to emphasize *the most to least important ideas* or *the least to most important ideas*.

Least to most important order example: There are several important things to keep in mind when buying a house. First, find a real estate agent you like. Also, set up tours of the houses you've viewed on the real estate Web site and decided that you like. It's very important to set up an inspection of the house you are interested in to make sure it is safe and in the condition the seller says it is. Finally, and most importantly, check that the houses you consider are in your price range by figuring out your finances and loan possibilities before you start looking seriously for a new home.

Of course, if you wanted to start with the most important steps and progress to least important, then you would reverse this order.

BASIC STRUCTURE FOR A PROCESS ESSAY

See the sample essay on pages 187–188.

INTRODUCTORY PARAGRAPH

Sets up background for the process and why you are describing it.

Thesis statement: A statement that describes what you are trying to explain, show, prove, or argue through describing a process. Do you want to instruct someone in how to perform a specific task? Do you want to explain how a process works? Or do you want to critique a process and propose an alternative?

BODY PARAGRAPHS (Two to five, depending on assignment and purpose)

Develop the process using time order or order of importance. Topic sentences should clarify the type of order and the categories or major stages of the process.

Use transitions within and between paragraphs to emphasize switching to the next step.

Provide concrete details and description.

Define terms when necessary, especially if your process involves parts or tools.

Add commentary and analysis about the steps, details, and descriptions to help develop the expository purpose/thesis statement.

CONCLUDING PARAGRAPH

Sum up and re-emphasize the thesis: the **purpose** for describing this process in the first place.

Structuring a Process Essay

You might structure a process essay around a natural process you have studied in a science course; a daily ritual such as getting ready for school, making your lunch, or studying for a test in order to show what you think is the best approach to accomplishing this ritual; or the best way to achieve a long-term goal such as saving money for college.

Topic

If your instructor has not assigned a topic for your process essay, then brain-storm ideas for a process you might want to describe. Then come up with some ideas for a purpose for describing the topic. What do you want your readers to understand through your description of the process?

Thesis Statements

The thesis statement in a process essay establishes what process you are describing or analyzing and for what purpose. For instance, if you were writing a basic essay in order to explain how to complete a task step by step, then this would be reflected in the thesis statement.

> In order to make a perfect homemade cake, complete each of the following steps in order.

If you were critiquing an existing process and proposing an alternative, you would set out both of these goals in your thesis statement.

> The combustion engine has been in use for over a century, but it is inefficient and bad for the environment; therefore, the hybrid engine's use of gas for starting and electricity for driving makes it better for the environment and an overall better choice for a new car.

ACTIVITY 8-2   Creating Thesis Statements

Directions: *Create a one-sentence thesis statement for each general topic. Make sure the thesis has a clear message or lesson to convey about why you would describe each process.*

1. **Topic:** Setting up a Facebook page

   Thesis sentence: _____

   _____

2. **Topic:** Writing an essay

   Thesis sentence: _____

   _____

3. **Topic:** Registering for classes

   Thesis sentence: _____

   _____

4. **Topic:** Finding an apartment to rent

   Thesis sentence: _____

   _____

5. **Topic:** Finding a part-time job

   Thesis sentence: _____

   _____

Cross Reference

See Chapter 6, pp. 104–115, Stage One: Prewrite to Generate Ideas.

Creating a Rough Outline

Once you have determined your topic and your thesis statement, you are ready to create a rough outline to determine your essay's structure and organizational plan. Use prewriting techniques such as brainstorming or clustering to generate supporting examples and concrete details. Then create a rough outline using this template:

Rough Outline Template for a Process Essay

    I. Introductory Paragraph
       A. A brief, general description of the process
       B. Thesis Statement: the purpose of your process essay (to inform, critique, suggest an alternative process, and so on).
   II. Body Paragraphs: Two to four paragraphs that explain the process in chronological order or order of importance
       A. Include concrete description and details for each step of the process
       B. Include transitions from one step to the next
       C. Include definitions and explanations when needed
  III. Concluding Paragraph
       A. Restate in a new way the process and purpose/thesis
       B. Add some general closing comments without introducing any new ideas

Introductory Paragraph

Begin your process essay with a general introduction that presents the process you'll be describing. End the introductory paragraph with your thesis statement.

Body Paragraphs

The body paragraphs in a process essay can be arranged in time order or order of importance, depending on the purpose of your thesis statement. Topic sentences should clarify the type of order and the categories or major stages of the process. You can describe one step in each paragraph, or you can arrange the body paragraphs so that you describe the process, critique it, and then propose an alternative. Regardless of which organizational pattern you choose, always include specific examples and definitions. For clarity, use transitions to introduce each new step in the process (see the list of transitions below). Other transitions common for process essays strengthen a point or show a summary, examples, purpose, place, and time.

Cross Reference
See also Chapter 5, p. 93, Transitions to. . . .

TRANSITIONS TO . . .

Show Addition of Another Point

again	but also	in addition	nor
also	equally important	last	plus the fact
and	finally	lastly	second
and then	first	likewise	then too
another	further	moreover	third
besides	furthermore	next	too

ACTIVITY 8-3   Creating Topic Sentences

Directions: *Create one possible topic sentence for each of the thesis statements you created in Activity 8-2.*

1. **Topic:** Setting up a Facebook page

   Topic sentence: _____

   _____

2. **Topic:** Writing an essay

   Topic sentence: _____

   _____

3. **Topic:** Registering for classes

   Topic sentence: _____

   _____

4. **Topic:** Finding an apartment to rent

   Topic sentence: _____

   _____

5. **Topic:** Finding a part-time job

   Topic sentence: _____

   _____

Support for your topic sentences should include examples and specific details that explain the process and all of its steps, as well as definitions of terms.

APPLYING CRITICAL THINKING

PURPOSE   IDEAS   SUPPORT   ASSUMPTIONS BIASES   CONCLUSIONS   POINT OF VIEW   ANALYSIS

When you write a process essay, you can't assume your reader will know what you mean. Carefully **analyze** the steps involved. Make sure you include each one, and describe exactly how to perform each one. For instance, if you are describing how to make a peanut butter sandwich and say, "Spread the peanut butter on the bread," you may want to add "using a knife," or the reader might use their bare hand. Obviously, most people will know to use a knife in the common process of making a peanut butter sandwich, but in more complex processes, such as the way a nuclear power plant works, you will need to be specific and define any technical terms you use so a general audience can understand you.

ACTIVITY 8-4   Using Examples, Definitions, and Other Details

Directions: *Now provide at least three possible examples or details you would include for each of the topic sentences you created in Activity 8-3.*

1. **Topic:** Setting up a Facebook page

   Examples: _____

   _____

2. **Topic:** Writing an essay

   Examples: _____

   _____

3. **Topic:** Registering for classes

   Examples: _____

   _____

4. **Topic:** Finding an apartment to rent

   Examples: _____

   _____

5. **Topic:** Finding a part-time job

   Examples: _____

   _____

Concluding Paragraph

The concluding paragraph in a process essay should restate both the process being described and the purpose for describing it: to instruct the reader on how to do something; to describe how a machine, experiment, or system works; or to critique the way something works and propose an alternative. The paragraph can also include some general concluding comments about the process.

ACTIVITY 8-5   Writing a Conclusion

Directions: *Choose one of the topics from the previous activities, and write a three-to five-sentence conclusion for the topic. Be sure to reiterate what you introduced in the thesis.*

_____

_____

_____

_____

_____

_____

ACTIVITY 8-6 Creating Your Outline and First Draft

Cross Reference
See Chapters 21–25,
pp. 515–648, for help with
the Editing section of the
critique form.

Directions: *Choose a topic from one of the activities you already completed in this chapter, from the assignment choices at the end of this chapter, or from a topic assigned by your instructor and create a rough outline using the template on page 181 of this chapter. Then, using your rough outline, write a first draft of your essay. After you have finished, use the critique form below to check for the basics in your essay draft.*

PROCESS ESSAY CRITIQUE FORM

PURPOSE   IDEAS   SUPPORT   ASSUMPTIONS BIASES   CONCLUSIONS   POINT OF VIEW   ANALYSIS

Overall	Done well	Needs work
1. Does the essay clearly describe a process with an **analytical** purpose (e.g., to inform, critique, etc.)?	_____	_____
2. Does the essay use time order or order of importance in the body paragraphs?	_____	_____
3. Are the paragraphs organized clearly and logically and are they a good length—5–15 sentences?	_____	_____

Introduction		
4. Is the title interesting and in the correct format?	_____	_____
5. Is there a general introduction that sets up the thesis?	_____	_____
6. Is there a clear thesis statement that explains the purpose of the process being described?	_____	_____

Continued ▶

Body

7. Do the body paragraphs develop the process logically and flow smoothly?   _____ _____
8. Are transitions used between and, when needed, within the paragraphs?   _____ _____
9. Do the **ideas** in the body paragraphs include **support**—descriptive details to show the process?   _____ _____

Conclusion

10. Does the **concluding** paragraph sum up the process and re-emphasize the **purpose** presented in the introductory paragraph and thesis, without adding new ideas?   _____ _____

Editing

11. Circle the following errors you think you see in this draft: spelling errors, fragments, run-ons/comma splices, errors in comma and semicolon/colon use, pronoun disagreement, pronoun reference errors, errors in parallelism, apostrophe use, verb use/tense, and passive voice construction.
12. Other types of grammar or sentence-level errors:

_____

Comments (For example: What works well in this draft? What needs to be added? Did you, or will your readers, understand each step of the process and could you duplicate it? Why or why not?):

_____

_____

_____

COMPLEMENTARY MODES FOR PROCESS ESSAYS

5 Use modes that complement process essays.

When writing a process essay, of course, the dominant mode will be process; however, you can create a more powerful message by weaving in sentences or paragraphs in other modes. For example:

- **Narration and description:** Specific description and details and stories bring relatable images and specificity to the process you are describing so your readers can follow along with the steps in their minds.
- **Examples and illustration:** Most effective process essays develop their purpose through specific examples and illustrations.
- **Cause and effect:** By offering the reasons for and results of each step in a process, the writer displays the logic of the steps in the process.
- **Comparison/contrast:** By comparing or contrasting the individual stages or tasks in a process, the writer helps the reader learn about an unfamiliar process or step through a connection to a more familiar one.
- **Argument:** Sometimes your reason for describing a process is to persuade your readers to learn a particular process or to critique an existing process and convince your readers to use it or avoid it.

Student Essay

The dominant mode used in this student's paper is process. Look for other modes used in this essay as well.

Michelle Rooney

Professor Hernandez

English 100

February 28, 2013

How to Pick the Right Courses

Being a college student poses many difficult challenges. One of the toughest parts of being in school is knowing which classes to take and how to register for the right courses once you have chosen them. It is essential to plan ahead, research your options and know your goals, and register on time if you want to pick the right courses for your degree in a timely manner.

Thesis statement

To begin with, many students make the mistake of waiting to the last minute to think about their courses for the next semester or quarter. However, it is essential to plan ahead. Choosing the right courses for your goals and your degree is not a matter that should be taken lightly or put off to the last minute. Begin thinking about the next quarter or semester's course offerings and what you might want to take at least two weeks before your scheduled registration date. You have to find out what the registration date is, or, if it is open registration, when that begins. Then, you need to mark your calendar and begin the next steps of getting ready to register.

Topic sentence

The next major component to picking your classes is to research your options carefully. Get a copy of the course schedule as soon as it becomes available. Then, research which courses you still need to take to achieve your educational goals

Topic sentence

Rooney 2

or meet your degree requirements. Also, research if you have
to take a prerequisite course before you can take any of the
courses you are interested in. Also, you will need to check the
available times for the courses you need and make sure they
do not conflict with each other or with your work schedule
if you work.

Topic sentence

Finally, the last step involved in getting the courses you
need is to register on time and not procrastinate. For some students, this step requires having enough money to afford tuition,
but other students who have no financial barriers still make the
mistake of putting off registering and therefore risk not getting
the classes they want and need. Remember, classes fill up quickly,
and the longer you wait, the less likely you are to receive your
first choices for classes. Be sure to have some back-up courses
in mind. For instance, if you plan to take a biology lab course, be
prepared to take a geology lab course if biology is full.

Restatement of thesis

If you follow these steps and avoid procrastination, you
should be successful in your quest to register for the right classes.
College is stressful enough, so why make the process for registering for classes another source of tension? Prepare, be ready, and
register on time.

ACTIVITY 8-7   Thinking Critically about the Student Essay

Directions: *Analyze the student essay above to identify the features and details characteristic of the process mode. Mark them on the essay. Then, reread the essay and make a list of specific revisions you would make to correct any problems with content, organization, transitions, and style.*

PROFESSIONAL PROCESS ESSAY

Making the Pitch in Print Advertising

Courtland L. Bovée, John V. Thill, George P. Dovel, and Marian Burk Wood

COPYWRITERS AND COPYWRITING

1   Given the importance of copy, it comes as no surprise that copywriters are key players in the advertising process. In fact, many of the most notable leaders and voices in the industry began their careers as copywriters, including Jane Maas, David Ogilvy, Rosser Reeves, Leo Burnett, and William Bernbach. As a profession, copywriting is somewhat unusual because so many of its top practitioners have been in their jobs for years, even decades (rather than moving up the management ranks as is usual in many professions). Copywriters can either work for agencies or set themselves up as freelancers, selling their services to agencies and advertisers. Because it presents endless opportunities to be creative, copywriting is one of those rare *Thesis statement* jobs that can be fresh and challenging year after year.

2   Although successful copywriters share a love of language with novelists, *Topic sentence* poets, and other writers, copywriting is first and foremost a business function, not an artistic endeavor. The challenge isn't to create works of literary merit, but to meet advertising objectives. This doesn't mean that copywriting isn't an art, however; it's simply art in pursuit of a business goal. Nor is it easy. Such noted literary writers as Stephen Vincent Benét, George Bernard Shaw, and Ernest Hemingway tried to write ad copy and found themselves unable to do it effectively. It's the combined requirements of language skills, business acumen, and an ability to create under the pressure of tight deadlines and *Example and illustration* format restrictions (such as the limited number of words you have to work *mode* with) that make copywriting so challenging—and so endlessly rewarding.

3   Copywriters have many styles and approaches to writing, but most *Topic sentence* agree on one thing: copywriting is hard work. It can involve a great deal of planning and coordinating with clients, legal staffers, account executives, researchers, and art directors. In addition, it usually entails hammering away at your copy until it's as good as it can be. David Ogilvy talked about doing 19 drafts of a single piece of copy and writing 37 headlines for a Sears ad in order to get 3 possibilities to show to the client. Actually, the chance to write and rewrite that many times is a luxury that most copywriters don't have; they often must produce copy on tight schedules with unforgiving deadlines (such as magazine publication deadlines).

4

Topic sentence

The task of copywriting is most often associated with the headlines and copy you see in an ad, but copywriters actually develop a wide variety of other materials, from posters to catalogs to press releases, as well as the words you hear in radio and television commercials.

Specific example of a step in the process

PRINT COPY

5

Copywriters are responsible for every word you see in print ads, whether the words are in a catchy headline or in the fine print at the bottom of the page. The three major categories of copy are headlines, body copy, and slogans.

Definition mode

Specific example of a step in the process

HEADLINES

6

The *headline*, also called a *heading* or a *head*, constitutes the dominant line or lines of copy in an ad. Headlines are typically set in larger type and appear at the top of the ad, although there are no hard-and-fast rules on headline layout. *Subheads* are secondary headlines, often written to move the reader from the main headline to the body copy.

Definition mode

7

Even if there is a pageful of body copy and only a few words in the headline, the headline is the most important piece of copy for two reasons: First, it serves as the "come-on" to get people to stop turning the page and check out your ad. Second, as much as 80 percent of your audience may not bother to read the body copy, so whatever message these nonreaders carry away from the ad will have to come from the headline.

8

Copywriters can choose from a variety of headline types, each of which performs a particular function.

Example and illustration mode

- **News headlines.** News headlines present information that's new to the audience, such as announcing a new store location, a new product, or lower prices. This approach is common because potential customers are often looking for new solutions, lower prices, and other relevant changes in the marketplace. For example, a newspaper ad from the Silo home electronics chain announced a recent sale using a news headline: "Everything on Sale! 4 Days Only! 5–20% Off Everything!" Headlines like this are typical in local newspaper advertising.

- **Emotional headlines.** The emotional appeal described earlier in the chapter is represented by emotional headlines. The quotation headline "I'm sick of her ruining our lives" was used in an ad for the American Mental Health Fund to echo the frustration some parents feel when they can't understand their teenagers' behavior. Combined with a photo of a sad and withdrawn teenage girl, the headline grabs any parent who has felt such frustration, and the body copy goes on to explain that families shouldn't get mad at people with mental illnesses but should help them get treatment for their conditions.

- **Benefit headlines.** The benefit headline is a statement of the key customer benefit. An ad for Quicken personal finance software used the question-form headline: "How do you know exactly where your money goes and how much you have?" followed by "It's this simple" above a photograph of the product package. The customer benefit is keeping better track of your money, and Quicken is the solution offered.

- **Directive headlines.** Headlines that direct the reader to do something, or at least suggest the reader do something, can motivate consumer action. Such headlines can be a hard sell, such as "Come in now and save," or they can be something more subtle, such as "Just feel the color in these black and whites," the headline in an ad for Ensoniq keyboards.

- **Offbeat and curiosity headlines.** Humor, wordplay, and mystery can be effective ways to draw readers into an ad. An ad promoting vacation travel to Spain used the headline "Sí in the dark," with a photo of a lively night-time scene. The word *Sí* is catchy because it first looks like an error, until the reader reads the body copy to learn that the ad is talking about Spain (*sí* is Spanish for "yes").

- **Hornblowing headlines.** The hornblowing headline, called "Brag and Boast" heads by the Gallup & Robinson research organization, should be used with care. Customers have seen it all and heard it all, and "We're the greatest" headlines tend to sound arrogant and self-centered. This isn't to say that you can't stress superiority; you just need to do it in a way that takes the customer's needs into account, and the headline must be honest. The headline "Neuberger & Berman Guardian Fund" followed by the subhead "#1 Performing Growth and Income Fund" blows the company's own horn but also conveys an important product benefit. Since investors look for top-performing mutual funds, the information about being number one is relevant.

- **Slogan, label, or logo headlines.** Some headlines show a company's slogan, a product label, or the organization's logo. Powerful slogans like Hallmark's "When you care enough to send the very best" can make great headlines because they click with the reader's emotions. Label and logo headlines can build product and company awareness, but they must be used with care. If the label or logo doesn't make some emotional or logical connection with the reader, the ad probably won't succeed.

Example and illustration mode

9   Headlines often have maximum impact when coupled with a well-chosen graphic element, rather than trying to carry the message with words alone. In fact, the careful combination of the two can increase the audience's involvement with the ad, especially if one of the two says something ironic or unexpected that has to be resolved by considering the other element. A magazine ad for Easter Seals had the headline "After all we did for Pete, he walked out on us." At first, you think the birth-defects organization is complaining. Then you see a photo of Pete with new artificial legs, walking away from a medical facility. It's a powerful combination that makes the reader feel good about the things Easter Seals can do for people.

Checklist for Producing Excellent Copy

❑ **A.** Avoid clichés.
  - Create fresh, original phrases that vividly convey your message.
  - Remember that clever wordplay based on clichés can be quite effective.

❑ **B.** Watch out for borrowed interest.
  - Make sure you don't use inappropriate copy or graphics since they can steal the show from your basic sales message.
  - Be sure nothing draws attention from the message.

❑ **C.** Don't boast.
  - Be sure the ad's purpose isn't merely to pat the advertiser on the back.
  - Tout success when you must convince nonbuyers that lots of people just like them have purchased your product; this isn't the same as shouting "We're the best!"

❑ **D.** Make it personal, informal, and relevant.
  - Connect with the audience in a way that is personal and comfortable. Pompous, stiff, and overly "businesslike" tends to turn people away.
  - Avoid copy that sounds like it belongs in an ad, with too many overblown adjectives and unsupported claims of superiority.

❑ **E.** Keep it simple, specific, and concise.
  - Make your case quickly and stick to the point. This will help you get past all the barriers and filters that people put up to help them select which things they'll pay attention to and which they'll ignore.
  - Avoid copy that's confusing, meandering, too long, or too detailed.

❑ **F.** Give the audience a reason to read, listen, or watch.
  - Offer a solution to your audience's problems.
  - Entertain your audience.
  - Consider any means possible to get your audience to pay attention long enough to get your sales message across.

BODY COPY

The second major category of copy is the *body copy*, which constitutes the words in the main body of the ad, apart from headlines, photo captions, and other blocks of text. The importance of body copy varies from ad to ad, and some ads have little or no body copy. Ads for easy-to-understand products, for instance, often rely on the headline and a visual such as a photograph to get their point across. In contrast, when the selling message needs a lot of supporting detail to be convincing, an ad can be packed full of body copy. Some advertisers have the impression that long body copy should be avoided, but that isn't always the case. The rule to apply here is to use the "right" number of words. You might not need many words in a perfume ad, but you might need a page or two to cover a complex industrial product.

11

Specific example of a step in the process

As with headlines, body copy can be built around several different formats. *Straight-line copy* is copy that takes off from the headline and develops the selling points for the product. *Narrative copy*, in contrast, tells a story as it persuades; the same selling points may be covered, but in a different context. *Dialog/monolog copy* lets one or two characters in the ad do the selling through what they are saying. *Picture-and-caption copy* relies on photographs or illustrations to tell the story, with support from their accompanying captions.

SLOGANS

12

Topic sentence

The third major category of copy includes *slogans*, or *tag lines*, memorable sayings that convey a selling message. Over the years, Coca-Cola has used such slogans as "Coke is it," "It's the real thing," and "Always Coca-Cola." Slogans are sometimes used as headlines, but not always. Their importance lies in the fact they often become the most memorable result of an advertising campaign. You've probably got a few slogans stuck in your head. Ever heard of "Quality is job 1," "Don't leave home without it," or "Melts in your mouth, not in your hand"?

13

The Korean automaker Hyundai recently switched back to the slogan "Cars that make sense," which is a great way of expressing its desired positioning as a lower cost but still reliable alternative to Japanese and U.S. cars. For several years, the company had used "Hyundai. Yes, Hyundai," but "Cars that make sense" has proved to be a much more effective way to define the value it offers consumers.

MyWritingLab™

Reading Reflection Questions

1. What is the main purpose in this article? Explain in your own words.

   _____

   _____

2. Explain how this article is an example of a process essay. What are some characteristics that distinguish it as describing a process?

   _____

   _____

3. T/F_____ According to the article, copywriters write all the words you see in print ads.

4. According to the article, the three major categories of copywriting include the following:

   a. Titles, information, and small print

   b. Slogans, titles, and print

   c. Headlines, body copy, and slogans

   d. Details, captions, and images

5. T/F_____ According to the article, most readers read all the body copy or words of an ad.

6. List two examples from the article of famous slogans for brands.

   _____

7. T/F_____ According to the article, using clichés is a good practice for producing good copywriting.

MyWritingLab™ **Checking Vocabulary**

Define each of the following words by figuring out their meaning using context clues in the reading selection. If you cannot work out the meaning of a word, use a dictionary.

8. practitioners (paragraph 1): _____

9. headline (paragraph 6): _____

10. slogans (paragraph 11): _____

   _____

CRITICAL THINKING CHECKLIST

PURPOSE

1. What is the **purpose** of this piece of writing? Is it clear?

   _____

   _____

IDEAS

2. What **ideas** and **background information** are provided to support the purpose of this piece of writing?

   _____

   _____

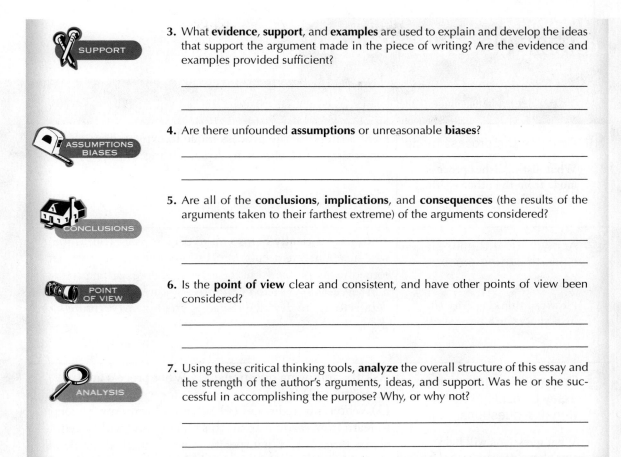

SUPPORT

3. What **evidence**, **support**, and **examples** are used to explain and develop the ideas that support the argument made in the piece of writing? Are the evidence and examples provided sufficient?

_____

_____

ASSUMPTIONS BIASES

4. Are there unfounded **assumptions** or unreasonable **biases**?

_____

_____

CONCLUSIONS

5. Are all of the **conclusions**, **implications**, and **consequences** (the results of the arguments taken to their farthest extreme) of the arguments considered?

_____

_____

POINT OF VIEW

6. Is the **point of view** clear and consistent, and have other points of view been considered?

_____

_____

ANALYSIS

7. Using these critical thinking tools, **analyze** the overall structure of this essay and the strength of the author's arguments, ideas, and support. Was he or she successful in accomplishing the purpose? Why, or why not?

_____

_____

MyWritingLab™ Essay Assignments

1. Using one of the topics you developed in this chapter, write a complete process essay on that topic. Use the critique form to check your draft.
2. Describe the process of making your favorite dish or sandwich. Include all the details you can, be very specific, and use the exact order to recreate this process.
3. Write a process essay explaining how to set up a Facebook page or create an online dating profile.
4. Pick an everyday routine, and write a process essay that shows someone who has never done this activity how to accomplish it step by step (for example, how to make a bed, how to change the oil in a car, how to clean a bathroom, how to do a task you complete routinely for your job, how to register for classes online, and so on).
5. Describe the process of applying and interviewing for a job.

Learning Objectives Review

MyWritingLab™   **Complete the chapter assessment questions at mywritinglab.com**

❶ Describe the process mode.

What distinguishes process mode from the other writing modes? (See p. 176.)

Essay writers use **the process mode** to explain how something works or how to do something.

❷ Apply critical thinking skills to writing process essays.

How can thinking critically help you write a process essay? (See p. 176.)

Thinking critically helps you to decide your purpose for writing about a particular process—to evaluate it, instruct someone how to perform it, or critique an existing process and suggest how it can be improved—and determine what details to use to describe the steps and how to organize them.

❸ Prepare to write a process essay by asking critical thinking questions.

What questions will help you plan a process essay? (See pp. 176–178.)

Ask the following questions: (1) What process am I describing? (2) What is my purpose for writing about it? (3) Who is my audience? (4) What do I want my readers to learn from reading about this process, and will I need to define terms? (5) What specific steps, examples, and details should I include? (6) How should I organize my essay, and how can I move smoothly from one step or detail to the next?

❹ Structure a process essay.

How do you structure a process essay? (See pp. 178–186.)

You **structure a process essay** by describing and analyzing a process with a clear thesis that explains the purpose of the process, and using concrete details and examples that illustrate the steps. Be sure to define any terms your audience needs to know.

❺ Use modes that complement process essays.

What modes complement a process essay? (See pp. 186–195.)

Modes that work well within a process structure include narration and description, example and illustration, cause and effect, comparison/contrast, and argument.

LEARNING OBJECTIVES

In this chapter, you will learn how to

1 Describe the classification mode.

2 Apply critical thinking skills to writing classification essays.

3 Prepare to write a classification essay by asking critical thinking questions.

4 Structure a classification essay.

5 Use modes that complement classification essays.

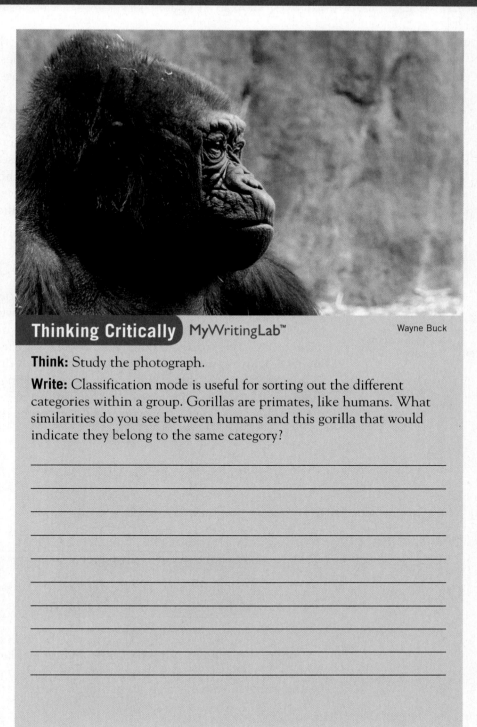

Wayne Buck

Thinking Critically MyWritingLab™

Think: Study the photograph.

Write: Classification mode is useful for sorting out the different categories within a group. Gorillas are primates, like humans. What similarities do you see between humans and this gorilla that would indicate they belong to the same category?

_____
_____
_____
_____
_____
_____
_____
_____
_____
_____

CLASSIFICATION ESSAYS

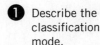

Describe the classification mode.

You use classification skills all the time in your daily life. When you write a grocery list, you may separate items into categories such as dairy, fruits and vegetables, and frozen foods so you can find things quickly in the store. In the academic world, classification enables you to divide large groups in order to analyze them or some aspect of them. As a writing mode, classification (sometimes also called "division") involves grouping, or dividing items into categories. This mode uses common characteristics to define categories within groups. Classification mode is often used in argument essays and story-analysis essays (categorizing an author's techniques or characters). Classification writing is also common in the workplace: Many tasks involve sorting items or people into particular groups or classifications for marketing or analysis purposes.

CRITICAL THINKING AND CLASSIFICATION

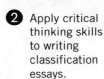

Apply critical thinking skills to writing classification essays.

Be sure you know your purpose in classifying information. Why do you want to sort and categorize your topic(s)? What purpose will it serve? Once you have determined your purpose for classifying subjects, next decide on the criteria you are going to use, and then sort, or *classify*, items accordingly. *Division* involves splitting items into distinct groups. When dividing or classifying, look at specific qualities of the people or items being classified. Then use those qualities as a basis for making your classification decisions. For instance, if you were classifying movies, you could sort them by genre: horror, action, adventure, romantic comedy, and so on.

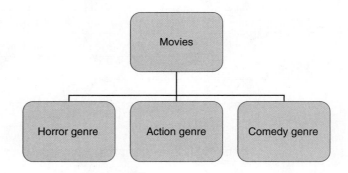

You must think critically to classify and divide, before and during your analysis. Use your analysis skills to create your categories. Ask yourself if you need to subdivide your categories in order to better define them.

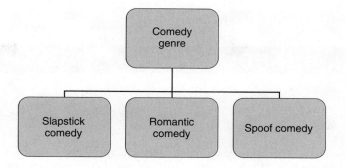

Moreover, you must think about how and why things or people are grouped together and what effects (positive or negative) grouping and classifying can have. Did you go too far? Do you have sound reasons and a **purpose** for classifying subjects a certain way? **Analyze** the reasoning and categories to make sure the **assumptions** you made are sound. You can easily make the following mistakes if you are not careful and thoughtful while classifying:

Hasty generalization fallacy: In this fallacy, the writer makes a generalization about a specific person or thing based on the category in which they belong, without providing evidence and reasoning for that conclusion. For example, if you put someone into a particular grouping such as "conservative" or "liberal" based on the way he or she was dressed, that would be illogical and a hasty generalization.

Begging the question fallacy: This fallacy involves stating and repeating claims but never giving support or evidence to develop them. For example, if you categorized someone or something without supporting your reasons for that decision, you would be "begging the question" why?

Equivocation: "Equivocation" means intentionally using vague words or phrases that mislead the reader. For example, if you said, "The *casualties* of this war were a needed sacrifice," you would be making an equivocation. ("Casualties" is a vague word that hides the truth: deaths.) If you use equivocal language when categorizing people or things, your readers realize that your vague language covers a lack of logic or support.

So ask yourself about each classification you make, your reasons for making it, and the effects of your classification.

APPLYING CRITICAL THINKING

| PURPOSE | IDEAS | SUPPORT | ASSUMPTIONS BIASES | CONCLUSIONS | POINT OF VIEW | ANALYSIS |

Analysis involves breaking down an idea and working out the meaning of the individual parts and how they relate to the whole. When you are classifying people or items, you want to look at the whole group and think carefully about what broad categories you could use to organize them accurately and then how you could break those categories down into more specific subgroups you can write about.

BEFORE WRITING A CLASSIFICATION ESSAY

❸ Prepare to write a classification essay by asking critical thinking questions.

Before you begin to write a classification essay, ask yourself these questions:

1. What basis or principles will I use to classify the topic?
2. How can I subdivide my categories or classifications?
3. What do I want to explain or prove as a result of this classification and division?
4. Have I unfairly or inaccurately classified my subjects or oversimplified complex divisions?
5. What do I want my readers to learn or understand after reading this essay?

Answering these questions will help you generate a thesis statement, help you determine what examples and details to include for support, and give you a general idea of how to organize your essay.

ACTIVITY 9-1   Practicing Classification

Directions: *For each topic, list two or three ways you could subdivide or classify it into categories.*

Topic: Carbohydrates

Categories: *Pasta, bread, crackers*

1. **Topic:** Websites
   Categories: _____

2. **Topic:** Jobs
   Categories: _____

3. **Topic:** College courses
   Categories: _____

4. **Topic:** Books
   Categories: _____

5. **Topic:** Phones
   Categories: _____

WRITING A CLASSIFICATION ESSAY

4 Structure a classification essay.

The paragraph structure of a classification essay is based on sorting a group into its particular parts in order to understand the whole better. For instance, you could choose to classify and divide college students on the basis of age, gender, race, economic background, and academic background. After classifying and studying the various parts of the college student body, you could reach a better understanding of the whole group. The purpose of a classification essay may also be to *critique* the categories set by someone else and argue against the decisions made in the process of categorizing those items or people. Often, classification essays involve a great deal of comparison and contrast, description, and narration, and they make an argument to persuade the reader to agree with the writer's point.

Organizational Pattern for Classification Essays

Most commonly, classification essays will organize categories by **order of importance**, most to least important or least to most, depending on your purpose and audience. If you were writing for your classmates and categorizing the class into groups, you could organize by the importance of the types you were describing such as class leaders, quiet classmates, disruptive classmates, disengaged classmates, and so on.

When you classify, think about what point you want to make about the group you've chosen for your topic and the best way to subdivide that group into categories. For instance, if you want to write about online classes, you might want to first subdivide online classes into specific types: online composition classes, online history classes, and online math classes. Be careful to avoid biased classifications that do not fairly represent the members of each subgroup or misrepresent the items, thoughts, or people within those groups. For example, you shouldn't claim that online students have particular habits or faults that on-campus students don't, if you don't have legitimate support for such a claim. Also, don't oversimplify your subdivisions into groups that don't fully represent the complexities of the subjects.

APPLYING CRITICAL THINKING

| PURPOSE | IDEAS | SUPPORT | ASSUMPTIONS BIASES | CONCLUSIONS | POINT OF VIEW | ANALYSIS |

Classification is something you do to make sense out of groups of things and people around you. When you classify, be extra careful not to overgeneralize, and be aware of your **biases** and **assumptions**.

1. A **bias** is a particular viewpoint that you have about an idea or a topic. Sometimes you are conscious of the biases in your ideas, and sometimes you are not. Having biases is not necessarily a bad thing, but when they are founded on misinformation they can get in the way of good critical thinking. When you classify people or things, think carefully about what ideas you already have about the group(s) you are discussing and whether they are based on fact.

    Example of unfounded bias: Girls are not as good at solving math problems as boys are.

2. An **assumption** is a belief or claim that you take for granted. Almost everything you believe and do is based on assumptions. Some of your assumptions, however, are ones that not everyone would agree with. It is important to learn to separate the assumptions that have a solid basis in fact from the ones that don't when you are making decisions about classifying.

    Example of unfounded assumption: Computer science majors are nerds.

In your introductory paragraph, identify your topic, and explain how you will divide and classify it. Also, clearly establish your purpose for classifying this group. What conclusion did you reach through the process of subdividing the group? Then, in the body paragraphs, focus on one subgroup at a time. Be sure to use transitions that show comparisons and contrasts. You may even subdivide the subcategories in separate paragraphs. Finally, in the concluding paragraph, re-emphasize the method of classification you used, state the conclusions you reached by subdividing the group, and emphasize the point you want to express to your readers. The chart below provides a brief overview of the structure of a classification essay.

BASIC STRUCTURE FOR A CLASSIFICATION ESSAY

See the sample essay on pages 211–212.

INTRODUCTORY PARAGRAPH

Sets up the **categories/subdivisions** of the larger topic you will discuss in your thesis.

Thesis statement: A statement that describes what you are trying to explain, show, prove, or argue by using classification—and what conclusions you reached by subdividing your topic.

BODY PARAGRAPHS (Two to five, depending on assignment and purpose)

Develop the separate subcategories, maybe even subdividing and classifying them—indicate with your **topic sentences**.

Use transitions within and between paragraphs to make the paragraphs flow smoothly.

Provide concrete examples/details and description about the categories.

Analyze the examples.

CONCLUDING PARAGRAPH

Sum up and re-emphasize the thesis: the conclusions reached by classifying your topic.

Structuring a Classification Essay

You can structure a classification essay around a grouping of types of people, classes, cars, exercise, music, films, and so on. It is necessary to use classification and division in order to understand the nuances and complexities within many groups. Be sure to have a purpose for categorizing: a conclusion related to the classifications you made that you want to explain to your readers.

Topic

To generate your topic and purpose for your classification essay, use the guidelines specified by your instructor. If you do not have a specific classification assignment, come up with a topic through brainstorming and decide how you could classify it into groups.

ACTIVITY 9-2   Breaking a Topic into Categories

Directions: *For each of the topics below, use one of the ways of classifying it that you chose in Activity 9-1 and come up with a list of subcategories.*

> **Topic:** Carbohydrates
>
> **Category:** Pasta
>
> Subcategories: *spaghetti, lasagna, macaroni* _____

1. **Topic:** Websites

   Category: _____

   Subcategories: _____

2. **Topic:** Jobs

   Category: _____

   Subcategories: _____

3. **Topic:** College courses

   Category: _____

   Subcategories: _____

4. **Topic:** Books

   Category: _____

   Subcategories: _____

5. **Topic:** Phones

   Category: _____

   Subcategories: _____

Thesis Statements

If you have a specific classification assignment that dictates what you will be trying to explain or prove through your essay, then customize your thesis using key words from that assignment. For instance, if you were asked to classify colleges and universities in order to explore which options were best for you, your thesis would specify which categories you have chosen to use and what conclusion you've reached as a result of this classification.

> College students can be grouped by the type of their living arrangements—those who live in on-campus dorms, those who share an apartment or house with other students, or those who stay with their parents while in college to save money—and each category has its own advantages and disadvantages.

ACTIVITY 9-3 Creating Thesis Statements

Directions: *Using the categories and subcategories you generated in Activities 9-1 and 9-2, create a one-sentence thesis statement for three of the general topics. Make sure the thesis statement has a clear message about what conclusion you reached using classification.*

1. Topic/Thesis statement: _____

_____

_____

_____

2. Topic/Thesis statement: _____

_____

_____

_____

3. Topic/Thesis statement: _____

_____

_____

_____

Creating a Rough Outline

Cross Reference

See Chapter 6, pp. 104–115, Stage One: Prewrite to Generate Ideas.

Once you have determined your topic and your thesis statement, you are ready to create a rough outline to determine your essay's structure and organizational plan. Use prewriting techniques such as brainstorming or clustering to generate supporting examples and concrete details. Then create a rough outline using this template:

Rough Outline Template for a Classification Essay

    I. Introductory Paragraph
        A. Start with a brief description of the categories in a general way
        B. Thesis Statement: the purpose of your classification (what you want to prove by grouping your subjects and how you chose to group them)
   II. Body Paragraphs: two to four body paragraphs that explain the categories and your reasons for these categories
        A. Include concrete description and details for each group
        B. Include clear transitions from one group to the next
        C. Include definitions and explanations when needed
  III. Concluding Paragraph
        A. Restate in a new way the classification and your purpose/thesis
        B. Add some general closing comments without introducing any new ideas

Introductory Paragraph

In the introductory paragraph of your classification essay, provide general information about the topic, the larger group that will be classified. Then present the subcategories you will use to create your classification. Finally, in the thesis statement, explain the purpose for your classification essay: what point you want your readers to understand as a result of your classification process.

Body Paragraphs

In your body paragraphs, individually develop each subcategory you created. Provide clear topic sentences that present each subcategory. Then, add specific examples and details to explain and develop the subcategories. You may need to further divide your subcategories, too. Use transitions when needed both within and between your paragraphs. Transitions indicating contrast and comparison are particularly useful in classification essays.

Cross Reference

For other useful transitions, see also Chapter 5, p. 93, Introduce Another Point, and p. 94, Explain a Purpose.

TRANSITIONS TO . . .

Show Contrast or a Change in Idea

although	even though	instead	on the other side
anyhow	for all that	nevertheless	otherwise
at the same time	however	notwithstanding	regardless
but	in any event	on the contrary	still
despite this	in contrast	on the other hand	yet

Show a Comparison

in like manner	in the same way	likewise	similarly

ACTIVITY 9-4 Creating Topic Sentences

Directions: *Now create two topic sentences for each of the thesis statements you created in Activity 9-3, addressing the different categories you would discuss in each paragraph.*

1. Topic sentences: _____

    _____

    _____

2. Topic sentences: _____

    _____

    _____

3. Topic sentences: _____

    _____

    _____

Definitions and Examples   Because in classification essays you explain and discuss a category in each paragraph, you need to provide clear definitions and examples to illustrate the differences and similarities between the categories. For example, if you were to classify trees into groups, you might use *evergreen* and *deciduous* as two of your subcategories, and then you would need to define both of these terms and provide examples of the types of trees they refer to:

TREES

Deciduous	Evergreen
(Leaves fall off in winter)	(Leaves/needles stay on year round)
Maple	Cedar
Oak	Fir
Elm	Pine

ACTIVITY 9-5 Providing Examples

Directions: *Now provide at least three possible examples or details you would include for three of the topic sentences you created in Activity 9-4.*

1. Topic sentence/details: _____

   _____

   _____

2. Topic sentence/details: _____

   _____

   _____

3. Topic sentence/details: _____

   _____

   _____

Concluding Paragraph

In your concluding paragraph, restate your thesis, emphasizing what conclusions you reached by classifying your topic. Touch on the categories you used and the main point you want your readers to realize after they read your essay.

ACTIVITY 9-6 Writing a Conclusion

Directions: *Choose one of the topics you've been developing in the preceding activities, and write a three- to five-sentence concluding paragraph* *that re-emphasizes the classification categories and the purpose you want to convey.*

_____

_____

_____

_____

_____

| **ACTIVITY 9-7** | **Creating Your Outline and First Draft** |

Cross Reference
See Chapters 21–25, pp. 515–648, for help with the Editing section of the critique form.

Directions: *Choose a topic from one of the activities you already completed in this chapter, from the assignment choices at the end of this chapter, or from a topic assigned by your instructor and create a rough outline using the template on page 206 of this chapter. Then, using your rough outline, write a first draft of your essay. After you have finished, use the critique form below to check for the basics in your essay draft.*

CLASSIFICATION ESSAY CRITIQUE FORM

PURPOSE   IDEAS   SUPPORT   ASSUMPTIONS BIASES   CONCLUSIONS   POINT OF VIEW   ANALYSIS

Overall

	Done well	Needs work
1. Does the essay categorize two or more subjects with specific characteristics?	_____	_____
2. Does the essay use specific categories consistently and clearly?	_____	_____
3. Are the paragraphs organized clearly and logically and are they a good length—3–15 sentences?	_____	_____

Introduction

4. Is the title interesting and in correct format?	_____	_____
5. Is there a general introduction that presents the thesis and categories?	_____	_____
6. Is there a clear thesis statement that explains the **purpose** of the classifications being made?	_____	_____

Continued ▶

Body

7. Do the **ideas** in the body paragraphs develop the categories and flow smoothly? _____ _____
8. Are transitions used between and, when needed, within the paragraphs? _____ _____
9. Do the body paragraphs include **support** (descriptive details and examples)? _____ _____

Conclusion

10. Does the **concluding** paragraph sum up the categories with **analysis** and re-emphasize the purpose developed in the introductory paragraph and thesis, without adding new ideas? _____ _____

Editing

11. Circle the following errors you think you see in this draft: spelling errors, fragments, run-ons/comma splices, errors in comma and semicolon/colon use, pronoun disagreement, pronoun reference errors, errors in parallelism, apostrophe use, verb use/tense, and passive voice construction.
12. Other types of grammar or sentence-level errors:

_____

Comments (For example, What works well in this draft? What needs to be added? Did you, or will your readers, feel drawn into the essay? Why or why not?):

_____

_____

COMPLEMENTARY MODES FOR CLASSIFICATION ESSAYS

5 Use modes that complement classification essays.

When writing a classification essay, of course, the dominant mode will be classification; however, you can create a more powerful message by weaving in sentences or paragraphs in other modes. For example:

- **Narration** and **description** can be used to develop the categories.
- **Illustration and examples** will further elaborate on the classifications.
- You can look at the **causes and effects** of classifications and divisions.
- You can **compare and contrast** among the categories.
- You can use classification to prove an **argument** or **persuade** your readers to agree with a particular point of view.

Student Essay

The dominant mode used in this student's paper is classification. Look for other modes used in this essay as well, such as comparison and contrast, narration and description, and example and illustration.

Hill 1

Lynne Hill

Professor Martinez

English 100

21 November 2012

TV People, Movie People, and Book People

Do you know people who love to watch TV, who go to the movies as much as possible, or who read books voraciously? Several of my friends fall into one of these categories, and some of them are so deeply devoted to their need for TV, movies, or books that that connection has become part of who they are. These people, let us call them the "TV people," "movie people," and "book people," have particular characteristics and particular personalities.

The TV people like to stay home on most nights, arranging their schedules as they consult *TV Guide*. They hate the sound of silence if they are home. They are drawn as if by a magnet to the lure of the box in the corner, calling them like a siren: "Come turn me on . . . you can watch just for a little while . . . Oprah misses you. . . ." The devoted TV people will forgo housecleaning, homework, and any type of creative project to ensure they do not miss a chance for some good passive TV watching. The TV people have a master plan to avoid engaging with their lives: They let the shows do the thinking, and the living, for them.

The movie people are one step above the TV people when it comes to social engagement. At least they will step out of their homes in the evenings from time to time . . . to see a movie. Some movie people have even studied cinematography and consider their fascination with movies a sign of their expertise; some will even actively critique the films—true artists in their medium.

Thesis statement

Topic sentence

Topic sentence

Hill 2

There are subcategories of movie people: the loner movie people, the social movie people, and the snobby movie people versus the nondiscriminating movie people. The loner movie people prefer to watch movies by themselves. They are easily irritated by friends who make comments during the show, and they are distracted by the sounds of people eating popcorn or snacks. The social movie people choose not to go to movies alone: they passively watch with someone or several people. Then, they like to engage in dialogue about the movies afterward. The snobby movie people will see only the highly critically acclaimed, "artsy" movies, while the nondiscriminating movie people will see anything—and love it! It's pricier to be a movie person than a TV person. Movies and the nearly mandatory accompanying snacks from the snack bar can set a person back $20 at a time.

Topic sentence

Finally, the book people are often the most creative, intelligent, and self-sufficient; however, that does not guarantee that they have any social graces. The book people are creative: they create movies in their own heads from the books they read, casting their own actors and blocking their own scenes. They are actively engaged in the stories they read, not just passive viewers. Also, book people are smart and can be great conversationalists, if you can tear them away from whatever book they are currently reading. In fact, book people can be downright antisocial on vacations, sneaking off to a beach or back room alone to delve into a juicy book.

Restatement of thesis

It's predictable that there are all levels of TV people, movie people, and book people out there. Certainly, each of these types has their own distinguishing characteristics. Which category do you fit in most closely?

ACTIVITY 9-8 Thinking Critically about the Student Essay

Directions: *Identify the features and details characteristic of the classification mode in the student essay. Mark them on the essay. Then, reread the essay and make a list of specific revisions you would make to correct any problems with content, organization, transitions, and style.*

PROFESSIONAL CLASSIFICATION ESSAY

Race in America

George Henderson

George Henderson is Dean of the College of Liberal Arts at the University of Oklahoma, where he is also Professor of Human Relations, Education, and Sociology. Henderson has served as a race relations consultant to many national and international organizations. He is author of *Our Souls to Keep: Black/White Relations in America* (1999) and coeditor with Grace Xuequin Ma of *Rethinking Ethnicity and Health Care: A Sociocultural Perspective* (1999). This essay appeared in a special issue of *National Forum* on race in America (spring 2000).

▶ NOTE   Some of the vocabulary in this essay is very high level, so make sure to use context clues and to consult a dictionary when you need to.

1   Because of intermarriage, most Americans have multiple ethnic and racial identities. Some persons of mixed lineage prefer to assume culturally nondescript identities. For example, they have become "white people," "black people," "Indians," "Latinos," "Asians," or just plain "Americans" in order to somehow deflect from themselves any connection with their ancestors. The task of tracing their families has become too taxing or too insignificant. Even so, the effects of ethnicity and race are pervasive: disparate patterns of community relationships and economic opportunities haunt us. At some time in their history, all ethnic groups in the United States have been the underclass. Also, at different times, all ethnic groups have been both the oppressed and the oppressors.

Thesis
2   Ethnicity is the most distinguishing characteristic of Americans, where we

Topic sentence   are sorted primarily on the basis of our cultural identities or nationalities. An ethnic group is a culturally distinct population whose members share a collective

Definition and category   identity and a common heritage. Historically, the overwhelming majority of ethnic groups emerged in the United States as a result of one of several responses to the following processes: (1) migration, (2) consolidation of group forces in the face of an impending threat from an aggressor, (3) annexation or changes in political boundary lines, or (4) schisms within a church. Hence, "ethnic minority" presupposes people different from the mainstream or dominant cultured persons.

3
Topic sentence

But it is the erroneous belief that people who come to America can be placed in categories based on their unique gene pools that has resulted in the most blatant instances of discrimination. Races, however defined, do not correspond to genetic reality because inbreeding world populations share a common gene pool. A much more practical dictum, and one that has often been ignored throughout American history, is that all people belong to the same species. Unfortunately, too few individuals believe that the only race of any significance is the human race.

A BRIEF HISTORY

4
Topic sentence and new category

At the time of the American Revolution, the American population was largely composed of English Protestants who had absorbed a substantial number of German and Scotch-Irish settlers and a smaller number of French, Dutch, Swedes, Poles, Swiss, Irish, and other immigrants. The colonies had a modest number of Catholics, and a smaller number of Jews. Excluding Quakers and Swedes, the colonists treated Native Americans with contempt and hostility, and engaged in wars against them that bordered on genocide. They drove natives from the coastal plains in order to make way for a massive white movement to the West. Although Africans, most of whom were slaves, comprised one-fifth of the American population during the Revolution, they, similar to Indians, were not perceived by most white colonists as being worthy of assimilation.

Specific examples to develop category

5
Topic sentence

The white peoples of the new nation had long since crossed Caucasian lines to create a conglomerate but culturally homogeneous society. People of different ethnic groups—English, Irish, German, Huguenot, Dutch, Swedish—mingled and intermarried. English settlers and peoples from western and northern Europe had begun a process of ethnic assimilation that caused some writers to incorrectly describe the nation as melted into one ethnic group: American. In reality, non-Caucasian Americans were not included in the Eurocentric cultural pot.

Specific examples to develop category

6
Topic sentence and new category

During the 150 years immediately following the Revolution, large numbers of immigrants came to the United States from eastern European countries. They were the so-called "new immigrants." During the latter part of that period, slaves were emancipated, numerous Indian tribes were conquered and forced to relocate to reservations, portions of Mexico's land were taken, and Asians began emigrating to the United States. The English language and English-oriented cultural patterns grew even more dominant. Despite a proliferation of cultural diversity within the growing ethnic enclaves, Anglo-conformity ideology spawned racist notions about Nordic and Aryan racial superiority. This ideology gave rise to nativist political agendas and exclusionist immigration policies favoring western and northern European immigrants.

7

Topic sentence

Specific examples to develop category

Non-English-speaking western Europeans and northern Europeans were also discriminated against. The slowness of some of those immigrants, particularly Germans, to learn English, their tendency to live in enclaves, and their establishment of ethnic-language newspapers were friction points. Such ethnic-oriented lifestyles prompted many Americanized people to chide: "If they don't like it here, they can go back to where they came from." But that solution was too simplistic. Immigrants from all countries and cultures, even those who were deemed socially and religiously undesirable, were needed to help build a nation—to work the farms, dig the ore, build railroads and canals, settle the prairies, and otherwise provide human resources.

8

Topic sentence

Beginning in the 1890s, immigrants from eastern and southern Europe were numerically dominant. That set the stage for racist statements about inferior, darker people threatening the purity of blond, blue-eyed Nordics or Aryans through miscegenation. Intermixture was perceived as a deadly plague. Although the immigrants from eastern and southern Europe were not suitable marriage partners, their critics stated, they could be properly assimilated and amalgamated. This kind of ethnocentrism prevented large numbers of other immigrants and indigenous peoples of color from becoming fully functioning citizens. And the legacy for the children of people denied equal opportunities was second-class citizenship. We can easily document the negative effects of second-class citizenship: abhorrent inequalities, unwarranted exclusions, and atmospheres of rejection.

9

Topic sentence

Immigrants who lived in remote, isolated areas were able to maintain some semblance of being ethnic nations within America. But the growth of cities brought about the decline of farming populations and ethnic colonies. A short time was required for the white immigrants who settled in cities to discard their native languages and cultures. But it is erroneous to think of any ethnic group as melting away without leaving a trace of its cultural heritage. All ethnic groups have infused portions of their cultures into the tapestry of American history.

10

Topic sentence

Specific examples to develop category

Early twentieth-century eastern European immigrants were a very disparate mixture of peoples. They came from nations that were trying to become states—Poland, Czechoslovakia, Lithuania, and Yugoslavia; from states trying to become nations—Italy, Turkey, and Greece; and from areas outside the Western concept of either state or nation. All of them included people such as Jews who did not easily fit into any of those categories. Through social and educational movements, laws, and superordinate goals such as winning wars and establishing economic world superiority, eastern Europeans and other white ethnic groups were able to enter mainstream America.

11

Topic sentence

The cultures and colors of Third World ethnic groups were in stark contrast to European immigrants. Those differences became obstacles to assimilation and, more importantly, to people of color achieving equal opportunities. Nonwhite groups in the United States occupied specific low-status niches in the workplace, which in turn resulted in similarities among their members in such things as occupations, standard of living, level of education, place of residence, access to political power, and quality of health care. Likenesses within those groups facilitated the formation of stereotypes and prejudices that inhibited the full citizenship of nonwhite minorities.

12

Topic sentence

Specific examples to
develop category

Immigrants who held highly esteemed occupations—lawyers, artists, engineers, scientists, and physicians—became Americanized much faster than those who held less esteemed positions—unskilled laborers, farm workers, coal miners, and stock clerks. But even in those instances there were pro-European biases and stereotypes. For example, French chefs, Italian opera singers, Polish teachers, German conductors, and Russian scientists were more highly recruited than Africans, Hispanics, and Asians who had the same skills. Racial and quasi-racial groups—including American Indians, Mexican Americans, Asian Americans, African Americans, and Puerto Ricans—were not nearly so readily absorbed as various Caucasian ethnic groups. And that is generally the situation today. Despite numerous and impressive gains during the past century, a disproportionate number of peoples of color are still treated like pariahs.

WHAT DOES THE FUTURE HOLD?

13

Topic sentence

Specific examples to
develop category

If U.S. Census Bureau population projections are correct, our nation is undergoing mind-boggling demographic changes: Hispanics will triple in numbers, from 31.4 million in 1999 to 98.2 million in 2050; blacks will increase 70 percent, from 34.9 million to 59.2 million; Asians and Pacific Islanders will triple, from 10.9 million to 37.6 million; Native Americans and Alaska Natives will increase from approximately 2.2 million to 2.6 million. During the same period, the non-Hispanic white population will increase from 196.1 million to 213 million. Also, the foreign-born population, most of them coming from Asia and Latin America, will increase from 26 million to 53.8 million. The non-Hispanic white population will decrease from 72 percent of the total population in 1999 to 52 percent in 2050, and the nation's workforce will be composed of over 50 percent racial and ethnic minorities and immigrants. Who then will be the pariahs?

14

Topic sentence

Without equal opportunities, the melting pot will continue to be an unreachable mirage, a dream of equality deferred, for too many people of color. This does not in any way detract from the significance of the things minorities have achieved. Ethnic-group histories and lists of cultural contributions support the contention that each group is an integral part of a whole nation. Although all American ethnic minority groups have experienced continuous socioeconomic gains, the so-called "playing field" that includes white participants is not yet level. Simply stated, the rising tide of economic prosperity has not yet lifted the masses of people of color. Whatever our life circumstances, the citizens of the United States are bound together not as separate ethnic groups but as members of different ethnic groups united in spirit and behavior and locked into a common destiny.

15

Topic sentence

There is little doubt that our nation is at a crossroads in its race relations. Where we go from here is up to all of us. We can try segregation again, continuance of the status quo, silence in the face of prejudice and discriminatory practices, or activism. The choice is ours.

16
Topic sentence

Segregation of ethnic minorities is not a redeeming choice for the United States. It did not work during earlier times, and it will not work now. There have never been separate but equal majority-group and minority-group communities in the United States. And the pretense of such a condition would once again be a particularly pernicious injustice to all citizens. Racial segregation diminishes both the perpetrators and their victims. Preserving the status quo in education, employment, health care, and housing, which so often is little more than codified racial discrimination, is not justice for minorities either.

17
Topic sentence

Cause-and-effect analysis

Inaction by people who witness oppressive acts is equally unacceptable. Even though they may be shocked and frustrated by the problems, standing in wide-eyed horror is not an adequate posture to assume. While they may be legally absolved of any wrongdoing, these silent people must come to terms with what others believe to be their moral culpability. Of course, silence may be prudent. Usually, there is a high price to be paid by those who would challenge racism in community institutions. Friends, jobs, promotions, and prestige may be lost. Furthermore, few victories come easily, and most of the victors are unsung heroes.

18
Restatement of purpose

Individuals who choose to challenge purveyors of bigotry and unequal opportunities must also take care that in their actions to redress racial injustices, they do not emulate the oppressors whom they deplore. That might makes right, that blood washes out injustices—these too are false strategies for achieving justice. "It does not matter much to a slave what the color of his master is," a wise black janitor once said. We, the descendants of migrants, immigrants, and slaves, can build a better nation—a place where all people have safe housing, get a top-quality education, do meaningful work for adequate wages, are treated fairly in criminal-justice systems, have their medical needs met, and in the end die a timely death unhurried by bigots. This is the kind of history that should be made.

MyWritingLab™   **Reading Reflection Questions**

1. What are the direct or indirect (implied) messages in this essay?

_____

_____

_____

2. What techniques, organizational patterns, and details distinguish this as a *classification* essay? _____

_____

_____

3. In your own words, what is Henderson's view of people who identify themselves by race? _____

_____

_____

MyWritingLab™ **Objective Questions**

4. T/F_____ As early white settlers in America, the Quakers treated Native Americans badly.

5. T/F_____ The author believes that segregation by race can be beneficial to society.

6. T/F_____ Nonwhite immigrants with higher-prestige jobs such as doctors or lawyers became Americanized faster.

7. Provide two examples of injustices that have happened in American society as a result of racial differences as mentioned by Henderson.

_____

_____

_____

MyWritingLab™ **Checking Vocabulary**

Define the following in your own words, or provide a dictionary definition if you don't know the word.

8. ethnicity: _____

9. migration: _____

10. ethnocentrism: _____

_____

CRITICAL THINKING CHECKLIST

PURPOSE

1. What is the **purpose** of this piece of writing? Is it clear?

_____

_____

IDEAS

2. What **ideas** and **background information** are provided to support the purpose of this piece of writing?

_____

_____

SUPPORT

3. What **evidence** and **examples** are used to explain and develop the ideas that support the argument made in the piece of writing? Are the evidence and examples provided sufficient?

_____

_____

ASSUMPTIONS BIASES

4. Are there unfounded **assumptions** or unreasonable **biases**?

_____

_____

CONCLUSIONS

5. Are all of the **conclusions**, **implications**, and **consequences** of the arguments (the results of the arguments taken to their farthest extreme) considered?

_____

_____

POINT OF VIEW

6. Is the **point of view** clear and consistent, and have other points of view been considered?

_____

_____

ANALYSIS

7. Using these critical thinking tools, **analyze** the overall structure of this essay and the strength of the author's arguments, ideas, and support. Was he or she successful in accomplishing the purpose? Why, or why not?

_____

_____

MyWritingLab™

Essay Assignments

1. Write a classification essay using any of the topics you developed in the activities in this chapter.

2. Classify college students into at least four categories (think of them as particular *types* of students). Then come up with an analytical conclusion based on the categories or stereotypes.

3. Pick one of the following types of establishments, and then subcategorize the types of businesses included in that category. Use specific examples and details. Then come to an analytical conclusion related to these subcategories.

   a. Fast-food restaurants

   b. Coffee shops

   c. Department stores

4. Categorize your coworkers by their skill levels and efficiency. Then come to an analytical conclusion as a result of your categories and criteria.

5. Categorize teachers at your college into types. Then come to an analytical conclusion related to the categories into which these teachers are grouped.

6. Categorize American cars versus imported cars. Then come to an analytical conclusion related to the details and categories you create.

Learning Objectives Review

MyWritingLab™ **Complete the chapter assessment questions at mywritinglab.com**

❶ Describe the classification mode.

What distinguishes classification mode from other writing modes? (See p. 198.)

Essay writers use **classification** (sometimes also called "division") to group or divide items into categories. This mode uses common characteristics to define categories within groups.

❷ Apply critical thinking skills to writing classification essays.

How can thinking critically help you write a classification essay? (See pp. 198–200.)

Thinking critically helps you classify and divide using logic and reasons. You must think about how and why things or people are grouped together and what effects (positive or negative) grouping and classifying can have. **Analyze** the reasoning and categories to make sure the **assumptions** you made are sound.

❸ Prepare to write a classification essay by asking critical thinking questions.

What questions will help you plan a classification essay? (See pp. 200–201.)

Ask the following questions: (1) What basis or principles will I use to classify the topic? (2) How can I subdivide my categories or classifications? (3) What do I want to explain or prove as a result of this classification and division? (4) Have I unfairly or inaccurately classified my subjects or oversimplified complex divisions? (5) What do I want my readers to learn or understand after reading this essay?

❹ Structure a classification essay.

How do you structure a classification essay? (See pp. 201–210.)

You **structure a classification essay** by placing the subjects into categories and analyzing those classifications and using an introductory paragraph with a thesis that draws a conclusion about the classifications, body paragraphs that support and develop the thesis, and a conclusion to restate the thesis and sum up the essay without adding any new ideas.

❺ Use modes that complement classification essays.

What other modes complement a classification essay? (See pp. 210–219.)

Modes that work well within a classification structure include narration and description, example and illustration, cause and effect, comparison and contrast, and argument or persuasion.

LEARNING OBJECTIVES

In this chapter, you will learn how to

1 Describe the definition mode.

2 Apply critical thinking skills to writing definition essays.

3 Prepare to write a definition essay by asking critical thinking questions.

4 Structure a definition essay.

5 Use modes that complement definition essays.

Thinking Critically   MyWritingLab™

Think: Study the photograph.

Write: Define these objects. Use specific descriptive words, as if your audience has no idea what the objects are and cannot see them.

_____

_____

_____

_____

_____

Write: Briefly define the significance of these objects. Explain any associations and connections to their cultural identity that you know.

_____

_____

_____

_____

DEFINITION ESSAYS

1 Describe the definition mode.

Definition essays explain, define, and clarify items, terms, and concepts. They are used to tell the reader what something is or what something means. Though you may need to use some description in a definition essay, make sure that when you are defining an object or concept you don't merely describe the subject: To *define*, you must explain what the object or concept *is* and what it *means*, not just what it looks like.

The purpose for a definition essay can be to provide your reader with a straightforward definition of a term or concept to increase their understanding of it or to explain the symbolic meaning or cultural and historic relevance of an item or idea. For instance, you might define a "tamale" as a type of food composed of cornmeal *masa* (dough) and fillings, such as meats, vegetables, or fruit, that is popular in Central American countries such as Mexico and El Salvador. Then you could define what this particular food represents in terms of the history, culture, or traditions of these countries.

CRITICAL THINKING AND DEFINITION

2 Apply critical thinking skills to writing definition essays.

As you develop your definition essay, assess the topic, your audience, and your purpose: **Analyze** your definition's **purpose** to assess the scope of your definition and to choose the best **ideas** and support to develop your purpose and draw meaningful **conclusions**.

An **extended definition** consists of one or more paragraphs that explain a complex term. In an extended definition, you might use synonyms (words that have the same or similar meanings), give examples, discuss the term's origins, provide comparisons, explain what the word is not, or create an anecdote to show the word in action. You can consult a dictionary, but do not use a dictionary quotation as the main part of your definition. You may, however, integrate information you learn from the dictionary into your extended definition (check with your instructor). Extended definitions can employ other methods of development—narration, description, process analysis, illustration, classification, comparison and contrast, and cause and effect. Also, they sometimes use contrast to define a subject by explaining what the term *does not mean*. Extended definitions can be purely personal, or they can be largely objective. A personal definition explains how a writer is using the term and allows the reader to see that term in a different light.

When choosing words to define your subject, be sure not to commit an **equivocation fallacy** or use **euphemisms**: Equivocation is intentionally using vague words or phrases that mislead the reader, and a euphemism is a word or phrase used to soften the effect of a more direct word in order to avoid addressing the severity of an issue or to minimize a harsh truth. For example, if you define an obese child as "a healthy boy" or "a husky boy," you mislead your readers.

APPLYING CRITICAL THINKING

BLUEPRINTS PURPOSE — IDEAS — SUPPORT — ASSUMPTIONS BIASES — CONCLUSIONS — POINT OF VIEW — ANALYSIS

You define words and concepts to make it easier to communicate with others. Some definitions are straightforward and rely on facts, while others require more **analysis** and explanation on your part—and maybe even some creative thought and comparisons. To write an effective definition essay, you will need to consider the following questions:

1. What is my **purpose** and plan for this definition essay? What point do I want to make? How will I convey that message?

2. What **ideas** should I include to make my definition clear to my reader? What **support** (descriptive details, terms, examples, creative comparisons) will help me develop my definition and its purpose?

BEFORE WRITING A DEFINITION ESSAY

3 Prepare to write a definition essay by asking critical thinking questions.

Before you begin to write a definition essay, ask yourself these questions:

1. What is the object or concept I want to define?
2. What general category does my subject belong in?
3. What distinguishing characteristics does it have?
4. Can I compare it with something similar to define it?
5. Can I explain it by saying what it is not?
6. Why am I defining this subject, and what purpose does it serve?
7. What do I want my readers to learn or understand after reading this essay?

Answering these questions will help you generate an expository thesis statement, help you determine examples and details to include for support, and give you a general idea of how to organize your essay.

APPLYING CRITICAL THINKING

| PURPOSE | IDEAS | SUPPORT | ASSUMPTIONS BIASES | CONCLUSIONS | POINT OF VIEW | ANALYSIS |

To define your subject, you can draw on your own personal knowledge of it. If you are defining an object, you can have it in front of you as you write your definition. Be careful, though, not to merely describe the object. Define what it is, its purpose, how it is used or what it is used for, or what relationship it has to society and human use. Use your well-founded **assumptions** and **biases**. Ask your instructor if you are allowed to look up definitions for an object or concept you are assigned to define. If you are allowed to include researched definitions from dictionaries, encyclopedias, or the Internet, make sure to give credit to any outside sources you use.

Cross Reference

For more on prewriting techniques, see Chapter 6, pp. 104–115, Step One: Prewrite to Generate Ideas.

ACTIVITY 10-1 Practicing Definition

Directions: *Prewrite on the following topics for a definition essay by brainstorming or clustering. Use a separate sheet of paper.*

1. Family
2. Tradition
3. Global warming
4. Discrimination
5. Social networking
6. Favoritism
7. Home
8. Logo of your choice
9. Meditation
10. Ceremony

WRITING A DEFINITION ESSAY

 Structure a definition essay.

In your introductory paragraph, identify the topic you will be defining. Then, on the basis of your prewriting, explain in your thesis statement how you will define the subject and what your purpose is for defining it.

In the body of your essay, you can define the item, term, or concept you have chosen by first discussing how your subject fits into a general category.

Then you can write about its distinguishing features in order to define it more specifically. For example, if you had to define a mango, you might first describe it as part of the general category of tropical fruit. Then you could specify the mango's distinguishing qualities: its taste, color, shape, size, texture, and so on.

In order to define your subject more precisely, you can also compare it with similar things. For instance, you could compare a hammer with a mallet, as they are similar kinds of tools, but then emphasize how they differ. Or you could compare something unfamiliar (the item you are defining) with something familiar to your audience. For example, you could explain that bouillabaisse is like a beef stew but made from several types of fish and shellfish. You can also define a term by saying what it is not. For instance, you could define the term "obesity" as follows: "Obesity is not just being a couple of pounds overweight; it is a condition in which is person carries and stores excess fat and has a body mass index of 30 or greater."

You might also want to create subcategories for the term you are defining. For example, if you were defining the term *schizophrenia* for a psychology course, you might want to talk about different types of schizophrenia such as disorganized, paranoid, and catatonic.

Conclude your definition essay by summing up what you have defined and your purpose for defining it. Here is a sample definition paragraph that provides a simple, clear definition of the term "flag." The topic sentence is in italics.

> *A flag is an object that is made of fabric and includes colors and possibly shapes, letters, or figures to represent a group, team, or even a country.* For example, many sports teams have flags dedicated to them that feature the team name and a picture of the team mascot. The Chicago Bulls, for instance, have a red and black team flag that shows a picture of a bull's head and the team name. Flags can also represent a country; for instance, the flag of the United States is red, white, and blue, with bold red and white stripes and a dark blue square in the upper left corner that contains 50 white stars to represent the 50 states.

If you wanted to add the dimension of cultural or symbolic significance to your paragraph, then you might make the topic sentence more analytical and add some examples of what the flag represents and what it embodies. For instance:

> *The American flag is more than just a piece of cloth representing the United States. It is also a symbol of our country's values, history, and identity.* The 50 stars that represent each state also indicate that America is made up of many unique states that join together to form one unified country. This unity is especially important symbolically because the American Civil War nearly tore the northern and southern states apart.

Organizational Pattern for a Definition Essay

You could organize your definition essay by **order of importance** (most to least or least to most important) based on the examples you use to define your subject. Or, if the subject is an unusual object that needs to be explained with visual details, such as a machine used for a specific purpose or a particular room or space, you could describe the subject using spatial order. **Spatial order** is used when you are describing a place, such as a town, city, or room in your house. Describe the space by one part at a time (from front to back, top to bottom, side to side, and so on) to give the whole picture. Spatial order helps you describe what something looks like and helps your reader create a mental picture of the space you are describing.

Whatever order pattern you choose, include many details in your body paragraphs to develop your definition through several examples or an extended one.

The chart below provides a brief overview of the structure of a definition essay.

BASIC STRUCTURE FOR A DEFINITION ESSAY

See the sample essay on pages 234–235.

INTRODUCTORY PARAGRAPH

Sets up background for your definition.

Thesis statement: States how you will define your chosen topic and your purpose for defining it.

BODY PARAGRAPHS (Two to five, depending on assignment and purpose)

Develop your definition by identifying the group the item or concept belongs to and discussing its distinguishing characteristics.

Topic sentences will set up the structure of your definition in each paragraph.

Provide concrete examples to illustrate and define your topic. Provide definitions of any unfamiliar terms you use to explain your topic. **Analyze** the examples.

Use transitions within and between paragraphs to make the paragraphs flow.

CONCLUDING PARAGRAPH

Sums up and re-emphasizes the thesis statement: the **conclusions** reached through your definition.

Structuring a Definition Essay

You can write a definition essay about a concept you learned in another class. You can define a term, position, or item from your job. Basically, anything you would need to define to your audience *in order to make a point* is a good topic for this essay mode.

Topic

If your instructor has not assigned a topic for your definition essay, brainstorm ideas for things, places, or people you might want to define. Then come up with some ideas for a purpose for defining the topic. What do you want your readers to understand through your definition?

Thesis Statements

The thesis statement in a definition essay states what item, concept, or term you are going to define and establishes your purpose for writing about it. Your purpose may be simply to define an object or concept for an audience unfamiliar with your subject.

> A mitral valve prolapse is a specific type of heart murmur that exhibits several distinct characteristics.

Often, though, a definition essay's purpose is to define something in order to reach a more complex conclusion related to the subject. For instance, in the tamale example used earlier in this chapter, the writer could first define what a *tamale* is and then use tamales as a cultural symbol of the tastes and traditions of the countries that prize them.

> The tamale is an important part of Mexican holiday traditions. It is more than a favorite food; it is part of a cultural tradition.

In your introductory paragraph, present the overall topic you will be defining. Then, on the basis of your prewriting, establish how you will define the subject and what the purpose is for defining it to create the right thesis statement for your topic and purpose.

ACTIVITY 10-2   Creating Thesis Statements

Directions: *Choose three of the topics from Activity 10-1 that you brainstormed about and two topics of your own choice (such as terms from other classes), and create a one-sentence thesis statement for each. Make sure each thesis statement identifies the item, concept, or term being defined and your purpose for defining it.*

1. Item, concept, or term: _____

   Thesis statement: _____

   _____

2. Item, concept, or term: _____

   Thesis statement: _____

   _____

3. Item, concept, or term: _____

   Thesis statement: _____

   _____

4. Item, concept, or term: _____

   Thesis statement: _____

   _____

5. Item, concept, or term: _____

   Thesis statement: _____

   _____

Creating a Rough Outline

Cross Reference
See Chapter 6,
pp. 104–115, Stage One:
Prewrite to Generate Ideas.

Once you have determined your topic and your thesis statement, you are ready to create a rough outline to determine your essay's structure and organizational plan. Use prewriting techniques such as brainstorming or clustering to generate supporting examples and concrete details. Then create a rough outline using this template:

Rough Outline Template for a Definition Essay

    I. Introductory Paragraph
       A. A brief description of the subject you will be defining and maybe a context for how it is used
       B. Thesis statement: the purpose of your definition (to simply define, to redefine or give an alternative definition, to use the term to express a larger argument)
   II. Body Paragraphs: two to four body paragraphs that explain your purpose(s) for your definition(s)
       A. Include concrete description, define terms, and provide examples
       B. Include clear transitions from one paragraph to the next

III. Concluding Paragraph
    A. Restate in a new way the definition and purpose/thesis
    B. Add some general closing comments without introducing any new ideas

Introductory Paragraph

Begin your definition essay with a general introduction to the subject or term you are defining. Give an overview of the term that you will elaborate on in your body paragraphs. You might also have to explain an item's uses or purpose in a particular field, depending on your subject. End with a thesis statement that presents the purpose for your definition essay.

Body Paragraphs

After creating a strong thesis statement for your definition essay, you need to organize your body paragraphs in the best way to develop your definition. For instance, using the tamale example from earlier, you could use the body paragraphs and topic sentences to further define the tamale and then develop the tamale's symbolic significance, giving specific details and explaining the traditions and cultural history that relate to the tamale in separate paragraphs. Transitions relating to comparison, contrast, and example are particularly useful in definition essays.

Cross Reference
For more transitions, see Chapter 5, pp. 93–94, Transitions to . . . .

TRANSITIONS TO . . .

Show Contrast or a Change in Idea

although	even though	instead	on the other side
anyhow	for all that	nevertheless	otherwise
at the same time	however	notwithstanding	regardless
but	in any event	on the contrary	still
despite this	in contrast	on the other hand	yet

Show a Comparison

in like manner	in the same way	likewise	similarly

Illustrate or Give Examples/Specifics

a few include	essentially	in particular	the following
an example	for example	let us consider	specifically
especially	for instance	the case of	you can see this in

ACTIVITY 10-3   Creating Topic Sentences

Directions: *Choose three of the thesis statements you created in Activity 10-2, and write two topic sentences for each that could be used to develop two body paragraphs for that thesis statement in an essay.*

1. Thesis statement: _____

   _____

   Topic sentence 1: _____

   _____

   Topic sentence 2: _____

   _____

2. Thesis statement: _____

   _____

   Topic sentence 1: _____

   _____

   Topic sentence 2: _____

   _____

3. Thesis statement: _____

   _____

   Topic sentence 1: _____

   _____

   Topic sentence 2: _____

   _____

Develop your body paragraphs by providing concrete details and examples.

ACTIVITY 10-4   Supporting Details

Directions: *Now provide at least three possible examples or details for three of the topic sentences you created in Activity 10-3.*

1. Topic sentence: _____

   _____

Example/detail 1: _____

_____

Example/detail 2: _____

_____

Example/detail 3: _____

_____

2. Topic sentence: _____

Example/detail 1: _____

_____

Example/detail 2: _____

_____

Example/detail 3: _____

_____

3. Topic sentence: _____

_____

Example/detail 1: _____

_____

Example/detail 2: _____

_____

Example/detail 3: _____

_____

Concluding Paragraph

The concluding paragraph in a definition essay should redefine the object or concept briefly and sum up your purpose for defining it.

ACTIVITY 10-5 Writing a Concluding Paragraph

Directions: *Choose one of the topics you've been developing in the preceding activities, and write a three- to five-sentence concluding paragraph that re-emphasizes the definition and your purpose for defining it.*

_____

_____

_____

_____

_____

_____

ACTIVITY 10-6 Creating Your Outline and First Draft

Cross Reference
See Chapters 21–25, pp. 515–648, for help with the Editing section of the critique form.

Directions: *Choose a topic from one of the activities you already completed in this chapter, from the assignment choices at the end of this chapter, or from a topic assigned by your instructor, and create a rough outline using the template on pages 228–229 of this chapter. Then, using your rough outline, write a first draft of your essay. After you have finished, use the critique form below to check for the basics in your essay draft.*

DEFINITION ESSAY CRITIQUE FORM

PURPOSE   IDEAS   SUPPORT   ASSUMPTIONS BIASES   CONCLUSIONS   POINT OF VIEW   ANALYSIS

Overall

	Done well	Needs work
1. Does the essay clearly define the subject?	_____	_____
2. Does the essay use specific details and **ideas** consistently and clearly?	_____	_____
3. Are the paragraphs organized clearly and logically and are they a good length—3–15 sentences?	_____	_____

Introduction

4. Is the title interesting and in correct format?	_____	_____
5. Is there a general introduction that gives background for the subject?	_____	_____
6. Is there a clear thesis statement that explains the **purpose** of the definition?	_____	_____

Body

7. Do the body paragraphs develop the definition and flow smoothly?	_____	_____
8. Are transitions used between and, when needed, within the paragraphs?	_____	_____
9. Do the body paragraphs include **support** (descriptive details and examples)?	_____	_____

Conclusion

10. Does the **concluding** paragraph sum up the definition with **analysis** and re-emphasize the **purpose** developed in the introductory paragraph and thesis, without adding new ideas? _____ _____

Editing

11. Circle the following errors you think you see in this draft: spelling errors, fragments, run-ons/comma splices, errors in comma and semicolon/colon use, pronoun disagreement, pronoun reference errors, errors in parallelism, apostrophe use, verb use/tense, and passive voice construction.

12. Other types of grammar or sentence-level errors:

_____

Comments (For example: What works well in this draft? What needs to be added? Did you, or will your readers, feel drawn into the essay? Why or why not?):

_____

_____

_____

COMPLEMENTARY MODES FOR DEFINITION ESSAYS

5 Use modes that complement definition essays.

When definition is used in an essay, it is often combined with several other modes:

- **Narration** and **description** can be used to develop a definition. You should use concrete and specific descriptions in a definition and sometimes include a story to explain the subject's purpose.
- **Example and illustration** is necessary to elaborate on the definition of a subject. You might provide examples of types of objects and uses for an object in a definition.
- **Classification** is usually part of the definition process itself: You have to classify items into broader groups to define them specifically.
- You can **compare and contrast** items to define your subject.
- You might use **argument** and **persuasion** in your essay to defend an unconventional definition.

Student Essay

The dominant mode used in this student's paper is definition. Look for other modes used in this essay, such as classification, narration and description, comparison and contrast, and example and illustration.

Figueroa 1

Rosie Figueroa

Professor Rosen

English 100

15 March 2013

The Importance of a Quinceañera

Many cultures have traditional rituals to represent a coming of age. In America, girls often celebrate their sixteenth birthday with a "Sweet 16" party. In Jewish culture, boys and girls celebrate their thirteenth birthday with a Bar or Bat Mitzvah. In my culture, which is Mexican-American, when girls turn fifteen they have an elaborate party called a quinceañera. This party and the rituals involved are a very important part of my culture and an important part of becoming a young woman.

A quinceañera is a specialized birthday celebration. The word "quinceañera" comes from the Spanish word "quince," which means "fifteen"; therefore, it is literally a celebration of a girl's fifteenth birthday. In some ways, it is more like a wedding than a normal birthday party. For example, in a quinceañera, the girl wears a beautiful white dress and, usually, a tiara. Also, as in a wedding, she chooses friends (up to 14 of them to make a total of 15) to be part of her quinceañera. If her court is made up of girls, these girls wear special matching dresses, much like bridesmaids, and are part of the formal ceremony acknowledging her coming of age before the reception to celebrate her coming out as a young woman to society. Sometimes, the formal ceremony is held in a church with a priest who gives a blessing, and sometimes it is held at a home or community hall. Always, family and friends are there to celebrate this special birthday.

Thesis statement

Topic sentence

Concluding sentence

Figueroa 2

Topic sentence

The last part of the quinceañera celebrates the importance of the girl's family and friends in her transition from childhood to adulthood and involves sharing good food, music, and dancing. Usually, close family members and godparents contribute money toward the celebration. Much planning goes into arranging the religious blessing as well as the reception afterward that provides food and entertainment for all the guests. Moreover, special invitations are sent out in advance, and these parties can be huge with hundreds of guests. That's why there are websites dedicated to buying supplies for a quinceañera celebration. Quinceañeras feature a banquet, often with rice, beans, carne asada, tamales, and enchiladas. Also, a mariachi band usually plays traditional Mexican dance music, and everyone, young and old, dances to celebrate the girl's coming out into society as a young adult. It's a

Concluding sentence

great chance to connect with family and friends and to celebrate Mexican traditions, food, music, and overall culture.

Restatement of thesis

The quinceañera is more than just a birthday party: it is an important part of my Mexican cultural identity. Young girls look forward to this special day, and family and friends see it as a way to celebrate both the girl's birthday and their pride in their culture's traditions and heritage. It celebrates the girl's transition into adulthood with the best combination of food, music, dancing, and family.

ACTIVITY 10-7 **Thinking Critically about the Student Essay**

Directions: *Identify the features and details characteristic of the definition mode in this essay. Mark them on the essay. Then, reread the essay and make a list of specific revisions you would make to correct any problems with content, organization, transitions, and style.*

PROFESSIONAL DEFINITION ESSAY

Cyberbullying: A Growing Problem

Science Daily, February 22, 2010

1

Example for support

Around 10 percent of all adolescents in grades 7–9 are victims of internet bullying. "This type of bullying can be more serious than conventional bullying. At least with conventional bullying the victim is left alone on evenings and weekends," says Ann Frisén, Professor of Psychology at the University of Gothenburg.

Cause-and-effect analysis

2

Definition

Victims of internet bullying—or cyberbullying—have no refuge. Victims may be harassed continuously via SMS and websites, and the information spreads very quickly and may be difficult to remove. In addition, it is often difficult to identify the perpetrator. Ann Frisén's research concerns body image, identity development and different types of bullying among children and adolescents. She is also part of an EU network of researchers studying cyberbullying and is since 1 January the national coordinator of this type of research.

WHAT IS CYBERBULLYING?

3

Definition

Cyberbullying occurs when new technologies such as computers and mobile phones are used to harass or bully somebody. The perpetrators often use SMS, e-mail, chat rooms and Facebook to spread their message. One example of this is the Facebook group "Vi som hatar Stina Johansson" (Those of us who hate Stina Johansson). "This Facebook group was very difficult to

Example

remove. It took Stina's parents almost one whole month," says Frisén.

A CLEAR LINK TO SCHOOL LIFE

4

Example

Cause-and-effect analysis

Who are the victims? Around 10 percent of all adolescents in grades 7–9 are victims of cyberbullying. There is a clear connection to school life—it usually calms down in the summer. The perpetrator is almost always from the same school as the victim. "It is a lot easier to be a perpetrator on the internet since it enables you to act anonymously. This also makes it possible for a weaker person to bully a stronger, which is uncommon in conventional bullying," says Frisén.

BLURRING OF BOUNDARIES IS ANOTHER IMPORTANT FACTOR

5

In these contexts, people take liberties they normally wouldn't. For example, nobody would ever think of starting a magazine called "Those of us

Example for support

who hate Stina Johansson." So how can cyberbullying among children and adolescents be prevented?

PARENTS HAVE AN IMPORTANT ROLE, ACCORDING TO FRISÉN

6

Argument

Adults shouldn't be so naive about what they put out about themselves on the internet, for example pictures. Kids get inspired by what adults do. In addition, it's good if parents show interest and ask their children to show them which sites they like to visit. But it's usually not a good idea to forbid them from visiting certain websites; they should instead teach them how to act when they are there.

Argument and persuasion

7

It is also important not to blame victimized children, since it's really not their fault. Our job is instead to help them end the harassment. Frisén feels that people in Sweden generally are a bit naive when it comes to these issues: "All school children in the UK are taught to 'zip it, block it and flag it'—don't share information, block contacts and tell an adult!"

MyWritingLab™ **Reading Reflection Questions**

1. What is the definition of cyberbullying that is given in paragraph 3?

   _____

   _____

2. Who do you think the article is written for—who is the target audience?

   _____

3. What are some of the Internet sites used for the cyberbullying that the author provides as examples?

   _____

MyWritingLab™ **Objective Questions**

4. T/F_____ Cyberbullying occurs less in the summertime when school is out.

5. T/F_____ The author thinks that parents do not have a role in helping prevent cyberbullying among teens.

6. T/F_____ The perpetrator is usually from the same school as the victim of cyberbullying.

7. According to the author, cyberbullying allows a weaker person to bully a stronger one. Why does the Internet make that possible?

   _____

MyWritingLab™   **Checking Vocabulary**

Define the following in your own words, or give a dictionary definition if you don't know the word.

8. conventional bullying: _____

_____

9. adolescents: _____

_____

10. naive: _____

_____

CRITICAL THINKING CHECKLIST

PURPOSE

1. What is the **purpose** of this piece of writing? Is it clear?

_____

_____

IDEAS

2. What **ideas** and **background information** are provided to support the purpose of this piece of writing?

_____

_____

SUPPORT

3. What **evidence** and **examples** are used to explain and develop the ideas that support the argument made in the piece of writing? Are the evidence and examples provided sufficient?

_____

_____

ASSUMPTIONS
BIASES

4. Are there unfounded **assumptions** or unreasonable **biases**?

_____

_____

CONCLUSIONS

5. Are all of the **conclusions**, **implications**, and **consequences** of the arguments (the results of the arguments taken to their farthest extreme) considered?

_____

_____

**POINT
OF VIEW**

6. Is the **point of view** clear and consistent, and have other points of view been considered?

_____

_____

ANALYSIS

7. Using these critical thinking tools, **analyze** the overall structure of this essay and the strength of the author's arguments, ideas, and support. Was he or she successful in accomplishing the purpose? Why, or why not?

_____

_____

MyWritingLab™   **Essay Assignments**

1. Write a definition essay using any of the topics you developed in the activities in this chapter.

2. Define a concept from one of your other classes (for example, a term from economics, history, or biology).

3. Combine definition with one other mode (see above, Complementary Modes for Definition Essays) and write an essay related to some aspect of your college campus. Narrow your topic down to some aspect of your campus that needs definition: the interlibrary loan option, the Career Center, the Writing Center, the Financial Aid Office, and so on.

4. Provide your own extended definition of the "ideal family."

5. Define the word "patriotism" using a dictionary definition of the word as well as the connotations it carries and your own personal associations with and opinions of the word.

Learning Objectives Review

MyWritingLab™   Complete the chapter assessment questions at mywritinglab.com

1 Describe the definition mode.

What distinguishes definition from other writing modes? (See p. 222.)

Essay writers use **definition mode** to explain, define, and clarify items, terms, and concepts. A definition essay does not merely describe its subject: To *define*, you must explain what the term or concept *is* and what it *means*, not just what it looks, feels, tastes, sounds, or smells like.

2 Apply critical thinking skills to writing definition essays.

How can thinking critically help you write a definition essay? (See pp. 222–223.)

Thinking critically helps you **analyze** your definition's **purpose** and assess the scope of your definition and the best **ideas** and support to develop your purpose and reach a **conclusion**.

3 Prepare to write a definition essay by asking critical thinking questions.

What questions help you plan a definition essay? (See pp. 223–224.)

Ask the following questions: (1) What is my purpose for defining this object or concept? (2) Who is my target audience, and what do I want them to learn? (3) What general category does my subject fall into, and what distinguishing characteristics does it have? (4) Can I compare it to something similar, or can I explain it by saying what it is *not*? (5) What support can I use? (6) What is the most effective order of development for my essay?

4 Structure a definition essay.

How do you structure a definition essay? (See pp. 224–233.)

You **structure a definition essay** by creating an introductory paragraph with a thesis that states the definition and purpose, body paragraphs that support and develop the thesis, and a conclusion to restate the thesis and sum up without adding new ideas.

5 Use modes that complement definition essays.

What modes complement a definition essay? (See pp. 233–239.)

Modes that work well with definition structure include narration and description, examples and illustration, classification, compare and contrast, and argument.

Thinking Critically MyWritingLab™

Are You Sleeping?
Cindy Small

Think: Study the painting.

Write: What is shown in this picture? Write a brief description using as many concrete details as possible. In your description, give two examples of the use of color, then describe what effect those colors have on your interpretation of the picture's mood.

_____

_____

_____

_____

_____

_____

_____

_____

EXAMPLE AND ILLUSTRATION ESSAYS

❶ Describe the example and illustration mode.

Example and illustration essays use examples to clarify, explain, illustrate, and support the purpose of the essay. Examples include facts, expert testimony, and personal experience. The examples illustrate your larger purpose and arguments. The examples provided can be combined to support a thesis; or a single, extended example can be used to develop a purpose.

CRITICAL THINKING AND EXAMPLE AND ILLUSTRATION

❷ Apply critical thinking skills to writing example and illustration essays.

Before you begin generating examples, you need to assess your audience and determine the message you want to express to them. When you write about any subject, the best way to illustrate your ideas and arguments is to provide concrete examples. If you wanted to write an essay that argued that people benefit from going to college, you would need to provide concrete examples of the kinds of skills you can learn at college, such as critical thinking skills, oral and written communication skills, group and collaboration skills, and so on. As you write an example and illustration essay, develop your **purpose** to decide on the right **ideas**, **support**, examples, and **conclusions**, and **analyze** the significance of your examples and how you illustrate your points and purpose. What do you want to illustrate through your use of examples? What is the purpose you will be developing through the use of examples and detailed illustrations?

When you provide examples, be sure to avoid **hasty generalizations** (jumping to conclusions about the examples provided that might not be supported, like using someone's age to determine a personality trait) about the examples and what they illustrate, and avoid using equivocal (vague and unclear) language or **euphemisms** (softened language to distract from a harsh truth) in your descriptions and examples. These logical fallacies will make your readers question the strength and validity of the examples you provide.

To make a convincing point to your readers, provide lots of examples or a strong extended example to illustrate and prove it. Your examples should be specific and descriptive and clearly relate to your purpose. To write a powerful example essay, consider the following questions:

1. What is the **purpose** of your essay? What point do you want to make through the use of examples? How will you convey that message and develop your **ideas**?

2. What **support** can you include? What are the best examples and details (descriptive details, examples, comparisons) you can include to develop your purpose?

3. What **assumptions and biases** have affected the examples you have provided? What do your choices for what to include or not include as examples say about your **point of view** and biases?

4. **Analyze** the examples you use and how much detail or background for the examples you will need to include. How should you break down the examples and organize them to best support your purpose?

BEFORE WRITING AN EXAMPLE AND ILLUSTRATION ESSAY

3 Prepare to write an example and illustration essay by asking critical thinking questions.

Before you begin to write an example essay, ask yourself these questions:

1. What point am I trying to make?
2. Which examples can I include to illustrate my purpose clearly?
3. What facts, testimony, and experiences can I tap into to develop my purpose in this essay?
4. What details should I provide to further illustrate my examples?
5. How should I organize this essay, and how should I conclude it?

ACTIVITY 11-1 Choosing Examples

Directions: *For each of the following topics, list three examples you could use to develop it.*

1. **Topic:** Internet sites

   _____

   _____

2. **Topic:** Smartphones

   _____

   _____

3. **Topic:** Fast food

   _____

   _____

4. **Topic:** Natural disasters

   _____

   _____

5. **Topic:** Peer pressure

_____

_____

WRITING AN EXAMPLE AND ILLUSTRATION ESSAY

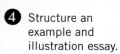 Structure an example and illustration essay.

All essays depend on examples and illustrations to develop and support their thesis statements. Examples support topic sentences in an essay, and extended examples can be used to develop the thesis statement of an essay. Always provide examples to illustrate your purpose and then comment on the examples given and explain how they support your purpose.

Organizational Pattern for an Example Essay

Organize your paper in a way that highlights your examples in the most powerful way to express your purpose. For instance, you might choose to organize your examples by order of importance (most to least or least to most important), or you might use chronological order if the examples happened in a particular sequence.

Examples illustrate your claims and purpose with concrete evidence and support. In your introductory paragraph, present the overall purpose of your essay, and in your thesis statement, explain what you will be illustrating through examples and your analytical purpose. In the body paragraphs, develop several simple examples or one or more extended examples to support your thesis. For instance, if you were explaining the progression of events at a typical wedding from your culture, you could use several different weddings you've attended as examples, or you could use your own wedding—or the wedding of someone close to you—as an extended example. Your examples should be vivid and interesting but not unfamiliar to your readers. Most important, the examples must clearly demonstrate the point(s) you have presented in your thesis. Be sure to incorporate as many details and concrete images as possible in your examples. Use transitions between examples within your body paragraphs and between paragraphs. Include key words and transitional phrases such as "for example," "to illustrate," and "for instance" to introduce your examples. Finally, in the concluding paragraph, re-emphasize the purpose you want to express to your readers though the examples.

The chart below provides a brief overview of the structure of an example and illustration essay.

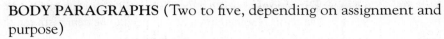

BASIC STRUCTURE FOR AN EXAMPLE AND ILLUSTRATION ESSAY

See the sample essay on pages 252–253.

PURPOSE

INTRODUCTORY PARAGRAPH

Sets up your subject and your purpose.

Thesis statement: A statement that defines your purpose and what example(s) you'll be using to illustrate it.

IDEAS

SUPPORT

BODY PARAGRAPHS (Two to five, depending on assignment and purpose)

Topic sentences set up the organization and focus of your examples or extended example.

Develop the examples, illustrations, and details. **Analyze** their significance.

Use transitions within and between paragraphs to make the paragraphs flow smoothly.

ANALYSIS

CONCLUSIONS

CONCLUDING PARAGRAPH

Sums up and **re-emphasizes** the thesis.

Structuring an Example and Illustration Essay

The most concrete way we can support our ideas and conclusions—whether it is in college, our careers, or our everyday interactions with others—is to provide examples. Many topics work well for structuring an example and illustration essay. You could write about the kinds of cars you can buy in America, the variety of food and interesting cuisines in this country, the latest advances in medicine, types of diabetes, new forms of alternative energy, political campaign ads, the types of clothing that are popular this decade, and so on.

Topic

If your instructor does not assign a topic for your example and illustration essay, then brainstorm ideas for things, places, or events you might want to describe. Come up with some ideas for a purpose for describing the topic. What do you want your readers to understand through your use of examples?

Thesis Statements

A thesis statement for an example and illustration essay clarifies your purpose for including specific examples or illustrations. It states what you want your readers to understand after reading your example essay, the message you want to impart.

> Sports fans go to many extremes to show support for their favorite teams. Technology has made being a college student easier in the last decade.

ACTIVITY 11-2   Creating Thesis Statements

Directions: *Create a thesis statement for each of the topics listed. Make sure that the thesis is something that will need to be demonstrated through examples.*

1. **Topic:** Prejudice

   Thesis sentence: _____

   _____

2. **Topic:** Interesting hobbies

   Thesis sentence: _____

   _____

3. **Topic:** Fast food

   Thesis sentence: _____

   _____

4. **Topic:** Bad habits

   Thesis sentence: _____

   _____

5. **Topic:** Video games

   Thesis sentence: _____

   _____

Creating a Rough Outline

Once you have determined your topic and your thesis statement, you are ready to create a rough outline to determine your essay's structure and organizational plan. Use prewriting techniques such as brainstorming or clustering

Cross Reference
See Chapter 6,
pp. 104–115,
Stage One: Prewrite
to Generate Ideas.

to generate supporting examples and concrete details. Then create a rough outline using this template:

Rough Outline Template for an Example and Illustration Essay

   I. Introductory Paragraph
      A. A brief, general description of the subject and examples
      B. Thesis Statement: the purpose of your examples and illustrations (what these examples will illustrate and your reason(s) for including them)
  II. Body Paragraphs: two to four body paragraphs that explain the purpose and provide examples and details
      A. Include concrete examples, descriptions, and details
      B. Include clear transitions from one paragraph to the next
      C. Include definitions and explanations
 III. Concluding Paragraph
      A. Restate the purpose/thesis in a new way
      B. Add some general closing comments without introducing any new ideas

Introductory Paragraph

Begin your example and illustration essay with a general introduction to the topic. End with the thesis statement to present the purpose of your example essay.

Body Paragraphs

The body paragraphs in an example and illustration essay provide specific details and examples organized to illustrate your purpose. For instance, in an essay about appropriate birthday parties for people of different ages, you could organize the examples chronologically and create topic sentences for each age-specific type of party. Or you might choose to organize your body paragraphs on the basis of the importance of each example: least to most important, or vice versa. Your topic sentences should introduce each specific example and its relevance to your thesis statement's purpose.

    Write a body paragraph for each separate example or write several body paragraphs for an extended example. Use at least two examples to illustrate each topic sentence and include analysis of the examples. For instance, the following sentences briefly outline an essay about birthday parties for three different age groups.

> **Thesis:** Birthday parties should be age appropriate.
>
> **Topic sentence 1:** Birthday parties for elementary school–age children should have interactive games that are supervised by adults.

> **Topic sentence 2:** For middle school–age children, birthday parties should skip organized games and focus on the kids just hanging out together, gifts, and food.
>
> **Topic sentence 3:** For high school kids, birthday parties are usually held at a place outside the home (at a restaurant, for example) and are attended by a small group of close friends.

ACTIVITY 11-3   Creating Topic Sentences

Directions: *For three of the thesis statements you created in Activity 11-2, create topic sentences with examples that support them.*

1. **Topic:** _____

   Thesis statement: _____

   Topic sentence:_____

   _____

2. **Topic:** _____

   Thesis statement: _____

   Topic sentence: _____

   _____

3. **Topic:** _____

   Thesis statement: _____

   Topic sentence: _____

   _____

ACTIVITY 11-4   Providing Examples

Directions: *Based on your answers in Activity 11-3, provide three detailed examples that would provide support for each topic sentence.*

1. **Topic:** _____

   Topic sentence: _____

   Examples: _____

   _____

2. Topic: _____

   Topic sentence: _____

   Examples: _____

   _____

3. Topic: _____

   Topic sentence: _____

   Examples: _____

   _____

Cross Reference
For other useful transitions, see also Chapter 5, p. 94, Strengthen a Point; p. 93, Introduce Another Point; and p. 94, Explain a Purpose.

Example transitions are especially useful in example and illustration essays.

TRANSITIONS TO . . .

Illustrate or Give Examples/Specifics

a few include	essentially	in particular	the following
an example	for example	let us consider	specifically
especially	for instance	the case of	one can see this in

Concluding Paragraph

The concluding paragraph for your example essay should recap your purpose and intended message using the examples and illustrations you chose.

ACTIVITY 11-5 Writing a Conclusion

Directions: *Based on your answers to Activities 11-2, 11-3, and 11-4, write a three- to five-sentence concluding paragraph for one of the topics you wrote about.*

_____

_____

_____

_____

_____

ACTIVITY 11-6   Creating Your Outline and First Draft

Cross Reference
See Chapters 21–25,
pp. 515–648 for help with
the Editing section of the
critique form.

Directions: *Choose a topic from one of the activities you already completed in this chapter, from the assignment choices at the end of this chapter, or from a topic assigned by your instructor and create a rough outline using the template on page 247 of this chapter. Then, using your rough outline, write a first draft of your essay. After you have finished, use the critique form below to check for the basics in your essay draft.*

EXAMPLE AND ILLUSTRATION ESSAY CRITIQUE FORM

BLUEPRINTS   PURPOSE   IDEAS   SUPPORT   ASSUMPTIONS BIASES   CONCLUSIONS   POINT OF VIEW   ANALYSIS

Overall

	Done well	Needs work
1. Does the essay provide **ideas**, examples, or illustrations and have an analytical **purpose?**	_____	_____
2. Does the essay include specific examples and analysis in the body paragraphs and provide a concluding paragraph?	_____	_____
3. Are the paragraphs organized clearly and logically and are they a good length—3–15 sentences?	_____	_____

Introduction

	Done well	Needs work
4. Is the title interesting and in correct format?	_____	_____
5. Is there a general introduction that gives background information for the essay's **purpose?**	_____	_____
6. Is there a clear thesis statement that explains the significance or message of the examples and illustrations provided—an expository **purpose?**	_____	_____

Body

	Done well	Needs work
7. Do the body paragraphs have **support**, develop the examples well, and flow smoothly?	_____	_____
8. Are transitions used between and, when needed, within the paragraphs?	_____	_____
9. Do the body paragraphs have descriptive details and **analysis** to enhance the examples?	_____	_____

Conclusion

10. Does the **concluding** paragraph sum up with an analytical frame that re-emphasizes the introductory paragraph and thesis, without adding new ideas?   _____   _____

Editing

11. Circle the following errors you think you see in this draft: spelling errors, fragments, run-ons/comma splices, errors in commas and semicolon/colon use, pronoun disagreement, pronoun reference errors, errors in parallelism, apostrophe use, verb use/tense, and passive voice construction.

12. Other types of grammar or sentence-level errors:

_____

Comments (For example: What works well in this draft? What needs to be added? Did you, or will your readers, feel drawn into this essay? Why or why not?):

_____

_____

COMPLEMENTARY MODES FOR EXAMPLE AND ILLUSTRATION ESSAYS

❺ Use modes that complement example and illustration essays.

Example and illustration mode is often combined with several other modes.

- **Narration** and **description** can be used to analyze the examples—you may even include a story as an example. Specific description and use of sensory details also heightens the effectiveness of your examples.
- **Definition** mode can be used to help explain objects or concepts used in the examples.
- **Cause-and-effect analysis** will further elaborate on the examples. You might choose to examine the reasons for and results of picking the examples you include to support your thesis and purpose.
- You can **compare and contrast** examples as you analyze your subject.
- You can use **argument** to persuade your readers to agree with the point of view you are using examples to support.

Student Essay

The dominant mode used in this student's paper is example and illustration. Look for other modes used in this essay, such as narration and description, definition, and comparison and contrast.

Brian Tobias

Professor Jacobson

English 100

26 September 2012

Seattle's Grunge Bands

Thesis statement

Seattle has always been recognized for having great musicians, but, in the late '80s and the early '90s, Seattle became the forefront for a new style of rock called grunge. Grunge combined elements of heavy metal, punk, and pop. The music featured screaming guitars, dissonant sounds, and wailing vocals, and it helped bring alternative rock into the mainstream. Pearl Jam, Soundgarden, and Nirvana are some of the best known grunge bands, opening the path to similar bands in the '90s and making a name for Seattle in music history.

Topic sentence

Pearl Jam consisted of Eddie Vedder (lead vocals and guitar); Stone Gossard (rhythm guitar); Jeff Ament (bass guitar); Mike McCready (lead guitar); and Dave Krusen (drummer), who was later replaced by Dave Abbruzzese. *Ten*, their first album, contained songs about loneliness, murder, suicide, and depression. The sound was a combination of classic rock, howling guitars, and Eddie Vedder's distinctive vocals. Pearl Jam released four other albums in the '90s: *Vs.*, *Vitalogy*, *No Code*, and *Yield*. Pearl Jam outsold Nirvana, making them the top-selling grunge band.

Concluding sentence

Although they were criticized for cashing in on the popularity of alternative rock, they did not play by the rules, refusing to make music videos and boycotting Ticketmaster.

Topic sentence

Another great band formed in Seattle was Soundgarden. In 1984, Kim Thayil (lead guitar); Hiro Yamamoto (bass); Scott Sundquist (drummer), replaced in 1986 by Matt Cameron; and Chris Cornell (lead singer, drummer) formed Soundgarden. Their

Tobias 2

music was a mix of punk, heavy metal, powerful guitar riffs, clear melodies, and Cornell's extraordinary and haunting vocals. Since 1984, the band recorded seven albums including *Screaming Life*, *FOPP*, *Ultramega OK*, *Louder than Love*, *Badmotorfinger*, *Superunknown*, and *Down on the Upside*. On April 9, 1997, Soundgarden broke up due to fighting among band members. Still, they will always remain an example of one of Seattle's finest grunge bands, with a sound all their own.

Finally, Nirvana is one of the best-known names in the grunge world. Nirvana consisted of Kurt Cobain (singer/guitarist), Chris Novoselic (bass), and Aaron Burkhart (drummer). Burkhart was replaced by Chad Channing in 1986, who was himself replaced by Dave Grohl in 1990. Their music was a powerful combination of hard rock, high-energy pop, strong melodies, screaming guitars, and Cobain's powerful and varied vocals. The band produced several albums between 1989 and 1996 including *Bleach, Silver Dive, Nevermind, Incesticide, In Utero*, and *From the Muddy Banks of the Wishkah*. *Nevermind* was their breakthrough album. By Christmas of 1991, 400,000 copies of the CD were being sold each week, and it became number one on the *Billboard* charts in January 1992. Nirvana's performances in the United States and abroad were sold out. Then, on April 8, 1994, Kurt Cobain was found dead in his home with a self-inflicted gunshot wound. The band members disbanded in 1996. However, Nirvana will always remain the ultimate Northwest grunge band example.

In conclusion, Pearl Jam, Soundgarden, and Nirvana were instrumental in starting the grunge era. Each one of the bands had its own style, which laid the foundation for the bands that followed them. They put Seattle on the musical map.

Marginal annotations:

Concluding sentence

Topic sentence

Concluding sentence

Restatement of thesis

ACTIVITY 11-7 Thinking Critically about
the Student Essay

Directions: *Identify the features and details characteristic of the example and illustration mode in this essay. Mark them on the essay. Then, reread the essay and make a list of specific revisions you would make to correct any problems with content, organization, transitions, format, and style.*

PROFESSIONAL EXAMPLE AND ILLUSTRATION ESSAY

Learning to Read and Write

Frederick Douglass

Frederick Douglass was born into slavery in 1818. He worked hard to learn how to read and write, using initiative and creative methods to succeed. As he educated himself, he became even more aware of and outraged by the injustices and immorality of slavery. Finally, he ran away and became an important figure in the abolitionist movement to end slavery. He became a world-class orator and author and his works are still relevant today in the fight for human rights.

▶ NOTE   For help with the essay's nineteenth-century vocabulary, consult a dictionary.

1   I lived in Master Hugh's family about seven years. During this time, I succeeded in learning to read and write. In accomplishing this, I was

Thesis   compelled to resort to various stratagems. I had no regular teacher. My mistress, who had kindly commenced to instruct me, had, in compliance with the advice and direction of her husband, not only ceased to instruct, but had set her face against my being instructed by any one else. It is due, however, to my mistress to say of her, that she did not adopt this course of treatment immediately. She at first lacked the depravity indispensable to shutting me up in mental darkness. It was at least necessary for her to have some training in the exercise of irresponsible power, to make her equal to the task of treating me as though I were a brute.

2   My mistress was, as I have said, a kind and tender-hearted woman; and in the simplicity of her soul she commenced, when I first went to live with her, to treat me as she supposed one human being ought to treat another. In entering upon the duties of a slaveholder, she did not seem to perceive that I sustained to her the relation of a mere chattel, and that for her to treat me

as a human being was not only wrong, but dangerously so. Slavery proved as injurious to her as it did to me. When I went there, she was a pious, warm, and tender-hearted woman. There was no sorrow or suffering for which she had not a tear. She had bread for the hungry, clothes for the naked, and comfort for every mourner that came within her reach. Slavery soon proved its ability to divest her of these heavenly qualities. Under its influence, the tender heart became stone, and the lamb-like disposition gave way to one of tiger-like fierceness. The first step in her downward course was in her ceasing to instruct me. She now commenced to practise her husband's precepts. She finally became even more violent in her opposition than her husband himself. She was not satisfied with simply doing as well as he had commanded; she seemed anxious to do better. Nothing seemed to make her more angry than to see me with a newspaper. She seemed to think that here lay the danger. I have had her rush at me with a face made all up of fury, and snatch from me a newspaper, in a manner that fully revealed her apprehension. She was an apt woman; and a little experience soon demonstrated, to her satisfaction, that education and slavery were incompatible with each other.

3   From this time I was most narrowly watched. If I was in a separate room any considerable length of time, I was sure to be suspected of having a book, and was at once called to give an account of myself. All this, however, was too late. The first step had been taken. Mistress, in teaching me the alphabet, had given me the *inch*, and no precaution could prevent me from taking the *ell*.

4   The plan which I adopted, and the one by which I was most successful, was that of making friends of all the little white boys whom I met in the street. As many of these as I could, I converted into teachers. With their kindly aid, obtained at different times and in different places, I finally succeeded in learning to read. When I was sent of errands, I always took my book with me, and by going one part of my errand quickly, I found time to get a lesson before my return. I used also to carry bread with me, enough of which was always in the house, and to which I was always welcome; for I was much better off in this regard than many of the poor white children in our neighborhood. This bread I used to bestow upon the hungry little urchins, who, in return, would give me that more valuable bread of knowledge. I am strongly tempted to give the names of two or three of those little boys, as a testimonial of the gratitude and affection I bear them; but prudence forbids:—not that it would injure me, but it might embarrass them; for it is almost an unpardonable offence to teach slaves to read in this Christian country. It is enough to say of the dear little fellows, that they lived on Philpot Street, very near Durgin and Bailey's ship-yard. I used to talk this matter of slavery over with them. I would sometimes say to them, I wished I could be as free as they would be when they got to be men. "You will be free as soon as you are twenty-one, *but I am a slave for life!* Have not I as good a right to be free as you have?" These words used to trouble them; they would express for me the liveliest sympathy, and console me with the hope that something would occur by which I might be free.

Marginal annotations:

Argument and persuasion

Cause and effect

Example

Example

Example

5

Example

I was now about twelve years old, and the thought of being *a slave for life* began to bear heavily upon my heart. Just about this time, I got hold of a book entitled "The Columbian Orator." Every opportunity I got, I used to read this book. Among much of other interesting matter, I found in it a dialogue between a master and his slave. The slave was represented as having run away from his master three times. The dialogue represented the conversation which took place between them, when the slave was retaken the third time. In this dialogue, the whole argument in behalf of slavery was brought forward by the master, all of which was disposed of by the slave. The slave was made to say some very smart as well as impressive things in reply to his master—things which had the desired though unexpected effect; for the conversation resulted in the voluntary emancipation of the slave on the part of the master.

Argument and example

6

In the same book, I met with one of Sheridan's mighty speeches on and in behalf of Catholic emancipation. These were choice documents to me. I read them over and over again with unabated interest. They gave tongue to interesting thoughts of my own soul, which had frequently flashed through my mind, and died away for want of utterance. The moral which I gained from the dialogue was the power of truth over the conscience of even a slaveholder. What I got from Sheridan was a bold denunciation of slavery, and a powerful vindication of human rights. The reading of these documents enabled me to utter my thoughts, and to meet the arguments brought forward to sustain slavery; but while they relieved me of one difficulty, they brought on another even more painful than the one of which I was relieved. The more I read, the more I was led to abhor and detest my enslavers. I could regard them in no other light than a band of successful robbers, who had left their homes, and gone to Africa, and stolen us from our homes, and in a strange land reduced us to slavery. I loathed them as being the meanest as well as the most wicked of men. As I read and contemplated the subject, behold! that very discontentment which Master Hugh had predicted would follow my learning to read had already come, to torment and sting my soul to unutterable anguish. As I writhed under it, I would at times feel that learning to read had been a curse rather than a blessing. It had given me a view of my wretched condition, without the remedy. It opened my eyes to the horrible pit, but to no ladder upon which to get out. In moments of agony,

Compare and contrast

I envied my fellow-slaves for their stupidity. I have often wished myself a beast. I preferred the condition of the meanest reptile to my own. Any thing, no matter what, to get rid of thinking! It was this everlasting thinking of my condition that tormented me. There was no getting rid of it. It was pressed upon me by every object within sight or hearing, animate or inanimate. The silver trump of freedom had roused my soul to eternal wakefulness. Freedom now appeared, to disappear no more forever. It was heard in every sound, and seen in every thing. It was ever present to torment me with a sense of my wretched condition. I saw nothing without seeing it, I heard nothing without hearing it, and felt nothing without feeling it. It looked from every star, it smiled in every calm, breathed in every wind, and moved in every storm.

7   I often found myself regretting my own existence, and wishing myself dead; and but for the hope of being free, I have no doubt but that I should have killed myself, or done something for which I should have been killed. While in this state of mind, I was eager to hear anyone speak of slavery. I was a ready listener. Every little while, I could hear something about the abolitionists. It was some time before I found what the word meant. It was always used in such connections as to make it an interesting word to me. If a slave ran away and succeeded in getting clear, or if a slave killed his master, set fire to a barn, or did any thing very wrong in the mind of a slaveholder, it

Example

was spoken of as the fruit of *abolition*. Hearing the word in this connection very often, I set about learning what it meant. The dictionary afforded me little

Definition

or no help. I found it was "the act of abolishing;" but then I did not know what was to be abolished. Here I was perplexed. I did not dare to ask any one about its meaning, for I was satisfied that it was something they wanted me to know very little about. After a patient waiting, I got one of our city papers, containing an account of the number of petitions from the north, praying for the abolition of slavery in the District of Columbia, and of the slave trade between the States. From this time I understood the words *abolition* and *abolitionist*, and always drew near when that word was spoken, expecting to hear something of importance to myself and fellow-slaves. The light broke in upon me by degrees. I went one day down on the wharf of Mr. Waters; and

Narration

seeing two Irishmen unloading a scow of stone, I went, unasked, and helped them. When we had finished, one of them came to me and asked me if I were a slave. I told him I was. He asked, "Are ye a slave for life?" I told him that I was. The good Irishman seemed to be deeply affected by the statement. He said to the other that it was a pity so fine a little fellow as myself should be a slave for life. He said it was a shame to hold me. They both advised me to run away to the north; that I should find friends there, and that I should be free. I pretended not to be interested in what they said, and treated them as if I did not understand them; for I feared they might be treacherous. White men have been known to encourage slaves to escape, and then, to get the reward, catch them and return them to their masters. I was afraid that these seemingly good men might use me so; but I nevertheless remembered their advice, and from that time I resolved to run away. I looked forward to a time at which it would be safe for me to escape. I was too young to think of doing so immediately; besides, I wished to learn how to write, as I might have occasion to write my own pass. I consoled myself with the hope that I should one day find a good

Example

chance. Meanwhile, I would learn to write.

8   The idea as to how I might learn to write was suggested to me by being in Durgin and Bailey's ship-yard, and frequently seeing the ship carpenters, after hewing, and getting a piece of timber ready for use, write on the timber the name of that part of the ship for which it was intended. When a piece of timber was intended for the larboard side, it would be marked thus—"L."

Examples

When a piece was for the starboard side, it would be marked thus—"S."

A piece for the larboard side forward, would be marked thus—"L. F." When a piece was for starboard side forward, it would be marked thus—"S. F." For larboard aft, it would be marked thus—"L. A." For starboard aft, it would be marked thus—"S. A." I soon learned the names of these letters, and for what they were intended when placed upon a piece of timber in the shipyard. I immediately commenced copying them, and in a short time was able to make the four letters named. After that, when I met with any boy who I knew could write, I would tell him I could write as well as he. The next word would be, "I don't believe you. Let me see you try it." I would then make the letters which I had been so fortunate as to learn, and ask him to beat that. In this way I got a good many lessons in writing, which it is quite possible I should never have gotten in any other way. During this time, my copy-book was the board fence, brick wall, and pavement; my pen and ink was a lump of chalk. With these, I learned mainly how to write. I then commenced and continued copying the Italics in Webster's Spelling Book, until I could make them all without looking on the book. By this time, my little Master Thomas had gone to school, and learned how to write, and had written over a number of copy-books. These had been brought home, and shown to some of our near neighbors, and then laid aside. My mistress used to go to class meeting at the Wilk Street meetinghouse every Monday afternoon, and leave me to take care of the house. When left thus, I used to spend the time in writing in the spaces left in Master Thomas's copy-book, copying what he had written. I continued to do this until I could write a hand very similar to that of Master Thomas. Thus, after a long, tedious effort for years, I finally succeeded in learning how to write.

Narration and example

Example

Narration and example

Repeat of thesis

MyWritingLab™ ## Reading Reflection Questions

1. List two examples that Douglass provides in this narrative to show the creative and determined ways he learned to read and write.

   _____

   _____

2. Why didn't his masters want him to read and write? What did they fear, according to Douglass?

   _____

   _____

3. Though this memoir is about his learning to read and write, it is also an argument against slavery. Provide one example he provides in support of an argument against slavery.

   _____

   _____

4. T/F_____ Douglass knew that his masters wanted to keep him from learning to read and write because knowledge brought power and would make him hate his situation.

5. T/F_____ As he read more and more about slavery and human rights, he did in fact become increasingly angry at his owners.

6. In your own words, explain what learning to read and write did for Douglass.

_____

_____

7. T/ F_____ Douglass never saw any redeeming qualities in his Mistress.

MyWritingLab™ **Checking Vocabulary**

Define each of the following words by figuring out their meanings, using context clues from the reading selection. If you cannot work out the meaning of a word, use a dictionary.

8. depravity (paragraph 1): _____

9. pious (paragraph 2): _____

10. abolitionist (paragraph 7): _____

_____

CRITICAL THINKING CHECKLIST

PURPOSE

1. What is the **purpose** of this piece of writing? Is it clear?

_____

_____

IDEAS

2. What **ideas** and **background information** are provided to support the purpose of this piece of writing?

_____

_____

Continued ▶

SUPPORT

3. What **evidence** and **examples** are used to explain and develop the ideas that support the argument made in the piece of writing? Are the evidence and examples provided sufficient?

_____

_____

ASSUMPTIONS BIASES

4. Are there unfounded **assumptions** or unreasonable **biases**?

_____

_____

CONCLUSIONS

5. Are all of the **conclusions**, **implications**, and **consequences** of the arguments (the results taken to their farthest extreme) considered?

_____

_____

POINT OF VIEW

6. Is the **point of view** clear and consistent, and have other points of view been considered?

_____

_____

ANALYSIS

7. Using these critical thinking tools, **analyze** the overall structure of this essay and the strength of the author's arguments, ideas, and support. Was he or she successful in accomplishing the purpose? Why, or why not?

_____

_____

MyWritingLab™   Essay Assignments

1. Choose one of the topics you developed in the activities in this chapter, and write a full example and illustration essay on that topic.

2. Write an essay about political campaigns. What trends have you seen? Provide specific examples and come up with your own analytical conclusion (judgment) about them for your thesis.

3. Write an essay about changes you have seen in Americans' overall health.

4. Write an essay about how the Internet has changed our lives. Provide at least three specific examples for support.

5. Write an essay about a particular sport, and include specific examples to illustrate the analytical purpose you present in your introduction.

6. Write an essay that explores magazine advertisements. Provide some description and examples and then analyze the ads' intentions and success.

Learning Objectives Review

MyWritingLab™ Complete the chapter assessment questions at mywritinglab.com

❶	Describe the example and illustration mode. **What distinguishes the example and illustration mode from other modes? (See p. 242.)**	**Example and illustration mode** supports an essay's purpose through examples that clarify, explain, and illustrate. Examples include facts, expert testimony, and personal experiences.
❷	Apply critical thinking skills to writing example and illustration essays. **How can thinking critically help you write an example and illustration essay? (See pp. 242–243.)**	**Thinking critically** helps you **assess your purpose**, develop your **ideas** and support, evaluate your **conclusions**, and **analyze** the overall effectiveness of your purpose and examples. Check for assumptions and biases in the examples you've included. Analyze the conclusions you've reached about these examples.
❸	Prepare to write an example and illustration essay by asking critical thinking questions. **What questions will help you plan an example and illustration essay? (See pp. 243–244.)**	**Ask the following questions:** (1) What point am I trying to make? (2) Which examples can I include to illustrate my purpose clearly? (3) What facts, testimony, and experiences can I tap into to develop my purpose in this essay? (4) What details should I provide to further illustrate my examples? (5) How should I organize this essay, and how should I conclude it?
❹	Structure an example and illustration essay. **How do you structure an example and illustration essay? (See pp. 244–251.)**	You **structure an example and illustration essay** by creating an introductory paragraph with a thesis that states your purpose, body paragraphs that support and develop the thesis with examples, and a conclusion to restate the thesis and sum up without adding new ideas.

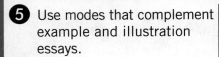 Use modes that complement example and illustration essays.

What modes complement an example and illustration essay? (See pp. 251–260.)

Modes that work well within an example and illustration structure include narration and description, definition, cause and effect, comparison and contrast, and argument and persuasion.

LEARNING OBJECTIVES

In this chapter, you will learn how to

1 Describe the cause and effect mode.

2 Apply critical thinking skills to writing cause-and-effect essays.

3 Prepare to write a cause-and-effect essay by asking critical thinking questions.

4 Structure a cause-and-effect essay.

5 Use modes that complement cause-and-effect essays.

Tide Pool

Thinking Critically   MyWritingLab™

Think: Study the photograph.

Write: How do you think the waves coming onto the ocean shore **cause** the formation of a tide pool? The tide pool above is a clean one, but what **causes** could endanger or pollute tide pools?

_____

_____

_____

_____

Write: What **effects** do you think pollution or human interaction would have on this tide pool?

_____

_____

_____

_____

CAUSE-AND-EFFECT ESSAYS

❶ Describe the cause and effect mode.

A **cause-and-effect essay** analyzes causes (what led to certain results or *why* something happens) and their effects (the consequences or the *results* of an action or event). We are constantly doing or witnessing actions that lead to specific consequences and reactions. Actions have a ripple effect, and those ripples can create a change in the overall dynamic of a situation. Cause-and-effect analysis is useful in academic and workplace writing to determine what led to a particular event and the consequences of that event.

Cause-and-effect essays examine causes that lead to specific results. They may discuss a single cause and a single effect, a series of effects resulting from a single cause, or a series of causes that led to one particular effect. For instance, trying a new hairstyle could be the single cause that leads to a compliment from a coworker (single effect), or overeating (single cause) could lead to several negative effects such as low self-esteem, diabetes, back pain, and heart disease. As another example, rainfall and dropping temperatures are two causes that lead to icy roads (single effect).

▶ **LANGUAGE TIP**   Use the word *effect* (a **noun**) when you write about results: She could immediately see the *effect* of her actions (although "effect" is used as a transitive verb in a few rare cases, such as "The citizens *effected* a new law."). Use the word *affect* (a **verb**) when you write about the action of the cause: The weather *affected* our travel plans. As a rule of thumb, "affect" is used as a verb and "effect" is used as a noun: When you *affect* a situation, you have an *effect* on it.

CRITICAL THINKING AND CAUSE AND EFFECT

❷ Apply critical thinking skills to writing cause-and-effect essays.

Cause-and-effect analysis is useful for helping your readers understand complicated events. The careful examination of the befores and afters of a specific event can help readers understand why it happened and how it might be avoided or repeated in the future. The **analysis** can also help convince your readers of an argument and the **conclusions** and the **purpose** you want to convey. For instance, one should stop smoking because of the negative health consequences or help stop the building of a new parking garage because it will destroy local wetlands.

Be careful when writing about causes and effects that you don't jump to unwarranted conclusions or connections: You can't conclude that an effect is the result of a specific cause simply because it happened after the event.

Do not make a cause-and-effect analysis without providing evidence to support the connection between two events. For example, if you were writing an essay about the number of students who drop out of college before finishing their degrees and you said that they dropped out because they received bad grades, you would need to do research to confirm that cause. There are several reasons students might drop out, including getting a good job.

APPLYING CRITICAL THINKING

| PURPOSE | IDEAS | SUPPORT | ASSUMPTIONS BIASES | CONCLUSIONS | POINT OF VIEW | ANALYSIS |

You see the causes and effects of actions and events around you all the time. You forget to put money in the parking meter (cause) and you get a ticket (effect). When analyzing a cause-and-effect pattern, you need to break down the parts of the cause(s) and the effect(s) of your topic. For example, maybe you forgot to put money in the meter because you saw someone fall while in a crosswalk and ran to help. Perhaps the judge waived the ticket because you took in the newspaper clipping applauding your rescue of the elderly woman who was almost run over by a truck. To write an effective cause-and-effect essay, you need to **analyze** all the *befores* and *afters* of an event.

BEFORE WRITING A CAUSE-AND-EFFECT ESSAY

❸ Prepare to write a cause-and-effect essay by asking critical thinking questions.

Before you begin to write a cause-and-effect essay, ask yourself these questions:

1. What process or event is the subject of my cause-and-effect analysis?
2. What are the benefits of doing a cause-and-effect analysis of my chosen topic?
3. Why did this process or event happen—what was the original cause(s)?
4. What is the result(s) (effect/s) of this process or event?
5. What do I want my readers to learn from reading about the cause(s) and/or effect(s) of this event or process?
6. How will I conclude this essay?

Answering these questions will help you generate an expository thesis statement, help you determine the causes and effects you want to focus on and the examples and details to include for support, and give you a general idea of how to organize your essay.

Cross Reference
See Chapter 6,
pp. 104–115,
Stage One: Prewrite
to Generate Ideas.

ACTIVITY 12-1   **Prewriting**

Directions: *Prewrite on the following broad subjects to come up with some ideas of causes and effects that could be analyzed in relation to each.*

Topic: Discrimination   *Self-esteem issues, unfair workplace practices,*
learned behavior, ignorance, school problems, therapy, cycle of discrimination,
institutionalized discrimination, education

1. **Topic:** Obesity _____
_____
_____

2. **Topic:** Political corruption _____
_____
_____

3. **Topic:** Bankruptcy _____
_____
_____

4. **Topic:** New laws _____
_____
_____

5. **Topic:** Being fired _____
_____
_____

ACTIVITY 12-2 Cause and Effect

Directions: *For each of the topics below, provide one cause and one effect.*

Cause		Effect
exercise	better sleep	*better health*
1. _____	war	_____
2. _____	prejudice	_____
3. _____	pollution	_____
4. _____	good grades	_____
5. _____	tooth decay	_____
6. _____	riots	_____
7. _____	economic crisis	_____
8. _____	paying bills	_____
9. _____	laughing	_____
10. _____	tears	_____

WRITING A CAUSE-AND-EFFECT ESSAY

4 Structure a cause-and-effect essay.

The point of analyzing causes and effects is to look at the reasons why things happen and/or the results of these events in order to understand them better and possibly to take action. When analyzing related events, you first need to make sure there is a causal relationship. Did one idea or event lead to another? What was the cause, and what was the effect? After you determine there is a cause-and-effect relationship in your topic, then you need to determine what you want to explain to your readers about it. Do you want to explain the causes and effects in order to inform your readers of a process or to critique the effects or the causes? For example, if you were writing about health and exercise, you could explain the effects of exercise on one's health in order to convince your readers to engage in more exercising. Or you could focus on the negative effects of too little exercise to accomplish the same goal.

Organization Pattern for Cause-and-Effect Essays

Be sure to organize your essay in the best way to build the analytical conclusion you establish in your thesis statement and introduction. Order of importance (most to least or least to most important) works very well as an organizational pattern for cause-and-effect essays. You will be focusing on the relationship between reasons and results.

When looking at the effects of one particular event or incident, it may help to think of the domino effect:

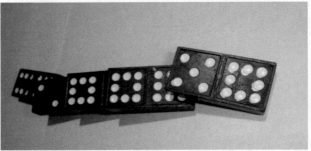

The dominos are lined up; then one is knocked over, and they fall one by one, leading to an overall change in the structure. The initial push of the first domino is the initial cause, and the dominos that fall one by one are the effects. It is a chain reaction: cause–effect–cause–effect.

Your body paragraphs should focus on the individual causes and/or effects you have presented in your introduction. Remember, again, depending on the assignment, you may analyze one cause and several effects, one effect and several causes, or several causes and several effects.

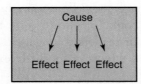

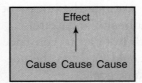

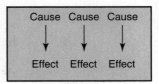

Use transitional words and phrases between the causes and/or effects you are providing as examples.

The chart below provides a brief overview of the structure of a cause-and-effect essay.

BASIC STRUCTURE FOR A CAUSE-AND-EFFECT ESSAY

See the sample essay on pages 276–277.

INTRODUCTORY PARAGRAPH

Sets up background for your cause/effect analysis.

Thesis statement: Establishes the causes and effects you will explain and your purpose for analyzing them.

BODY PARAGRAPHS (Two to five, depending on assignment and purpose)

Topic sentences set up the cause-and-effect subcategories.

Develop your analysis of the causal relationship by providing specific examples of the cause(s) and effect(s) and critiquing their importance.

Provide concrete examples and details.

Use transitions within and between paragraphs to make the paragraphs flow smoothly.

CONCLUDING PARAGRAPH

Sums up and re-emphasizes the thesis statement: the conclusions reached through your cause-and-effect analysis.

Structuring a Cause-and-Effect Essay

We are asked all the time to evaluate the reasons and results of actions or words. You can structure a cause-and-effect essay around pollution, political tension between two countries, depression, or any other cause that leads to a particular result. Or you can examine the effects of an event or condition such as a hurricane or other natural disaster, a world economic crisis, eating habits, or any action or event that leads to a particular result. The key is to analyze what caused something to occur, what happened after something occurred, or both.

Topic

If your instructor has not assigned a topic for your cause-and-effect essay, then brainstorm ideas for events or processes you might want to describe. Then come up with some ideas for a purpose for describing the topic. What do you want your readers to understand through your cause-and-effect essay?

Thesis Statements

The thesis statement in a cause-and-effect essay establishes whether you are focusing on just the causes of something, just the effects of something, or both. It also establishes the purpose for the cause-and-effect analysis: what you want your readers to understand. For example, if you were writing about diet and exercise, your thesis might establish both a causal relationship and an argument:

> Watching your diet and increasing your weekly exercise will create significant positive health results within weeks.

ACTIVITY 12-3   Creating Thesis Statements

Directions: *Develop a thesis statement for each of the topics you brainstormed about in Activity 12-1. Be sure the thesis focuses on the causes, effects, or both related to the topic and has a purpose to convey.*

1. **Topic:** Obesity

   Thesis statement: _____

   _____

2. **Topic:** Political corruption

   Thesis statement: _____

   _____

3. **Topic:** Bankruptcy

   Thesis statement: _____

   _____

4. **Topic:** New laws

   Thesis statement: _____

   _____

5. **Topic:** Being fired

   Thesis statement: _____

   _____

Creating a Rough Outline

Once you have determined your topic and your thesis statement, you are ready to create a rough outline to develop your essay's structure and organizational plan. Use prewriting techniques such as brainstorming or clustering

Cross Reference

See Chapter 6, pp. 104–115, Stage One: Prewrite to Generate Ideas.

to generate supporting examples and concrete details. Then create a rough outline using this template:

Rough Outline Template for a Cause-and-Effect Essay

    I. Introductory Paragraph
       A. A brief, general description of the cause(s), effect(s), or both causes and effects you will explore
       B. Thesis statement: the purpose of your cause-and-effect analysis
    II. Body Paragraphs: two to four paragraphs that explain the causes and/or effects
       A. Include concrete description and details for each cause or effect
       B. Include clear transitions from one cause and/or effect to the next and from each paragraph to the next
       C. Include definitions and explanations of the causes and effects when needed
    III. Concluding Paragraph
       A. Restate the causes and effects and purpose/thesis in a new way
       B. Add some general closing comments without introducing any new ideas

Introductory Paragraph

Begin your cause-and-effect essay with a general introduction to the topic, and end your introductory paragraph with a thesis statement that presents the purpose for your essay.

Body Paragraphs

The body paragraphs and topic sentences introduce the order of the examples you will develop for your cause-and-effect analysis. You could arrange the causes and/or effects in separate paragraphs from least to most important (or vice versa) or arrange them in the order in which they take place (chronologically). For example, if you were writing about Hurricane Katrina, you could look at the effects chronologically (by which place was hit first, second, and so on) or by order of importance (such as "New Orleans is the city that suffered the most loss," and so on). Use transitional words and phrases to lead your readers from one cause or effect to the next.

Cross Reference

For other useful transitions, see also Chapter 5, p. 93, Illustrate or Give Examples/ Specifics, and p. 94, Explain a Purpose.

TRANSITIONS TO . . .

Show Result and/or Cause-and-Effect Relationships

accordingly	consequently	since	therefore
as a result	for this reason	so	thereupon
because	hence	then	thus

Be sure to use plenty of specific examples and details to illustrate the particular causes (high winds and torrential rainfall) or effects (such as the breaking of the levees in New Orleans, the loss of property, and so on) in your body paragraphs. Your topic sentences will indicate which causes or effects you will be explaining in each paragraph.

In New Orleans, many lifelong residents lost their homes in the floods.

ACTIVITY 12-4 Creating Topic Sentences

Directions: *Develop a topic sentence for each of the thesis statements you generated in Activity 12-3. You need to decide whether to focus on causes, effects, or both, as if you were writing this essay.*

1. **Topic:** Obesity

   Topic sentence: _____

   _____

2. **Topic:** Political corruption

   Topic sentence: _____

   _____

3. **Topic:** Bankruptcy

   Topic sentence: _____

   _____

4. **Topic:** New laws

   Topic sentence: _____

   _____

5. **Topic:** Being fired

   Topic sentence: _____

   _____

After you have come up with your topic sentences, you need to support them with examples and details. Always illustrate your points!

ACTIVITY 12-5 Providing Examples

Directions: *For three of the topic sentences you generated in Activity 12-4, provide at least two examples that would help demonstrate your cause-and/or-effect analysis.*

1. Topic sentence: _____

   Examples: _____

   _____

2. Topic sentence: _____

   Examples: _____

   _____

3. Topic sentence: _____

   Examples: _____

   _____

Concluding Paragraph

Your essay will need a concluding paragraph that briefly recaps your cause-and-effect analysis and your purpose for studying this causal relationship. Re-emphasize what you want your readers to realize about the cause-and-effect connection(s).

ACTIVITY 12-6 Writing a Concluding Paragraph

Directions: *Create a three- to six-sentence concluding paragraph for any one of the topics from the previous activities.*

Topic chosen: _____

Concluding paragraph:

_____

_____

_____

_____

ACTIVITY 12-7 Creating Your Outline and First Draft

Cross Reference

See Chapters 21–25, pp. 515–648 for help with the Editing section of the critique form.

Directions: *Choose a topic from one of the activities you already completed in this chapter, from the assignment choices at the end of this chapter, or from a topic assigned by your instructor, and create a rough outline using the template on page 271 of this chapter. Then, using your rough outline, write a first draft of your essay. After you have finished, use the critique form below to check for the basics in your essay draft.*

CAUSE-AND-EFFECT ESSAY CRITIQUE FORM

PURPOSE   IDEAS   SUPPORT   ASSUMPTIONS BIASES   CONCLUSIONS   POINT OF VIEW   ANALYSIS

	Done well	Needs work
Overall		
1. Does the essay clearly develop cause-and-effect **analysis** with a clear **purpose**?	_____	_____
2. Does the essay use a clear order in the body paragraphs?	_____	_____
3. Are the paragraphs organized clearly and logically and are they a good length—3–15 sentences?	_____	_____
Introduction		
4. Is the title interesting and in correct format?	_____	_____
5. Is there a general introduction that gives the **purpose** for the cause-and-effect **analysis**? Is the process clear?	_____	_____
6. Is there a clear thesis statement that explains the results of the cause(s) and effect(s) and the overall **purpose**?	_____	_____
Body		
7. Do the body paragraphs develop the **ideas** and **analysis** well and flow smoothly?	_____	_____
8. Are transitions used between and, when needed, within the paragraphs?	_____	_____
9. Do the body paragraphs include **support** and descriptive details for development?	_____	_____
10. Does the essay demonstrate the relationship of the cause(s) and the effect(s) and the importance of this relationship?	_____	_____

Conclusion

11. Does the **concluding** paragraph sum up the essay with an analytical frame that re-emphasizes the introductory paragraph and thesis, without adding new ideas?

_____   _____

Editing

12. Circle the following errors you think you see in this draft: spelling errors, fragments, run-ons/comma splices, errors in comma and semicolon/colon use, pronoun disagreement, pronoun reference errors, errors in parallelism, apostrophe use, verb use/tense, and passive voice construction.

13. Other types of grammar or sentence-level errors:

_____

Comments (For example: What works well in this draft? What needs to be added? Did you, or will your readers, feel drawn into this essay? Why or why not?):

_____

_____

COMPLEMENTARY MODES FOR CAUSE-AND-EFFECT ESSAYS

5 Use modes that complement cause-and-effect essays.

Cause-and-effect mode is often combined with several other modes.

- **Narration** and **description** can be used to develop the analysis. You might have to include narrative to explain an action (cause) and what effect (reaction) that created. Specific descriptions will strengthen your reader's ability to visualize the causes and effects.

- **Definition** mode can be used to help explain objects or concepts used in the cause-and-effect analysis.

- **Example and illustration** can further elaborate on the cause-and-effect analysis of the subject. You should include specific examples of causes and effects to determine their relationships and the results of those interactions.

- You can use **classification mode** to group causes and effects and analyze them by category. For example, if you were looking at the causes and effects of pollution, you could classify types of pollution, then analyze cause(s) or effect(s) by type.

- You can **compare and contrast** items or the causes or effects themselves as you analyze your subject in order to develop your purpose for the causal analysis.

- You can use **argument** to persuade your readers to accept a particular point of view related to the cause-and-effect analysis.

Student Essay

The dominant mode used in this student's paper is cause and effect. Look for other modes used in this essay, such as example and illustration, comparison and contrast, and argument and persuasion.

Kunitz 1

Michelle Kunitz

Professor Archer

English 100

3 November 2012

The Dangers of Too Much TV

Television is a great invention, and it is a great element of most homes, as long as it is watched in moderation. Unfortunately, these days, too many children are watching too much TV every day. Studies show that students watch an average of two to four hours of TV a day. There are several negative effects of watching too much TV.

The first negative effect for children who watch too much TV is lack of exercise due to sitting passively in front of the tube all day. Unfortunately, many children do not spend as much time outside playing with their friends as children did in the past. With the constant availability of kid's programming, such as cartoons played 24 hours a day, more children choose to stay on the couch watching shows than to go outside and play with their friends. It used to be that cartoons were only available at certain times, so the fact that they are on 24/7 may have added to the increase in TV watching.

A direct result of increased TV watching has been the increase in childhood obesity in America. Many children are more

Thesis statement

Topic sentence

Concluding sentence

Topic sentence

Kunitz 2

inactive due to increased TV watching, and, in addition, they tend to snack more when they are indoors watching TV all day.

Concluding sentence — Both of these reasons lead to children becoming overweight and obese.

Topic sentence — Another negative effect of too much TV is a decrease in reading and imaginative play by children. When children spend hours watching TV, they spend a lot less time reading or engaging in imaginative play. For instance, many children these days rarely play board games or work on puzzles. These interactive

Concluding sentence — types of play are much more intellectually stimulating than passive TV viewing.

Restatement of thesis — Overall, the increase in TV viewing by children over the last couple of decades has led to negative consequences for many of them. Their health and intelligence are put in jeopardy when they watch too much TV. Hopefully, parents will take these negative effects seriously and take action to decrease the amount of time their kids spend in front of the tube and strongly encourage them to participate in physical activities, imaginative play, and reading.

ACTIVITY 12-8 Thinking Critically about the Student Essay

Directions: *Identify the features and details characteristic of the cause-and-effect mode in this essay. Mark them on the essay. Then, reread the essay and make a list of specific revisions you would make to correct any problems with content, organization, transitions, and style.*

PROFESSIONAL CAUSE-AND-EFFECT ESSAY

The Columbine Syndrome: Boys and the Fear of Violence

William S. Pollack

William S. Pollack is Assistant Clinical Professor in the Department of Psychiatry at Harvard Medical School and a clinical psychologist. He is the author of *Real Boys: Rescuing Our Sons from the Myths of Masculinity* (1999), *Real Boys' Voices* (2000), and *Real Boys Workbook* (2001). Pollack serves as an advisor to the President's National Campaign against Youth Violence. This essay appeared in the fall 2000 issue of *National Forum*.

"I don't want to be that type of kid who comes to school and just takes out a gun and starts shooting."—*Bobby, age 12, from a city in the West*

"The other day I walked into school and a girl was carrying balloons and one of them popped. Everyone in the whole school got really terrified."—*Errol, age 17, from a suburb in the West*

"I think there are people at my school who have the potential for doing something similar."—*Jules, age 17, from a suburb in the South*

"People were coming up to me and begging me not to kill them. I felt like telling them: 'Cut it out; I'm not going to do anything.'"—*Cody, age 14, from a suburb in New England*

"You can't say 'them' or 'you.' You have to say 'us.'"—*Jimmy, age 16, from a small town in the West*

1   Probably no risk other than violence has made America more afraid of boys and made boys more afraid of being male and living in this country. Though it has been understood for decades that the perpetrators of most violent crimes in our nation are male, the recent spate of school shootings, culminating in the heinous massacre of teachers and students recently carried out in suburban Littleton, Colorado, has made the public even more frightened and confused about the threat of extreme violence and its connection, in particular, with boys. Boys of adolescent age, boys just like the ones who have contributed to my research, are the ones pulling the triggers and injuring, sometimes killing, their peers and school teachers. What many people do not realize—and what the media isn't following as well as they might—is that most of the victims of teenage violence, indeed the vast majority, are also boys.

Thesis

CONSEQUENCES OF THE COLUMBINE SYNDROME

2

Topic sentence and exploration of an effect

Definition

In my travels across our country, listening to boys and doing research for my latest book, *Real Boys' Voices* (Random House, 2000), I have come to see that the effect of these terrible crimes has been immense. It has led to the "Columbine Syndrome": Across our nation students, parents, and teachers are absolutely terrified—sometimes to an extreme degree—about which boys amongst them are violent, who the next perpetrators might be, and who their victims will become. Paranoia is rampant. School children and the adults around them are constantly canvassing the student body and worrying, often inappropriately, that particular students may be murderous. Grady, age seventeen, from a school in the South, says, "When a kid's wearing a trenchcoat and he's going for something in his jacket, you learn from watching the news that more than likely he might have a gun."

3

Topic sentence and exploration of an effect

The consequence is that boys themselves are becoming increasingly afraid. They are frightened not only of being victimized by the rage and violence of other boys, but also of being accused, or falsely accused, of having the disposition it takes to snap into hyper-violent action and embark on a murderous rampage. Boys fear that despite their true nature, they will automatically, because they are boys, be seen as somehow toxic, dangerous, and culpable. As one young preadolescent boy said, "I think women like small kids. Girls like newborn babies. They don't like big people. We bigger guys scare everybody, and then we get blamed even when we've done nothing wrong."

Example for support

4

Topic sentence and exploration of an effect

Boys are also afraid of the violence they may feel inside themselves and of whether it is safe to talk with us about it. As they internalize this fear of being misunderstood—and of being charged with having a violent temperament they genuinely do not have—boys themselves are beginning to worry if maybe, just maybe, the demon is within, if lurking underneath their conscious understanding of themselves are uncontrollable urges to do depraved, violent acts. The Columbine Syndrome means that America's boys today are as confused about violence as they are afraid of it. They fear each other and they fear their own selves.

THE "BOY CODE"

5

Topic sentence and exploration of an effect

While the statistics indicate that teenage boys not only commit a considerable percentage of the nation's violent juvenile crimes but also become the frequent victims of those crimes, in reality there seems to be no inherent biological factor that makes boys more violent than their female counterparts. Violence committed by and acted out upon boys seems to stem, more often than not, from what we teach (or do not teach) boys about the behavior we expect from them. It comes from society's set of rules about masculinity, the Boy Code that says, "To be a man, you must show your strength and your power. You must show that you can hold your own if challenged by another male. You can show your rage, but you must not show any other emotions. You must protect your honor and fight off shame at all costs."

6
Topic sentence and exploration of an effect

Think of it yourself. A boy gets slightly angry as a way to express his pain, and there will be mixed emotions. Some of us may show some fear, but if the anger is in control, we are unlikely to respond in a drastic manner. So long as it is "within bounds," society tends to approve of, if not encourage, aggression by and among boys. Violence in boys is widely (although, as I have said, incorrectly) seen as inevitable, if not biologically pre-ordained. As long as nobody is seriously hurt, no lethal weapons are employed, and especially within the framework of sports and games—football, soccer, boxing, wrestling—aggression and violence are widely accepted and even encouraged in boys. Boys are constantly trying to prove their masculinity through aggression, and society is complicit; winning a game, or even a fight, helps many boys gain society's respect.

7
Topic sentence and exploration of an effect and a cause

The corollary to this message, simply enough, is that soft, gentle, non-violent boys are "feminine" and therefore losers. While we often pay lip service to helping boys "put feelings into words" and even create multi-million dollar educational programs to address this, if you're "a big guy" and start to express your vulnerable emotions too openly, people crawl back in fear. Or imagine the boy who misses a goal and bursts into tears on the soccer field. He is not considered masculine. Peers call him a "girl," "sissy," or "fag." Parents cringe. It is precisely in this environment that even the most hearty boy soon learns to avoid showing his pain in public. He may want to cry, he may wish he could speak of his fear, sadness, or shame; but he holds it back. He resists. Instead, the boy displays anger, aggression, and violence.

8
Topic sentence and exploration of an effect

Perhaps it should not shock us, then, when we hear from the boys who say that while they overwhelmingly condemn extreme violence, and to a large extent do not engage in it, they can understand, empathize with the boys who hit, hurt, and even kill. They tell us about what the teasing and razzing "can do to your head," how alone and isolated some boys can become, and how rage is indeed often the only sanctioned emotion that does not bring further ridicule to them. We are all afraid of boys and violence, but boys, it turns out, are the most in fear. Gun detectors, violence screening tools or "profiles," armed guards, and "zero tolerance" only goad our sons into the very aggression we, and they, are afraid of; by expecting boys to be angry, rambunctious, and dangerous, we push boys to fulfill these prophecies. This is the essence, I believe, of the Columbine Syndrome. By living in fear and expecting danger, that is exactly what we produce.

9
Topic sentence and exploration of a cause

To compound the risk to all of us, society is now giving boys another complex and confusing message, what I call the "No Black Shirts" response. Because the Columbine killers were outcast boys, spiteful nonconforming boys who wore dark clothing and were estranged from their peers, society has now rushed to the conclusion that adolescent boys who seem "different," especially ones who seem quiet, distant, and in pain, are the likely perpetrators of the next ghastly Columbine-like crime. Sadly, what the huge majority of outcast boys needs most—in fact what many so-called "popular" boys, boys on the "inside" often desperately need as well—is not to have their pain suppressed and disregarded, but rather to have it listened to and understood.

CURBING THE SYNDROME

10
Topic sentence
Argument and persuasion

Boys in pain require immediate intervention. As soon as we detect that a boy is experiencing emotional distress, we need to stop what we are doing, turn towards him, and hear him out. Whether he is wearing a black hood or Brooks Brothers sweater, whether he is well-liked or an outcast, he needs us to come toward him, embrace and affirm him, and assuage his hurt feelings before they push him to the edge. Boys are simply not inherently violent or dangerous, and the emotional distress that they may feel, in the first instance, does not make them any more so. But if we continue to give boys the message that expressing their distress is forbidden, that we will ignore their vulnerable feelings when we see them, and that we actually expect them to act out angrily and violently, we should not be surprised that the world becomes, for all of us, a mighty frightful place.

11

Topic sentence

As the voices I heard (sampled in brief above) and published in detail in *Real Boys' Voices* exemplify, only a tiny percentage of boys are capable of egregious acts of violence. In truth, as aggressive as they can perhaps be pushed to become, most boys are quite anxious about and revolted by the prevalence of violence in society. They feel powerless to do anything about it, though, because they simply feel too much shame, too concerned about how other people will respond to their confessions of fear.

12
Topic sentence
and addition to
the purpose/thesis

The solution, I believe, is for society to commit to a whole new way of seeing boys and violence. First, as a society we need to decide, unequivocally, that as much as we will not exalt boys who fight, we also will not punish or ostracize those who show their vulnerability. By defending and actually providing positive reinforcement to boys who openly exhibit their moments of fear, longing, anxiety, and despair, by telling these boys and men that they are fully "masculine" no matter what emotions they share with us, we can help them avoid the repression and resistance that may make them bottle up their emotions and then spill them out in irrational acts. Second, because society may not change overnight, we need to be on the lookout for the signs of sadness and depression that in boys and men so often seem harder to see, or more difficult to believe and accept. In my book, I outlined these many signs. If we are attentive to them, and if we help boys overcome the pain and disaffection that gives rise to them, much of the aggression and violence we now see will evaporate, or be directed towards safe, appropriate channels.

13

Finally, we must simply decide, as a society, that most boys, as angry or aggressive as they may become, are highly unlikely to become dangerous in any way. The boys' voices quoted at the beginning of this piece are

Conclusion and restatement of the purpose/thesis

overwhelming proof that most of our sons have a non-violent nature and that, in reality, their greater struggle is with sadness and the fear of violence rather than with violence itself. Together we must create prophecies that their gentle nature will triumph over old pressures to act tough and lash out. Perhaps if we hear boys' fears about violence in a new light, read their stories with a new empathy, we may be able to reach across the boundaries of fear and create a new dialogue of peace. For boys and for the rest of us, the only cure for the Columbine Syndrome, in the end, is to develop safe spaces that are friendly to boys and thereby create genuine security. The time is now!

MyWritingLab™   **Reading Reflection Questions**

1. What are the direct or indirect (implied) messages in this story? _____

_____

_____

_____

2. In your own words, define what the author means by the "Columbine Syndrome." _____

_____

MyWritingLab™   **Objective Questions**

3. T/F_____ Most of the perpetrators and victims of teenage violence are boys.

4. T/F_____ Many boys are afraid of their own potential for violence.

5. T/F_____ Many boys are afraid they will be feared just for being boys.

6. Explain what the author means by the "Boy Code." _____

_____

7. What solution does this author propose to this problem? _____

_____

_____

MyWritingLab™   **Checking Vocabulary**

Define the following in your own words, or provide a dictionary definition if you don't know the word.

8. heinous: _____

9. perpetrators: _____

10. corollary: _____

CRITICAL THINKING CHECKLIST

PURPOSE

1. What is the **purpose** of this piece of writing? Is it clear?

_____

_____

IDEAS

2. What **ideas** and **background information** are provided to support the purpose of this piece of writing?

_____

_____

SUPPORT

3. What **evidence** and **examples** are used to explain and develop the ideas that support the argument made in the piece of writing? Are the evidence and examples provided sufficient?

_____

_____

POINT OF VIEW

4. Are there unfounded **assumptions** or unreasonable **biases?**

_____

_____

ASSUMPTIONS BIASES

5. Are all of the **conclusions**, **implications**, and **consequences** of the arguments (the results of the arguments taken to their farthest extreme) considered?

_____

_____

CONCLUSIONS

6. Is the **point of view** clear and consistent, and have other points of view been considered?

_____

_____

ANALYSIS

7. Using these critical thinking tools, **analyze** the overall structure of this essay and the strength of the author's arguments, ideas, and support. Was he or she successful in accomplishing the purpose? Why, or why not?

_____

_____

MyWritingLab™ **Essay Assignments**

1. Write an essay that illustrates the negative effects of stress on a college student.

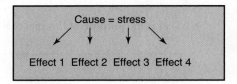

2. Write an essay that focuses on the causes of stress for college students.

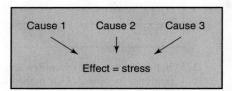

3. Write an essay that explores a chain reaction, or domino effect, where there is a sequence of one cause leading to an effect that starts a second cause that leads to a second effect, and so on.

4. Write a cause-and-effect essay about any of the subjects you worked on in the activities in this chapter.

5. Write a cause-and-effect essay about the increased use of cell phones and the classroom.

6. Write a cause-and-effect essay about the new technology teaching tools and student learning tools available in the college classroom.

Learning Objectives Review

MyWritingLab™ Complete the chapter assessment questions at mywritinglab.com

1 Describe the cause and effect mode.

What distinguishes cause and effect from other writing modes? (See p. 264.)

Cause-and-effect mode is used to examine causes that lead to specific results. These essays may discuss a single cause and a single effect, a series of effects resulting from a single cause, or a series of causes that led to a particular effect.

2 Apply critical thinking skills to writing cause-and-effect essays.

How can thinking critically help you write a cause-and-effect essay? (See pp. 264–265.)

Thinking critically helps you **assess** your purpose, **analyze** the "befores and afters" of what you are analyzing, **develop** your ideas and support, evaluate your **conclusions**, and **analyze** the overall effectiveness of your purpose and examples.

3 Prepare to write a cause-and-effect essay by asking critical thinking questions.

What questions will help you plan a cause-and-effect essay? (See pp. 265–267.)

Ask the following questions: (1) What process or event is the subject of my cause-and-effect analysis? (2) What are the benefits of doing a cause-and-effect analysis of my chosen topic? (3) Why did this process or event happen—what was the original cause(s)? (4) What is the result(s) (effect/s) of this process or event? (5) What do I want my readers to learn by reading about the cause(s) and/or effect(s) of this event or process? (6) How will I conclude this essay?

4 Structure a cause-and-effect essay.

How do you structure a cause-and-effect essay? (See pp. 267–275.)

You **structure a cause-and-effect essay** by creating an introductory paragraph with a thesis that states the causes and effects you will explore and the purpose for that exploration, body paragraphs that support and develop the thesis with examples and cause-and-effect analysis, and a conclusion to restate the thesis and sum up without introducing any new ideas.

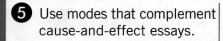 Use modes that complement cause-and-effect essays.

What modes complement a cause and effect essay? (See pp. 275–284.)

Modes that work well within a cause-and-effect structure include narration and description, definition, example and illustration, classification, comparison and contrast, and argument and persuasion.

LEARNING OBJECTIVES

In this chapter, you will learn how to

1 Describe the comparison and contrast mode.

2 Apply critical thinking skills to writing comparison and contrast essays.

3 Prepare to write a comparison and contrast essay by asking critical thinking questions.

4 Structure a comparison and contrast essay.

5 Use modes that complement comparison and contrast essays.

Thinking Critically MyWritingLab™

Think: Look carefully at these two chairs.

Write: Describe in detail some of the similarities and differences between the two chairs.

Similarities: _____

_____

_____

_____

_____

_____

_____

Differences: _____

_____

_____

_____

_____

_____

COMPARISON AND CONTRAST ESSAYS

1 Describe the comparison and contrast mode.

Comparison essays look at the *similarities* between two subjects, and **contrast essays** look at the *differences* between two subjects. A comparison *and* contrast essay looks at both the similarities and differences between two subjects. People have written essays comparing and contrasting two leaders, two countries, two musicians or authors, two periods in history, two scientific theories, and so on. Sometimes, your comparison and contrast will explore more than two subjects; in that case, establish your categories for comparison and be consistent in exploring those categories for all of your subjects.

CRITICAL THINKING AND COMPARISON AND CONTRAST

2 Apply critical thinking skills to writing comparison and contrast essays.

Using comparison and contrast lets you explore characteristics of two subjects by examining their similarities and differences. Through the process, you gain a better, deeper, and more detailed understanding of both subjects and can draw some conclusions based on your comparisons and contrasts. Think about your **purpose** for comparing the two subjects. **Analyze** whether to focus on similarities, differences, or both. If you have established your analytical purpose and then followed through by using concrete, specific examples to make your points, then you will inform your readers in the process.

Be careful not to make logical fallacies in your comparisons. Don't jump to a conclusion about a subject based on a characteristic of that subject without providing the evidence and reasoning that led to that conclusion. For example, saying that John must be a bad driver because he is a teenager, not based on evidence related to the way John drives, is a hasty generalization. This type of mistake is easy to make when comparing two subjects. Don't generalize about your subjects and use support for the comparisons and contrasts you draw between them. Also, avoid presenting only two sides of a complex issue or subject that may have many sides (known as the "false dilemma" fallacy). All examples or definitions for your two subjects must be legitimate and fully thought-out to avoid these fallacies. For example, rarely is a politician, from any particular party, completely in support of all issues of the party they identify with (such as Republican or Democrat)—so check your facts and examples.

BEFORE WRITING A COMPARISON/ CONTRAST ESSAY

3 Prepare to write a comparison and contrast essay by asking critical thinking questions.

Before you begin to write a comparison/contrast essay, ask yourself these questions:

1. What two or more objects, people, or concepts am I going to compare and/or contrast?

2. Are they in the same general category?

3. Am I going to focus on similarities, differences, or both? Are the two subjects mostly alike, mostly different, or some of each?

4. How will I set up my comparisons/contrasts, and how will I structure my paragraphs?

5. What examples and details should I include for support?

6. What do I want my readers to learn or understand after reading this comparison and/or contrast essay?

7. How will I conclude my essay?

Answering these questions will help you generate an expository thesis statement, help you determine what you will be comparing and/or contrasting, help you develop examples and details to include for support, and give you a general idea of how to organize your essay.

APPLYING CRITICAL THINKING

PURPOSE   IDEAS   SUPPORT   ASSUMPTIONS BIASES   CONCLUSIONS   POINT OF VIEW   ANALYSIS

We use comparisons and contrasts to make sense of the world and put things into perspective. Comparing is a way to find the familiar or common ground between or among subjects and explore it to understand these subjects better. Contrasting helps us to see the differences between or among things in order to better understand them. To write an effective comparison/contrast essay, you need to use your **analytical** skills to identify how things are similar and different, determine your **purpose** for writing about those similarities and differences, and decide which **ideas**, **support**, and details will best illustrate and explain the point you want to make.

For example, if you were comparing two grocery stores, what similarities would you point out? What differences? What possible **conclusions** could you reach? Will your comparison lead to a recommendation?

ACTIVITY 13-1   Generating Topics for a Comparison/
Contrast Essay

Directions: *Generate three possible topics for a comparison/contrast essay: List the two items, concepts, people, and so on. Then explain whether you would focus on similarities, differences, or both.*

1. Two subjects: _____

   Similarities, differences, or both: _____

   _____

2. Two subjects: _____

   Similarities, differences, or both: _____

   _____

3. Two subjects: _____

   Similarities, differences, or both: _____

   _____

WRITING A COMPARISON/CONTRAST ESSAY

❹ Structure a comparison and contrast essay.

First, make sure that the two subjects you compare and/or contrast are in the same general group or category. The adage "It's like comparing apples and oranges" (a saying usually used when people think two things can't be compared because they are too different) isn't necessarily accurate; you can compare apples with oranges: They are both in the "fruit" category, and there are similarities between them. However, you probably wouldn't want to write a compare/contrast essay about an orange and your best friend, unless your best friend is particularly orange and round. And, after that, an orange and your best friend probably wouldn't have enough categories in common to make for an interesting or developed analytical comparison.

Organizational Pattern for a Comparison/Contrast Essay

Once you have chosen your subjects, you need to decide whether you are focusing on similarities, differences, or both and determine the purpose of your essay. Then you have to choose an organizational plan for your comparison/contrast essay. In general, you should use the order of importance pattern for your comparisons and contrasts. However, due to the complexity of arranging comparison and contrast essays (which involve a great deal of jumping back and forth, potentially making the organization confusing), there are two specialized comparison and contrast organization patterns you could use: a subject-by-subject approach or a point-by-point approach.

Subject-by-Subject Organization Pattern

In a **subject-by-subject** organization pattern, you first present all aspects of one subject; then you transition and present all aspects of the second subject. For example:

> **Subject A = compact cars; Subject B = SUVs**
>
> > **Point 1** = Size/comfort
> > **Point 2** = Gas mileage/cost
> > **Point 3** = Image/personality

An outline of a paper on compact cars versus SUVs, using this pattern, would look like this:

> **General introductory comments**
>
> **Thesis:** Compact cars and SUVs offer very different options for a consumer when it comes to size and comfort, gas mileage and cost, and the type of image or personality the cars project.
>
> **Subject A: Compact Cars**
> > **Point 1:** Compact cars' size and comfort
> > **Point 2:** Compact cars' gas mileage and cost
> > **Point 3:** Compact cars' image and personality
>
> **Subject B: SUVs**
> > **Point 1:** SUVs' size and comfort
> > **Point 2:** SUVs' gas mileage and cost
> > **Point 3:** SUVs' image and personality
>
> **Conclusion:** Re-emphasize thesis. Provide closing comments.

Point-by-Point Organization Pattern

In a **point-by-point** organization pattern, you discuss both subjects at the same time, categorized point by point. For example:

	Subject A: Compact cars	**Subject B: SUVs**
Point 1	Size/comfort	Size/comfort
Point 2	Gas mileage/cost	Gas mileage/cost
Point 3	Image/personality	Image/personality

An outline of a paper on compact cars versus SUVs, using this pattern, would look like this:

General introductory comments

Thesis: Compact cars and SUVs offer very different options for a consumer when it comes to size and comfort, gas mileage and cost, and the type of image or personality the cars project.

Point 1: Size and comfort for subjects A and B (compact cars and SUVs)

Point 2: Gas mileage and cost for subjects A and B (compact cars and SUVs)

Point 3: Image and personality for subjects A and B (compact cars and SUVs)

Conclusion: Re-emphasize thesis. Provide closing comments.

▶ **NOTE** These patterns do not necessarily indicate the number of paragraphs you would use in an essay. It might take more than one paragraph to develop each point.

Pick the organizational pattern that works best for your subject and purpose. Also, be sure that you give a balanced comparison, and provide an equal number of details to support both subjects. Create topic sentences that will highlight the categories for comparison or contrast and the points you want to make. Provide plenty of examples and details to illustrate these points in the body paragraphs. Use transitions between paragraphs or examples to help the flow of your essay.

Finally, be sure that you reach an analytical conclusion through your comparison/contrast and that your thesis and your concluding paragraph sum up that analytical conclusion.

The chart below provides a brief overview of the structure of a comparison and contrast essay.

BASIC STRUCTURE FOR A COMPARISON/CONTRAST ESSAY

See the sample essay on pages 300–301.

INTRODUCTORY PARAGRAPH

Sets up your subject and your purpose.

Thesis statement: A statement that defines your purpose and what subjects(s) and main categories you'll be using to illustrate your purpose.

BODY PARAGRAPHS (Two to five, depending on assignment and purpose)

Choose the subject-by-subject or point-by-point organization pattern.

Create **topic sentences** to support your thesis.

Develop the comparisons and contrasts through illustrations, details, and **analysis**.

Provide **examples and concrete details** to illustrate the examples vividly.

Use **transitions** within and between paragraphs to make the paragraphs flow smoothly.

CONCLUDING PARAGRAPH

Sums up and re-emphasizes the thesis.

Structuring a Comparison/Contrast Essay

Comparing and contrasting ideas, objects, and people is a natural and effective way to draw conclusions. Any two subjects that you want to evaluate side by side in order to emphasize similarities or differences or both make for a good topic for structuring this type of essay. You could compare and contrast two or more historical figures, political figures, people you know, restaurants, musicians, paintings, photographs, cities, and so on. Just make sure they have enough in common to make for worthwhile explorations.

Topic

If your instructor has not assigned a topic for your comparison/contrast essay, then brainstorm ideas for things, places, people, or ideas you might want to compare and contrast. Then come up with some ideas for a purpose for comparing/contrasting your subjects. What do you want your readers to understand through your comparison/contrast?

Thesis Statements

After you have done some prewriting and determined your subjects and whether you will focus on similarities, differences, or both, come up with the purpose for your comparison/contrast essay and write your thesis statement. What conclusion did you reach by comparing and contrasting these subjects? What do you want your readers to understand after reading this essay?

> The technology of the Xbox game system is very different from the Wii game system's.
>
> Cooking at home and going out to restaurants result in diverse dining experiences.

ACTIVITY 13-2   Creating Thesis Statements

Directions: *For each of the topics you generated in Activity 13-1, create a thesis statement.*

1. **Topic:** _____

    Thesis statement: _____

    _____

2. **Topic:** _____

    Thesis statement: _____

    _____

3. **Topic:** _____

    Thesis statement: _____

    _____

Creating a Rough Outline

Cross Reference
See Chapter 6,
pp. 104–115, Stage One:
Prewrite to Generate Ideas.

Once you have determined your topic and your thesis statement, you are ready to create a rough outline to develop your essay's structure and organizational plan. Use prewriting techniques such as brainstorming or clustering to generate supporting examples and concrete details. Then create a rough outline using this template:

Rough Outline Template for a Comparison and Contrast Essay

    I. Introductory Paragraph
        A. A brief, general description of the subjects you will be comparing and contrasting
        B. Thesis Statement: the purpose of your comparison/contrast
    II. Body Paragraphs: two to four body paragraphs that develop the categories and details for comparison
        A. Include concrete descriptions and details for each comparison or contrast
        B. Include clear transitions from one paragraph to the next
        C. Include definitions and explanations when needed for the comparisons
    III. Concluding Paragraph
        A. Restate the subjects, comparison/contrast categories, and purpose/thesis in a new way
        B. Add some general closing comments without introducing any new ideas

Introductory Paragraph

Begin your comparison/contrast essay with a general introduction of the two subjects you are comparing/contrasting in order to demonstrate your analytical conclusion. End with the thesis statement to present the purpose for your comparison/contrast essay.

Body Paragraphs

The body paragraphs in a comparison/contrast essay are structured either by focusing on one subject at a time or on one category or point for both of the subjects at a time. For each paragraph, be sure you have a clear topic sentence that spells out the subject(s) and category you are exploring and the point you want to make. Then use specific evidence and examples to illustrate the comparisons or contrasts. Analyze the examples. Use comparison and contrast transitions to show your readers when you are comparing and contrasting items. Then frame your examples with a concluding sentence that relates to your topic sentence.

Cross Reference
For other useful transitions, see also Chapter 5, p. 93, Show Summary or Repetition; p. 93, Illustrate or Give Examples/Specifics; and p. 94, Explain a Purpose.

TRANSITIONS TO . . .

Show Contrast or a Change in Idea

although	even though	instead	on the other side
anyhow	for all that	nevertheless	otherwise
at the same time	however	notwithstanding	regardless
but	in any event	on the contrary	still
despite this	in contrast	on the other hand	yet

Show a Comparison

in like manner	in the same way	likewise	similarly

ACTIVITY 13-3   Creating Topic Sentences

Directions: *Create one topic sentence for each of the thesis statements you generated in Activity 13-2.*

1. **Topic:** _____

   Topic sentence:_____

   _____

2. **Topic:** _____

   Topic sentence:_____

   _____

3. **Topic:** _____

   Topic sentence:_____

   _____

After you have created your topic sentences, develop the ideas using examples and details for support.

ACTIVITY 13-4   Providing Details

Directions: *Now, come up with at least two examples or details you could use to develop each of the topic sentences you came up with in Activity 13-3.*

1. Topic sentence: _____

   Examples: _____

   _____

   _____

2. Topic sentence: _____

   Examples: _____

   _____

   _____

3. Topic sentence: _____

   Examples: _____

   _____

   _____

Concluding Paragraph

The concluding paragraph for a comparison/contrast essay should remind your readers what the purpose of your comparison/contrast was—why you compared and/or contrasted the subjects you chose.

ACTIVITY 13-5 **Writing a Conclusion**

Directions: *Now choose one of the topics you've been developing in the previous activities and write a three- to six-sentence concluding paragraph that could finish that essay.*

_____

_____

_____

_____

_____

ACTIVITY 13-6 **Creating Your Outline and First Draft**

Directions: *Choose a topic from one of the activities you already completed in this chapter, from the assignment choices at the end of this chapter, or from a topic assigned by your instructor, and create a rough outline using the template*

Cross Reference
See Chapters 21–25,
pp. 515–648 for help with
the Editing section of the
critique form.

on page 295 of this chapter. Then, using your rough outline, write a first draft of your essay. After you have finished, use the critique form below to check for the basics in your essay draft.

COMPARISON/CONTRAST ESSAY CRITIQUE FORM

PURPOSE   IDEAS   SUPPORT   ASSUMPTIONS BIASES   CONCLUSIONS   POINT OF VIEW   ANALYSIS

Overall

	Done well	Needs work
1. Does the essay clearly develop a comparison and/or contrast of two or more subjects with a clear **purpose**/analytical conclusion?	_____	_____
2. Does the essay use a clear order (subject by subject or point by point or an effective combination of the two) in the body paragraphs and have an analytical conclusion drawn from the comparison or contrast?	_____	_____
3. Are the paragraphs organized clearly and logically and are they a good length—3–15 sentences?	_____	_____

Introduction

4. Is the title interesting and in correct format?	_____	_____
5. Is there a general introduction that gives the purpose for the comparison and contrast analysis? Is the process and organization clear?	_____	_____
6. Is there a clear thesis statement that explains the purpose of the comparisons and/or contrasts and the overall purpose?	_____	_____

Body

7. Do the body paragraphs develop the **ideas** and **analysis** well and flow smoothly?	_____	_____
8. Are transitions used between and, when needed, within the paragraphs?	_____	_____
9. Do the body paragraphs include **support** and descriptive details for development?	_____	_____
10. Does the writer demonstrate the significance of the similarities and differences?	_____	_____

Conclusion

11. Does the **concluding** paragraph sum up the essay with an analytical frame that re-emphasizes the introductory paragraph and thesis, without adding new ideas?   _____   _____

Editing

12. Circle the following errors you think you see in this draft: spelling errors, fragments, run-ons/comma splices, errors in comma and semicolon/colon use, pronoun disagreement, pronoun reference errors, errors in parallelism, apostrophe use, verb use/tense, and passive voice construction.

13. Other types of grammar or sentence-level errors:

_____

Comments (For example: What works well in this draft? What needs to be added? Did you, or will your readers, feel drawn into this essay? Why or why not?):

_____

_____

COMPLEMENTARY MODES FOR COMPARISON/CONTRAST ESSAYS

❺ Use modes that complement comparison and contrast essays.

Compare/contrast mode is often combined with several other modes.

- You can develop analysis with **narration** and **description**. Narrating a story and describing it in detail enhances your comparisons.
- Use the **definition** mode to help define and describe objects or concepts used in the examples.
- Use concrete **examples** to help illustrate the comparisons.
- Use **cause-and-effect analysis** to look at the causal relationship of two or more subjects you are comparing.
- **Classification** is usually part of the comparison itself: You have to classify items into broad groups to analyze them specifically.
- Use the **argument** mode to persuade your readers to agree with a particular point of view related to the comparison and contrast analysis and the conclusions you've drawn through the process of comparing the two subjects.

Student Essay

The dominant mode used in this student's paper is comparison and contrast. Look for other modes used in this essay, such as classification, narration and description, and example and illustration.

White 1

Todd White

Professor James

English 100

23 May 2013

Softball and Baseball: Serious Differences

Softball and baseball are both popular sports in America. At first glance, they seem very similar. However, there are some major differences between the two sports, not just in how they are played, but also in how much respect and attention sports fans give them.

Thesis statement

Topic sentence

Both sports use similar equipment, but there are differences in their design. Softball equipment is very basic. The ball is the size of a grapefruit and somewhat soft. The bats and gloves are a little larger than those used in baseball. Baseball is also played with a ball, a bat, and gloves. However, there are some differences in the equipment. To begin with, the baseball itself is smaller (the size of a small orange) and harder than a softball. The gloves are similar to softball gloves, but a bit smaller, and the bats are a bit narrower than the ones used for softball.

In both softball and baseball, players hit the ball and run from base to base, and the goal of the game is to get as many players as possible onto home base to score runs (points). However, a major difference between these two sports is how the pitcher pitches the ball. In softball, the pitcher pitches underhand. There is slow-pitch softball and fast-pitch softball. Though both pitches are done underhand, the slow-pitch has a much higher arch. Moreover, in softball, there are not different types of pitches: The throw is consistently the same.

Topic sentence

White 2

Concluding sentence

Topic sentence

Concluding sentence

Restatement of thesis

In baseball, the pitcher throws overhand, and it is always fast-pitch. Also, in baseball, there are many types of pitches, such as a curve ball, a slider, and so on. Much of baseball depends on the speed and unpredictability of the pitch.

Finally, the most interesting difference between softball and baseball is the amount of recognition, popularity, and respect the two sports receive. Though both are enjoyed and played at most high schools and colleges, baseball is far more popular and is funded and attended at much higher levels. Also, there are more major and minor leagues for baseball, while there are no major leagues for softball. Most importantly, baseball is often called "America's pastime" and is considered a major component of our American heritage. The same prestige is not attributed to softball.

Obviously, there are major differences between softball and baseball, even though these two sports seem so similar on the surface. Most likely, softball will never reach the level of esteem that baseball has earned as a beloved part of our American culture. It just doesn't have the history. However, both of these sports are played every day on fields and in parks around the country.

ACTIVITY 13-7 Thinking Critically about the Student Essay

Directions: *Identify the features and details characteristic of the comparison and contrast mode in this essay. Mark them on the essay. Then reread the essay and make a list of specific revisions you would make to correct any problems with content, organization, transitions, and style.*

PROFESSIONAL COMPARISON AND CONTRAST ESSAY

American Space, Chinese Place

Yi-Fu Tuan

Yi-Fu Tuan was born in 1930 in Tianjin, China. He received a Ph.D. in Geography from the University of California, Berkeley, in 1957. He is a retired professor emeritus of the University of Wisconsin, Madison. One of his most important publications is the book *Place, Art and Self*. In his book *Space and Place: The Perspective of Experience*, Tuan explores human movement from place to place and the need for a person to have a sense of space. In this excerpt, he compares and contrasts how Americans and Chinese relate to their physical space.

1   Americans have a sense of space, not of place. Go to an American home in exurbia, and almost the first thing you do is drift toward the picture window. How curious that the first compliment you pay your host inside his house is to say how lovely it is outside his house! He is pleased that you should admire his vistas. The distant horizon is not merely a line separating earth from sky, it is a symbol of the future. The American is not rooted in his place, however lovely: his eyes are drawn by the expanding space to a point on the horizon, which is his future. By contrast, consider the traditional Chinese home. Blank walls enclose it.

Thesis and establishment of the two subjects to be compared and the category

2   Step behind the spirit wall and you are in a courtyard with perhaps a miniature garden around the corner. Once inside the private compound you are wrapped in an ambiance of calm beauty, an ordered world of buildings, pavement, rock, and decorative vegetation. But you have no distant view: nowhere does space open out before you. Raw nature in such a home is experienced only as weather, and the only open space is the sky above. The Chinese is rooted in his place. When he has to leave, it is not for the promised land on the terrestrial horizon, but for another world altogether along the vertical, religious axis of his imagination.

3   The Chinese tie to place is deeply felt. Wanderlust is an alien sentiment. The Taoist classic *Tao Te Ching* captures the ideal of rootedness in place with these words: "Though there may be another country in the neighborhood so close that they are within sight of each other and the crowing of cocks and barking of dogs in one place can be heard in the other, yet there is no traffic between them; and throughout their lives the two peoples have nothing to do with each other." In theory if not in practice, farmers have ranked high in

Topic sentence

Classification

Chinese society. The reason is not only that they are engaged in the "root" industry of producing food but that, unlike pecuniary merchants, they are tied to the land and do not abandon their country when it is in danger.

Nostalgia is a recurrent theme in Chinese poetry. An American reader of translated Chinese poems will be taken aback—even put off—by the frequency as well as the sentimentality of the lament for home. To understand the strength of this sentiment, we need to know that the Chinese desire for stability and rootedness in place is prompted by the constant threat of war, exile, and the natural disasters of flood and drought. Forcible removal makes the Chinese keenly aware of their loss. By contrast, Americans move, for the most part, voluntarily. Their nostalgia for home town is really longing for childhood to which they cannot return: in the meantime the future beckons and the future is "out there," in open space. When we criticize American rootlessness we tend to forget that it is a result of ideals we admire, namely, social mobility and optimism about the future. When we admire Chinese rootedness, we forget that the word "place" means both location in space and position in society: to be tied to place is also to be bound to one's station in life, with little hope of betterment. Space symbolizes hope; place, achievement and stability.

Margin notes:
Example for support
4
Topic sentence

Contrast and example for support

Classification

Definition, example, and argument
Restatement of thesis/purpose

MyWritingLab™

Reading Reflection Questions

1. What are the direct or indirect (implied) messages in this story?

_____

_____

2. List two characteristics of this article that distinguish it as a contrast article. _____

_____

_____

_____

3. Who do you think is the intended audience for this article: Americans or Chinese? Why? _____

_____

_____

4. Provide one reason suggested in the article for the different perspectives of the Chinese and Americans toward their homes. _____

_____

_____

MyWritingLab™ **Objective Questions**

5. T/F_____ The author suggests that Americans love open spaces.

6. T/F_____ The author suggests that Americans are more rooted to their homes than are the Chinese.

7. T/F_____ The author suggests that the American desire for home is really longing for a return to childhood.

MyWritingLab™ **Checking Vocabulary**

Define the following in your own words, or provide a dictionary definition if you don't know the word.

8. ambiance: _____

9. wanderlust: _____

10. pecuniary: _____

CRITICAL THINKING CHECKLIST

PURPOSE

1. What is the **purpose** of this piece of writing? Is it clear?

_____

_____

IDEAS

2. What **ideas** and **background information** are provided to support the purpose of this piece of writing?

_____

_____

SUPPORT

3. What **evidence** and **examples** are used to explain and develop the ideas that support the argument made in the piece of writing? Are the evidence and examples provided sufficient?

_____

_____

ASSUMPTIONS BIASES

4. Are there unfounded **assumptions** or unreasonable **biases**?

_____

_____

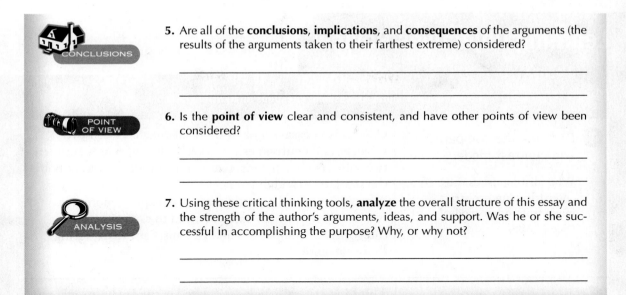

5. Are all of the **conclusions**, **implications**, and **consequences** of the arguments (the results of the arguments taken to their farthest extreme) considered?

_____

_____

6. Is the **point of view** clear and consistent, and have other points of view been considered?

_____

_____

7. Using these critical thinking tools, **analyze** the overall structure of this essay and the strength of the author's arguments, ideas, and support. Was he or she successful in accomplishing the purpose? Why, or why not?

_____

_____

MyWritingLab™ **Essay Assignments**

1. Write a comparison/contrast essay about two teachers you've had. Determine at least three points you want to use for your comparison/contrast. Pick either subject-by-subject or point-by-point organization to construct your essay.

2. Compare and contrast two musicians (or musical groups).

3. Compare and contrast two countries that you have visited or lived in. Determine at least three points you want to use for your comparison/ contrast. Pick either subject-by-subject or point-by-point organization to construct your essay.

4. Compare and contrast two Internet sites that you visit frequently. Determine at least three categories you want to use for your comparison/ contrast. Pick either subject-by-subject or point-by-point organization to construct your essay.

5. Choose any of the subjects you worked on in the activities from this chapter, and write a complete comparison/contrast essay about that topic.

Learning Objectives Review

My WritingLab™ Complete the chapter assessment questions at mywritinglab.com

❶ Describe the comparison and contrast mode.

What distinguishes the comparison and contrast mode from other modes? (See p. 288.)

Comparison essays look at the *similarities* between two subjects, and **contrast essays** look at the *differences* between two subjects. A comparison *and* contrast essay looks at both the similarities and differences between two subjects. A comparison and contrast essay may explore more than two subjects, in which case you need to establish your categories for comparison and be consistent in exploring those categories.

❷ Apply critical thinking skills to writing comparison and contrast essays.

How can thinking critically help you write a comparison and contrast essay? (See p. 288.)

Thinking critically helps you **assess your purpose**, analyze the categories you will use for your comparisons and contrasts, decide if you will emphasize similarities or differences or a balance of both, develop your **ideas** and support, evaluate your **conclusions**, and **analyze** the overall effectiveness of your comparison's purpose and the examples you use.

❸ Prepare to write a comparison and contrast essay by asking critical thinking questions.

What questions will help you plan a comparison and contrast essay? (See pp. 289–290.)

Ask the following questions: (1) What objects, people, or concepts am I going to compare and/or contrast? (2) Are they in the same general category? (3) Am I going to focus on similarities, differences, or both? Are the subjects mostly alike, mostly different, or some of each? (4) How will I set up my comparisons/contrasts, and how will I structure my paragraphs? (5) What examples and details should I include for support? (6) What do I want my readers to learn or understand after reading this comparison and/or contrast essay? (7) How will I conclude my essay?

4 Structure a comparison and contrast essay.

How do you structure a comparison and contrast essay? (See pp. 290–299.)

You **structure a comparison and contrast essay** by creating an introductory paragraph with a thesis that states your analytical purpose, body paragraphs that support and develop the thesis using either a subject-by-subject approach or a point-by-point approach, and a conclusion to restate the thesis and sum up without adding any new ideas.

5 Use modes that complement comparison and contrast essays.

What modes complement a comparison and contrast essay? (See pp. 299–305.)

Modes that work well within a comparison and contrast structure include narration and description, definition, example and illustration, cause-and-effect, classification, and argument and persuasion.

LEARNING OBJECTIVES

In this chapter, you will learn how to

1 Describe the argument and persuasion mode.

2 Apply critical thinking skills to writing argument and persuasion essays.

3 Prepare to write an argument and persuasion essay by asking critical thinking questions.

4 Structure an argument and persuasion essay.

5 Use modes that complement argument and persuasion essays.

Second hand smoke kills

CANCER
PATIENTS AID
ASSOCIATION

Thinking Critically MyWritingLab™

Think: Look closely at this advertisement.

Write: Briefly describe the ad and what it is trying to persuade you to do. Then describe any secondary arguments the ad makes.

_____

_____

_____

_____

_____

_____

_____

_____

_____

_____

_____

_____

_____

ARGUMENT AND PERSUASION ESSAYS

① Describe the argument and persuasion mode.

Some students hear the term *argument paper* and assume that they will have to use anger and harsh tones. But in this case, argument does not mean quarrel. **Argument essays** state a claim, support the claim with valid and fair-minded reasoning, provide supporting examples and evidence, and give an even-handed presentation of counterarguments to a proposed solution in order to persuade your readers to agree with your position. The best argumentative and persuasive writing uses logic and fair-minded appeals to the audience in order to sway them to the writer's point of view.

Becoming skilled in clear, logical reasoning and arguments will help you see through the faulty arguments and logic in books, newspaper articles, political speeches, and other kinds of persuasive writing you encounter in the everyday world. Most advertisements have embedded arguments within them: the most common argument, of course, is "Buy me!" Often, other arguments are hinted at, too, such as "If you buy a certain car you will seem more good-looking." Argumentative and persuasive writing is one of the most common types of writing in college. You will be asked to write argumentative and persuasive pieces in the workplace, too. Even a memo to your boss asking for a raise is a type of argument essay.

CRITICAL THINKING AND ARGUMENT

② Apply critical thinking skills to writing argument and persuasion essays.

You must have clear **ideas**, a clear **purpose**, and **conclusion**s and **analysis** with support to create a strong argument. You need to check your **biases and assumptions** especially carefully when constructing your argument(s).

One of the most important elements of a good argument and persuasion essay is credibility, so use logic in your arguments instead of emotion. Provide clear support and examples to defend your point of view and convince the reader of your ideas (or at least give your reader a better understanding of your side, even if he or she still disagrees with your argument). Providing **counterarguments** (what others would say in response to your arguments) or alternative solutions to a problem shows that you are being fair-minded and not presenting an issue in a **biased** way. Evidence and support can include facts, statistics, detailed examples, firsthand accounts and/or interviews, and observations. Counterarguments require meticulous critical thinking. You have to anticipate what others would say to refute your argument.

Be careful! Argument essays are the easiest essays in which to fall prey to **logical fallacies** (common errors in logic, which weaken your reasoning— see the list below) and the use of emotion over reason. Maintaining your credibility through the use of a fair-minded tone and good logic in your essay's arguments is essential to persuading your readers of your point. Of course, you are arguing from your own point of view, but your reasoning should be detailed, logical, and free from fallacies. You need to assess your intended audience carefully in order to choose the most effective tone, approach, and evidence to provide in support of your claims. Moreover, you need to make sure you haven't oversimplified the subject, your arguments, or your opposition's arguments.

Logical Fallacies

Check to make sure you haven't damaged your credibility by including any logical fallacies, or errors in reasoning, in your essay. Here are eight of the most common logical fallacies that students commit in essay writing (they are also common in speeches and debates).

Ad hominem fallacy: Attacking the person or group of people who make the argument instead of criticizing the claims, reasoning, or evidence within the argument (from *ad hominem*, Latin for "to the man").

> Those tree-hugging hippies should stop interfering with progress.

Post-hoc fallacy: Mistakenly thinking that because one event happened first, it must be the cause of the event that followed it even though there is no support for this claim (from *post hoc*, Latin for "after this"). One should not make a cause-and-effect analysis without providing evidence to support the connection between two events.

> I wore my striped shirt the day I aced my chemistry exam, so if I wear it again today, I should do great on my English test.

Hasty generalization fallacy: Jumping to a conclusion based on examples that are not representative.

> I see drivers of red sports cars speeding on the interstate all the time. All drivers of red sports cars must speed on the interstate.

Begging the question fallacy: Stating and repeating claims but never giving support or evidence to develop them.

Good parenting would have prevented all of these social problems. All of our society's major problems are a direct result of bad parenting.

Equivocation: Intentionally using vague words or phrases that mislead the reader.

The *casualties* of this war were a needed sacrifice. ("Casualties" is a vague word that hides the truth: deaths.)

Some equivocations can be funny:

Thank you for your manuscript. I shall lose no time in reading it. (The writer may or may not read the mansucript.)

Euphemism: Substituting a word or phrase to soften the effect of a more direct word, to avoid addressing the severity of an issue or to minimize a harsh truth.

Those casualties were actually a result of *friendly fire*.

Red herring fallacy: Using details, examples, or other language that distract the reader from the real argument.

I hear that many soldiers suffer from depression after returning home from Iraq. Has anyone looked into why these soldiers signed up for the military in the first place?

False dilemma *or* either/or fallacy: Presenting only two sides of a complex issue that may have many sides. "You're either with us or against us" is a classic false dilemma. One may actually be somewhere in the middle.

If you don't support our request for more library funding, then you are against student success.

APPLYING CRITICAL THINKING

PURPOSE   IDEAS   SUPPORT   ASSUMPTIONS BIASES   CONCLUSIONS   POINT OF VIEW   ANALYSIS

To write an effective argument essay, consider these questions:

1. What is my **purpose** for writing this essay? What **ideas** and point or points do I want to make to my audience?

2. What biases do I have? What are they based on? Are they logical? What **biases or assumptions** might my audience have that I will need to address as I make my arguments?

3. What is my **point of view** on the subject? Is it based on credible information? How will I best present it?

4. Have I thoroughly **analyzed** my argument? How will I break it down into its basic parts, and how will I present them?

5. What **support** do I need to include? What details (descriptive details, facts, evidence, examples) can I include to develop my argument(s) and **conclusions**?

BEFORE WRITING AN ARGUMENT ESSAY

3 Prepare to write an argument and persuasion essay by asking critical thinking questions.

Before you begin to write an argument essay, ask yourself these questions:

1. What is my stand on this issue?

2. Is there a plan of action I can propose to solve a problem?

3. Who would disagree with my stand or solution, and why? (What are the counterarguments?)

4. What examples and evidence can I provide to support my arguments and claims?

5. How will I organize my arguments and evidence?

6. How will I conclude my essay?

Answering these questions will help you generate an expository thesis statement, help you determine which language and details will provide vivid description and images for support, and give you a general idea of how to organize your essay.

ACTIVITY 14-1 Brainstorming for Potential Arguments

Directions: *Brainstorm a list of problems that exist in your neighborhood or in the country as a whole that need action to be resolved.*

_____

_____

_____

_____

_____

_____

_____

_____

WRITING AN ARGUMENT ESSAY

4 Structure an argument and persuasion essay.

When instructors ask you to take a stand on a particular issue and argue for that stand, you will need to provide reasons to support your position. You will also need to address possible counterarguments both to your overall stand and to the individual reasons or support statements and examples in your paper.

In some argument/persuasion essays, you will be arguing for a proposed *solution* to a perceived *problem*. This type of argument paper goes beyond just explaining your viewpoint on an issue and your reasons for that view; it also includes proposing an action—arguing for a change to address a perceived problem. Often, the thesis statement for this type of argument paper will include the words "should," "needs to," "ought to," or "must."

When writing an argument paper, you must know your audience and customize your approach based on that audience. For example, if you were writing a position paper on the issue of gun control, you would modify your approach depending on your audience. How you would present your views to a parent–teacher association would be very different from how you would present them to the National Rifle Association.

Also, in all argument/persuasion essays, your tone should be respectful and fair-minded. Of course, you will have a bias, which is the nature of an argument paper. Your stand on the issue must be clear from beginning to end, but do not make the mistake of oversimplifying the counterarguments or underestimating your readers' knowledge about the issue. You may even point out the merits of others' arguments against your proposed solution in order to convince your readers that your solution is best.

Keep these basic tips in mind when writing argument essays.

Ten Argument Basics

1. Clearly define your argument and **purpose**.

2. Be aware of your audience, and adjust your style and tone appropriately; use tactful and fair language.

3. Provide evidence, **ideas**, examples, **support**, and **conclusions** for your claims and arguments.

4. Check for logical fallacies and oversimplifications in your reasoning.

5. Acknowledge and **analyze** differing **points of view** and present counterarguments.

6. Point out common ground, and, when appropriate, point out the merits of another view, or make a concession to a well-put counterargument.

7. Refute (address and disagree with) counterarguments and claims from the opposing view—again using fair and respectful language.

8. Use the Critical Thinking Checklist on pages 330–331 to check for your own **assumptions**, **biases**, and inferences, and for the consequences of your argument and overall point of view.

9. Use the critique form on pages 321–322 to check the structure and components of your essay.

10. Revise and proofread your argument essay carefully.

Organizational Pattern for an Argument Essay

Organize your arguments, reasons, support, and counterarguments using order of importance, least to most or most to least, depending on if you are building up your arguments or starting with the argument that has the biggest impact: your strongest reason for the change.

The chart below provides a brief overview of the structure of an argument essay.

BASIC STRUCTURE FOR AN ARGUMENT ESSAY

See the sample essay on pages 323–326.

INTRODUCTORY PARAGRAPH

Sets up the background for the problem and establishes the need for a change or action.

Thesis statement: Presents what you are arguing for: what you want to persuade your readers about.

BODY PARAGRAPHS (Two to five, depending on assignment and purpose)

Create topic sentences to develop your thesis.

Develop your arguments with reasoning and evidence.

Use transitions within and between paragraphs to smoothly move from one argument or idea to the next.

Provide examples and concrete details for support.

Present counterarguments to be fair.

Add analysis and commentary about the examples used to help develop the arguments/thesis statement.

CONCLUDING PARAGRAPH

Sums up and re-emphasize the thesis: your arguments and reasons.

Structuring an Argument Essay

As soon as babies start talking, they learn how to use argument and persuasion to influence others. You can structure an argument essay around any issue that needs changing, from a personal issue to a global one. You could write about a problem in your neighborhood: the need for stoplights or stop signs or more streetlights; the need for a neighborhood watch program; pet control; noise control; or any other problem that occurs in a neighborhood. You could also write about the need for improvements in your school such as a need for increased diversity awareness and celebration or about student services issues such as tuition and book prices, food available on campus, parking issues, cell phone use in the classroom, smoking on campus, and student rights. You could write about unfair scheduling, pay, and other issues at your place of employment. Finally, you could write about a national or international issue such as global warming, migration legislation, institutionalized racism and sexism, war and poverty, technological advances and issues, and so on.

Topic

The only real rule for topics for argumentative essays is that you must be trying to persuade your readers about something. Usually, you will begin by explaining a problem—something that is wrong with the status quo (the way things are now), and then argue for resolving that problem through action or a change in perspective, depending on the subject.

ACTIVITY 14-2   Narrowing Argument Topics

Directions: *Choose three of the broad subjects listed on page 315, and create a cluster or brainstorm on a separate sheet of paper to narrow them down into more manageable topics. Then choose a broad topic of your own and narrow it down in the same way.*

Subject 1: _____

Possible narrowed topics: _____

_____

_____

Subject 2: _____

Possible narrowed topics: _____

_____

_____

Subject 3: _____

Possible narrowed topics: _____

_____

_____

Subject 4, your choice: _____

Possible narrowed topics: _____

_____

_____

Thesis Statements

Write one to three sentences that explain the problem and give the basic facts and background (see Introductory Paragraph below). Your thesis will be your plan for solving the problem (the proposed change you are arguing for). Try to use "should," "must," or "needs to" in your thesis statement to indicate that you want to make a change.

> My employer should contribute half of the cost of my family's health care. My local grocery store needs to offer a greater selection of organic produce.

ACTIVITY 14-3   Creating Thesis Statements

Directions: *Create a thesis statement for each of the topics you narrowed in Activity 14-2.*

1. Subject 1: Thesis statement: _____
   _____

2. Subject 2: Thesis statement: _____
   _____

3. Subject 3: Thesis statement: _____
   _____

4. Subject 4: Thesis statement: _____
   _____

Creating a Rough Outline

Cross Reference
See Chapter 6, pp. 104–115, Stage One: Prewrite to Generate Ideas.

Once you have determined your topic and your thesis statement, you are ready to create a rough outline to determine your essay's structure and organizational plan. Use prewriting techniques such as brainstorming or clustering to generate supporting examples and concrete details. Then create a rough outline using this template:

Rough Outline Template for an Argument Essay

    I. Introductory Paragraph
        A. A brief, general description of the subject focusing on the problem
        B. Thesis statement: the purpose of your argument (what you are arguing for)

II. Body Paragraphs: two to four body paragraphs that explain
the problem and your plan of action for solving it and provide
examples and details
  A. Include concrete examples, descriptions, and details
  B. Include clear transitions from one paragraph to the next
  C. Include definitions and explanations
  D. Include counterarguments and address the counterarguments
III. Concluding Paragraph
  A. Restate the purpose/thesis in a new way
  B. Add some general closing comments without introducing any
  new ideas

Introductory Paragraph

You will need an introduction of one or two paragraphs. Your argument essay
may begin with a call to action or some other type of attention grabber to
interest your readers in your subject, such as "Our neighborhood's pets and
children are in danger on our street." It can be a rhetorical question (a question that does not need an answer) or a powerful statement. Next, you need
to give a two- or three-sentence general explanation of your argument and
any background information the readers need in order to understand it. Here
are some examples of attention grabbers:

1. **Rhetorical question:** "Have you ever experienced the frustration of
   spending your whole paycheck on your textbooks?"
2. **A powerful piece of information or fact:** "On average, books for only
   one quarter will cost a student $100–$200."
3. **An anecdote or story:** "When I started college, I only had $100 set
   aside to buy my books . . ."
4. **A call to action:** "It's time for students to take a stand against our
   campus bookstore's prices."
5. **A background/explanation of the problem:** "For over twenty years,
   our campus bookstore has charged students too much for and made too
   high a profit on our textbooks."

Then you need to narrow down your topic to create your thesis statement,
which should explain exactly what you are arguing for and why. If you propose
a change, remember that using the words "should" or "must" or the phrase
"needs to" indicates to your reader that you are arguing for a change (see
Thesis Statements above).

> My neighborhood needs to petition the city for speed bumps, and the city should respond to our neighborhood's request for the sake of our children's safety.

Body Paragraphs

The first body paragraph should explain in more detail the problem you see and the solution you are arguing for. Give specific examples and details to illustrate the problem.

The following body paragraphs should explain how your plan will solve the problem or at least be the first step toward changing the problem. Provide reasons, evidence, and examples to support your proposed argument. The topic sentences will present those reasons and your supporting examples. Predict, evaluate, and address what people might say *against* your plan (the counterargument[s]). Address those counterarguments, and explain why you don't agree with them. Be fair-minded and thorough to maintain your credibility and your readers' respect. If the solution involves spending money, many counterarguments have to do with who will *pay* for the changes. So be sure to address *who* would pay and *how* the money would be raised. If the counterarguments are about something other than money such as a moral concern or a political difference, make sure that you present the counterargument(s) fairly and thoroughly. If you discount the real counterarguments, your paper loses credibility.

Transitions to introduce another point and show purpose are useful in argument essays.

Cross Reference
For other useful transitions, see also Chapter 5, p. 94, Strengthen a Point, and p. 93, Show Contrast or a Change in Idea (for introducing counterarguments).

TRANSITIONS TO . . .

Introduce Another Point

again	but also	in addition	nor
also	equally important	last	plus the fact
and	finally	lastly	second
and then	first	likewise	then too
another	further	moreover	third
besides	furthermore	next	too

Show Purpose

all things considered	for this reason	to accomplish	with this in mind
for this purpose	in order to	to this end	with this objective

ACTIVITY 14-4   Creating Topic Sentences

Directions: *Create a possible topic sentence you could use to develop a body paragraph that would provide reasons and support for each of the thesis statements you created in Activity 14-3.*

1. Subject 1: Topic sentence: _____

_____

2. Subject 2: Topic sentence: _____

_____

3. Subject 3: Topic sentence: _____

_____

4. Subject 4: Topic sentence: _____

_____

ACTIVITY 14-5   Providing Support

Directions: *List one specific reason that provides support for each of the topic sentences you created in Activity 14-4.*

1. Subject 1: Reason to support topic sentence: _____

_____

2. Subject 2: Reason to support topic sentence: _____

_____

3. Subject 3: Reason to support topic sentence: _____

_____

4. Subject 4: Reason to support topic sentence: _____

_____

Concluding Paragraph

The conclusion should sum up the problem and restate your plan to solve the problem and its effectiveness. Be sure not to introduce any new ideas, arguments, or evidence in the conclusion.

ACTIVITY 14-6 Writing a Conclusion

Directions: *Now choose one of the topics you've been developing in the preceding activities, and write a three- to six-sentence concluding paragraph for that topic/argument.*

_____

_____

_____

_____

_____

ACTIVITY 14-7 Creating Your Outline and First Draft

Cross Reference
See Chapters 21–25, pp. 515–648 for help with the Editing section of the critique form.

Directions: *Choose a topic from one of the activities you already completed in this chapter, from the assignment choices at the end of this chapter, or from a topic assigned by your instructor and create a rough outline using the template on pages 317–318 of this chapter. Then, using your rough outline, write a first draft of your essay. After you have finished, use the critique form below to check for the basics in your essay draft.*

ARGUMENT ESSAY CRITIQUE FORM

| BLUEPRINTS | PURPOSE | IDEAS | SUPPORT | ASSUMPTIONS BIASES | CONCLUSIONS | POINT OF VIEW | ANALYSIS |

Overall   Done well   Needs work

1. Is the chosen problem clearly described?   _____   _____
2. Is there a clear **purpose** and argument for change—a plan for a solution?   _____   _____
3. Is the plan for change reasonable—not too extreme? Is it specific?   _____   _____

Introduction

4. Is the title interesting and in correct format?   _____   _____
5. Is there a good attention grabber and general explanation of the problem?   _____   _____

Continued ▶

6. Is the thesis statement a brief and specific summary of the plan for change—a solution? Are the words "should," "must," or "needs to" used to help clarify the proposed plan of action? _____ _____

Body

7. Do the body paragraphs have clear topic sentences? Underline them. _____ _____

8. Does the body of the paper develop, explain, and elaborate the problem with **ideas**, examples, **analysis**, and **support**? _____ _____

9. Does the body explain in detail exactly how the plan for change will resolve the problem and make a positive change? Also, does the body address the major counterargument(s)? _____ _____

10. Does the solution include all details for how the solution will work, and who will be involved (including who will pay for the change, if necessary)? _____ _____

11. Does each body paragraph have a strong concluding sentence? _____ _____

12. Are transitions used both within and between paragraphs? _____ _____

Conclusion

13. Does the **concluding** paragraph sum up the argument with an analytical frame that re-emphasizes the introductory paragraph and thesis, without adding new ideas? _____ _____

Editing

14. Circle the following errors you think you see in this draft: spelling errors, fragments, run-ons/comma splices, errors in comma and semicolon/colon use, pronoun disagreement, pronoun reference errors, errors in parallelism, apostrophe use, verb use/tense, and passive voice construction.

15. Other types of grammar or sentence-level errors:

_____

Comments (For example: What works well in this draft? What needs to be added? Did you, or will your readers, feel drawn into this essay? Why or why not?):

_____

_____

COMPLEMENTARY MODES FOR ARGUMENT ESSAYS

5 Use modes that complement argument and persuasion essays.

Argument mode is often combined with several other modes:

- **Narration** and **description** can be used to develop the argument(s).
- **Definition** mode can be used to explain objects or concepts used in the examples provided.
- **Example and illustration** is essential to providing good reasoning and support for your argument.

- **Cause-and-effect analysis** will further elaborate on the arguments and reasons.
- **Definition** helps explain the problem(s) and potential solutions.
- You can **compare and contrast** your arguments and counterarguments.

Student Essay

The dominant mode used in this student's paper is argument and persuasion. Look for other modes used in this essay, such as example and illustration, narration and description, and cause-and-effect analysis.

Beeds 1

John Beeds

Professor Furness

English 101

25 January 2013

Danger Around Every Corner

Have you ever heard the screech of car tires in front of your house, the kind that makes your heart instantly skip a beat or two? We send our children out to play in our front yards. We tell them not to talk to strangers and to watch for cars. I used to think that in most neighborhoods, drivers watch for children, and they drive slower down residential streets just in case a child runs out between two parked cars. However, in my neighborhood, the number of speeding cars is staggering. My neighborhood, specifically my street, has many families with children. However, even though children are on the sidewalks at all times of the day, cars race down our street in excess of 30 mph. It is time to take action and create a petition for speed bumps or a round-about in our neighborhood in order to slow cars down and increase

Thesis statement

our children's safety. Our neighborhood needs to take action to protect the safety of our families: We need to petition for speed

Beeds 2

bumps or a round-about, and our city needs to listen to and then respond to our concerns and make the required changes.

Topic sentence

The risk of a child on my street being hurt by a car on any given day, at any given time, day or night, is high: I hear cars speeding down my street at all hours. In reaction, some of my neighbors have walked door-to-door asking people to slow down as they drive on our street. The response seemed good at first; *Concluding sentence* however, the speeding started again soon afterward. I can thankfully say that no child has been hurt yet, but there have been too many narrow escapes.

Topic sentence

Even my own family has had a close call. Early this year when we had snow, my daughter and I were sledding down a hill half a block from our home. We had a terrific time playing in the snow until, as we were walking back to our house, a car slid around the corner almost hitting us as we were crossing the street. Even though we are very aware of the dangers on our street, the *Concluding sentence* car came so fast that we had to jump out of its path. The most troubling part was that not only did we come close to getting hurt, but the driver also never looked back to see if we were okay.

Topic sentence

These scary near-misses happen frequently on our block. On one sunny day this summer, my daughter and her friend were rollerblading on the sidewalk across from my house. My daughter's friend hit a rock, tripped, and fell partially into the street. At the same time, a car came down the street, swerved to miss a dog and nearly hit her. The girl's experience of nearly being hit by the car was far more traumatic than the fall she had experienced. Sadly, the driver did not look back or stop to see if there were any injuries. I asked myself, "Do people just not care anymore?"

Beeds 3

Topic sentence

However, several people in my neighborhood do care and are ready to take action. Some neighbors have attempted to solve the issue in less than desirable ways. Two doors down from me, my neighbor rolled a tire out into the street when a repeat offender sped down our street at what had to be 40 mph. The tire hit the car on the driver's door, and the scene got ugly. A fist fight broke out on the sidewalk. When the fight ended, each man went to his corner, and, needless to say, those neighbors to this day do not speak to each other. Even though I do not agree with the tactics my neighbor used, that driver does not speed down the

Concluding sentence

street anymore. However, we do not want to be vigilantes: We just want our children to be safe.

Topic sentence

Instead of resorting to violent or ugly acts, we have other means of dealing with this issue. My neighbors and I have been working on getting signatures for a petition to put in speed bumps and/or a round-about on our street. The irony is that some of the people who are signing the petition are some of the people that are speeding down the street in the first place. From what I have researched and been told, getting the signatures will be the

Concluding sentence

easiest part. Having the petition approved and asking the city to allocate money for this project will be the difficult part, but all of the residents are committed to the success of this project.

Process

In order to get the Department of Transportation to pay for a speed bump or round-about, a survey of the street or streets in question must be done. The Department of Transportation will evaluate the areas in three categories: number of accidents, volume of traffic, and average speed of the drivers. The Department of Transportation's evaluation will directly influence how

Beeds 4

Counterargument

much money they will allocate to the project. If the Department of Transportation allocates only half of the money, one quarter of the money, or no money, the neighborhood residents will have to pay to complete the project, which will be $8,000 to $14,000 depending on which speed control device the Department of Transportation advises. Many people would argue that that is a lot of money, but the value of our children's lives far outweighs this cost. Also, if we held a neighborhood fundraiser, the price per person could be quite small. At this stage, our neighborhood must wait its turn for the construction of the speed bumps or round-about.

Concluding sentence

Restatement of thesis

To summarize, our goal is to keep our children safe. Our neighborhoods and our homes should be where we can feel safe, and our children need to be able to walk, run, and play outside their homes in a safe environment. Installing speed bumps and/or a round-about is a relatively inexpensive deterrent for speeders, especially when one weighs it against the possible loss of a child's life. Our lives are not that busy, nor is what we have to do that important or urgent. Do you remember the old commercial "Speed Kills"? We must take action in our neighborhood before we get to that point.

ACTIVITY 14-8   Thinking Critically about the Student Essay

Directions: *Identify the features and details characteristic of the argument/ persuasion mode in this essay. Mark them on the essay. Then reread the essay and make a list of specific revisions you would make to correct any problems with content, organization, transitions, and style.*

PROFESSIONAL ARGUMENT ESSAY

Can You Be Educated from a Distance?

James Barszcz

1   By almost any measure, there is a boom in Internet-based instruction. In just a few years, thirty-four percent of American colleges and universities have begun offering some form of what's called "distance learning" (DL), and among the larger schools, it's closer to ninety percent. If you doubt the popularity of the trend, you probably haven't heard of the University of Phoenix. It grants degrees entirely on the basis of online instruction. It enrolls 90,000 students, a statistic used to support its claim to be the largest private university in the country.

2

Definition

Examples

   While the kinds of instruction offered in these programs will differ, DL usually signifies a course in which the instructors post syllabi, reading assignments, and schedules on websites, and students send in their written assignments by e-mail. Other forms of communication often come into play, such as threaded messaging, which allows for posting questions and comments that are publicly viewable, as a bulletin board would, as well as chat rooms for real-time interchanges. Generally speaking, face-to-face communication with an instructor is minimized or eliminated altogether.

3

Example

Argument

   The attraction for students might at first seem obvious. Primarily, there's the convenience promised by courses on the Net: you can do the work, as they say, in your pajamas. But figures indicate that the reduced effort results in a reduced commitment to the course. While the attrition rate for all freshmen at American universities is around twenty percent, the rate for online students is thirty-five percent. Students themselves seem to understand the weaknesses inherent in the setup. In a survey conducted for eCornell, the DL division of Cornell University, less than a third of the respondents expected the quality of the online course to be as good as the classroom course.

4

Counterargument

   Clearly, from the schools' perspective, there's a lot of money to be saved. Although some of the more ambitious programs require new investments in servers and networks to support collaborative software, most DL courses can run on existing or minimally upgraded systems. The more students who enroll in a course but don't come to campus, the more the school saves on keeping the lights on in the classrooms, paying custodians, and maintaining parking lots. And, while there's evidence that instructors must work harder to run a DL course for a variety of reasons, they won't be paid any more, and might well be paid less.

5

Counterargument

But as a rule, those who champion distance learning don't base their arguments on convenience or cost savings. More often, they claim DL signals an advance in the effectiveness of education. Consider the vigorous case made by Fairleigh Dickinson University (FDU), in Madison, New Jersey, where students—regardless of their expectations or desires—are now required to take one DL course per year. By setting this requirement, FDU claims that it recognizes the Internet as "a premier learning tool" of the current technological age. Skill in using online resources "prepares our students, more than others, for life-long learning—for their jobs, their careers, and their personal growth."

6

Examples

Moreover, Internet-based courses will connect FDU students to a "global virtual faculty," a group of "world-class scholars, experts, artists, politicians, and business leaders around the world."

7

Sounds pretty good. But do the claims make much sense? First, it should be noted that students today and in the future might well use the Internet with at least as much facility as the faculty. It's not at all clear that they need to be taught such skills. More to the point, how much time and effort do you suppose "world-class scholars" (much less politicians and business leaders) will expend for the benefit of students they never meet or even see? Probably

Refutation of counterarguments

a lot less than they're devoting to the books, journal articles, and position papers that are already available to anyone with access to a library.

8

Counterargument

Another justification comes from those who see distance learning as the next step in society's progress toward meritocracy. A recent article in *Forbes* magazine cites Professor Roger Schank of Northwestern University, who predicts that soon "students will be able to shop around, taking a course from any institution that offers a good one. . . . Quality education will be available to all. Students will learn what they want to learn rather than what some faculty committee decided was the best practical compromise." In sum, says Professor Schank, who is also chairman of a distance-learning enterprise called CognitiveArts, "Education will be measured by what you know rather

Example for support

than by whose name appears on your diploma."

9

Statements like these assume education consists in acquiring information ("what you know"). Accept that and it's hard to disagree with the conclusions. After all, what does it matter how, or through what medium, you get the information? But few truly educated people hold such a mechanistic view. Indeed, traditionally, education was aimed at cultivating intellectual and moral values, and the "information" you picked up was decidedly secondary. It was commonplace for those giving commencement speeches to note that, based on etymology, education is a drawing out, not a putting in. That is, a true education *educes*, or draws out, from within a person qualities of intellect

Refutes counterargument

and character that would otherwise have remained hidden or dormant.

10

Exactly how this kind of educing happens is hard to pin down. Only in part does it come from watching professors in the classroom present material

Argument

and respond to student questions, the elements of education that can be translated to the Net with reasonable fidelity. Other educational experiences include things like watching how professors joke with each other (or not!) in the hallways, seeing what kinds of pictures are framed in a professor's office, or going out for coffee after class with people in your dorm. Such experiences, and countless others, are sometimes labeled (and dismissed) as "social life on campus." But they also contribute invaluably to education. Through them, you learn a style, in the noblest sense of that term, a way of regarding the information you acquire and the society you find yourself in. This is what the philosopher Alfred North Whitehead meant when he called style the ultimate acquisition of a cultivated mind. And it's the mysterious ways of cultivating that style that the poet Robert Frost had in mind when he said that all that a

Argument and thesis

11

college education requires is that you "hang around until you catch on."

Hang around campus, that is, not lurk on the Net.

MyWritingLab™

Reading Reflection Questions

1. What is the main purpose in this article? Explain in your own words.

   _____

2. T/F _____ According to the essay, the dropout (attrition) rate for distance learning (online) students is higher than traditional students.

3. What counterarguments does Barszcz provide to his arguments against distance learning (what his opponents might say in defense of distance learning)?

   _____

   _____

4. Give an example of one of the author's refutations to one of the counterarguments (he addresses counterarguments with refutations).

   _____

   _____

   _____

   _____

5. T/F _____ The author agrees that good education is mostly about "what you know" or acquiring facts and information.

6. T/F _____ The author thinks that education includes more than learning information and that even an instructor's office and behavior can be educational.

7. In your own words, what does the author mean, in the last paragraph of the article, when he talks of the importance of learning a "style" in college?

_____

_____

MyWritingLab™ **Checking Vocabulary**

Define each of the following words by figuring out their meaning using context clues in the reading selection. If you cannot work out the meaning of a word, use a dictionary.

8. distance learning (paragraph 1): _____

9. minimized (paragraph 2): _____

10. attrition (paragraph 3): _____

CRITICAL THINKING CHECKLIST

PURPOSE

1. What is the **purpose** of this piece of writing? Is it clear?

_____

_____

IDEAS

2. What **ideas** and **background information** are provided to support the purpose of this piece of writing?

_____

_____

SUPPORT

3. What **evidence** and **examples** are used to explain and develop the ideas that support the argument made in the piece of writing? Are the evidence and examples provided sufficient?

_____

_____

ASSUMPTIONS BIASES

4. Are there unfounded **assumptions** or unreasonable **biases**?

_____

_____

5. Are all of the **conclusions**, **implications**, and **consequences** of the arguments (the results of the arguments taken to their farthest extreme) considered?

_____

_____

6. Is the **point of view** clear and consistent, and have other points of view been considered?

_____

_____

7. Using these critical thinking tools, **analyze** the overall structure of this essay and the strength of the author's arguments, ideas, and support. Was he or she successful in accomplishing the purpose? Why, or why not?

_____

_____

MyWritingLab™

Cross Reference
See Chapter 16, pp. 345–383, for information on using sources with integrity.

Essay Assignments

1. Choose one of the subjects under Structuring an Argument Essay on page 315, and narrow that subject to a manageable topic. Then take a stand on that issue (for or against or proposing a change). Be sure to include the opposition's view and counterarguments and address them thoroughly. Don't do any secondary research unless your instructor tells you to do so. If you do include secondary research in your essay, be sure to examine your sources with care and document them according to your professor's preferred style.

2. Choose a problem from the following list to create your argument (plan for change or solution):

   a. A problem you see at your school (such as not enough parking, high bookstore prices, high cafeteria prices and few offerings, conflicts with class scheduling)

   b. A problem where you work (such as not enough parking, difficulty scheduling shifts, problems with coworkers, low pay)

   c. A problem from your neighborhood that you'd like to see fixed (such as a needed stop sign/stoplight, parking problems, a needed park)

   After you have chosen a problem, you'll need to create a plan to solve the problem (your thesis). Remember, using the words "should" or "must" or the phrase "needs to" indicates to your reader that you are arguing for a change.

After you finish your draft of this essay, use the critique form for self- and peer reviews of your essay draft.

3. Choose a topic from one of the activities you worked on in this chapter, and write an argument essay about it.

4. Other possible subjects to narrow down and write an argument essay about:

Technology
social networking

Legislation and politics
drunk driving laws
sex offender laws
smoking laws
immigration laws
sexism and racism in legislation

Sports
performance-enhancing drugs
players' salaries

Money and price
gas prices
tuition costs
medication/medical costs

Environment
global warming
overfishing
overpopulation
traffic problems

Education
mandatory foreign language
    classes
online education
tuition and student fees

Health
obesity in children
addiction

Learning Objectives Review

MyWritingLab™   **Complete the chapter assessment questions at mywritinglab.com**

❶ Describe the argument and persuasion mode.

What distinguishes the argument and persuasion mode from other modes? (See p. 309.)

Essay writers use **argument and persuasion mode** when they state a claim, support the claim with valid and fair-minded reasoning, provide supporting examples and evidence, and give an even-handed presentation of counterarguments to their proposed solution to persuade their readers.

❷ Apply critical thinking skills to writing argument and persuasion essays.

How can thinking critically help you write an argument essay? (See pp. 309–312.)

Thinking critically helps you **assess your purpose**, analyze your biases and assumptions and the logic in your arguments, develop your **ideas** and support, evaluate your **conclusions**, and **analyze** the overall effectiveness of your argument and support.

Check your reasons and support for **logical fallacies**, such as ad hominem, post hoc, hasty generalization, begging the question, equivocation, euphemism, red herring, and false dilemma.

❸ Prepare to write an argument and persuasion essay by asking critical thinking questions.

What questions will help you plan an argument essay? (See pp. 312–313.)

Ask the following questions: (1) What is my stand on this issue? (2) Is there a plan of action I can propose to solve a problem? (3) Who would disagree with my stand or solution, and why? (What are the counterarguments?) (4) What examples and evidence can I provide to support my arguments and claims? (5) How will I organize my arguments and evidence? (6) How will I conclude my essay?

❹ Structure an argument and persuasion essay.

How do you structure an argument essay? (See pp. 313–322.)

You **structure an argument essay** by creating an introductory paragraph with a thesis that states your argument (purpose) and main reasons, body paragraphs that support and develop the thesis with examples and address the counterarguments(s), and a conclusion to restate the thesis and sum up without adding any new ideas.

5 Use modes that complement argument and persuasion essays.

What modes complement an argument and persuasion essay? (See pp. 322–332.)

Modes that work well within an argument structure include narration and description, definition, example and illustration, cause-and-effect analysis, or comparison and contrast.

LEARNING OBJECTIVES

In this chapter, you will learn how to

1 Apply critical thinking strategies to taking essay exams or writing timed essays.

2 Prepare for an essay exam.

3 Follow standard essay-writing steps for essay exams.

4 Define terms used in many essay exam writing prompts.

5 Practice timed writing or essay exams.

Thinking Critically   MyWritingLab™

Think: What effect does writing with a time limit have on your ability to write well?

_____

_____

Write:

1. How can you condense the writing process to make the most of your time?

_____

_____

2. What can you do to generate ideas and develop a purpose quickly?

_____

_____

3. How much time out of an hour would you allow for generating ideas and planning? How much time out of that hour would you dedicate to proofreading and revising?

_____

_____

STRATEGIES FOR TAKING ESSAY EXAMS OR WRITING TIMED ESSAYS

❶ Apply critical thinking strategies to taking essay exams or writing timed essays.

Essay exams and timed in-class essays have the same basic rules as take-home essays. Added pressure, of course, is caused by the time restriction and the nervousness it creates. Unfortunately, you will often have a limited time to organize your ideas and support into a concise essay, both in college and on the job. Timed essays or in-class essay exams provide great practice for writing under pressure in the real world and in your future career. Prospective employers may ask you to write something for them during the interview process, and in many jobs, you'll need to be able to generate a memo, email, or other form of writing with no notice.

Like all essays, a timed essay or a focused essay exam with an instructor's prompt will ask you to narrow your focus and state a purpose. You need to stay focused and organized and provide adequate support and examples to illustrate your points. The basic essay structure is the same, too: a focused introduction that states the purpose for your essay, body paragraphs that develop your thesis and focus on particular aspects of your topic, and a conclusion that wraps up your points in a concise way without introducing any new ideas.

Critical Thinking and Timed Essays

You'll do much better on a timed in-class essay if you use critical thinking from the moment you receive the writing prompt. First, you need to interpret and analyze what the prompt is asking you to write about. Look for clues in the writing prompt itself and check for specific directions as well as key words. Then, you need to create a thesis statement (a purpose to explain in your timed essay) and a plan for writing your essay. It helps to brainstorm first and jot down a brief outline. Finally, you need to leave some time to assess what you've written and make revisions before submitting your essay.

BEFORE THE ESSAY EXAM OR TIMED ESSAY

❷ Prepare for an essay exam.

You can improve your timed essays or essay exams by remaining calm. If you are panicked or have severe test anxiety, it will interfere with your ability to think clearly and write well. In order to alleviate that panic, you need to do some of the same things you do to perform well on a regular exam.

Study and Prepare in Advance

First, be sure that you are well prepared by reading any required materials long before the day of the test. It might mean that you have to study for several days, so make sure to leave enough time. If the timed essay is an analysis of assigned readings, you'll have to study them and prepare notes as you would for a regular exam. Whether or not the essay prompt requires analyzing assigned readings, review the basics of essay writing below.

Also, be sure to get a good night's sleep the night before an essay exam or timed in-class essay. Eat a healthy, but not heavy, meal an hour or so before the test. If you are hungry or tired, it is harder to concentrate and think clearly, and your essay will suffer. Finally, be on time to class on test day; arrive early, if possible, because anxiety increases if you are running late. Sometimes instructors issue verbal directions right at the beginning of class; if you are late, you could miss crucial directions or tips.

What to Bring to Class

1. **Pens and sharpened pencils.** Even if you will be writing directly on a computer, it is still a good idea to have a pen or pencil for brainstorming or in case of printer/computer problems. Instructors prefer black or blue ink for handwritten exams. Avoid unusual colors such as purple or green.

2. **Paper** or a **composition notebook**, unless paper is provided by the instructor or you will be typing in a computer lab or classroom.

3. A **dictionary**, if it is allowed by the instructor; check before the day of the essay exam.

4. A **memory stick**, if you will be writing on a computer in class—always save a copy of your work, and save regularly as you type your essay, every 10 minutes or so.

5. A **watch**, if there is no clock in your classroom, so you can monitor your time as you write.

DURING THE ESSAY EXAM OR TIMED ESSAY

❸ Follow standard essay-writing steps for essay exams.

If you are particularly nervous before the exam, try some relaxation techniques such as deep breathing before you go into the classroom. Use positive thinking to tell yourself you are ready. After all, you've studied, right?

The five basic steps of the writing process still apply to an essay exam:

1. **Prewriting:** Generate ideas and your paper's purpose

2. **Organizing:** Develop a plan for presenting your purpose and ideas

3. **Drafting:** Create a first draft of your essay based on your plan and the pattern(s) of organization you have chosen; develop support for your essay's purpose

4. **Revising:** Reassess the draft for content, development, organization, and support (examples and details)

5. **Editing:** Check for sentence-level effectiveness, style, diction, grammar, and spelling errors

Remember to quickly assess your subject, purpose, and audience from the writing prompt. The **subject** of your essay is the topic you are writing about, which you need to focus into a manageable **topic** for the length of your essay. The **purpose** is what you want to explain or prove related to that topic, so your **thesis** is a statement of your overall goal. Your **audience** is the intended reader(s) for your essay—who you are addressing, usually your instructor (unless he or she indicates otherwise), so use a semiformal tone for your essay.

Common Terms Used in Writing Prompts

❹ Define terms used in many essay exam writing prompts.

As you review your writing prompt or question, check for indicator words, clues for specific tasks your instructor wants you to accomplish in the essay. Here are some of the common terms used in writing prompts that are clues that you are being asked to provide specific information.

Analyze	Interpret the significance of something; divide the topic into individual components and analyze its parts; look at cause-and-effect relationships; look for purpose, messages, or meanings.
Argue	Take a stand on an issue, and develop your argument with reasoning and support.
Compare/contrast	Explore similarities and/or differences among two or more subjects.
Defend	Provide evidence to support a stand or conclusion.
Define	Provide a definition (or set of definitions).
Discuss	Write about the subject—be sure to focus on a particular purpose and not just randomly brainstorm on the topic.
Enumerate	List specific points, ways of doing something, steps in a process, and so on.
Examine	Analyze and explore an issue thoroughly.
Identify	Specifically identify what is required.
Illustrate	Show with examples, support, and analysis.
Interpret	Translate and analyze the significance of the material.
List/include	Provide a list of examples, support, and/or reasons.
Provide/support	Provide examples and details for support and explanation.
Summarize	Sum up the main ideas in your own words.
Trace	In chronological order, detail events or situations related to the subject.

APPLYING CRITICAL THINKING

The best way to make the most of your limited time during an essay exam is to:

1. **Make sure that you understand the writing prompt, or question,** that has been given to you. Read it carefully (see the list of terms above for clues about what you are being asked to do). It helps to revise the given *question* into a thesis statement *answer* before you prewrite.

2. **Allow at least five minutes for brainstorming** after you receive your topic or prompt. Brainstorm on paper with a pen or pencil or on the computer, depending on your preference or the instructor's directions. If you prefer, you can freewrite instead. Develop the **support**, **purpose**, and **analysis** for your essay.

3. **Come up with a brief plan for organization.** Try a rough outline to organize your ideas.

4. **Focus more on ideas and details** than on spelling and style (although do use complete sentences and paragraph structure).

5. **Allow at least five minutes for a quick revision** of glaring problems after you draft your essay. Be sure to check for spelling (this is the time to use the dictionary you brought, if allowed) or grammar mistakes, and check your tone and diction.

Remember "ATODE"

Use this memory trick to check for the five basic requirements for a successful in-class essay:

A   **Address** the writing prompt and reuse key terms from the question

T   Present a clear **thesis** that states your purpose at the end of your introductory paragraph

O   Use overall **organization** and clear transitions from paragraph to paragraph

D   Use **details** and examples to support your thesis

E   **Edit** your essay for grammar and spelling errors

ACTIVITY 15-1 Identifying Word Clues in Prompts

Directions: *In each of these sample essay prompts, identify what the italicized words are asking the writer to do. What modes can the writer draw on?*

1. Write a two- to three-page essay that *defines* civic duty and *examines* why people tend to uphold it.

   _____

   _____

2. *Identify* a recurring problem in your neighborhood, and then *illustrate* why it is a problem.

   _____

   _____

3. *Trace* the events that led to the creation of the North Atlantic Treaty Organization (NATO).

   _____

   _____

4. *Examine* the following poem, and *interpret* the meaning and messages within it.

   _____

   _____

5. *Summarize* a current debate or controversy in the news, and then *argue* your viewpoint on that controversy.

   _____

   _____

PRACTICE TIMED IN-CLASS ESSAYS AND ESSAY EXAMS

5 Practice timed writing or essay exams.

In order to get better at taking timed essays or writing essay exams, you need to practice. Taking timed exams becomes easier as you practice and continually assess your performance and skills.

Review the tips throughout this chapter and then practice using the prompts that follow.

MyWritingLab™   **ACTIVITY 15-2** **Timed Essay Exam Practice I**

Directions: *Give yourself one hour to write this essay from start to finish.*

Prompt Questions: *Write about a time when someone treated you unfairly. Explain what happened. How did it make you feel, and why? Examine your memories of the experience. Interpret this event's significance in your life and for your identity. Provide specific examples. What did you learn from this experience? (What you learned will become the thesis statement of your essay.)*
Complete the following:

1. *Brainstorm, prewrite, and outline for five minutes to find a thesis and generate ideas.*
2. *Begin with an introductory paragraph to present your thesis; be sure to provide a thesis statement that addresses the questions above.*
3. *Arrange the rest of your paragraphs to develop your points, and describe what happened. Use narration and description to develop your thesis.*
4. *Write a concluding paragraph that sums up your experience.*
5. *Do a quick review for needed organization and details; check quickly for spelling and grammar errors.*

MyWritingLab™   **ACTIVITY 15-3** **Timed Essay Exam Practice II**

Directions: *Write for one hour on the following prompt:* Do you think that cigarette smoking should be illegal? Why, or why not? *Be sure to give reasons for your position, provide support and examples for your reasons, and define and analyze the counterarguments or positions.*

MyWritingLab™   **ACTIVITY 15-4** **Timed Essay Exam Practice III**

Directions: *Write for one hour on the following prompt:* Do you think that social networking should be banned from the workplace (e.g., the office network shouldn't allow users to sign on to Facebook)? Why, or why not? *Be sure to give reasons for your position, provide support and examples for your reasons, and define and analyze the counterarguments or positions.*

MyWritingLab™   **ACTIVITY 15-5**   Self-Assessment Essay

Directions: *Write a 250- to 500-word self-assessment essay. In the essay, address the following questions.*

1. *Assess your improvement over the span of this writing course in planning, drafting, and revising essays. How exactly has your essay writing improved? Be specific. Some of the categories to consider include organization, details and examples, development, flow/coherence/transitions, introductory paragraphs and thesis statements, concluding paragraphs, and, finally, grammar and editing (spelling, fragments, run-ons, comma splices, commas, semicolon/ colon use, pronoun agreement, pronoun reference errors, parallelism, apostrophe use, verb use/tense, passive voice construction, and so on).*
2. *In your opinion, what are your strengths as a writer? What do you do well in essay writing?*
3. *In your opinion, what are your weaknesses in writing essays? What do you need to continue to work on?*
4. *Anything else you've noticed?*

Learning Objectives Review

MyWritingLab™ Complete the chapter assessment questions at mywritinglab.com

1 Apply critical thinking strategies to taking essay exams or writing timed essays.

How do you strategize when taking essay exams and writing timed essays? (See p. 336.)

A good strategy when taking essay exams and writing timed essays is to use your critical thinking skills to analyze the writing prompt before you start and address it with care as you develop your essay.

2 Prepare for an essay exam.

How can you prepare for an essay exam? (See pp. 336–337.)

To prepare for an essay exam, start studying several days in advance. Get a good night's sleep the night before, and eat a balanced meal an hour before the exam. Also, arrive at class on time or early on exam days to decrease your stress.

3 Follow standard essay-writing steps for essay exams.

How can you apply the writing process to an essay exam? (See pp. 337–338.)

In essay-exam writing, remember ATODE! Address the writing prompt and reuse key terms from the question; present a clear **thesis** that states your purpose at the end of your introductory paragraph; use overall **organization** and clear transitions from paragraph to paragraph; use **details** and examples to support your thesis; and **edit** your essay for grammar and spelling errors.

4 Define terms used in many essay exam writing prompts.

What terms often used in essay writing prompts should you know? (See pp. 338–340.)

Instructors commonly use the following terms in essay writing prompts: analyze, argue, compare/contrast, defend, define, discuss, enumerate, examine, identify, illustrate, interpret, list/include, provide, support, summarize, and trace.

5 Practice timed writing or essay exams.

How and why should you practice timed writing or writing essay exams? (See pp. 340–342.)

Practice makes perfect! Learning common prompts and key words will help you **know what to do** when you see those key words on an in-class exam. Use the tips, the activities, and the timed practice exercises in this chapter to practice your timed test-taking skills.

CONTENTS

16 **Using Sources with Integrity**

17 **Writing Essays about Visuals**

18 **Writing Essays about Readings**

INTRODUCTION TO PART IV

Throughout college and your career, you will be asked to incorporate sources or data into your writing, evaluate other people's work, and follow certain standards for crediting the work of others. In college, professors across the disciplines will ask you to write about a wide range of assigned readings, including articles, case studies, stories, argumentative essays, and textbook chapters. Part IV prepares you to incorporate and document sources, textual or visual, in your own writing and to critique other people's work.

To write critically about what you have read or seen, you will need to use the critical thinking and active reading and summary skills you learned in Part I and the essay-writing techniques from Parts II and III. Several of the modes covered in Part III (Narration and Description, Classification, Definition, and Argument and Persuasion) can help you analyze source material. Part V will help you pull all these techniques together using correct mechanics and grammar so your sentences have authority and clarity.

LEARNING OBJECTIVES

In this chapter, you will learn how to

1 Write a documented paper.

2 Distinguish types of sources.

3 Find, evaluate, and integrate sources.

4 Avoid plagiarism.

5 Use correct MLA format.

6 Use correct APA format.

Thinking Critically MyWritingLab™

Think: How might using sources in your writing make your ideas more convincing?

_____

_____

_____

_____

_____

Write: How do you use sources effectively and give proper credit for other people's ideas?

_____

_____

_____

_____

_____

WRITING A DOCUMENTED PAPER

1 Write a
documented
paper.

Writing a **documented paper** requires that you use sources to strengthen and support your ideas. You first determine your argument, the point you want to make, and then research sources to find evidence to explain and support it. Before you begin to write, you should also examine any assumptions or biases you might have about the subject.

> **Documented Paper:** Write your own arguments/conclusion on a topic of your choice → research for support → integrate sources → document sources

APPLYING CRITICAL THINKING

PURPOSE   IDEAS   SUPPORT   ASSUMPTIONS BIASES   CONCLUSIONS   POINT OF VIEW   ANALYSIS

When you look for sources to support your argument, ask yourself the following questions:

1. What do I want to explain, show, or prove related to my topic? What is my **purpose**?

2. What information—**ideas**—do I need to research to develop my argument?

3. What **support** (information, facts, and data) will I need to explain and illustrate my ideas?

4. What concepts or principles will I need to include and define?

5. Where should I look for the kinds of information I need, and how will I know if these sources are reliable? How do I evaluate and **analyze** them?

6. What is my **point of view** about the topic, and what **conclusions** have I reached?

7. What are my **biases and assumptions** about the topic? Are they fair?

Ten Steps for Writing a Documented Paper

The following guidelines will help you work through the process of writing a documented paper.

Step One: **Select your subject and prewrite to narrow it down to a manageable topic.** Unless your topic is assigned, pick a subject that interests you and can be easily researched.

Then narrow the subject down by prewriting and thinking about it.

▶ **NOTE** If you do not know a great deal about your chosen subject, you may have to complete Step Two before you can adequately prewrite.

Step Two: **Get an overview of your topic.** Read background articles and get a sense of the issues and subtopics related to it. You may find you need to narrow your topic and the scope of your paper even further after you have done some preliminary research.

Step Three: **Brainstorm, freewrite, and organize your ideas to develop a preliminary thesis statement.** This is a chance to think about *how* you will structure your paper and *what* kind of information you will need to find to support your thesis statement.

Step Four: **Prepare a working outline.** Taking the ideas you generated in Step Three, create a rough outline and determine the main subheadings for your paper. Ask yourself, *What do I want to say? How will I develop my arguments? What support will I provide?* Be sure to put your preliminary thesis at the top of your outline.

Step Five: **Conduct research and take notes.** Be sure to record in your notes all the bibliographical information for each source you locate. You can use notecards, a research notebook, or your laptop or tablet to record your working (not complete) list of sources and notes. (See p. 359 for guidelines on how to accurately record source information.)

▶ **TIP** Keep your notes sorted alphabetically by the authors' last names to make it easier to create your bibliography, Works Cited, or References page later.

Step Six: **Review your notes carefully to see if there are any information gaps.** Use your preliminary thesis and rough outline to assess whether you need to look for further support. If you do, continue to research your topic.

Step Seven: **Re-outline your paper, fine-tuning the structure and organization and modifying your arguments and your thesis (if necessary) based on any newly discovered information.** Add more details to your outline if necessary, noting carefully which sources you will use in which sections of your paper.

Step Eight: **Write the first draft of your documented paper.** Your introduction should lead into and then present your thesis statement (argument). The body of your paper should develop and support your thesis using the sources you have identified. Be sure to cite all your sources, using the documentation format required by your instructor, to avoid plagiarism (see "How to Avoid Plagiarism" on pp. 358–359). Your conclusion should sum up and reiterate your thesis.

Step Nine: **Prepare your Works Cited page.** Follow the instructions for the documentation format assigned. See "Using Modern Language Association Format" on pages 360–375 for MLA format or "Using American Psychological Association Format" on pages 375–381 for APA format; for other styles, consult the respective handbooks or style guides.

Step Ten: **Revise, edit, and proofread your paper.** Check for unity, coherence, organization, support, and details, and then fine-tune your introduction, thesis, and conclusion. Double-check the format and accuracy of all references (summary, paraphrase, or direct quotes). Check especially for punctuation errors within your citations. Use a dictionary and spell-check and consult a thesaurus to find synonyms for words you have overused. Add transitions where needed within and between paragraphs.

▶ **TIP**   If you can put your draft away for at least two days before completing Step Ten, you will see errors you did not see before and get a clearer and more accurate assessment of your paper. Also, you may want to visit your college's tutoring or writing center to get some objective feedback on your ideas, organization, and use of sources.

TYPES OF SOURCES

❷ Distinguish types of sources.

When you research a subject for a paper, you need to look for sources of information about your subject that will provide relevant and credible support for your ideas. Three general sources of information are:

- **Reference sources**, such as dictionary or encyclopedia entries that you can use to explain or develop a term or concept in your paper.

- **Primary sources**, which are original materials such as journals, letters, novels, poems, stories, historical accounts, newspapers, and so on.
- **Secondary sources**, which are materials that are written about or in response to primary sources such as summaries, bibliographies, critical analyses, and reviews.

When using information from other writers, be sure to evaluate what you find and be alert for signs of author bias. Use your critical thinking skills to evaluate the credibility of other writers' interpretations and evaluations.

FINDING, EVALUATING, AND INTEGRATING SOURCES

 Find, evaluate, and integrate sources.

When you conduct research, you should decide which sources would be most useful and how and where to find them; evaluate whether the sources are reliable and credible; and then integrate the information from the sources into your paper and correctly document it.

Finding Sources

Students today are fortunate to have easy access, at home or on campus, to the most amazing source of information since the beginning of civilization: the Internet. However, don't forget that some of the old-fashioned techniques for finding sources still have merit. Your campus or local library, databases, and personal interviews are all excellent resources too.

Libraries

Books and reference texts (such as specialized dictionaries and encyclopedias), as well as periodicals, magazines, and newspapers, are treasures that you'll find in any library, but libraries also hold valuable collections of DVD, CD-ROM, print, and database resources. Moreover, libraries pay for access to online databases that you might not be able to access from your home computer or would be charged for accessing. Libraries offer two major features that can make your research easier:

1. **Web sites designed to help you efficiently search the libraries' complete holdings (print, CD-ROM, database, online subscriptions, and so on).** Often, you can access your college library's Web site from home, using your student ID and password. College library Web sites also include helpful links to other online resources that you might not find on your own. Both college and local library Web sites have search engines designed to help you customize a search through their holdings (and even the holdings of other local libraries in your area) for the

topic you are writing about. Another common feature on a library Web site is an "Ask a Librarian" link that will allow you to post questions to the librarian on duty who will respond to you.

2. **Helpful staff and trained research librarians who are experts at conducting customized searches can help you find exactly what you are looking for in a fraction of the time it would take you on your own.** It's not cheating to get help from librarians: that's what they're there for and most of the time they are eager to help you discover the perfect sources for your topic. They can even help you narrow and fine-tune the scope of your topic and the purpose for your research. Therefore, it helps to have a preliminary outline of the main ideas for your paper on hand when you visit your local or college librarian. Remember, you can also check to see if your college or local libraries have online access to librarians so you can email questions from home.

Databases

Databases are digital collections of information. They are available as CD-ROMs stored in libraries or as online databases (such as Infotrac, Pro-Quest, EbscoHost, and CQ Researcher) accessible through your library's subscription service. Go to your local or college library to check which databases they subscribe to (or check their Web site). Databases are valuable because they are field- or subject-specific and have search functions that allow for quick and easy access to reliable and credible sources. For instance, Infotrac is a database containing articles on academic subjects that can be searched either by subject or by author name.

Interviews with Experts

You can conduct interviews with experts on your subject in person, by telephone, or via email. Be sure to check with your instructor first to see if interviews from experts are allowed as sources for your paper. Also, be sure that the person interviewed is a credible authority in the field or subject. Evaluate the expertise of interviewees by finding out if they have the right credentials for your subject. What degrees do they hold? What have they published in relation to the subject? Are they known authorities on the subject?

The Internet and Search Engines

The World Wide Web has changed the way we conduct research and opened up possibilities we could never have imagined. The easiest way to navigate the Web and find sources related to your subject is to use a search engine. A **search engine** allows you to use key words to search a database or the

Web for information on specific topics. Some of the more prominent search engines include the following:

Google (www.google.com)

Google Scholar (www.scholar.google.com)

Yahoo (www.yahoo.com)

Bing (www.bing.com)

Ask.com (www.ask.com)

Dictionary.com (www.dictionary.com)

You can do either a basic search using a key word or phrase, or you can do an **advanced search** that allows you to target more specific articles. All of the sites above, as well as more specialized discipline-specific databases, provide information on how to most effectively search their sites. When you do a basic search on your topic, if you get over 500 "hits" (articles or entries related to the key word or phrase you entered), do an advanced search to narrow the scope of the search to articles that more specifically address your topic.

The Internet contains a wealth of credible, up-to-date, and easily accessible sources for your paper. However, there are many Web sites and online articles and studies that contain inaccurate or even false information. You must be on guard, particularly when evaluating a source or research study online (see the questions on pp. 353–354 for evaluating your sources).

Sample Google Page for a Search on the Subject of "Plagiarism"

pla·gia·rism

noun \\plā-jə-ˌri-zəm *also* -jē-ə-\\

Definition of PLAGIARISM

1

: an act or instance of plagiarizing

2

: something plagiarized

— **pla·gia·rist** *noun*

— **pla·gia·ris·tic** *adjective*

⌐ See plagiarism defined for English-language learners »

See plagiarism defined for kids »

Examples of PLAGIARISM

1. The student has been accused of *plagiarism*.

First Known Use of PLAGIARISM

1621

Other Literature Terms

apophasis, bathos, bildungsroman, bowdlerize, caesura,coda, doggerel, euphemism, poesy, prosody

Rhymes with PLAGIARISM

absurdism, activism, Adventism, alarmism, albinism, alpinism,anarchism, aneurysm, anglicism, animism, aphorism, Arabism,archaism, asteri...
[+]more

Learn More About PLAGIARISM

Spanish-English Dictionary: Translation of "plagiarism"
Britannica.com: Encyclopedia article about "plagiarism"

Evaluating Potential Sources

Whenever you do research for a paper, you need to make sure that the sources you use are legitimate. Inaccurate, biased, or even false information can be found in all forms of print or electronic material. Here is a set of questions to use as guidelines for evaluating whether to include specific sources in your documented paper.

QUESTIONS TO ASK WHEN CHECKING THE RELIABILITY OF A SOURCE

PURPOSE   IDEAS   SUPPORT   ASSUMPTIONS BIASES   CONCLUSIONS   POINT OF VIEW   ANALYSIS

If you answer "no" to any of these questions about a source, you may want to reject it or consider other sources; you should at least check with a librarian to see if the source is legitimate. You do not want the sources you use in your paper to damage your credibility: You are using them to support and strengthen your claims so **analyze** them carefully using these questions.

1. **Is the source completely up-to-date?** It is essential to use the most up-to-date and legitimate sources in your paper to **support** your **ideas**. If your sources don't have credibility, then neither do you.

2. **Is this a scholarly or academic resource?** Check the origin of your source and make sure the information is objective and not slanted in order to sell a product or promote a particular point of view on a controversial issue. Is the source privately or publicly funded? In general, you are better off using sites that end in "**.edu**" (education sites), "**.gov**" (government sites), or "**.org**" (sites run by reputable companies or nonprofit organizations) rather than for-profit "**.com**" sites.

Continued ▶

3. **Does the author have the correct credentials to write knowledgeably on the subject?** Do not assume that having an MD or PhD automatically gives a person credibility. Check an author's degree to make sure he or she is writing about his or her field of expertise. You can also see what job an expert holds to see if it relates to the subject and even conduct a Google or Yahoo! search to check his or her background. If the author's background seems unrelated to your subject, then he or she is probably not an expert on the subject.

4. **If statistics and numbers are included in a source, who commissioned the study or conducted the research?** For instance, if you are researching the effects of tobacco industry advertising on middle school students, you should look for **unbiased** sources of information and carefully evaluate the accuracy of studies commissioned by the tobacco industry itself.

5. **Can you verify the information contained in a source?** If numbers and statistics are involved, double-check the facts using at least one other source.

6. **Does the author provide secondary research to support his or her ideas and claims?** Are these sources credible? Choose a few key facts and run a Google search to test them against what other sources say.

7. **Does the author present different sides of an issue even if strongly advocating a particular stance?** Check your source against other sources found through an Internet search on the subject. Many authors have a particular **bias** on a subject, and, if they oversimplify an issue or do not address counterarguments, using these sources could hurt your credibility.

QUESTIONS TO ASK WHEN EVALUATING THE CONTENT OF A SOURCE

| PURPOSE | IDEAS | SUPPORT |  ASSUMPTIONS BIASES | CONCLUSIONS | POINT OF VIEW | ANALYSIS |

Once you have determined a source is reliable, you want to ask specific questions in order to evaluate whether it provides unbiased information.

1. What **assumptions** does the author make in his or her arguments?

2. What **point of view** is the author putting forward?

3. What **biases** are evident in the author's argument and point of view?

4. Who paid for or sponsored the author's research?

5. Has the author included the major counterarguments and objections to the claims he or she is making?

Integrating Sources into Your Paper

As you begin to incorporate sources into your writing, be sure that they serve as backup for your own ideas and the purpose of your essay. You want expert opinions, statistics, and other valuable information you gleaned from your research to work for you: Don't let your voice, your purpose, your ideas, or your argument get lost in the background. The research is support; it should not speak for you.

When you incorporate ideas from other sources into your paper, you should smoothly weave them together with your own ideas. To do this effectively, use the concept of the analytical ice cream sandwich: Each time you include a piece of information from a source, first introduce it (the bottom cookie) and then follow it with your critical analysis of what it means (the ice cream filling) and your explanation of how it supports your point (the top cookie).

Incorporating Quotations

All quotations must be cited. This means you need to include the name of the author and the page number(s) of the work from which you took the quoted information in parentheses immediately after the quote. In general, end punctuation goes *after* the parenthetical citation, except in the case of a block quotation (see "In-Text Citations" on pp. 361–365 for further details).

Quotations from Prose or Text

Four lines or fewer: If a quotation is four lines or fewer in length, include the quoted lines within the body of your text, surrounded by double quotation marks and followed by a parenthetical citation before the period. For quotations within a quotation, use single quotation marks.

> **Single quotation:** In Mortimer Adler's "How to Mark a Book," he writes, "There are two ways in which one can own a book" (1).
>
> **Quotation within a quotation:** According to Suzan Shown Harjo, "There is doubt as to whether permanent curation of our dead really benefits Indians. Dr. Emery A. Johnson, former assistant surgeon general, recently observed, 'I am not aware of any current medical diagnostic or treatment procedure that has been derived from research on such skeletal remains. Nor am I aware of any during the 34 years that I have been involved in American Indian . . . health care'" (2).

More than four lines (block quotation): If a quotation is more than four lines long, set it off from the main body of your text in a block indented 1 inch, or 10 spaces, from the left margin. Double-space the quotation, and do not use quotation marks. Place the parenthetical citation after the period at the end of a long quotation.

> **Block quotation:** Jackson Jodie Daviss describes her character's joy for dancing in "Gotta Dance":
>> I tapped an oh-so-easy, wait-a-minute time-step while I lifted the sneakers from around my neck. I gripped the laces in my right hand and gave the shoes a couple of overhead, bola-style swings, tossing them to land beside the tape player, neat as you please. I didn't miss a beat. The audience liked it; I knew they would. Then I let the rhythm take me and I started to fly. Everything came together. I had no weight, no worries, just the sweet, solid beat. Feets, do your stuff. (2)

Quotations from Poetry

Three lines or fewer: If you are quoting three lines or fewer from a poem, include the lines within the body of your text, with each line break indicated by a slash with a space on either side of it, and place the parenthetical citation *before* the final period. In the citation, include the line numbers for the lines you are quoting. The first time you do this, use the word *line* or *lines* before the number(s). For subsequent citations, just include the line number(s).

> In Suzanne Paola's poem "Genesis," she writes, "First, there was nothing. / In that, a severe beauty—" (lines 1–2).

Three lines or more: If you are quoting three lines or more from a poem, set the quotation off from the main text in a block indented 1 inch or 10 spaces from the left margin. Double-space the quoted lines, and do not use quotation marks. The parenthetical citation should follow the final period or word of the poem you are quoting.

> In Suzanne Paola's poem "Genesis," she writes about life and alludes to the Bible:
>> First, there was nothing.
>> In that, a severe beauty—
>> Then
>> The geometry of being,
>> Circle & angle, thorax
>> & horn.
>> The Word,
>> Life after life. (lines 1–8)

Indicating Editorial Information

Sometimes when you quote writers and cite information, you need to insert notes to explain some of the information or to note existing errors within the quoted material. Certain conventions for doing this are outlined below.

1. **Indicating errors in an original source:** If there is an error in a quotation you are using (grammar, spelling, etc.), indicate that you are aware of the error by placing the word "sic" (Latin for "thus") in brackets immediately after it, so your readers will know it is not your error.

2. **Omitting words, phrases, or sentences from a direct quotation:** Make sure that the word(s), phrase(s), or sentence(s) you are omitting from the direct quotation does not change the author's intended meaning, and use the following guidelines.

   - **To omit one or more words or a part of a sentence from an original quotation,** use an ellipsis (a series of three spaced periods). So the following passage,

   "The tension between them had started to grow even more intense. They knew that money was tight and that the rent was due, bills were waiting, the kids were hungry. However, now he had lost his job too, and they didn't speak of it, but their eyes met with a stressful exchange whenever they stopped for a moment."

   minus parts of two sentences, becomes

   "The tension between them had started to grow even more intense. They knew that money was tight and that the rent was due . . . now he had lost his job too, and they didn't speak of it, but their eyes met with a stressful exchange whenever they stopped for a moment."

   - **To omit one or more sentences from a quotation,** use an ellipsis with an extra period (a total of four periods):

   "The tension between them had started to grow even more intense. . . . However, now he had lost his job too, and they didn't speak of it, but their eyes met with a stressful exchange whenever they stopped for a moment."

- **To insert clarifying words or information.** Use brackets around words or phrases that must be added within a quotation to provide clarification for the reader or make the verb tense or form consistent.

> "They had not seen [his daughter] in three years."
> "She want[ed] a new life."

PLAGIARISM

4 Avoid plagiarism.

Plagiarism is taking someone else's words, ideas, or concepts and using them as if they were your own without giving credit to the original source. Some people cheat by copying information, even full papers, from the Internet. Others unintentionally present someone else's work as their own by not correctly documenting and citing the source(s). Ignorance of the rules for citing sources is no excuse: Whether a student has used someone else's work by accident or on purpose, he or she is committing plagiarism. Even if a professor does not immediately realize that a student's work is plagiarized, this plagiarism can be discovered later in the student's academic or professional career, damaging his or her academic credibility and resulting in severe consequences. *Always* give credit for other people's ideas or words!

How to Avoid Plagiarism

You can avoid plagiarism by being aware of what it is and taking the following precautions:

1. **Do not use the annotated instructor's edition of a course textbook.** It will have answers to most of the exercises in the book and insights for teaching that are meant for your instructors only. Reading the sample answers before you write your own answers, or rewriting the answers in your own words, is plagiarizing. If you are caught using an instructor's edition, you may be subject to disciplinary action by the college.

2. **Do not use phrases, passages, or visuals from a source—print or electronic—without citing it.** Whether you quote, paraphrase, or summarize content, always cite its source.

3. **Do not use *ideas or concepts* from a source—print or electronic— without citing it.** Except for ideas you came up with on your own *before* you read anything about a subject, you need to cite the source of every idea you use in a paper—even if you phrase the ideas in your own words. Instead of claiming that you just "coincidentally" came up with the same idea as a noted scholar, cite the scholar and add credibility to your claim.

Be careful, too, that the brilliant idea you put in your paper didn't come from something you read a while ago. Research to find the original source, and give credit where credit is due. The only exception is when you include a "common knowledge" fact, information that most people know. For example, if you mention that George Washington was our first president and his home was in Mount Vernon, you don't have to cite a source. Rule of thumb: When in doubt, always cite the source.

4. **Be very careful when you paraphrase, even when you cite your source.** When you paraphrase too much content from a source, and/ or your overall writing style and use of words and phrases is too close to the original (without using quotation marks), **you are plagiarizing**, *even if you cite the source.* Be careful not to rely too much on other people's words or ideas.

Guidelines for Accurately Recording Source Information

Here are some guidelines for accurately recording print, online, and other media sources in your notes.

Cross Reference
See Chapter 3, "Six Steps for Paraphrasing Material" (pp. 47–48) or "Eight Steps for Writing a Summary" (pp. 50–51).

1. **Write a summary of the information you want to use, with specific sections that are particularly relevant paraphrased in more detail.** Make sure that you use your own words and sentence construction when you paraphrase or summarize the ideas of others and that you clearly credit the original source.

2. **Enclose any quotations you may want to use in your paper in quotation marks followed by page numbers.**

3. **Record all relevant source information as listed below.**

   - **Book:** author name(s), title (and edition if relevant), city of publication, publisher, year of publication, page number(s)

   - **Journal article:** author name(s), title, journal name, volume and issue numbers, year of publication, and page number(s)

   - **Magazine article:** author name(s); title; magazine name; day, month, and year of publication; and page number(s)

   - **Newspaper article:** author name(s); title; newspaper name; day, month, and year of publication; section letter or number; and page number(s)

   - **Online sources:** name(s) of author, if credited; title of article; name of Web site; version or edition number, if provided; publisher or sponsor of the site; date of publication; URL; and date you accessed the site

   ▶ **NOTE** As you search for sources online, remember to consult the checklist provided earlier in this chapter in order to evaluate their credibility.

MyWritingLab™ ** ACTIVITY 16-1 ** Avoiding Plagiarism

Directions: *Go to your library either in person or online and find an academic article or essay. Use the "Guidelines for Accurately Recording Source Information" above and write in the correct source documentation below.*

_____

_____

Then, on a separate sheet of paper, either summarize the article in one to two paragraphs, using your own words, or paraphrase one paragraph of it. After you have summarized or paraphrased, review your draft and make sure that you have used your own words, style, and sentence constructions, not those of the original author.

USING MODERN LANGUAGE ASSOCIATION (MLA) FORMAT

5 Use correct MLA format.

MLA style is the standard documentation format used in the United States for writing in the humanities (literature, philosophy, history, art, etc.). For a more detailed and complete description of MLA style, consult the *MLA Handbook for Writers of Research Papers* (7th ed., 2009), or a current writer's handbook that includes a full section on MLA documentation. You can also access information about MLA format online at www.mla.org.

Two main features of MLA format are in-text citations and a Works Cited list that provides detailed publication information for each source cited in the body of the paper, both of which are discussed in more detail later. First, here are some guidelines for formatting an MLA style paper.

Formatting Your Paper

Here are guidelines for formatting your paper using MLA style:

Paper	8½ × 11-inch white paper.
Line Spacing	Use double-spacing throughout the entire paper, including the heading and title—with no extra spaces between them or between paragraphs.
Margins	Leave one-inch margins on all sides, and justify left margins.
Page Numbering	Number every page, including the first page and the Works Cited page. Numbers should be in the upper right corner one-half inch from the top of the page and aligned flush with the right margin. Include your last name, a space, and then the page number. Do not use a comma or *p* or *page* between your name and the number.

Font	Use an easy-to-read font and font size, for example, 12 point Times Roman (check with your instructor).
Title page	Do not create a separate title page unless your instructor requests one; ask your instructor for specific formatting directions.
First page	In the top left corner, 1 inch from the top of the page, type your full name, your instructor's name, the course name, and the date, each on a separate line. Double-space these lines. Double-space again, and then center your paper's title (see sample paper on p. 371).
Title	Capitalize the first, last, and all significant words in the title. Do not italicize the title; only use italics or quotation marks if you are including the name of another published work in your title. Double-space all titles longer than one line. If you have a title and a subtitle, separate the title from the subtitle with a colon.
Italics	Italicize the titles of books. For shorter works such as short stories or magazine articles, uses quotation marks around the titles.
Clarifying words	Use brackets around words or phrases that must be added within a quotation to clarify meaning or make verb tense or form consistent.

In-Text Citations

For every piece of information, idea, or reference used in your paper that comes from someone else, you must include a parenthetical citation. This means providing the name of the author(s) and/or the title of the work and the relevant page number(s) in parentheses immediately after the information you use. This brief citation refers to an entry in the Works Cited list at the end of the paper; this list provides the reader with detailed information about each source. Here is an overview of the most common in-text citations.

Print Sources

Text by one author

- **Author named in text:** If you name the author in your introduction to a quotation, paraphrase, or summary, include both his or her first and last names the first time you mention him or her, and include only the page number(s) in the parenthetical citation:

> Michael Dorris, in his novel *A Yellow Raft in Blue Water*, writes, "My school in Seattle was better than the Mission, and I know more than anyone expects" (46).

If you mention the author again in your text, use only his or her last name.

▶ **NOTE** If you use more than one work by the same author, include an abbreviated version of the title in your citation.

> When the character first realizes she's in love, she struggles with the emotion: "Your love is newly born, the first page in a blank notebook" (Allende, *Paula*, 77).

- **Author not named in text:** If you do not name the author in your introductory sentence, list the last name of the author and the page number(s) of the source in your citation:

> The character is very self-aware: "My school in Seattle was better than the Mission, and I know more than anyone expects" (Dorris 46).

Text by two or three authors If a text is by two or three authors, you can include their full names in the body of the text:

> Julie Moore, Lori Vail, and Amanda Schaefer write that the "students in composition classes at our university are looking for solid information and explicit examples" (51).

Or include their last names in the citation:

> In contrast, the "students in composition classes at our university are looking for solid information and explicit examples" (Moore, Vail, and Schaefer 51).

Text by three or more authors For three or more authors, either list the authors' names in your introductory sentence or include the first author's last name followed by the Latin term "et al." (meaning "and others") and the page number(s) in the parenthetical citation:

> In contrast, the "students in composition classes at our university are looking for solid information and explicit examples" (Moore et al. 51).

Two different authors with the same last name Distinguish between two authors with the same last name by using their first initials, or by using their whole first names if they share the same first initial:

> (B. Smith 22) or (Brenda Smith 22)

Works with no author listed   Include the first one to three words of the title (or the whole title if it is short enough) in the parentheses followed by the page number(s):

> Many people "learn by getting involved, by putting their hands in and engaging in a task with another" ("Learning by Touch" 38).

Work from an anthology   When you quote a selection from an anthology, cite the name of the author, not the name of the editor of the anthology; you will provide the editor and anthology information in the Works Cited list. For example, if you were quoting the short story "In Roseau" by Jamaica Kincaid from the *Best American Short Stories* anthology, your citation would look like this:

> She writes, "My father had inherited the ghostly paleness of his own father" (Kincaid 196).

Works by a corporation, government agency, or other group author   If you mention the name of an organization in your introductory sentence, only include the page number(s) in parentheses:

> According to a study conducted in 2007 by the Department of Transportation, "Most people who carpool do so less than four times a week" (4).

If you do not mention the organization in your sentence, include its name and the page number in your parenthetical citation:

> In fact, "Most people who carpool do so less than four times a week" (Department of Transportation 4).

Verse dramas/plays   Provide the title of the play in the sentence, and then cite the act, scene, and line number(s), separated by periods, in the parenthetical citation. Do not use Roman numerals.

> In Sam Shepard's play, *Action*, one of the main characters, Jeep, starts the play with an intriguing statement: "I'm looking forward to my life. I'm looking forward to uh—me. The way I picture me" (1.1.1–2).

Poetry   If you use the name of the poet in your introductory sentence, list just the line number(s) in the citation:

> In Sylvia Plath's poem "Daddy," she writes these powerful lines: "Daddy, I have had to kill you. / You died before I had time—" (lines 6–7).

If you do not mention the author in your introductory sentence, then cite the author's last name and the line number(s) in your citation:

> The narrator in the poem says, "Daddy, I have had to kill you. / You died before I had time—" (Plath 6–7).

Indirect citations   If you quote someone quoting someone else, use the abbreviation "qtd. in" to indicate that it is an indirect quote. Use the full name of the person you are quoting in the body of the sentence before the quote and place the name of the author of the source in the parenthetical citation, preceded by "qtd. in":

> Connor Murphy asserts, "One must always portray pride in his or her heritage, no matter what happened in the past" (qtd. in Kennedy 228).

Reference entry from a dictionary or encyclopedia   If the entry does not credit a specific author, use the title of the entry in your citation:

> Bioluminescence is "light produced by a chemical reaction within an organism" ("Bioluminescence" 203).

Sacred/religious texts   When you quote from a religious text, use the title of the book in your introductory sentence or in the citation the first time you refer to it. Identify specifically where a quotation came from using book, verse, and line numbers. For example, if you quote from the Bible, include the name of the book and the chapter and verse number(s) in the citation: (Revelation 10:14). It is also acceptable to include an abbreviated code for the version of the Bible you are citing, for instance, *KJV* stands for King James Version:

> (KJV, Genesis 1:1–5)

Electronic Sources

You must cite information found in databases, on CD-ROMs, or on the Internet. Give the author's name(s), if provided; if not, give the title of the material. If the electronic source is paginated, then provide a page number.

Author named in source   If the work has an author and uses page numbers, then follow the rules for parenthetical citations outlined above:

> In fact, "The housing market is so dismal that sellers are desperate for any halfway decent offer" (Cranston 1).

Author not named in source   If the work has no author but does have a title and page numbers, then use a shortened version of the title in the citation:

> In fact, "The housing market is so dismal that sellers are desperate for any halfway decent offer" ("Hostile Housing Market" 1).

Page numbers not included in source   If the source does not include page numbers but does use paragraph numbers, include the relevant paragraph number(s) in your parenthetical citation. If there are no page or paragraph numbers, just use the author's name in the citation:

> In fact, "The housing market is so dismal that sellers are desperate for any halfway decent offer" ("Hostile Housing Market" para. 5).

No information available   If there is no article name, no author, and no page number or other information and you are using just a fact or statistic from a Web site, then include the address of the Web site in your parenthetical citation:

> In fact, 23.1 million homeowners have refinanced since April 9, 2013 (www.HUD.gov).

Compiling a Works Cited List

Every work or idea that you cite parenthetically in your paper must also be included in the Works Cited section at the end of your paper. Here are some guidelines for formatting your Works Cited page.

Formatting Your Works Cited Page

1. **Start your list on a new page at the end of your paper.** Center the title, Works Cited, 1 inch below the top of the page (but be sure to put your last name and the page number in the upper right-hand corner as on the other pages of your paper). Do not bold the Works Cited title, put it in quotation marks, or make it a larger font.

2. **Double-space everything.** Double-space between the title and the first entry and between and within all entries.

3. **Align and indent entries.** Align the first line of each entry flush with the left margin of the page, and indent each subsequent line of the entry five spaces (one tab) from the margin (sometimes called "hanging indent format"). Do not number the entries.

4. **Alphabetize the Works Cited list by authors' last names.** If a work has a corporate or group author, list it alphabetically by the first word of the name of the organization. If a work does not have an author, alphabetize it by the first word of the title (but ignore *A*, *An*, or *The*).

5. **If you have two or more works by the same author**, use three hyphens ("---") in place of the author's name in the second and subsequent entries by the same author. Alphabetize by title.

Erdrich, Louise. *Love Medicine*. New York: Bantam, 1984. Print.
---. *Tracks*. New York: Harper, 1989. Print.

6. **If a work has an editor or translator, be sure to include that information.** If a work has a named author, list that name first, then the title, followed by either the abbreviation "Ed." for editor or "Trans." for translator and then that person's first and last name, followed by a period.

Ibsen, Henrik. *Three Plays: The Pillars of the Community, The Wild Duck, Hedda Gabler*. Trans. Una Ellis-Fermor. London: Penguin, 1950. Print.

If there is no author, list the name of the editor or translator first, followed by either the abbreviation "ed." or "trans." then the title and the publication information.

Galmish, Hank, ed. *White Whale Symbolism*. Auburn: Green River P, 2009. Print.

Common Works Cited Entries for Print Sources

Print sources such as books, magazines, journals, and newspapers usually provide thorough publication information. Use the following guidelines for Works Cited entries. For sources not included here, check the *MLA Handbook*, MLA Web site, or a composition handbook with a comprehensive MLA section.

Books There are six basic units of information to include for book entries: (1) name of author(s), last name first; (2) full title (italicized; if there is a subtitle include it after a colon); (3) city of publication; (4) name of publisher; (5) year of publication; (6) medium of publication.

Book by one author

> Erdrich, Louise. *Love Medicine*. New York: Bantam, 1984. Print.

Book by two or three authors: Reverse the name of the first author only:

> Moore, Julie, and Pamela Dusenberry. *Crossroads*. New York: Pearson, 2010. Print.

Book by four or more authors: Name only the first author listed and then add "et al." or you may list all the authors in the order they appear in the original source:

> Moore, Julie, et al. *Outcomes Assessment in the Community College*. New York: Pearson, 2009. Print.

Book with no author (alphabetize by the work's title):

> *A Complete Concordance to Shakespeare*. New York: Macmillan, 1969. Print.

Articles from Scholarly Journals There are seven basic units of information needed for journal articles: (1) name of the author(s), last name first; (2) full title of the article in quotation marks; (3) full name of the journal in italics; (4) volume and issue number; (5) year of publication; (6) page number(s) of the article; (7) medium of publication.

> Martin, Joann. "Teens in College." *Community College News* 18.5 (2009): 22–34. Print.

Magazine Articles   There are six basic units of information needed for magazine articles: (1) name of the author(s), last name first; (2) full title of the article in quotation marks; (3) full title of the magazine in italics; (4) day, month, and year of publication with no punctuation between them (abbreviate all months except for May, June, and July); (5) page number(s) of the article; (6) medium of publication.

> Perkins, Connor. "The Dynamics of Machoism." *Gendered Times* 24 May 2008: 48–63. Print.

Articles, Editorials, and Letters from Newspapers   There are six basic units of information needed for newspaper articles: (1) name of author(s), last name first; (2) full title of the article in quotation marks; (3) full title of newspaper in italics; (4) day, month, and year of publication with no punctuation between them (abbreviate all months except for May, June, and July); (5) section letter or number and page number(s) of the article; (6) medium of publication.

> Musselmann, Rachel. "A New Park for Dogs." *Monrovia Times* 12 May 2009: A5. Print.

▶ **NOTE**   If the entry from a newspaper is an editorial, type the word "Editorial" after the name of the article followed by a period and a space. If it is a letter to the editor, type the word "Letter" after the author's name, followed by a period and a space.

Selection from an Anthology   There are nine basic units of information needed for a selection from an anthology (a poem, story, play, essay, or article): (1) name of author(s), last name first; (2) title of the selection in quotation marks; (3) title of the anthology, italicized; (4) name(s) of the editor(s), preceded by "Ed." or "Eds."; (5) city of publication; (6) name of publisher; (7) year of publication; (8) page numbers; (9) medium of publication.

> Shelley, Percy Bysshe. "Ozymandias." *The Longman Anthology of British Literature, Volume 2A.* Eds. David Damrosch and Keven J. H. Dettmar. New York: Pearson Longman, 2006. 823. Print.

Articles in Reference Books   Use the following guidelines for citing articles in reference books:

- **Author named in text:** If the author's name is given, list that first, then the title of the article in quotation marks, followed by the title of the work from which it came (in italics). If the entries are arranged alphabetically, do not list the volume or page numbers. For commonly used reference works, particularly ones that are regularly revised, just give the edition number and years of publication followed by the medium, *Print.*

> Wells, Cathy. "Chinese Civil War." *Encyclopædia Britannica.* 15th ed. 2010. Print.

- **Author not named in text:** If the author is not named, begin the entry with the article title.

> "Chinese Civil War." *Encyclopædia Britannica.* 15th ed. 2010. Print.

Common Works Cited Entries for Electronic Sources

Three different kinds of electronic sources are databases supplied on CD-ROM or DVD, databases accessed online, and Web sites accessed through search engines like Google.

CD-ROM and DVD-ROM Databases   Use the following guidelines for citing information accessed from CD-ROM or DVD-ROM databases:

- **Nonperiodical CD-ROM or DVD databases:** Information accessed from a single-issue CD-ROM (one that is only produced once, like a print version dictionary, book, or encyclopedia) should be cited in the same way as a book, with the medium "Print" replaced by "CD-ROM" or "DVD-ROM." If the disc is produced by a vendor other than the publisher of the material, provide the vendor's name and the date of electronic publication after the medium.

> "Aristotle." *The Complete Works of Aristotle: The Revised Oxford Translation.* Ed. Jonathan Barnes. 2 vols. Princeton: Princeton UP, 1984. CD-ROM. Auburn: Proquest, 2010.

- **Periodical CD-ROM or DVD databases:** Information accessed from a periodical CD-ROM (one that contains newspaper, journal, and other articles and is issued once or twice a year) should be cited the same way as the equivalent print version, but "Print" should be replaced by CD-ROM or DVD-ROM, followed by the title of the database (in italics), the vendor's name, and the date of publication (month and year).

> Marshall, Patrick. "Cybersecurity: Are US Military and Civilian Computer Systems Safe?" *CQ Press.* Feb. 2010: 16+ CD-ROM. *GRCC-CQ Researcher Online.* Feb. 2010.

Online Databases   When you cite sources from online databases, include as many of the following elements as possible:

1. **Name of author(s):** If the name of the author (or authors) is provided, start the citation with it, last name first.

2. **Name of article or entry:** Provide the title of the article. If no author is listed, alphabetize the entry by the title.

3. **Name of source:** Include the name of the source (magazine, newspaper, and so on).

4. **Date of publication:** Next, list the date the material was first published, using the format day month year.

5. **Page numbers:** If the page numbers are given, place them after the date and a colon. If pages are all in sequence, list them all: for example, 1–10. If page numbers aren't in sequence, give just the first page number followed by a plus sign with no space between them: 2+. If no page numbers are listed, use the abbreviation *n. pag.*

6. **Name of database:** Provide the name of the database in italics.

7. **Medium of publication:** Then list the medium of publication: Web.

8. **Date the source was accessed:** Include the date you accessed the source, for example, 7 Dec. 2008. Abbreviate the names of all months except May, June, and July.

> Barrera, Rebeca María. "A Case for Bilingual Education." *Scholastic Parent and Child* 12.3 (2004): 72–73. *EBSCOhost.* Web. 1 Feb. 2009.

Web Sites   Give as much information as necessary to direct the reader to the original online source. Include all of the following information that is available:

1. **Names of the author(s):** If there is an author (or authors) credited, start the citation with it, last name first.

2. **Title of the article:** Provide the full title. If there is no author listed, alphabetize the Works Cited entry by the title.

3. **Name of Web site:** Provide the name of the Web site, in italics, if it is different from the title of the article.

4. **Version or edition number:** If such a number is given, provide it. "Rev. ed.," for instance, means "revised edition."

5. **Publisher or sponsor of the Web site:** If not given, use the abbreviation *n.p.* for "no publisher."

6. **Date of electronic publication:** If not given, use the abbreviation *n.d.* for "no date."

7. **Medium of publication:** Web.

8. **Date of access:** Give the date you accessed the site. Use the day month year format.

9. **URL:** Only provide the URL for sources that readers won't be able to find using the information provided in the citation. For example, if you can type the name of the Web site into the Google search box, go to that site, and search the Web site to find the particular page you are citing, then you don't need to include the URL in your citation.

> Bernstein, Mark. "10 Tips on Writing the Living Web." *A List Apart: For People Who Make Websites.* A List Apart Magazine, 16 Aug. 2002. Web. 4 May 2009.

Many professional and nonprofessional, private Web sites do not provide all the information listed above. The key is to include as many of the nine elements as possible in the order they are listed. For complicated or difficult-to-access online sources, go to www.mla.org for more information on citing online and Internet-based sources.

MLA-Style Student Paper

Willey 1

Acacia Willey

Professor Moore

English 100

11 May 2009

Students or Objects?

When was the last time you walked into a school and didn't see a soda machine? Six years ago, the first soda machine was installed on my middle school campus. Kids from every building raced to the cafeteria the second the recess bell rang. They were all waiting for the same thing: to pay a dollar for a twenty-ounce sugar drink. Kids darted to the cafeteria as if their clothes were on fire. Teachers rewarded good behavior by allowing kids to go to recess early, letting them get a better spot in line. Forget the "no running indoors rule." All that mattered was getting in that line. Michael Moore, a filmmaker and author, wrote *Stupid White Men* to criticize the hold corporations have on the young people of this country. Another man, John Gatto, who has been named New York City teacher of the year three times, quit teaching recently, claiming that he didn't want to hurt children anymore. He has since become a public speaker about school reform, expressing his opinions on the school system through books and media appearances. One thing that Gatto and Moore agree on is that corporations should not be allowed to play such a big role in children's education.

Michael Moore points out the huge role of corporations in schools, starting with one of the biggest corporate involvements, the agreements made between schools and the three biggest soda companies. He writes, "Two hundred and forty school districts in thirty-one states have sold exclusive rights to one of the big three soda companies (Coca Cola, Pepsi, Dr. Pepper) to push their product in schools" (Moore 165). Due to these agreements, schools are obligated to sell a certain amount of soda. This is good for the soda companies because they can sell their products at higher prices, and, more importantly, they can heavily promote their product to students. Many students will drink whatever is available, regardless of whether they really enjoy it, but after drinking the soda every day they start to like it, get addicted to the sugar, and begin to crave it. Moore continues, explaining how Pizza Hut targets students: "When students meet the monthly reading goal, they are rewarded with a certificate for a Pizza Hut personal pan pizza" (165). Pizza Hut does encourage students to read, but

Willey 3

they are far from good: They reward students with a pizza, a not very healthy food. Like soda, the free pizza hooks students to the product and the company, and soon they will spend their own money (or their parents') for Pizza Hut pizzas.

Gatto agrees with Moore's argument that corporations play too big a role in education. He writes, "The experts make all the important choices; only I, the teacher, can determine what my kids must study, or rather, only the people who pay me can make those decisions" (176). Therefore, if the principal encourages the selling of soda, then that is what the teachers teach, urging their students to purchase it. The soda companies pay the schools to teach their students to drink the soda companies' products. Schools make these agreements with soda companies and other corporations because they get great deals, and they just don't think about how badly it affects their students' long-term eating habits and health.

Moore also explains how schools force their students to support the corporation. He writes, "When Mike Cameron wore a Pepsi shirt on 'Coke Day' . . . he was suspended for a day. . . . Cameron was suspended for 'being disruptive and trying to ruin a school photo' . . . the shirt was visible all day, but he didn't get in trouble until posing for the picture" (166). The school officials explained that he was suspended for ruining a photo of students spelling out the word "Coke." However, it seems more like the majority of the students did exactly as they were told and supported Coca Cola, but school officials felt there was one bad seed who did not. This occurrence made the school look bad in front of their "boss," also known as the Coca Cola Company. Companies like Coca Cola often obtain power over schools (become "the boss") because they donate money to schools for supplies or become a "corporate sponsor" for a school, as long as the school visibly promotes their product. In this case, to prevent bad feelings between their school and Coca Cola, officials suspended the student who expressed a different, but nonharmful opinion.

Gatto also discusses in his article how students are forced to believe what they are told. He writes, "I teach kids to surrender their will to the predestined chain of command. Rights may be granted or withheld by any authority without appeal because rights do not exist inside a school" (178). Gatto feels that students are not allowed the right to form their own opinions; teachers explain exactly what they want the students to know. In this case, it is that Coca Cola, Pepsi, or Dr. Pepper are the best soft drinks, and they should drink whichever is approved by the school. Failure to agree results in the student being labeled as "the bad kid" by their classmates and teachers. Rejection of these brands can also possibly result in trips to the principal's office.

Corporations have been involved with children's education for too long. As the years go by, children become adults who believe it is necessary to buy from large corporations. Why do you think "The Astrodome," home of the Houston Astros, was renamed "Minute Maid Park"? The point of education is to teach children to be successful in life by giving them the skills they need, including the ability to think for themselves. Being told that one company is better because it gives you the most money is not a skill children should learn or a skill they need. Schools need to find other sources of funding. Parents should get more involved in fundraising, and companies should sponsor schools anonymously, without expecting their products to be visible on campus. Students' opinions and tastes should not be for sale.

Willey 5

Works Cited

Gatto, John Taylor. *Dumbing Us Down*. New York: New Society
   Publishers, 1992. Print.

Moore, Michael. *Stupid White Men*. Los Angeles: Regan Books,
   2001. Print.

USING AMERICAN PSYCHOLOGICAL ASSOCIATION (APA) FORMAT

6 Use correct APA format.

APA (American Psychological Association) format is a documentation style used most often for the social sciences. Like the MLA-style format, the APA style has two main components: in-text citations and a References page at the end that lists all sources cited in your paper.

In-Text Citations

APA style in-text citations include the author and date. If you use the author name(s) in your running text, place just the date in parentheses.

Without author name(s) in your sentence:

Victims of emotional abuse often will emotionally abuse their own children later (Jones & Perkins, 2010).

With author name(s) in your sentence:

Jones and Perkins (2010) find that victims of emotional abuse often will emotionally abuse their own children later.

Two or more references cited within the same parentheses: If you cite two or more works by different authors within the same parentheses, list them alphabetically in the same order in which they appear in your References list, and separate the citations with semicolons:

Several studies (Johnson & Bahl, 2011; Wood, 2012) show that this syndrome is a cycle that is difficult to overcome.

Print Sources

Author(s) listed: In-text citations consist of the last name(s) of the author(s) and the year of publication.

No author listed: If there is no author, use the title (if the title is long, use a short form of the title) and the year. Titles that are italicized in the References list are italicized in text; titles that are not italicized in the References list appear in quotation marks in the text.

No date listed: If there is no date, use "n.d." (without quotation marks) instead.

Web Sites

For a casual, general reference to a Web site in text (no specific information shared), the URL is sufficient; also, no References entry is needed.

> Some people even meet in online chat rooms to discuss their love of cats (http://www.catcraze.com).

However, when you cite a particular document or piece of information from a Web site, include both an in-text citation and an entry in your References list.

The **in-text citation** should include the author and date, as with any other APA-style citation.

> The city of Monrovia, California, is considering adding a new dog park that will cost the city over half a million dollars (Musselman, 2012).

References List

Your References list should appear at the end of your paper, and it must include all the sources you cited in your paper. Like the Works Cited list in MLA style, the References section provides the information necessary for a reader to locate any source you cite in the body of the paper. Also, your References list should begin on a new page separate from the text of the essay. Center the title "References" at the top of the page (do not bold, underline, italicize, or use quotation marks for the title). All text in the References should be double-spaced just like the rest of your essay.

Basic Rules for an APA References Page

- Double-space the entire list.
- Use the hanging indentation format: The first line of each entry should align flush with the left margin and all subsequent lines should be indented one-half inch from the left margin.
- Authors' names are inverted (last name first). List the last name and initials for all authors of a work, up to and including seven authors. If the work has more than seven authors, list the first six authors, an ellipsis, and the last author's name.
- Alphabetize entries by the last name of the first author of each work.
- For multiple articles by the same author(s), list the entries in chronological order, from earliest to most recent.
- Give the full journal titles.
- Maintain the punctuation and capitalization that is used in the original book, article, or journal title.
- When the original title is not formatted, capitalize only the first word of the title.
- Italicize titles of books and journals. Do not italicize, underline, or put quotes around the titles of journal articles or essays in edited collections.
- Proofread and edit your References for correct spelling and punctuation.

For more information, see the *Publication Manual of the American Psychological Association, Sixth Edition*, or go to www.apastyle.org.

Basic Information for References Entries

There are four basic units of information that should always be included in a References entry, no matter the type of source:

1. **Names of the author(s):** If there is an author's name (or authors'), start the citation with it, last name first.
2. **Date of publication:** If not given, use the abbreviation *n.d.* for "no date."
3. **Title of the article:** Provide the full title. If there is no author listed, alphabetize the entry by the title.
4. **Source of publication:** publisher, journal or magazine name, Web site, and so on.

▶ **NOTE** The following rules for handling works by a single author or multiple authors apply to all APA-style references in your References list, regardless of the type of work (book, article, electronic resource, etc.).

Here are a few examples of the most common sources for References page entries:

Book by a single author List by author's last name, first initial. Then add year/date in parentheses, the italicized name of the book set in lowercase (except the first word, proper nouns, and the first word after a colon), the city and state or country, and name of the publisher.

> Sims, M. (2014). *The write stuff: Thinking through essays*. Upper Saddle River, NJ: Pearson.

Book by two authors List authors by their last names and initials. Use the ampersand between authors' names instead of "and."

> Moore, J., & Dusenberry, P. (2010). *Crossroads*. Upper Saddle River, NJ: Pearson.

Article by a single author Authors are listed by last name followed by initials; place the year of publication in parentheses, followed by a period. In the title of the article, only the first word and proper nouns are capitalized. The periodical title is followed by the volume number, and both are italicized.

> Martin, J. (2009). Teens in college. *Community College News, 18*(22), 22–34.

Article by two authors List authors by their last names and initials. Use the ampersand between authors' names instead of "and."

> Martin, J., & Petersen, L. (2009). Teens in college. *Community College News, 18*(22), 22–34.

Work by three to seven authors   List authors by their last names and initials; use commas to separate author names; place an ampersand before the last author name.

> Moreno, M., Katims, K., Hoene, J., Johanson, S., Howe, B. H., & Wood, J. S. (2011).

Two or more works by the same author   Use the author's name for all entries and list entries chronologically (earliest comes first).

References that have the same first author and different second or third authors are arranged alphabetically by the last name of the second author, or the last name of the third if the first and second authors are the same.

> Mommer, E., & Murphy, T. C. (2012). Small group dynamics. *Journal of Higher Education, 108*, 101–112.
> Mommer, E., & Paul, R. T. (2012). Interactive sociology classrooms. *Journal of Higher Education, 106*, 63–71.

Organization as author

> American Psychological Association. (2010).

Article in a magazine

> Peters, W. B. (2010, April 16). Looking at elections. *Time, 182*, 16–24.

Article in a newspaper   Unlike other periodicals, *p.* or *pp.* precedes page numbers for a newspaper reference in APA style. Single pages take *p.*, for example, *p. B2*; multiple pages take *pp.*, for example, *pp. B2, B4* or *pp. C1, C3–C4.*

> Miller, Jordan. (2012, February 20). Evaluating the texting debate. *USA Today*, pp. 2A, 3B.

Article from an Online Periodical Online articles follow the same guidelines for printed articles. Include all information the online host makes available, including volume and issue numbers and digital object identifiers (DOIs).

> Szalavitz, M. (2013, June 27). Unique brain pattern could predict autism in youngest children. *Time*. doi:10.xxxx/xxxxxxxx

If no digital object identifier is available, give the URL instead.

> Szalavitz, M. (2013, June 27). Unique brain pattern could predict autism in youngest children. *Time*. Retrieved from http://healthland .time.com/2013/06/27/unique-brain-pattern-could-predict-autism-in-youngest-children/

Electronic books Electronic books may include books found on Web sites, in online classes, databases, or even in audio form. As with print books, include the publication date in parentheses after the author's name. At the end of the entry, give the digital object identifier (DOI) or, if no DOI is available, the URL.

> Sims, M. (2011). *The write stuff: Thinking through paragraphs.* doi:10.xxxx/xxxxxxxx
> Sims, M. (2011). *The write stuff: Thinking through paragraphs.* Retrieved from http://digital.library.grcc.edu/thewritestuff.html

Online Encyclopedias, Dictionaries, and Bibliographies Often encyclopedias, dictionaries, and bibliographies do not provide bylines (authors' names). If an author is named, list the author(s) first. When no author is credited, start the citation with the article title. Provide publication dates if available or use (n.d.) if the source gives no date. At the end of the entry, give the digital object identifier (DOI) or URL if no DOI is available.

> Blogging. (n.d.). In Encyclopædia Britannica online. doi:10.xxxx/xxxxxxxx
> Blogging. (n.d.). In Encyclopædia Britannica online. Retrieved from http://www.britannica.com/blogging

ACTIVITY 16-2   Using APA Style

Directions: *Using the MLA-Style Student Paper on pages 371–375, locate the first three in-text citations and rewrite them in APA style.*

1. MLA: _____

   APA: _____

2. MLA: _____

   _____

   _____

   APA: _____

   _____

   _____

3. MLA: _____

   _____

   _____

   _____

   APA: _____

   _____

   _____

   _____

Now revise the Works Cited list on page 375 into an APA-style References list.

_____

_____

_____

Learning Objectives Review

❶ Write a documented paper.

What are the ten steps for writing a documented paper? (See pp. 347–349.)

The **ten steps for writing a documented paper** are (1) select a subject and narrow it to a manageable topic; (2) do preliminary reading; (3) write a preliminary thesis; (4) prepare a working outline; (5) research and take notes; (6) check notes for information gaps; (7) fine-tune the essay's proposed structure and organization and modify your arguments and thesis, if necessary; (8) write a first draft; (9) prepare the Works Cited page; and (10) revise, edit, and proofread.

❷ Distinguish types of sources.

What are the three general types of sources? (See pp. 349–350.)

Three types of sources include: (1) **Reference sources,** such as dictionary or encyclopedia entries that you can use to explain or develop a term or concept in your paper. (2) **Primary sources,** which are original sources such as journals, essays, novels, poems, stories, historical accounts, blogs, and so on. (3) **Secondary sources,** materials written about or in response to primary, original sources such as summaries, critical analyses, and reviews.

❸ Find, evaluate, and integrate sources.

How do you find, evaluate, and integrate sources? (See pp. 350–358.)

You can **find sources** by searching *libraries, databases,* and the *Internet;* you can **evaluate sources** by asking questions about their reliability and content; and you can **integrate sources** using *paraphrasing, summary,* and *quotation,* as well as the ice cream sandwich technique.

4 Avoid plagiarism.

What is plagiarism, and how can you avoid it? (See pp. 358–360.)

Plagiarism is taking someone else's words, ideas, or concepts and using them as if they are your own. You can **avoid plagiarism** by carefully documenting all sources of information in your notes (enclose direct quotes in quotation marks and note page numbers); citing your sources every time you quote, paraphrase, summarize, or discuss another person's ideas in your papers; using your own words and style when you paraphrase; and providing a complete Works Cited list.

5 Use correct MLA format.

What is the MLA documentation format? (See pp. 360–375.)

MLA (Modern Language Association) format is a documentation style used in the humanities that provides specific guidelines for formatting papers. It has two main features: in-text parenthetical citations and a Works Cited list that provides detailed source information and is arranged in alphabetical order.

6 Use correct APA format.

What is the APA documentation format? (See pp. 375–381.)

APA (American Psychological Association) format is a documentation style used most often for the social sciences. The two main features of the APA documentation style are in-text citations (author name(s) and year of publication) and a References list that provides detailed source information and is arranged in alphabetical order.

LEARNING OBJECTIVES

In this chapter, you will learn how to

1 Write critically about images.

2 Identify similarities between analyzing an image and analyzing a text.

3 Actively read visuals.

4 Ask critical thinking questions about a variety of visuals.

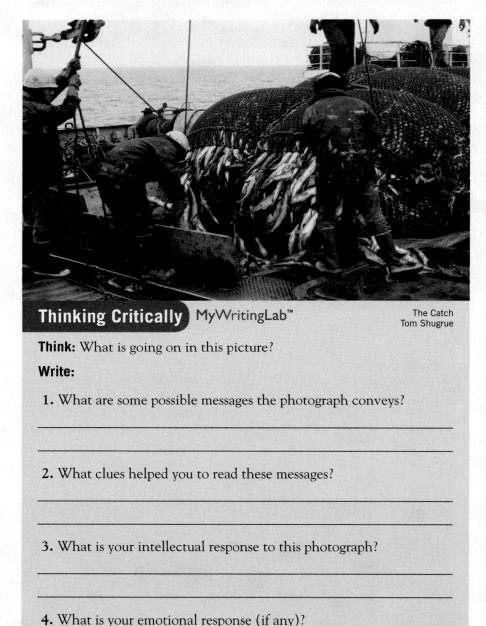

Thinking Critically MyWritingLab™

The Catch
Tom Shugrue

Think: What is going on in this picture?

Write:

1. What are some possible messages the photograph conveys?

_____

_____

2. What clues helped you to read these messages?

_____

_____

3. What is your intellectual response to this photograph?

_____

_____

4. What is your emotional response (if any)?

_____

_____

VISUAL COMMUNICATION AND CRITICAL THINKING

1 Write critically about images.

Pictures are an essential part of human communication. They are a universal language. From ancient cave paintings and petroglyphs to modern emoticons, visuals communicate quickly, and more complex visuals like photographs or cartoons can have several layers of meaning. Platforms for visual communication abound: magazines, TV, movies, billboards, and the Internet. Some visuals deliver a more effective argument or evoke a more immediate emotional response than a sentence or essay so read them as actively as you would a passage of text.

Like words, images can be thoughtful, truthful, misleading, or even deceitful in representing ideas and arguments. Visuals often have a clear thesis, or argument, that the creator wants you to infer. Graphic designers, photographers, advertisers, and so on employ particular approaches and include specific clues to help impart their intended messages. Therefore, when you write about visuals, use the same critical thinking and analysis skills you use to write about readings. When you write an essay about a single visual or a set of visuals, pay attention to the same elements that you use in writing other essays—purpose, organization, support, examples, and details—in order to present an argument.

Visuals *imply* the messages their creators intend, and viewers of the images *infer* these meanings from the visuals.

Visual (and sender)

↕

Implies a message

Viewer (receiver)

↕

Infers a message (based on clues)

APPLYING CRITICAL THINKING

| PURPOSE | IDEAS | SUPPORT | ASSUMPTIONS BIASES | CONCLUSIONS | POINT OF VIEW | ANALYSIS |

Since visuals are created to send a message—sometimes simple, sometimes quite complex—you need to read below the surface and look carefully at both the direct and indirect messages. Advertisements or political campaign ads can even try to manipulate their viewers with propaganda and biased premises.

Imply/implication: To imply information means to hint at something, to say it indirectly. When advertisers imply what they want to say in an ad, they make choices about what they will and will not include in order to convey their message. They might present an image from an unusual angle, place contrasting images together, omit parts of an object, or add elements you would not expect to see.

Continued ▶

Inference:	To infer information from a visual involves tapping into your ability to "read between the lines" and figure out what an image means based on the clues contained within it. When you think critically about a visual, you need to look for clues that indicate the point its creator is making.
Assumptions and biases:	Check what **assumptions** are embedded in the visual. Also, what **biases** does the artist demonstrate in this image?

Use your **analysis** skills to break down all parts of the image and evaluate the implications, inferences, and biases.

Visuals invite a dialogue with the viewers. An image sends a message, but the viewers create their own versions of the message through their intellectual and emotional responses to it. Viewers bring their own personal history, knowledge, and associations to the reading of visual clues just as they do to reading written text.

When you study visuals, you must study all the clues they present. Like words, visuals can have clear **denotative**, or exact, meanings, and they can have **connotative**, or implied, meanings and associations. You need to fill in the blanks, draw conclusions, and determine your intellectual and emotional responses (if any) to the image. You must also study the form and conventions of the image and the medium the creator has chosen in order to interpret its messages and implied arguments. Sometimes, you must even study what is left out and why.

SIMILARITIES BETWEEN ANALYZING TEXT AND VISUALS

2 Identify similarities between analyzing an image and analyzing a text.

There are many parallels between analyzing a visual and analyzing text:

1. Visuals have a message: a thesis or argument. They have a **purpose**. Ask yourself, "What is this visual's message or implied argument?"

2. Visuals express a particular **point of view** and can display the **biases** of the creator. Ask yourself, "What is the artist's point of view, and what biases, if any, does he or she expose in the visual?"

3. Visuals include clues (or details) related to their main point and are designed to impart those clues as effectively as possible. Ask yourself, "What support and details are included in the visual to support its purpose?" and "What clues in this visual provide evidence for my interpretation of the messages and biases?"

4. Visuals may need to be viewed in their historical or cultural contexts in order to be fully understood. You must **analyze** their parts.

5. Visuals can appeal both to the viewer's intellect and emotions. The artist may intentionally manipulate the viewers' emotions to change their point of view on a subject.

Just as logos and pathos apply to arguments made in writing, they are also at work in visual arguments. **Logos** is an appeal to reasoning and logic; therefore, most academic writing contains logos. Many photographs, especially documentary or news photographs, also contain logos. **Pathos** is an appeal to emotion. Many photographs contain pathos. Advertisements and political campaigns and cartoons, for example, are notorious for using visuals to appeal to our emotions in order to sell products or ideas.

Cross Reference
See Chapter 14, pp. 310–311, Logical Fallacies.

READ VISUALS ACTIVELY

3 Actively read visuals.

Images can be straightforward or complex. They can scream a message like "Buy me!" or they can work more subtly on your brain or your emotions to achieve their desired effect. When you analyze images, ask specific questions such as *What? How? Why? Who? When? Where?* and *So what?* Look for clues as a good visual detective should; don't just look at images passively. Also, pay attention to every detail within the image: size, color, shape, medium, approach, content, and historical or cultural background.

VISUAL DETECTIVE CHECKLIST

This Visual Checklist gives you some basic questions to ask when you analyze the techniques used to convey direct and implied messages in all types of visuals.

1. What is the purpose of this image (for example, to inform, to persuade, to move viewers emotionally).

2. What support did the artist use to create the message (what artistic choices and details are included in the image)? What clues are visual evidence of the intended message(s)?

3. Who is the intended audience for this image (general? specific? if so, list)?

4. Does the image appeal to logic (logos), emotions (pathos), or both? How so? What did you think when you first viewed this image? What did you feel?

5. What are the strengths or advantages of the type of image chosen?

Continued ▶

6. What are the weaknesses or limitations, if any?

7. What are the *direct* messages of the image?

8. What are the *indirect* or implied messages of this visual?

9. Ask *What? How? Why? Who? When? Where?* questions to check for all the clues. Include any historical or social context you may know about the image.

10. What is the image's overall thesis or argument? Did it achieve its goal?

ACTIVITY 17-1   Applying Questions to an Image

Directions: *Look at the advertisement and answer the questions that follow. If needed, refer to the information provided earlier in this chapter for help.*

1. Does this advertisement appeal more to your sense of logos (logic), pathos (emotion), or both? Explain your answer.

_____

2. Answer briefly (in a few words or a short sentence) each of these analytical questions for this advertisement: *What* is being advertised and what is the message? *How* did you determine that? *Why* is the image arranged this way? *Who* is the intended audience? *What* details stand out, and why?

_____

3. How do the color, shapes, and background of this photograph add to the message?

_____

ANALYZING VARIOUS TYPES OF VISUALS

4 Ask critical thinking questions about a variety of visuals.

Like essays, visuals such as political cartoons, photographs, advertisements, and video and film have ideas and arguments, and you can study their messages and techniques.

Political Cartoons

Political cartoons are powerful visual statements that always have a purpose: a political statement (message) with a clear bias. Usually, they reflect current political trends and conflicts. Since the printing press was invented, cartoons have been used to express political viewpoints, biases, and arguments. Most political cartoons try to sway or inform viewers.

Thinking Critically about Political Cartoons

Benjamin Franklin created the cartoon at the top of the next page in 1754, when some American colonies were still hesitant about joining the Revolution. Some critical thinking questions to ask about this image are

1. What do the labeled parts of the snake represent (be sure to look at the initials)?
2. How do the words (text) relate to the image?
3. What is Ben Franklin's message in this political cartoon?

Here's a modern example of a political cartoon. What are the direct and implied messages in this cartoon?

Monte Wolverton, The Wolverton, April 2006 TIC/Cagle Cartoons, Inc.

Critical Thinking Questions to Ask about Political Cartoons

1. What is the direct message of the cartoon?
2. What are the indirect or implied messages?
3. What are the visual details that serve as clues to the direct and/or implied messages? List them.
4. What intellectual response (logos) do you have to this ad?
5. What emotional response (pathos) do you have to this ad?

6. What arguments or appeals are embedded in this image?
7. How do the text (words) and the visuals work together to create the overall message?
8. In your opinion, is this an effective cartoon? Why, or why not?

ACTIVITY 17-2   Analyzing a Political Cartoon

Directions: *Look at the cartoon and answer the Critical Thinking Questions above on a separate sheet of paper. Then write a short essay analyzing the cartoon that first describes it in detail, then identifies its intended audience and direct and implied messages, and finally evaluates the overall effectiveness of its arguments.*

Mike Lane, *The Baltimore Sun*, October 2004 TIC/Cagle Cartoons, Inc.

Photographs

Photographs are a powerful form of visual communication. In many ways, they are like paragraphs: They pack a big message into a small space and develop the message through details and structure. Photographs can be art, or they can be used in news stories (print and online) to impart a visual message. Reactions to and interpretations of photographs are as varied as their viewers. The photographer, like a writer, determines what information you receive. He or she makes decisions about what to include and what not to include in a photograph. Also, photographers can digitally edit and manipulate photographs to show anything they want so photographs can easily deceive, although we often assume they show the truth. Thus, you view an image that has been created to make a specific point or to evoke a particular emotional response.

Thinking Critically about Photographs

A photograph should be analyzed for its composition (the arrangement of visual elements) and content (what's in it and the meaning evoked by it). The historical and social context of a photograph should also be carefully examined.

Critical Thinking Questions to Ask about Photographs

When you look at a photograph, ask these questions:

1. What is the purpose of this photograph (to inform, persuade, move emotionally)?

2. What is my overall reaction to this image? Is the photographer appealing to logos (logic), pathos (emotion), or both?

3. What details or elements has the photographer used to support the purpose (composition, lighting, background, setup, setting, featured subjects)?

4. Is there a particular social or historical context for this picture? If so, what effect does that have on your reaction to or understanding of the message(s)?

5. Does there seem to be an intended audience for this photo, or does it appeal to a broad audience?

ACTIVITY 17-3 Analyzing a Photograph

Directions: *Look at the photograph. Then answer the questions that follow. Also write a short essay about the photograph—see the writing prompt below.*

Small-Town Parade

1. What is happening in this photograph? Describe the subjects and their emotional state based on clues from the image.

2. What is the purpose of this photograph, and what details (support) from the picture create that impression?

3. **Essay Prompt:** Now, write a short essay that includes narration and description of the scene and your own analysis of the mood and potential messages of the photograph.

Advertisements

Advertisements come in many forms: television commercials, billboards, magazine and newspaper ads, ads at the movie theater, and so on. All advertisements have one basic thing in common: They attempt to sell a product to a carefully targeted audience. So analyzing an advertisement is similar to analyzing an author's argument in a piece of persuasive writing: You employ the same analysis skills. Advertisements use various visual details and techniques to generate conscious and sometimes subconscious (below the surface) responses from viewers. They can combine text and visuals or focus solely on either visuals or text.

Thinking Critically about Advertisements

In order to think critically about advertisements and analyze both their messages and the techniques used to impart those messages, you need to pay close attention to details and ask questions about everything included in the ad, as well as think about what is not included. All advertisements try to sell something, so most of them have a direct argument, but many also have implied arguments. Most advertisements use pathos, an appeal to your emotions, to sell their product. Most ads also sell a particular image and are intended for specific audiences.

Note the difference in approaches in advertisements and how they target audiences by gender, social class, economic status, race, age, region, political affiliations, and other factors, depending on the products they are selling. When analyzing advertisements, check for errors in logic or implied messages that deceive people into thinking that the product might do more than it actually can, such as a new car increasing one's sex appeal.

Critical Thinking Questions to Ask about Ads

Here are some questions to ask when analyzing ads:

1. What product or person (e.g., political candidate) is this advertisement designed to sell?

2. Who is the target audience for the ad? How do you know?

3. What is the direct message of the ad?

4. What are the indirect or implied messages of the ad?

5. What are the visual details that serve as clues to the direct and/or implied messages in this ad? List them.

6. What intellectual response do you have to this ad?

7. What emotional response do you have to this ad?

8. What arguments or appeals are embedded in this ad? Are deceptive or illogical messages implied by this ad?

9. To what cultural or historical ideas or norms does the ad allude? Look especially for references to race, gender, age, economic class, and region.

10. In your opinion, is this an effective ad? Why, or why not?

ACTIVITY 17-4 Analyzing an Advertisement

Directions: *Find an advertisement in a magazine or newspaper, and answer the Critical Thinking Questions above on a separate sheet of paper. Then write a short essay that analyzes the advertisement: first describe it in detail; then identify its intended audience and direct and implied messages; and finally evaluate the overall effectiveness of its arguments.*

Campaign Ads

Like political cartoons, campaign ads have clear biases and messages they want to convey to their audience. However, over the years, political campaign ads have become more and more about smearing the reputation of the opposing candidate and less about the issues or about the politician being endorsed by the campaign ad.

Thinking Critically about Campaign Ads

When viewing a political cartoon or campaign ad, ask the following questions: (1) What is this ad's **purpose?** (2) What **assumptions and biases** are obvious in this ad? Are those biases and assumptions logical and sound? (3) What **conclusions** does this ad draw about the candidate and/or his or her opponent? (4) Whose **point of view** does the ad express (the political party's? the candidate's? other?)? (5) Use your **analysis** skills to break down the parts of this ad. Is the ad guilty of any logical fallacies?

ACTIVITY 17-5 Analyzing a Campaign Ad

Directions: *Find a campaign ad from the last presidential election on the Internet and answer the Critical Thinking Questions above on a separate sheet of paper. Then write a short essay that analyzes the campaign ad: first describe it in detail; then identify its intended audience and direct and implied messages; and finally evaluate the overall effectiveness of its arguments.*

Video and Film

Video and film are complex visuals. You have to think critically in order to move from being a *passive* watcher to an *active* "reader" if you want to understand the messages they convey and the techniques used to impart those messages. Television shows and film communicate important social messages and serve as mirrors of society; whether in the form of documentaries, reality shows, or dramas, they reflect values and culture. Therefore, they should be read the same way you would read an essay: with the intention of exploring the author's (the director's and producer's) messages and techniques for delivering those messages.

Thinking Critically about Video and Film

How the camera records the scenes being acted out or happening in real life is an important part of understanding video and film. As in photographs, the video or film camera limits what is shown in a particular scene. Directors convey certain messages and evoke intellectual and emotional responses from viewers by making decisions about what they will and will not show. Be sure to question what you see on the screen, to think about what does not appear there, and to consider your intellectual and emotional responses to the content. Also, if it is a YouTube video, is it a real event or is it staged? Who made the video and for what purpose? To entertain? To persuade? By looking at the techniques used and the point of view and style choices directors make, you'll get a more thorough understanding of the message being presented.

Critical Thinking Questions to Ask about Video and Film

Here are some general questions to ask as you watch a video or a film. Be sure to take notes as you watch any video or film that you will write about later:

1. What are the messages or purpose of the film or video?
2. What support is used to create the purpose? What elements and techniques are used to develop the messages (e.g., plot, camera techniques, music, lighting, characters)?
3. Who do you think is the intended audience for this piece? What evidence or details lead you to that conclusion?

4. When was the video or film made? Does it reflect current events and values, or is it set in a specific period in the past?

5. What is your intellectual response to this film or video? Why? What is your emotional response to this film or video? Why?

ACTIVITY 17-6 Analyzing a YouTube Video

Directions: *Watch a YouTube video and take notes as you watch. Then answer the following questions. Be sure to read through these questions before you watch so you can take notes that will help you answer them.*

1. What type of YouTube video did you watch? Describe it. Does it seem to be a real event caught on video or a staged one? What led you to this conclusion?

_____

_____

2. What happened in the video? Provide a brief summary.

_____

_____

3. What seems to be the purpose of the video (e.g., to entertain, advocate, criticize)? What themes or social concepts were touched on or developed?

_____

_____

4. What support for the purpose and techniques stood out?

_____

_____

5. What effect did these choices and techniques have on your intellectual and emotional responses to the video?

_____

_____

6. Now, review your notes and write an essay critiquing the video; explore its strengths and weaknesses and describe the messages and the techniques used to convey those messages. Be sure to incorporate specific examples and details, using your notes.

ACTIVITY 17-7   Analyzing a Film

Directions: *Watch a film and take notes as you watch. Then answer the following questions. Be sure to read through these questions before you watch so you can take notes that will help you answer them.*

1. What type of film did you watch (documentary, comedy, romance, drama, etc.)? _____

2. What happened in the film (plot or event)? Provide a brief summary.

   _____

   _____

3. What purpose, messages, themes, or social concepts were touched on or developed?

   _____

   _____

4. What techniques used by the director/producer stood out?

   _____

   _____

5. What effect did these choices and techniques have on your intellectual and emotional responses to the film?

   _____

   _____

6. Now write a short essay about this film focusing on one of these two options:

   a. Write a critique of the film you watched analyzing the film's social messages. Use specific terms and examples of film techniques used by the director, and discuss whether or not those techniques were successful in creating a good film or conveying the intended message(s).

   b. Choose a film that is based on a book you have read. Then compare the way you saw the characters and the story in your head as you read the book to the director's vision of the same story as imparted through the film. Critique the choices made by the director as he or she recreated the story on film. Were those choices effective? Why, or why not?

MyWritingLab™ | **ACTIVITY 17-8**   **General Visual Analysis**

Directions: *Choose one of the visuals from this chapter. Then follow these steps to reach analytical conclusions about the image you chose. After you have answered all the questions below, write a short essay about the visual using ideas generated by your answers to this activity.*

1. Describe the image/visual objectively. What do you see (just the facts, not your opinions or judgments)? Don't include what you *think* and *feel* about the visual, just what is literally represented. Include details about the medium or type of visual, the format, size, shape, texture(s), colors, and so on.

   _____

   _____

   _____

2. Can you provide any background information: historical context, cultural clues, visual type, or genre?

   _____

   _____

   _____

3. Now focus on your subjective response to the image. What thoughts are provoked by it? What feelings (if any) are evoked?

   _____

   _____

   _____

4. What associations come to mind when you look at this visual? Why?

   _____

   _____

   _____

5. Focus on the details of the image and the conscious choices made by the creator. What effects do these details and choices have on you?

   _____

   _____

   _____

6. List a couple of specific examples of the details that served as visual clues that led you to a particular thought or emotion.

_____

_____

_____

7. What ideas or concepts are represented in this image?

_____

_____

_____

8. What is the purpose, thesis, or argument implied by this visual?

_____

_____

_____

9. After considering all of your answers so far, what do you think are the main messages of this image, and who is the intended audience?

_____

_____

_____

10. Is the visual successful or unsuccessful in imparting its message? Why?

_____

_____

_____

Learning Objectives Review

My WritingLab™ **Complete the chapter assessment questions at mywritinglab.com**

❶ Write critically about images.

How do you write critically about an image? (See pp. 385–386.)

In order to present an argument about a visual, you must infer its purpose by analyzing its organization, support, examples, and details.

❷ Identify similarities between analyzing an image and analyzing a text.

What are some critical thinking skills used in analyzing a text that you can also apply to analyzing visuals? (See pp. 386–387.)

There are many **parallels between analyzing a visual and analyzing a text:** You look at the purpose, details, and choices the artist or designer has made in order to analyze it, just as in text. Also, you can assess it for biases, just like any other argument, and determine the artist's point of view and assumptions. Finally, visuals can have both intellectual (logos) and emotional (pathos) appeals, just as in argumentative writing.

❸ Actively read visuals.

What does it mean to "actively read" an image, and how do you do that? (See pp. 387–389.)

To actively read an image, study the image and ask these questions: (1) What is the purpose of this image (e.g., to inform, to persuade, to move viewers emotionally)? What are the direct and indirect messages? (2) What support did the artist use to create the message (what artistic choices and details are included in the image)? What clues are present as visual evidence of the intended message(s)? (3) Who is the intended audience for this image?

4 Ask critical thinking questions about a variety of visuals.

What types of questions should you ask about political cartoons, photographs, advertisements, and video and film? (See pp. 389–399.)

Just like good expository writing, visuals such as political cartoons, photographs, advertisements, and video and film present ideas and arguments, and you can study their messages and techniques. Whatever the medium, always ask: (1) What is this image's **purpose?** (2) What are its obvious **assumptions and biases?** Are those biases and assumptions logical and sound? (3) What **conclusions** can you draw from this image? (4) What **point of view** does the image express? (5) Use your **analysis** skills to break down the parts of this image. Is it guilty of any logical fallacies?

LEARNING OBJECTIVES

In this chapter, you will learn how to

1 Write analytically about readings.

2 Structure an analysis essay.

3 Incorporate text references into body paragraphs.

4 Apply the same critical reading and analysis skills to a variety of reading selections.

Thinking Critically MyWritingLab™

Think: When critics review a play, they not only comment on whether the play was enjoyable, they also discuss the classic elements it contains (the writing, the acting, the sets, the costumes, the lighting, and so on) and whether these elements were executed well.

Write: How is a critic's job of reviewing a play similar to a student's task of critiquing a reading? What kinds of things should you consider when writing about a reading?

_____

_____

_____

_____

_____

_____

_____

_____

WRITING ABOUT READINGS

1 Write analytically about readings.

Throughout your college career, you will be asked to write critically about what you have read for your classes. You may or may not need to summarize in such essays (if you are writing for your instructor and classmates about a piece you have all read, then you do not need to summarize the reading because your audience is already familiar with it). But you must always *interpret* and *analyze* the author's intended **purpose** and the techniques the author used to convey that message. To write about a reading with clarity, accuracy, and depth, be sure to look at its overall meaning and the connections between its parts.

APPLYING CRITICAL THINKING

PURPOSE   IDEAS   SUPPORT   ASSUMPTIONS BIASES   CONCLUSIONS   POINT OF VIEW   ANALYSIS

When writing about readings, whether you are paraphrasing, summarizing, analyzing, or a combination of those, you must think about certain elements of the reading. What is the author's **purpose**? What are the main ideas and major supporting examples in the reading? Has the author accomplished the intended purpose? How so? Why or why not? Are the author's **ideas** clear? Do they develop the purpose well? Why or why not? Is there enough **support**, and is the support valid? Did the author have unfounded **assumptions** or **biases**? How so? What effect did they have on your reading? Are the author's **conclusions** sound? Are they built upon the purpose, ideas, and support? Why or why not? What is the author's **point of view**? How does that affect his or her purpose or support? Finally, evaluate the writing overall by **analyzing** each piece of the author's argument and purpose and how he or she arranged and supported the ideas and purpose. Is the writing successful? Why or why not?

Interpret and Infer Meaning

Sometimes, you will have to make inferences and interpretations about the messages and ideas in a reading. To **infer** means to figure out what someone means based on evidence found in what they say or write. For instance, in a short story, you would use information about the setting, the characters, the plot, and maybe repeated images as clues to *infer* the message and **purpose** the author wants to convey through the story. To **interpret** means to **analyze** an idea so you understand its meaning. When you interpret an author's ideas, you explain them using your own words. In an analysis essay, you need to interpret an author's ideas before you can evaluate them.

STRUCTURE OF AN ANALYSIS ESSAY

2 Structure an analysis essay.

To structure your critical analysis, ask yourself the following questions:

1. What is the most important **purpose** the author wants to convey to the reader?
2. What are some of the **secondary messages** or ideas developed in this piece?
3. Are there any **implied messages** or ideas? If so, what are they?
4. What **support** does the author supply to develop his or her ideas and purpose? What specific examples and details are used and are they effective? Why or why not?
5. How does the author's **tone** affect the overall impression made by the reading?
6. What specific writing **techniques** did the author use?
7. Are the style and writing techniques used **effective** or not? Why, or why not?

Introductory Paragraph

Begin with a general introduction to the subject and to the direct or implied message(s) (two to four sentences). Then, add an analytical thesis statement that presents your opinion of what the main messages of the piece are.

Body Paragraphs

3 Incorporate text references into body paragraphs.

Each body paragraph should have an analytical topic sentence based on your thesis and elements of the reading. For instance, if your essay focuses on analyzing the main characters of a short story, you could have a topic sentence that relates to the thesis statement for each main character. If you write an analysis based on the progression of events in the story, you could explain how the author leads us step by step to a core message. Similarly, if you focus on the author's writing techniques, you could discuss style and language choices, such as the use of particular words or symbols, in order of their importance.

After the topic sentence, you should provide support statements, examples from the reading, and analysis of those examples. For each example, you should interpret (translate to explain what the passage illustrates) and analyze its meaning (the direct and implied messages). You need to comment on the significance of the passage to the overall purpose as well as analyze the author's stylistic choices in terms of his or her purpose, ideas, and arguments.

In general, you need about two quotations or examples from a reading for each body paragraph in order to provide adequate support for your thesis. Every time you use a summary, paraphrase, or quotation, you need to

Cross Reference

If your analysis essay is for an audience who may not have read the original work, include a brief summary of the reading. See Chapter 3, pp. 50–51, Eight Steps for Writing a Summary.

Cross Reference
See Chapter 16,
pp. 360–375, Using
Modern Language
Association (MLA) Format,
and pp. 375–381, Using
American Psychological
Association (APA) Format.

document its source using your instructor's preferred documentation format—either Modern Language Association (MLA) or American Psychological Association (APA).

The Ice Cream Sandwich Technique for Framing Quotations

Whenever you use a quotation from a reading, you need to frame that quotation on both sides with your own commentary. Picture assembling an ice-cream sandwich as you incorporate quotations. Take care to cite references and format each quotation correctly. The examples below are from an analysis of a short story by Richard Selzer, a doctor and writer. The citations in this example follow MLA format. The selection, titled "The Discus Thrower," is one of the readings you will find later in this chapter.

- **Top cookie:** First, introduce the quotation with a general analytical statement of one or two sentences.

> In "The Discus Thrower," by Richard Selzer, the doctor in the story is intrigued by his patient's sense of pride.

- **Ice cream filling:** Next, incorporate the quotation and add a citation.
  Use a colon: You may connect a quotation that is one to three sentences long to your general analysis sentence (top cookie) by a colon.

When you use a colon to introduce a direct quotation, the sentence before the colon must be a complete sentence and must present the idea(s) within the quotation that follows:

> In "The Discus Thrower," by Richard Selzer, the doctor in the story is intrigued by his patient's sense of pride: "His face is relaxed, grave, dignified" (96).

Use a tag: You may use a simple tag:

> Selzer writes, "His face is relaxed, grave, dignified" (96).

Weave the quotation: Or you may weave a quotation from the reading (usually less than a full sentence) into your own sentence:

> The doctor describes the patient's face as "relaxed, grave, dignified" (96).

- **Bottom cookie:** Finally, in one or two sentences, interpret the quotation and analyze its significance (what this excerpt demonstrates; why it's important).

> This description of the patient creates an image of dignity and grace. The doctor realizes this poor patient still has dignity and pride and a need for respect, even though there is little left to him physically.

Again, it's a good rule of thumb to include at least two full ice cream sandwiches (with specific references to the reading) to support your thesis in each body paragraph.

Concluding Paragraph

You will need a concluding paragraph that restates your thesis in a new way and sums up and concludes your essay's main points without adding any new information.

Student Essay

First, read Richard Selzer's essay "The Discus Thrower," on pages 425–428. Then actively read this student's analysis of the piece. The citations are documented using MLA format.

Martin Smith

Professor Johnson

English 090

11 October 2013

An Unlikely Hero

Sometimes, people forget to see others in the way they should, with understanding and respect. In Richard Selzer's essay, "The Discus Thrower," the readers see a patient through his doctor's eyes and learn to admire him as the doctor does. The doctor uses heroic images and comparisons throughout the essay to describe the blind and legless patient. In this essay, Selzer shows that even people who seem completely broken still have a sense of human dignity and still want to be respected.

To begin with, the title for this essay, though puzzling at first, compares the patient to an athletic hero from the Olympic Games—a discus thrower; this comparison emphasizes that the doctor sees this patient as admirable. Selzer describes in detail the patient's daily ritual of ordering scrambled eggs for breakfast and then throwing the eggs against the wall: he touches the plate first, fingering "across the plate until he probes the eggs" (2), and then he balances the plate before throwing it at a specific spot on the wall. The doctor sees how the man laughs afterwards, a joyous laugh that could "cure cancer" (2). The doctor is impressed with the man's determination to make his existence more meaningful through this detailed ritual.

Furthermore, Selzer uses other details and comparisons to impart a sense of admiration for this patient in spite of his harsh circumstances. In his first sentence, the doctor confesses that he spies on his patients, and this blind and legless patient particularly intrigues him because he doesn't fade away without a fight.

Thesis

Topic sentence

Concluding sentence

Topic sentence = top cookie

Smith 2

The patient's constant request for his shoes and for eggs to throw against the wall only annoys the poor nurses, but the doctor is curious and fascinated by this behavior. Early in the story, the doctor compares the patient to a bonsai tree, "roots and branches pruned" (1) to signify the man's amputated legs. However, the comparison to a bonsai is telling because the bonsai is also a noble and rare object, which reflects the doctor's impression of this poor man. The doctor also compares the patient to a sailor and says he "remains impressive" (2). It is obvious from this doctor's fascination with the patient and from the comparisons and descriptive words he uses for the patient that he sees this man as a type of hero, fighting for dignity in spite of his poor circumstances.

Even after the patient dies, he has a lasting impression on the doctor. When the doctor describes the dead man in his hospital bed, he describes the man's face as "relaxed, grave, dignified" (3). The man seems to be at peace, and the doctor sees him as a digni-fied human being who deserves his respect. In addition to leaving a lasting impression on the doctor, this patient leaves an impres-sion on his wall: "My gaze sweeps the wall at the foot of the bed, and I see the place where it has been repeatedly washed, where the wall looks very clean and very white" (3). This patient, though blind, legless, and alone, has certainly left his mark.

In this essay, Selzer's portrayal of this patient creates an image of dignity and grace and paints him as a hero, despite his unheroic condition. The doctor realizes that this poor patient still has dignity and pride and a need for respect, even though there is little left to him physically. Through the doctor's spying, we, too, learn an important lesson, see the patient through the doctor's eyes, and understand this patient better.

Margin annotations:

Quotation = ice cream

Bottom cookie

Analysis

Topic sentence = top cookie

Quotation = ice cream

Bottom cookie

Analysis + concluding sentence

Restatement of thesis

MyWritingLab™

Cross Reference
See Chapter 2,
pp. 34–36, The T-KED
Method for Marking
Textbooks and Articles.

ACTIVITY 18-1   **Critical Analysis Assignment**

Directions: *Choose a reading from this chapter or a different reading that your instructor has assigned. Then, using an active reading technique such as T-KED, read the piece. Next, write an analytical essay using the suggestions in this section for structuring and developing your essay. Finally, use the critique form in this chapter for self- and peer reviews of your essay draft.*

ANALYTICAL ESSAY CRITIQUE FORM

Overall	Done well	Needs work
1. Is the essay analytical (does it include interpretation, commentary, and analysis of the message/s)?	_____	_____
2. Does the essay avoid merely summarizing the reading?	_____	_____
3. Does the essay stay focused on proving the thesis?	_____	_____

Introduction

4. Is the title interesting, appropriate, and typed in the correct format?	_____	_____
5. Does the general introduction lead smoothly into the thesis?	_____	_____
6. Is the thesis statement clear (is it a clear presentation of the reading's message)?	_____	_____
7. Is a plan of development included in the thesis (for example, did you organize your paragraphs by themes or ideas, characters, the author's style and writing techniques, etc.)?	_____	_____

Body

8. Do the body paragraphs have clear topic sentences?	_____	_____
9. Does each body paragraph include support, examples, and quotes from the reading (about two quotations per body paragraph)?	_____	_____
10. Is each quotation tagged or woven into your own sentence?	_____	_____
11. Is each quotation framed with your analysis—introduced and then interpreted (the ice cream sandwich technique)?	_____	_____
12. Are quotation marks and punctuation handled correctly?	_____	_____
13. Is there a concluding analytical sentence in each body paragraph?	_____	_____
14. Are transitions used well, both within and between paragraphs?	_____	_____

Continued ▶

Conclusion

15. Does the concluding paragraph sum up your points well without
introducing new ideas or analysis?   _____   _____

Citation Format (MLA)/Grammar/Spelling

16. Citation format: Every time a quotation is used, is it followed by
parentheses containing the author's name and/or a page number?   _____   _____

17. Circle grammar errors you see in this paper: spelling errors; fragments; run-ons/comma splices;
pronoun disagreement; pronoun reference errors; errors in verb use; commas, semicolons/colons,
quotation marks, and apostrophes; point-of-view shifts; faulty parallelism; passive voice
constructions.

18. Other types of grammar or sentence-level errors you noticed in this draft:

_____

Comments:

_____

_____

READING SELECTIONS FOR ANALYSIS

4 Apply the same
critical reading
and analysis
skills to a variety
of reading
selections.

The rest of this chapter features essays and short stories from professional
writers. When you read these selections, be sure to use active reading techniques and annotations.

Each reading is followed by a set of reading comprehension questions that
check your understanding of what you have read (both ideas and vocabulary
from the readings), a set of critical thinking questions that help you analyze
the author's purpose and writing techniques, and prompts for writing analysis
essays about these selections.

Gotta Dance

Jackson Jodie Daviss

The author, Jackson Jodie Daviss, writes this story about a true passion that
must be acted upon. The story was originally published in *Story Magazine* in
1992. This story is predominantly written in *narration/description* mode, but
there is also some implied *cause and effect* and *argument*.

1   Maybe I shouldn't have mentioned it to anyone. Before I knew it, it was all through the family, and they'd all made it their business to challenge me. I wouldn't tell them my plans, other than to say I was leaving, but that was enough to set them off. Uncle Mike called from Oregon to say, "Katie, don't do it," and I wouldn't have hung up on him except that he added, "Haven't you caused enough disappointment?" That did it. Nine people had already told me no, and Uncle Mike lit the fire under me when he made it ten. Nine-eight-seven-six-five-four-three-two-one. Kaboom.

2   On my way to the bus station, I stopped by the old house. I still had my key and I knew no one was home. After ducking my head into each room, including my old one, just to be sure I was alone, I went into my brother's room and set my duffel bag and myself on his bed.

3   The blinds were shut so the room was dim, but I looked around at all the things I knew by heart and welcomed the softening effect of the low light. I sat there a very long time in the silence until I began to think I might never rise from that bed or come out of that gray light, so I pushed myself to my feet. I eased off my sneakers and edged the rug aside so I could have some polished floor, then I pushed the door shut.

4   Anyone passing in the hall outside might've heard a soft sound, a gentle sweeping sound, maybe a creak of the floor, but not much more as I danced a very soft shoe in my stocking feet. Arms outstretched but loose and swaying, head laid back and to one side, like falling asleep, eyes very nearly closed in that room like twilight, I danced to the beat of my heart.

5   After a while, I straightened the rug, opened the blinds to the bright day and walked out of what was now just another room without him in it. He was the only one I said good-bye to, and the only one I asked to come with me, if he could.

6   At the bus station, I asked the guy for a ticket to the nearest city of some size. Most of them are far apart in the Midwest and I liked the idea of those long rides with time to think. I like buses—the long-haul kind, anyway— because they're so public that they're private. I also like the pace, easing you out of one place before easing you into the next, no big jolts to your system.

7   My bus had very few people on it and the long ride was uneventful, except when the little boy threw his hat out the window. The mother got upset, but the kid was happy. He clearly hated that hat; I'd seen him come close to launching it twice before he finally let fly. The thing sailed in a beautiful arc, then settled on a fence post, a ringer, just the way you never can do it when you try. The woman asked the driver if he'd mind going back for the hat. He said he'd mind. So the woman stayed upset and the kid stayed happy. I liked her well enough, but the boy was maybe the most annoying kid I've come across, so I didn't offer him the money to buy a hat he and his mother could agree on. Money would have been no problem. Money has never been my problem.

8   There are some who say money is precisely my problem, in that I give it so little thought. I don't own much. I lose things all the time. I'm told I dress lousy. I'm told, too, that I have no appreciation of money because I've never had to do without it. That may be true. But even if it is, it's not all there is to say about a person.

9   There is one thing I do well, and money didn't buy it, couldn't have bought it for me. I am one fine dancer. I can dance like nobody you've ever seen. Heck, I can dance like everybody you've ever seen. I didn't take lessons, not the usual kind, because I'm a natural, but I've worn out a few sets of tapes and a VCR. I'd watch Gene Kelly and practice until I had his steps. Watch Fred Astaire, practice, get his steps. I practice all the time. Bill Robinson, Eleanor Powell, Donald O'Connor, Ginger Rogers. You know, movie dancers. I'm a movie dancer. I don't dance in the movies, though. Never have. Who does, anymore? I dance where and when I can.

10   My many and vocal relatives don't think much, have never thought much, of my dancing—largely, I believe, because they are not dancers themselves. To be honest, they don't think much of anything I do, not since I left the path they'd set for me, and that's been most of my twenty-three years. These people, critical of achievement they don't understand, without praise for talent or dreams or the elegant risk, are terrified of being left behind but haven't the grace to come along in spirit.

11   Mutts and I talked a lot about that. He was a family exception, as I am, and he thought whatever I did was more than fine. He was my brother, and I backed everything he did, too. He played blues harmonica. He told bad jokes. We did have plans. His name was Ronald, but everyone's called him Mutts since he was a baby. No one remembers why. He never got his chance to fly, and I figure if I don't do this now, I maybe never will. I need to do it for both of us.

12   The bus depot was crowded and crummy, like most city depots seem to be. I stored my bag in a locker, bought a paper and headed for where the bright lights would be. I carried my tap shoes and tape player.

13   When I reached the area I wanted it was still early, so I looked for a place to wait. I found a clean diner, with a big front window where I could read the paper and watch for the lines to form. I told the waitress I wanted a long cup of coffee before ordering. After a half hour or so, she brought another refill and asked if I was ready. She was kind and patient and I wondered what she was doing in the job. It seems like nothing takes it out of you like waitress work. She was young; maybe that was it. I asked her what was good and she recommended the baked chicken special, said it was what she'd had on her break. That's what I had, and she was right, but I only picked at it. I wanted something for energy, but I didn't want to court a side ache, so the only thing I really ate was the salad. She brought an extra dinner roll and stayed just as pleasant the whole time I was there, which was the better part of two hours, so I put down a good tip when I left.

14   While I was in the diner, a truly gaunt young man came in. He ordered only soup, but he ate it like he'd been hungry a long time. He asked politely for extra crackers and the waitress gave them to him. When he left, he was full of baked chicken special with an extra dinner roll. He wouldn't take a loan. Pride, maybe, or maybe he didn't believe I could spare it, and I didn't want to be sitting in a public place pushing the idea that I had plenty of money. Maybe I don't know the value of money, but I know what discretion is worth. The guy was reluctant even to take the chicken dinner, but I convinced him if he didn't eat it, nobody would. He reminded me of Mutts, except that Mutts had never been hungry like that.

15   When the lines were forming I started on over. While I waited, I watched the people. There were some kids on the street, dressed a lot like me in my worn jeans, faded turtleneck, and jersey warm-up jacket. They were working the crowd like their hopes amounted to spare change. The theater patrons waiting in line were dressed to the nines, as they say. There is something that makes the well-dressed not look at the shabby. Maybe it's guilt. Maybe it's embarrassment because, relatively, they're overdressed. I don't know. I do know it makes it easy to study them in detail. Probably makes them easy marks for pickpockets, too. The smell of them was rich: warm wool, sweet spice and alcohol, leather, peppermint and shoe polish. I thought I saw Mutts at the other edge of the crowd, just for a moment, but I remembered he couldn't be.

16   I was wearing my sneakers, carrying my taps. They're slickery black shoes that answer me back. They're among the few things I've bought for myself and I keep them shiny. I sat on the curb and changed shoes. I tied the sneakers together by the laces and draped them around my shoulders.

17   I turned on my tape player and the first of my favorite show tunes began as I got to my feet. I waited a few beats, but no one paid attention until I started to dance. My first taps rang off the concrete clear and clean, measured, a telegraphed message: *Takka-takka-takka-tak! Takka-takka-takka-tak! Takka-takka-takka-tak-tak-tak!* I paused; everybody turned.

18   I tapped an oh-so-easy, wait-a-minute time-step while I lifted the sneakers from around my neck. I gripped the laces in my right hand and gave the shoes a couple of overhead, bola-style swings, tossing them to land beside the tape player, neat as you please. I didn't miss a beat. The audience liked it; I knew they would. Then I let the rhythm take me and I started to fly. Everything came together. I had no weight, no worries, just the sweet, solid beat. Feets, do your stuff.

19   Didn't I *dance*. And wasn't I *smooth*. Quick taps and slow rolling, jazz it, swing it, on the beat, off the beat, out of one tune right into the next and the next and I never took one break. It was a chill of a night, but didn't I sweat, didn't that jacket just have to come off. Didn't I feel the solid jar to the backbone from the heavy heel steps, and the pump of my heart on the beat on the beat on the beat.

20   Time passed. I danced. A sandy-haired man came out of the theater. He looked confused. He said, "Ladies and gentlemen, curtain in five minutes." I'm sure that's what he said. Didn't I dance, and didn't they all stay. The sandy-haired man, he was tall and slim and he looked like a dancer, and didn't he stay, too.

21   Every move I knew, I made, every step I'd learned, I took, until the tape had run on out, until they set my rhythm with the clap of their hands, until the sweet sound of the overture drifted out, until I knew for certain they had held the curtain for want of an audience. Then I did my knock-down, drag-out, could-you-just-die, great big Broadway-baby finish.

22   Didn't they applaud, oh honey, didn't they yell, and didn't they throw money. I dug coins from my own pockets and dropped them, too, leaving it all for the street kids. Wasn't the slender man with sandy hair saying, "See me after the show." I'm almost sure that's what he said as I gripped my tape player, grabbed my sneakers, my jacket, and ran away, ran with a plan and a purpose, farther with each step from my beginnings and into the world, truly heading home.

23   The blood that drummed in my ears set the rhythm as I ran, ran easy, taps ringing off the pavement, on the beat on the beat on the beat. Everything was pounding, but I had to make the next bus, that I knew, catch that bus and get on to the next town, and the next, and the next and the next. Funeral tomorrow, but Mutts will not be there, no, and neither will I. I'm on tour.

My**Writing**Lab™   Reading Reflection Questions

1. What are the direct and implied messages of this story?

_____

_____

2. In your own words, why does Katie, the narrator, "gotta dance"?

_____

_____

3. Money is a prominent subject in this story. What is Katie's opinion about money? Give an example from the story to support your answer.

_____

4. Why is Katie's brother, Mutts, such a prominent part of her story even though he is not directly in the story?

_____

_____

5. T/F _____ Katie's whole family supported her dance dreams.

6. T/F _____ Katie danced for money.

7. T/F _____ Katie learned how to dance from formal lessons at a dance school.

MyWritingLab™   **Checking Vocabulary**

Define each of the following words by figuring out their meaning using context clues from the reading selection. If you cannot work out the meaning of a word, refer to a dictionary.

8. depot (paragraph 12): _____

9. gaunt (paragraph 14): _____

10. reluctant (paragraph 14): _____

READING CRITICALLY

1. What is the author's **purpose** or goal in this reading selection?

_____

_____

_____

2. What are the implied or stated messages?

_____

_____

_____

3. What specific **support**, details, and examples does the author use to develop the reading's purpose or goal?

_____

_____

_____

Continued ▶

4. What inferences does the author include in this reading? (Inferences imply cause-and-effect analysis.)

_____

_____

_____

5. Who is the intended audience, and how did you reach that **conclusion?**

_____

_____

_____

MyWritingLab™ **Writing Assignments**

Cross Reference
See Chapter 7,
pp. 142–174, "Narration
and Description";
Chapter 12, pp. 263–286,
"Cause and Effect";
or Chapter 14,
pp. 308–334, "Argument
and Persuasion."

1. Write a narration and description essay that tells about a time you tried to follow a dream that your family and/or friends didn't support.

2. Write a cause-and-effect analysis essay about choosing a traditional job versus choosing a career that you love but that does not pay.

3. Write an argument essay that proposes including free dance classes as part of the curriculum for public schools.

What Adolescents Miss When We Let Them Grow Up in Cyberspace

Brent Staples

Brent Staples is an editorial writer for the _New York Times_. He has a Ph.D. in Psychology from the University of Chicago. He won the Anisfield Book Award for his memoir, _Parallel Time: Growing Up in Black and White._ This essay is predominantly written in _argument_ mode, but there is also a great deal of _cause and effect_ and _comparison and contrast._

1   My 10th-grade heartthrob was the daughter of a fearsome steelworker who struck terror into the hearts of 15-year-old boys. He made it his business to answer the telephone—and so always knew who was calling—and grumbled in the background when the conversation went on too long. Unable to make time

by phone, the boy either gave up or appeared at the front door. This meant sub-mitting to the first-degree for which the girl's father was soon to become famous.

2   He greeted me with a crushing handshake, then leaned in close in a transparent attempt to find out whether I was one of those *bad* boys who smoked. He retired to the den during the visit, but cruised by the living room now and then to let me know he was watching. He let up after some weeks, but only after getting across what he expected of a boy who spent time with his daughter and how upset he'd be if I disappointed him.

3   This was my first sustained encounter with an adult outside my family who needed to be convinced of my worth as a person. This, of course, is a crucial part of growing up. Faced with the same challenge today, however, I would probably pass on meeting the girl's father—and outflank him on the Internet.

4   Thanks to e-mail, online chat rooms and instant messages—which permit private, realtime conversations—adolescents have succeeded at last in shield-ing their social lives from adult scrutiny. But this comes at a cost. The paradox is that teenagers nowadays are both more connected to the world at large than ever, and more cut off from the social encounters that have historically prepared young people for the move into adulthood.

5   The Internet was billed as a revolutionary method of enriching our social lives and expanding our civic connections. This seems to have worked well for elderly people and others who were isolated before they got access to the World Wide Web. But a growing body of research is showing that the heavy use of the Net actually isolated younger socially connected people who are unwittingly allowing time online to replace face-to-face interaction with their families and friends.

6   Online shopping, checking e-mail and Web surfing—mainly solitary activities—have turned out to be more isolating than watching television, which friends and family often do in groups. Researchers have found that the time spent in direct contact with family members drops by as much as half for every hour we use the Net at home.

7   This should come as no surprise to two-career couples who have seen their domestic lives taken over by e-mail and wireless tethers that keep people working around the clock. But a startling body of research from the Human–Computer Interaction Institute at Carnegie Mellon has shown that heavy Internet use can have a stunting effect outside the home as well. Studies show that gregarious, well-connected people actually lose friends and experience symptoms of loneliness and depression, after joining discussion groups and other activities. People who communicated with disembodied strangers online found the experience empty and emotionally frustrating but were nonetheless seduced by the novelty of the new medium. As Prof. Robert Kraut, a Carnegie Mellon researcher, told me recently, such people allowed low-quality relationships developed in virtual reality to replace higher-quality relationships in the real world.

8   No group has embraced this socially impoverishing trade-off more enthusias-
tically than adolescents, many of whom spend most of their free hours cruising
the Net in sunless rooms. This hermetic existence has left many of these
teenagers with nonexistent social skills—a point widely noted in stories about
the computer geeks who rose to prominence in the early days of Silicon Valley.

9   Adolescents are drawn to cyberspace for different reasons than adults.
As the writer Michael Lewis observed in his book *Next: The Future Just
Happened*, children see the Net as a transformational device that lets them
discard quotidian identities for more glamorous ones. Mr. Lewis illustrated the
point with Marcus Arnold, who, as a 15-year-old, adopted a pseudonym a few
years ago and posed as a 25-year-old legal expert for an Internet information
service. Marcus did not feel the least bit guilty, and was deterred, when real-
world lawyers discovered his secret and accused him of being a fraud. When
asked whether he had actually read the law, Marcus responded that he found
books "boring," leaving us to conclude that he had learned all he needed to
know from his family's big-screen TV.

10   Marcus is a child of the Net, where everyone has a pseudonym, telling a
story makes it true and adolescents create older, cooler, more socially powerful selves any time they wish. The ability to slip easily into a new, false self is
tailor-made for emotionally fragile adolescents, who can consider a bout of
acne or a few excess pounds an unbearable tragedy.

11   But teenagers who spend much of their lives hunched over computer
screens miss the socializing, the real world experience that would allow
them to leave adolescence behind and grow into adulthood. These vital
experiences, like much else, are simply not available in a virtual form.

MyWritingLab™   Reading Reflection Questions

1. Explain exactly what Brent Staples means by his title to this piece.
   Explain how this title relates to his message in the essay.

   _____

   _____

2. Why does Staples start the essay with a story from his childhood?

   _____

   _____

3. Paragraphs 4 and 11 provide a strong viewpoint. In your own words, what
   is Staples's argument in these paragraphs?

   _____

   _____

4. What is the purpose for the example about Marcus (the 15-year-old he describes)? What did Marcus do, and why does Staples include this example?

_____

_____

5. T/F _____ Staples thinks the Internet is a good tool for improving teens' social skills and maturity.

6. T/F _____ Staples points out that even adults can face negative consequences due to spending too much time on the Internet.

7. Why does Staples think that spending less time on the Internet will benefit adolescents? How so?

_____

_____

MyWritingLab™   ### Checking Vocabulary

Define each of the following words by figuring out their meaning using context clues from the reading selection. If you cannot work out the meaning of a word, refer to a dictionary.

8. transparent (paragraph 2): _____

9. unwittingly (paragraph 5): _____

10. disembodied (paragraph 7): _____

READING CRITICALLY

1. What is the author's **purpose** or goal in this reading selection?

_____

_____

_____

Continued ▶

2. What are the implied or stated messages?

_____

_____

_____

3. What specific **support**, details, and examples does the author use to develop the reading's purpose or goal?

_____

_____

_____

4. What inferences does the author include in this reading? (Inferences imply cause-and-effect analysis.)

_____

_____

_____

5. Who is the intended audience, and how did you reach that **conclusion?**

_____

_____

_____

MyWritingLab™   **Writing Assignments**

Cross Reference
See Chapter 7,
pp. 142–174, "Narration
and Description";
Chapter 13, pp. 287–307,
"Comparison and
Contrast"; or Chapter 14,
pp. 308–334, "Argument
and Persuasion."

1. Write a narration/description essay that describes a period when you spent too much time in front of a computer. What did you notice about yourself?

2. Write a comparison and contrast essay that compares hanging out with your friends in person versus using social media or playing an interactive online game.

3. Write an argument essay that refutes Staples's assumption that the Internet is not good for social interaction skills.

One Man's Kids

Daniel R. Meier

Daniel R. Meier is a teacher and a writer. He has written articles and books related to teaching, including *Learning in Small Moments: Life in an Urban Classroom* and *Scribble Scrabble—Learning to Read and Write: Success with Diverse Teachers, Children, and Families*. This essay is predominantly written in *narration and description* mode, but there is also a great deal of *cause and effect*, *comparison and contrast*, and *argument*.

1   I teach first graders. I live in a world of skinned knees, double-knotted shoelaces, riddles that I've heard a dozen times, stale birthday cakes, hurt feelings, wandering stories, and one lost shoe ("and if you don't find it my mother'll kill me"). My work is dominated by 6-year-olds.

2   It's 10:45, the middle of snack, and I'm helping Emily open her milk carton. She has already tried the other end without success, and now there's so much paint and ink on the carton from her fingers that I'm not sure she should drink it at all. But I open it. Then I turn to help Scott clean up some milk he has just spilled onto Rebecca's whale crossword puzzle.

3   While I wipe my milk- and paint-covered hands, Jenny wants to know if I've seen that funny book about penguins that I read in class. As I hunt for it in a messy pile of books, Jason wants to know if there is a new seating arrangement for lunch tables. I find the book, turn to answer Jason, then face Maya, who is fast approaching with a new knock-knock joke. After what seems like the 10th "Who's there?" I laugh and Maya is pleased.

4   Then Andrew wants to know how to spell "flukes" for his crossword. As I get to "u," I give a hand signal for Sarah to take away the snack. But just as Sarah is almost out the door, two children complain that "we haven't even had ours yet." I stop the snack mid-flight, complying with their request for graham crackers. I then return to Andrew, noticing that he has put "flu" for 9 Down, rather than 9 Across. It's now 10:50.

5   My work is not traditional male work. It's not a singular pursuit. There is not a large pile of paper to get through or one deal to transact. I don't have one area of expertise or knowledge. I don't have the singular power over language of a lawyer, the physical force of a construction worker, the command over fellow workers of a surgeon, the wheeling and dealing transactions of a businessman. My energy is not spent in pursuing, climbing, achieving, conquering, or cornering some goal or object.

6   My energy is spent in encouraging, supporting, consoling, and praising my children. In teaching, the inner rewards come from without. On any

given day, quite apart from teaching reading and spelling, I bandage a cut, dry a tear, erase a frown, tape a torn doll, and locate a long-lost boot. The day is really won through matters of the heart. As my students groan, laugh, shudder, cry, exult, and wonder, I do, too. I have to be soft around the edges.

7   A few years ago, when I was interviewing for an elementary-school teaching position, every principal told me with confidence that, as a male, I had an advantage over female applicants because of the lack of male teachers. But in the next breath, they asked with a hint of suspicion why I chose to work with young children. I told them that I wanted to observe and contribute to the intellectual growth of a maturing mind. What I really felt like saying, but didn't, was that I loved helping a child learn to write her name for the first time, finding someone a new friend, or sharing in the hilarity of reading about Winnie the Pooh getting so stuck in a hole that only his head and rear show.

8   I gave that answer to those principals, who were mostly male, because I thought they wanted a "male" response. This meant talking about intellectual matters. If I had taken a different course and talked about my interest in helping children in their emotional development, it would have been seen as closer to a "female" answer. I even altered my language, not once mentioning the word "love" to describe what I do indeed love about teaching. My answer worked; every principal nodded approvingly.

9   Some of the principals also asked what I saw myself doing later in my career. They wanted to know if I eventually wanted to go into educational administration. Becoming a dean of students or a principal has never been one of my goals, but they seemed to expect me, as a male, to want to climb higher on the career stepladder. So I mentioned that, at some point, I would be interested in working with teachers as a curriculum coordinator. Again, they nodded approvingly.

10   If those principals had been female instead of male, I wonder whether their questions, and my answers, would have been different. My guess is that they would have been.

11   At other times, when I'm at a party or a dinner and tell someone that I teach young children, I've found that men and women respond differently. Most men ask about the subjects I teach and the courses I took in my training. Then, unless they bring up an issue such as merit pay, the conversation stops. Most women, on the other hand, begin the conversation on a more immediate and personal level. They say things like "those kids must love having a male teacher" or "that age is just wonderful, you must love it." Then, more often than not, they'll talk about their own kids or ask me specific questions about what I do. We're then off and talking shop.

12   Possibly, men would have more to say to me, and I to them, if my job had more of the trappings and benefits of more traditional male jobs. But my job

has no bonuses or promotions. No complimentary box seats at the ball park. No cab fare home. No drinking buddies after work. No briefcase. No suit. (Ties get stuck in paint jars.) No power lunches. (I eat peanut butter and jelly, chips, milk, and cookies with the kids.) No taking clients out for cocktails. The only place I take my kids is to the playground.

13   Although I could have pursued a career in law or business, as several of my friends did, I chose teaching instead. My job has benefits all its own. I'm able to bake cookies without getting them stuck together as they cool, buy cheap sewing materials, take out splinters, and search just the right trash cans for useful odds and ends. I'm sometimes called "Daddy" and even "Mommy" by my students, and if there's ever a lull in the conversation at a dinner party, I can always ask those assembled if they've heard the latest riddle about why the turkey crossed the road. (He thought he was a chicken.)

MyWritingLab™   **Reading Reflection Questions**

1. What is it that Daniel Meier loves about teaching first graders? Give some specific examples from his essay.

   _____

   _____

2. What does Meier mean by the phrase "The day is really won through matters of the heart" (paragraph 6)? Explain.

   _____

   _____

3. Provide some examples from the essay that prove that Meier is, as he says in his essay, "soft around the edges" (paragraph 6) with his students.

   _____

   _____

4. T/F _____ The majority of first-grade teachers are male.

5. T/F _____ Meier hopes to become his school's principal.

6. List two of the "benefits" Meier sees as part of his job (see final paragraph).

   _____

   _____

7. T/F _____ Some people question Meier's motives as a male working with young children.

MyWritingLab™   **Checking Vocabulary**

Define each of the following words by figuring out their meaning using context clues from the reading selection. If you cannot work out the meaning of a word, refer to a dictionary.

8. dominated (paragraph 1): _____

9. transactions (paragraph 5): _____

10. consoling (paragraph 6): _____

READING CRITICALLY

1. What is the author's **purpose** or goal in this reading selection?

_____

_____

_____

2. What are the implied or stated messages?

_____

_____

_____

3. What specific **support**, details, and examples does the author use to develop the reading's purpose or goal?

_____

_____

_____

4. What inferences does the author include in this reading? (Inferences imply cause-and-effect analysis.)

_____

_____

_____

5. Who is the intended audience, and how did you reach that **conclusion?**

_____

_____

_____

MyWritingLab™

Cross Reference
See Chapter 7,
pp. 142–174, "Narration
and Description";
Chapter 11, pp. 241–262,
"Example and Illustration";
Chapter 14, pp. 308–334,
"Argument and
Persuasion"; or
Chapter 12,
pp. 263–286,
"Cause and Effect."

Writing Assignments

1. Write a narration/description essay about one of your favorite elementary school teachers. What makes that teacher stick out in your memory?

2. Write an example/illustration essay about what makes Meier's job more "female" or "feminine" than "male" or "masculine." Provide examples from Meier's essay to back up your analysis.

3. Write an argument/persuasion essay that argues for the need for more male teachers in elementary schools. You may want to use some cause-and-effect analysis to explain why many men don't choose to teach younger children _and_ what effects (benefits) could come from encouraging more men to teach young children.

The Discus Thrower

Richard Selzer

Richard Selzer was born in Troy, New York, in 1928. He is both a practicing surgeon and a writer. In 1974, after years of being a doctor, he wrote _Rituals of Surgery_, a collection of short stories. He has also published several essays and stories in magazines such as _Redbook, Esquire,_ and _Harper's_. Many of his essays and stories are in two collections: _Mortal Lessons_ (1977) and _Confessions of a Knife_ (1979). This essay is written predominantly in _narration and description_ mode, but there is also a great deal of _cause and effect, comparison and contrast,_ and _argument_.

1   I spy on my patients. Ought not a doctor to observe his patients by any means and from any stance that he might the more fully assemble evidence? So I stand in the doorways of hospital rooms and gaze. Oh, it is not all that furtive an act. Those in bed need only look up to discover me. But they never do.

2   From the doorway of Room 542 the man in the bed seems deeply tanned. Blue eyes and close-cropped white hair give him the appearance of vigor and good health. But I know that his skin is not brown from the sun. It is rusted, rather, in the last stage of containing the vile repose within. And the blue eyes are frosted, looking inward like the windows of a snowbound cottage. This man is blind. This man is also legless—the right leg missing from midthigh down, the left from just below the knee. It gives him the look of a bonsai, roots and branches pruned into the dwarfed facsimile of a great tree.

3   Propped on pillows, he cups his right thigh in both hands. Now and then he shakes his head as though acknowledging the intensity of his suffering. In all of this he makes no sound. Is he mute as well as blind?

4   The room in which he dwells is empty of all possessions—no get-well cards, small, private caches of food, day-old flowers, slippers, all the usual kickshaws of the sickroom. There is only the bed, a chair, a nightstand, and a tray on wheels that can be swung across his lap for meals.

5   "What time is it?" he asks.

6   "Three o'clock."

7   "Morning or afternoon?"

8   "Afternoon."

9   He is silent. There is nothing else he wants to know.

10   "How are you?" I say.

11   "Who is it?" he asks.

12   "It's the doctor. How do you feel?"

13   He does not answer right away.

14   "Feel?" he says.

15   "I hope you feel better," I say.

16   I press the button at the side of the bed.

17   "Down you go," I say.

18   "Yes, down," he says.

19   He falls back upon the bed awkwardly. His stumps, unweighted by legs and feet, rise in the air, presenting themselves. I unwrap the bandages from the stumps, and begin to cut away the black scabs and the dead, glazed fat with scissors and forceps. A shard of white bone comes loose. I pick it away. I wash the wounds with disinfectant and redress the stumps. All this while, he does not speak. What is he thinking behind those lids that do not blink? Is he remembering a time when he was whole? Does he dream of feet? Of when his body was not a rotting log?

20   He lies solid and inert. In spite of everything, he remains impressive, as though he were a sailor standing athwart a slanting deck.

21   "Anything more I can do for you?" I ask. For a long moment he is silent.

22   "Yes," he says at last and without the least irony. "You can bring me a pair of shoes."

23   In the corridor the head nurse is waiting for me.

24   "We have to do something about him," she says. "Every morning he orders scrambled eggs for breakfast, and, instead of eating them, he picks up the plate and throws it against the wall."

25   "Throws his plate?"

26   "Nasty. That's what he is. No wonder his family doesn't come to visit. They probably can't stand him any more than we can."

27   She is waiting for me to do something.

28   "Well?"

29   "We'll see," I say.

30   The next morning I am waiting in the corridor when the kitchen delivers his breakfast. I watch the aide place the tray on the stand and swing it across his lap. She presses the button to raise the head of the bed. Then she leaves.

31   In time the man reaches to find the rim of the tray, then on to find the dome of the covered dish. He lifts off the cover and places it on the stand. He fingers across the plate until he probes the eggs. He lifts the plate in both hands, sets it on the palm of his right hand, centers it, balances it. He hefts it up and down slightly, getting the feel of it. Abruptly he draws back his right arm as far as he can.

32   There is the crack of the plate breaking against the wall at the foot of his bed and the small wet sound of the scrambled eggs dropping to the floor.

33   And then he laughs. It is a sound you have never heard. It is something new under the sun. It could cure cancer.

34   Out in the corridor, the eyes of the head nurse narrow.

35   "Laughed, did he?"

36   She writes something down on her clipboard.

37   A second aide arrives, brings a second breakfast tray, puts it on the night-stand, out of his reach. She looks over at me shaking her head and making her mouth go. I see that we are to be accomplices.

38   "I've got to feed you," she says to the man.

39   "Oh, no you don't," the man says.

40   "Oh, yes I do," the aide says, "after the way you just did. Nurse says so."

41   "Get me my shoes," the man says.

42   "Here's oatmeal," the aide says. "Open." And she touches the spoon to his lower lip.

43   "I ordered scrambled eggs," says the man.

44   "That's right," the aide says.

45   I step forward.

46   "Is there anything I can do?" I say.

47   "Who are you?" the man asks.

48   In the evening I go once more to that ward to make my rounds. The head
nurse reports to me that Room 542 is deceased. She has discovered this quite
by accident, she says. No, there had been no sound. Nothing. It's a blessing,
she says.

49   I go into his room, a spy looking for secrets. He is still there in his bed.
His face is relaxed, grave, dignified. After a while, I turn to leave. My gaze
sweeps the wall at the foot of the bed, and I see the place where it has been
repeatedly washed, where the wall looks very clean and very white.

MyWritingLab™   ## Reading Reflection Questions

1. What are the direct or indirect (implied) messages in this story?

   _____

   _____

2. Describe the conflict between the doctor and the nurse with regard to
   the patient.

   _____

   _____

3. What is it about this patient that intrigues the doctor so? Provide specific
   examples.

   _____

   _____

4. T/F _____ The doctor is curious about this patient's unusual ritual.

5. T/F _____ The doctor is annoyed by this patient's stubbornness.

6. T/F _____ The nurse admires the patient's pride.

7. T/F _____ The patient and the doctor become good friends.

MyWritingLab™   ## Checking Vocabulary

*Define each of the following words by figuring out their meaning using context clues
from the reading selection. If you cannot work out the meaning of a word, refer to
a dictionary.*

8. furtive (paragraph 1): _____

9. facsimile (paragraph 2): _____

10. inert (paragraph 20): _____

READING CRITICALLY

1. What is the author's **purpose** or goal in this reading selection?

_____

_____

_____

2. What are the implied or stated messages?

_____

_____

_____

3. What specific **support**, details, and examples does the author use to develop the reading's purpose or goal?

_____

_____

_____

4. What inferences does the author include in this reading? (Inferences imply cause-and-effect analysis.)

_____

_____

_____

5. Who is the intended audience, and how did you reach that **conclusion?**

_____

_____

_____

MyWritingLab™   Writing Assignments

1. Write a story analysis essay (see the beginning of this chapter) that addresses both Selzer's writing techniques and style as well as his analytical message (the purpose) of the story.

Cross Reference
See Chapter 7,
pp. 142–174, "Narration
and Description"; or
Chapter 8, pp. 175–196,
"Process."

2. Write a narration/description essay about someone you know who displayed pride and dignity in the face of an awkward or uncomfortable event or circumstance.

3. Write a process essay that describes step by step a ritual or habit that you have or that someone you know has. Include specific details. What purpose does this ritual serve?

The Mystery of Mickey Mouse

John Updike

John Updike (1932–2009) wrote novels, essays, stories, and poetry, and began publishing in the 1950s. He also was a regular writer for *The New Yorker* early in his career. He won two Pulitzer Prizes and is still considered one of the most important American authors. This essay is predominantly written in *argument* mode, but there is also a great deal of *cause and effect*, *process*, *comparison and contrast*, and *narration and description*.

1   It's all in the ears. When Mickey Mouse was born, in 1927, the world of early cartoon animation was filled with two-legged zoomorphic humanoids, whose strange half-black faces were distinguished one from another chiefly by the ears. Felix the Cat had pointed triangular ears and Oswald the Rabbit— Walt Disney's first successful cartoon creation, which he abandoned when his New York distributor, Charles Mintz, attempted to swindle him—had long floppy ears, with a few notches in the end to suggest fur. Disney's Oswald films, and the Alice animations that preceded them, had mice in them, with linear limbs, wiry tails, and ears that are oblong, not yet round. On the way back to California from New York by train, having left Oswald enmeshed for good in the machinations of Mr. Mintz, Walt and his wife Lillian invented another character based—the genesis legend claims—on the tame field mice that used to wander into Disney's old studio in Kansas City. His first thought was to call the mouse Mortimer; Lillian proposed instead the less pretentious name Mickey. Somewhere between Chicago and Los Angeles, the young couple concocted the plot of Mickey's first cartoon short, *Plane Crazy*, costarring Minnie and capitalizing on 1927's Lindbergh craze. The next short produced by Disney's fledgling studio—which included, besides himself and Lillian, his brother Roy and his old Kansas City associate Ub Iwerks—was *Gallopin' Gaucho*, and introduced a fat and wicked cat who did not yet wear the prosthesis that would give him his name of Pegleg Pete. The third short, *Steamboat Willie*, incorporated that brand-new novelty a sound track, and was released first, in 1928. Mickey Mouse entered history, as the most persistent and pervasive figment of American popular culture in this century.

2   His ears are two solid black circles, no matter the angle at which he holds his head. Three-dimensional images of Mickey Mouse—toy dolls, or the papier-mâché heads the grotesque Disneyland Mickeys wear—make us uneasy, since the ears inevitably exist edgewise as well as frontally. These ears properly belong not to three-dimensional space but to an ideal realm of notation, of symbolization, of cartoon resilience and indestructibility. In drawings, when Mickey is in profile, one ear is at the back of his head like a spherical ponytail, or like a secondary bubble in a computer-generated Mandelbrot set. We accept it, as we accepted Li'l Abner's hair always being parted on the side facing the viewer. A surreal optical consistency is part of the cartoon world, halfway between our world and the plane of pure signs, of alphabets and trademarks.

3   In the sixty-four years since Mickey Mouse's image was promulgated, the ears, though a bit more organically irregular and flexible than the classic 1930s appendages, have not been essentially modified. Many other modifications have, however, overtaken that first crude cartoon, born of an era of starker stylizations. White gloves, like the gloves worn in minstrel shows, appeared after those first, to cover the black hands. The infantile bare chest and shorts with two buttons were phased out in the forties. The eyes have undergone a number of changes, most drastically in the late thirties, when, some historians mistakenly claim, they acquired pupils. Not so: the old eyes, the black oblongs that acquired a nick of reflection in the sides, were the pupils; the eye whites filled the entire space beneath Mickey's cap of black, its widow's peak marking the division between these enormous oculi. This can be seen clearly in the face of the classic Minnie; when she bats her eyelids, their lashed shades cover over the full width of what might be thought to be her brow. But all the old animated animals were built this way from Felix the Cat on; Felix had lower lids, and the Mickey of *Plane Crazy* also. So it was an evolutionary misstep that, beginning in 1938, replaced the shiny black pupils with entire oval eyes, containing pupils of their own. No such mutation has overtaken Pluto, Goofy, or Donald Duck. The change brought Mickey closer to us humans, but also took away something of his vitality, his alertness, his bugeyed cartoon readiness for adventure. It made him less abstract, less iconic, more merely cute and dwarfish. The original Mickey, as he scuttles and bounces through those early animated shorts, was angular and wiry, with much of the impudence and desperation of a true rodent. He was gradually rounded to the proportions of a child, a regression sealed by his fifties manifestation as the genius of the children's television show *The Mickey Mouse Club*, with its live Mouseketeers. Most of the artists who depict Mickey today, though too young to have grown up, as I did, with his old form, have instinctively reverted to it; it is the bare-chested basic Mickey, with his yellow shoes and oval buttons on his shorts, who is the icon, beside whom his modified later version is a mere mousy trousered pipsqueak.

4   His first, iconic manifestation had something of Chaplin to it; he was the little guy, just over the border of the respectable. His circular ears, like two

minimal cents, bespeak the smallest economic unit, the overlookable democratic man. His name has passed into the language as a byword for the small, the weak—a "Mickey Mouse operation" means an undercapitalized company or minor surgery. Children of my generation—wearing our Mickey Mouse watches, prying pennies from our Mickey Mouse piggy banks (I won one in a third-grade spelling bee, my first intellectual triumph), following his running combat with Pegleg Pete in the daily funnies, going to the local movie-house movies every Saturday afternoon and cheering when his smiling visage burst onto the screen to introduce a cartoon—felt Mickey was one of us, a bridge to the adult world of which Donald Duck was, for all of his childish sailor suit, an irascible, tyrannical member. Mickey didn't seek trouble, and he didn't complain; he rolled with the punches, and surprised himself as much as us when, as in *The Little Tailor*, he showed warrior resourcefulness and won, once again, a blushing kiss from dear, all but identical Minnie. His minimal, decent nature meant that he would yield, in the Disney animated cartoons, the starring role to combative, sputtering Donald Duck and even to Goofy, with his "gawshes" and Gary Cooper–like gawkiness. But for an occasional comeback like the "Sorcerer's Apprentice" episode of *Fantasia*, and last year's rather souped-up *The Prince and the Pauper*, Mickey was through as a star by 1940. But as with Marilyn Monroe when her career was over, his life as an icon gathered strength. The American that is not symbolized by that imperial Yankee Uncle Sam is symbolized by Mickey Mouse. He is America as it feels to itself—plucky, put-on, inventive, resilient, good-natured, game.

5   Like America, Mickey has a lot of black blood. This fact was revealed to me in conversation by Saul Steinberg, who, in attempting to depict the racially mixed reality of New York streets for the supersensitive and race-blind *New Yorker* of the sixties and seventies, hit upon scribbling numerous Mickeys as a way of representing what was jauntily and scruffily and unignorably there. From just the way Mickey swings along in his classic, trademark pose, one three-fingered gloved hand held on high, he is jiving. Along with round black ears and yellow shoes, Mickey has soul. Looking back to such early animations as the early Looney Tunes' Bosko and Honey series (1930–36) and the Arab figures in Disney's own *Mickey in Arabia* of 1932, we see that blacks were drawn much like cartoon animals, with round button noses and great white eyes creating the double arch of the curious peaked skullcaps. Cartoon characters' rubberiness, their jazziness, their cheerful buoyance and idleness, all chimed with popular images of African Americans, earlier embodied in minstrel shows and in Joel Chandler Harris's tales of Uncle Remus, which Disney was to make into an animated feature, *Song of the South*, in 1946.

6   Up to 1950, animated cartoons, like films in general, contained caricatures of blacks that would be unacceptable now; in fact, *Song of the South* raised objections from the NAACP when it was released. In recent reissues of *Fantasia*, two Nubian centaurettes and a pickaninny centaurette who shines

the others' hooves have been edited out. Not even the superb crows section of *Dumbo* would be made now. But there is a sense in which all animated cartoon characters are more or less black. Steven Spielberg's hectic tribute to animation, *Who Framed Roger Rabbit?*, has them all, from the singing trees of Silly Symphonies to Daffy Duck and Woody Woodpecker, living in a Los Angeles ghetto, Toonville. As blacks were second-class citizens with entertaining qualities, so the animated shorts were second-class movies, with unreal actors who mocked and illuminated from underneath the real world, the live-actor cinema. Of course, even in a ghetto there are class distinctions. Porky Pig and Bugs Bunny have homes that they tend and defend, whereas Mickey started out, like those other raffish stick figures and dancing blots from the twenties, as a free spirit, a wanderer. As Richard Schickel has pointed out, "The locales of his adventures throughout the 1930s ranged from the South Seas to the Alps to the deserts of Africa. He was, at various times, a gaucho, teamster, explorer, swimmer, cowboy, fireman, convict, pioneer, taxi driver, castaway, fisherman, cyclist, Arab, football player, inventor, jockey, storekeeper, camper, sailor, Gulliver, boxer," and so forth. He was, in short, a rootless vaudevillian who would play any part that the bosses at Disney Studios assigned him. And though the comic strip, which still persists, has fitted him with all of a white man's household comforts and headaches, it is as an unencumbered drifter whistling along on the road of hard knocks, ready for whatever adventure waits at the next turning, that he lives in our minds.

7   Cartoon characters have soul as Carl Jung defined it in his *Archetypes and the Collective Unconscious:* "soul is a life-giving demon who plays his elfin game above and below human existence." Without the "leaping and twinkling of the soul," Jung says, "man would rot away in his greatest passion, idleness." The Mickey Mouse of the thirties shorts was a whirlwind of activity, with a host of unsuspected skills and a reluctant heroism that rose to every occasion. Like Chaplin and Douglas Fairbanks and Fred Astaire, he acted out our fantasies of endless nimbleness, of perfect weightlessness. Yet withal, there was nothing aggressive or self-promoting about him, as there was about Popeye. Disney, interviewed in the thirties, said, "Sometimes I've tried to figure out why Mickey appealed to the whole world. Everybody's tried to figure it out. So far as I know, nobody has. He's a pretty nice fellow who never does anybody any harm, who gets into scrapes through no fault of his own, but always manages to come up grinning." This was perhaps Disney's image of himself: for twenty years he did Mickey's voice in the films, and would often say, "There's a lot of the Mouse in me." Mickey was a character created with his own pen, and nurtured on Disney's memories of his mouse-ridden Kansas City studio and of the Missouri farm where his struggling father tried for a time to make a living. Walt's humble, scrambling beginnings remained embodied in the mouse, whom the Nazis, in a fury against the Mickey-inspired Allied legions (the Allied code word on D-Day was "Mickey Mouse"), called "the most miserable ideal ever revealed . . . mice are dirty."

8   But was Disney, like Mickey, just "a pretty nice fellow"? He was until crossed in his driving perfectionism, his Napoleonic capacity to marshal men and take risks in the service of an artistic and entrepreneurial vision. He was one of those great Americans, like Edison and Henry Ford, who invented themselves in terms of a new technology. The technology—in Disney's case, film animation—would have been there anyway, but only a few driven men seized the full possibilities and made empires. In the dozen years between *Steamboat Willie* and *Fantasia*, the Disney studios took the art of animation to heights of ambition and accomplishment it would never have reached otherwise, and Disney's personal zeal was the animating force. He created an empire of the mind, and its emperor was Mickey Mouse.

9   The thirties were Mickey's conquering decade. His image circled the globe. In Africa, tribesmen painfully had tiny mosaic Mickey Mouses inset into their front teeth, and a South African tribe refused to buy soap unless the cakes were embossed with Mickey's image, and a revolt of some native bearers was quelled when the safari masters projected some Mickey Mouse cartoons for them. Nor were the high and mighty immune to Mickey's elemental appeal— King George V and Franklin Roosevelt insisted that all film showings they attended include a dose of Mickey Mouse. But other popular phantoms, like Felix the Cat, have faded, where Mickey has settled into the national collective consciousness. The television program revived him for my children's generation, and the theme parks make him live for my grandchildren's. Yet survival cannot be imposed through weight of publicity; Mickey's persistence springs from something unhyped, something timeless in the image that has allowed it to pass in status from a fad to an icon.

10   To take a bite out of our imaginations, an icon must be simple. The ears, the wiggly tail, the red shorts, give us a Mickey. Donald Duck and Goofy, Bugs Bunny and Woody Woodpecker are inextricably bound up with the draftsmanship of the artists who make them move and squawk, but Mickey floats free. It was Claes Oldenburg's pop art that first alerted me to the fact that Mickey Mouse had passed out of the realm of commercially generated image into that of artifact. A new Disney gadget, advertised on television, is a camera-like box that spouts bubbles when a key is turned; the key consists of three circles, two mounted on a larger one, and the image is unmistakably Mickey. Like yin and yang, like the Christian cross and the star of Israel, Mickey can be seen everywhere—a sign, a rune, a hieroglyphic trace of a secret power, an electricity we want to plug into. Like totem poles, like African masks, Mickey stands at that intersection of abstraction and representation where magic connects.

11   Usually cartoon figures do not age, and yet their audience does age, as generation succeeds generation, so that a weight of allusion and sentimental reference increases. To the movie audiences of the early thirties, Mickey Mouse was a piping-voiced live wire, the latest thing in entertainment; by the time of *Fantasia* he was already a sentimental figure, welcomed back. *The Mickey*

Mouse Club, with its slightly melancholy pack leader, Jimmie Dodd, created a Mickey more removed and marginal than in his first incarnation. The generation that watched it grew up into the rebels of the sixties, to whom Mickey became camp, a symbol of U.S. cultural fast food, with a touch of the old rodent raffishness. Politically, Walt, stung by the studio strike of 1940, moved to the right, but Mickey remains one of the thirties proletariat, not uncomfortable in the cartoon-rickety, cheerfully verminous crash pads of the counterculture. At the Florida and California theme parks, Mickey manifests himself as a short real person wearing an awkward giant head, costumed as a ringmaster; he is in danger, in these nineties, of seeming not merely venerable kitsch but part of the great trash problem, one more piece of visual litter being moved back and forth by the bulldozers of consumerism.

12   But never fear, his basic goodness will shine through. Beyond recall, perhaps, is the simple love felt by us of the generation that grew up with him. He was five years my senior and felt like a playmate. I remember crying when the local newspaper, cutting down its comic pages to help us win World War II, eliminated the Mickey Mouse strip. I was old enough, nine or ten, to write an angry letter to the editor. In fact, the strips had been eliminated by the votes of a readership poll, and my indignation and sorrow stemmed from my incredulous realization that not everybody loved Mickey Mouse as I did. In an account of my boyhood written over thirty years ago, "The Dogwood Tree," I find these sentences concerning another boy, a rival: "When we both collected Big Little Books, he outbid me for my supreme find (in the attic of a third boy), the first Mickey Mouse. I can still see that book. I wanted it so badly, its paper tan with age and its drawings done in Disney's primitive style, when Mickey's black chest is naked like a child's and his eyes are two nicked oblongs." And I once tried to write a short story called "A Sensation of Mickey Mouse," trying to superimpose on adult experience, as a shiver-inducing revenant, that indescribable childhood sensation—a rubbery taste, a licorice smell, a feeling of supernatural clarity and close-in excitation that Mickey Mouse gave me, and gives me, much dimmed by the years, still. He is a "genius" in the primary dictionary sense of "an attendant spirit," with his vulnerable bare black chest, his touchingly big yellow shoes, the mysterious place at the back of his shorts where his tail came out, the little cleft cushion of a tongue, red as a valentine and glossy as candy, always peeping through the catenary curves of his undiscourageable smile. Not to mention his ears.

MyWritingLab™   ## Reading Reflection Questions

1. What are Updike's direct or indirect (implied) messages in this essay and his overall purpose in writing about Mickey Mouse?

_____

_____

2. Paragraphs 2 and 3 describe how Mickey's image has been modified over the years. However, Updike also compares and contrasts the early Mickey and the more modern Mickey. Based on his comments in those paragraphs, which version of Mickey does Updike prefer and why?

   _____

3. Explain in your own words what Updike means by this statement from paragraph 4: "The American that is not symbolized by that imperial Yankee Uncle Sam is symbolized by Mickey Mouse. He is America as it feels to itself—plucky, put-on, inventive, resilient, good-natured, game."

   _____

   _____

4. In your opinion, why does Updike bring up the question of Mickey's race and roots? What are his direct and implied arguments?

   _____

   _____

5. In paragraphs 9–12, Updike defines what makes an icon and what specifically makes Mickey a successful icon. Give two of his definitions for an icon and one reason he gives for Mickey being a successful icon.

   _____

   _____

6. T/F _____ Updike sees Mickey as an important and successful American icon.

7. T/F _____ Updike particularly admires the version of Mickey Mouse found at the theme parks (such as Disneyland).

MyWritingLab™   **Checking Vocabulary**

Define each of the following words by figuring out their meaning using context clues from the reading selection. If you cannot work out the meaning of a word, refer to a dictionary.

8. prosthesis (paragraph 1): _____

9. grotesque (paragraph 2): _____

10. irascible (paragraph 4): _____

READING CRITICALLY

1. What is the author's **purpose** or goal in this reading selection?

_____

_____

_____

2. What are the implied or stated messages?

_____

_____

_____

3. What specific **support**, details, and examples does the author use to develop the reading's purpose or goal?

_____

_____

_____

4. What inferences does the author include in this reading? (Inferences imply cause-and-effect analysis.)

_____

_____

_____

5. Who is the intended audience, and how did you reach that **conclusion?**

_____

_____

_____

MyWritingLab™   Writing Assignments

Cross Reference
See Chapter 13,
pp. 287–307, "Comparison
and Contrast."

1. Write an essay that compares and contrasts Mickey Mouse and another, more modern, cartoon character.

Cross Reference

See Chapter 7, pp. 142–174, "Narration and Description"; Chapter 8, pp. 175–196, "Process"; Chapter 9, pp. 197–220, "Classification"; or Chapter 12, pp. 263–286, "Cause and Effect."

2. Write a narration/description essay that describes an icon from your childhood and what that icon meant to you and why.

3. Write a process, classification, or cause-and-effect essay that traces a modern symbol or logo found in our culture and discuss how it represents more than just a simple logo.

Thread

Stuart Dybek

Stuart Dybek (1942–) writes fiction and poetry and teaches writing at Northwestern University. Many of his stories, like "Thread," are based on his childhood. His work is often featured in *Harper's*, *The New Yorker*, and *Poetry* magazines. This essay is predominantly written in *narration and description* mode, but there is also a great deal of *cause and effect*, *comparison and contrast*, and *argument*.

1   The year after I made my first Holy Communion, I joined the Knights of Christ, as did most of the boys in my fourth-grade class. We'd assemble before mass on Sunday mornings in the sunless concrete courtyard between the convent and the side entrance to the sacristy. The nuns' courtyard was private, off-limits, and being allowed to assemble there was a measure of the esteem in which the Knights were held.

2   Our uniforms consisted of the navy blue suits we'd been required to wear for our first Holy Communion, although several of the boys had already outgrown them over the summer. In our lapels we wore tiny bronze pins of a miniature chalice engraved with a cross, and across our suit coats we fit the broad satin sashes that Sister Mary Barbara, who coached the Knights, would distribute. She had sewn them herself. At our first meeting Sister Mary Barbara instructed us that just as in the days of King Arthur, the responsibility of the Knights was to set an example of Christian gentlemanliness. If ever called upon to do so, each Knight should be ready to make the ultimate sacrifice for his faith. She told us that she had chosen her name in honor of Saint Barbara, a martyr whose father had shut her up in a tower and, when she still refused to deny her Christian faith, killed her. I'd looked up the story of Saint Barbara in *The Lives of the Saints*. After her father had killed her—it didn't say how—he'd been struck by lightning, and so Saint Barbara had become the patron of fireworks and artillery, and the protectress against sudden death.

3   Our sashes came in varying shades of gold, some worn to a darker luster and a bit threadbare at the edges and others crisp and shining like newly minted coins. We wore them diagonally in the swashbuckling style of the Three Musketeers. It felt as if they should have supported the weight of silver swords ready at our sides.

4   Once outfitted, we marched out of the courtyard into the sunlight, around St. Roman Church, and through its open massive doors, pausing to dip our fingers in the marble font of holy water and cross ourselves as if saluting our Lord—the bloodied, lifesized Christ crowned with thorns and crucified in the vestibule. Then we continued down the center aisle to the front pews that were reserved for the Knights.

5   In the ranking order of the mass we weren't quite as elite as the altar boys, who got to dress in actual vestments like the priest, but being a Knight seemed an essential step up the staircase of sanctity. Next would be torchbearer, then altar boy, and beyond that, if one had a vocation, subdeacon, deacon, priest.

6   Though I couldn't have articulated it, I already understood that nothing was more fundamental to religion than hierarchies. I was sort of a child prodigy when it came to religion, in the way that some kids had a gift for math or were spelling whizzes. Not only did I always know the answer in catechism class, I could anticipate the question. I could quote Scripture and recite most any Bible story upon command. Although I couldn't find my way out of our parish, the map of the spiritual world was inscribed on my consciousness. I could enumerate the twelve choirs of angels. From among the multitude of saints, I could list the various patrons—not just the easy ones like Saint Nicholas, patron of children, or Saint Jude, patron of hopeless cases, but those whom most people didn't even know existed: Saint Brendan the Navigator, patron of sailors and whales; Saint Stanislaus Kostka, patron of broken bones; Saint Anthony of Padua, whose name, Anthony, I would take later when I was confirmed, patron of the poor; Saint Bonaventure of Potenza, patron of bowel disorders; Saint Fiacre, an Irish hermit, patron of cabdrivers; Saint Alban, patron of torture victims; Saint Dismas, the Good Thief who hung beside Christ, patron of death row inmates; Saint Mary Magdalen, patron of perfume.

7   I could describe their powers with the same accuracy that kids described the powers of superheroes—Batman and Robin, Green Lantern, the Flash— but I knew the difference between saints and comic book heroes: the saints were real.

8   I didn't doubt either their existence or their ability to intercede on behalf of the faithful with God. In the dimension of the spiritual world there was the miraculous and the mysterious, but never the impossible. At each mass, we would witness the miraculous in the transubstantiation of bread and wine into the body and blood of Christ. And when I encountered mysteries such as the mystery of the Trinity, I believed. Mystery made perfect sense to me.

9   My holy medal turning green around my neck, I practiced small rituals: wore a thumbed cross of ashes on my forehead on Ash Wednesday as a reminder of mortality, wore a scapular wool side against the skin of my chest as a reminder of Christ's suffering, and I offered up my own small suffering as I offered up the endless ejaculations I kept careful count of for the poor souls in Purgatory.

10   That was an era for ceremony, a time before what my aunt Zosha came to derisively refer to as Kumbaya Catholicism, when the mass was still in Latin and on Good Fridays weeping old women in babushkas would walk on their knees up the cold marble aisle to kiss the glass-encased sliver of the True Cross that the priest presented at the altar rail. After each kiss, he would wipe the glass with a special silk kerchief for sanitary purposes.

11   It was a time of cold war, when each Sunday mass ended with a prayer "for the conversion of Russia," a more severe time when eating meat on Friday, the day of Christ's crucifixion, could send a soul to Hell. Before receiving Communion, one was required to fast from the night before. To receive Communion without fasting was a mortal sin, and there could be no greater blasphemy than to take the body and blood of Christ into one's mouth with mortal sin on the soul. Sometimes at Sunday mass, women, weak from fasting, would faint at church.

12   Once mass began, the Knights would rise in unison and stand and kneel to the ebb and flow of the ceremony with a fierce attention that should have been accompanied by the rattling of our sabers and spurs against the marble. Our boyish, still unbroken voices were raised in prayer and hymn. At Communion time, it was the privilege of the Knights to be the first to file from the pews, leading the rest of the congregation to the Communion rail. There we would kneel in a long row of navy blue slashed with diagonals of gold, awaiting the priest. Often the priest was Father Fernando, the first Mexican priest at our parish. He'd served as a chaplain in the Marine Corps and lost an eye to shrapnel while administering the last rites to dying soldiers in Korea, and he distributed the Eucharist to us as if reviewing the troops. Usually Father Fernando wore a brown glass eye, but he'd been shattering glass eyes lately—the rumor was he'd been going out drinking with Father Boguslaw— and when he'd break one he'd wear a pair of sunglasses with the lens over the good eye popped out.

13   Sometimes, approaching the Communion rail, I'd be struck by the sight of my fellow Knights already kneeling, by their frayed cuffs and the various shades of socks and worn soles. It never failed to move me to see my classmates from the perspective of their shoes.

14   One Sunday, sitting in the pew, watching flashes of spring lightning illuminate the robes of the angels on the stained glass windows, my mind began to drift. I studied my gold sash, upon which the tarnishing imprint of raindrops had dried into vague patterns—it had begun to rain just as we marched in off

the street. There was a frayed edge to my sash, and I wrapped a loose thread around my finger and gently tugged. The fabric bunched and the thread continued to unwind until it seemed the entire sash might unravel. I pinched the thread and broke it off, then wound it back around my finger tightly enough to cut off my circulation. When my fingertip turned white, I unwound the thread from my finger and weighed it on my open hand, fitting it along the various lines on my palm. I opened my other palm and held my hands out to test if the balance between them was affected by the weight of the thread. It wasn't. I placed the thread on my tongue and let it rest there, where its weight was more discernible. I half expected a metallic taste of gold, but it tasted starchy, like any other thread. Against the pores of my tongue, I could feel it growing thicker with the saliva that was gathering in my mouth. I swallowed both the saliva and the thread.

15   Immediately after, when it was already too late, it occurred to me that I had broken my fast.

16   It would be a mortal sin for me to receive the host. Yet the primary duty of a Knight was to march to the Communion rail leading the congregation. Not only was the enormous humiliation I would feel if I remained seated while the others filed up to the altar more than I was willing to face, but in a sudden panic I worried that I'd be kicked out of the Knights, my ascent up the staircase of sanctity over almost before it had begun. I sat trying to figure a way out of the predicament I'd created, feeling increasingly anxious, a little sick, actually, as if the thread were winding around my stomach. I thought about how not a one of my classmates would have even realized that his fast had been broken by swallowing a thread, and since he wouldn't have realized it was a sin, then it wouldn't have been one. It didn't seem quite fair that my keener understanding made me more culpable. Perhaps a thread didn't count as food, I thought, but I knew I was grasping for excuses—it seemed a dubious distinction to risk one's soul upon. The choir was singing the *Agnus Dei;* Communion would be next. My suit coat felt pasted to my back by a clammy sweat as I thought up various plans at what seemed a feverish pace and rejected them just as feverishly. Maybe I could pretend to be even sicker than I was feeling and run from church with my hand over my mouth as if I were about to vomit; or I could pretend to faint. But not only did the notion of making up a lie in order not to receive Communion seem too devious, I didn't have the nerve to carry off a spectacle like that. To do so would probably be a mortal sin against the Eighth Commandment; I'd just be getting myself in deeper.

17   Then a detail mentioned in passing by Sister Aurelia back in third grade when we practiced for our first Holy Communion occurred to me. She'd told us that if, at the Communion rail, one should ever realize he had a mortal sin on his soul that he'd somehow forgotten about until that moment, then he was merely to clasp a hand in a *mea culpa* over his heart and bow his head, and the priest would understand and move on.

18   Communion time arrived, and on trembling legs I marched to the rail with the other Knights. How fervently I wished that I were simply going to receive Communion. I felt alone, separated from the others by my secret, and yet I became aware of an odd kind of excitement bordering on exhilaration at what I was about to do. Father Fernando wearing his one-eyed pair of dark glasses approached, an altar boy at his elbow, holding a paten to catch the host in case it should slip from the priest's hand. I could hear their soles on the carpet as they paused to deliver a host and moved to the next Knight. I could hear Father Fernando muttering the Latin prayer over and over as he deposited a host upon each awaiting tongue. *Corpus domini nostri Jesu Christi . . . May the body of our Lord, Jesus Christ, preserve your soul in everlasting life.*

19   So this is the aching flush of anticipation, I thought, that a penitent sinner would feel, a murderer, perhaps, or a thief, someone who had committed terrible crimes and found himself at the Communion rail.

20   Father Fernando paused before me, and I clapped a fist against my heart and bowed my head. He stopped and squinted down at me through the missing lens of his dark glasses, trying to catch my eyes and having a hard time doing it with his single good eye. Finally he shrugged and moved on, wondering, I was sure, what grievous sin I had committed.

21   I never told him, nor anyone else. I had swallowed a thread. No one but God would ever be the wiser. It was my finest hour as a theologian. Only years later did I realize it would be that moment I'd think back to when I came to wonder how I'd lost my faith.

MyWritingLab™   ## Reading Reflection Questions

1. What are the direct or indirect (implied) messages in this story?

_____

_____

2. How does Dybek use specific details and description to enhance his narrative? Give one example.

_____

_____

3. Provide two examples of the young narrator's dedication to his church's religious rituals found in the first two-thirds of the story.

_____

_____

4. The author ends the narrative with a surprise that changes the message and focus of the story completely. What is that surprise announcement, and how does it affect the rest of the story?

_____

_____

5. T/F _____ The majority of the story focuses on a fourth grader who is extremely devoted to his religion.

6. T/F _____ The swallowed thread made him throw up.

7. T/F _____ The narrator has a change of heart and mind by the end of the story.

MyWritingLab™   **Checking Vocabulary**

Define each of the following words by figuring out their meaning using context clues from the reading selection. If you cannot work out the meaning of a word, refer to a dictionary.

8. sacristy (paragraph 1): _____

_____

9. vestibule (paragraph 4): _____

10. hierarchy(ies) (paragraph 6): _____

READING CRITICALLY

1. What is the author's **purpose** or goal in this reading selection?

_____

_____

_____

2. What are the implied or stated messages?

_____

_____

_____

Continued ▶

3. What specific **support**, details, and examples does the author use to develop the reading's purpose or goal?

_____

_____

_____

4. What inferences does the author include in this reading? (Inferences imply cause-and-effect analysis.)

_____

_____

_____

5. Who is the intended audience, and how did you reach that **conclusion?**

_____

_____

_____

MyWritingLab™   **Writing Assignments**

1. Write an analysis essay that examines Dybek's writing techniques and style as well as his analytical message (the purpose) of the story.

Cross Reference
See Chapter 7, pp. 142–174, "Narration and Description" or Chapter 8, pp. 175–196, "Process."

2. Write a narration/description essay about a time you had a complete change of heart about something important to you. What happened? Why did you have the change of heart? What was the effect of that change?

3. Write a process essay that describes step by step a ritual or habit that you have or that someone you know has. Include specific details. What purpose does this ritual serve?

Mute in an English Only World

Chang Rae Lee

Chang Rae Lee is an essayist and novelist whose 1995 novel, _Native Speaker_, won the American Book Award. Lee explores the challenges of nonnative speakers and the power of language. This essay is predominantly written in _narration and description_ mode, but it also has _cause and effect_, _process_, and _argument_.

1   When I read of the troubles in Palisades Park, New Jersey, over the prolif-eration of Korean-language signs along its main commercial strip, I unexpect-edly sympathized with the frustrations, resentments and fears of the longtime residents. They clearly felt alienated and even unwelcome in a vital part of their community. The town, like seven others in New Jersey, has passed laws requiring that half of any commercial sign in a foreign language be in English.

2   Now I certainly would never tolerate any exclusionary ideas about who could rightfully settle and belong in the town. But having been raised in a Korean immigrant family, I saw every day the exacting price and power of language, especially with my mother, who was an outsider in an English-only world.

3   In the first years we lived in America, my mother could speak only the most basic English, and she often encountered great difficulty whenever she went out.

4   We lived in New Rochelle, New York, in the early 1970s, and most of the local businesses were run by the descendants of immigrants who, generations ago, had come to the suburbs from New York City. Proudly dotting Main Street and North Avenue were Italian pastry and cheese shops, Jewish tailors and cleaners, and Polish and German butchers and bakers. If my mother's marketing couldn't wait until the weekend, when my father had free time, she would often hold off until I came home from school to buy the groceries.

5   Though I was only 6 or 7 years old, she insisted that I go out shopping with her and my younger sister. I mostly loathed the task, partly because it meant I couldn't spend the afternoon playing catch with my friends but also because I knew our errands would inevitably lead to an awkward scene, and that I would have to speak up to help my mother.

6   I was just learning the language myself, but I was a quick study, as children are with new tongues. I had spent kindergarten in almost complete silence, hearing only the high nasality of my teacher and comprehending little but the cranky wails and cries of my classmates. But soon, seemingly mere months later, I had already become a terrible ham and mimic, and I would crack up my father with impressions of teachers, his friends and even himself. My mother scolded me for aping his speech, and the one time I attempted to make light of hers I rated a roundhouse smack on my bottom.

7   For her, the English language was not very funny. It usually meant trouble and a good dose of shame, and sometimes real hurt. Although she had a good reading knowledge of the language from university classes in South Korea, she had never practiced actual conversation. So in America, she used English flashcards and phrase books and watched television with us kids. And she faithfully carried a pocket workbook illustrated with stick-figure people and compound sentences to be filled in.

8   But none of it seemed to do her much good. Staying mostly at home to care for us, she didn't have many chances to try out sundry words and phrases. When she did, say, at the window of the post office, her readied speech would stall, freeze, sometimes altogether collapse.

9   One day was unusually harrowing. We ventured downtown in the new Ford Country Squire my father had bought her, an enormous station wagon that seemed as long—and deft—as an ocean liner. We were shopping for a special meal for guests visiting that weekend, and my mother had heard that a particular butcher carried fresh oxtails, which she needed for a traditional soup.

10   We'd never been inside the shop, but my mother would pause before its window, which was always lined with whole hams, crown roasts and ropes of plump handmade sausages. She greatly esteemed the bounty with her eyes, and my sister and I did also, but despite our desirous cries she'd turn us away and instead buy the packaged links at the Finast supermarket, where she felt comfortable looking them over and could easily spot the price. And, of course, not have to talk.

11   But that day she was resolved. The butcher store was crowded, and as we stepped inside the door jingled a welcome. No one seemed to notice. We waited for some time, and people who entered after us were now being served. Finally, an old woman nudged my mother and waved a little ticket, which we hadn't taken. We patiently waited again, until one of the beefy men behind the glass display hollered our number.

12   My mother pulled us forward and began searching the cases, but the oxtails were nowhere to be found. The man, his big arms crossed, sharply said, "Come on, lady, whaddya want?" This unnerved her, and she somehow blurted the Korean word for oxtail, soggori.

13   The butcher looked as if my mother had put something sour in his mouth, and he glanced back at the lighted board and called the next number.

14   Before I knew it, she had rushed us outside and back in the wagon, which she had double-parked because of the crowd. She was furious, almost vibrating with fear and grief, and I could see she was about to cry.

15   She wanted to go back inside, but now the driver of the car we were blocking wanted to pull out. She was shooing us away. My mother, who had just earned her driver's license, started furiously working the pedals. But in her haste she must have flooded the engine, for it wouldn't turn over. The driver started honking and then another car began honking as well, and soon it seemed the entire street was shrieking at us.

16   In the following years, my mother grew steadily more comfortable with English. In Korean, she could be fiery, stern, deeply funny and ironic; in English, just slightly less so. If she was never quite fluent, she gained enough confidence to make herself clearly known to anyone, and particularly to me.

17   Five years ago, she died of cancer, and some months after we buried her I found myself in the driveway of my father's house, washing her sedan. I liked taking care of her things; it made me feel close to her. While I was cleaning out the glove compartment, I found her pocket English workbook,

the one with the silly illustrations. I hadn't seen it in nearly 20 years. The yellowed pages were brittle and dog-eared. She had fashioned a plain-paper wrapping for it, and I wondered whether she meant to protect the book or hide it.

18 I don't doubt that she would have appreciated doing the family shopping on the new Broad Avenue of Palisades Park. But I like to think, too, that she would have understood those who now complain about the Korean-only signs.

19 I wonder what these same people would have done if they had seen my mother studying her English workbook—or lost in a store. Would they have nodded gently at her? Would they have lent a kind word?

MyWritingLab™ **Reading Reflection Questions**

1. What are the direct or indirect (implied) messages in this story?

_____

_____

2. With what real-life/current event does the author begin his essay? How does that opening connect to his mother's story?

_____

_____

_____

3. What happens to the author's mother in the butcher shop, and why does he include that example in his story?

_____

_____

4. What are some things the author's mother did to try to learn English? Provide a couple of examples.

_____

_____

5. T/F _____ The author's mother was physically mute.

6. T/F _____ The author sympathizes both with the people who are against the Korean signs and with the nonnative speakers.

7. T/F _____ The author's mother eventually learned English well enough to get by.

MyWritingLab™   **Checking Vocabulary**

Define each of the following words by figuring out their meaning using context clues from the reading selection. If you cannot work out the meaning of a word, refer to a dictionary.

8. alienated (paragraph 1): _____

9. exclusionary (paragraph 2): _____

10. harrowing (paragraph 9): _____

READING CRITICALLY

1. What is the author's **purpose** or goal in this reading selection?

_____

_____

_____

2. What are the implied or stated messages?

_____

_____

_____

3. What specific **support**, details, and examples does the author use to develop the reading's purpose or goal?

_____

_____

_____

4. What inferences does the author include in this reading? (Inferences imply cause-and-effect analysis.)

_____

_____

_____

5. Who is the intended audience, and how did you reach that **conclusion?**

_____

_____

_____

MyWritingLab™

Cross Reference
See Chapter 7,
pp. 142–174, "Narration
and Description"
or Chapter 14,
pp. 308–334, "Argument
and Persuasion."

Writing Assignments

1. Write a story analysis essay (see "Writing about Readings" at the beginning of this chapter) that examines Lee's writing techniques and style as well as his analytical message (the purpose) of the story.

2. Write a narration/description essay about a time you or someone you know was discriminated against based on race or culture.

3. Write an argument essay in favor of or against dual-language signs in your neighborhood.

On Being a Cripple

Nancy Mairs

Nancy Mairs (1943–) writes stories and articles about women's issues, spirituality, and living with multiple sclerosis. She was diagnosed with the disease when she was 28 years old and has navigated through her life supported by her family and her sense of humor. This story is predominantly in _narration and description_ mode, but there is also some implied _cause and effect_ and _argument_.

> To escape is nothing. Not to escape is nothing.   —Louise Bogan

1   The other day I was thinking of writing an essay on being a cripple. I was thinking hard in one of the stalls of the women's room in my office building, as I was shoving my shirt into my jeans and tugging up my zipper. Preoccupied, I flushed, picked up my book bag, took my cane down from the hook, and unlatched the door. So many movements unbalanced me, and as I pulled the door open I fell over backward, landing fully clothed on the toilet seat with my legs splayed in front of me: the old beetle-on-its-back routine. Saturday afternoon, the building deserted, I was free to laugh aloud as I wriggled back to my feet, my voice bouncing off the yellowish tiles from all

directions. Had anyone been there with me, I'd have been still and faint and hot with chagrin. I decided that it was high time to write the essay.

2   First, the matter of semantics. I am a cripple. I choose this word to name me. I choose from among several possibilities, the most common of which are "handicapped" and "disabled." I made the choice a number of years ago, without thinking, unaware of my motives for doing so. Even now, I'm not sure what those motives are, but I recognize that they are complex and not entirely flattering. People—crippled or not—wince at the word "cripple," as they do not at "handicapped" or "disabled." Perhaps I want them to wince. I want them to see me as a tough customer, one to whom the fates/gods/viruses have not been kind, but who can face the brutal truth of her existence squarely. As a cripple, I swagger.

3   But, to be fair to myself, a certain amount of honesty underlies my choice. "Cripple" seems to me a clean word, straightforward and precise. It has an honorable history, having made its first appearance in the Lindisfarne Gospel in the tenth century. As a lover of words, I like the accuracy with which it describes my condition: I have lost the full use of my limbs. "Disabled," by contrast, suggests any incapacity, physical or mental. And I certainly don't like "handicapped," which implies that I have deliberately been put at a disadvantage, by whom I can't imagine (my God is not a Handicapper General), in order to equalize chances in the great race of life. These words seem to me to be moving away from my condition, to be widening the gap between word and reality. Most remote is the recently coined euphemism "differently abled," which partakes of the same semantic hopefulness that transformed countries from "undeveloped" to "underdeveloped," then to "less developed," and finally to "developing" nations. People have continued to starve in those countries during the shift. Some realities do not obey the dictates of language.

4   Mine is one of them. Whatever you call me, I remain crippled. But I don't care what you call me, so long as it isn't "differently abled," which strikes me as pure verbal garbage designed, by its ability to describe anyone, to describe no one. I subscribe to George Orwell's thesis that "the slovenliness of our language makes it easier for us to have foolish thoughts." And I refuse to participate in the degeneration of the language to the extent that I deny that I have lost anything in the course of this calamitous disease; I refuse to pretend that the only differences between you and me are the various ordinary ones that distinguish any one person from another. But call me "disabled" or "handicapped" if you like. I have long since grown accustomed to them; and if they are vague, at least they hint at the truth. Moreover, I use them myself. Society is no readier to accept crippledness than to accept death, war, sex, sweat, or wrinkles. I would never refer to another person as a cripple. It is the word I use to name only myself.

5   I haven't always been crippled, a fact for which I am soundly grateful. To be whole of limb is, I know from experience, infinitely more pleasant and useful than to be crippled; and if that knowledge leaves me open to bitterness at MY loss, the physical soundness I once enjoyed (though I did not enjoy it half enough) is well worth the occasional stab of regret. Though never any good at sports, I was a normally active child and young adult. I climbed trees, played hopscotch, jumped rope, skated, swam, rode my bicycle, sailed. I despised team sports, spending some of the wretchedest afternoons of my life, sweaty and humiliated, behind a field-hockey stick and under a basketball hoop. I tramped alone for miles along the bridle paths that webbed the woods behind the house I grew up in. I swayed through countless dim hours in the arms of one man or another under the scattered shot of light from mirrored balls, and gyrated through countless more as Tab Hunter and Johnny Mathis gave way to the Rolling Stones, Credence Clearwater Revival, Cream. I walked down the aisle. I pushed baby carriages, changed tires in the rain, marched for peace.

6   When I was twenty-eight I started to trip and drop things. What at first seemed my natural clumsiness soon became too pronounced to shrug off. I consulted a neurologist, who told me that I had a brain tumor. A battery of tests, increasingly disagreeable, revealed no tumor. About a year and a half later I developed a blurred spot in one eye. I had, at last, the episodes "disseminated in space and time" requisite for a diagnosis: multiple sclerosis. I have never been sorry for the doctor's initial misdiagnosis, however. For almost a week, until the negative results of the tests were in, I thought that I was going to die right away. Every day for the past nearly ten years, then, has been a kind of gift. I accept all gifts.

7   Multiple sclerosis is a chronic degenerative disease of the central nervous system, in which the myelin that sheathes the nerves is somehow eaten away and scar tissue forms in its place, interrupting the nerves' signals. During its course, which is unpredictable and uncontrollable, one may lose vision, hearing, speech, the ability to walk, control of bladder and/or bowels, strength in any or all extremities, sensitivity to touch, vibration, and/or pain, potency, coordination of movements—the list of possibilities is lengthy and, yes, horrifying. One may also lose one's sense of humor. That's the easiest to lose and the hardest to survive without.

8   In the past ten years, I have sustained some of these losses. Characteristic of MS are sudden attacks, called exacerbations, followed by remissions, and these I have not had. Instead, my disease has been slowly progressive. My left leg is now so weak that I walk with the aid of a brace and a cane; and for distances I use an Amigo, a variation on the electric wheelchair that looks rather like an electrified kiddie car. I no longer have much use of my left hand. Now my right side is weakening as well. I still have the blurred spot in my right eye. Overall, though, I've been lucky so far. My world has, of

necessity, been circumscribed by my losses, but the terrain left me has been ample enough for me to continue many of the activities that absorb me: writing, teaching, raising children and cats and plants and snakes, reading, speaking publicly about MS and depression, even playing bridge with people patient and honorable enough to let me scatter cards every which way without sneaking a peek.

9   Lest I begin to sound like Pollyanna, however, let me say that I don't like having MS. I hate it. My life holds realities—harsh ones, some of them—that no right-minded human being ought to accept without grumbling. One of them is fatigue. I know of no one with MS who does not complain of bone-weariness; in a disease that presents an astonishing variety of symptoms, fatigue seems to be a common factor. I wake up in the morning feeling the way most people do at the end of a bad day, and I take it from there. As a result, I spend a lot of time in extremis and, impatient with limitation, I tend to ignore my fatigue until my body breaks down in some way and forces rest. Then I miss picnics, dinner parties, poetry readings, the brief visits of old friends from out of town. The offspring of a puritanical tradition of exceptional venerability, I cannot view these lapses without shame. My life often seems a series of small failures to do as I ought.

10   I lead, on the whole, an ordinary life, probably rather like the one I would have led had I not had MS. I am lucky that my predilections were already solitary, sedentary, and bookish—unlike the world-famous French cellist I have read about, or the young woman I talked with one long afternoon who wanted only to be a jockey. I had just begun graduate school when I found out something was wrong with me, and I have remained, interminably, a graduate student. Perhaps I would not have if I'd thought I had the stamina to return to a full-time job as a technical editor; but I've enjoyed my studies.

11   In addition to studying, I teach writing courses. I also teach medical students how to give neurological examinations. I pick up freelance editing jobs here and there. I have raised a foster son and sent him into the world, where he has made me two grandbabies, and I am still escorting my daughter and son through adolescence. I go to Mass every Saturday. I am a superb, if messy, cook. I am also an enthusiastic laundress, capable of sorting a hamper full of clothes into five subtly differentiated piles, but a terrible housekeeper. I can do italic writing and, in an emergency, bathe an oil-soaked cat. I play a fiendish game of Scrabble. When I have the time and the money, I like to sit on my front steps with my husband, drinking Amaretto and smoking a cigar, as we imagine our counterparts in Leningrad and make sure that the sun gets down once more behind the sharp childish scrawl of the Tucson Mountains.

12   This lively plenty has its bleak complement, of course, in all the things I can no longer do. I will never run again, except in dreams, and one day I may have to write that I will never walk again. I like to go camping, but I can't follow George and the children along the trails that wander out of a campsite through

the desert or into the mountains. In fact, even on the level I've learned never to check the weather or try to hold a coherent conversation: I need all my attention for my wayward feet. Of late, I have begun to catch myself wondering how people can propel themselves without canes. With only one usable hand, I have to select my clothing with care not so much for style as for ease of ingress and egress, and even so, dressing can be laborious. I can no longer do fine stitchery, pick up babies, play the piano, braid my hair. I am immobilized by acute attacks of depression, which may or may not be physiologically related to MS but are certainly its logical concomitant.

13   These two elements, the plenty and the privation, are never pure, nor are the delight and wretchedness that accompany them. Almost every pickle that I get into as a result of my weakness and clumsiness—and I get into plenty—is funny as well as maddening and sometimes painful. I recall one May afternoon when a friend and I were going out for a drink after finishing up at school. As we were climbing into opposite sides of my car, chatting, I tripped and fell, flat and hard, onto the asphalt parking lot, my abrupt departure interrupting him in mid-sentence. "Where'd you go?" he called as he came around the back of the car to find me hauling myself up by the door frame. "Are you all right?" Yes, I told him, I was fine, just a bit rattly, and we drove off to find a shady patio and some beer. When I got home an hour or so later, my daughter greeted me with "What have you done to yourself?" I looked down. One elbow of my white turtleneck with the green froggies, one knee of my white trousers, one white kneesock were blood-soaked. We peeled off the clothes and inspected the damage, which was nasty enough but not alarming. That part wasn't funny: The abrasions took a long time to heal, and one got a little infected. Even so, when I think of my friend talking earnestly, suddenly, to the hot thin air while I dropped from his view as though through a trap door, I find the image as silly as something from a Marx Brothers movie.

14   I may find it easier than other cripples to amuse myself because I live propped by the acceptance and the assistance and, sometimes, the amusement of those around me. Grocery clerks tear my checks out of my checkbook for me, and sales clerks find chairs to put into dressing rooms when I want to try on clothes. The people I work with make sure I teach at times when I am least likely to be fatigued, in places I can get to, with the materials I need. My students, with one anonymous exception (in an end-of-the-semester evaluation), have been unperturbed by my disability. Some even like it. One was immensely cheered by the information that I paint my own fingernails; she decided, she told me, that if I could go to such trouble over fine details, she could keep on writing essays. I suppose I became some sort of bright-fingered muse. She wrote good essays, too.

15   The most important struts in the framework of my existence, of course, are my husband and children. Dismayingly few marriages survive the MS test, and why should they? Most twenty-two- and nineteen-year-olds, like George

and me, can vow in clear conscience, after a childhood of chicken pox and summer colds, to keep one another in sickness and in health so long as they both shall live. Not many are equipped for catastrophe: the dismay, the depression, the extra work, the boredom that a degenerative disease can insinuate into a relationship. And our society, with its emphasis on fun and its association of fun with physical performance, offers little encouragement for a whole spouse to stay with a crippled partner. Children experience similar stresses when faced with a crippled parent, and they are more helpless, since parents and children can't usually get divorced. They hate, of course, to be different from their peers, and the child whose mother is tacking down the aisle of a school auditorium packed with proud parents like a Cape Cod dinghy in a stiff breeze jolly well stands out in a crowd. Deprived of legal divorce, the child can at least deny the mother's disability, even her existence, forgetting to tell her about recitals and PTA meetings, refusing to accompany her to stores or church or the movies, never inviting friends to the house. Many do.

16   But I've been limping along for ten years now, and so far George and the children are still at my left elbow, holding tight. Anne and Matthew vacuum floors and dust furniture and haul trash and rake up dog droppings and button my cuffs and bake lasagna and Toll House cookies with just enough grumbling so I know that they don't have brain fever. And far from hiding me, they're forever dragging me by racks of fancy clothes or through teeming school corridors, or welcoming gaggles of friends while I'm wandering through the house in Anne's filmy pink babydoll pajamas. George generally calls before he brings someone home, but he does just as many dumb thankless chores as the children. And they all yell at me, laugh at some of my jokes, write me funny letters when we're apart—in short, treat me as an ordinary human being for whom they have some use. I think they like me. Unless they're faking. . . .

17   Faking. There's the rub. Tugging at the fringes of my consciousness always is the terror that people are kind to me only because I'm a cripple. My mother almost shattered me once, with that instinct mothers have—blind, I think, in this case, but unerring nonetheless—for striking blows along the fault-lines of their children's hearts, by telling me, in an attack on my selfishness, "We all have to make allowances for you, of course, because of the way you are." From the distance of a couple of years, I have to admit that I haven't any idea just what she meant, and I'm not sure that she knew either. She was awfully angry. But at the time, as the words thudded home, I felt my worst fear, suddenly realized. I could bear being called selfish: I am. But I couldn't bear the corroboration that those around me were doing in fact what I'd always suspected them of doing, professing fondness while silently putting up with me because of the way I am. A cripple. I've been a little cracked ever since.

18   Along with this fear that people are secretly accepting shoddy goods comes a relentless pressure to please—to prove myself worth the burdens I impose, I guess, or to build a substantial account of goodwill against which I may write drafts in times of need. Part of the pressure arises from social expectations. In our society, anyone who deviates from the norm had better find some way to compensate. Like fat people, who are expected to be jolly, cripples must bear their lot meekly and cheerfully. A grumpy cripple isn't playing by the rules. And much of the pressure is self-generated. Early on I vowed that, if I had to have MS, by God I was going to do it well. This is a class act, ladies and gentlemen. No tears, no recriminations, no faint-heartedness.

19   One way and another, then, I wind up feeling like Tiny Tim, peering over the edge of the table at the Christmas goose, waving my crutch, piping down God's blessing on us all. Only sometimes I don't want to play Tiny Tim. I'd rather be Caliban, a most scurvy monster. Fortunately, at home no one much cares whether I'm a good cripple or a bad cripple as long as I make vichyssoise with fair regularity. One evening several years ago, Anne was reading at the dining-room table while I cooked dinner. As I opened a can of tomatoes, the can slipped in my left hand and juice spattered me and the counter with bloody spots. Fatigued and infuriated, I bellowed, "I'm so sick of being crippled!" Anne glanced at me over the top of her book. "There now," she said, "do you feel better?" "Yes," I said, "yes, I do." She went back to her reading. I felt better. That's about all the attention my scurviness ever gets.

20   Because I hate being crippled, I sometimes hate myself for being a cripple. Over the years I have come to expect—even accept—attacks of violent self-loathing. Luckily, in general our society no longer connects deformity and disease directly with evil (though a charismatic once told me that I have MS because a devil is in me) and so I'm allowed to move largely at will, even among small children. But I'm not sure that this revision of attitude has been particularly helpful. Physical imperfection, even freed of moral disapprobation, still defies and violates the ideal, especially for women, whose confinement in their bodies as objects of desire is far from over. Each age, of course, has its ideal, and I doubt that ours is any better or worse than any other. Today's ideal woman, who lives on the glossy pages of dozens of magazines, seems to be between the ages of eighteen and twenty-five; her hair has body, her teeth flash white, her breath smells minty, her underarms are dry; she has a career but is still a fabulous cook, especially of meals that take less than twenty minutes to prepare; she does not ordinarily appear to have a husband or children; she is trim and deeply tanned; she jogs, swims, plays tennis, rides a bicycle, sails, but does not bowl; she travels widely, even to out-of-the-way places like Finland and Samoa, always in the company of the ideal man, who possesses a nearly identical set of characteristics. There are a few exceptions. Though usually white

and often blonde, she may be black, Hispanic, Asian, or Native American, so long as she is unusually sleek. She may be old, provided she is selling a laxative or is Lauren Bacall. If she is selling a detergent, she may be married and have a flock of strikingly messy children. But she is never a cripple.

21   Like many women I know, I have always had an uneasy relationship with my body. I was not a popular child, largely, I think now, because I was peculiar: intelligent, intense, moody, shy, given to unexpected actions and inexplicable notions and emotions. But as I entered adolescence, I believed myself unpopular because I was homely: my breasts too flat, my mouth too wide, my hips too narrow, my clothing never quite right in fit or style. I was not, in fact, particularly ugly, old photographs inform me, though I was well off the ideal; but I carried this sense of self-alienation with me into adulthood, where it regenerated in response to the depredations of MS. Even with my brace I walk with a limp so pronounced that, seeing myself on the videotape of a television program on the disabled, I couldn't believe that anything but an inchworm could make progress humping along like that. My shoulders droop and my pelvis thrusts forward as I try to balance myself upright, throwing my frame into a bony S. As a result of contractures, one shoulder is higher than the other and I carry one arm bent in front of me, the fingers curled into a claw. My left arm and leg have wasted into pipe-stems, and I try always to keep them covered. When I think about how my body must look to others, especially to men, to whom I have been trained to display myself, I feel ludicrous, even loathsome.

22   At my age, however, I don't spend much time thinking about my appearance. The burning egocentricity of adolescence, which assures one that all the world is looking all the time, has passed, thank God, and I'm generally too caught up in what I'm doing to step back, as I used to, and watch myself as though upon a stage. I'm also too old to believe in the accuracy of self-image. I know that I'm not a hideous crone, that in fact, when I'm rested, well dressed, and well made up, I look fine. The self-loathing I feel is neither physically nor intellectually substantial. What I hate is not me but a disease.

23   I am not a disease.

24   And a disease is not—at least not single-handedly—going to determine who I am, though at first it seemed to be going to. Adjusting to a chronic incurable illness, I have moved through a process similar to that outlined by Elizabeth Kubler-Ross in *On Death and Dying*. The major difference—and it is far more significant than most people recognize—is that I can't be sure of the outcome, as the terminally ill cancer patient can. Research studies indicate that, with proper medical care, I may achieve a "normal" life span. And in our society, with its vision of death as the ultimate evil, worse even than decrepitude, the response to such news is, "Oh well, at least you're not going to die." Are there worse things than dying? I think that there may be.

25   I think of two women I know, both with MS, both enough older than I to have served me as models. One took to her bed several years ago and has been there ever since. Although she can sit in a high-backed wheelchair, because she is incontinent she refuses to go out at all, even though incontinence pants, which are readily available at any pharmacy, could protect her from embarrassment. Instead, she stays at home and insists that her husband, a small quiet man, a retired civil servant, stay there with her except for a quick weekly foray to the supermarket. The other woman, whose illness was diagnosed when she was eighteen, a nursing student engaged to a young doctor, finished her training, married her doctor, accompanied him to Germany when he was in the service, bore three sons and a daughter, now grown and gone. When she can, she travels with her husband; she plays bridge, embroiders, swims regularly; she works, like me, as a symptomatic-patient instructor of medical students in neurology. Guess which woman I hope to be.

26   At the beginning, I thought about having MS almost incessantly. And because of the unpredictable course of the disease, my thoughts were always terrified. Each night I'd get into bed wondering whether I'd get out again the next morning, whether I'd be able to see, to speak, to hold a pen between my fingers. Knowing that the day might come when I'd be physically incapable of killing myself, I thought perhaps I ought to do so right away, while I still had the strength. Gradually I came to understand that the Nancy who might one day lie inert under a bedsheet, arms and legs paralyzed, unable to feed or bathe herself, unable to reach out for a gun, a bottle of pills, was not the Nancy I was at present, and that I could not presume to make decisions for that future Nancy, who might well not want in the least to die. Now the only provision I've made for the future Nancy is that when the time comes—and it is likely to come in the form of pneumonia, friend to the weak and the old—I am not to be treated with machines and medications. If she is unable to communicate by then, I hope she will be satisfied with these terms.

27   Thinking all the time about having MS grew tiresome and intrusive, especially in the large and tragic mode in which I was accustomed to considering my plight. Months and even years went by without catastrophe (at least without one related to MS), and really I was awfully busy, what with George and children and snakes and students and poems, and I hadn't the time, let alone the inclination, to devote myself to being a disease. Too, the richer my life became, the funnier it seemed, as though there were some connection between largesse and laughter, and so my tragic stance began to waver until, even with the aid of a brace and a cane, I couldn't hold it for very long at a time.

28   After several years I was satisfied with my adjustment. I had suffered my grief and fury and terror, I thought, but now I was at ease with my lot. Then one summer day I set out with George and the children across the desert for a vacation in California. Part way to Yuma I became aware that my right leg

felt funny. "I think I've had an exacerbation," I told George. "What shall we do?" he asked. "I think we'd better get the hell to California," I said, "because I don't know whether I'll ever make it again." So we went on to San Diego and then to Orange, up the Pacific Coast Highway to Santa Cruz, across to Yosemite, down to Sequoia and Joshua Tree, and so back over the desert to home. It was a fine two-week trip, filled with friends and fair weather, and I wouldn't have missed it for the world, though I did in fact make it back to California two years later. Nor would there have been any point in missing it, since in MS, once the symptoms have appeared, the neurological damage has been done, and there's no way to predict or prevent that damage.

29   The incident spoiled my self-satisfaction, however. It renewed my grief and fury and terror, and I learned that one never finishes adjusting to MS. I don't know now why I thought one would. One does not, after all, finish adjusting to life, and MS is simply a fact of my life—not my favorite fact, of course—but as ordinary as my nose and my tropical fish and my yellow Mazda station wagon. It may at any time get worse, but no amount of worry or anticipation can prepare me for a new loss. My life is a lesson in losses. I learn one at a time.

30   And I had best be patient in the learning, since I'll have to do it like it or not. As any rock fan knows, you can't always get what you want. Particularly when you have MS. You can't, for example, get cured. In recent years researchers and the organizations that fund research have started to pay MS some attention even though it isn't fatal; perhaps they have begun to see that life is something other than a quantitative phenomenon, that one may be very much alive for a very long time in a life that isn't worth living. The researchers have made some progress toward understanding the mechanism of the disease: It may well be an autoimmune reaction triggered by a slow-acting virus. But they are nowhere near its prevention, control, or cure. And most of us want to be cured. Some, unable to accept incurability, grasp at one treatment after another; no matter how bizarre: megavitamin therapy, gluten-free diet, injections of cobra venom, hypothermal suits, lymphocytopharesis, hyperbaric chambers. Many treatments are probably harmless enough, but none are curative.

31   The absence of a cure often makes MS patients bitter toward their doctors. Doctors are, after all, the priests of modern society, the new shamans, whose business is to heal, and many an MS patient roves from one to another, searching for the "good" doctor who will make him well. Doctors too think of themselves as healers, and for this reason many have trouble dealing with MS patients, whose disease in its intransigence defeats their aims and mocks their skills. Too few doctors, it is true, treat their patients as whole human beings, but the reverse is also true. I have always tried to be gentle with my doctors, who often have more at stake in terms of ego than I do. I may be frustrated,

maddened, depressed by the incurability of my disease, but I am not diminished by it, and they are. When I push myself up from my seat in the waiting room and stumble toward them, I incarnate the limitation of their powers. The least I can do is refuse to press on their tenderest spots.

32   This gentleness is part of the reason that I'm not sorry to be a cripple. I didn't have it before. Perhaps I'd have developed it anyway—how could I know such a thing?—and I wish I had more of it, but I'm glad of what I have. It has opened and enriched my life enormously. This sense that my frailty and need must be mirrored in others, that in searching for and shaping a stable core in a life wrenched by change and loss, change and loss, I must recognize the same process, under individual conditions, in the lives around me. I do not deprecate such knowledge, however I've come by it.

33   All the same, if a cure were found, would I take it? In a minute. I may be a cripple, but I'm only occasionally a loony and never a saint. Anyway, in my brand of theology God doesn't give bonus points for a limp. I'd take a cure; I just don't need one. A friend who also has MS startled me once by asking, "Do you ever say to yourself, 'Why me, Lord?' " "No, Michael, I don't," I told him, "because whenever I try, the only response I can think of is 'Why not?' " If I could make a cosmic deal, whom would I put in my place? What in my life would I give up in exchange for sound limbs and a thrilling rush of energy? No one. Nothing. I might as well do the job myself. Now that I'm getting the hang of it.

MyWritingLab™   **Reading Reflection Questions**

1. What are the direct and implied messages of this essay?

_____

_____

2. Why does Mairs refer to herself as a "cripple" (see paragraphs 2–4)?

_____

_____

3. List two symptoms/disabilities that Mairs says multiple sclerosis can cause (see paragraph 7).

_____

_____

4. In your own words, what is Mairs's attitude to this disease?

_____

_____

5. T/F _____ Mairs is in denial about her disease.

6. T/F _____ Mairs has been disabled her whole life.

7. T/F _____ Over time, her condition will only get worse.

MyWritingLab™   **Checking Vocabulary**

Define each of the following words by figuring out their meaning using context clues from the reading selection. If you cannot work out the meaning of a word, refer to a dictionary.

8. chagrin (paragraph 1): _____

9. semantics (paragraph 2): _____

10. euphemism (paragraph 3): _____

_____

READING CRITICALLY

1. What is the author's **purpose** or goal in this reading selection?

_____

_____

_____

2. What are the implied or stated messages?

_____

_____

_____

3. What specific **support**, details, and examples does the author use to develop the reading's purpose or goal?

_____

_____

_____

4. What inferences does the author include in this reading? (Inferences imply cause-and-effect analysis.)

_____

_____

_____

5. Who is the intended audience, and how did you reach that **conclusion?**

_____

_____

_____

MyWritingLab™   Writing Assignments

Cross Reference
See Chapter 7,
pp. 142–174, "Narration
and Description";
Chapter 12, pp. 263–286,
"Cause and Effect";
or Chapter 14,
pp. 308–334, "Argument
and Persuasion."

1. Write a narration and description essay about a time you felt like you were treated differently based on how you look or act.

2. Write a cause-and-effect analysis essay about discrimination against the disabled.

3. Write an essay that argues in favor of or against mandatory nondiscrimination training in the workplace.

Learning Objectives Review

MyWritingLab™ **Complete the chapter assessment questions at mywritinglab.com**

---

1 Write analytically about readings.

How do you write analytically about readings? (See p. 403.)

To write analytically about a reading, focus on interpreting its meaning. Show what the author's main messages are, and analyze the techniques and style choices the author used to convey those messages.

---

2 Structure an analysis essay.

How do you structure an analysis essay? (See p. 404.)

Structure an analysis essay with an introductory paragraph, body paragraphs, and a conclusion. In your body paragraphs, include quotations from the original work as evidence and use interpretation, analysis, and commentary.

---

3 Incorporate text references into body paragraphs.

What are the three main components of the Ice Cream Sandwich method for incorporating quotations into your essay? (See pp. 404–410.)

The three main components of the **Ice Cream Sandwich method** are: (1) the top cookie, a sentence or two that introduces the point you want to make; (2) the ice cream filling, which is a direct quotation, paraphrase, or summary with a page citation; and (3) the bottom cookie, which provides interpretation and analysis.

---

4 Apply the same critical reading and analysis skills to a variety of reading selections.

How do I apply critical reading and analysis skills to various reading selections? (See pp. 410–461.)

To apply critical reading and analysis skills to readings, use active reading techniques and annotations. Then, answer the reading comprehension and critical thinking questions, along with the essay writing prompts, at the end of the reading selections.

PART V SENTENCE CONSTRUCTIONS AND COMMON SENTENCE ERRORS

CONTENTS

19 **Sentence Parts**

20 **Sentence Variety**

21 **Correcting Major Sentence Errors**

INTRODUCTION TO PART V

Part V of this text gives you the keys you need to unlock the parts of sentences and to put those parts together to make varied and thoughtful sentences that are complete and grammatically correct according to the conventions and rules for English. But you should also use the critical thinking and reading skills you learned in Part I to evaluate your sentence constructions and grammar. Refer to Part V as you work on your paragraph and essay skills and the revision process covered in Parts II, III, and IV. Your ability to spot and fix sentence construction errors, as well as the types of grammar errors covered in Part VI, will improve the clarity of your ideas and facilitate good communication.

These chapters lay the foundation for solid sentence skills that will allow you to construct grammatically correct paragraphs and essays. Reviewing the basics of what makes a sentence, how to create more complex and varied sentences, and how to create complete sentences that aren't run together will enhance your writing in all your courses and in your day-to-day life.

In this chapter, you will learn how to

1 Use sentence building blocks correctly and identify the parts of speech.

2 Use various phrases and phrase types.

3 Use articles and other noun determiners.

4 Use conjunctions to combine sentences.

Thinking Critically MyWritingLab™

Think: Sentence parts are like tiles in a mosaic: Individual pieces fit together to make a coherent whole and create an overall message, each piece adding to the meaning. What sentence parts do you already know before reading this chapter? List all the sentence parts you can think of.

Write: Write a sentence using all the sentence parts you listed.

_____

_____

_____

_____

_____

_____

_____

_____

_____

THE BUILDING BLOCKS OF SENTENCES

1 Use sentence building blocks correctly and identify the parts of speech.

A **sentence** is a group of words that expresses a complete thought. The individual components of sentences are the building blocks. In order to convey a complete thought, all sentences must have at least a **subject** (the *what* or *who* the sentence is about) and a **predicate** (the action of the sentence). However, there are many other parts to sentences—phrases, articles, noun determiners, coordinating and subordinating conjunctions, and conjunctive adverbs—which, like building blocks, can be put together to express what you want to say. **Grammar** means the basic rules or principles of a language, specifically how words combine to form correct sentences. Sentences in college-level essays should be constructed using correct grammar.

Subjects and Predicates (Verbs)

When a word describes another word, it is called a modifier. A subject consists of a noun or a noun plus its modifiers and a predicate consists of a verb, or a verb plus its modifiers. When the modifiers are stripped from the subject and the predicate, leaving only the noun and the verb, the noun is called the **simple subject** and the verb is called the **simple predicate**. The simple subject and the simple predicate are the two most basic building blocks of a sentence.

SUBJECT	PREDICATE
The gray-haired **dog** *limped* slowly to its dog bed.	
SIMPLE SUBJECT	SIMPLE PREDICATE
dog	*limped*

The Subject

The main, or simple, subject of the sentence is *dog*. *Gray-haired* modifies the word *dog*. *The* describes the rest of the words in the subject. *The gray-haired dog* is the complete subject.

The Predicate

What did the dog do? It *limped*. That action is the verb, the simple predicate. How did it limp? *Slowly*. This word describes how the dog limped; it modifies the verb. The verb plus the modifier and the other words that complete the meaning of the verb make up the complete predicate: *limped slowly to its bed*.

ACTIVITY 19-1   Simple Subjects and Predicates

Directions: *Underline the simple subject in each sentence, and mark it with an S. Then double-underline the simple predicate (the verb) in each sentence, and mark it with a V.*

1. The old dog slept peacefully.

2. My husband's snoring sounded throughout the house.

3. The toddler's legs were stretched, out in front of him.

4. Based on the tracks, a car must have driven by this house.

5. Suddenly, his whole body jerked.

6. The problem was simple.

7. Noisy squirrels jetted around the yard.

8. The rooftops were covered with leaves.

9. The students cheered at the end of the day.

10. Trina marked special events on the calendar.

Subjects: Who or What It's All About

A **subject** can be a noun or noun phrase, a pronoun, a gerund phrase, or the implied *you* of a command. In the following sentences, the subjects are in **bold** font, and the verbs are in *italics*:

> **Kenneth** *called* the fire department last night. (noun as subject)
>
> **She** *didn't use* a recipe for the cake. (pronoun as subject)
>
> **The old theater building** *created* the old-fashioned feel of the neighborhood. (noun phrase as subject)
>
> **Its stubby legs** *took* it slowly across the room. (noun phrase as subject)
>
> *Grab* the keys. (implied *you* as subject)
>
> **Knowing she could change** *kept* her motivated. (gerund phrase as subject)

To be able to assess the subject in a sentence, you will need to be familiar with different types of subjects.

The four types of subjects are listed below.

1. **The subject can be a noun, a noun phrase, or an infinitive.**
   - **Noun as subject.** A **noun** can be a person, place, thing, idea, or state of existence. Also, there are different categories of nouns.

Noun Categories at a Glance

Common nouns	Name general categories or types: *refrigerator, boy, tornado*
Proper nouns	Name specific people or items: *The Lincoln Memorial, Sherman Alexie, Auburn High School*
Abstract nouns	Not related to specific details: *love, happiness, beauty*
Concrete nouns	Related to specific sensory details: *blue, ice cream, stone*
Singular nouns	Name one of something: *child, Tom, Columbia River*
Plural nouns	Name more than one of something: *children, tables, clouds*
Collective nouns	Name several items grouped as one collective item: *team, family, group*
Count nouns	Can be counted as individual units: *girl, friend, dog*
Noncount (mass) nouns	Cannot be counted as individual units: *sand, flour, blood*

- **Noun phrase as subject.** A **noun phrase** is a noun plus its modifiers, the words that describe it.

> **Most people** *sleep* at night. (The noun is *people*. The word that describes it is *Most*.)

- **Infinitive as subject.** Phrases beginning with *to* (infinitives) can be subjects.

> *To be happy* is something most people want.

- **Nouns and noun phrases can be joined to form a *compound subject*.** A **compound subject** is made of two or more nouns or noun phrases joined by the word *and* or *or*.

> **Clara and Soroa** *caught* the morning train. (compound subject)
>
> **Either the eastbound train or the westbound train** *will arrive* first. (compound subject)

2. **The subject can be a pronoun.** A **pronoun** is a word that replaces a noun: *I, you, he, she, it, we, they, this, that, these,* and *those* are pronouns. A pronoun may replace a previously mentioned noun, or a pronoun may be indefinite, that is, it refers to one or more unspecified beings, objects, or places; for example, *everyone, someone, anybody, both, few,* and *many.*

> The couple was married in Hawaii. **They** *had planned* the wedding a full year in advance. (The pronoun *They* replaces the words *The couple* from the first sentence.)

3. **The subject can be a gerund phrase** (an *-ing* phrase that serves as the subject of the sentence).

> **Taking the test early** *is* sometimes a bad idea. (*Taking the test early* is the subject, a gerund phrase; *is* is the main verb of the sentence.)

4. **All sentences must have a subject, and, in commands, the subject (you) is implied.**

> **(You)** *Run!* (*You* is implied. *Run* is the verb.)
> **(You)** *Eat* the cake. (*You* is implied. *Eat* is the verb.)

▶ **NOTE**   The subject doesn't always come first in the sentence. Sometimes other words come before the subject of a sentence. For instance, the second sentence in the example below starts with a **transition**, that is, a word or phrase that shows the relationship between the two sentences. The subject follows the transition. To find the subject, identify the verb, and then ask who or what performed the action of the verb.

> **The laundry** *needed* to be washed. Next to the basket, **the washing machine** *sat waiting.*

▶ **ELL TIP**   Identifying types of nouns can be especially challenging for English language learners. Here are three tips to help you use nouns correctly:

1. **Check for Count versus Noncount Nouns**

   Count nouns name items that can be counted as individual units:

   > dog/dogs, cat/cats, boy/boys, girl/girls, flower/flowers, window/windows, cracker/crackers, street/streets, nut/nuts

Noncount (or **mass**) **nouns** name items that cannot be counted as individual units:

> food, rice, flour, water, sugar, peace, life, death, furniture, milk, wood, cotton, leather, beauty, chess, evidence

2. **Use Subject Pronouns.** If you have used a noun subject in a sentence and don't want to repeat the subject in the next sentence, use a pronoun to represent the original noun in your second sentence.

> **Incorrect:** I'm taking upper-level physics this semester. *Is* a challenging course. [no subject pronoun]
>
> **Correct:** I'm taking upper-level physics this semester. *It is* a challenging course. [subject pronoun added]

3. **Use *It* or *There* Correctly with Deferred Subjects.** In English, when a subject is deferred (placed later in the sentence than is usual), the sentence should start with *it* or *there*.

> **Incorrect:** *Is* not good to use a cell phone while driving.
>
> **Correct:** *It is* not good to use a cell phone while driving.
>
> **Incorrect:** *Are* risks even when drivers use hands-free cell phones.
>
> **Correct:** *There are* risks even when drivers use hands-free cell phones.

ACTIVITY 19-2 **Identifying Subjects**

Directions: *Underline the subjects in the following sentences. Be careful not to underline* all *the nouns—only the nouns functioning as subjects. If the subject is implied, write "implied" at the end of the sentence.*

1. Martha likes to mow the lawn in the spring.

2. She says mowing can be more difficult when the grass gets longer.

3. My friends, Mary and Mike, like to mow their lawn once a week.

4. However, Ben and Chris mow their lawn once every two weeks.

5. Just to be safe, mow the lawn at least semi-regularly.

6. Some people prefer electric mowers.

7. Some prefer gas mowers.

8. Others prefer to use old-fashioned push mowers.

9. Knowing the art of lawn care is important to many people.

10. Then again, many could care less about the state of their lawns.

Predicates (Also Known as Verbs): Action Words

All sentences must have at least one verb or verb phrase. A **verb** is the action of a sentence—it can be a physical action, a mental action, or a state of being.

> **Physical Action**
>
> Hannah *kicked* the ball. (*Kicked* is the simple predicate; *the ball* describes what she kicked. The complete predicate is *kicked the ball.*)
>
> Hannah *kicked* the ball and *ran* behind it. (Compound predicate; the two verbs are in italics. The complete compound predicate is *kicked the ball and ran behind it.*)
>
> **Mental Action**
>
> I *thought* about taking a trip. (*thought* is the simple predicate)
>
> **State of Being**
>
> I *am.* (simple predicate)

Verbs function in different ways, depending on their role in a particular sentence:

1. Some verbs can stand on their own.

> **My dog** *eats* three times a day. (simple present tense verb)
>
> **Clara's sisters** *called* all their friends to invite them to the party. (simple past tense verb)

2. Some verb forms need auxiliary, or helping, verbs to complete them.

A **verb phrase** is two or more words working together to create the action (verb) for the sentence.

> The new campaign *was created* today. (*Created* can't be a main verb on its own in this sentence.)
>
> She *has been waiting* for a new mission. (*Waiting* can't be a main verb on its own.)
>
> When *will* he *arrive?* (*Will* adds the meaning of "the future" to the verb *arrive.*)

There are three verb forms that can't be the main verb of a sentence without some helping verbs. They are the *to* form (infinitives), the *-ed* form in certain cases (past participles), and the *-ing* form (present participles):

- **to + Verb (Infinitives).** In an infinitive, the word *to* comes before the plain form of the verb: *to walk, to run, to eat*. The infinitive can't be used alone as the main verb of a sentence—you wouldn't write, *The child to eat cake*. Infinitives don't give enough information about what is happening to be used as the main verb.

> ▶ **ELL TIP** In English, the verb indicates the tense or time in addition to describing the action.

In predicates, infinitives normally follow the main verb.

> Emily *had promised to cook* dinner for Kyle. (*Had promised to cook* is the whole verb phrase.)
>
> The meeting *was scheduled to occur* at noon on Tuesday.

▶ **NOTE** Avoid *splitting your infinitive*, that is, putting a word in between *to* and the verb:

> **Incorrect:** Phoebe wanted *to quickly solve* the math problem.
>
> **Correct:** Phoebe wanted *to solve the math problem quickly*.

To verbs can also act as the subject of a sentence:

> **To run a marathon** *takes* true determination.

- **-ed Verbs (Past Participles).** To indicate the past tense of most verbs, *-ed* or *-d* is added to the base form. If there is no helping verb (such as *was, has,* or *had*), then the verb is in simple past tense form. A verb in the simple past can act as the main verb of a sentence. But the *-ed* form of a verb must always be helped by an auxiliary verb. A helping verb plus an *-ed* verb forms a perfect tense (see "Applying Critical Thinking" on p. 473).

Simple past tense:	She *cooked* lasagna. She also *made* a nice salad.
Present perfect:	She *has wanted* to have a party for all her friends for years. (*has* adds the meaning of "the present" to *wanted*)
Past perfect:	She *had planned* to throw a party for her colleagues, too. (*had* adds the meaning of "the past" to *planned*)

- **-ing Verbs (Present Participles).** Verbs that end with *-ing* are called participles. An *-ing* form is never a complete verb by itself—you wouldn't say *My boyfriend washing his car*. In predicates, a form of the verb *to be* is needed before the participle to indicate an action that *was*, *is*, or *will be* continuing.

> He *is having* a hard time understanding. (*is* adds the meaning of "the present")
>
> Yesterday, he *was hoping* to take the test. (*was* adds the meaning of "the past")
>
> He *will be studying* for the test all night long. (*will be* adds the meaning of "the future")

3. **Verb tense indicates time—past, present, and future.** (See "Verb Tense at a Glance," below, for more information.)

Verb Tense at a Glance

Think of tense as a timeline that starts on the left, in the past, and moves to the right, the future.

Here's a chart that shows the past, present, and future tenses of the verb *walk*:

Tense	Past	Present	Future
Simple	She walked.	She walks.	She will walk.
Perfect	She had walked.	She has walked.	She will have walked.
Progressive	She was walking.	She is walking.	She will be walking.
Perfect Progressive	She had been walking.	She has been walking.	She will have been walking.

▸ **NOTE**   For most verbs in the present tense, use the base form (as found in the dictionary) for the first person subjects *I* and *we*, the second person subject *you*, and the third person plural subject *they*. For the third person singular subjects *he*, *she*, and *it*, add *-s* or *-es*.

> base form: *walk*.
>
> **First person, second person, third person plural:** I walk. You walk. They walk.
>
> **Third person singular:** He walks. She walks. It walks.

Base Forms: *To Be* Verbs   Since there are many irregular verbs in English that don't follow this pattern, be sure to consult a dictionary or grammar handbook for correct verb forms. Here is a chart showing how three common irregular verbs change depending on the tense and number.

Base Verb	Present Singular	Present Plural	Past Singular	Past Plural
be	I am	We are	I was	We were
	You are	You are	You were	You were
	He/she/it is	They are	He/she/it was	They were
have	I have	We have	I had	We had
	You have	You have	You had	You had
	He/she/it has	They have	He/she/it had	They had
do	I do	We do	I did	We did
	You do	You do	You did	You did
	He/she/it does	They do	He/she/it did	They did

APPLYING CRITICAL THINKING

 PURPOSE   IDEAS   SUPPORT   ASSUMPTIONS BIASES   CONCLUSIONS   POINT OF VIEW   ANALYSIS

Analysis involves breaking down an **idea** and working out the meaning of the individual parts and how they relate to the whole. Ask the following analytical questions to ensure that you have used the correct tense.

1. Am I writing about something that happened in the past and then stopped?

   If so, use the **simple past tense**: Manny **went** to the store yesterday.

2. Am I writing about something that happened and stopped before another past event?

   If so, use the **past perfect tense**: Although he **had brought** a grocery list, he still **forgot** to buy milk.

3. Am I writing about something that started in the past and is still happening?

   If so, use the **present perfect tense**: She **has wondered** for a long time what it would be like to be married.

4. Am I writing about something that is happening now?

   If so, use the **present or present progressive tense**: She **is leaving** now.

5. Am I writing about something that hasn't happened yet but will happen in the future?

   If so, use the **future tense**: By tomorrow, I **will know** how it feels to be married!

6. Am I writing about something that will start in the future, continue, and then stop at a particular time?

   If so, use the **future perfect tense**: According to her grand plan, she **will have been married** for a couple of years before she has children.

Irregular Verbs   One of the most difficult aspects of English (for both new learners of English and native speakers) is the large number of irregular verbs (verbs that change form in an unconventional way when they change tense). Here is a chart to help you with some irregular verb forms.

Base Form	Simple Past Tense	Past Participle
awake	awoke	awoken
be	was, were	been
bear	bore	borne
beat	beat	beat
become	became	become
begin	began	begun
bend	bent	bent
beset	beset	beset
bet	bet	bet
bid	bid/bade	bid/bidden
bind	bound	bound
bite	bit	bitten
bleed	bled	bled
blow	blew	blown
break	broke	broken
breed	bred	bred
bring	brought	brought
broadcast	broadcast	broadcast
build	built	built
burn	burned/burnt	burned/burnt
burst	burst	burst
buy	bought	bought
cast	cast	cast
catch	caught	caught
choose	chose	chosen
cling	clung	clung
come	came	come
cost	cost	cost
creep	crept	crept
cut	cut	cut

Base Form	Simple Past Tense	Past Participle
deal	dealt	dealt
dig	dug	dug
dive	dived/dove	dived
do	did	done
draw	drew	drawn
dream	dreamed/dreamt	dreamed/dreamt
drink	drank	drunk
drive	drove	driven
eat	ate	eaten
fall	fell	fallen
feed	fed	fed
feel	felt	felt
fight	fought	fought
find	found	found
fit	fit	fit
flee	fled	fled
fling	flung	flung
fly	flew	flown
forbid	forbade	forbidden
forget	forgot	forgotten
forgive	forgave	forgiven
forsake	forsook	forsaken
freeze	froze	frozen
get	got	gotten
give	gave	given
go	went	gone
grind	ground	ground
grow	grew	grown
hang	hung	hung
hear	heard	heard
hide	hid	hidden
hit	hit	hit
hold	held	held
hurt	hurt	hurt

Continued ▶

Base Form	Simple Past Tense	Past Participle
keep	kept	kept
kneel	knelt	knelt
knit	knit	knit
know	knew	know
lay	laid	laid
lead	led	led
leap	leaped/leapt	leaped/leapt
learn	learned/learnt	learned/learnt
leave	left	left
lend	lent	lent
let	let	let
lie	lay	lain
light	lighted/lit	lighted
lose	lost	lost
make	made	made
mean	meant	meant
meet	met	met
misspell	misspelled/misspelt	misspelled/misspelt
mistake	mistook	mistaken
mow	mowed	mowed/mown
overcome	overcame	overcome
overdo	overdid	overdone
overtake	overtook	overtaken
overthrow	overthrew	overthrown
pay	paid	paid
plead	pled	pled
prove	proved	proved/proven
put	put	put
quit	quit	quit
read	read	read
rid	rid	rid
ride	rode	ridden
ring	rang	rung
rise	rose	risen

Base Form	Simple Past Tense	Past Participle
run	ran	run
saw	sawed	sawed/sawn
say	said	said
see	saw	seen
seek	sought	sought
sell	sold	sold
send	sent	sent
set	set	set
sew	sewed	sewed/sewn
shake	shook	shaken
shave	shaved	shaved/shaven
shear	sheared	shorn
shed	shed	shed
shine	shone	shone
shoe	shoed	shoed/shod
shoot	shot	shot
show	showed	showed/shown
shrink	shrank	shrunk
shut	shut	shut
sing	sang	sung
sink	sank	sunk
sit	sat	sat
slay	slew	slain
sleep	slept	slept
slide	slid	slid
sling	slung	slung
slit	slit	slit
smite	smote	smitten
sow	sowed	sowed/sown
speak	spoke	spoken
speed	sped	sped
spend	spent	spent
spill	spilled/spilt	spilled/spilt
spin	spun	spun

Continued ▶

Base Form	Simple Past Tense	Past Participle
spit	spit/spat	spit
split	split	split
spread	spread	spread
spring	sprang/sprung	sprung
stand	stood	stood
steal	stole	stolen
stick	stuck	stuck
sting	stung	stung
stink	stank	stunk
stride	strode	stridden
strike	struck	struck
string	strung	strung
strive	strove	striven
swear	swore	sworn
sweep	swept	swept
swell	swelled	swelled/swollen
swim	swam	swum
swing	swung	swung
take	took	taken
teach	taught	taught
tear	tore	torn
tell	told	told
think	thought	thought
thrive	thrived/throve	thrived
throw	threw	thrown
thrust	thrust	thrust
tread	trod	trodden
understand	understood	understood
uphold	upheld	upheld
upset	upset	upset
wake	woke	woken
wear	wore	worn
weave	weaved/wove	weaved/woven
wed	wed	wed
weep	wept	wept

Base Form	Simple Past Tense	Past Participle
win	won	won
wind	wound	wound
withhold	withheld	withheld
withstand	withstood	withstood
wring	wrung	wrung
write	wrote	written

▸ **ELL TIP**   Two of the verb forms that cause confusion for learners of English are infinitive and participle verbs.

An **infinitive** is a verb with the word *to* in front of it. It indicates action *after* the main verb, indicates an *effort*, or indicates a *purpose or intention:*

> **Infinitive (action after):** I decided *to paint* the garage.
>
> **Infinitive (indicates effort):** I tried *to paint* the whole garage in one day.
>
> **Infinitive (indicates purpose):** I went downtown *to buy* more paint.

A **participle** is a verb that ends with *-ing*. Generally speaking, participles present facts rather than intentions. A participle may also indicate an experiment:

> **Participle (fact):** I finished *painting* the garage before dark.
>
> **Participle (experiment):** Try *painting* an entire garage in a single day.

Check to make sure you've used the infinitive and participle forms of verbs correctly.

ACTIVITY 19-3   Identifying Verbs

Directions: *Underline the verbs in the following sentences. If there is an auxiliary verb, be sure to underline that as well.*

1. In grade school, dodge ball is a popular game.

2. Dodge ball can be fun, too.

3. My friends, Avis and Andrea, like dodge ball the most.

4. However, Marta and Beatrice say dodge ball is a mean sport.

5. Just to be safe, be sure not to throw the ball at people's feet.

6. Some people aim at others' feet and cause injuries.

7. My buddy Bryan used to show his aggressive nature in dodge ball.

8. He would aim at people with too much gusto.

9. He threw the ball so hard that it would sting.

10. Many people dislike the game of dodge ball for these very reasons.

ACTIVITY 19-4   Correct Verb Forms and Tenses

Directions: *In the following paragraph, fill in each blank with the correct form and tense of the verb in brackets.*

Last summer, I [to go] _____ to the Grand Canyon. The views from the top [to be] _____ amazing. I [to feel] _____ overwhelmed by the sheer size of the canyon. I remember I [to be] _____ a little queasy because I [to be] _____ afraid of heights. Having a fear of heights [to be] _____ normal in my family. Almost all of us [to have] _____ it. I didn't [to realize] _____ how bad my fear [to be] _____ until I [to look] _____ down into that immense canyon. I must [to admit] _____ that I [to be] _____ a bit intimidated. Finally, when it was time to leave, I [to think] _____ about the importance of taking the opportunity [to see] _____ this amazing natural wonder.

In the following paragraph, fill in the blanks with appropriate verbs.

Knowing how to make the best of a tough situation takes practice and patience. People _____ bad situations. If a person first _____ a decision, then he or she _____ succeed. However, if a person _____ without considering the consequences, then he or she _____ fail. Whenever I _____ in a situation like this, I _____ my options carefully. Last week, I _____ a bad choice, and this week I _____ for it. _____ in mind this simple fact: _____ first, and then _____. You'll _____ happier if you _____ this advice.

Inside the Predicate: Objects

An **object** in grammar is part of the predicate because it is the receiver of the action. A **direct object** is the receiver of the action in a sentence, as in "He hit the ball." The ball is hit, so the ball is the direct object.

The **indirect object** identifies to or for whom or what the action of the verb is performed. In the sentence, "She sent Anders the letter," "letter" is the *direct object* (the letter is sent), and "Anders" is the *indirect object* (she sent the letter *to* Anders).

▸ **NOTE**

1. Some verbs, called intransitive, describe an action that doesn't include a receiver:

   The sun **rises**. The moon **sets**.

2. Other verbs, called transitive, do require (or can have) a receiver:

   The potential employer **took** new applications once a month.

The verb *took* needs a receiver, which is the **object of the verb**. What did the potential employer take? New applications. *Applications* is the object of the verb *took*.

APPLYING CRITICAL THINKING

| PURPOSE | IDEAS | SUPPORT | ASSUMPTIONS BIASES | CONCLUSIONS | POINT OF VIEW | ANALYSIS |

Use your **analysis** skills to break down the sentence into its parts and figure out both the direct and indirect objects.

Too much exercise *can cause* **problems** for one's back.

To find the direct object, ask "What can too much exercise cause?" The direct object is *problems*.
To find the indirect object, ask "Problems to or for whom?" In this case, the word *for* is in the sentence. The indirect object is *one's back*.

ACTIVITY 19-5   Identifying Direct and Indirect Objects

Directions: *Underline the direct objects and indirect objects in the following sentences. Mark DO over the direct objects and IO over the indirect objects.*

1. Martha tossed the magazine to the floor.

2. Manny gave her a cake.

3. Sandy provided an argument in favor of the proposed bill.

4. Angelo kissed her suddenly.

5. Jen gave the old dress to her.

6. Thuy spent four dollars.

7. Du Lan gave Omar the correct answer.

8. Rica passed the note to Margaret.

9. Latosha ate the whole cake.

10. The Board of Directors passed the motion.

PHRASES

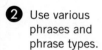 **2** Use various phrases and phrase types.

A **phrase** is a group of related words without a subject and a predicate.

Noun Phrases

A noun phrase includes a noun and all its modifiers.

> *The sparkling ocean* stretched for miles in every direction.

A noun phrase can also act as the object of a verb:

> She wanted to swim in *the blue green sea.*

> ▶ **NOTE**   A noun phrase can also be the object of a preposition, which is discussed in the next section.

Forms of verbs that function as other parts of speech (gerunds and infinitives) can also be noun phrases.

Gerund Noun Phrase
Swimming in the ocean is refreshing.

Infinitive Noun Phrase
To swim in the ocean takes strength and skill.

Prepositions and Prepositional Phrases

Prepositions are words that connect nouns and pronouns to other parts of a sentence. Prepositions indicate relationships in time, place, and direction and also signal connections such as cause and effect or addition: *before, after, above, below, across, because of,* and *in addition to.* A **prepositional phrase** begins with a preposition (see the chart on page 484) and ends with a noun, pronoun, gerund, or clause, the "object" of the preposition.

The **subject** of the film *is* the problem of child labor in some countries.

The prepositional phrases underlined above help guide you through the meaning of the sentence. (The subject of the sentence above is bold, and the verb is italicized.)

Visualization/Memory Tip: Think of a cat and a pair of pipes: Prepositions are anything the cat can do in relation to the two pipes (for instance, the cat can go *around* the pipes, *toward* the pipes, *over* the pipes, *on* the pipes, *in* the pipes, *between* the pipes, and so on). Of course, not every preposition works with this example; for instance, a cat cannot be "of" the pipes. But, as a rule of thumb, this memory tip may help you recognize many common prepositions.

The Most Common Prepositions in English

about	down	outside
above	during	over
according to	except	past
across	except for	plus
after	excepting	regarding
against	for	respecting
along	from	round
along with	in	since
among	in addition to	than
apart from	in case of	through
around	inside	throughout
as	in spite of	till
at	instead of	to
because of	into	toward
before	like	under
behind	near	underneath
below	next	unlike
beneath	of	until
beside(s)	off	unto
between	on	up
beyond	on top of	up to
by	onto	upon
concerning	opposite	with
considering	out	within
despite	out of	without

▶ **NOTE** Avoid ending your sentences with prepositions.

> Cara is who Steve is having dinner with.
> **Rearranged:** Cara is the one with whom Steve is having dinner.
> **Or even better:** Steve is having dinner with Cara.

Prepositional phrases include a preposition, the object of the preposition, and any modifiers of the object. The entire prepositional phrase functions as a modifier in the sentence.

> That mean mother *of hers* is always looking *for more to be mad about.*

Of hers modifies *mother,* a noun, so it is an adjective. *For more to be mad about* modifies a verb, so it is an adverb. Adjectives and adverbs are discussed later in the chapter.

▶ **ELL TIP**   Prepositions and prepositional phrases can be particularly confusing because they sometimes don't have any logic. You will often need memorize them; however, using them should get easier with practice.

Choose the Right Preposition or Prepositional Phrase

Getting prepositions right is difficult because many are learned through use and familiarity with a language, but logical rules do apply to some prepositions. The most easily confused prepositions are those related to *space* and *time.*

1. **Space:** Think location versus direction.

   Location: Use *at, on,* or *in*

   > They had a picnic *at* [location] the park.
   > They sat *on* [surface] a blanket because the grass was damp.
   > He put the leftover food *in* [enclosed space] the basket.

   Direction: Use *to, onto,* or *into*

   > They ran *to* [direction] the car when it started to rain.
   > Muddy water splashed *onto* [surface] her new jeans when she got out of the car.
   > They carried the picnic basket and other gear *into* [enclosed space] the house.

2. **Time:** Use *at* for an exact point in time, *on* for a particular day or date, and *in* for months, years, centuries, and longer periods.

   > The baby was born *at* 1:30 A.M. *on* Sunday.
   > My parents were married *in* 1974.
   > The play is a period drama set *in* the nineteenth century.

Don't Use a Prepositional Phrase as a Subject

A prepositional phrase cannot be used as the subject of a sentence. Instead, use a noun or add a subject pronoun after the prepositional phrase.

> **Incorrect:** *In my apartment complex* has a nice community room.
> **Correct:** My apartment complex has a nice community room.   OR   *In my apartment complex*, there is a nice community room.

Become Familiar with Idioms

Idioms are phrases that develop in a regional language that don't translate directly or easily into another language. Idioms are learned over time through immersion in a language, and the incorrect use of an idiom often indicates that the writer is not a native speaker. Many mistakes in idiom usage come from the misuse of prepositions or verbal phrases.

Verbal phrases are formed when a verb is combined with an adverb or preposition to create a new meaning. Most verbal phrases are idioms, and they are used more in informal conversation or informal writing than in formal essays. However, even when used in informal writing, verbal phrases must be written in a particular order.

Here's a list of the most common idioms in English.

Common English Idioms

ask out	fill in	put away/back/off/on/out/up
break down	fill out	
break up (with)	fill up	quiet down
bring up	find out	run across/into/out
burn down	get along (with)	show off/up
burn out	get away (from or with)	shut off/up
burn up	get back in/on	speak out/up
call back	get out/over/up	stand up (for)
call off	give back/in/up	stay in/off/up
call up	go out (with)	stop up
catch up (with)	go over	take after/in/off/out/over
check in	grow up	take care (of)
check out	hand in/out	tear down/up
check up (on)	hang out/up	think about/over
come out	have on	throw out/up
cross out	help out	try on/out (for)
cut (it) out	keep on/out/up	tune in/out/up
cut up	leave out	turn down/off/on/out/up
drop in	look after/into/out/over/up	wake up
drop off	make up	watch out (for)
drop out (of)	pass out	
figure out	pick out/up	

ACTIVITY 19-6 Identifying Prepositional Phrases

Directions: *Underline all the prepositions and prepositional phrases in the following sentences.*

1. Fadumo came along with the girls because she was fast becoming one of the group.

2. She arrived at the back door of his house looking for food.

3. Aubrey changed her mind because of the reasons that Brandon gave her.

4. She had thought differently before he spoke to her.

5. She decided to stay instead of leaving for the week.

6. Grandmother decided to vacuum the entire house, and then she took the dusty vacuum bag to the trash bin outside.

7. I looked longingly toward the hills.

8. She kept her feelings buried deeply within her heart.

9. Kenji put his shoes beside the front door stoop.

10. Hiroko preferred to keep her shoes with her at all times.

Participles and Participial Phrases

Participles are verb forms that can either be part of the main verb or can function as adjectives. Present participles end in *-ing*: *leaving, heaving, ringing*. Past participles usually end in *-ed* or *-d*: *hated, performed, laid*. However, some participles are formed irregularly with endings such as *-n* and *-t*: *forgiven, taken, spent, brought*.

> **Part of main verb:** Chester *was having* second thoughts.
> Daniel *was defeated* in the tennis match.
> **As adjective:** The *defeated* player shook hands graciously with his opponent.

Participial phrases use the *-ing* form for the present participle, and the past participle form usually ends in *-ed, -d, -n,* or *-t*: *elected, deleted, chosen,* and *sent*.

> I saw Daniel *trying to hit* her serve.
> The *elected* official will take her office in the fall.

ACTIVITY 19-7 Identifying Participles
and Participial Phrases

Directions: *Underline the participles and participial phrases in the following
sentences.*

1. Ranjit was exhausted after the race.

2. Gurpreet was encouraging him to keep it up.

3. I saw Latara asking for advice from Miwa.

4. Miwa watched Omar spending so much time trying to get the answer.

5. Midori was wondering if she could solve the problem.

6. Ian caught Christina staring at her watch during the lecture.

7. Masa had said no before, thinking that it wasn't worth it.

8. Defeated, Peter gave up.

9. Cory had taken too long to answer.

10. The distracted student wasted too much of her allotted time.

Adjectives and Adjective Phrases

Adjectives are words that modify nouns and pronouns (the adjectives below
are italicized; the nouns they modify are in bold).

Modifying nouns: The *skinny* **dog** looked scared.
Modifying pronouns: They were very *thin*.

Descriptive adjectives can take three forms:

1. **The positive form**, used to express simple descriptions, such as *red,
heavy, tiny, flat, beautiful*:

   The *new* **car** looked good.

2. **The comparative form**, used to compare two things, such as *lower,
smarter, more functional, less useful*:

   Trina has a *newer* **car** than her boyfriend's.

3. **The superlative form**, used to compare three or more things, such as *largest*, *dirtiest*, *most functional*, *least useful*:

> She had the *newest* **car** on the block: newer than any of her neighbors' cars.

An **adjective phrase** is a phrase that modifies a noun or pronoun:

> The **woman** *parking the car* is my mother.

The adjective phrase modifies *woman*, a noun.

ACTIVITY 19-8   Identifying Adjectives and Adjective Phrases

Directions: *Underline all the adjectives and adjective phrases in the following sentences.* **Tip:** *It might help to circle all the nouns first.*

1. The old clock on the antique dresser kept time like a reliable friend.

2. The moldy cheese from Gina's refrigerator smelled like a wet sock.

3. The happy child sitting in the worn leather chair looked pleased with her tiny furry puppy by her side.

4. The large blue luxury car pulling into the station took only expensive premium gas.

5. The loud obnoxious buzzing was coming from inside the stranger's handbag, and we were sure it was an overactive and overly loud cell phone.

6. The man handing out the balloons overlooked some of the smaller children.

7. The blazing sun kept Monica moving quickly to find refreshing shade.

8. The woman sneezing over and over was allergic to long-haired dogs.

9. The too-tight shirt and high pants told Mustafa he had washed his clothes in the wrong temperature.

10. The slippery fish popped out of the boy's wet hands.

Adverbs and Adverb Phrases

Adverbs are words that modify verbs, verb forms, adjectives, and other adverbs to indicate *how, where, when,* or *how much.* Many adverbs end with *-ly,* but not all. The adverbs below are in italics; the words they modify are in bold.

> **Modifying verbs:** Tito **spoke** *loudly.*
>
> **Modifying verb forms:** Troy had *barely* **noticed** the child hiding in the back.
>
> **Modifying adjectives:** It was a *very* **fancy** dinner.
>
> **Modifying other adverbs:** The dog ran *very* **quickly.** Who knew he could run *this far?*

Like adjectives, adverbs have three forms. The adverbs below are in italics; the words they modify are in bold.

1. **Positive:** *quietly, smoothly, slow, awkwardly, intensely*

   > She **limped** *awkwardly.*

2. **Comparative:** *quieter, smoother, slower, more awkwardly, more intensely*

   > She **limped** even *more awkwardly* when she noticed she was being watched.

3. **Superlative:** *quietest, smoothest, slowest, most awkwardly, most intensely*

   > She **limped** the *most awkwardly* after a few people laughed.

An **adverb phrase** is a phrase that begins with a preposition and functions as an adverb:

> The casserole was **full** *of vegetables from her garden.*

The adverb phrase *of vegetables from her garden* modifies *full,* an adjective.

ACTIVITY 19-9   Identifying Adverbs and Adverb Phrases

Directions: *Underline the adverbs and adverb phrases in the following sentences.*

1. The hamsters dashed happily through the see-through tubes.

2. Knowing the crowd was very hungry, the wait staff served the customers extremely quickly.

3. The ants fought mightily and valiantly against the termites' attack.

4. The meeting went well.

5. Students sometimes get the tickets for free.

6. The ice cream was loaded with roasted almonds.

7. The cat swam quicker than the dog.

8. In fact, it swam the quickest of all the animals in the pool.

9. The paper was ruined by typos and grammar errors.

10. Larry jumped higher than Tony in the competition.

ACTIVITY 19-10 **Identifying Adjectives and Adverbs**

Directions: *Underline the adjectives and adverbs in the following sentences. Then circle the nouns, verbs, verb forms, or adverbs they modify.*

1. Leslie's brand-new convertible car raced quickly along the highway.

2. The family nobly honored the recently departed head of the extended family.

3. The sandy beaches and warm breezes of Hawaii easily calmed the weary traveler.

4. The man with the eye patch made the imaginative child nervous as he looked very cautiously from behind the building.

5. The last movie played promptly at 7:00 in the remodeled theater.

ARTICLES AND OTHER NOUN DETERMINERS

3 Use articles and other noun determiners.

The **articles** *a*, *an*, and *the* are a type of **noun determiner**—a word that signals a noun is to follow; the context and the type of noun that follows determine which article, if any, is used. Articles are divided into two categories: the **definite**, or specific, article (*the*) and the **indefinite**, or nonspecific, articles (*a* or *an*). In some cases, you should use a noun determiner such as *some* instead of an article.

1. A and *an* are indefinite articles used for general description nouns.

- Use *a* when the noun that follows starts with a consonant or a consonant sound: *a car, a sheep, a place, a united front* (the *u* sounds like the consonant *y*, so use *a*).

- Use *an* when the noun that follows starts with a vowel or a vowel sound: *an Englishman, an orange, an elevator, an honor* (the *h* is silent; the word begins with the sound of *o*, so use *an*).

2. ***The* is a definite article.**

   Use *the* when the word that follows is a specific noun (not a general descriptor): **the** *best place to shop,* **the** *champion racehorse,* **the** *movie to watch.*

3. **Other noun determiners** include:

   - **Demonstratives:** *this, that, these, those*
   - **Possessives:** *my, our, your, his, her, their, its*
   - **Cardinal numbers:** *one, two, three,* and so on.
   - **Miscellaneous:** *all, another, each, every, much, some,* and so on.

▶ **ELL TIP**　Articles are one of the most challenging aspects of the English language for new speakers.

1. **No noun determiner:** If a noun is used in a general sense and not as a specific subject, it doesn't need an article.

   > Cats love to drink milk. (cats in general = no article)
   > The cats on my street like to attack squirrels. (particular cats = article needed)

2. **Definite articles:** Use *the* to refer to particular or specific common nouns (singular or plural) and noncount nouns that are specific because the noun was previously identified:

   > *The* sandwiches we ordered were delicious.
   > Let me pay for *the* food this time.

   Use *the* with superlatives:

   > *The* best vegetarian pizza has caramelized onions on it.

   The is also used with some proper nouns:

   > *The* Smiths just moved to New Mexico.
   > They used to live in *the* Midwest.
   > We took a riverboat cruise on *the* Mississippi.
   > *The Columbia Tribune* is known for its lively editorials.

3. Indefinite articles: Use *a* or *an* with generic singular count nouns:

> She asked if he would like to get *a* cup of coffee sometime.

4. Noun determiners: Use *some* with plural nouns or noncount nouns that refer to a particular or specifiable quantity:

> *Some* roses are very fragrant, but others have no fragrance at all.
> The orchids need *some* water, but not too much.

ACTIVITY 19-11 Identifying Articles and Noun Determiners

Directions: *Underline the articles and noun determiners in the following sentences.*

1. The math teacher in room five held a set of keys.
2. Spotting every type of error in writing is difficult.
3. That chair over there is broken.
4. One of these will work better.
5. Your sister is a very nice person.
6. An apple a day keeps the doctor away.
7. The best way to get your vitamins is a healthy diet.
8. The only thing you need to remember tonight is to get a good night's rest.
9. All the students decided to take the train.
10. Three heads are better than the usual two.

CONJUNCTIONS

❹ Use conjunctions to combine sentences.

A **clause** is a group of words containing a finite verb (a finite verb works on its own with a subject to help create an independent clause: it doesn't need a helping verb). A clause can be **dependent**, which means it cannot stand on its own as a complete sentence, or **independent**, which means it is a complete sentence. *Coordinating conjunctions, subordinating conjunctions,* and *conjunctive adverbs* help correctly join two clauses. If the clauses are both independent (two complete sentences, each with its own subject and verb), use a coordinating conjunction with a comma or a conjunctive adverb with a semicolon to join the clauses. If one of the clauses is dependent on the other, use a subordinating conjunction to join them.

Coordinating Conjunctions

Coordinating conjunctions are seven words that can connect two independent clauses (along with a comma):

For	And	Nor	But	Or	Yet	So

A simple mnemonic device for remembering these seven words is the acronym **FAN BOYS**.

▶ **NOTE**   Don't assume that whenever you use one of these seven words in a sentence, they are serving as a coordinating conjunction. You may use the word *and*, for instance, in a list of items such as *bread, cheese,* **and** *mustard,* in which case the word *and* does not join two independent clauses.

ACTIVITY 19-12   Identifying Coordinating Conjunctions

Directions: *Underline the coordinating conjunctions in the following sentences.*

1. *It must be one of the seven words listed above.*
2. *It must be preceded by a comma.*
3. *It must be between two independent clauses.*

1. The neighborhood decided to take action, so they started a clean-up campaign.
2. People said they were interested, but only a few volunteered at first.
3. Several of the neighbors were willing to work, and that was enough to get the ball rolling.
4. The strongest and youngest took the job of clearing the debris, for that task required physical strength.
5. They agreed not to let the children lift big objects, nor would they let them handle sharp debris.
6. Their neighborhood had been used as a dumping ground, so they had a lot to do.
7. They could take things to the dump, or they could pay someone to move the trash.

8. They decided to take the debris to the dump, but they needed a truck.

9. The truck rental was very expensive, so they could not pay the dump fees.

10. The children sold lemonade for two days, and they raised the money needed.

Subordinating Conjunctions

Subordinating conjunctions connect dependent (or subordinate) clauses to independent clauses. If the dependent clause is first, place a comma after it. Do not use a comma if the dependent clause follows the independent clause.

> **Dependent clause first:** *Because* she always supported her students, Jaeney decided to contribute to the scholarship fund.
>
> **Dependent clause second:** Jaeney decided to contribute to the scholarship fund *because* she always supported her students.

The twenty most common subordinating conjunctions are listed below.

Twenty Common Subordinating Conjunctions

after	before	though	whether
although	if	unless	which
as	once	until	while
as though	since	when	who
because	that	whereas	whose

> ▶ **ELL TIP** Sometimes, new speakers of English use both coordination and subordination in the same sentence by mistake.
>
> **Avoid Mixing Coordination and Subordination**
>
> Use a subordinating clause with a comma or connect two clauses with a coordinating conjunction, but do not do both.
>
> > **Incorrect:** *Although* I went to bed early, *but* I was still tired in the morning.
> >
> > **Correct:** *Although* I went to bed early, I was still tired in the morning.
> >
> > OR
> >
> > I went to bed early, *but* I was still tired in the morning.

Conjunctive Adverbs

Conjunctive adverbs are words that can connect two independent clauses, but they are not coordinating conjunctions. Conjunctive adverbs are transitions that can be used at the beginning of a sentence to help connect it to a preceding sentence or paragraph. Here is a list of the most common conjunctive adverbs:

Common Conjunctive Adverbs		
consequently	moreover	therefore
furthermore	nevertheless	thus
however	otherwise	

When a conjunctive adverb appears between two independent clauses, a semicolon sets it off from the clause that comes before it, and a comma sets it off from the clause that comes after it.

> Kathleen wanted to win the race; *consequently*, she trained for weeks.
> Salman wanted to compete, too; *however*, he had injured his knee.

ACTIVITY 19-13　Identifying Subordinating Conjunctions and Conjunctive Adverbs

Directions: *Underline the subordinating conjunctions and/or conjunctive adverbs in the following sentences.*

1. When the sequel comes out in the theaters, I will be the first one in line.
2. Although Emma wanted to see the play, Debbie had her heart set on seeing the baseball game.
3. The school track team had a great season; however, they did not win the championship.
4. She wanted to buy a new umbrella because her old one was coming apart.
5. I have decided to run for office; furthermore, I want you to be my campaign manager.
6. While I waited in line, I thought about my tasks for the day.

7. I knew it was just a matter of time before she arrived; therefore, I bought a coffee and began to read the paper.

8. I read the paper and drank my coffee until she finally arrived.

9. I knew she was usually late; nevertheless, I still arrived at the agreed-upon time.

10. Before I knew it, she was sitting beside me and grinning sheepishly.

ACTIVITY 19-14 **Create Your Own Sentences Using Coordination and Subordination**

Directions: *Create five sentences of your own on the subject of weather using both co-ordination and subordination. Three should include either a* coordinating conjunction, *a* subordinating conjunction, *or a* conjunctive adverb. *The other two are your choice. Refer to the tables shown earlier to identify possibilities.*

1. Use a **coordinating conjunction:**

   _____

   _____

2. Use a **subordinating conjunction:**

   _____

   _____

3. Use a **conjunctive adverb:**

   _____

   _____

4. Your choice:

   _____

   _____

5. Your choice:

   _____

   _____

APPLYING CRITICAL THINKING

| PURPOSE | IDEAS | SUPPORT | ASSUMPTIONS BIASES | CONCLUSIONS | POINT OF VIEW | ANALYSIS |

When you are making choices about which elements to include when constructing a sentence, you need to ask yourself the following questions:

1. What is my **purpose** for this particular sentence? What do I want to say?

2. What **ideas** and information do I need to include in this sentence?

3. Who is my target audience? How can I best arrange the parts of the sentence to convey my ideas to this audience?

Then, use your **analysis** skills to break the sentence down into its parts and make sure that you have constructed it correctly. Check that the sentence contains a verb and a subject, expresses a complete thought, and is written in the correct tense.

MyWritingLab™   **Mastery Test: Identifying Coordinating and Subordinating Conjunctions and Conjunctive Adverbs**

Directions: *On the lines provided, label the bold word in each sentence as either a coordinating conjunction (CC), a subordinating conjunction (SC), or a conjunctive adverb (CA).*

_____ 1. **Although** I know it's bad for me, I allow myself the indulgence.

_____ 2. Chocolate has sugar; **nevertheless**, it has healthy properties, too.

_____ 3. Chocolate has antioxidants, **and** dark chocolate has a lot of them.

_____ 4. Chocolate is certainly one of my favorite treats; **however**, other candy tempts me as well.

_____ 5. Sugar contributes to tooth decay, **yet** candy is a favorite treat.

_____ 6. I try to maintain a healthy diet; **however**, I crave dessert at night.

_____ **7.** I could try eating more fruit, **but** that's just not the same somehow.

_____ **8.** **Because** most candy features sugar or corn syrup, it is full of calories.

_____ **9.** I think I will still allow myself these treats **because** we're all entitled to one vice in life.

_____**10.** **As** far as vices go, candy is low on the dangerous list.

Mastery Test: Identifying Parts of Speech

Directions: _In this excerpt from Diane Ackerman's "Chocolate Equals Love," mark the various parts of speech in the following way: Circle all subjects, underline all verbs, and double-underline all prepositions or prepositional phrases._

We can thank the Indians of Central and South America for chocolate's bewitching lusciousness. As the Spanish explorer Hernán Cortés found, the Aztecs worshipped chocolate (which they named _cacahuatl_) as a gift from their wise god Quetzalcoatl. Aztec soldiers and male members of court drank as many as 2,000 pitchers of chocolate every day. They spiked their drink with vanilla beans and spices, and they drank it bubbly thick from golden cups. Adding chili peppers gave it bite. The Aztec leader Montezuma required a chocolate ice, made from pouring syrup over snow that runners brought to him from the nearest mountain.

Learning Objectives Review

My**Writing**Lab™ Complete the chapter assessment questions at mywritinglab.com

❶ Use sentence building blocks correctly and identify the parts of speech.

What are the primary building blocks of a sentence? (See pp. 465–482.)

The primary components of a sentence are the **subject** (*who* or *what* is doing the action) and the **predicate** or verb (the action of the sentence). All sentences must have at least a subject and a verb and convey a complete thought.

❷ Use various phrases and phrase types.

What is a phrase, and what are some specific types of phrases? (See pp. 482–491.)

A **phrase** is a group of related words without a subject and a predicate. There are several types of phrases including prepositional phrases, participial phrases, and adjective and adverb phrases.

❸ Use articles and other noun determiners.

What are articles and other noun determiners? (See pp. 491–493.)

Articles (*a*, *an*, and *the*) are a type of **noun determiner**, a word that signals that a noun is to follow. The context and the type of noun that follows determine which article, if any, is used. **Noun determiners** also include **demonstratives** (*this, that, these, those*); **possessives** (*my, our, your, his, her, their, its*); **cardinal numbers** (*one, two, three, etc.*); and **miscellaneous** (*all, another, each, every, much, etc.*).

❹ Use conjunctions to combine sentences.

What are conjunctions, and how are they used to combine dependent and independent clauses in sentences? (See pp. 493–499.)

Conjunctions are words or phrases that can link together words, phrases, or clauses in sentences. Clauses can be **dependent** (they cannot stand on their own as a complete sentence) or **independent** (they are complete sentences). Two or more independent clauses can be joined by a *coordinating conjunction* and a comma or a *conjunctive adverb* and a semicolon. A dependent (or subordinate) clause can be joined to an independent clause by a *subordinating conjunction*.

20 Sentence Variety

LEARNING OBJECTIVES

In this chapter, you will learn how to

❶ Use coordination and subordination.

❷ Write sentences that have specific purposes.

❸ Write sentences using the four basic structures.

❹ Revise sentences to increase sentence variety.

Thinking Critically MyWritingLab™

Think: Sentence parts can be combined to create different sentence structures and to achieve sentence variety, which keeps writing interesting. Once you know the parts, you can arrange them in different ways to achieve your desired effect.

Write: In the lines below, write three sentences that describe the photograph. Then, rewrite those three sentences as one sentence.

_____

_____

_____

_____

_____

_____

_____

_____

_____

_____

_____

_____

COORDINATION AND SUBORDINATION

❶ Use coordination and subordination.

Coordination and subordination allow you to combine clauses in different ways in order to make sentences more effective and interesting.

Coordination

When two independent clauses of equal importance are joined, they form a **coordinate sentence**. They can be joined in two ways:

1. **Coordinating conjunctions:** Use one of the **FANBOYS** (*for, and, nor, but, or, yet, so*) and a **comma** to combine the two independent clauses.

> The news report said the weather was turning blustery, *so* Hannah went back for her hat and gloves.

2. **Conjunctive adverbs:** Use one of the conjunctive adverbs (preceded by a semicolon and followed by a comma) to combine two independent clauses. Some commonly used conjunctive adverbs include *however, therefore, thus, moreover, furthermore, otherwise, nevertheless,* and *consequently*.

> Mahmoud slammed the oven door; *consequently*, the cake fell.

Subordination

When one clause is less important (needs less emphasis), then it is **subordinate** or *dependent* on the independent clause. Use subordinating conjunctions to mark the beginning of the dependent or subordinate clause. If the dependent clause is placed before the independent clause, add a comma after the dependent clause. Some of the most common subordinating conjunctions are *because, since, if, after, although, until, while, as, as though, before, once, that, who, whose, which,* and *whereas*.

> The map indicated we were getting close *although* we couldn't see a sign of civilization.
>
> *Even though* we were starving, we decided to keep driving to the next town.
>
> *Since* Trinh ate all the eggs, we couldn't have pancakes this morning.

ACTIVITY 20-1 **Sentence Combining Using Coordination and Subordination**

Directions: *Combine the following pairs of sentences into one grammatically correct sentence using either coordination or subordination as indicated.*

Example	A. The Capitol Building is located in Washington, DC.
	B. The Capitol Building is a beautiful and symbolic building.
Coordination	The Capitol Building is located in Washington, DC, **and** it is a beautiful and symbolic building.
Conjunctive adverb	The Capitol Building is located in Washington, DC; **moreover**, the Capitol Building is a beautiful and symbolic building.
Subordination	The Capitol Building, **which** is located in Washington, DC, is a beautiful and symbolic building.

The Capitol Dome in Winter

1. The US Capitol Building was designed in 1792.
   The designer, Dr. William Thornton, decided to create a dome for the Capitol.
   Use **coordination:**

   _____

   _____

2. Dr. Thornton submitted his plan in a contest for the Capitol building design.
   He was only an amateur architect.
   Use **subordination:**

   _____

   _____

3. The first cornerstone was laid by George Washington on September 18, 1793.

   The original north wing wasn't fully constructed until November 17, 1800.

   Use a **conjunctive adverb with a semicolon:**

   _____

   _____

4. British troops marched on Washington, DC, during the War of 1812.

   Unfortunately, on August 24, 1814, British troops set fire to the building.

   Use **coordination:**

   _____

   _____

5. The new architect, Benjamin Latrobe, used the opportunity to make changes to the interior because most of the exterior was spared.

   He added more marble and a more ornate interior design.

   Use a **conjunctive adverb with a semicolon:**

   _____

   _____

   _____

6. Charles Bulfinch took over as head architect in 1818.

   Bulfinch worked on the restoration and the Senate and House chambers until his position was terminated in 1829.

   Use **coordination:**

   _____

   _____

   _____

7. By 1850, the Capitol needed to be expanded to accommodate the growing number of senators.

   Another competition, offering $500 for the best expansion design, was held.

   Use **coordination:**

   _____

   _____

   _____

8. In 1856, the old dome was removed.

Work began on a new dome that was cast iron and fireproof.

Use **subordination:**

_____

_____

9. In 1861, construction was halted due to the Civil War.

In 1862, construction was resumed as a symbol of the strength of the Union.

Use **coordination:**

_____

_____

10. The work on the dome and extensions was completed in 1868 under the new architect, Edward Clark.

Clark held the post of Architect of the Capitol until his death in 1902.

Use **coordination:**

_____

_____

_____

SENTENCE TYPES AND PURPOSES

2 Write sentences that have specific purposes.

A **sentence** is a group of words that expresses a complete thought and contains at least one independent clause. An independent clause includes, at a minimum, an implied or stated subject and a main verb. Sentences can have the following four purposes:

1. Declarative: They make a statement or declaration.

> The new hybrid cars are better than ever.
> Both the hybrid sedans and the SUVs drive well and get good mileage.

2. Interrogative: They ask a question.

> Will you buy a hybrid car?

3. Imperative: They give a command.

> Try a test drive of one of the new models.

4. Exclamatory: They express a strong emotion or sentiment.

> The newest hybrids are spectacular!

ACTIVITY 20-2   Practicing Sentence Types

Directions: *Write one sentence of your own for each of the four sentence types. Be sure to punctuate your sentences correctly.*

Declarative:

_____

Interrogative:

_____

Imperative:

_____

Exclamatory:

_____

SENTENCE STRUCTURES

3 Write sentences using the four basic structures.

There are four basic sentence structures in English:

1. **Simple Sentences:** Simple sentences have one independent clause.

> The banks are lowering interest rates.

2. **Compound Sentences:** Compound sentences have two or more independent clauses.

> The banks are lowering interest rates, and people are beginning to buy new houses again.

3. **Complex Sentences:** Complex sentences have at least one independent clause and at least one dependent clause.

> The housing market is starting to get busy again since interest rates decreased.

4. **Compound-Complex Sentences:** Compound-complex sentences have at least two independent clauses and at least one dependent clause.

> The realtors in my neighborhood have joined the buying craze, and they are pushing for even more sales because interest rates will surely rise again soon.

ACTIVITY 20-3 Practicing with Sentence Structures

Directions: *Create a sentence for each sentence structure indicated.*

Simple Sentence:

_____

Compound Sentence:

_____

_____

Complex Sentence:

_____

_____

Compound-Complex Sentence:

_____

_____

To make your writing interesting, you can combine dependent clauses with independent clauses (using coordination and subordination) in various patterns to achieve a variety of sentence types.

Use critical thinking to choose the best sentence type to express your ideas in the context of your writing assignment. The types of sentences you write will depend on your topic and your audience. If you just write a series of independent clauses in your paragraphs, your writing will be choppy and uninteresting. By using coordination and subordination to combine those shorter sentences, you will keep your readers engaged. Here are a few possible combinations (DC = dependent clause, IC = independent clause):

1. **Two independent clauses (joined by a coordinating conjunction)**

> IC   +   IC
>
> Selling a home is stressful, *but* it helps to hire a realtor.

2. **A dependent clause in front of an independent clause**

> DC   +   IC
>
> When I sold my home, I tried doing it on my own at first.

3. **Independent clause followed by a dependent clause**

> IC   +   DC
>
> The stress of waiting for an offer was intense when I first advertised the sale of my house.

4. **A dependent clause followed by an independent clause and a dependent clause**

> DC   +   IC   +
>
> When I didn't get an offer for over a month, I finally hired a realtor
>   DC
> *because* I needed professional help.

See how many types of sentences you can create as you experiment with coordination and subordination.

ACTIVITY 20-4   Sentence Combining Practice

Directions: *Step One: Write a paragraph that describes where you live using 8–15 simple sentences. Step Two: Go back and revise your original paragraph, and combine some of your sentences using coordination and subordination to achieve sentence variety.*

Original Version

_____

_____

_____

_____

_____

_____

_____

Revised Version

_____

_____

_____

_____

_____

_____

_____

SENTENCE VARIETY

4 Revise sentences to increase sentence variety.

When crafting longer pieces of writing, such as paragraphs and essays, you should vary your sentences in length, type, and rhythm. Readers get tired of short, choppy sentences, and your style and tone suffer, too. Use a variety of sentence lengths to keep your readers interested and your style strong. Similarly, change the structure of your sentences in your paragraphs and essays to avoid a monotonous style, tone, and rhythm.

One way to achieve sentence variety is to go back to some of your original, simple sentences and add more details and examples. For instance, if you had a sentence that read *I like to snorkel*, you could vary it in length and style by simply adding more details: *I like to snorkel because it gives me an intense connection with nature through the many sea plants and animals I get to observe firsthand.*

Another way to vary your sentences is to use coordination and subordination to combine sentences, making them more complex. For example:

> **Original sentences:** I like to snorkel. Sea turtles are the most exciting creatures to see while snorkeling.
>
> **Revised with coordination:** I like to snorkel, and sea turtles are the most exciting creatures to see underwater.
>
> **Revised with subordination:** Though I like to see all kinds of plants and animals when I snorkel, sea turtles are my favorite.

You can also achieve more variety in your writing by including sentences that are *declarative, interrogative, imperative,* and *exclamatory.* (However, be careful not to overuse exclamatory sentences.)

> I really enjoy snorkeling. Have you ever tried it? You have to try snorkeling in Hawaii. It is the best spot to snorkel by far!

APPLYING CRITICAL THINKING

PURPOSE IDEAS SUPPORT ASSUMPTIONS BIASES CONCLUSIONS POINT OF VIEW ANALYSIS

To revise your writing for sentence variety, employ your **analysis** skills. Go through your draft, reading each sentence carefully. Make sure you have expressed your **ideas** clearly, used correct grammar, and created sentences in which all the parts work together to convey what you want to say. Then see if you can incorporate some of the following suggestions for making your sentences more interesting and eloquent:

Five Tips for Achieving Sentence Variety

1. Double-check the entire piece to make sure you have a good balance of short and long sentences.

2. Try adding some additional information (words or phrases) to your shorter, simpler sentences.

3. Try using different types of sentences: statements (declarative), questions (interrogative), commands (imperative), and exclamations.

4. Try combining some of your simple sentences to create compound, complex, or even compound-complex sentences through the use of coordination and subordination.

5. Vary the style and rhythm of your sentences. Read the sentences aloud to determine if they sound interesting or could benefit from some of the changes listed above.

Before and After Revising for Sentence Variety

Before (no variety)

Making soap at home is a fun hobby and can be used to make beautiful gifts. Soap making involves following a step-by-step process and using caution. Most soap is made by combining fats with lye. Some soaps use animal fat and some use vegetable fat. Also, some soap is cold processed some hot processed. In the cold process, lye is dissolved in water, and then fatty oils are stirred in. However, the cold process requires very exact measurements for the lye and oils. In the hot process, the lye and the oils are boiled together to a temperature of 80–100 degrees Celsius. The measurements don't have to be as exact in the hot process because the heat will adjust the balance until saponification occurs (the fat changes into soap). Next, the soap starts to thicken. At that point, one can add essential oils or fragrances to the soap. Finally, the liquid is poured into a mold and allowed to cure for a day to up to a month, depending on the process used.

After (revised using the five tips for achieving sentence variety)

Change in sentence type for variety
Coordination to combine two sentences

Subordination to combine two sentences
Subordination

Coordination

Coordination to combine two sentences

Have you ever thought of making your own soap? Making soap at home is a fun hobby and can be used to make beautiful gifts. Soap making involves following a step-by-step process, and one needs to use extreme caution when working with harsh ingredients such as lye. In fact, most soaps are made by combining fats, animal fats or vegetable fats such as olive oil, with lye. Also, some soaps are cold processed, while some are hot processed. In the cold process, lye is dissolved in water, and then fatty oils are stirred in; however, the cold process requires very exact measurements of the lye and the oils. In the hot process, the lye and the oils are boiled together to a temperature of 80–100 degrees Celsius, and the measurements don't have to be as exact as in the cold process because the heat will adjust the balance until saponification occurs (the soap sets up). Next, the soap starts to thicken, and, at that point, one can add other essential oils such as moisturizing jojoba oil or fragrant oils such as peppermint oil to the soap. Finally, the liquid is poured into a mold, and the soap is allowed to cure for a day to up to a month depending on the process used. Try making your own soap today! Beautiful, handmade soap makes a perfect gift.

ACTIVITY 20-5 **Practicing Sentence Variety**

Directions: *Using the five tips on page 510, rewrite the following paragraph to achieve more sentence variety.*

Alfred Hitchcock made many classic American movies. Most of his films were in the horror genre. However, many would say they should be considered psychological thrillers. One of his most famous films is *Psycho*. However, some would argue that either *Vertigo* or *Rear Window* could also be judged his best film. Two more films by Hitchcock that stand out are *North by Northwest* and *The Birds*. Two of his lesser-known films are *Strangers on a Train* and *Shadow of a Doubt*. These two lesser-known films are actually two of his best. Almost all of his films feature an everyday person who has to overcome unusual, often deadly, circumstances. Sometimes Hitchcock even has us rooting for the bad guys.

Without a doubt, the most noteworthy aspect of Hitchcock's films is the tension and the eerie atmosphere he creates on film.

_____

_____

_____

_____

_____

MyWritingLab™   ## Mastery Test I: More Sentence Combining Using Coordination and Subordination

Directions: _On the lines provided, combine the sets of sentences into one sentence using either_ **coordination** _or_ **subordination**.

1. The houses in the neighborhood were well designed and pleasing to the eye. Most of them were new construction.

   _____

2. The children were eager for summer to arrive. Many of them planned to attend summer camp.

   _____

3. The fish were brightly colored. Some sported exotic blues and yellows.

   _____

4. Baseball is truly an all-American pastime. Spring and baseball go together.

   _____

5. Dogs are very popular pets in America. Cats are also very popular pets in America.

   _____

6. Drinking coffee is a morning ritual for Mary. Specialty coffees with added flavors such as vanilla or cinnamon delight her.

   _____

7. Bagels and cream cheese are a weekend morning favorite breakfast. Bagels with lox and onions are delicious, too, but not for everyone.

_____

8. Swimming is a great cardio workout. Walking daily is also great for one's heart.

_____

9. The neighborhood voted to add a new park. The funds for the park will come from the city and private donations.

_____

10. Red roses are considered the flowers of romance. Yellow roses are the flowers of friendship.

_____

MyWritingLab™   ## Mastery Test II: More Practice with Sentence Variety

Directions:

1. _Write a short paragraph about your family on the lines below. Create at least 10 simple sentences._
2. _Then revise the paragraph using a combination of the five tips to vary the sentence types and lengths._

Original paragraph

_____

_____

_____

_____

_____

Revised paragraph

_____

_____

_____

_____

_____

Learning Objectives Review

MyWritingLab™ Complete the chapter assessment questions at mywritinglab.com

❶ Use coordination and subordination.

What are coordination and subordination, and why are they important in creating sentences? (See pp. 502–505.)

Coordination means combining independent clauses using a comma and a coordinating conjunction (*for, and, nor, but, or, yet, so*—FANBOYS) or a semicolon and a conjunctive adverb (*however, therefore, consequently*, etc.) followed by a comma. **Subordination** involves joining an independent clause to a dependent clause using a subordinating conjunction (*because, since, if, after*, etc.). Coordination and subordination are crucial because they allow you to combine dependent and independent clauses in different ways to make sentences more effective and interesting.

❷ Write sentences that have specific purposes.

What are the four main types of sentences, and what are their purposes? (See pp. 505–506.)

The **four main types of sentences** are: (1) **declarative** (they make a statement), (2) **interrogative** (they ask a question), (3) **imperative** (they give a command), and (4) **exclamatory** (they express a strong emotion or sentiment).

❸ Write sentences using the four basic structures.

What are the four basic sentence structures? (See pp. 506–509.)

The **four basic sentence structures** are (1) the **simple sentence** (consists of one independent clause), (2) the **compound sentence** (has two or more independent clauses), (3) the **complex sentence** (has at least one independent clause and one dependent clause), and (4) the **compound-complex sentence** (has at least two independent clauses and one dependent clause, in any order).

❹ Revise sentences to increase sentence variety.

What are five tips for achieving greater sentence variety? (See pp. 509–513.)

The **five tips** for achieving greater sentence variety are: (1) ensure you have a good balance of short and long sentences and sentence types; (2) add additional words or phrases to shorter, simpler sentences; (3) use different types of sentences; (4) combine some sentences to create compound, complex, or compound-complex sentences using coordination and subordination; and (5) vary the style and rhythm of your sentences.

LEARNING OBJECTIVES

In this chapter, you will learn how to

1 Identify and correct sentence fragments.

2 Identify and correct run-ons and comma splices.

Thinking Critically MyWritingLab™

Think: What are the two main sentence parts that determine if you have a complete sentence?

_____

Write: Write four to five complete sentences describing the dishes in this photograph.

_____

_____

_____

_____

_____

_____

_____

_____

FRAGMENTS

1 Identify and correct sentence fragments.

Like individual dishes that make a complete meal, the parts of a sentence come together to make a complete sentence. But you can't just put the parts together randomly. If you don't have all the necessary parts, or if you have too many parts without the correct punctuation, you can end up with a major construction error. If you are missing a necessary sentence part, you will have a sentence fragment; if you have enough parts for more than one sentence but improper or no punctuation, you will have a comma splice or a run-on sentence.

A **sentence fragment** starts with a capital letter and ends with a period, but it does not express a complete thought. A fragment is a piece of a sentence posing as a complete sentence. Though we often use fragments in everyday speech and in written dialogue, college essays generally require the use of grammatically complete sentences.

Common Errors That Create Fragments

1. **Missing subject:** leaving out the *subject* of the sentence

2. **Missing, incomplete, or incorrect form of verb:** leaving out the *verb,* using an *incomplete verb,* or using the *wrong form of a verb*

3. **Including a subordinating word or phrase before the subject and the verb:** adding a word or phrase that makes a clause *dependent* on another clause for meaning

---

Check your writing carefully for these three common errors that lead to sentence fragments.

1. **Missing a subject**

> **Forgot to close the car door.**
> [Subject missing: *Who* forgot to close the car door?]
> *Mahad* forgot to close the car door.

2. **Missing the verb, using an incomplete verb, or using the wrong form of a verb**

> **A good variety of dining options available in the cafeteria.**
> [No verb. Add one to make the sentence complete.]
> A good variety of dining options *is* available in the cafeteria.

> **Margaret studying for the test.**
> [Incomplete verb: add the helping verb *is* or *was* before *studying*.]
> Margaret *is studying* for the test.
> Margaret *was studying* for the test.

> **The machine running the elevator.**
> [Wrong form of verb: change to *runs* or *ran*.]
> The machine *runs* the elevator.
> The machine *ran* the elevator.

3. **Including a subordinate word or phrase before the subject and verb (makes the word group a dependent clause)**

> **Since she travels every spring.**
> [Subordinating word: the word *Since* makes this a dependent clause. Either delete the word *Since*, or add an independent clause before or after it.]
> ~~Since~~ She travels every spring.
> Since she travels every spring, she has accrued a great deal of frequent flyer miles.

Identifying Sentence Fragments

A complete sentence contains a subject and a verb and does not have a subordinating word or phrase before the subject. Here are three steps you can use to identify sentence fragments:

Three Steps for Identifying Sentence Fragments

1. Find the verb.

2. Find the subject.

3. Check for a subordinating word or phrase.

---

1. **Find the verb.** The verb is usually easy to spot because it indicates the action or state of being in a sentence, so find it first. If there is no verb or if an auxiliary verb is needed, then you have a sentence fragment. Ask yourself, "What is happening in this sentence?" For example:

   > **The kitten in the living room.**
   >
   > [*What* is the kitten doing in the living room? The sentence needs a verb.]
   >
   > The kitten *is sleeping* in the living room.

   If the verb is an *-ing* form (verbal), make sure there is an auxiliary or helping verb (a *to be* verb such as *is*, *was*, *are*, or *were*) in front of it. For instance:

   > **Tom *taking* a nap.**
   >
   > [The above sentence needs a helping verb.]
   >
   > Tom *is taking* a nap.
   >
   > OR, change the *-ing* form to a regular verb:
   >
   > Tom *takes* (or *took*) a nap.

2. **Find the subject.** Ask yourself, "Who or *what* is the subject of the action/verb I found?" If there is no noun serving as the subject, then the word group is a sentence fragment. For example:

   > **Takes the bus almost every day.**
   >
   > [*Who* is taking the bus? *Who* is the subject of this sentence?]
   >
   > *Lori* takes the bus almost every day.

   Exception: The one exception is when the subject is implied, as in the word *you* in a command. For example:

   > **Don't drop that glass.**
   >
   > [Although not stated, the subject of this sentence is the implied "you."]
   >
   > (You) Don't drop that glass.

3. **Check for a subordinating word or phrase that creates a dependent clause.** When you put a subordinating conjunction such as *whenever* in front of the subject of a sentence, the sentence becomes a dependent

clause. It is incomplete because it now depends on the addition of more information to make sense. For example:

> **Whenever she works on weekends.**
>
> [The word *whenever* makes this a dependent clause. Either delete the subordinating word *whenever*, or add an independent clause before or after the phrase.]
>
> ~~Whenever~~ She works on weekends.
>
> *Her partner complains* whenever she works on weekends.
>
> Whenever she works on weekends, *her kids don't see her much.*

Here are a few of the most common words that indicate the beginning of a dependent clause or subordinate phrase:

because	as	believing that
since	on	hoping that
when	in	especially
whenever	every time	
if	knowing that	

Correcting Sentence Fragments

When you spot a fragment, identify the error and use it as a key to fixing the problem.

1. **Missing verb**

   > **Fragment:** Rainfall on the streets. [Missing a verb, so add one.]
   > **Revised:** Rainfall *puddles* on the streets.

   > **Fragment:** The kids playing on the lawn.
   > [Not a complete verb, so add an auxiliary verb or change the verb form.]
   > **Revised:** The kids are playing on the lawn.
   >   The kids play on the lawn.

2. **Missing subject**

   > **Fragment:** Needs to find a good career. [Missing a subject, so add one.]
   > **Revised:** *Clay* needs to find a good career.

3. Dependent clause

> **Fragment:** Because I rowed yesterday.
>
> [Dependent clause due to the word *because*: delete the word *because* or add an independent clause.]
>
> **Revised:** ~~Because~~ I rowed yesterday.
>
>   Because I rowed yesterday, *I will rest today.*
>
>   *I will rest today* because I rowed yesterday.

ACTIVITY 21-1   Identifying and Correcting Fragments I

Directions: *Using the three-step test for fragments, list which type or types of error created each fragment below. Some items may have more than one error.*

1. *Missing a subject*

2. *A missing, incomplete, or incorrect form of verb*

3. *Subordinate word or phrase before the subject and verb*

Then, add or delete words to fix the fragment and rewrite it as a complete sentence. You may need to add more information for the sentence to make sense.

> **Example:** Ate the salad.   Error Type(s) _____ *#1* _____
>
> Corrected: *Cameron ate the salad.* _____

1. Having several fish in one tank.   Error Type(s) _____

   Corrected: _____

2. Because the fish were exotic.   Error Type(s) _____

   Corrected: _____

   _____

3. The fish having several bright colors.   Error Type(s) _____

   Corrected: _____

4. Because the fish were in a large tank.   Error Type(s) _____

   Corrected: _____

   _____

5. Fish observing people who observe fish. Error Type(s) _____

   Corrected: _____

6. Whenever the fish are agitated.   Error Type(s) _____

Corrected: _____

_____

7. The fish being disturbed and anxious.   Error Type(s) _____

Corrected: _____

8. Move quickly from side to side.   Error Type(s) _____

Corrected: _____

9. In several quick patterns.   Error Type(s) _____

Corrected: _____

10. Being that they are easily disturbed. Error Type(s) _____

Corrected: _____

ACTIVITY 21-2 **Identifying and Correcting Fragments II**

Directions: *Review the following word groups. If a word group is a complete sentence, write S on the line provided. If it is a fragment, write F, and then revise it to make it into a complete sentence. You may add or delete words to fix the fragments.*

_____ **1.** San Francisco's Golden Gate Bridge, a miraculous engineering achievement.

_____

_____

_____ **2.** The bridge, completed in 1937, spanning 1.7 miles, linking Marin County and San Francisco.

_____

_____

_____ **3.** The bridge's two towers are 746 feet high.

_____

_____ **4.** Making the towers 191 feet taller than the Washington Monument.

_____

_____ 5. Featuring an art deco design.

_____

_____ 6. The bridge having five lanes for traffic.

_____

_____ 7. The bridge itself a San Francisco landmark.

_____

_____ 8. It's a very recognizable sight, too.

_____

_____ 9. Beneath the bridge, the Golden Gate Strait body of water, 400 feet deep.

_____

_____

_____10. The beautiful bridge, taking four years to complete and $35 million in expenses.

_____

_____

The Golden Gate Bridge

ACTIVITY 21-3 Identifying and Correcting
Fragments III

Directions: *In the spaces provided after the paragraph, mark* F *for a fragment and* S *for a complete sentence. You should find ten fragments.*

> [1]The Golden Gate Bridge is a beautiful site. [2]A long suspension bridge, spanning 4,200 feet. [3]It is a stunning sight in the skyline. [4]Because of the spectacular view. [5]Visitors will travel over the bridge to see it from the other side as well. [6]Fort Point, built at the beginning of the Civil War, sitting at the south end of the bridge. [7]The fort designated a National Historic Monument in 1970. [8]It is built of brick. [9]The bridge and its surrounding areas are some of the most photographed spots of California. [10]Lighthouses visible from the bridge in the distance. [11]One of the lighthouses situated on Alcatraz Island. [12]Alcatraz Island also was home to an infamous prison. [13]It, too, a tourist attraction. [14]Every day, boats take tourists from the mainland to the island. [15]The boats loading at the waterfront. [16]Then, they take people to Alcatraz. [17]It's a short ride. [18]Once there, tourists exploring the old prison. [19]However, the Golden Gate Bridge is the most celebrated San Francisco site. [20]Its marvelous orange towers raised to the sky in beauty.

1. _____   6. _____   11. _____   16. _____

2. _____   7. _____   12. _____   17. _____

3. _____   8. _____   13. _____   18. _____

4. _____   9. _____   14. _____   19. _____

5. _____   10. _____   15. _____   20. _____

Now, pick five of the fragments you found above, and rewrite them below to make them complete sentences by adding the needed subject, by fixing or adding the needed verb, or by removing the subordinating word.

1. _____

_____

2. _____

_____

3. _____

_____

4. _____

_____

5. _____

_____

ACTIVITY 21-4 Identifying and Correcting Fragments IV

Directions: _Correct the verb, add the needed words, or revise the dependent clauses in the following fragments to make them complete sentences._

1. Knowing it was the third Monday of the month.

_____

2. Running as fast as she could.

_____

3. Believing in something strongly.

_____

4. Finding his keys in the nick of time.

_____

5. Deciding it was too late after all.

_____

6. Finding the right path.

_____

7. Moving in a straight line.

_____

8. Eating too much.

_____

9. As the panic set in.

_____

10. Ending the class on time.

_____

RUN-ONS AND COMMA SPLICES

2 Identify and correct run-ons and comma splices.

Run-on sentences and comma splices are grammatical errors that occur when independent clauses are not connected properly.

Run-On Sentences

A **run-on** sentence, sometimes called a *fused sentence*, occurs when you combine two or more independent clauses (complete sentences) with no punctuation to separate them. Use your analysis skills to make sure you don't have two or more independent clauses that need punctuation to join them.

> Rain brings flowers spring is stunning.
>
> [This group of words is a run-on because it includes two full sentences, each with a subject and a verb.]

Rain	**brings**	**flowers**	**spring**	**is stunning.**
(subj)	(verb)	(obj)	(subj)	(verb)

Four Ways to Fix Run-Ons

1. Add a comma and a coordinating conjunction (**F**or, **A**nd, **N**or, **B**ut, **O**r, **Y**et, **S**o—FANBOYS) after the first independent clause.

2. Add end punctuation (a period, an exclamation point, or a question mark) after each independent clause.

3. Add a semicolon (;) after the first independent clause if the content of the two clauses is closely related. If the second clause *answers* or *explains* the first, use a colon.

4. Make one of the independent clauses into a dependent clause by adding a subordinating word. Remember: If the dependent clause comes first, place a comma after it.

Comma Splices

A **comma splice** occurs when you combine two or more independent clauses (two complete sentences, each with a subject and a verb) with just a comma.

> Rain brings flowers, spring is stunning.
>
> [This word group is a comma splice because it contains two full sentences, each with its own subject and verb, separated only by a comma.]

Four Ways to Fix Comma Splices

1. **Add a coordinating conjunction** (FANBOYS—**F**or, **A**nd, **N**or, **B**ut, **O**r, **Y**et, **S**o) after the comma.

> Rain brings flowers, and spring is stunning.

2. **Change the comma into a period** (or an exclamation point or a question mark if the first independent clause is a question).

> Rain brings flowers. Spring is stunning.

3. **Change the comma into a semicolon or a colon**. A semicolon can be used to combine two independent clauses that have closely related content, but use semicolons sparingly.

> Rain brings flowers; spring is stunning.

A colon can also be used between two independent clauses if the second clause *answers* or *explains* the first one.

> I like spring rain for one reason: It brings flowers.

4. Turn one of the independent clauses into a dependent clause by adding a subordinating word.

> Because it rains a great deal in the spring, we get stunning flowers.

ACTIVITY 21-5   Correcting Run-ons

Directions: *Fix the following run-on (fused) sentences by (1) adding a comma and a coordinating conjunction (*For, And, Nor, But, Or, Yet, So*), (2) adding a period, or (3) adding a semicolon.*

1. The airplane was made of wood it also had painted wings.

_____

2. The cat saw the mouse she immediately ran to catch it.

_____

3. At first, the children were scared of the snake after awhile, they became more comfortable handling it.

_____

_____

4. The store owner wanted to attract new customers he added a big new sign out front.

_____

5. It's amazing the trick is to believe it.

_____

6. The appeal of his photographs was strong people admired his work in galleries.

_____

7. Grilling vegetables is a good idea it brings out their natural flavor.

_____

8. Taking notes in class is a good idea it helps with retention.

_____

9. My history teacher requires us to take notes during lectures my grades have improved in that class as a result.

_____

_____

10. I plan to start taking notes in all my classes I think it will pay off.

_____

_____

ACTIVITY 21-6 **Correcting Comma Splices**

Directions: _Fix the following comma splices by (1) adding a coordinating conjunction (For, And, Nor, But, Or, Yet, So) after the comma, (2) changing the comma to a period and capitalizing the first letter in the second sentence, or (3) changing the comma to a semicolon._

1. The air was calm, the wind wasn't blowing at all.

_____

2. Middle school is a tough time for kids, many of the students are uncomfortable at this age.

_____

3. The dog ate the last of the cookies, they had been sitting on the counter.

_____

4. The job interview was tough, Karla didn't think she would get the position.

_____

5. My friend Neal has applied for a new job, he'll hear if he got it soon.

_____

6. Fumitaka's cat liked only him, she was mean to other people.

_____

7. Emma watched from a distance, she tends to be cautious.

_____

8. The smell of the pie baking brought all to the kitchen, it smelled delicious.

_____

9. Baking bread takes time, waiting for the dough to rise is essential.

_____

10. It is worth the wait, what tastes better than fresh bread?

_____

ACTIVITY 21-7   **Correcting Run-ons and Comma Splices I**

Directions: _Mark each sentence RO for run-on (no punctuation between two independent clauses), CS for a comma splice (two independent clauses joined with only a comma), or C if the sentence is correct. Then fix the run-ons and comma splices using one of the methods listed on pages 525–526._

_____   1. The Eiffel Tower is one of the most beloved monuments in the world it is the most well-known monument in Europe.

_____

_____ **2.** The Eiffel Tower was built in 1889, its first year it hosted two million visitors.

_____

_____ **3.** From 1889 to the present, more than 200 million people have visited the Eiffel Tower.

_____

_____ **4.** The Eiffel Tower was built for the Universal Exhibition in celebration of the French Revolution it has come to symbolize France.

_____

_____ **5.** The architect of the Eiffel Tower was Stephen Sauvestre, the construction took two years, two months, and five days.

_____

_____ **6.** The total weight of the Eiffel Tower is 10,100 tons, the height is 324 meters.

_____

_____ **7.** The Eiffel Tower contains over 18,038 pieces of metal, and there are 2,500,000 rivets.

_____

_____ **8.** The Tower is open 365 days a year more than 6 million visitors come each year.

_____

_____ **9.** There are several elevators servicing different levels of the Tower, one elevator is exclusively for guests dining at the Jules Verne Restaurant at the Tower.

_____

_____**10.** The Eiffel Tower is under surveillance 24 hours a day, security is essential for a world-class monument such as this.

_____

The Eiffel Tower

ACTIVITY 21-8 **Correcting Run-ons and Comma Splices II**

Directions: *In the spaces provided below the paragraph, mark RO for run-ons, CS for comma splices, and C for correct sentences.*

[1]According to a survey hosted by the Eiffel Tower website, visitors from five countries consisting of Italy, England, Spain, Germany, and the United States all listed the Eiffel Tower as the most well-known European monument. [2]The Italian responses listed three other popular European monuments after the Eiffel Tower, they were the Coliseum, the Dome of Milan, and the Louvre. [3]The British respondents listed several other monuments the Tower of Pisa, the Arc de Triomphe, Big Ben, and the Tower of London were among their answers. [4]Similarly, the Spanish respondents listed other monuments, but none were above the Eiffel Tower. [5]Spanish tourists also included the Tower of Pisa as a monument that was high on their list. [6]German visitors also listed the Eiffel Tower as number one, they also mentioned the Tower of London and the Tower of Pisa. [7] The German tourists included a few lesser-known sites including the Cologne Dome they also listed the Brandenburg Gate and the Atomium. [8]The American respondents listed the most monuments of all, they, like the other tourists, put the Eiffel Tower at the top of their

list. ⁹They also included the Tower of Pisa and Big Ben on their list the Tower of London ranked high as well. ¹⁰Like the British, the Americans also listed the Arc de Triomphe; it's interesting to see how people around the world view Europe's most famous landmarks.

1. _____   5. _____   9. _____

2. _____   6. _____   10. _____

3. _____   7. _____

4. _____   8. _____

Pick three of the run-ons and three of the comma splices you found above and revise them by adding the needed punctuation or joining word.

1. _____

_____

2. _____

_____

3. _____

_____

4. _____

_____

5. _____

_____

6. _____

_____

MyWritingLab™   ## Mastery Test I: Identifying and Correcting Fragments

Directions: *In the spaces provided below the paragraph, mark* F *for fragment and* S *for complete sentence for each of the numbered word groups.*

¹The Empire State Building in New York City. ²Rises more than a quarter mile into the sky above Manhattan. ³The Observatory is located on the 86th floor. ⁴Because of the panoramic views. ⁵Visitors flock to the glass-enclosed pavilion and the open-air promenade. ⁶Since 1931, almost 110 million visitors having made the visit to the Empire State Building. ⁷There are several businesses within the Empire State

Building. ⁸Including two restaurants, a sushi bar, and three coffee shops. ⁹It's incredible. ¹⁰The building is like a mini city in itself.

1. _____   5. _____   9. _____

2. _____   6. _____   10. _____

3. _____   7. _____

4. _____   8. _____

MyWritingLab™   ## Mastery Test II: Identifying and Correcting Run-ons and Comma Splices

Directions: *In the spaces provided below the paragraph, mark RO for run-ons, CS for comma splices, and C for correct sentences.*

¹The St. Louis Memorial Arch commemorates westward expansion. ²The arch is an amazing accomplishment each leg of the arch is an equilateral triangle. ³At the bottom of the triangle, each leg has sides that are 54 ft. long, tapering to 17 ft. at the top. ⁴The legs also have double walls of steel these walls are three feet apart at ground level and 7 1/2 inches apart at the 400-foot level. ⁵The double-walled triangular sections were welded together, then they were placed one on top of the other to form the arch. ⁶The stairways are for emergencies also the stairways have 1,076 steps. ⁷The arch's legs can withstand strong winds, they are oriented in a north–south line. ⁸There are also tendons for support that go below ground they extend 34 feet below the top of the foundations. ⁹Moreover, the foundation for the arch was pre-stressed, it was essential that the ground could securely withhold the weight of the massive structure. ¹⁰Over the years, the arch has proven its stability, even in a strong wind storm, for the St. Louis Arch is a miraculous achievement of engineering.

1. _____   5. _____   9. _____

2. _____   6. _____   10. _____

3. _____   7. _____

4. _____   8. _____

Learning Objectives Review

MyWritingLab™ Complete the chapter assessment questions at mywritinglab.com

❶ Identify and correct sentence fragments.

What are sentence fragments, and how can you recognize and correct them? (See pp. 516–524.)

Sentence fragments start with a capital letter and end with a period but do not express a complete thought. The **three common errors** that create fragments are (1) a missing subject; (2) a missing, incorrect, or incomplete form of the verb; and (3) the inclusion of a subordinating word that creates a dependent clause. You can **correct fragments** by adding a subject, adding or fixing a verb, or either deleting a subordinating conjunction or adding an independent clause.

❷ Identify and correct run-ons and comma splices.

What are run-ons and comma splices, and what are the four ways to fix these errors? (See pp. 525–532.)

A **run-on** occurs when you combine two or more independent clauses (complete sentences) with no punctuation to separate them. A **comma splice** occurs when you combine two or more independent clauses with just a comma. The **four ways to properly connect independent clauses** are to: (1) use a comma followed by a coordinating conjunction between the two clauses; (2) use a final punctuation mark after each independent clause; (3) put a semicolon or colon between the two clauses; or (4) make one independent clause into a dependent clause by adding a subordinating conjunction.

PART VI HANDBOOK OF GRAMMAR, MECHANICS, AND STYLE

CONTENTS

22 Comma, Semicolon, and Colon

23 Other Punctuation

24 Correcting Common Shift and Construction Errors

25 Spelling and Mechanics

26 Tone, Style, and Word Choice

27 Vocabulary in Context

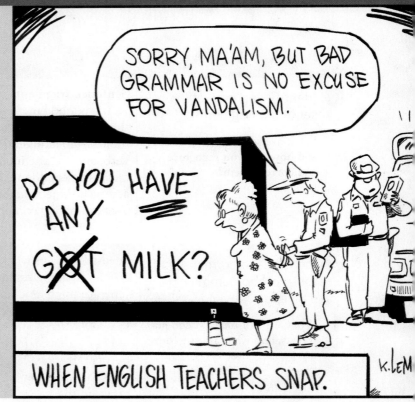

© Kathryn Lemieux

INTRODUCTION TO PART VI

In Part II, you learned how to use the writing process to create stronger paragraphs and essays. The last steps in that writing process are the editing and revision stages, which are covered in Part VI. This part of the book focuses on how to use correct English grammar (the rules of a language), with proper punctuation and spelling and appropriate tone, style, and word choices. In order to write well, you need to check your spelling, punctuation, and grammar—every detail!

These chapters are the final step for taking all you have learned about constructing sentences, paragraphs, and essays in the other parts of this text. They provide you with the tools to write using correct grammar, spelling, and mechanics and to make the right word choices so your ideas are clearly communicated to your readers.

22 Comma, Semicolon, and Colon

LEARNING OBJECTIVES

In this chapter, you will learn how to

1 Use the comma correctly.

2 Use the semicolon correctly.

3 Use the colon correctly.

THE GRAMMARIANS AT HOME

NOTHING BOTHERED ARNOLD MORE THAN A MISPLACED COMMA.

Thinking Critically   MyWritingLab™

Think: What do you imagine it would be like to read a page of writing with misused or missing punctuation marks?

_____

_____

_____

_____

_____

_____

_____

_____

_____

Write: Why?

_____

_____

_____

_____

_____

_____

_____

_____

COMMA

❶ Use the comma correctly.

Punctuation is essential to imparting meaning. The comma (,) is the most common form of punctuation. It serves several functions in writing and helps your readers understand your ideas and sentences. **Commas** clarify, make distinctions, or create the pauses that help your readers digest your sentences and ideas.

Five Comma Rules

There are five basic rules of comma use, and if you keep them in mind, the mystery of comma use will be solved. Do not insert a comma every place you pause as you read your writing; follow the comma rules.

When you edit your writing, check to see if the commas you have used fall into one of these categories, and if they do not, then remember the old saying: "When in doubt, leave it out." Unnecessary commas usually cause more confusion than missing commas.

Rule 1

Use a comma before a coordinating conjunction in order to combine two independent clauses to create a compound sentence.

> **Independent clause + , + FANBOYS + independent clause**
>
> ▼
>
> **(Coordinating conjunctions)**

Use the memory trick FANBOYS (**F**or, **A**nd, **N**or, **B**ut, **O**r, **Y**et, **S**o) to recall the coordinating conjunctions. These are the only seven words in the English language that can be used after a comma to combine two independent clauses (when you use any other word, you end up with a comma splice).

> The computer graphics course is fun, and the professor is excellent. Many students want to take the course, but it is already full.

▶ **TIP**   The comma comes *before* the coordinating conjunction. Also, be careful not to add a comma whenever you see one of the FANBOYS. The comma is only necessary if there is an independent clause (with a subject and a verb) on *both* sides of the word.

Otherwise, the word is part of a compound subject or a compound predicate, and, in that case, you don't use a comma:

> Maya took the course last year and said it was great.

There is only one subject in this sentence: *Maya*. There are two verbs that both relate to the subject: *took* and *said*. The word *and* links two parts of a compound predicate, so no comma is needed.

Rule 2

Use a comma to separate the items in a series (a list of three or more items) or a list of coordinate adjectives.

1. **Using commas with items in a series.** Commas help separate distinct items within a list of items:

> **Item + , + item + , + item + , + and item**

> Maya has taken several other computer courses, including Computer Programming, Software Tools, and Web Site Development.

Placing the last comma before the "and" is one of the comma rules currently being debated. Some people argue that a comma replaces the word "and," so the comma before the last item in a series isn't necessary. However, there are cases when a reader could get confused by the absence of a comma before the last item in a series, so it's usually a good idea to use this comma. Consistency and clarity are the rules of thumb. For example:

> I went to the movie with my cousins, Marco, and Sofia.

Without the second comma, the reader would not know whether Marco and Sofia are the names of the speaker's cousins or the names of two other people who accompanied the speaker and the speaker's cousins to the movie. As this sentence is now punctuated, it means that the speaker went with both his or her cousins *and* Marco and Sofia (two friends).

2. **Using commas with coordinate adjectives versus cumulative or compound adjectives**
   - **Coordinate adjectives:** If two or more adjectives before a noun indicate separate and equal qualities, use a comma between them:

> Marco thought it was a poignant, thought-provoking, inspiring movie.

▶ **TIP**   If you can change the order of the adjectives and replace each comma with the word *and*, then you are dealing with coordinate adjectives:

> Marco thought it was a thought-provoking and inspiring and poignant movie.

- **Cumulative adjectives:** If the adjectives work together to describe something or modify each other in stages, then *do not* use commas:

> Author Betty Friedan pointed out the inequities of traditional gender roles.

No comma should come between *traditional* and *gender roles* because the words function as cumulative adjectives. "Gender roles" functions as a single unit, and "traditional" describes that unit.

▶ **TIP**   Try adding *and* between the adjectives or reversing their position. If the sentence changes meaning or sounds wrong, then the adjectives are cumulative adjectives and should not be separated by a comma:

> Author Betty Friedan pointed out the inequities of traditional and gender roles.
>
> Author Betty Friedan pointed out the inequities of gender traditional roles.

Inserting *and* between *traditional* and *gender* changes the meaning of the sentence, and "gender traditional roles" sounds wrong because "gender" is a noun being used as an adjective in this phrase and also because "traditional" is an adjective that modifies "gender roles." Cumulative adjectives should sound right in the particular order in which they appear in the original sentence: They are not interchangeable.

- **Compound adjectives:** If two adjectives are used together to make one descriptor, then they become a compound adjective, and you should use a hyphen between them instead of a comma.

> **Coordinate adjectives:** The lilac bushes were covered with lavender, blue, and pink blossoms. [Three separate qualities/colors, so use commas]
>
> **Compound adjective:** The lilac bushes were covered with lavender-blue and pink blossoms. [Lavender-blue is one color, so use a hyphen, not a comma]

Coordinate adjectives: The small, modern hospital provides excellent care for patients. [Small and modern are two separate qualities, so use a comma]

Compound adjective: The small-animal hospital provides excellent care for dogs and cats. [Small-animal is one quality, so use a hyphen]

Rule 3

Use a comma after introductory material (an introductory dependent clause, an introductory prepositional or participial phrase, a single introductory word for emphasis or transition, direct address, or a tag line).

Introductory dependent clause + , + remainder of sentence
Introductory phrase + , + remainder of sentence
Introductory word + , + remainder of sentence

A comma sets off the introductory word, phrase, or clause from the rest of the sentence. To find introductory material, look for the main subject and verb and see what comes before them.

1. **Introductory dependent clause**

   Use a comma between the end of an introductory dependent clause and the remainder of the sentence. A dependent clause begins with a subordinating word, such as *though, because, since, when,* or *if.*

   If the weather is good, I go jogging in the park.

   However, if a dependent clause comes after an independent clause, then a comma is not required:

   I go jogging in the park *if the weather is good.*

2. **Introductory prepositional phrase**

   Use a comma after a prepositional phrase that comes at the beginning of the sentence. A prepositional phrase begins with a preposition such as *on, in, before,* or *after:*

   Before heading out to jog, I do some warm-up exercises.

If, however, a prepositional phrase comes after an independent clause, *do not* use a comma:

> I do some warm-up exercises *before heading out to jog.*

3. **Introductory participial phrase**

   Use a comma after a participial phrase that comes at the beginning of the sentence. A participial phrase begins with a word ending in *-ing*:

   > *Jogging through the park,* I feel a little creaky at first.

4. **Introductory word for emphasis or transition**

   Use a comma after a transitional or emphatic word that comes at the beginning of the sentence:

   > *Eventually,* I hit my stride and feel totally energized.
   > *Yes,* I was proud to serve as a juror.

5. **Direct address**

   When you begin a sentence by directly addressing someone by name or title, use a comma after the name or title:

   > *Daniel,* have you ever served on a jury?

   ▶ **TIP**   If the direct address comes at the end of the sentence, you will need a comma before the name or title. If the direct address comes in the middle of the sentence, use two commas, one before and one after the name or title:

   > Have you ever served on a jury, *Daniel?*
   > With all due respect, *Your Honor,* the prosecution objects.
   > *Dear Ashley,* I hope you win the case.
   > [Also used in an informal letter greeting]

6. **Tag lines for dialogue or quotations**

   Use a comma after a tag word or phrase that comes before a quotation in your sentence:

   > *The lawyer asked,* "What caused you to trip and fall?"
   > *Walt Whitman wrote,* "Justice is always in jeopardy."

▶ **NOTE** Sometimes the comma can be omitted after introductory material if there is a short clause or a phrase that causes no danger of misreading.

> *Without a doubt* jury duty is a solemn responsibility.

However, it's acceptable to use the comma there, too.

> *Without a doubt,* jury duty is a solemn responsibility.

Rule 4

Use a comma to set off interrupters—words, phrases, or clauses that "interrupt" an independent clause (IC).

> **Beginning of IC + , + interrupter + , + end of IC**

1. **Dependent clause interrupter**

   Use commas before and after a dependent clause that interrupts an independent clause:

   > Mary decided, *after she discovered the high cost of housing,* to share an apartment.

   ▶ **TIP** Imagine taking the middle clause out of the sentence by using the two commas like two handles you can grab to remove the interrupting clause. The sentence should still make sense if you remove the interrupting clause.

   > Mary decided to share an apartment.

2. **Transitional words and phrases or parenthetical interrupters**

   Use commas before and after transitional words or parenthetical interrupters.

   > Most of her friends, *however,* had already made other housing arrangements.

▶ **TIP**   You can also imagine these commas as handles you can use to remove the transitional word or phrase or the parenthetical interrupter. Test to make sure your sentence still makes sense without the deleted word(s).

> Most of her friends had already made other housing arrangements.

▶ **NOTE**   Use commas around parenthetical or side information instead of using parentheses when the information is still fairly important and when you are already using parenthetical citations in research papers.

3. **Appositive interrupters**

Use commas before and after appositive interrupters (nouns or phrases that rename or categorize nearby nouns):

> Mary heard that Brianna, *a friend from college*, was looking for a roommate.

4. **Nonrestrictive clauses**

A nonrestrictive adjective clause starts with a relative pronoun (*who, whom, whose,* or *which*) or with a relative adverb (*where* or *when*). The information conveyed by this type of clause is not essential for identifying the subject of the sentence. That is, the clause doesn't *restrict* the subject.

> Mary, *who had always enjoyed Brianna's company*, was delighted to learn that she was interested in sharing an apartment.

In this instance, the relative pronoun *who* introduces a nonrestrictive clause; you do not need the information in this clause to identify the subject, Mary. The clause provides extra, nonrestrictive information.

▶ **NOTE**   When the information in the relative pronoun statement or adverb statement is necessary in order to *restrict* or identify the noun/subject, then *do not* use commas:

> The friend *whom Brianna had been sharing an apartment with* was moving to a different town.

The clause "whom Brianna had been sharing an apartment with" *restricts* the noun, "friend," by clearly identifying a particular person.

5. **Tag lines that interrupt a dialogue or a quotation**

Two commas are used to set off tag lines that interrupt dialogue or a quotation.

> "My friend is leaving next month," *Brianna explained*, "so you could move in then, if you like."

▶ **TIP**   You also need a comma if the tag comes at the end of the sentence:

> "That should work out perfectly," *Mary said*.

▶ **NOTE**   Place the comma *inside* the quotation marks in both cases. Do not use quotation marks or a comma with an indirect quotation:

> Brianna *said that* she was looking forward to sharing the apartment with Mary.

Rule 5

Use commas according to conventions for dates, locations, numbers, and titles and to avoid confusion. Here are some examples of commas used in dates, locations, numbers, and titles.

1. **Dates**

> Abraham Lincoln was born *February 12, 1809*.
>
> Charles Darwin was born *February 12, 1809*, the same day Abraham Lincoln was born. [If more information follows, put a comma after the year, too.]

2. **Addresses/Locations**

> Darwin grew up in a large, comfortable home in *Shrewsbury, England*. Lincoln grew up in *Hardin County, Kentucky*, in a one-room log cabin. [Notice the comma after *Kentucky*.]

3. **Numbers**

> There are more than *10,000* species of birds in the world.

4. Formal Titles

> Don Kroodsma, *Ph.D.*, analyzes how and why birds sing.

Use commas to prevent confusion and to distinguish between repeated words or phrases:

> The recent oil spill can only be described as *a disaster, a disaster* that seriously damaged the environment and cost the lives of many birds.
>
> Because of bird-rescue efforts after the oil spill, some oil-coated birds that were not expected to *survive, survived*.

When Not to Use a Comma

- Do not use a comma to separate a subject from its verb.
- Do not use a comma to separate verbs that share the same subject.
- Do not automatically place a comma before every *and* and *but*. Check that these words have a subject and a verb on both sides (in other words, that they link two independent clauses).
- Do not place a comma between the verb and the direct object.
- Do not place a comma before a dependent clause that follows an independent clause (unless the comma is necessary for clarity).
- Do not place a comma after *especially* or *such as*.

APPLYING CRITICAL THINKING

PURPOSE   IDEAS   SUPPORT   ASSUMPTIONS BIASES   CONCLUSIONS   POINT OF VIEW   ANALYSIS

As you construct sentences and make choices about using commas, ask yourself the following critical thinking questions:

- What is my **purpose** for this particular sentence, and how can I best construct my sentence and use commas to achieve my purpose?
- How can commas make my meaning clearer?

Then break down the parts of the sentence and **analyze** them to make sure that you have constructed the sentence and used commas correctly.

ACTIVITY 22-1 **Correcting Misused Commas**

Directions: *Delete the misused or unnecessary commas in the following sentences.*

1. The weather is turning, and getting colder.
2. Actually, the fall, is ending too soon, not to our liking.
3. The winter is beginning to show its silvery start, and is sure to stay too long.
4. With an intense winter come consequences, such as, snow, wind, and power outages.
5. I plan to be prepared, and stock up on supplies, because I want to be ready for the worst.

ACTIVITY 22-2 **Adding Commas and Comma Rules**

Directions: *Each of the ten sentences below needs one or more commas. Place the commas where they belong in the sentences. Then, write the number of the rule that applies for each added comma or commas.*

1. In the 1890s, in Chicago Illinois, there was a great Ferris wheel.

Rule _____

2. Each of the cars on the wheel weighed 26 000 pounds.

Rule _____

3. The Ferris wheel was named after an engineer named George Ferris who designed and built bridges railroads and then the Ferris wheel.

Rule _____

4. The Chicago Ferris wheel one of the largest and heaviest ever created was built for the Columbian Exposition of 1893 in Chicago.

Rule _____

5. When the wheel first opened for visitors many lined up for a ride and spread the word.

Rule _____

6. Many visitors helped make the wheel world famous from tourists to locals to international journalists.

Rule _____

7. Though it opened later than scheduled it had a successful run from June 21 to November 6.

Rule _____

8. It was the talk of the nation but soon problems arose.

Rule _____

9. Building cost overruns mechanical difficulties and maintenance costs for the heavy and complicated wheel contributed to a loss in profits.

Rule _____

10. On May 11, 1906 the giant wheel was blown up with over 300 pounds of dynamite.

Rule _____

ACTIVITY 22-3   Add, Delete, and Move Commas I

Directions: *Add, delete, and move commas as necessary in each sentence below. If you add or move a comma, write the rule that applies in the space provided. If you delete a comma, briefly explain why in the space provided.*

1. The need for a new bridge according to the Mayor, was first on her agenda.

Reason for change: _____

2. Manpreet wanted a new apartment and, he didn't want roommates.

Reason for change: _____

3. Tammie on the other hand thought roomates were the best option to save money.

Reason for change: _____

4. Tammie said "It can cut your bills in half, Manpreet."

Reason for change: _____

5. The following day Tammie helped Manpreet advertise for a roommate.

Reason for change: _____

6. The department felt that they needed a new leader, and that their current chair wasn't organized.

Reason for change: _____

7. Maria knowing that her rent was overdue decided to get a loan from her parents.

Reason for change: _____

8. Kelly wanted to get a puppy and her sister was set on getting a kitten.

Reason for change: _____

9. Fumitaka said, that he wanted to get a ride to the airport.

Reason for change: _____

10. A good friendship requires patience trust, and reliability.

Reason for change: _____

ACTIVITY 22-4 **Add, Delete, and Move Commas II**

Directions: *Add, delete, and move commas as necessary. Consult the Five Comma Rules on pages 536–544 if you need help.*

In many different ways the Internet has changed the way higher education works. The Internet is clearly here to stay, but it has really only been an active part of our lives since the 1990s. Especially when writing research papers students have come to rely heavily on information, available on the Internet. This amazing wealth of information though comes with certain risks. For instance, a great deal of information, that is found, on the Internet is inaccurate. Many people rely on the facts statistics and expert testimonials they find online. Students should be cautious however because some sources are unreliable. It is important to double-check all sources for credibility, and accuracy. Another problem arises when students fail to cite Internet sources or cite them incorrectly, and, commit plagiarism, a serious academic crime.

SEMICOLON

❷ Use the semicolon correctly.

The **semicolon(;)** is a stronger mark of punctuation than the comma. The semicolon separates related clauses and phrases that are of equal importance, clarifies meaning, or provides emphasis. The semicolon is one of the most abused, misused, and neglected punctuation marks in the English language, but when used correctly (and sparingly), it can greatly enhance your writing.

There are only two rules for using the semicolon.

Rule 1

Use a semicolon between two independent clauses when the second clause has a strong connection to the first, and they are equally important.

Use a semicolon instead of a comma and a coordinating conjunction when you want to emphasize the connection between the two related independent clauses.

Independent clause   +   ;   +   independent clause

Angel Falls <u>is</u> a scenic wonder; from the top of a mountain in
(SUBJ) (VERB)
Venezuela, the <u>waterfall</u> <u>plunges</u> more than 2,640 feet.
        (SUBJ)   (VERB)

Each of the two independent clauses in the example could function as a complete sentence; however, the semicolon emphasizes the connection between the two independent clauses more than a period or coordinating conjunction would. Here is another example:

The remote <u>location</u> of Angel Falls <u>enhances</u> its mystique; the <u>waterfall</u>
<u>is hidden</u> deep in the jungle.

Sometimes a student will mistakenly use a comma to link two independent clauses in a sentence, thus creating a comma splice. To correct the comma splice, the student can either add a coordinating conjunction after the comma or replace the comma with a semicolon.

Often, a semicolon is followed either by a transitional expression or word (such as *however* or *therefore*) or by a conjunctive adverb (such as *consequently*), followed by a comma.

Angel Falls is the tallest waterfall in the world; however, Victoria Falls in Zimbabwe is known as the world's largest waterfall.

CONJUNCTIVE ADVERBS OFTEN USED AFTER A SEMICOLON (AND FOLLOWED BY A COMMA)

however	therefore	furthermore	moreover	consequently
also	finally	certainly	next	then
besides	conversely	likewise	subsequently	similarly
otherwise	indeed	meanwhile	thus	specifically

▶ **TIP** The semicolon should be used sparingly for maximum effect. It is a gem, so use it when it is the perfect punctuation mark, not when a period would do.

Rule 2

Use a semicolon to separate complex items in a series.

When a sentence contains a list with items that already have commas in them, use semicolons to separate the items in the list.

> **Item 1, with internal punctuation; item 2, with internal punctuation; and item 3, with internal punctuation.**

Rule 2 for commas says to use commas to separate items in a series (see p. 537). This semicolon rule is very similar except that you use semicolons when the items you are listing already have subcomponents separated by commas:

> In the United States, travelers can observe impressive waterfalls in Yosemite National Park, California; Colonial Peak, Washington; Glacier National Park, Montana; and Niagara Falls, New York.

If only commas had been used, a reader might become confused and think the sentence listed eight waterfalls instead of four.

▶ **TIP 1** Include a semicolon before the *and* that comes before the final item listed.

▶ **TIP 2** If the sentence did not include the states in which the waterfalls are located, you would use commas: Yosemite National Park, Colonial Peak, Glacier National Park, and Niagara Falls.

Here's another example:

> Other dramatic waterfalls include Dettifoss, a glacier-fed waterfall in Iceland; Kaieteur Falls, a broad waterfall in the rainforest of Guyana; and Iguazu Falls, a cascading waterfall on the border between Brazil and Argentina.

When Not to Use a Semicolon

- Do not use a semicolon after the phrases *especially* and *such as*.
- Do not use a semicolon after a coordinating conjunction (FANBOYS).
- Do not use a semicolon before a dependent clause that follows an independent clause.
- Do not use a semicolon before a list of words or items that follows an independent clause (use a colon).

ACTIVITY 22-5 Adding a Semicolon

Directions: *Add semicolons where they belong in the following sentences.*

1. The artwork was unique many unusual objects made it stand out.
2. The artwork included objects from nature such as seeds, rocks, and leaves objects from the kitchen such as forks, knives, and spoons and objects from clothing such as buttons, zippers, and pieces of cloth.
3. Most children love puppies puppies usually love children as well.
4. Water is a precious resource it is getting scarce in many countires around the world.
5. We went to the soccer game it was a sell-out crowd.

ACTIVITY 22-6 Adding or Deleting a Semicolon

Directions: *In each of the following sentences, add or delete a semicolon, or change the semicolon to a comma.*

1. I started a new hobby I took up stand-up paddleboarding.
2. The sport is really fun; and it is easy to learn.
3. It works many muscle groups such as; abdominals and calves.
4. It only takes a couple of pieces of equipment including; the board itself and a paddle and possibly a wetsuit.
5. It is easy to learn how to do it however, if the water is choppy or there are waves, expect to fall in as you learn.

APPLYING CRITICAL THINKING

PURPOSE — IDEAS — SUPPORT — ASSUMPTIONS BIASES — CONCLUSIONS — POINT OF VIEW — ANALYSIS

As you construct sentences and make choices about using the semicolon, ask yourself the following critical thinking questions:

- What is my **purpose** for this particular sentence, and how can I best construct my sentence and use a semicolon to achieve my purpose?
- Will a semicolon make my meaning clearer or add emphasis to a relationship between two clauses?

Then break down the parts of the sentence and **analyze** them to make sure that you have constructed the sentence and used semicolons correctly.

COLON

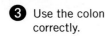 Use the colon correctly.

The **colon (:)** is used to clarify meaning, provide emphasis, or introduce information. There are several rules for using a colon, but it usually indicates that a list or explanation is to follow.

Rule 1

Use a colon between two independent clauses when the second clause explains, summarizes, or answers the first one.

> The <u>contestants</u> in the singing contest all <u>had</u> the same dream: <u>They</u>
> (SUBJ)   (VERB)   (SUBJ)
> <u>wanted</u> to become famous.
> (VERB)

Each independent clause in the example could function as a complete sentence. The second clause explains the first one. It's true that a period, a semicolon, or a comma followed by a coordinating conjunction would work here. The colon, however, is the *best choice* of punctuation in this case because it helps the reader see the explanatory relationship between the two clauses. Here's another example:

> The contestant had two choices: She could sing a popular song or perform a song she had composed herself.

▶ **NOTE**   When a colon separates two independent clauses, the second independent clause should begin with a capital letter.

Rule 2

Use a colon after an independent clause that is followed by a word or phrase that answers or explains the idea presented in the independent clause.

The contestants in the singing contest all had the same dream: to become famous. [Colon followed by a phrase]

The contestants in the singing contest all had the same dream: becoming famous. [Colon followed by a phrase]

The contestants in the singing contest all had the same dream: fame. [Colon followed by a single word]

The contestant had two choices: to sing a popular song or perform her own song. [Colon followed by a phrase]

▶ **TIP**   An independent clause must come before the colon.

Incorrect: Two main factors for judging: the originality of the winner's song and the energy of her performance.

Correct: The <u>judges</u> <u>cited</u> two main factors: the originality of the winner's song and the energy of her performance.

Rule 3

Use a colon after an independent clause that introduces a list of items.

When planning our trip to Montana, I started a list of things to take on hikes: water, energy bars, first-aid kit, raingear, insect repellent, and sunscreen.

We also started getting in shape for mountain climbing: taking long walks, lifting weights, eating healthy foods, and getting enough sleep.

▶ **TIP 1**   Be sure that the clause that comes before the colon is independent. It should have both a subject and a verb and not be introduced by a subordinating conjunction.

> **Incorrect:** Several mountains to climb in Montana: Blue Mountain, Heaven's Peak, and Rising Wolf Mountain.
>
> **Correct:** We wanted to climb several mountains in Montana: Blue Mountain, Heaven's Peak, and Rising Wolf Mountain.

▶ **TIP 2**   Don't use a colon after words and phrases like *such as* and *including*. Think of these words as replacements for a colon; they serve the same function.

> **Incorrect:** We also scheduled other activities, such as: fishing excursions, horseback riding, and museum visits.
>
> **Correct:** We also scheduled other activities, such as fishing excursions, horseback riding, and museum visits.

Rule 4

Use a colon before a quotation if an independent clause is used to introduce the quotation.

> In *Travels with Charley*, John Steinbeck wrote about the state he admired greatly: "Montana is a great splash of grandeur."

Miscellaneous Uses

There are several miscellaneous uses for the colon.

- In greetings:

> To Whom It May Concern:
> Dear Mr. Ortiz:

- To show hours and minutes:

> 6:05 P.M.

- Between titles and subtitles:

> *Angels and Ages: A Short Book about Darwin, Lincoln, and Modern Life*

- To show ratios:

> The odds were 4:1 that the new drug would be effective.

- In Works Cited format:

> Upper Saddle River: Pearson, 2010.

When Not to Use a Colon

- Do not use a colon after *especially, such as, consisted of, including,* and other words or phrases that indicate a list will follow.
- Do not use a colon after a verb that sets up a list of objects.

> **Incorrect:** We wanted to climb: Blue Mountain, Heaven's Peak, and Rising Wolf Mountain.
> **Correct:** We wanted to climb Blue Mountain, Heaven's Peak, and Rising Wolf Mountain.

- Do not use a colon between book and verse or act and scene (in MLA style). Use periods instead:

> **Incorrect:** Genesis 4:2
> **Correct:** Genesis 4.2
> **Incorrect:** *Phantom of the Opera,* 1:3 (or I:III)
> **Correct:** *Phantom of the Opera,* 1.3 (or I.III)

APPLYING CRITICAL THINKING

| PURPOSE | IDEAS | SUPPORT | ASSUMPTIONS BIASES | CONCLUSIONS | POINT OF VIEW | ANALYSIS |

As you construct sentences and make choices about using colons, ask yourself the following critical thinking questions:

- What is my **purpose** for this particular sentence, and how can I best construct my sentence and use a colon to achieve my purpose?
- Will colons make my meaning clearer? Do I use a colon after an independent clause to list items? Do I use a colon to separate two independent clauses if the second clause answers the first?

Then break down the parts of the sentence and **analyze** them to make sure that you have constructed the sentence and used colons correctly.

ACTIVITY 22-7 Adding a Colon

Directions: *Add colons where they belong in the following sentences.*

1. Mohammed had to remember one important concept to succeed he needed to study.
2. The odds were 4 1 that there would be money to construct the new building.
3. Miles wanted to do one thing before his trip fill his car's gas tank.
4. There is something much more important in life than making money family.
5. Alicia had a secret She was afraid of heights.

ACTIVITY 22-8 Adding or Deleting a Colon

Directions: *Add or delete colons where needed in the following sentences.*

1. She brought: sleeping bags, food, and bicycles on the camping trip.
2. She forgot two important items matches and a tent.
3. When I go camping, I like to bring activities to do at the campsite, such as: dominos, Scrabble, and cards.
4. The book was called *Monsters of the Deep A History of Sea Monsters and Myths*.
5. To have a successful first day of school, be sure to bring the following items pen or pencil, paper, your textbooks, and a good backpack to carry everything.

Mastery Test I: Adding a Semicolon or a Colon

Directions: *Add a semicolon or a colon to the following sentences where needed. Make the best, most specific choice for each.*

1. All students will benefit from one piece of advice improve time management skills.
2. Organization is a big part of success most leaders are very organized.
3. Shari bought a self-help book called *Getting the Grade Time Management and Organization Advice for Students*.
4. All of the supplies were ready pencils, pens, paper, a notebook, a calendar, and a laptop.

5. On Friday, the university is sponsoring a Success Workshop led by many key faculty and staff, including Linda Foss, school counselor Roberto Gonzales, research librarian Marina Cruz, Professor of Business and Jamie Fitzgerald, Writing Center Director.

MyWritingLab™   ## Mastery Test II: Adding Comma, Semicolon, and Colon

Directions: *For each sentence in the following passage, insert the correct punctuation mark—comma, semicolon, or colon—in the appropriate blank. Review the rules if you get stumped.*

, (comma)   ; (semicolon)   : (colon)

Stress _____ and all of its symptoms _____ can take a toll on the body and the mind _____ the way one's body handles stress has an overall effect on a person's physical and mental health. To begin with _____ recognizing the various signs of stress can help one manage it. The body releases two hormones when stressed _____ adrenaline and cortisol. Sometimes, one's body needs these hormones to avoid danger _____ however _____ in the modern world _____ these hormones are often caused by work-related pressures or daily life stresses _____ and it is important to learn to manage stress.

Deep breathing _____ for example _____ is a great way to combat stress _____ many people find that meditation and deep breathing can help calm the body almost immediately. Two other factors are also crucial in combating stress _____ diet and exercise. In a WebMD survey of over 90,000 people _____ only 40 percent of them said they exercised at least once a day. Moreover _____ more than half of the American public is now overweight _____ lack of exercise and weight gain are accompanied by increased stress factors _____ so these issues are closely related. Therefore, calming techniques, diet, and exercise are all essential to combating stress _____ improving these things will create healthier bodies and minds.

Learning Objectives Review

MyWritingLab™ Complete the chapter assessment questions at mywritinglab.com

❶ Use the comma correctly.

What are commas used for, and what are five rules for using them correctly? (See pp. 536–547.)

Commas (,) clarify, make distinctions, or create the pauses needed to let your readers follow your sentences and ideas. **Five rules for correctly using commas are:** (1) use a comma before a coordinating conjunction to combine two independent clauses and create a compound sentence; (2) use a comma to separate the items in a series or a list of coordinate adjectives; (3) use a comma after introductory material; (4) use a comma to set off interrupters; and (5) use commas according to conventions for dates, locations, numbers, titles, and to avoid confusion.

❷ Use the semicolon correctly.

What are semicolons used for, and what are two rules for using them correctly? (See pp. 547–551.)

Semicolons (;) separate related clauses and phrases that are of equal importance. **Two rules for using semicolons are:** (1) use a semicolon between two independent clauses when the second clause has a strong connection to the first and they are equally important, and (2) use a semicolon to separate complex items in a series.

❸ Use the colon correctly.

What are colons used for, and what are four rules for using them correctly? (See pp. 551–556.)

Colons (:) clarify meaning, provide emphasis, or introduce information. **Four rules for using colons are:** (1) use a colon between two independent clauses when the second clause explains, summarizes, or answers the first one; (2) use a colon after an independent clause that is followed by a word or phrase that answers or explains the idea presented in the independent clause; (3) use a colon after an independent clause that introduces a list of items; and (4) use a colon before a quotation if an independent clause is used to introduce the quotation.

LEARNING OBJECTIVES

In this chapter, you will learn how to

1 Recognize and use the three end-punctuation marks correctly.

2 Use apostrophes correctly.

3 Use quotation marks correctly.

4 Use other punctuation correctly.

Thinking Critically MyWritingLab™

Thinking About Punctuation
Tom Shugrue

Think: Do you think punctuation is important?

Write: Why, or why not? What function does it serve for the reader?

_____

_____

_____

_____

_____

_____

_____

_____

_____

_____

_____

_____

END PUNCTUATION

1 Recognize and use the three end-punctuation marks correctly.

End punctuation comes, naturally, at the end of a sentence. There are three types of end punctuation: the period, the question mark, and the exclamation point.

Period

A **period (.)** ends a statement. You should use a period under the following circumstances:

1. **Use a period at the end of a complete sentence (independent clause).** The sentence can be a statement or an indirect question:

> Macklemore is his favorite musician. [Statement]
>
> He asked me if I'd like to go to the Macklemore concert. [Indirect question]

2. **Use periods with some abbreviations (not all abbreviations require periods; check a dictionary if you are unsure).**

Mr.   Ms.   Mrs.   etc.   e.g.   Dr.   Ph.D.

APPLYING CRITICAL THINKING

| PURPOSE | IDEAS | SUPPORT | ASSUMPTIONS BIASES | CONCLUSIONS | POINT OF VIEW | ANALYSIS |

As you construct sentences and make choices about punctuation, ask yourself the following critical thinking questions:

- How can punctuation make my meaning and **purpose** clearer?
- What are the best choices I can make for punctuation in this sentence? A period? An apostrophe? Quotation marks? An exclamation point?
- Have I used this punctuation correctly?

Then, break down the parts of the sentences using your **analysis** skills to make sure that you have constructed the sentence correctly.

ACTIVITY 23-1   Adding the Period

Directions: *Add periods where needed in the following passage.*

When I wake up in the morning, the first thing I have to do is brush my teeth I can't stand the feeling of fuzzy teeth Also, brushing my teeth right away helps prevent someone noticing my morning breath I wish everyone was that considerate My boss, Mr Smith, definitely forgets to brush

Question Mark

A **question mark** (**?**) indicates that a question is being asked. Use a question mark when a sentence is a direct question.

> Do you think it will rain today?

Do not use a question mark if the sentence is an indirect question:

> I asked my friend if she thought it would rain today. [Period, not a question mark]

Using the Question Mark with Quotations or Dialogue

When you are using a quotation or dialogue, check if a question mark is part of the quotation or dialogue or if you are asking a question about the quotation or dialogue. If the question mark is part of the quotation or dialogue, it goes inside the closing quotation marks.

> She asked, "Are the Radiohead tickets already sold out?"

If you are asking a question about a quotation, the question mark comes after the closing quotation marks:

> Who was it that said, "Music is the universal language"?

ACTIVITY 23-2 Adding, Moving, or Changing
the Question Mark

Directions: *Add or move the question mark, or change it to another form of punctuation as necessary in the following passage.*

"Did you see the 2012 Olympics" Roberto asked. Maria looked at him.
She replied that she didn't like to watch the Olympics on TV and wondered
why he did? Later he asked her if she wanted to watch his tape of the swimming events? She said she would be interested.

Then she asked, "When should I come by."

He asked her if 7:00 the next day would work? They agreed on that time.

Exclamation Point

Use an **exclamation point** (**!**) to show emphasis, to express strong emotion—
excitement, surprise, disbelief—or to indicate a strong command.

> I'm starving, and that stew smells delicious!
> You scared me to death!
> I can't believe he gave us a pop quiz the day before spring break!
> Stop—it's a red light!

▶ **NOTE** Don't overuse the exclamation point, or it will lose its
power! See what I mean?! Too much!

ACTIVITY 23-3 Adding or Replacing
the Exclamation Point

Directions: *Add the exclamation point, or replace it with a different type of punctuation mark as needed in the following passage.*

"Run," my father shouted. I wondered what was happening!

"It's a wild boar coming right at us" my father said, grabbing my arm and
pulling me along even faster. After we had gotten clear of the boar, my father
explained that wild boars are common in Mexico and that it is best to stay

clear of them. "They just are protecting their territory," he said! Then he told me they usually don't actually attack, just chase.

APOSTROPHE

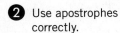 Use apostrophes correctly.

The **apostrophe** (') indicates contractions (words in which certain letters have been omitted) and possession (who or what owns something).

Apostrophe and Contractions

Use an apostrophe to indicate the omission of one or more letters when words are combined to form a contraction. Place the apostrophe where the missing letter(s) would be: *it's* (*it is*) or *haven't* (*have not*) or *would've* (*would have*). Contractions may not be appropriate for formal, academic writing. **Check with your instructor to see if contractions are allowed or if a more formal tone is required. It may depend on the assignment or type of essay you are writing or on your target audience.**

Common Contractions	
aren't	are not
can't	cannot
could've	could have
couldn't	could not
didn't	did not
doesn't	does not
don't	do not
hadn't	had not
hasn't	has not
haven't	have not
he'd	he had/he would
he'll	he will
he's	he is
I'm	I am
isn't	is not
it'd	it had/it would
it'll	it will

it's	it is
let's	let us
mightn't	might not
might've	might have
mustn't	must not
she'd	she had/she would
she'll	she will
she's	she is
shouldn't	should not
should've	should have
there'd	there had/there would
there'll	there will
they're	they are
'twas	it was
wasn't	was not
we'll	we will
we're	we are
weren't	were not
what'd	what had/what would
what's	what is
won't	will not
wouldn't	would not
would've	would have
you'll	you will
you're	you are

Cross Reference
See Chapter 25,
pp. 614–628, "Commonly
Confused Words."

▶ **NOTE**   Be careful with the following contractions. They sound like other words that have different meanings.

they're = they are	vs.	their	= possessive pronoun
you're = you are		your	= possessive pronoun
who's = who is		whose	= possessive pronoun
it's = it is		its	= possessive pronoun

▶ **SIMPLE TEST**   If the word can be said aloud as two words, then it is probably the contraction you want.

> **Incorrect:** The car needs new brake pads, and *it's* windshield is cracked. [The car needs new brake pads, and *it is* windshield—oops, wrong word; use "its," possessive pronoun, instead—*its* windshield is cracked.]
>
> **Correct:** The car needs new tires, and *it's* not getting good mileage. [The car needs new tires, and *it is* not getting good mileage.]

Apostrophe and Possession

Add an apostrophe to a noun or indefinite pronoun to indicate possession. (But don't add an apostrophe to an already possessive pronoun such as *his*, *hers*, or *its*.)

> Sam's essay about her most embarrassing moment was hilarious. [The apostrophe indicates the essay belongs to Sam.]
>
> Someone's dirty dishes are in the sink. [The apostrophe indicates that dirty dishes in the sink belong to someone.]

1. **Singular possession.** Use an apostrophe before the added *s* to indicate possession if the noun is singular.

> A hummingbird's wings can beat up to 78 times per second. [The apostrophe indicates that the wings of a hummingbird can beat up to 78 times per second.]
>
> *History's* lessons are always being relearned. [The apostrophe indicates that the lessons of history are always being relearned.]
>
> Dr. Ortega is *everyone's* favorite professor. [The apostrophe indicates that the favorite professor of everyone is Dr. Ortega.]

If the singular noun already ends with the letter *s*, then add an apostrophe and another *s*.

> Each of the *octopus's* eight arms has two rows of suction cups.

▶ **NOTE**   Don't use apostrophes with pronouns that are already possessive.

> **Incorrect:** Is this textbook *your's* or mine? *It's* cover is torn.
>
> **Correct:** Is this textbook yours or mine? Its cover is torn.

2. **Plural possession.** Use an apostrophe after the *s* that indicates a plural, possessive noun.

> Many of the *trees'* branches broke during the ice storm. [Refers to two or more trees—the only way to know this is by the placement of the apostrophe.]
>
> The *artists'* paintings are on display in the main gallery. [The placement of the apostrophe indicates that there is more than one artist.]

▶ **NOTE**   If the form of the noun is already plural, add an apostrophe and an *s*.

> The *women's* locker rooms are on your right.

▶ **NOTE**   Don't use an apostrophe to make nouns plural.

> **Incorrect:** There are several news Web site's that I check every day.
> **Correct:** There are several news Web sites that I check every day.

3. **Possessive and compound nouns.** Place an apostrophe at the end of compound nouns in order to indicate possession.

> My *brother-in-law's* jokes are pretty lame.
> [The apostrophe goes at the end of the compound noun; you do not write *brother's-in-law*.]

With two brothers-in-law, make the word "brother" plural by adding an *s*; then just use apostrophe and an *s* after "law" (only one law but two brothers).

> My *brothers-in-law's* favorite joke is so lame that they are the only ones who laugh.

4. **Possession and proper names.** As with other singular nouns, add an apostrophe and an *s* to single proper names to show possession.

> *Shanika's* job interview went very well.
> [There is only one Shanika, so the apostrophe goes before the *s*.]
> *Professor Wang's* letter of recommendation helped Shanika get the job.

Even if a proper name ends in *s*, you still show possession by adding an apostrophe and an *s*.

> *Chris's* dream is to become a marine biologist.
> *Henry James's* novels are psychologically complex.

However, if the pronunciation would be awkward with the added *s*, it is acceptable to omit the extra *s* (both ways are acceptable).

> The New Testament includes descriptions of *Jesus'* [or *Jesus's*] disciples.

If the proper name is plural, put the apostrophe after the *s*.

> *The Steinbergs'* house is always full of neighborhood kids.
> [Adding the *s* to the name *Steinberg* indicates the whole family, not just one person, and the apostrophe after it indicates their joint possession of the house.]

5. **Joint possession.** If two or more people share a possession, then add an apostrophe and an *s* only after the last name.

> Are you riding in *Lamont* and *Whitney's* car?
> [The car belongs to both of them, so the apostrophe goes after *Whitney*.]

If people individually (separately) possess things, use an apostrophe and an *s* for each one.

> Are you riding in *Lola's*, *Ethan's*, or *Kenji's* car?
> [There are three cars, so the apostrophes indicate individual possession.]

Apostrophe and Plurals

You may use an apostrophe to indicate plural numbers, letters, and symbols and to indicate the plurals of words used as terms. (Due to the dynamic nature of grammar, it is now acceptable to use an apostrophe or to omit the apostrophe in many of these cases. You may choose to add the apostrophe or leave it out, but be consistent.)

> The Federal Aviation Association announced that mechanical defects on two *747's* had been corrected.
> [It's acceptable to use *747s*.]

> My preschooler, who is learning to write, complains that *M*'s and *N*'s look too much alike.
>
> The two *A*'s I got last semester raised my GPA.
>
> For the arithmetic worksheet, the kindergarten teacher printed the +'s and −'s in different colors.
>
> When making an oral presentation, try to avoid nervous verbal mannerisms such as *uh*'s, *um*'s, and *you know*'s.

Apostrophe and Missing Letters or Numbers

You can use an apostrophe to indicate letters or numbers that are missing from words in dialogue, slang, or colloquial speech. Remember, you should only include slang or colloquial words in dialogue; these words are inappropriate in academic writing.

> "*Y*'*all* come in now. I'm *fixin*' to serve up some three-alarm chili."
>
> My grandmother said, "We went through some tough times during the '30s, but we never doubted that things would get better."

When Not to Use an Apostrophe

- Do not use an apostrophe with possessive pronouns (*his, hers, its, ours, yours, theirs, whose*).
- Do not use an apostrophe to form plurals that do not indicate possession (*cats, trees,* etc.)

ACTIVITY 23-4 Apostrophe Practice I

Directions: *Add, delete, or move the apostrophe in the following sentences as needed. Write C for correct if the use of the apostrophe is correct.*

_____ **1.** We're heading for the coast the next day, so pack your' bag's.

_____ **2.** Wednesday's specials at my school's cafeteria are the best.

_____ **3.** I did'nt want to order the meatloaf surprise though.

_____ **4.** The Smith's house was the target of the burglars.

_____ **5.** The women's hats were red, and they wouldn't take them off in the restaurant.

_____   **6.** The friends' treated each other to the movies.

_____   **7.** Hers' was the best car on the block.

_____   **8.** The A's on her transcripts stood out.

_____   **9.** Both bosses' vacations were during the same week.

_____   **10.** It's not what you can't do; it's what you can.

ACTIVITY 23-5 **Apostrophe Practice II**

Directions: *Place the apostrophe where needed in the following passage.*

I wanted to visit the Eiffel Tower when I was in Paris. It is one of the citys most famous landmarks. However, when I got to the Tower, the line was extremely long. I was'nt sure I could wait in what looked like a three-hour line. The peoples faces were red, and it was getting hotter. Its a tough decision to not make it to the top of the famous tower, but I decided to just take some picture's of it from the ground. My camera takes good picture's. So, Im satisfied with the pictures, and my memories' are good, too.

QUOTATION MARKS

3 Use quotation marks correctly.

Quotation marks (" ") indicate direct quotations or dialogue (written or spoken), some types of titles, definitions, and irony.

1. **Use quotation marks around direct quotations.** Use quotation marks when you are directly quoting someone else's words in your writing. Enclose all quoted words in a pair of **double quotation marks**, one set at the beginning of the quotation and one set at the end:

> John Sawhill said, "In the end, our society will be defined not only by what we create but by what we refuse to destroy" (56).

▶ **NOTE**   Remember to include either a page citation for a source if you use MLA format or the year of publication if you use APA format.

When there is a quotation within a quotation, use **single quotation marks** around the internal quotation:

> Describing her rival writer Lillian Hellman, Mary McCarthy said, "Every word she writes is a lie, including 'and' and 'the.'"

2. **Use quotation marks to quote prose or poetry.**

- **Introducing quotations.** If you are quoting a complete sentence, use a tag to introduce the quotation followed by a comma. If, however, you use a complete sentence to introduce a quotation, use a colon. Be sure to start the quotation with a capital letter.

  > **Tag:** James Baldwin said, "The challenge is in the moment; the time is always now" (83).
  >
  > **Introductory sentence:** James Baldwin said it best: "The challenge is in the moment; the time is always now" (83).

- **Quoting partial sentences.** If you quote only part of a sentence, then don't start the quotation with a capital letter.

  > James Baldwin said that "the time is always now" (83).

- **Leaving words out of a quotation.** If you leave out part of a quotation, use an ellipsis (three spaced dots) to indicate where the omitted word or words were deleted.

  > Federico García Lorca wrote, "There is nothing more poetic and terrible than the skyscrapers' battle with the heavens that cover them. Snow, rain, and mist highlight, drench, or conceal the vast towers, but those towers . . . shine their three thousand swords through the soft swan of the fog."

- **Adding words and phrases.** If you add a word or phrase for clarification within a direct quotation, put brackets around the insertion.

  > Tom Paine wrote, "What we obtain too cheap, we esteem too lightly; it is dearness [high cost] only that gives everything its value."

- **Quoting fewer than four lines of poetry.** If you quote fewer than four lines of poetry, use slashes to indicate the line breaks.

> Poet Maya Angelou wrote, "The caged bird sings with a fearful trill / Of things unknown but longed for still" (1).

- **Quoting four or more lines of poetry.** If you quote four or more lines of poetry or prose, indent the quotation 10 spaces from the left margin and omit quotation marks; place punctuation before the citation.

> Bruce Beasley wrote:
>> so, go
>> little poem, little
>>
>> ink-smudge-on-fingertip
>> & -print, mimicker
>>
>> & camouflage,
>> self-getaway, cloud-
>>
>> scribble, write
>> out my dissipating
>>
>> name on the water,
>> emptied sac of self-elusive ink . . . (*Theophobia* 61)

3. **Use quotation marks with dialogue.** Quotation marks indicate that someone is speaking. Here are some tips for using quotation marks with dialogue.

   - Put the actual words spoken by the person in quotation marks.
   - Use commas to set off tags at the beginning, middle, or end of the dialogue.
   - Start a new paragraph whenever you switch speakers or characters in dialogue, even if the line is only one word long.

> "So what did you think?" she asked.
> "The special effects were awesome!" he said. "I was surprised that the 3-D glasses worked so well."
> "I know," she said. "The 'look' of the movie was very original. The plot—not so much."
> "I hear you," he said. "Been there, done that."

4. **Use quotation marks for specific types of titles.** Use quotation marks around the titles of short stories and poems (not book-length epic poems, though), chapter titles, essay titles, magazine article titles, titles of television episodes from series, and song titles.

> **Story title:** "What You Pawn I Will Redeem" by Sherman Alexie
> **Poem title:** "Where the Sidewalk Ends" by Shel Silverstein
> **Magazine article title:** "Four Ways of Looking at Breakfast" by Thomas Fuller
> **Television episode title:** "No More Mister Nice Guy" from *Family Guy*
> **Song title:** "I Will Always Love You" by Dolly Parton

▶ **NOTE**   Titles of books, epic poems, plays, movies, CDs/albums, TV shows, and magazines are all italicized.

5. **Use quotation marks around defined or ironic words.** When you define a word or want to indicate that you are speaking ironically, use quotation marks.

> The word "miscreant" refers to a person who is dishonest or unkind.
>
> School and work leave little time for anything else: My "free time" is for running errands and doing chores.

Punctuation and Quotation Marks

Place commas and periods inside quotation marks if you do not include a page citation.

> "Wildwood," a short story by Junot Díaz, won the O. Henry Award.
> William Strunk said, "Omit needless words."

However, if you include a citation, the punctuation goes after the citation.

> In his eulogy for Eleanor Roosevelt, Adlai Stevenson said, "She would rather light candles than curse the darkness, and her glow has warmed the world" (McCarthy 63).
> [The period should not go inside the closing quotation: Place the period after the citation and after the last parenthesis.]

▶ **NOTE**   When you use the semicolon and the colon in your writing, they should be placed after the quotation marks. For instance:

> The ad described the apartment as "dirt cheap": It turned out to be more dirty than cheap.

Review the rule on page 560 about placing the question mark inside or outside quotation marks.

ACTIVITY 23-6   Adding Quotation Marks

Directions: *Add or delete quotation marks where needed in the following sentences. Write a C if the sentence is correct.*

_____ 1. In the classic novel *Moby Dick*, Ishmael introduces himself in the famous opening line, "Call me Ishmael."

_____ 2. Stop now, said the mother, trying to keep her children safe, and look both ways before crossing.

_____ 3. Trish said, I was terrified when the police officer yelled Stop from behind my car.

_____ 4. Which poet said A thing of beauty is a joy forever?

_____ 5. Robert Frost's poem "Stopping by Woods on a Snowy Evening" is a powerful poem.

_____ 6. He asked "when she had to leave."

_____ 7. Watching the Market was the article she was assigned to read in her economics class.

_____ 8. The Beatles' song She Loves You caused a sensation in America in the 1960s.

_____ 9. What should we have for dinner? Fernando asked. I can cook anything, he added.

_____ 10. He told her he "didn't want to see her anymore."

PARENTHESES

4 Use other punctuation correctly.

Parentheses (()) set off information or citations. Parentheses can be used in a number of ways:

1. **Use parentheses to set off nonessential information** in the middle of a sentence.

> The school's science teacher (who also coaches the soccer team) has really gotten the kids excited about science.

If the information in a side comment is relatively important, it is preferable to use parenthetical commas to set it off (use commas around an interrupting comment).

> The storm, which included high winds and hail, caused widespread power outages.

2. **Use parentheses to set off numbers or letters in a list or series.**

> If your clothes catch on fire, follow these three simple steps: (1) Stop moving, (2) drop to the ground, and (3) roll to extinguish the flames.
>
> When administering CPR, remember your ABC's: (A) **A**irway (check the airway), (B) **B**reathing (provide rescue breathing), and (C) **C**irculation (check pulse to determine if chest compressions are needed).

▶ **NOTE** Only certain style formats, such as business or science writing, encourage the use of cardinal numbers or letters with parentheses. To list items in the humanities, use ordinal numbers or other descriptive words (such as "first," "second," "next," and so on).

3. **Use parentheses to indicate formal citations.** Use parentheses for in-text citations when documenting sources.

> As H. L. Mencken observed, "The cure for the evils of democracy is more democracy" (Corcoran 36).

Cross Reference
For information about parenthetical citations, see Chapter 16, pp. 361–365, Using MLA Format: In-Text Citations, and pp. 375–376, Using APA Format: In-Text Citations.

4. **Use parentheses to indicate abbreviations.** If you use an abbreviation or acronym in your paper, spell out the full name or term the first time it's mentioned. Then follow it with the abbreviation or acronym in parentheses so that readers know what the initials stand for when you use them again:

> The Federal Drug Administration (FDA) has not yet approved the new medication.

ACTIVITY 23-7   Adding or Deleting Parentheses

Directions: *Add or delete parentheses as needed in the following passage.*

When I see a (good) book at the bookstore, I can't resist though I probably should. I tell myself I deserve to buy it for three reasons: 1 I have been working hard. 2 Books are a good indulgence, and 3 I am bettering my mind when I read. I read a famous line once about a good book: "Books are like never failing friends" Southey 12. I think I will head to the bookstore now and look for (and buy) another friend.

HYPHEN

4 Use other punctuation correctly.

The **hyphen (-)** combines or divides words. Here are some uses for the hyphen.

1. **Use a hyphen (-) to form compound words.** Check your dictionary to be sure that the compound word you're using is hyphenated. Some are not. Here are some commonly hyphenated compound words:

> **Fractions** such as *one-third, two-thirds, one-fourth*
> **Numbers** that are spelled out between twenty-one and ninety-nine
> **Compound nouns** such as *mother-in-law* or *brother-in-law*

2. **Use a hyphen with compound modifiers.** Use a hyphen with compound modifiers, usually adjectives, which are used together as one descriptor before a noun.

> The bank approved the store owners' application for a *short-term* loan. [Here *short-term*—a compound adjective—modifies the word *loan*.]
> The *well-liked* professor was awarded tenure.

▶ **NOTE** If a compound modifier is not followed by a noun, then omit the hyphens.

> The bank loan would enable them to keep the store open in the *short term*.
> The tenured professor was *well liked*.

3. **Use a hyphen to join letters, prefixes, and suffixes to a word.** Here are some examples of common prefixes that require a hyphen:

> **Letters before words:** T-shirt, B-team, S-curve, A-frame, J-bar, C-note
> *Self-* **before words:** self-addressed, self-control
> *All-* **before words:** all-knowing, all-seeing
> *Ex-* **before words:** ex-husband, ex-mayor

Usually the prefixes *anti-, pro-, co-,* and *non-* do not require hyphens unless the prefix ends in a vowel and the root word begins with one, too: for example, *anti-inflammatory, co-owner, de-emphasize,* and *co-ed*. Also use a hyphen after a prefix to avoid confusion between two similar words, for example, *re-cover* (to cover again) vs. *recover* (to bring back to normal or regain) and *re-create* (to create again) vs. *recreate* (to relax and enjoy).

4. **Use a hyphen to divide words at the end of a line.** It is preferable not to divide words at all, but if you must, follow these guidelines:

- Divide words at syllable breaks.
- Don't leave fewer than three letters at the end of a sentence before the hyphen or put two or fewer letters on the next line.

Dividing words is rare these days because word-processing programs automatically bring whole words down to the next line. You may still see this in books, but, in your papers, you should avoid it by letting the word processor format your lines.

ACTIVITY 23-8 Adding Hyphens

Directions: *Add a hyphen where needed in the following sentences. If the sentence is correct, then write C on the line provided.*

_____ **1.** She had to reemphasize the severity of the situation.

_____ **2.** The preamble to the new faculty contract included their mission statement.

_____ **3.** His antisocial behavior was putting a strain on their relationship.

_____ **4.** The everfaithful dog waited on the porch.

_____ **5.** Josh's seventyyearold mother was coming for a visit.

_____ **6.** She rewarded all the active five year olds.

_____ **7.** She has a coowner for her shop.

_____ **8.** Hannah's eyes were bluegreen like the ocean.

_____ **9.** The preformed patties were very convenient.

_____**10.** Previewing the schedule before you register is a good idea.

DASH

4 Use other punctuation correctly.

Dashes (—) make information stand out—they add emphasis. (If your word processor doesn't include a dash (—), use two hyphens together to create one.)

Dashes are placed around a phrase in the middle of a sentence or at the end of a sentence. They enclose material like parentheses do—but dashes emphasize the material inside them (whereas parentheses de-emphasize it). At the end of a sentence, a dash can work much like a colon, but it is more informal.

> Generally speaking, I'm a strong supporter of tradition, but I draw the line—and I suspect I'm not alone in this—at the tradition of spring cleaning.
>
> Early autumn—when the morning air is crisp, and the first red leaves appear—is my favorite time of year.

▶ **NOTE**   Material enclosed by dashes can be removed, and the sentence will still make sense.

▶ **NOTE**   Dashes are considered an informal punctuation mark. In more formal writing, use commas or colons instead of a dash.

ACTIVITY 23-9 **Adding or Deleting Dashes**

Directions: *Add or delete dashes in the following passage.*

Fly fishing a classic technique for fishing in rivers requires patience and skill. One must learn how to tie the fake "fly" a particular art passed down for decades. Also—it can be a calming hobby. There are many guidebooks on fly-fishing—and many articles about how to do it on the Internet.

SLASH

 Use other punctuation correctly.

A **slash** (/) is a diagonal line slanting from right to left that indicates a choice between words or line breaks in quoted excerpts from poems.

1. **Use a slash between two words to indicate a choice.**

   yes/no   and/or   either/or

2. **Use a slash to indicate line breaks when you quote two or three lines of poetry within your sentence.**

   > The first three lines of "Juke Box Love Song," a poem by Langston Hughes, are: "I could take the Harlem night / and wrap around you, / Take the neon lights and make a crown" (24).

ACTIVITY 23-10 **Using a Slash**

Directions: *Write three sentences that use words that are sometimes combined with a slash to show that either could be used.*

> **Example:** *The test featured a yes/no answer format.*

_____

_____

_____

_____

_____

ELLIPSIS

4 Use other punctuation correctly.

An **ellipsis** (. . .) indicates that words, phrases, or even complete sentences have been left out of a quotation or dialogue. An ellipsis consists of three periods with spaces between them, with a space before the first one and a space after the last one.

1. **Use an ellipsis to signify where words have been omitted in a quotation.** An ellipsis indicates where you have omitted words within material you are quoting. Be careful not to change the author's meaning when omitting a word or words in the middle of a phrase or sentence. An ellipsis is not needed at the beginning or end of a quotation if you are quoting part of a sentence or a phrase.

   For example, here is an excerpt from Amy Tan's novel *Joy Luck Club*:

   > My mother believed you could be anything you wanted to be in America. You could open a restaurant. You could work for the government and get good retirement. You could buy a house with almost no money down. You could become rich. You could become instantly famous.

   Here is the same passage with some of the text removed as indicated by the use of an ellipsis:

   > My mother believed you could be anything you wanted to be in America. You could open a restaurant. You could work for the government and get good retirement. . . . You could become instantly famous.

2. **In dialogue, use an ellipsis to indicate a sentence that trails off.**

   > Noticing her frown, he hastily added, "Oh, never mind . . ."
   > OR
   > "Hold on a minute . . . ," Eliot interrupted. "That doesn't make sense!"

ACTIVITY 23-11 Using Ellipses

Directions: *Choose a reading from Chapter 18 or another class, and copy five sentences from it. Then remove at least three words from one of the sentences using an ellipsis without changing the original meaning of the passage.*

_____

_____

_____

_____

_____

_____

_____

BRACKETS

❹ Use other punctuation correctly.

Brackets ([ ]) are similar to parentheses (but square not curved), and they also set off information.

1. **Use brackets to add a word or comments to a direct quotation.**

> In the words of Thomas Wolfe, "It [New York City] was a cruel city, but it was a lovely one."
>
> One of the goals stated in the first sentence of the U.S. Constitution is to "provide for the common defence [*sic*]."

▶ **NOTE** The word *sic* (Latin for "as is") in brackets shows that a word in a quotation has been quoted exactly, even if it is incorrect or misspelled.

2. **Use brackets when you need to set off material within a sentence or phrase that is already in parentheses.**

> (The conductor reminded the orchestra to play *sotto voce* [quietly] during the vocalist's solo.)

ACTIVITY 23-12 **Using Brackets**

Directions: *Choose a reading from Chapter 18 or another class and quote two sentences from it, adding a word or phrase of your own in brackets.*

_____

_____

_____

_____

_____

_____

_____

_____

MyWritingLab™

Mastery Test: Practicing with Punctuation

Directions: *Choose the appropriate punctuation mark from the list below to fill in each of the blanks in the paragraph that follows.*

.	period	""	quotation marks	/	slash
?	question mark	( )	parentheses	[ ]	brackets
!	exclamation point	-	hyphen		
'	apostrophe	—	dash		

When writing a paper, be sure to cite all of your sources _____ You can use Modern Language Association format _____ MLA _____ or American Psychological Association format (APA). Most teachers are extremely antiplagiarism. Don't risk getting expelled from college _____ Do you know the rule of thumb for citing sources _____ Basically, if you didn't know the information before you started your paper, then you need to cite a source. Ask yourself, "Did I know this before I began working on this paper _____ If you didn't, then give credit where credit is due _____ It is essential. It_____s an either_____or situation: either you knew it _____ the rule, that is _____ or you didn't. Save yourself the shame, and when in doubt, cite it.

Learning Objectives Review

MyWritingLab™   **Complete the chapter assessment questions at mywritinglab.com**

❶ Recognize and use the three end-punctuation marks correctly.

What is end punctuation, and how is it used? (See pp. 559–562.)

Three types of **end punctuation** end a sentence. **Periods** (.) end a statement or indicate an abbreviation; **question marks** (?) indicate a direct question; and **exclamation points** (!) provide emphasis, express strong emotion, or indicate a strong command.

❷ Use apostrophes correctly.

What are the main uses of apostrophes? (See pp. 562–568.)

Apostrophes (') indicate (1) the omission of one or more letters; (2) possession; or (3) plural numbers, titles, symbols, and the plurals of words used as terms.

❸ Use quotation marks correctly.

What are the main uses of quotation marks? (See pp. 568–572.)

Quotation marks ("") indicate (1) direct quotations from prose or poetry; (2) dialogue; (3) titles of short stories, poems, articles, songs, and television episodes; and (4) words that are being defined or used ironically.

❹ Use other punctuation correctly.

What are the six other punctuation marks discussed in this chapter, and how are they used? (See pp. 573–580.)

The six other punctuation marks are **parentheses** (()), which set off information or citations; **hyphens** (-), used to combine or divide words; **dashes** (—), which add emphasis; **slashes** (/), used to indicate a choice between words or line breaks in quoted poetry; **ellipses** (. . .), which indicate that words, phrases, or even complete sentences have been omitted; and **brackets** ([]), similar to parentheses (but square not curved), which also set off information.

LEARNING OBJECTIVES

In this chapter, you will learn how to

1 Define construction and shift errors.

2 Identify and correct subject-verb agreement errors.

3 Ensure pronouns agree with their antecedents.

4 Identify and correct pronoun reference errors.

5 Identify and correct point-of-view shifts.

6 Identify and correct faulty parallelism.

7 Identify and correct dangling and misplaced modifiers.

8 Avoid unnecessary passive voice construction.

Thinking Critically MyWritingLab™

Think: Study the photograph. How would looking at these sails from another angle or perspective change your understanding of this image? Also, how does seeing just part of this sailboat affect your comprehension of the image? What if you could see the whole sailboat?

Write: Shifting point of view in your writing can cause confusion. Write a paragraph that describes the room you are sitting in without changing your point of view from the first person (I).

_____

_____

_____

_____

_____

_____

CONSTRUCTION AND SHIFT ERRORS

1 Define construction and shift errors.

What you see depends on who you are and your relationship to what you are viewing. In writing, a sudden change in the structure of your sentences or a shift in point of view can interfere with your readers' ability to understand your point or can change the meaning of the sentence completely. Life is confusing enough! Don't confuse your readers with mistakes such as this one: *She love to write in a confusing way.* Let's fix the verb to fit the subject: *She loves to write in a confusing way.*

Sometimes, the errors are much more subtle and may lead a reader to assume a meaning that wasn't intended, which can be much more confusing. Think about the following example: *Wanda noticed that Ellen looked sad and wondered if it was because her mother had died.* We are not sure whose mother died—Wanda's or Ellen's—because the pronoun "her" in the phrase *her mother* could mean either one's mother. Rewrite the sentence like this: *Wanda noticed that Ellen looked sad and wondered if it was because Ellen's mother had recently died.* Now it is clear! Grammatical errors that result when parts of the sentence don't match up are called construction and shift errors.

SUBJECT-VERB AGREEMENT

2 Identify and correct subject-verb agreement errors.

A verb must agree with its subject in number. A singular subject requires a singular verb, and a plural subject requires a plural verb.

> **Singular subject:** The *restaurant* **is** open until 10:00 P.M.
> **Plural subject:** Most *restaurants* **are** open until 10:00 P.M.

Subjects composed of collective nouns, singular nouns ending in *s*, or certain nouns that refer to measurements require singular verbs.

- **Collective nouns** (words that include a group but can act as a singular noun) take singular verbs:

> The *band* **plays** during halftime.

- **Singular nouns** ending in *s* still take singular verbs:

> *Physics* **is** a field that demands math skills.
> *Measles* **is** a serious illness in children.

- **Nouns referring to measurements** such as time, weight, and money take singular verbs:

> The twenty *dollars* **belongs** to Beth.
> The extra five *pounds* **looks** good on her.

Subject-Verb Agreement Errors

A **subject-verb agreement** error occurs when a writer uses a singular noun with a plural verb or a plural noun with a singular verb. For the subject and the verb to agree, both must be in singular form or both in plural form. In the following cases, it's easy for a writer to make mistakes in subject-verb agreement:

- When a verb comes before the subject
- When words come between the subject and the verb
- When the subject is an indefinite pronoun
- When a sentence has a compound subject

Here are some examples of these cases:

1. **Verb before the subject creates the error** (the verb is in bold font, and the subject is in italics).

   > **Incorrect:** There **is** many *birds* in our yard.
   > **Correct:** There **are** many *birds* in our yard.

2. **Words coming between the subject and the verb (often prepositional phrases) create the error.**

   > **Incorrect:** *One* of the students **were** in the bookstore this morning.
   > **Correct:** *One* of the students **was** in the bookstore this morning.

   The subject of the sentence is *one*, and, because the subject *one* is singular, the verb should also be singular. The subject is not *students*. A noun at the end of a prepositional phrase, such as *students*, can never be the subject of a sentence.

▶ **TIP** To avoid mistaking part of a prepositional phrase for the subject, try crossing out all the prepositional phrases in a sentence to find the subject, then check if the verb agrees with it. For example, you could cross out the prepositional phrase "of the students" in the incorrect example shown above.

> *One* ~~of the students~~ **were** in the bookstore this morning.

This clearly shows the disagreement between the singular subject *one* and the plural verb *were*.

3. **Indefinite pronouns as subjects taking singular or plural verbs create the error.** Indefinite pronouns function as general nouns rather than as substitutes for specific nouns. Some indefinite pronouns take singular verbs, and other indefinite pronouns take plural verbs. Some of the most common indefinite pronouns that require singular verbs are:

another	everybody	no one
anybody	everyone	nothing
each	everything	one
either	neither	something

> *Everybody* **is** going to the concert.

Common indefinite pronouns that require plural verbs include:

all	many
both	most
few	some

> *All* **are** welcome to attend the reception.

Even experienced writers can make the mistake of using plural verbs with singular indefinite pronouns.

> **Incorrect:** *Everyone* **like** to eat good food.
>   *Each* of the customers **order** food from the menu.
> **Correct:** *Everyone* **likes** to eat good food.
>   *Each* of the customers **orders** food from the menu.

4. **Compound subjects taking plural or singular verbs create the error.** Compound subjects can take either singular or plural verbs, depending on the subjects. Subjects joined by *and* generally take a plural verb:

> **Incorrect:** *Fruit and cheese* **tastes** good together.
> **Correct:** *Fruit and cheese* **taste** good together.

When subjects are joined by *either . . . or, neither . . . nor,* or *not only . . . but also,* the verb agrees with the subject closer to the verb:

> **Incorrect:** Neither Rob nor *Jim* **want** to wash the dishes.
> Neither the kids nor *Jim* **want** to wash the dishes.
> Neither Jim nor the *kids* **wants** to wash the dishes.
> **Correct:** Neither Rob nor *Jim* **wants** to wash the dishes.
> Neither the kids nor *Jim* **wants** to wash the dishes.
> Neither Jim nor the *kids* **want** to wash the dishes.

ACTIVITY 24-1 Subject-Verb Agreement

Directions: *Correct the error in subject-verb agreement in each of the following sentences. Cross out the incorrect word(s), and write the correction above the word(s) you deleted.*

1. One of my favorite restaurants are Palisades.

2. Though he doesn't want to admit it, the teacher, always in control of his classes, feel like the class is chaotic today.

3. The book contain facts about rugby and other European sports.

4. The chapters of the book features both the history and the definitions of various sports.

5. Neither the pilot nor the flight attendant want to make the announcement.

6. Anyone who is a citizen and over the age of 18 are allowed to vote.

7. There is several different issues one should review before voting for the first time.

8. Neither Ella nor Clara want to take the trip.

9. Overall, cake and ice cream fits the occasion at birthday parties.

10. Each of the scouts want to earn a merit badge.

PRONOUN-ANTECEDENT AGREEMENT

3 Ensure pronouns agree with their antecedents.

A **pronoun** (such as *he, she, it, we, they*) takes the place of another noun or pronoun used earlier in a sentence or in a preceding sentence. The noun or pronoun to which it refers is called the **antecedent**.

> My *boss* communicates well, and *she* is always fair.

In this example, the pronoun *she* refers to the noun *boss*; *boss* is the antecedent of *she*. A pronoun must agree with its antecedent in **number** (singular/plural), **gender** (male/female), and **person** (first, second, or third).

> My *great-grandfathers* were farmers, and *they* both raised dairy cattle.

The plural, third-person pronoun *they* agrees with its antecedent, the plural noun *great-grandfathers*.

> My *great-grandfather* was a farmer, and *he* raised dairy cattle.

In this example, the singular, third-person, masculine pronoun *he* agrees with its antecedent, the singular noun *great-grandfather*.

Pronoun-Antecedent Agreement Errors

Pronoun agreement errors occur when a pronoun "disagrees" with its antecedent. If the noun is singular, then the pronoun that refers to that noun must be singular. If the noun is plural, then the pronoun must be plural. Often writers create pronoun agreement errors in an attempt to avoid using gender-specific language.

> **Incorrect:** A <u>student</u> can get *their* books at the campus bookstore.

The subject *student* is singular; therefore, using the pronoun *their* (which is plural) creates a pronoun error. There are two ways to fix this error.

1. **Make the pronoun singular:**

   > A <u>student</u> can get *his or her* books at the campus bookstore.

2. **Make the subject plural:**

   > <u>Students</u> can get *their* books at the campus bookstore.

   ▶ **NOTE**   Making the subject plural helps avoid two problems related to sexist language: using unnecessarily gender-specific language, and using the more awkward split pronoun, *his or her*.

   ▶ **NOTE**   If the singular subject *is* gender-specific, then be sure to use a gender-specific pronoun.

   > A <u>boy scout</u> must keep *his* uniform clean.
   > A <u>ballerina</u> must have *her* shoes custom-made.

   It's a matter of logic: When gender *is* specific, use a gender-specific pronoun. When gender *is not* specific, don't use a gender-specific pronoun.

ACTIVITY 24-2   Pronoun Agreement

Directions: *Fix the pronoun agreement error in each of the following sentences. Cross out the error, and write the correction above it. If you change a pronoun or antecedent, remember that you may have to change the verb, too.*

1. Breaking the ice on the first day helps a student relax and lets them feel less intimidated.

2. In the summer, movies are top-notch, and it makes the summer a little more exciting.

3. Teaching a child to play soccer helps him work on team skills.

4. Communication skills are valuable, too, as it provides essential basics for school, career, and life in general.

5. Reading magazines is a great way to exercise the mind. They stimulates the mind with both words and images.

6. A farmer must know what all of his tools can do and how to use them.

7. A preschool teacher must have a great deal of patience, and she must have a sense of humor too.

8. College sports builds life-long skills.

9. One of the rules are hard to follow.

10. An adult must accompany a child learning to drive because they need guidance and instruction.

PRONOUN REFERENCE

4 Identify and correct pronoun reference errors.

A pronoun should clearly refer to its antecedent, the noun it is replacing.

Pronoun Reference Errors

A **pronoun reference error** occurs when a pronoun does not have a clear connection to its antecedent (the noun it refers to). The antecedent can be *ambiguous* (it is unclear which noun is the antecedent), *vague* (the antecedent is often completely missing), or *too broad* (there is no specific antecedent).

1. **An ambiguous pronoun reference error** occurs when there are two or more possible antecedents for a pronoun. To fix this type of reference error, revise the sentence to distinguish which antecedent you meant to refer to.

> **Incorrect:** Julie told Mayra that she needed to take her test at the Testing Center. [Who needs to take the test, Julie or Mayra?]
>
> **Correct:** Julie told Mayra that she *was planning* to take *the* test at the Testing Center.

2. **A vague pronoun reference error** occurs when the antecedent for the pronoun is completely missing. To fix this type of reference error, you need to fill in the missing noun or subject.

> **Incorrect:** At this coffee shop, *they* never provide enough free coffee refills. [Who does *they* refer to? *Coffee shop* is not the antecedent.]
>
> **Correct:** At this coffee shop, *the servers* are always very busy, and *they* never provide enough free coffee refills.

3. **A broad pronoun reference error** occurs when a relative pronoun (*who, whom, whose, which, these, those, that,* and *this*) is used without a clear noun to refer to. The relative pronoun may refer to a whole group of words, or even a whole sentence, instead of referring back to one clear noun antecedent. To fix this type of pronoun reference error, supply the missing noun or replace the relative pronoun with a noun.

> **Incorrect:** The landlord did not allow pets, which many tenants did not like. [The relative pronoun *which* refers to the entire situation of pets being prohibited and creates ambiguity. Do the tenants not like pets or not like the policy prohibiting pets? In order to correct this broad pronoun reference error, an antecedent for *which* must be supplied or the sentence must be restructured to indicate a clear subject.]
>
> **Correct:** The landlord did not allow pets, a policy that many tenants did not like.
>
> OR
>
> The landlord did not allow pets because many tenants objected to them.

The pronouns *this, that, these,* or *those* can cause pronoun reference errors when they are used to refer to a whole sentence or a situation described in a previous sentence. The error occurs because the pronoun has no clear, specific noun antecedent. Usually, this type of reference error requires you to insert a noun or a noun phrase after the pronoun.

> **Incorrect:** *This* is the reason for our trouble. [What is the *this* that is the reason for our trouble?]
>
> *That* is the one I want. [What is the *that*?]
>
> *These* (or *those*) are the ones I want. [What are the *these*?]
>
> **Correct:** *This* <u>lack of funding</u> is the reason for our trouble.
>
> *That* <u>puppy</u> is the one I want.
>
> *These* (or *those*) <u>puppies</u> are the ones I want.

▶ **TIP**   When a reference error is caused by a pronoun such as *this* or *that*, think of adding a "fill in the blank" answer after it. Answer the question, "This *what?*" or "That *what?*"

ACTIVITY 24-3   Correcting Pronoun Reference Errors

Directions: *Rewrite the sentences below to correct pronoun reference errors. You may need to add nouns or rewrite sentences completely to fix the errors.*

1. Before finishing the whole thing, he skimmed it.

_____

_____

2. That is what I was hoping for.

_____

_____

3. When the dog wouldn't stop chewing her purse, she moved it to the bedroom.

_____

_____

4. The cat chased a bird and terrified a toddler, but we knew it would be fine.

_____

_____

5. I checked a traffic website and I listened to the news, but it didn't have an up-to-date traffic report.

_____

_____

POINT-OF-VIEW SHIFTS

5 Identify and correct point-of-view shifts.

In reading and writing, the term *point of view* refers to a writer's perspective on a subject. In grammar, however, **point of view** determines the pronouns you use in writing. While it is possible to switch among points of view within an essay, you generally use personal pronouns associated with a single point of view: *first person*, *second person*, or *third person*.

1. **First person**

   Singular: *I, me, my, mine, myself*

   Plural: *we, us, our, ours, ourselves*

   First-person point of view is most commonly used in narrative writing.

   > *I* went on a vacation with *my* family this summer. *We* took *our* favorite car, but two days into the trip, *our* car broke down.

2. **Second person**

   Singular and plural: *you, yours*, or implied *you*/imperative (command form)

   Second-person point of view is most commonly used for rhetorical questions (a question you ask to interest your readers) in an essay introduction. In general, avoid using second-person point of view when writing essays except in rhetorical questions. Be careful not to use the pronoun *you* to refer to people in general. Use the second person only when specifically addressing the reader.

   > Do you think you pay too much for your college textbooks?

3. **Third person**

   Singular: *he, she, him, her, his, hers, himself, herself, it, its*

   Plural: *they, them, their, theirs, themselves*

   Third person is the preferred point of view for most essays.

   > Author Alice Walker met Martin Luther King Jr. during the early 1960s. *He* inspired *her* to become active in the civil rights movement, and *she* participated in the 1963 March on Washington.

Indefinite Pronouns

For all indefinite pronouns except *one*, third-person personal pronouns may be used to maintain a consistent point of view.

> *Anyone* who wants to use a gym locker is required to bring *his or her* own padlock.
>
> Michael and Janine joined the other musicians for a jam session; *both* brought *their* own guitars.

The indefinite pronoun *one* can refer to the writer or people in general.

> *One* would think that the library would stay open all night during finals.

This sentence suggests that the writer thinks the library should stay open all night. The sentence also implies that other people are likely to agree.

The possessive form of one is *one's*. *One's*—unlike *hers*, *ours*, or *theirs*—includes an apostrophe.

> One should be attentive to *one's* personal hygiene.

Do not mix the indefinite pronoun *one* with personal pronouns or general nouns such as *a person*, especially in the same sentence.

> **Incorrect:** *One* should not neglect *his or her* studies.
>
> *One* should not neglect *their* studies.
>
> *A person* should not neglect *one's* studies.
>
> **Correct:** *One* should not neglect *one's* studies.

Avoid Incorrect Point-of-View Shifts

Though it is possible to employ more than one point of view in an essay, be sure that the switch is logical and actually needed grammatically. The most common point-of-view shift error involves switching to the second-person pronoun *you*. In casual speech, people often use the generic *you* to mean "people in general." However, in formal writing, this substitution is not acceptable.

Incorrect: *I* had a wonderful time collecting shells on the beach. When *a person* looks carefully at low tide, *you* can see many different kinds of shells.

Correct: *I* had a wonderful time collecting shells on the beach. When *I* looked carefully at low tide, *I* could see many different kinds of shells.

▶ **NOTE**   Many teachers suggest using the third-person-plural point of view in most college writing to avoid both point-of-view shifts and other agreement errors.

POV shift error (indefinite pronoun shift to second person):

One can receive *your* degree within two years.

Pronoun agreement error (plural pronoun for singular noun):

A *student* can receive *their* degree within two years.

Both errors fixed by substituting a plural noun for the subject and using a third-person plural pronoun:

Students can receive *their* degrees within two years.

ACTIVITY 24-4   Correcting POV Shifts

Directions: *Correct the POV shift errors in the following sentences. Be sure to stay in the point of view that is used first in the sentence.*

1. When the day is hot, you can always head to water.

2. As you learn how to cope with stress, one's overall health improves.

3. As people gain weight, you tend to have lower self-esteem.

4. Many people take up a group sport, but few decide to give up one's entire weekend for that sport.

5. Anyone who wants to join us should send us an email with their contact information.

FAULTY PARALLELISM

6 Identify and correct faulty parallelism.

Parallelism (or parallel structure) means keeping the grammatical form or word form in a series of verbals or phrases consistent. Faulty parallelism occurs when the same grammatical form or structure is not used throughout.

> **Incorrect:** When we're on vacation, we *swim* in the ocean, *run* on the beach, and *hiking* in the mountains.

The last verb in this list of three verbs is *hiking*, which uses an *-ing* form of the verb, while the first and second verbs use the base forms. To correct this error, simply change *hiking* to *hike*. Or, if you prefer to use *-ing* verbs, change *swim* and *run* to *-ing* verb forms by restructuring the sentence.

> **Correct:** When we're on vacation, we *swim* in the ocean, *run* on the beach, and *hike* in the mountains.
>
> **Correct:** When we're on vacation, we like *swimming* in the ocean, *running* on the beach, and *hiking* in the mountains.

Sometimes, problems with parallelism occur with whole phrases, especially when comparisons are being made.

> **Incorrect:** Page didn't know *whether to give* Jacob her new toy or *if she should keep* it for herself.

The phrases *whether to . . .* and *if she should . . .* are not parallel constructions. Choose one or the other to create the comparison. Here is one way to correct the sentence.

> **Correct:** Page didn't know *whether to give* Jacob her new toy or *keep* it for herself.

▶ **NOTE**   When there are two infinitive phrases (*to give, to keep*), the *to* does not need to be repeated.

Here are two other ways to correct the parallelism error in the original sentence.

> **Correct:** Page didn't know *if she should give* Jacob her new toy or *if she should keep* it for herself.
>
> **Correct:** Page didn't know if she should *give* Jacob her new toy or *keep* it for herself.

ACTIVITY 24-5 Correcting Faulty Parallelism

Directions: *Rewrite the following sentences to correct errors in parallelism.*

1. Saving for college can be a challenge, but to work while attending college is worse.

   _____

   _____

2. Driving a car for the first time can be scary: Be sure to practice with someone you trust, to forgive simple mistakes you make, and put safety first.

   _____

   _____

3. Whether you are buying a new car or are to buy a used car, check with a few dealerships to find the best value.

   _____

   _____

4. You can find good deals on textbooks by shopping on the Internet, buying books from other classmates, or to buy used copies of textbooks in the campus bookstore.

   _____

   _____

5. Food on campus is not always the best, often lacking variety, costs too much, and tasting bland.

   _____

   _____

DANGLING AND MISPLACED MODIFIERS

7 Identify and correct dangling and misplaced modifiers.

A **modifier** is a word or word group that *refers to* or *modifies* a nearby word or word group. Errors in modifiers occur when the nearby word or word group is not directly stated (so the modifier is "dangling" without anything to connect to) or the modifier isn't close enough to the word or word group it is supposed to modify (a misplaced modifier).

Dangling Modifiers

Dangling modifiers are missing a home base: The word they're intended to modify is missing from the sentence. As a result, dangling modifiers are often unintentionally funny. This example illustrates the dangers, and the humor, of dangling modifiers:

> **Incorrect:** Galloping across the finish line, the crowd cheered loudly.
> **Correct:** The crowd cheered loudly as the horses galloped across the finish line.
> **Correct:** As the horses galloped across the finish line, the crowd cheered loudly.

▶ **NOTE** Dangling modifiers often occur when an introductory phrase is not followed by the correct subject.

> **Incorrect:** After examining the patient, the doctor's recommendation was to continue the prescribed treatment. [The doctor's recommendation did not examine the patient.]
> **Correct:** After examining the patient, the doctor recommended continuation of the prescribed treatment.

ACTIVITY 24-6 Correcting Dangling Modifiers

Directions: *Edit the following sentences to correct dangling modifiers. You may need to add a subject, change words, or rearrange the sentence.*

1. While flying across country, the seats became a little uncomfortable.

_____

_____

2. Knowing that the movie was starting, it was a relief that we only missed the previews.

_____

_____

3. Starting to burn in the hot sun, the sunscreen came in handy.

_____

_____

4. Surfing the Internet, my computer suddenly went blank.

_____

_____

5. Laughing uncontrollably, the commercial was very funny.

_____

_____

Misplaced Modifiers

A **misplaced modifier** is in the wrong place in a sentence, so the reader thinks it modifies the wrong word or cannot figure out what it is modifying.

Incorrect: I was chased by a dog wearing my pajamas.

Okay, it's bad enough to be chased by a dog, but it adds insult to injury if he's wearing my pajamas! The modifier _wearing my pajamas_ is in the wrong spot: It is closer to _dog_ than to _I_.

Revised: Wearing my pajamas, I was chased by a dog.

Single-word modifiers such as _often_ and _almost_ are often misplaced:

Example: I almost made $200 for the lawn-mowing job.

So did the job not happen? If the writer means that he or she made almost $200 for the job, then the modifier needs to be placed immediately before the word (or words) being modified:

Revised: I made almost $200 for the lawn-mowing job.

ACTIVITY 24-7 Correcting Misplaced Modifiers

Directions: *Rewrite each of the following sentences to correct the misplaced modifier. You may need to completely restructure the sentence.*

1. I almost drank the entire pot of coffee while studying for my exam.

_____

_____

2. She stood beside the silver car dressed in a bright blue sweater, which made a nice backdrop for her.

_____

_____

3. Drenched in hot fudge sauce, I love ice cream sundaes.

_____

_____

4. She bought a new dress weighing only 120 pounds, thanks to her diet.

_____

_____

5. He decided to be a math teacher only when he was ten years old.

_____

_____

ACTIVITY 24-8 Correcting Dangling and Misplaced Modifiers

Directions: *On the line before each sentence, write DM if the sentence includes a dangling modifier and MM if it includes a misplaced modifier. Then revise the sentences to correct the errors.*

_____ **1.** We were given the choice of three entrees, but my friend only said the salmon would do for her.

_____

_____

_____ **2.** Resting in the grass, my bicycle almost hit the baby squirrel.

_____

_____

_____   **3.** Hungry after playing tennis, the fast-food restaurant caught my eye.

_____

_____

_____   **4.** The lost cat was picked up by the passerby without an ID tag.

_____

_____

_____   **5.** Wearing a crazy outfit, the audience didn't know what to make of the lead character of the play.

_____

_____

PASSIVE VOICE CONSTRUCTION

8 Avoid unnecessary passive voice construction.

As a grammatical term, "voice" refers to verbs. Verbs can be in the active or passive voice. When a verb is in the **active voice**, the subject performs the action. When a verb is in the **passive voice**, the subject experiences the effect of the action. Passive voice uses a form of the verb "to be" and a past participle.

Whenever possible, avoid using *passive* voice and opt for *active* voice to write clear, powerful sentences. Sometimes, the passive voice will leave out the agent (the doer of the action) completely and make the sentence vague. An active verb construction is easier for readers to understand because the active voice places the emphasis on *who* is doing the action:

> **Passive voice:** The ball *was thrown.*
>
> OR
>
> The ball *was thrown* by Thomas.
>
> **Revised to active voice:** Thomas *threw* the ball.

Not only does the active voice construction sound cleaner, it is also clearer because the "doer" of the action (Thomas) is emphasized and not buried at the end of the sentence or left out of the sentence completely. Here is another example of passive voice construction:

> **Passive:** The puppy that was selected by the children was wagging its tail.
>
> **Changed to active:** The children selected the puppy that was wagging its tail.

ACTIVITY 24-9 Changing Passive Voice to Active Voice

Directions: *Rewrite each of the following sentences in the space provided, changing the sentence from the passive voice to the active voice.*

1. The potato salad was made by Linda for the big neighborhood barbeque.

   _____

   _____

2. After the long race, a meal was inhaled by the runner.

   _____

   _____

3. The dandelions were pulled out.

   _____

   _____

4. The performers were greeted with a warm, welcoming applause by the audience.

   _____

   _____

5. The recording contract offer was rejected by the new young band.

   _____

   _____

ACTIVITY 24-10 Correcting Subject-Verb and Pronoun Agreement Errors, Passive Voice Construction, and Point-of-View Shifts

Directions: *Fix errors in subject-verb agreement, pronoun agreement, point of view, and passive voice construction in the following passage. Cross out the errors and write corrections above them. You will find a total of six errors.*

A local businesswoman who started her own business making cupcakes a few years ago offers some advice to potential new business owners. The successful businesswoman, Mary Taylor, say that opening a business of one's own is tricky. You have to be careful. She discusses the need to plan ahead. Advice was given to her by many friends. One of the pieces of advice she got were to find investors for the business. Money was invested by a few friends. One has to keep track of their debts, too. Overall, she suggests getting help and being careful in each step of the process.

Mastery Test I: Correcting Dangling and Misplaced Modifiers

Directions: *Underline misplaced and dangling modifiers in the following paragraph. Then write MM over the underlined word or phrase if it is a misplaced modifier or DM over the phrase if it is a dangling modifier. You should find seven modifier errors.*

My nephew, now full grown, is a very tall person. He nearly stands 6'9" tall. Towering over many people, the ceiling seems close to my nephew's head. Born in a small hospital, the staff was surprised by the size of my nephew even at birth. He almost was 24 inches long. Today, when walking down the street, the cars will honk as they go by sometimes just to acknowledge his size. He almost realizes everyone sees him as a giant. However, making everyone smile at first meeting, the town knows him as a lovable giant.

MyWritingLab™

Mastery Test II: Changing Passive Voice to Active Voice

Directions: *Rewrite the following passage, changing each sentence from the passive to the active voice.*

A perfect game was pitched by the pitcher. The pitches thrown by him were impressive during all nine innings. Credit was also given to the rest of the team for the perfect game. Balls were caught in the infield or outfield, so they didn't count. However, most of the victory was due to the amazing pitching. His arm didn't give out. The score was seen. A standing ovation was given by the crowd at the end of the game.

_____

_____

_____

_____

_____

_____

_____

_____

_____

APPLYING CRITICAL THINKING

| PURPOSE | IDEAS | SUPPORT | ASSUMPTIONS BIASES | CONCLUSIONS | POINT OF VIEW | ANALYSIS |

After you have drafted and revised your work, use your **analysis** skills to break your sentences down into their parts to make sure you have constructed them correctly and haven't made any of the errors discussed in this chapter.

Ask yourself the following questions:

- **Have I switched point of view when I shouldn't have** (from first person—*I, me, us;* to second person—*you;* or to third person—*he, she, they*)?
- **Does each verb agree with its subject** (are the verb and the subject both singular or both plural)?
- **Do pronouns agree with their subjects** (are the pronoun and the subject both singular or both plural)?
- **Are pronoun references clear** (is it clear to which noun a pronoun refers)?
- **Are my sentences parallel** (do grammatical forms or structures stay consistent throughout the sentence)?
- **Are my modifiers attached and in the right place** (are the words they modify included in the sentence)?
- **Did I avoid passive voice construction?**

MyWritingLab™   ## Mastery Test III: Recalling and Applying

Directions: *After reading this chapter, perform the following tasks.*

Recall: Explain the difference between a dangling modifier and a misplaced modifier.

_____

_____

Apply: Which of these two sentences is not parallel? Explain why.

    A. I decided to go to college, to graduate early, and to get a good job.

    B. I love to eat while I am driving, to listen to music as I drive, but not texting while driving.

_____

_____

_____

_____

_____

Write: Now, rewrite the sentence that wasn't parallel to correct it.

_____

_____

_____

_____

_____

Learning Objectives Review

MyWritingLab™ Complete the chapter assessment questions at mywritinglab.com

❶ Define construction and shift errors.

What are construction and shift errors? (See p. 583.)

Grammatical errors that result when parts of the sentence don't match up are called **construction and shift errors**.

❷ Identify and correct subject-verb agreement errors.

What is subject-verb agreement, and how do you correct subject-verb agreement errors? (See pp. 583–587.)

Subject-verb agreement means that a verb agrees with its subject in number: a singular subject requires a singular verb, and a plural subject requires a plural verb. A **subject-verb agreement error** occurs when a singular noun is used with a plural verb or a plural noun with a singular verb. **Correct** subject-verb agreement errors by (1) ensuring the verb and subject are both singular or both plural; (2) if the pronoun is indefinite, check if it takes a singular or plural verb; and (3) if there is a compound subject joined by *and*, use a plural verb, and if it is joined by *either/or, neither/nor,* or *not only . . . but also,* make the verb agree with the closest subject.

❸ Ensure pronouns agree with their antecedents.

What is pronoun-antecedent agreement? (See pp. 587–589.)

A **pronoun** (*he, she, it, we, they*) takes the place of another noun or pronoun (the **antecedent**) used earlier in a sentence or in a preceding sentence. A pronoun must agree with its antecedent in **number** (singular/plural), **gender** (male/female), and **person** (first, second, or third).

❹ Identify and correct pronoun reference errors.

What are pronoun reference errors, and how can you correct them? (See pp. 589–591.)

Pronoun reference errors occur when a pronoun does not have a clear connection to its antecedent. There are three types: (1) The antecedent can be *ambiguous* (it is unclear which noun is the antecedent). **Revise to clarify** which antecedent is being referred to. (2) The antecedent can be *vague* (the antecedent is often completely missing). **Add** the missing noun or subject. (3) The antecedent can be *too broad* (there is no specific antecedent). **Add** a noun or **replace** a relative pronoun with a noun.

5 Identify and correct point-of-view shifts.

What is point of view, and how can you avoid point-of-view errors? (See pp. 592–595.)

In grammar, **point of view** determines the pronouns you use in your writing: *first person, second person,* or *third person.* Be sure that your use of pronouns is consistent; making pronouns plural can help.

6 Identify and correct faulty parallelism.

What is parallelism, and how can you correct faulty parallelism? (See pp. 595–596.)

Parallelism involves using a consistent grammatical form or structure in a series of related words, phrases, or clauses. **Faulty parallelism** occurs when the same grammatical form or structure is not used throughout a sentence. **Correct** it by revising all the elements to have the same grammatical structure.

7 Identify and correct dangling and misplaced modifiers.

What is a modifier, and how can you correct a dangling or misplaced modifier? (See pp. 597–600.)

A **modifier** is a word or word group that *refers to* or *modifies* a nearby word or word group. A **dangling modifier** is created when the word the modifier is intended to modify is missing. **Correct it** by adding the missing subject to the main clause or revising the dangling modifier to include the missing subject and a verb. A **misplaced modifier** is in the wrong place in a sentence, so the reader thinks it modifies the wrong word or cannot figure out what it is modifying. **Correct it** by moving the modifier closer to the word or words it modifies.

8 Avoid unnecessary passive voice construction.

What is passive voice construction, and why should you avoid it? (See pp. 600–604.)

Passive voice construction is a type of sentence construction in which the subject of the sentence experiences the effect of the action. Active verb construction (in which the subject of the sentences *does* the action) is easier for readers to understand because it places the emphasis on *who* is doing the action; you should avoid using the passive voice.

LEARNING OBJECTIVES

In this chapter, you will learn how to

1 Improve your spelling.

2 Use spell-check effectively.

3 Distinguish between commonly confused words.

4 Use a dictionary.

5 Use a thesaurus.

6 Capitalize correctly.

7 Format numbers correctly.

8 Use abbreviations correctly.

© J. Lemon/Lemonworld

Thinking Critically MyWritingLab™

Think: Explain this cartoon.

Write: What is funny about it?

_____

_____

_____

_____

_____

_____

_____

_____

_____

_____

_____

_____

_____

_____

_____

_____

_____

_____

TEN TIPS TO IMPROVE YOUR SPELLING

① Improve your spelling.

My friend Walter, who teaches composition, always says to his students, "I don't take off for spelling in essays, but I do take off for misspelling!" If you make spelling mistakes in a final draft, your readers will probably understand what you mean, but they may lose respect for your ideas and consider your arguments less credible. If you want to be taken seriously as a writer, then *you* have to take spelling seriously. In fact, every detail in your essay counts. Writers call spelling, word usage, and the conventions for numbers, capitalization, and abbreviations "mechanics."

Mechanics are essential to the correct use of language, and none is more important to your credibility as a writer than spelling.

Spelling Tip 1: Use a Dictionary

During the revision and editing stage of your writing process, use a dictionary to double-check any word that you are not 100 percent sure is spelled correctly. *When in doubt, look it up.*

Spelling Tip 2: Check for Correct Pronunciation

Some spelling errors occur because some words are not spelled the way they sound or are pronounced. Here are a few examples of words that are commonly mispronounced and, consequently, misspelled: *accidentally* (not "accidently"), *athletics* (not "atheletics"), *disastrous* (not "disasterous"), *February* (not "Febuary"), *government* (not "goverment"), *mathematics* (not "mathmatics"), *publicly* (not "publically"), *temperament* (not "temperment"), and *wondrous* (not "wonderous").

Spelling Tip 3: Do Not Confuse Homophones

Some spelling mistakes occur as the result of confusing two **homophones**, words that sound the same, or nearly the same, but have different meanings and sometimes are spelled differently. Here are some examples:

affect/effect

complement/compliment

break/brake

right/write/rite

See "Commonly Confused Words" later in this chapter (pp. 614–628) for a more complete list of homophones, and use the list to avoid spelling errors.

Spelling Tip 4: Use Rules for Making Words Plural

Some plural forms of words are commonly misspelled. Watch for them. Here are a few rules that will help you spell plurals correctly:

1. **Most nouns are made plural by adding a final s:** *cat/cats*, *dog/dogs*, and *apple/apples*.

2. **Singular nouns ending with s, x, ch, or sh need es to form the plural:** *boss/bosses*, *ax/axes*, *crutch/crutches*, and *dish/dishes*.

3. **If a noun ends with a y preceded by a consonant, change the y to an i, and add es to form the plural:** *beauty/beauties* and *city/cities*. However, always keep the y when you are making a family's name plural: *the Murphys*.

4. **If a noun ends with y preceded by a vowel, then keep the y and add an s to form the plural:** *boy/boys* and *ray/rays*.

5. **If a noun ends with an o, add either an s or es.** It's best to consult a dictionary if you're not sure whether the word you're spelling ends in s or es: *solo/solos*, *piano/pianos*, *hero/heroes*, and *tomato/tomatoes*.

6. **If a noun ends with an f or an f followed by a silent e, then change the f to a v, and add es (for words ending with an f) or s (for words ending with an f followed by a silent e):** *leaf/leaves*, *self/selves*, *wife/wives*, and *knife/knives*. However, for some words ending with an f, the plural is formed just by adding s: *chief/chiefs* and *proof/proofs*. Consult a dictionary if you are not sure which spelling is correct.

7. **There are many irregular plurals in English, and most of them are well known from regular usage.** Here are a few examples: *child/children*, *man/men*, *woman/women*, *tooth/teeth*, *mouse/mice*, *deer/deer*, *moose/moose*, *sheep/sheep*, *datum/data*, and *medium/media*. When in doubt, consult a dictionary.

Spelling Tip 5: Distinguish Between *ei* and *ie*

Learn the correct spelling of words containing *ei* or *ie*. Pay attention to the previous letter and the sound of the word to figure out whether "i" goes before "e" or vice versa. There are some simple rules you can follow.

1. **When the sound you want to make is ee as in see, then use i before e:** *believe*, *chief*, *grief*, and *yield*.

2. **When the combination is preceded by a c, the spelling is almost always ei:** *receive*, *deceiving*, *ceiling*, and *conceit*.

3. **When the word has an ay sound, as in bay or way, then the spelling is almost always ei:** *neigh/neighborhood*, and *weigh/weight*.

▶ **TIP**   Memorize this little rhyme:

"I" before "e" except after "c,"
or when it sounds like *ay*
as in *neighbor* or *weigh*.

Even this rule has exceptions: *caffeine* and *seize*, for example. So, remember to consult a dictionary when you have any doubts.

Spelling Tip 6: Learn the Rules for Adding Suffixes and Prefixes

Adding Suffixes

1. **When adding the *-ing* suffix, in general, drop the silent *e* at the end of a word:** *become/becoming, come/coming, hope/hoping, scare/scaring,* and *surprise/surprising.* However, there are a few exceptions, such as *dye/dyeing* and *shoe/shoeing.*
   When the word ends with a *y*, then retain the *y: cry/crying, enjoy/enjoying, lay/laying,* and *study/studying.*

2. **When adding the *-ible* suffix, drop the silent *e*:** *force/forcible.*

3. **When adding the *-able* suffix, the silent *e* may be dropped or kept, so consult a dictionary if you are unsure:** *advise/advisable, argue/arguable, manage/manageable,* and *change/changeable.*

4. **A final silent *e* that is preceded by another vowel is always dropped when adding any suffix:** *argue/arguable* and *true/truly.*

5. **When a word ends with a *y* preceded by a consonant (and the suffix added is not *-ing*), then change the *y* to an *i* before adding the suffix:** *happy/happiest/happier, pity/pitiful,* and *ugly/uglier/ugliest.* However, when the *y* is preceded by a vowel, keep the *y* and add an *s: delay/delays, enjoy/enjoys, toy/toys,* and *valley/valleys.*

6. **When you are adding a suffix to a word that ends in a consonant, you often need to double the consonant first:** *cancel/cancelled, grip/gripping, grip/gripped, sad/saddest, occur/occurrence, refer/referred,* and *scar/scarring.* But there are exceptions (such as *deep/deepened, travel/traveling,* and *crawl/crawler*), so consult your dictionary when in doubt.

Adding Prefixes

Adding a prefix to a word does not typically require a change in the spelling of the base word, but if the base word starts with a vowel, a hyphen may be needed. Again, when in doubt, consult your dictionary.

appear/disappear	eminent/preeminent
operate/cooperate	educate/re-educate
spell/misspell	emphasize/re-emphasize
usual/unusual	

Spelling Tip 7: Keep a List of Your Errors

Keep a list of your own frequently misspelled words in a spelling log or journal. Just being aware of your most frequent errors will help you eradicate them eventually.

Spelling Tip 8: Be Familiar with Commonly Misspelled Words

Consult the following list for some of the most commonly misspelled words in college essays: *believe, conceive, curiosity, definitely, disastrous, environment, forty, friend, interrupt, irrelevant, license, mathematics, medieval, necessary, occasion, precede, professor, receive, tendency, themselves, thorough,* and *weird.*

Spelling Tip 9: Be Aware of Common Letter Groupings

Be aware of common letter groupings, such as *qu, ei, ie, au, ch, ou, th, sh,* and *gh.* Note patterns, and keep them in mind: *qu*iet, *qu*ite, rece*i*ve, d*i*et, l*au*nch, *th*ose, *sh*ould, and tou*gh.* Use these patterns as spelling cues.

Spelling Tip 10: Use Spell-Check

Use the spell-check function on your computer, but be careful. See "The Rewards and Dangers of Spell-Check" on page 612.

ACTIVITY 25-1 Trying Out the Spelling Tips

Directions: *Correct the spelling errors in the following paragraph. Refer to the ten spelling tips above for help. You should find eight spelling errors in this paragraph.*

Last fall, I was able to take a trip to Japan with my good freind Keiko. When I showed her my passport picture, she laughed right away because of my wierd expression and crazy hairstyle. Then, we recieved some good news from our parents: it was time to baord our flight. We went thorough the long security lines and made it to the gate with plenty of time to spare.

There were alot of people waiting to board. Keiko told me she would run and get us some coffee because caffiene would help with the long trip. She didn't take to long and got back just in time. We got on the plane without any issues and knew this was defiantly going to be one of the best trips of our lives.

THE REWARDS AND DANGERS OF SPELL-CHECK

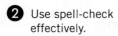 **Use spell-check effectively.**

Spell-check is certainly helpful to writers, but don't fall into the habit of always accepting what spell-check suggests. You need to be sure you are using the right word in the right context. Spell-check will always suggest a correctly spelled word, but it might not be the word you intended, and the word suggested by spell-check may mean something completely different. Many spell-check programs automatically indicate (by a red underline, for example) a misspelled word as soon as you've finished typing it. In some word processing programs, you can use your computer mouse to right-click on the word, and spell-check will offer possible correct spellings. When in doubt, though, consult your dictionary. Here is a list of the rewards and dangers of using spell-check programs.

The Rewards

1. **The spell-check function can help you spot many of your spelling errors**.
2. **The spell-check function is convenient**, requiring just a mouse click. In some word processing programs or computer systems, spell-check operates automatically.
3. **The spell-check function offers a fairly extensive collection of correctly spelled words.**

The Dangers

1. **Spell-check may not point out words in your essay that are spelled correctly but not used correctly.** For example, spell-check would not identify these two errors:

> **Incorrect:** My brother suggested that we play Monopoly, but I get *board* with *bored* games.

These two italicized words should be interchanged.

> **Corrected:** My brother suggested that we play Monopoly, but I get *bored* with *board* games.

2. **Spell-check may suggest words that are correctly spelled but do not fit the context of your sentence.**

> I'm not sure whether I should take a biology course, but I'm <u>*definantly*</u> taking physics.
>
> **Spell-check suggestion:** I'm not sure whether I should take a biology course, but I'm <u>*defiantly*</u> taking physics.
>
> **Intended correct spelling:** I'm not sure whether I should take a biology course, but I'm *definitely* taking physics.

In this example, the writer misspelled the word *definitely*, meaning "without a doubt," but spell-check incorrectly substituted the word *defiantly*, meaning "in a challenging or disobedient manner."

▶ **NOTE**   Be careful not to automatically click "Replace" for words suggested by spell-check. Look carefully, and when in doubt, consult a dictionary to make sure you choose the right word for the context of your sentence.

3. **Spell-check does not include every word you might use.** Sometimes spell-check wrongly identifies correctly spelled words (such as proper names with unusual spellings) as errors. Consult a dictionary or other resource, as needed.

As you can see, spell-check is a wonderful tool. Far too often, however, students rely too heavily on spell-check and run into trouble. Use this tool with caution: Apply critical thinking, and have a good dictionary handy as a backup.

ACTIVITY 25-2   Testing Spell-Check

Directions: *Using a word processor that has spell-check, write a paragraph of your own and deliberately misspell five words, preferably words with difficult or uncommon spellings. Then, use spell-check to fix the spelling of the words. Use a dictionary to double-check a word's spelling, if necessary. Then answer the following questions in the spaces below.*

1. Was spell-check's first suggestion for each of your misspelled words accurate? If not, list the inaccurate suggestions, and explain why they were wrong.

   _____

   _____

2. When you mistyped the word, did spell-check automatically identify it (for example, by underlining it in red)? Did it provide suggestions for the correct spelling? If so, were the suggestions appropriate?

   _____

   _____

3. Did you use a dictionary? If so, how did it help?

   _____

   _____

COMMONLY CONFUSED WORDS

3 Distinguish between commonly confused words.

Often, spelling mistakes result from writers confusing one word with another that sounds like it (a homonym), as we learned in Spelling Tip 3 on page 608. Some confusion also results from using the wrong form of a word, using slang, or using a word that is spelled correctly but in the wrong context. For example, many people misuse a common phrase by saying, "For all intensive purposes" when the real saying is "For all intents and purposes." If an instructor ever writes "wrong word" or "ww" on your paper, you have confused one word with another.

Here is a list of some of the commonly confused words that most often show up in student writing.

a/an

Both these words are indefinite articles (words that come before a general noun). Use *a* when the word following it starts with a consonant sound, and use *an* when the word following it starts with a vowel sound (*a, e, i, o, u*) or a silent *h*. When the *h* is not silent, use *a*. Sometimes an initial vowel has a consonant sound; when this is the case, use *a*.

> Lil ate *an* apple from Hallie's fruit bowl, and Hallie thought it was *an* honor to provide her with a treat. Neither was interested in eating *a* banana.

> The author is currently writing *a* history of the Iditarod, *a* unique dog sled race that began in 1973.

a lot/allot/alot (misspelling)

a lot is a two-word phrase (an article and a noun) that means *a great deal* or *many*. The phrase should be used only in informal writing.

allot is a transitive verb meaning *to divide something up* or *to portion* or *to allow*.

alot is a common misspelling of "a lot." It is not a legitimate word.

> Marge didn't want *a lot* from life: She just wanted what was *allotted* to her.

accept/except

accept is a transitive verb that means *to agree* or *to receive*.

except is either a verb meaning *to exclude* or *leave out* or a preposition meaning *other than* or *apart from*.

> Sandy decided to *accept* all the gifts from Sam *except* the new pet lizard.

adapt/adopt

adapt is a verb meaning *to adjust* or *to fit or make suitable*.

adopt is a verb meaning to make something or someone one's own.

> Martin had to *adapt* his viewpoint to match his wife's state of mind so they could *adopt* the newborn kittens.

advice/advise

advice is a noun meaning *a suggestion or recommendation*.

advise is a verb meaning *to suggest, give a recommendation*.

> I *advise* you not to listen to all of your parents' *advice* when you have a new baby.

affect/effect

affect is a verb meaning *to influence* (think "a" for action).

effect is a noun meaning *a result* (think "e" for ending), or it can be a verb if used to mean *to bring about*.

> Monique's strong academic goals *affected* her success and created long-lasting, positive career *effects*. The new rules *effected* a change in policy.

afraid/frightened

afraid is an adjective, usually followed by the preposition *of* or the word *that*; *afraid* means "filled with fear, regret, or concern."

> As a child, I was *afraid of* the dark.
> He was *afraid that* he would not have enough time to study.

frightened can be an adjective, meaning "filled with fear" or "alarmed"; *frightened* can also function as a verb, meaning "made afraid."

> The *frightened* dog hid under the bed.
> The loud crack of thunder *frightened* the dog.

aggravate/irritate

aggravate is a verb meaning "to make worse."
irritate is a verb meaning "to annoy, anger, inflame, or to chafe."

> Winston was *irritated* by the rash on his arm, but he *aggravated* the itching by constantly scratching it.

all ready/already

all ready is an adjective phrase meaning "prepared."
already is an adverb used in expressions of time.

> We were *all ready* to leave for the airport, but we realized that our ride had *already* left.

all right/alright (misspelling)

all right is an adjective or an adverb, depending on the context, and means "agreeable, satisfactory."
alright is a misspelling of "all right" and should not be used.

> Kelly was *all right* after she found out that many students confused words and their spellings.

allude/refer

allude is a verb meaning "to call attention to something *indirectly*."
refer is a verb meaning "to describe something in a particular way."

> In her speech, Susan didn't *refer* directly to the Bible, but she *alluded* to it.

allusion/illusion

allusion is a noun meaning "an indirect or casual reference" or "a specific reference to a well-known artistic or literary work."

illusion is a noun meaning "an unreal perception" or a "visual trick."

> Houdini often made *allusions* to famous lines from Shakespeare before he performed one of his famous *illusions*.

among/between

among is a preposition used to refer to *more than two* people or things.

between is a preposition used to refer to *two* people or things.

> The money was divided *among* the nieces and nephews, but the furniture was divided equally *between* the son and the daughter.

bad/badly

bad is an adjective used to describe a negative attribute of a person or a thing.

badly is an adverb used to describe a verb or action in a negative light. A descriptive linking verb—such as *look, seem, smell, sound*, or a form of the verb *to be* (*am, is, were*, etc.)—uses *bad* instead of *badly*, but other verbs require the adverb *badly*.

> It was a *bad* idea to act *badly* on the first day at my new job.
>
> I felt *bad* about complaining, but the office refrigerator smelled *bad*, and something needed to be done about it.

beside/besides

beside is a preposition meaning "by the side of" or "next to."

besides is an adverb meaning "in addition to."

> *Besides* waiting for him for over two hours, she had to stand *beside* a smelly dumpster.

board/bored

board is a noun meaning "a wooden plank."

bored is a verb meaning "being in a disengaged mindset, uninterested."

> Sharif was so *bored* by the lecture that he wanted to hit his head against a *board*.

brake/break

brake is a noun meaning "an instrument for stopping a vehicle" or a verb meaning "to stop a vehicle."

break is a noun meaning either "a rest period" or "a fractured bone or object," or a verb meaning "to separate something(s) into two or more pieces" or "to exceed a record or violate a rule."

> Mohammad decided to *brake* suddenly so he didn't *break* the bumper on his car or any of his bones as a result.

can/may

can is a verb meaning "to be able to."

may is a verb meaning "permission to do" or "possible to do."

> Because Valery *can* eat anything he wants, he *may* ask you if he *may* have more cookies.

cannot/can not (misspelling)/can't

cannot is the correct spelling of the negative form of "can."

can not is a common misspelling of "cannot."

can't is the contraction for "cannot"; it is less formal and is used mostly in dialogue.

> Marisela *cannot* believe her ears whenever her daughter Soroa says, "I *can't* do it, Mom."

capital/capitol

capital is a noun meaning "the location or seat of a government (states and countries)"; the word also can refer to wealth, or an uppercase letter, or the death penalty (capital punishment).

capitol means the actual building where the state or country's government meets.

> When Jane visited an elementary school in Washington, D.C., she learned that students had taken a tour of the U.S. *Capitol* building and had also memorized all of the *capital* cities of the United States.

coarse/course

coarse is an adjective meaning "rough" either in texture or attitude.

course is a noun that can mean "a class," "a curriculum," "a direction for a journey," or "one part of a several-part meal."

> Lee didn't accept *coarse* language in his workshop. He did let people work with *coarse* material like sandpaper, though.
>
> Ilona took a special *course* on French cooking and learned to make a full five-*course* meal. She now wants to continue on her *course* to receive a full culinary degree.

complement/compliment

complement is a noun meaning "something that completes or coordinates with something else" or a verb meaning "to complete."

compliment is a noun meaning "a positive statement about something or someone" or a verb meaning "to give a positive statement about something or someone."

> Craig gave Joan a *compliment* about the way her aqua-colored blouse *complemented* her eyes.

conscious/consciousness/conscience/conscientious

conscious is an adjective meaning "able to feel, think, or be aware."

consciousness is the noun form meaning "awareness" or "knowledge."

conscience is a noun meaning "a person's sense of right or wrong, morals."

conscientious is an adjective meaning "governed by or conforming to the dictates of conscience" or "meticulous; careful."

> Lily had a guilty *conscience* about what she had done, but Shima wasn't even *conscious* of her inappropriate behavior.
>
> Mikhail's acute *consciousness* allowed for him to become a more *conscientious* student.

could have/could've/could of (misspelling)

could have is the helping verb *could*, meaning either "might" or "having the ability to," plus the main verb *have*.

could've is the correct contraction for "could have" and should be used in informal writing only.

could of is a misuse/misspelling of "could've"; do not use it.

> Kate decided her students needed a reminder not to use "*could of*" in their papers instead of "*could have*." After class, Marta declared, "I *could've* done without that lesson!"

desert/dessert

desert can be a noun meaning "a dry, arid place, usually with sand and little vegetation"; as a verb, desert means "to leave or abandon."

dessert is a noun meaning "the last course in a meal, usually sweet."

> The Mojave *Desert* is prominently featured in Hollywood movies. Often, the hero is *deserted*—wounded and horseless—in this *desert* by his enemy.
>
> Bev enjoyed a delicious New York cheesecake as *dessert* after dinner.

▶ **TIP**   You want *two* helpings of it after dinner. So, remember to use the *s* twice when you spell *dessert*.

device/devise

device is a noun that means "an object, mechanical, electric, or electronic, created for a particular purpose."

devise is a verb meaning "to create a plan or think up something."

> The spy *devised* a way to escape that involved creating a *device* that would blow up the lock on his cell door.

effect/affect (see affect/effect)

either/neither

either can be an adjective or pronoun meaning "one of two people, things, or concepts"; *either* can also be an adverb introducing the first of two alternatives.

neither is the negative version of "either": "not one of . . ."

> Nguyen planned to order *either* a taco or a burrito for lunch but later decided to have *neither*, asking instead for a hamburger.

▶ **NOTE** If more than two things or people are involved, use *any* instead of *either*—for example, Nguyen wasn't sure he liked *any* of the choices on the menu.

except/accept (see **accept/except**)

explicit/implicit

explicit is an adjective meaning "directly expressed."

implicit is an adjective meaning "implied but not directly expressed."

> The rules of board games are usually *explicit*, but the rules of life tend to be *implicit*.

farther/further

farther is an adjective, adverb, or noun meaning "more distance."

further is an adjective or noun meaning "more."

> Francisca needed *further* proof that walking improves heart health before she would commit to walking a little bit *farther* every day.

fewer/less

fewer is an adjective or noun meaning "less" and is used only for things that can be counted.

less is an adjective or noun that refers to an "amount" or "specific value or degree." It is used with nouns that cannot be counted.

> To diet successfully, it helps to consume *fewer* calories and take in *less* fat.

good/well

good can be an adjective used to describe a person or thing in a positive way; *good* can also be a noun meaning "positive."

well is an adverb, noun, or adjective used to describe positive attributes. When used to describe a person, *well* focuses on health or state of being and feelings, while *good* focuses on character or personality.

> Sibyl is a *good* person. She is feeling *well* now, after her long bout with pneumonia. She can dance almost as *well* as she used to before her illness.

hanged/hung

Both *hanged* and *hung* are past-tense forms of *hang*.

Use **hanged** only as a past tense of the verb *hang* when referring to an execution.

Use **hung** for all other past-tense forms of "hang."

> In the novel, the prisoner was *hanged*, and, afterward, a sign that listed his crimes was *hung* over the gallows.

hear/here

hear is a verb meaning the physiological act of *hearing*.

here is a noun that indicates a physical or symbolic place.

> Eduardo, did you *hear* that loud noise? I think it is coming from over *here*.

▶ TIP   The word *hear* has the word *ear* in it.

hole/whole

hole is a noun that means "an opening."

whole is a noun or an adjective that means "complete."

> Pedro, there must be a *hole* in Napoleon's stomach; I can't believe he ate the *whole* pie.

imply/infer

imply is a verb meaning "to suggest a secondary meaning, to suggest indirectly."

infer is a verb meaning "to deduce, or to draw a conclusion."

> I didn't mean to *imply* that he was stingy, but I did *infer* from his comments that he won't be joining us on the trip.

its/it's

its is a possessive pronoun indicating ownership.

it's is a contraction of "it is."

> *It's* a fact that this dog loves *its* bone.

lay/lie

lay is a transitive verb meaning "to put or place." It is followed by a direct object. *Lay* is the present-tense form of the verb. *Laid* is the past-tense form and the past participle.

lie can be a noun meaning "false statement," but it also can be an intransitive verb meaning "to recline or rest." *Lie* is the present-tense form of the verb. *Lay* is the past-tense form, and *lain* is the past participle.

> The robber *had laid* his gun on the floor of the car, but he grabbed the gun out of the car when the police officer approached. The officer ordered the robber to *lay* down the gun and *lie* on the ground with his hands behind his back. After handcuffing the robber, the officer *laid* the gun in the trunk of his cruiser, while the robber *lay* on the ground. The robber *had lain* there for only a few minutes before back-up arrived.

lead/led

lead has two pronunciations and two meanings: (1) pronounced *led*, it is a noun meaning a "type of metal" and (2) pronounced *leed*, it is a noun or verb meaning to "show the way" or "to make follow."

led (rhymes with *bed*) is a verb and is the past-tense form of definition 2 of *lead* above.

> David asked Traci to *lead* the way to the kitchen so he could inspect the *lead* pipes, so Traci *led* him there.

loose/lose

loose (pronounced *loohs*, with a final s sound) is a noun or adjective meaning "not attached," "roomy, unbinding," or "not exact."

lose (pronounced *loohz*, with a final z sound) is a verb meaning "to fail" or "to not be able to keep or to find something."

> We knew we would *lose* the match since Iliana managed to *lose* her lucky socks and her confidence the day before the match.
>
> She must have a *loose* interpretation of sports fashion to wear such *loose* shorts.

passed/past

passed is a past-tense verb meaning "to go by" or "to have achieved," such as a goal or test.

past is a noun or adjective meaning "in a previous time, not current."

> Sophia *passed* Brad on the way to take her last test. Later, she told him that she had *passed* the exam. Now her *past* fears related to passing the test have been laid to rest.

precede/proceed

precede is a verb or adjective meaning "something that comes before."

proceed is a noun or a verb meaning "to go forward" (action).

> Winter *precedes* spring, but when spring arrives, we will *proceed* with wearing lighter clothing.

principal/principle

principal is a noun for "the head of a school" or an adjective meaning "first, most important."

principle is a noun meaning "a basic truth, moral law, or assumption."

> Andy always acts on the *principles* he learned from his parents. Because of his good moral sense, he would make a great *principal* for my son's elementary school.

▶ **TIP**   The princi*pal* is the one you hope would be your "pal."

quiet/quit/quite

quiet is a noun, verb, adjective, or adverb meaning "silent, or with little or no sound."

quit is a verb meaning "to stop or give up."

quite is an adverb meaning "very, entirely, completely."

> The crowd suddenly went *quiet* as the band walked onstage. Saito *quit* talking to Dolly and turned toward the stage, and it was all *quite* magical.

raise/rise

raise is a noun or a verb. The noun *raise* means "an increase in salary." The transitive verb *raise* means "to move or lift something up to a higher position."

rise is a noun meaning "an increase," and it is an intransitive verb meaning "to go (or come) up."

> After Val decided to *raise* her expectations and work her hardest, she finally got her *raise*.
>
> We *rise* at sunrise and hope not to see another *rise* in gas prices.

right/rite/write

right is a noun meaning "a moral," "guaranteed condition," or "the opposite of left"; it can also be an adjective meaning "appropriate" or "correct"; it can even be a verb meaning "to make something correct, fix."

rite is a noun for a "ritual or ceremonial act, literal or symbolic."

write is a verb meaning "the creation of words or symbols on a surface."

> Lisa knew she had the *right* to make the *right* choice for her own life and to set things *right* with Sam, so she made a sharp *right* turn into the next street to go back and talk with him again.
>
> In California, learning to surf is a *rite* of passage for many teens.
>
> The textbook title *The Write Stuff* is based on a pun—learning to *write* stuff (essays) the *right* way.

than/then

than is a conjunction used for comparison of two or more unequal items.

then is an adverb related to a particular period in time or a conjunction meaning "therefore."

> My three-year-old daughter first asked if I was older *than* Grandpa; *then* she asked if I was older *than* Grandma.

that/which/who

that can function as a relative pronoun that introduces a restrictive clause—a clause that limits or restricts the meaning of the words that are modified. The clause is essential to the meaning of the sentence.

> Did you try the new restaurant *that* Will told us about?

which can function as a relative pronoun that introduces a nonrestrictive clause, a clause that is not essential to the meaning of the sentence.

> Washington, D.C., *which* is lovely in the fall, is not really a state or a city: It's a district.

who is a relative pronoun used to refer to a person; *who* is used to convey both essential (restrictive) and nonessential (nonrestrictive) information.

> **Restrictive:** Maria is the one *who* knows how to make perfect Mexican wedding cookies from scratch.
>
> **Nonrestrictive:** Maria, *who* grew up in Mexico, knows how to make perfect Mexican wedding cookies from scratch.

their/there/they're

their is a plural possessive pronoun.

there is a noun, an adverb, or an impersonal pronoun. Use it to indicate a place or direction and as a pronoun to start sentences.

they're is a contraction for the words "they are."

> Did Anna and Liz finish *their* paperwork so we can go to lunch?
>
> Do you want to go *there* for lunch? *There* is an excellent lunch menu.
>
> Cindy and Allen are my cousins; *they're* the ones who live in Virginia.

threw/through/thru (misspelling)

threw is the past tense form of the verb "throw."

through is a preposition indicating passage or movement, often from one side to another; and it is also an adverb meaning "finished" or "done."

thru is a common misspelling of "through," and it should not be used.

> Heather *threw* the pen to Abby.
>
> Sothera is *through* with love since she has gone *through* the rocky passage of heartbreak too many times.

to/too/two

to is a preposition used to indicate direction or movement.

too is an adverb meaning "also," "in addition," or "very." With the first two usages, it is always preceded by a comma at the end of a sentence or surrounded by parenthetical commas in the middle of a sentence.

two is a noun or adjective used to indicate the number that comes after one and before three.

> Jim went *to* his new classroom.
>
> After Emma and Dominic moved *to* Arizona, Ann and Dale moved there, *too*. Carlene and John were *too* happy to complain about them all coming at once.
>
> It was lucky that Becky, *too*, was able *to* get *two* weeks of vacation during the busiest time of the year.

waist/waste

waist is a noun meaning the middle part of a person's body.

waste can function as a noun or a verb. The noun can refer to a failure to use something wisely; the verb can mean "to squander something."

> Juliette, even though she has had two children, has a tiny *waist*.
>
> It is a *waste* of time to watch television.
>
> I ordered the gift online because I didn't want to *waste* my energy by checking a bunch of different stores.

weather/whether

weather is a noun used to indicate climate conditions.

whether is a conjunctive adverb, similar to *if*, used in clauses to indicate conditions.

> The *weather* conditions for the Labor Day weekend in Lake Chelan were favorable.
>
> *Whether* he liked it or not, Josh's parents made him stick with his piano lessons.

were/we're/where

were is a past-tense form of the verb *to be* (the plural form of *was*).

we're is a contraction for the words "we are" or "we were."

where is a noun indicating a direction or a place.

> The kindergarteners *were* eager for snack time.

> *We're* ready to serve the milk and cookies now.
> *Where* do you want us to set the cookies?
> Home is *where* the heart is.

who/whom

Both *who* and *whom* are used to refer to people. Use **who** as the subject of a sentence (subjective case) and **whom** as the object (objective case). To test whether **who** or **whom** should begin a question, try answering the question by using a personal pronoun.

> *Who* was William Shakespeare? [*He* was a playwright.]

The pronoun *he* is in the subjective case, so *who* is correct.

> *Whom* did you invite to the party? [I invited *him*.]

The pronoun *him* is in the objective case, so "whom" is correct.

▶ **TIP**   The *m* in *whom* is like the *m* in *him*.

who's/whose

who's is a contraction for "who is" or "who has," and **whose** is used to indicate possession.

> *Who's* ready to read *Hamlet? Whose* book is this?

would have/would've/would of (misuse)

would have is the correct spelling for this verb tense phrase, **would've** is the contraction (use it only in informal writing), and **would of** is an incorrect spelling of *would've* (never use it).

> Caroline *would have* been sad if she had missed the concert.

your/you're

your is the second-person possessive pronoun.

you're is the contraction for the words "you are."

> Did you take *your* medicine yet?
> *You're* not looking too well.
> *You're* welcome.

ACTIVITY 25-3 Commonly Confused Words

Directions: *Underline the correct word for each bracketed choice below.*

I'm not a morning person, and getting ready for school on time used to seem like [a, an] overwhelming challenge. When my alarm clock rang, I usually hit the snooze button and [lay, laid] in bed for another 20 minutes. Especially when I'd gotten less [then, than] six hours of sleep, I needed several cups of coffee just to get going. While drinking my coffee, I'd [waist, waste] time watching news shows on television. Before I knew it, it was almost time to leave, so I'd skip my shower and frantically rummage [threw, through, thru] my drawers to find some clothes. As I ran out the door to catch the bus, I made a wild grab for my books and papers, which never seemed to be where I had [lay, laid, lain] them the previous day. I was always [frightened, afraid] of forgetting something important, and I often did. Since I hadn't showered, I worried all day that I looked [bad, badly] and maybe even smelled [bad, badly], [to, two, too]!

I'm happy to report that I have found a way to [brake, break] these bad habits by following a few simple time management strategies. I try to get [a, an] hour more sleep each night than I used to, which helps me wake up in the morning. Most importantly, I get organized the night before, making sure that I am [already, all ready] for school the following morning. After checking the weather forecast, I [lay, lie] out my clothes and collect my school materials. When everything is properly organized, morning chores no longer seem like such [a, an] heavy burden. I also have found [a, an] use for the kitchen timer in the mornings: When I pour my coffee, I set the timer for 15 minutes so I don't [lose, loose] track of time. When the timer dings, I make myself turn off the television, [whether, weather] I want to or not, and take a shower. Then I have plenty of time to get dressed and catch the bus. I no longer have to run the [hole, whole] way to the bus stop.

It may sound silly, but my entire outlook has changed because of this new morning ritual; [its, it's] enabled me to take charge and feel in control. I [cannot, can not] believe how these time management strategies have [effected, affected] the rest of my life. When I get off to a good start in the morning, I seem to have [fewer, less] problems all day. I only wish that I'd made this change in my morning routine years ago; I could [of, have] spared myself [a lot, alot, allot] of anxiety. Of [course, coarse], my particular time management strategies might not work for everyone, but I think it would be worthwhile for any student to get organized and [device, devise] his or her own morning ritual.

TIPS FOR USING A DICTIONARY

4 Use a dictionary.

A **dictionary** is a reference text (either print or online) that gives the pronunciations and definitions of words. It is a good idea to buy a comprehensive college dictionary and/or to use an online version. Make sure that your print dictionary is no more than five years old and that it features American spellings and usage.

There are also specialized dictionaries available in both hard copy and online for particular subjects such as biology, history, or psychology, as well as dictionaries that give a word in one language and then the word in another language, for instance a Spanish–English dictionary (be careful not to depend on these for accurate translations, however).

During the writing process, it is best to postpone using the dictionary until the revision and editing steps. If you are writing your first draft and keep stopping to look up words, you may lose your train of thought, and the delay may impede your ability to generate ideas and details. Instead, after you have written at least one full draft, go back and use a dictionary to check your spelling and usage. See if the words you're using are appropriate in terms of their denotations (exact meanings) and connotations (associated meanings), spelling, tone and style, and context.

Anatomy of a Dictionary Entry

A dictionary entry has several parts: the word's pronunciation, part(s) of speech, meaning(s), origin(s) (etymology), related forms, synonyms, and antonyms. Here is an example of a typical dictionary entry from merriamwebster.com for the word *formidable*.

for·mi·da·ble 🔊 *adjective* \'fȯr-mə-də-bəl;
fȯr-'mi-, fər-'mi-\

Definition of FORMIDABLE ···························· 🗎+1

1 : causing fear, dread, or apprehension <a *formidable* prospect>

2 : having qualities that discourage approach or attack

3 : tending to inspire awe or wonder : IMPRESSIVE

— **for·mi·da·bil·i·ty** 🔊 *noun*
— **for·mi·da·ble·ness** 🔊 *noun*
— **for·mi·da·bly** 🔊 *adverb*

🖻 See formidable **defined for English-language learners** »
See formidable **defined for kids** »

Examples of FORMIDABLE ·····································

• The mountains were a *formidable* barrier.

• He has mastered a *formidable* amount of material.

• She was known throughout Manchester as a *formidable* woman, and being educated had only piled more formidability on top of what she had been born with.
—Edward P. Jones, *The Known World*, 2003

[+]more

Origin of FORMIDABLE ·····································

Middle English, from Latin *formidabilis,* from *formidare* to fear, from *formido* terror, bogey; akin to Greek *mormō* bogey

First Known Use: 15th century

Related to FORMIDABLE ·····································

Synonyms

alarming, dire, direful, dread, dreadful, fearsome, forbidding, fearful, frightening, frightful, ghastly, hair-raising, horrendous, horrible, horrifying, intimidating, redoubtable, scary, shocking, spine-chilling, terrible, terrifying

Antonyms

cheap, easy, effortless, facile, light, mindless, simple, soft, <u>undemanding</u>

TIPS FOR USING A THESAURUS

5 Use a thesaurus. A **thesaurus** is a text that provides **synonyms** (words that have very similar meanings) and sometimes **antonyms** (words that have opposite meanings). You can buy a hard copy or use an online version.

When revising your writing, you may find that you have used certain words too often in your essay or that you need a better, more precise, or just more interesting word than the one you have used. At those times, a thesaurus can be a great help.

When using a thesaurus, you have to be particularly careful to check the connotations (associated meanings or more subtle meanings) of a word to make sure you have used the *best* word for your intended meaning. It's a good idea to use a dictionary in tandem with a thesaurus to check the synonyms listed and make sure the one you choose has the right meaning.

Anatomy of a Thesaurus Entry

A thesaurus entry lists the word in bold, names its part of speech, and then lists its synonyms and sometimes its antonyms. Here is an example of a typical thesaurus entry:

Main Entry:	formidable
Part of Speech:	*adjective*
Definition:	horrible, terrifying
Synonyms:	appalling, awful, dangerous, daunting, dire, dismaying, dreadful, fearful, fierce, frightful, horrific, imposing, impregnable, intimidating, menacing, redoubtable, shocking, terrible, terrific, threatening
Antonyms:	feeble, friendly, harmless, nice, pleasant, powerless, weak
Main Entry:	formidable
Part of Speech:	*adjective*
Definition:	difficult, overwhelming
Synonyms:	all-powerful, arduous, awesome, challenging, colossal, dismaying, effortful, great, hard, impressive, indomitable, intimidating, labored, laborious, mammoth, mighty, murder*, onerous, overpowering, powerful, puissant, rough go, rough*, staggering, strenuous, tall order, toilsome, tough proposition, tough*, tremendous, uphill
Antonyms:	easy, not hard, pleasant, trivial

* = informal/nonformal usage from Thesaurus.com

Sometimes a thesaurus will list words that are not clear synonyms or antonyms of the target word but have related or contrasting meanings. If you are not sure how to interpret an entry, make sure to check the key provided in the thesaurus.

A thesaurus can come in very handy when you are revising your essay draft and you want to replace some of the words that you have overused. For instance, consider the following synonyms for the word *said*:

acknowledged	disclosed	proclaimed
added	divulged	professed
addressed	droned	ranted
admitted	elaborated	reassured
advised	emphasized	refuted
advocated	entreated	related
affirmed	exclaimed	repeated
agreed	explained	replied
alleged	exposed	responded
announced	expressed	resumed
answered	implied	retorted
argued	indicated	returned
asserted	inferred	reveal
assured	instructed	snapped
attested	lectured	sneered
avowed	maintained	solicited
began	mentioned	specified
called	moaned	spoke
claimed	mumbled	stated
commented	murmured	stressed
complained	muttered	suggested
confided	narrated	thought
cried	noted	threatened
debated	objected	told
decided	observed	urged
declared	petitioned	uttered
denounced	pleaded	vowed
described	pled	whispered
dictated	pointed out	yelled
directed	predicted	

Each of these words describes *how* a person *said* something.

ACTIVITY 25-4 Using Synonyms

Directions: *Fill in each blank using the most appropriate synonym for* said *listed above.*

1. "Where are some places in the city we can visit that will be free?" Loren _____.

2. "There are a lot of things to do for free in the city," Fernando _____.

3. Loren smiled. "I know of a few," she _____. "But what were you thinking?"

4. "Well, to start with," Fernando _____, "you could go to the art galleries."

5. "Good idea!" Loren _____. "What else?"

6. "The botanical gardens are free too," Fernando _____.

7. "Another good idea!" she _____.

8. "Tell me more," she _____.

9. Fernando laughed and _____, "OK, how about a walk along the waterfront?"

10. "You are full of great ideas!" she _____. "Thanks."

ACTIVITY 25-5 Using a Dictionary and a Thesaurus in Combination

Directions: *First use a thesaurus to look for an alternative word for each of the words listed below. Then, use a dictionary to provide the meaning for the new word you chose. Write your findings in the spaces provided.*

1. **Ridiculous**

   Thesaurus word you chose: _____

   Dictionary meaning: _____

   _____

   _____

2. **Intriguing**

   Thesaurus word you chose: _____

   Dictionary meaning: _____

   _____

   _____

3. Boisterous

Thesaurus word you chose: _____

Dictionary meaning: _____

_____

_____

4. Beautiful

Thesaurus word you chose: _____

Dictionary meaning: _____

5. Intimidating

Thesaurus word you chose: _____

Dictionary meaning: _____

_____

_____

SPELLING CHECKLIST

✓ **Use a dictionary**. If you are not sure how a word is spelled, use the spelling tips in this chapter and/or consult a dictionary.

✓ **Beware of homophones**. If the word you are using is a homophone (a word that sounds like another word), check that you have used the correct spelling. Consult a dictionary or the list of commonly confused words in this chapter.

✓ **Keep a list of your most common spelling errors**. Be aware of the spelling errors you most commonly make (keep a list of corrections received from instructors), and check for them when you proofread your writing.

✓ **Use spell-check**. Use the spell-check feature on your computer, but keep in mind that spell-check will not indicate if a word is *spelled correctly* but *used incorrectly*.

CAPITALIZATION

6 Capitalize correctly.

Capital letters indicate the first word of a sentence and proper nouns, of course, but there are other basic rules for capitalization that you should know.

Capitalization Basics

The basic rule is that capital letters are needed when you use a specific name or label. So, if a word describes a general object or category, the initial letter of the word is not capitalized, but if the word describes a specific person, place, or thing—one particular, named object—the initial letter is capitalized. Therefore, common nouns are not capitalized, and proper nouns are capitalized.

Here are some general categories of words that need to be capitalized.

1. **Capitalize the first word of a sentence and the first word of a sentence used in a direct quotation.**

> In *The Waste Land*, T. S. Eliot described April as the cruelest month.
>
> Edna St. Vincent Millay said, "April comes like an idiot, babbling and strewing flowers."

- *Do not capitalize* the first word of the second part of an interrupted or continuing quotation:

> "April," said Edna St. Vincent Millay, "comes like an idiot, babbling and strewing flowers."

2. **Capitalize the pronoun *I* and the names of specific people.**

> Here are some famous people I'd love to meet: Toni Morrison, Jimmy Page, Mae C. Jemison, Bill Gates, Sandra Day O'Connor, and Stephen Hawking.

3. **Capitalize the names of nationalities, cultural or ethnic groups, and languages.**

> Cambodian, Italian, Canadian, Mexican American, Nigerian, Hebrew, Asian American, Swahili, Japanese, Portuguese, African American, Greek, Russian

If a prefix comes in front of a word that is usually capitalized, insert a hyphen after the prefix and keep the first letter of the word capitalized: *un-American*, *anti-American*, and so on.

4. Capitalize titles that precede proper names.

> Chancellor Merkel, Uncle Robert, Senator Feinstein, United Nations Secretary-General Ban Ki-moon, Father Morris, Reverend Adams, Rabbi Hirshfeld, Dr. Bialik, Mr. Skinner, Professor Nylan

- *Do not capitalize* a title if it follows a proper name.

> Angela Merkel, chancellor; Robert, my uncle; Dianne Feinstein, senator

- *Do not capitalize* nouns that refer to family relationships—for example, *mother, father, mom, dad, grandfather, grandmother, aunt,* and *uncle*—unless they are being used as proper names:

> My *grandfather* was a real character. He used to play tricks on *Grandmother* to make her laugh. My *father* was their only child. I love to hear *Dad* tell stories about his childhood. I also love the story of how my mom and dad met. He says it was love at first sight, but *Mom* said it took awhile. My *mother's* sister, *Aunt Rose*, claims my *mother* had a crush on my *father* before he even noticed her. My *uncle*, Ed, says it took months for *Dad* to get up the courage to ask her out.

5. Capitalize names of specific places (including continents, countries, regions, states, counties, cities, parks, and streets).

> Antarctica, Europe, Ghana, Brazil, the Middle East, New England, North Dakota, Oregon, Boone County, Hong Kong, Seville, Tampa, Forest Park, Hollywood Boulevard, Bourbon Street

6. Capitalize the names of days, months, and holidays.

> Tuesday, August, Thanksgiving, Valentine's Day, Memorial Day, Mother's Day, Veterans Day, Presidents Day

- In general, *do not* capitalize the seasons (summer, winter, spring, and fall). However, if they are part of a specific event or title, they are capitalized: *Spring Fling, Winter Festival,* and so on.

7. **Capitalize the names of religions, religious figures (and pronouns for them), titles of holy texts, and holy days.**

> Buddhism/Buddhists, Christianity/Christians, Hinduism/Hindus, Islam/Muslims, Judaism/Jews, Taoism/Taoists, Tipitaka, Bible, New Testament, Rig Veda, Qur'an, Talmud, Tao Te Ching, Easter, Ramadan, Yom Kippur

- *Lord* and *God* are usually capitalized and so are pronouns that refer to particular supreme beings: the *Lord* and *His* teachings, the *Goddess* and *Her* ways.

8. **Capitalize the names of specific organizations (including businesses, government institutions, political groups, and academic or cultural institutions).**

> General Motors, Whole Foods, Cub Scouts, Democratic Party, Republican Party, Parent-Teacher Association (PTA)

- Capitalize abbreviations (or acronyms) for companies, institutions, and organizations:

> NBC, AARP, NATO, FDA, UPS

9. **Capitalize the names of historical periods or events.**

> Iron Age, Renaissance, Cultural Revolution, Aztec Empire, Six Day War, Cold War, Battle of Gettysburg, Fall of Constantinople, Norman Invasion, Apartheid

- Do not capitalize *centuries*: the seventeenth century and so on.

10. **Capitalize the names of monuments, buildings, and famous objects.**

> Eiffel Tower, St. Louis Arch, Stonehenge, Empire State Building, Taj Mahal, Alhambra, Rockbridge High School, Crown Jewels, Great Wall of China

- *High school*, *middle school*, and *elementary school* are not capitalized if they are not part of the name of a specific school.

> Next year my brother will be a senior at Rockbridge *High School*. The year after next, he will graduate from *high school*.

11. Capitalize the names of specific brands or trademarks.

> Levi's, Mercedes-Benz, Dunkin' Donuts, Betty Crocker, Black & Decker, Disneyland, Apple Inc., Google

12. Capitalize the titles of books, magazines, articles, stories, poems, plays, films, TV shows, albums, CDs, songs, works of art, and official documents. In titles, capitalize the first and last word and all significant words in between except articles (*a, an,* and *the*), prepositions (*of, in, on,* etc.), and conjunctions (*and, but, or,* etc.):

> *The Brief Wondrous Life of Oscar Wao, US Weekly,* "Three Quick and Easy Meals," "The Tell-Tale Heart," "The Road Not Taken," *A Streetcar Named Desire, Avatar, Survivor, Led Zeppelin IV,* "We Are the World," *The Scream,* Emancipation Proclamation, Treaty of Versailles

ACTIVITY 25-6   Capitalization Practice

Directions: *In the following paragraphs, underline the letters that should be capitalized. Refer to the rules above for help.*

Every summer our family attends the fourth of july celebration organized by the local branch of veterans of foreign wars (vfw). It is the most popular celebration in springfield county, and people from many small towns come to enjoy the food, the music, and the fireworks. The greenfield high school athletic field provides ample space and parking for the festivities.

The celebration opens with a few short speeches by local citizens. One year a high school principal, ms. higuchi, spoke about her parents. As asian immigrants to the united states, principal higuchi's mother and father cherished the freedoms of their adopted country and inspired their daughter to follow her dreams. Another year one of our neighbors, a former hippie who has an american flag painted on his volkswagon van, spoke about the importance of free speech. He pointed out that it is not un-american to disagree with government policies, as diversity of opinion strengthens, rather than undermines, democracy. Last year, professor ashley jackson, a professor of history at a local college, gave a short presentation about the history and symbolism of the liberty bell.

This year, the president of the springfield historical society, who was dressed in an eighteenth-century costume, kicked off the celebration by reading aloud quotations from heroes of the american revolution. He ended by quoting benjamin franklin, who said, "without freedom of thought there can be no such thing as wisdom; and no such thing as liberty without freedom of speech." Then a popular local singer, who performed on the television show american idol, led the crowd in a stirring rendition of the song "god bless america."

NUMBERS

7 Format numbers correctly.

The correct format for numbers varies depending on context. The following standards work for most academic writing.

1. **Spell out the numbers zero through ten and numbers that can be written using one or two words.**

> At the bakery, we had to choose among ten different kinds of cookies and eight kinds of cake.
> So far, twelve hundred citizens have signed the petition.

▶ **NOTE** For business or technical writing, use numbers for all numerals ten and above.

2. **Spell out numbers that begin a sentence, no matter how large the number.** If possible, however, revise the sentence so you don't need to start with a number. Make sure to use commas correctly in numbers over one thousand.

> Twenty-seven hundred and fifty fans clapped and cheered loudly when the band came onstage.
> When the band came onstage, 2,750 fans clapped and cheered loudly.

3. **For extremely large numbers, use a combination of figures and words.**

> The national debt now stands at $16.4 trillion.

However, if it is not a round number, you'll have to use all figures.

> If the national debt were divided equally among U.S. citizens, each person's share would be $40,315.65.

4. **Use figures for dates, years, and times.**

> July 6, 2013, 11:25 A.M.

5. **Use figures in addresses.**

> The White House
> 1600 Pennsylvania Avenue NW
> Washington, D.C. 20500

6. **Use figures for exact measurements and specific identifications.**

> The General Sherman Tree in Sequoia National Park is 274 feet tall; at the base of the tree, the trunk is 36 feet wide.
>
> The football player is 6'5" tall and weighs 265 pounds.
>
> Tonight we're staying in room 274 at the Holiday Inn on Interstate 91.
>
> The Channel 22 meteorologist predicts a foot of snow for our area.
>
> I have to finish reading Chapter 12 of the textbook because there may be a pop quiz tomorrow.
>
> Please turn to page 74, and read Act 3, Scene 2 of the play.
>
> For homemade salad dressing, use a 1:3 ratio of oil to vinegar—for example, 1/4 cup oil and 3/4 cup vinegar.
>
> Nearly 65 percent of people polled say that the governor is doing a good job.
>
> Because of the two A's I earned last semester, I now have a 3.7 GPA.
>
> The icy roads remained treacherous, as the temperature hovered around 32°F.
>
> The job has a 40-hour workweek but sometimes requires overtime.

ACTIVITY 25-7　Numbers Practice

Directions: *Correct the errors in numbers usage in the following sentences. Underline the error(s) in each sentence, and then write the correct form(s) in the space provided. If the sentence has no errors in numbers usage, write "correct."*

1. The entire budget was over two hundred million dollars.

   _____

2. I found out that the mortgage was going to be two thousand dollars a month.

   _____

3. I went to six or seven different open houses before I decided which house to buy.

   _____

4. Finally, I signed an agreement on the twenty-third of May 2012.

   _____

5. 70,000,000 Americans are obese.

   _____

ABBREVIATIONS

8 Use abbreviations correctly.

Although abbreviations are common in casual writing, they are less acceptable in academic writing. Below are the most commonly accepted categories of abbreviations in formal writing.

1. **Titles or Academic Degrees**

   - **Mr./Mrs./Ms.** These abbreviations are acceptable when used as titles before a person's last name.
   - **Academic Titles/Degrees.** Abbreviated academic titles and/or degrees are used *after* a person's name:

   > B.A. (Bachelor of Arts), M.A. (Master of Arts), B.S. (Bachelor of Science), M.F.A. (Master of Fine Arts), Ph.D. (Doctor of Philosophy), R.N. (Registered Nurse), M.D. (Doctor of Medicine), C.P.A. (Certified Public Accountant)
   >
   > W. E. B. DuBois, Ph.D.; Shan Shan Sheng, M.F.A.; Christiaan Barnard, M.D.

▸ **NOTE**   The title *Professor* should always be spelled out: Professor George C. Gross. Writing "Prof." may turn your teacher off!

• **Government/Military/Religious Titles.** Abbreviate government, military, and religious titles when they are used before someone's complete name. If only a person's last name is given, then use his or her full title.

> Sen. Daniel Inoue of Hawaii served eight terms in the U.S. Senate. Senator Inoue served as Chairman of the U.S. Senate Committee on Appropriations.
>
> Rev. Martin Luther King Jr. was a civil rights leader and humanitarian who, in the 1960s, fought for justice and equality for all races.

2. **Countries or States.**   In addresses, abbreviate the state and country. In sentences, spell out the names of states.

> Johnson Space Center, 2101 NASA Parkway, Houston, TX 77058 U.S.A.
>
> Astronauts are trained at the Johnson Space Center in Houston, Texas.

▸ **NOTE**   Abbreviate "United States" only in addresses or adjectives.

> In the United States, astronauts are trained at the Johnson Space Center.
>
> NASA, the National Aeronautics and Space Administration, manages the U.S. Space Program.

3. **Common Acronyms.**   **Acronyms** are composed of the first letter of each word of a name that includes two or more words. Acronyms designating agencies, businesses, or institutions are commonly used in writing and speech. These types of abbreviations do not require periods between the letters.

> AAA (American Automobile Association), AP (Associated Press), CEO (Chief Executive Officer), CIA (Central Intelligence Agency), PIN (Personal Identification Number)

Use the following abbreviations with **numbers:**

> A.M. or a.m. (ante meridian), P.M. or p.m. (post meridian), and MPH or mph (miles per hour)

4. **Latin Expressions.** The following abbreviations of Latin terms appear only inside parentheses:

> c. or ca. (*circa*, approximately), cf. (*confer*, compare), e.g. (*exempli gratia*, for example), etc. (*et cetera*, and so forth), et al. (*et alia*, and all others), i.e. (*id est*, that is), re (*res*, concerning), and vs. or v. (versus).
>
> The Great Pyramid (completed c. 2580 BCE) is the largest of the pyramids.
>
> Perennial flowers (e.g., iris, peonies, and daylilies) bloom again each spring.
>
> In the winter, outdoor activities (sledding, skiing, ice skating, etc.) can combat cabin fever and chase away the blues.

In the main body of a sentence, use complete words and/or their English equivalents.

> Many items are on sale now: clothes, linens, kitchenware, furniture, and more.

5. **Documentation Formats (such as Modern Language Association or American Psychological Association).** The following abbreviations are commonly used when documenting sources in MLA, APA, or other styles.

> vol. for "volume," vols. for "volumes," trans. for "translator" or "translated by," p. or pp. for "pages," ed. for "editor"

ACTIVITY 25-8 Abbreviation Practice

Directions: *Underline the correct word(s) or abbreviation for each bracketed choice. Refer to the rules above for help.*

1. [Reverend, Rev.] Adam Clayton Powell Jr., an influential civil rights leader during the 1930s, was elected to the [United States, U.S.] House of Representatives in 1944.

2. *Masterpiece Classic*, a popular [Public Broadcasting Service, PBS] television show, often features dramatizations of Jane Austen novels.

3. Women's Medical College was founded in 1867 by Elizabeth Blackwell, [Medical Doctor, M.D.].

4. High-protein plant-based foods—[for example, e.g.,] legumes, tofu, and other soy products—play an essential role in a healthy vegan diet.

5. Barbery, Muriel. *The Elegance of the Hedgehog.* [Translated by, Trans.] Alison Anderson. New York, NY: Europa Editions, Inc., 2008.

MyWritingLab™   **Mastery Test I: More Commonly Confused Words Practice**

Directions: *Circle the correct word for each bracketed choice below.*

The Library of Congress is [a/an] amazing place. It has more holdings [then/than] any other library. However, the Library of Congress also has [alot/allot/a lot] of other things besides books in [there/they're/their] collection. The LOC has practically everything [accept/except] books from other planets! If you know [whose/who's] book [your/you're] looking for, [then/than] you can search by author. If you know the title but not the author, you can search [threw/through/thru] the holdings by title. If you've forgotten the title, [to/two/too], you can search by subject. Some people don't realize the benefits of a computer search and so [waist/waste] [allot/alot/a lot] of time. They [could of/could have] saved a great deal of time if they had started at the computer. This [device/devise] was [deviced/devised] for making one's job easier. Why [loose/lose] precious time?

In the [past/passed], before computers, patrons of the LOC used card catalogs. Going [through/thru/threw] these cards would [precede/proceed] going to the shelves. This process was not [quite/quiet] as efficient as a modern computer search. Also, the reader would have to [write/right/rite] the call number and location on paper.

Now most readers have [already/all ready] gotten used to the ease of computer searches. You can find even the most inexperienced computer users [among/between] the people [that/who/which] frequent the Library of Congress. These smart searchers of information may find a way to [lead/led] others to their needed books. The Library of Congress is known for [it's/its] incredible and comprehensive collection. The pleasant [affects/effects] of finding a rare book can [affect/effect] even the most seasoned reader. It is a [good/well] place to search for information [weather/whether] [your/you're] an avid reader or an occasional one.

Mastery Test II: Capitals, Numbers, and Abbreviations

Directions: *Underline any errors in capitalization, numbers usage, or abbreviations in the following paragraph.*

I was traveling to Houston, Txs, last week, when I realized that I had never been to Texas before. I travel a lot for my business, so I was surprised to realize that I had never been asked to go on a trip to such a big and important state such as Texas. 2000 miles from my own home, Texas is a different place completely. After landing at the airport, I used my Triple A membership to get a rental car. I asked the rental car company clerk how many people lived in Texas, and he told me that twenty-six million people lived in that state. Wow! I bet the irs has its hands full with that many people. So, it is a big state, both in size and in population—one of the biggest in the us.

Learning Objectives Review

MyWritingLab™   **Complete the chapter assessment questions at mywritinglab.com**

❶ Improve your spelling.

Why is correct spelling important, and how can you improve your spelling? (See pp. 608–612.)

Correct spelling is important, as spelling mistakes can cause your readers to lose respect for your ideas and find your arguments less credible. Improve your spelling by using the Ten Tips for Spelling Improvement: (1) use a dictionary, (2) check pronunciation, (3) do not confuse homophones, (4) pluralize correctly, (5) distinguish between *ei* and *ie*, (6) learn the rules for adding suffixes and prefixes, (7) keep an error list, (8) become familiar with commonly misspelled words, (9) be aware of common letter groups, and (10) use spell-check.

❷ Use spell-check effectively.

What are three reasons to be cautious when using spell-check? (See pp. 612–614.)

Three dangers of using spell-check are: (1) Spell-check may not point out words in your essay that are spelled correctly but not used correctly; (2) spell-check may suggest words that are correctly spelled but do not fit the context of your sentence; and (3) spell-check does not include every word you might use.

❸ Distinguish between commonly confused words.

Why are some words commonly confused? (See pp. 614–630.)

Often, **spelling mistakes occur** when writers confuse one word with another that sounds like it (a homonym), use the wrong form of a word, use slang, or misuse a word that is spelled correctly.

❹ Use a dictionary.

What information does a dictionary contain, and when should you use it? (See pp. 630–631.)

A **dictionary entry** has several parts: the word's pronunciation, part(s) of speech, meaning(s), origin(s) (etymology), related forms, synonyms, and antonyms. **Wait until the revision stage** to use a dictionary to check spelling, tone, and context and whether the words you are using are appropriate in terms of their denotation and connotation.

5 Use a thesaurus.

What is a thesaurus, how do you use it, and what information does an entry contain? (See pp. 632–635.)

A **thesaurus** is a text that provides **synonyms** (words that have very similar meanings) and sometimes **antonyms** (words that have opposite meanings) of the original word. A **thesaurus entry** lists the word in bold, names its part of speech, and then lists its synonyms and antonyms. A thesaurus can help you find better, more precise or expressive words when you are revising your writing.

6 Capitalize correctly.

What is the general rule for capitalization? (See pp. 635–640.)

The general rule is that you should **capitalize** proper nouns (words naming a specific person, place, or thing) and **not capitalize** common nouns (words describing a general object or category).

7 Format numbers correctly.

What are the six rules for writing numbers? (See pp. 640–642.)

The **six rules for writing numbers** are: (1) spell out the numbers zero through ten and numbers that can be written using one or two words; (2) spell out numbers that begin a sentence; (3) use a combination of figures and words for very large numbers; (4) use numbers for dates, years, and time; (5) use numbers for addresses; and (6) use numbers for exact measurements.

8 Use abbreviations correctly.

What are the most commonly accepted categories of abbreviations? (See pp. 642–646.)

The **most commonly accepted categories of abbreviations** are: (1) titles or academic degrees; (2) countries or states; (3) common acronyms; (4) Latin terms; and (5) terms used in documentation formats such as MLA or APA.

26 Tone, Style, and Word Choice

LEARNING OBJECTIVES

In this chapter, you will learn how to

1 Adjust your tone and style according to your audience and purpose.

2 Improve your word choices.

3 Avoid using sexist language.

Thinking Critically   MyWritingLab™

Think: Look closely at the cartoon above.

Write: Tone, style, and word choice greatly affect how readers understand ideas in writing. How do the tone, style, and word choice of the text on the bearded man's sign make this cartoon funny?

_____

_____

_____

_____

_____

_____

_____

_____

_____

_____

_____

_____

_____

_____

_____

_____

THINKING CRITICALLY ABOUT TONE AND STYLE

① Adjust your tone and style according to your audience and purpose.

Writing styles can be as distinct as fingerprints. In fact, some teachers say that after a few weeks of class, students could turn in their essays without names, and the teachers would be able to figure out who wrote each paper based on the distinctive voices. Voice is a function of **tone**—your manner or attitude—and **style**—the choices you make about language, diction, and sentence structure.

Your tone and style affect the way a reader comprehends or responds to your ideas as well as the credibility and effectiveness of your ideas. Some writers create style, tone, and voice patterns in their essays unconsciously; they don't think about the distinctive voice they have created through their choices. However, becoming aware of these choices and *evaluating critically* whether these are the best choices for your assignment and audience will make you a more sophisticated writer and turn your writing into a conscious dialogue with your audience.

When deciding on a particular tone for an assignment, be sure to think about your audience. Your tone may be formal, serious, informal, playful, mocking, sarcastic, or impartial and detached.

Emailing, Texting, and Audience

When you are composing a work- or school-related email, do not use the kind of language or spelling you would use while texting a friend. For example, when you email a friend, you will most likely use a casual, informal tone and

APPLYING CRITICAL THINKING

| BLUEPRINTS | PURPOSE | IDEAS | SUPPORT | ASSUMPTIONS BIASES | CONCLUSIONS | POINT OF VIEW | ANALYSIS |

Before you begin writing, consider the following questions; then, as you write your drafts, make conscious choices about tone and language:

1. What is my topic, and what kind of tone would be most appropriate for the subject matter, **ideas**, and arguments that I want to make?

2. What attitude do I want to portray in this essay (for example, serious/formal, playful/informal, sarcastic/mocking, and so on)?

3. Who is my intended audience? What tone would be most effective for expressing my message to my intended audience?

4. What is my **purpose** in this essay? What tone and style choices would be most effective for the messages and arguments I want to convey?

word choice (maybe even texting shortcuts such as "cuz" or "B4"). However, when you email your instructor, your tone should be more formal, polite, and respectful (yes, even in an email).

As you revise your essay draft, check again to make sure that the style and tone of your writing are appropriate and are the most effective choices for your topic, your audience, and your arguments and conclusions. For instance, a formal research paper about breast cancer would require a serious tone. However, a personal narrative essay about the first time you snowboarded might be more casual and informal.

Here is an example of inappropriate tone in an academic paper evaluating Diane Ackerman's essay "Chocolate Equals Love":

> Diane's essay talked about how awesome chocolate is.

Here is the revised sentence:

> Diane Ackerman's essay "Chocolate Equals Love" explores the benefits, the pleasures, and the history of chocolate.

Formal Style and Tone versus Academese

Even when you are writing a more formal academic paper, avoid **academese:** writing that uses pompous multisyllabic words and unnecessarily complicated sentence structures. Academese uses passive voice constructions and contains overly complex language or jargon. Here is an example:

> Facilitation of the deliberations of the collaborative, strategic-planning body was assumed by individuals possessing requisite levels of professional expertise and relevant experience.

Here is a translation in a more reasonable tone and style:

> Senior staff led the meetings of the planning committee.

The bottom line is that academese doesn't make you sound smarter if your readers don't understand what you are trying to say. Successful writing communicates ideas clearly. Strengthen your tone and style by consciously choosing the best voice and language for your arguments and your intended audience.

▶ **NOTE**   Using a complex word is not necessarily a bad idea. Just be sure that the word you choose is the best one to convey your intended meaning and that the passage is not too complex for your intended audience.

Doublespeak, a kind of language that deliberately distorts or disguises meaning, can be similar to academese. Doublespeak typically contains *euphemisms*, deliberately vague or indirect words used in place of words that might be considered overly direct, unpleasant, or offensive. For example:

> **Corporate downsizing and outsourcing have resulted in job flexibility or termination.** (Employees have been fired or have lost their job security because the management is restructuring the business or using cheaper labor.)
>
> **The mission to neutralize the target resulted in some collateral damage.** (A government operation to kill an enemy agent caused unintended deaths or injuries of innocent bystanders.)

ACTIVITY 26-1   Tone

Directions: *Revise the following sentences to create a more appropriate tone for a general, academic audience.*

1. That dance was happening and totally off the hook.

   _____

2. He was an ugly guy with an ugly dude haircut.

   _____

3. She better get outta that life before it eats her up.

   _____

4. The idea of that philosopher is just stupid.

   _____

5. It was a totally lame class with bogus content.

   _____

ACTIVITY 26-2   Revising to Eliminate Academese

Directions: *Read the following paragraph about methods for coping with the stresses of a new job. In the space provided, rewrite the paragraph to eliminate academese and make the passage readable for a general audience. You may need to look up some of the words in a dictionary.*

Visualization of successful workplace performance is a prerequisite for actualization of professional goals. Systematic analysis of the relative urgency of work-related tasks is necessary for the development of an effective strategy for fulfilling professional obligations in a timely manner. An incremental approach is recommended for assignments characterized by significant breadth or complexity. For documents that are deemed critical for the implementation of a given project, it is considered prudent to make appropriate arrangements for duplication of such documentation. Avoidance of lapses in punctuality is achieved through strict compliance with contractually specified arrival times.

_____

_____

_____

_____

WORD CHOICE

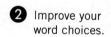 Improve your word choices.

Word choice, sometimes referred to as **diction,** is crucial to creating your tone and voice: Make a conscious *choice* when you select each word. Pick the best word for the idea you are expressing based on the content of the sentence and where the word will appear. Think about your intended audience as you choose your words. Will you need a formal word or an informal word? Will you need to use language that a general audience can understand, or should you use discipline-specific terms for a specialized audience? Is your tone academic or more casual? How should that affect your word choices? For example:

> **Intended audience:** Local school board
>
> **Inappropriate diction:** The school board is crazy to even think about cutting art classes. There are lots of better ways to solve our money problems.
>
> **Revised:** I urge the school board to preserve the arts program and to seek alternative strategies for balancing the budget.

Many words have both literal and implied meanings. Primary, or literal, meanings are called **denotations,** and secondary, or implied, meanings are called **connotations.** Think of the denotation of a word as the exact, or surface, meaning of a word; think of connotations as the "baggage," or associations, that come with that word. The denotation of a word is like the tip of an iceberg above the surface of the water, and the connotations, which often impart the most meaning, are the base of the iceberg under the water's surface. Some words have very few connotations, while others are rich with connotative associations. For instance, consider the following two signs:

Which language is more effective? Both signs advertise a residence for sale, but *house* is a more denotative word while *home* is full of connotations. *Home* is where the heart is; it's cozy, Mom, comfort food, and everything we associate with the bigger concept of *home*. So, make word choices carefully in order to get the maximum effect, and be sure the words you choose convey (both on the surface and more subtly) exactly what you mean to say.

Choose language that gives your sentence and your whole essay clarity and accuracy. When you use effective diction, you communicate your ideas successfully.

Slang

Slang is casual language used at home or among friends. The old saying "*Ain't* ain't a word 'cause it ain't in the dictionary" is partially true: *Ain't* is listed in most dictionaries—as slang. It's fine to use slang in casual speech or in emails between friends or even in dialogue. However, in college or professional essays, you should convert slang into more conventional words.

> **Slang:** The author's first novel was a bust, and the critics were cold, but her next novel was kickin', and the critics were blown away.
>
> **Revised:** The author's first novel was unsuccessful, and the critics judged it harshly, but her next novel was excellent, and the critics were impressed.
>
> **Slang:** At the beginning of the story, the guy is all hung up on this hottie, but he majorly blows it, and she tells him to hit the road.
>
> **Revised:** At the beginning of the story, the main character is in love with a beautiful woman, but he makes a serious mistake, and she ends the relationship.

Jargon

Jargon is the language used in a specific field. Jargon has its place, and if one is writing for an audience familiar with the jargon of that field, then it's fine to use it. Otherwise, jargon needs to be translated into more general language. For instance, if you worked in a computer repair store, you could leave your coworkers a list of instructions that included jargon that they would understand; however, a new computer owner would not necessarily understand the jargon in your list.

> **Jargon:** His megabite storage allowed him to download JPEGs loaded with megapixels onto his hard drive.
>
> **Revised:** His computer's large memory capability allowed him to save extremely large picture files on his computer.

Dialect

Dialect is language that reflects the speech (word choice and accent) of a certain region or culture. Dialect can reflect a specific region of a country such as a Southern dialect in the United States, or it can reflect a particular cultural background.

> **Dialect:** I reckon the dogs are fussin' at a critter down yonder.
>
> **Revised:** I think the dogs are barking at some animal over there.

Although you would not use dialect in an academic paper, it would certainly be appropriate to use it in dialogue to communicate information about the person or character speaking.

Foreign Words

Foreign words that are used without a specific purpose can be confusing. If you decide to use a foreign term in your sentence, be sure it is one your intended audience will recognize. Otherwise, use English or provide a translation in parentheses:

> **Foreign term:** When he saw his friend from home during his trip to Paris, he realized *¡Que pequeno es el mundo!*
>
> **Revised:** When he saw his friend from home during his trip to Paris, he realized *it's a small world!*
>
> **With definition:** When he saw her about to fall from the top of the escalator, he yelled, *"Cuidado!"* (Be careful!).

There are places where it is appropriate to use slang, dialect, technical jargon, and foreign words, such as in dialogue or in direct quotations, but, in general, you should not use these types of language in formal academic writing.

ACTIVITY 26-3 Slang, Dialect, Foreign Words, and Tone

Directions: *Read the following student paragraph. In the space provided, rewrite the paragraph so it has a more appropriate tone and more appropriate word choices for a general audience. Make sure to eliminate slang and translate foreign words. If necessary, consult a dictionary or online resources.*

My teacher really blew it last semester. I had a teacher the semester before who rocked. She was nice and good. She had a certain *je ne sais quoi* as they say. But this other guy really bites. His assignments were really lame, and his attitude really sucked. He totally played favorites too. He handed out A's like candy to the teacher's pets. In the meantime, the rest of us got screwed and treated like dirt. I think he was just lazy and mean. He never told us what he wanted us to do. It's like we had to be psychic to get an assignment done. Then, he'd rag about how bad the assignments were. Overall, this dude and this class really blew.

_____

_____

_____

_____

_____

_____

Clichés

Clichés are expressions that have been used so often that they have become stale and no longer communicate their intended meanings.

Most clichés are metaphors or similes. Both **similes** and **metaphors** make implied or direct comparisons between two things in order to convey an idea.

Emily Dickinson wrote, " 'Hope' is the thing with feathers— / That perches in the soul."

In the above example, the metaphor implicitly compares "hope" to a "bird." Similes use the specific words *like* or *as* in the comparisons:

> William Shakespeare, in *Romeo and Juliet*, wrote, "Death lies upon her like an untimely frost."

This simile uses *like* to compare Juliet's death to an unexpected, early frost.

> In "The Mystery of Mickey Mouse," John Updike describes Mickey's tongue as a "little cleft cushion of a tongue, red *as* a valentine and glossy *as* candy."

This simile uses *as* to compare Mickey's cartoon tongue to positive red images such as a valentine and glossy candy. It creates both an image and a positive association.

Students often use famous metaphors and similes from literature in their writing. However, many of these similes have lost their effect over time and become clichés. You should avoid them. Instead, create a fresh comparison of your own. Who knows, maybe it will be so good that everyone will want to use it, and it, too, will become a cliché one day. Here are some of the most overused clichés:

> I've been *busy as a bee* preparing for the party.
> For a moment, he didn't respond to the insult, but it was the *calm before the storm*.
> She never gets stage fright; she's always *cool as a cucumber*.
> My grandmother exercises every day, so she's *fit as a fiddle*.
> After his girlfriend broke up with him, he was *sadder but wiser*.
> Wearing old jeans, he *stuck out like a sore thumb* at the fancy reception.
> Sitting close to the cozy fire, I was *snug as a bug in a rug*.
> He describes his volunteer work at the shelter as a *labor of love*.
> She reached down to pick up her briefcase, but it had *vanished into thin air*.
> I checked once again to make sure I had my car keys: *better safe than sorry!*
> The high school reunion was a real *trip down memory lane*.
> As a lawyer, she's *tough as nails* and *drives a hard bargain*.
> The plant he had forgotten to water was *dead as a doornail*.
> My husband *slept like a log*, but I *didn't sleep a wink*.

In the revision stage of your writing process, check to make sure that clichés haven't crept into your writing—you can write them automatically, and you can have difficulty spotting them as you revise. Here is a list of some of the most common clichéd phrases in English—be sure to look again at the very common clichés used in the sentences listed previously, too.

Common Clichés

add(ing) insult to injury	heavy as lead	sharp as a tack
better half	hit the nail on the head	sink or swim
beyond a shadow of a doubt	in this day and age	smart as a whip
bottom line	last but not least	sneaking suspicion
brave as a lion	light as a feather	straight and narrow
cold, hard facts	nose to the grindstone	tears streamed down
come to grips with	paint the town red	tried and true
crazy as a loon	pale as a ghost	untimely death
crying over spilled milk	pass the buck	walk the line
deep, dark secret	pretty as a picture	wax eloquent
drunk as a lord	quick as a flash	white as a sheet
face the music	red as a rose	work like a dog
few and far between	right as rain	worth its weight in gold
flat as a pancake	rise and shine	
green with envy	rise to the occasion	

ACTIVITY 26-4   Revising Clichés

Directions: *Rewrite each of the following sentences to eliminate the cliché, replacing it with fresh imagery.*

> **Example:** After their narrow escape, his face was white as a sheet.
> **Revised:** After their narrow escape, his face was pale as moonlight on a frozen lake.

1. I knew what was going on because I could *read him like a book.*

_____

2. Our meeting went badly because *the bottom line is our leader couldn't rise to the occasion.*

3. Tina was *playing with fire* by choosing that outfit.

_____

4. Erin decided not *to stick her neck out* for that promotion.

_____

5. We'll just have to *go with the flow* to do well on this project.

_____

6. Sharon said her mother was *as sharp as a tack* even at the age of 95.

_____

7. Midori was *as pale as a ghost* after watching the horror flick.

_____

8. Lisa and Maria thought their English teacher was *as nutty as a fruitcake*.

_____

9. Mick tried to *pass the buck* when asked to do his chores.

_____

10. Matt *hit the nail on the head* when he said that the homework was hard.

_____

AVOIDING SEXIST LANGUAGE

3 Avoid using sexist language.

Language is dynamic: It evolves with culture. It used to be acceptable to use gender-specific terms such as *man* or *mankind* to stand for all people, but due to political and societal changes in the last few decades, the use of such language is outdated at best, sexist at worst.

Use Gender-Specific Terms Only When Appropriate

The key to avoiding sexist language is to use logic: Use gender-specific terms only when the subject really is gender specific. **Gender-specific terms** are words that refer to a specific gender. For instance, the terms *men* and *he* refer to males, and the terms *women* and *she* refer to females.

Each member of the women's basketball team put on *her* uniform.

The man with the clipboard raised a whistle to *his* lips.

If your subject is not gender specific, use inclusive (non-gender-specific) language.

> The dedicated fans roared with joy as the home team scored another point.

Non-gender-specific terms are neither male nor female; they are neutral and therefore include both sexes. Some examples of gender-neutral terms are *people*, *one*, *humanity*, and *humankind*. Plural pronouns such as *they*, *them*, or *their* are also gender neutral. When you use terms like *people* or *humans*, you can use the plural pronoun *their*. If you use singular terms such as *a person* or *one* as your subject, then you'll need to use *he or she* instead of *they* to avoid a different type of mistake, a pronoun agreement error. In general, the easiest way to avoid a pronoun agreement error is to use the plural forms of non-gender-specific terms and the corresponding plural pronouns.

> **Singular:** Any student who wishes to change majors should consult *his or her* faculty advisor.
>
> **Plural:** Students who wish to change majors should consult *their* faculty advisors.

Don't Assume an Occupation Is Exclusively Male or Female

Another kind of sexist language use arises from stereotyping certain occupations as being primarily for women or for men. Consider the following example:

> **Sexist language:** Demand for qualified nurses remains high, and a student who graduates with the R.N. degree can be optimistic about *her* job prospects.
>
> **Revised:** Demand for qualified nurses remains high, and students who graduate with the R.N. degree can be optimistic about *their* job prospects.

Here's another example:

> **Sexist language:** When you discuss treatment options with a physician, make sure that *he* answers all of your questions about possible side effects.
>
> **Revised:** When you discuss treatment options with a physician, make sure that *he or she* answers all of your questions about possible side effects.

Both sentences stereotype men and women. Similarly, be careful not to write *male nurse* or *woman doctor*—just write *nurses* or *doctors*, and then use the plural pronoun *their*.

Use Parallel Terms for Men and Women

Be careful not to use double standards. For example, if you are writing about high school students, don't call the males *men* and the females *girls*. Instead, call them *boys and girls* or *men and women*. Be consistent and fair in your use of terms.

Here are some gender-specific terms that are already obsolete and some non-gender-specific terms that can be used to replace them.

Gender-Specific Term	Inclusive Term
man or mankind	humans, humanity, people, humankind, human beings
fireman	firefighter
policeman	police officer
mailman	mail carrier, postal carrier
weatherman	meteorologist, weather forecaster
salesman	sales associate
congressman	representative, senator, legislator
foreman	supervisor
chairman	chairperson, chair
businessman	business person or exact title (for example, sales manager)
manpower	staff, personnel, workers
to man	to operate, to staff
man-made	handcrafted, human-made
male nurse	nurse
female doctor	doctor

ACTIVITY 26-5 Revising Sexist Language

Directions: *Rewrite each of the following sentences to eliminate sexist or inappropriately gender-specific terms.*

A clever student of science will know how to move forward in his classes and in his career.

A student majoring in dance will have to monitor her diet and exercise routine.

_____

_____

In the 1960s, mankind entered the space age.

_____

_____

The secretary of the union is responsible for taking accurate notes for her fellow union workmen.

_____

_____

I'm not sure what I want to be when I grow up, maybe a policeman or a fireman.

_____

_____

MyWritingLab™ ## Mastery Test I: More Cliché Revision

Directions: *Rewrite the following paragraph to revise the clichés (italicized).*

My big brother would always *pass the buck* when we had to do chores. First, he would try to get me to *do his dirty work*, and if I wouldn't, he'd try to get my little sister who was innocent and *cute as a button* to do the work. He didn't realize that if he'd just *put his nose to the grindstone* and get busy that the chores would be done *as quick as a flash*. One time, my mom got the *sneaking suspicion* that my brother was pushing his chores onto us, and when she caught him *red-handed* coaxing my sister to take out the trash, he turned *white as a sheet*. She told him he better *walk the line* and take responsibility for his own work. After that, everything was *right as rain* when it came to sharing the chores.

_____

_____

_____

_____

_____

MyWritingLab™   Mastery Test II: More Revision of Sexist Language

Directions: *Rewrite the following paragraph to eliminate sexist or unnecessary words or phrases.*

Last week my family and I had to make an unexpected visit to the emergency room of our local hospital in the middle of the night. When we got there, a male nurse greeted us at the doorway when he saw how much blood was on my little brother's shirt. After the male nurse helped us get signed in, an intern asked us to wait in an examination room. My mom was so nervous while we were waiting that she was making small talk with everyone who came into the room. She asked one intern what it takes if a person wants to become a doctor including what classes he would have to take to become a doctor. The intern explained what classes a person would have to take and that he would have to be in college for at least eight years. Then my mom said no wonder so many students want to be businessmen. Then, after about 20 minutes, a female doctor came into the room and introduced herself as Dr. Larson. She fixed up my little brother and sewed up his cuts, and we were happy to be able to go back home.

_____

_____

_____

_____

_____

_____

_____

_____

_____

_____

_____

_____

_____

Learning Objectives Review

MyWritingLab™   **Complete the chapter assessment questions at mywritinglab.com**

❶ Adjust your tone and style according to your audience and purpose.

What are tone and style, and why are they important? (See pp. 650–653.)

Tone reflects your manner or attitude toward a subject, and **style** reflects the choices you make about language, diction, and sentence structure. It is **important to** *critically evaluate* your choices to ensure they are the best ones to communicate your message to your audience.

❷ Improve your word choices.

Why is it important to have strong and appropriate word choices in your writing? (See pp. 653–659.)

Smart word choices (good diction) allow you to communicate effectively. Pick the best word for the idea you are expressing based on the content of the sentence and your intended audience. Be sure to consider both the *denotation* and *connotation* of the words you choose. In academic writing avoid using *slang, dialect, jargon, foreign words,* and *clichés.*

❸ Avoid using sexist language.

What is sexist language, and what are some ways to avoid it? (See pp. 659–663.)

Sexist language unnecessarily uses gender-specific terms when referring to people's work, behavior, and skills. Only use gender-specific terms when referring directly to men or women. Use **inclusive language, plural pronouns,** or **parallel terms,** and do not assume an occupation is exclusive to men or women.

LEARNING OBJECTIVES

In this chapter, you will learn how to

1 Build your vocabulary.

2 Pronounce words correctly.

3 Use context clues to determine the meanings of unfamiliar words.

Pearls Before Swine © 2012 Stephan Pastis. Reprinted by permission of Universal Uclick for UFS. All rights reserved.

Thinking Critically MyWritingLab™

Think: Look at the comic strip above. What effect does word choice and level of vocabulary have on your impressions of people, their ideas, or their level of intelligence?

Write: Give an example of a time when someone's vocabulary choices positively or negatively affected your impression of him or her. Then explain why.

_____

_____

_____

_____

_____

_____

_____

_____

_____

_____

_____

_____

_____

_____

_____

VOCABULARY BUILDING

① Build your vocabulary.

Did you know that the average educated person knows about 20,000 words and uses about 2,000 different words a week? William Shakespeare, arguably the greatest English-speaking writer, had a vocabulary of between 18,000 to 25,000 words, back when most people only knew approximately 5,000 words. Why is improving your vocabulary important? Studies have shown that having a better vocabulary increases your success in school and in your career. It also improves your understanding of other people's ideas and arguments, both verbal and written. Having command of language is a form of power. Most highly successful business and world political leaders have impressive vocabularies and a clear command of language.

The best way to build your vocabulary is to make a conscious decision to work on it daily. Write new words and their definitions in a notebook as you learn them and then use them when you speak and write. The more you use new words in your day-to-day life, the faster your personal vocabulary will grow. Don't be afraid to take some risks and make some mistakes as you try out new words. However, try not to use an awkward or overly formal or complex word where a simpler one would be better, or, as Mark Twain once said, "Never use a five dollar word when a fifty cent one will do." However, using too many simple words won't necessarily generate more complex arguments and reasoning. Find the right balance for your purpose and audience.

Five Tips for Building Your Vocabulary

Tip 1: Keep a Vocabulary Log or Vocabulary Journal. Every time you read or hear a new word, write it in your log, note where it came from (a textbook, lecture, the radio, and so on), write down what you think it means, look it up in a dictionary (immediately or as soon as you get a chance), and write down the relevant definition(s). Using a new word helps you remember its meaning, so write a sentence using the new word. Be sure to review your log regularly to brush up on your list of new words.

> **Sample Entry**
>
> **pseudonym:** I heard this word in my Victorian literature class when my teacher explained that George Eliot was the <u>pseudonym</u> of Mary Anne Evans.
>
> **My definition:** a fake name
>
> **Dictionary definition:** pseu·do·nym (**sood**-do-nim) *n.* bearing a false name; a fictitious name; *esp*: PEN NAME
>
> **Used in a sentence:** Mary Anne Evans used the pseudonym George Eliot because she was a woman writing in a man's world.

Tip 2: Make a conscious effort to use new words. If you use a word more than a few times, it becomes a natural part of your vocabulary. Be sure that you are using the new words correctly.

Tip 3: Make friends with your dictionary and your thesaurus. Consult a dictionary and a thesaurus regularly to learn new words and to find synonyms for words you habitually use so you can add variety to your vocabulary.

Tip 4: Learn Latin roots, prefixes, and suffixes. Many words in English are derived from Latin word parts. Becoming familiar with the meanings of these common **prefixes** (word beginnings), **roots** (word bases), and **suffixes** (word endings) makes it easier to understand new words. For instance, the Latin prefix *de*, meaning *away* or *from*, is used in words such as *derail* (go off the tracks) and *depart* (go away from); the Latin root *tact* means *touch*, as in *tactile* (relating to the sense of touch); and the Latin suffix *-ation* forms nouns from verbs, so the verb *create* becomes the noun *creation*.

Tip 5: Use the Internet. The Internet puts a world of vocabulary tools and vocabulary-building resources at your fingertips. You can look up roots, prefixes, and suffixes as well as definitions of words and **homonyms** (words that sound alike but don't mean the same thing), **synonyms** (different words that mean the same thing), and **antonyms** (words that have opposite meanings, such as *good* and *evil*) in various online dictionaries and thesauruses. Just use your favorite search engine (such as Google or Yahoo!) and plug in a word to see what happens!

ACTIVITY 27-1 Keeping a Log

Directions: *Begin your own vocabulary log. Keep track of new words that you hear or read this week. Look up the meanings of the new words in your dictionary, and then use them in sentences of your own. Use a separate notebook for your vocabulary log, and try to keep it with you throughout the day: You never know when a good word will come along.*

ACTIVITY 27-2 Vocabulary Practice

Directions: *Write down two words that appear somewhere in this chapter that you did not know before reading them.*

1. _____

2. _____

Look up their meanings in a dictionary (online or print):

3. _____

4. _____

Use each word in a sentence of your own:

5. _____

6. _____

ACTIVITY 27-3   Vocabulary-Building Techniques

Directions: *Complete the following tasks for each word listed below.*

1. *Use an Internet search engine (Google, Ask, or Yahoo!) to look up the meaning of the word.*
2. *Briefly summarize the definition(s) of the word that you find online.*
3. *Write your own definition(s) of the word.*
4. *Create a sentence of your own using the word.*
5. *Try to use the word in conversation or in your writing this week.*

1. Retaliate

   Online definition(s): _____

   _____

   _____

   My definition(s): _____

   Used in a sentence: _____

   _____

2. Scintillating

   Online definition(s): _____

   _____

My definition(s): _____

Used in a sentence: _____

_____

3. Nonchalant

Online definition(s): _____

_____

My definition(s): _____

Used in a sentence: _____

4. Beguile

Online definition(s): _____

_____

My definition(s): _____

Used in a sentence: _____

_____

5. Vacillate

Online definition(s): _____

_____

My definition(s): _____

Used in a sentence: _____

_____

PRONUNCIATION

❷ Pronounce words correctly.

Pronouncing words correctly takes a little effort on your part. You might have to look up their pronunciations and develop some good habits to get it right. **Syllables** are the number of sounds in a word. For instance, the word *dog* has only one syllable, but the word *Labrador* has three syllables: *Lab-ra-dor*. Syllables help you pronounce words correctly. When you look up a word in the dictionary, you will see it broken down into syllables through the use of hyphens, dots, or slashes. For example, the word *irritable* could be shown in several ways: *ir-ri-ta-ble*, *ir.ri.ta.ble*, or *ir/ri/ta/ble*.

However, pronouncing words correctly isn't just about breaking a word into syllables. Dictionaries also provide phonetic (spelling by how a word sounds) pronunciation guides to help you pronounce words correctly. The following pronunciation guide will help you identify the most common consonant and vowel sounds in English.

PRONUNCIATION GUIDE

Consonant sounds		Short vowel sounds		Long vowel sounds	
b	bed	a	ham	a	say
d	dog	e	ten	e	she
f	fur	i	if	i	hi
g	goat	o	lot	o	go
h	her	oo	look	oo	school
j	jump	u	up	u (yoo)	use
k	kick				
l	leaf				
m	man				
n	no				
p	power				
r	row				
s	saw				
t	tea				
v	vase				
w	way				
y	yes				
z	zero				
ch	channel				
sh	shop				
th	that				
th	thick				

ACTIVITY 27-4   Practicing Pronunciation

Directions:

1. *Pronounce* each of the following words aloud.
2. *Break the word into syllables* using dashes or dots, and write it in the space provided.

3. **Look up the word in a dictionary**. *Make sure you have pronounced it correctly and divided it into syllables correctly. Then read the definition(s) of the word.*

4. **Write a brief definition** *in your own words.*

1. **Incandescent** _____

My definition: _____

_____

2. **Reconnaissance** _____

My definition: _____

_____

3. **Phlegmatic** _____

My definition: _____

4. **Alleviate** _____

My definition: _____

5. **Supercilious** _____

My definition: _____

CRITICAL THINKING AND CONTEXT CLUES

3 Use context clues to determine the meanings of unfamiliar words.

Sometimes when you are reading it's not possible to stop and look up a word you don't know in a dictionary or on the Internet. Also, it may be impractical to look up *every* word you don't know at first glance. At those times, it is best to try to figure out a word's meaning by using the context clues that surround it.

As you are reading, when you come across a word you don't know, don't skip over it or get frustrated. Use **context clues**, hints or clues from the text surrounding the unfamiliar word, and your reasoning and critical thinking skills to figure out the word's meaning. Figuring out a word's meaning using context clues is a skill that you get better at with practice. Moreover, you'll remember the new word better if you have to figure out its meaning yourself, and this will help build your personal vocabulary.

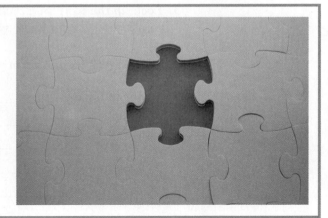

Critical Thinking and Visualization

A word you don't know is like a missing puzzle piece. By studying the pieces surrounding the missing piece, you can figure out what that missing piece should look like.

Using Context Clues

To figure out the meaning of a word, ask yourself the following questions:

1. **Does the word have a prefix, root, or suffix I know** that will give me a partial clue to its meaning?

2. **What part of speech is the word** functioning as in the sentence? Is it a noun? A verb? An adverb? An adjective?

3. **Is the word followed by an explanation or an example?**

4. **Is there a word near the unfamiliar word that may mean the same (a synonym) or the opposite (an antonym)** that I can use as a clue?

5. **What details or descriptive words are used in the sentence?** Do they give me clues to the unfamiliar word's meaning?

6. **What idea is being articulated in the sentence that contains the unfamiliar word?**

7. **What is the subject of the whole reading?** How does the sentence that contains this word develop the subject?

8. **What purpose is being developed in this piece of writing?** Does the word in question relate to the overall theme? Does it make sense in that context?

If you are *not* able to work out the meaning of the unfamiliar word using these questions, read the next few sentences in the passage, then come back to the word and try again. Sometimes clues appear later in a paragraph or even in the next one. Even if you *are* able to work out a word's meaning, it is always useful to later consult a dictionary to make sure you were correct.

ACTIVITY 27-5 Using Context Clues in Sentences

Directions: *Use the context clue questions above to figure out the meanings of the words in bold print in the following sentences. In the spaces provided after each sentence, write the meaning of each word, and explain how you used context clues to figure it out. Then double-check your answers using a dictionary.*

1. The new plan he proposed for updating our website was **ludicrous** and made no sense at all.

   ludicrous: _____

   Context clues used: _____

   _____

2. I love her **vivacious** personality, so outgoing.

   vivacious: _____

   Context clues used: _____

   _____

3. Wearing my shirt inside out at work today was **unintentional**.

   unintentional: _____

   Context clues used: _____

   _____

4. The **trinkets** at the fair were interesting. I went though many of them looking for something to buy my sister.

   trinkets: _____

   Context clues used: _____

   _____

5. To repair the stereo, he **spliced** the wires together so that they made contact again.

   spliced: _____

   Context clues used: _____

   _____

MyWritingLab™   **Mastery Test: Using Context Clues in Paragraphs**

Directions: *Use the context clue questions to figure out the meanings of the words in bold print in the following passage. In the spaces provided after the passage, write the meaning of each word, and explain how you used context clues to figure it out. Then double-check your answers using a dictionary.*

In (1) **retrospect**, I clearly recognize the mistakes I made that morning, but at the time I had no (2) **premonition** of disaster. Hank, my faithful dog and (3) **unwitting** companion in catastrophe, was equally clueless. It was Saturday, and both of us were impatient to get outdoors, so I ignored the (4) **ominous** clouds (that was my first mistake), threw on some baggy jeans (that was my second mistake), and grabbed Hank's leash. Outside, I hastily cuffed my jeans, jumped on my bike, and headed for the park, Hank trotting contentedly by my side.

As we neared the park, a flash of lightning split the sky, releasing a deluge of rain. We had no (5) **recourse** but to turn around and return home. Tail plastered between his legs, Hank whined nervously, hanging back as I struggled to pull the leash without overturning the bike.

Ten minutes later, only halfway home, it happened: As I maneuvered through (6) **inundated** potholes, one (7) **sodden** cuff of my baggy jeans unrolled and caught in the spokes of the bike. The next thing I knew, I was sprawled in a puddle, Hank's muddy paws on my chest as he licked the rainwater from my face. Stunned, I lay (8) **immobile** for a moment, contemplating my (9) **ignominious** plight, before cautiously moving my arms and legs, testing for injuries.

Escaping with nothing worse than a few scrapes and a bruised ego, I gingerly walked my bike and Hank the rest of the way home. Later that day, from the comfort of the couch, enjoying a few doggy treats and a cup of cocoa, Hank and I agreed to be a little less (10) **impetuous** when planning future excursions.

1. retrospect: _____

Context clues used: _____

_____

2. premonition: _____

Context clues used: _____

_____

3. unwitting: _____

Context clues used: _____

_____

4. ominous: _____

Context clues used: _____

_____

5. recourse: _____

Context clues used: _____

_____

_____

6. inundated: _____

Context clues used: _____

_____

7. sodden: _____

Context clues used: _____

_____

8. immobile: _____

Context clues used: _____

_____

9. ignominious: _____

Context clues used: _____

_____

10. impetuous: _____

Context clues used: _____

_____

Learning Objectives Review

MyWritingLab™ Complete the chapter assessment questions at mywritinglab.com

1 Build your vocabulary.

What are five tips for building your vocabulary?
(See pp. 666–669.)

The **five tips for building your vocabulary** are (1) keep a vocabulary log or journal; (2) make a conscious effort to use new words; (3) use a dictionary and thesaurus; (4) learn Latin roots, prefixes, and suffixes; and (5) use the Internet.

2 Pronounce words correctly.

What can you use to pronounce words correctly?
(See pp. 669–671.)

Syllables are the units of sound in a word, and once you know how many syllables are in a word and where the syllable breaks are, it is easier to figure out **how to pronounce the word.** You can also use the phonetic pronunciation guides in dictionaries to help you pronounce words.

3 Use context clues to determine the meanings of unfamiliar words.

What are the questions you can ask to figure out meanings of words using context clues?
(See pp. 671–675.)

Context clues—clues that appear before and after words, in the same sentence or surrounding ones—can help you figure out the meaning of unfamiliar words. **Ask:** (1) Does the word have a prefix, root, or suffix I know that will give me a partial clue to its meaning? (2) What part of speech is the word functioning as in the sentence? Is it a noun? A verb? An adverb? An adjective? (3) Is the word followed by an explanation or an example? (4) Is there a word near the unfamiliar word that may mean the same (a synonym) or the opposite (an antonym) that I can use as a clue? (5) What details or descriptive words are used in the sentence? Do they give me clues to the unfamiliar word's meaning? (6) What idea is being articulated in the sentence that contains the unfamiliar word? (7) What is the subject of the whole reading? How does the sentence that contains this word develop the subject? (8) What purpose is being developed in this piece of writing? Does the word in question relate to the overall theme? Does it make sense in that context?

Credits

Index

A

Abbreviations, 559, 574, 642–45, 646, 647
Abstract nouns, 467
Academese, 651–53
Acronyms, 643–44
Action words, 470
Active reading, 23–28
  background knowledge, 25
  passive *versus*, 23
  previewing, 24–25
  professional essay examples, 28–33
  questions, 26
  reading in blocks, 26
  reading log, writing in, 27
  reviewing and answering questions, 27–28
  steps in, 23–28, 43
  of visuals, 387–89, 400
Active voice, 600–602
Adjectives, 488–89
  comparative form of, 488
  compound, 538, 539
  coordinate, 537, 538, 539
  cumulative, 538
  phrases, 488–89
  positive form of, 488
  superlative form of, 489
Adler, Mortimer J., 36, 38–42
Advanced search, 352
Adverbs, 490–91
  comparative form of, 490
  conjunctive, 496–97, 502, 548
  phrases, 490–91
  positive form of, 490
  superlative form of, 490
Advertisements, 308, 393–94
Agreement
  pronoun-antecedent, 587–89
  subject-verb, 583–87
American Psychological Association (APA) format. *See* APA format

"American Space, Chinese Place" (Yi-Fu Tuan), 302–303
Analysis, 15
  critical, 45, 53–55
  in expository paragraphs, 64–69
  skills, 462
  summary *versus*, 53
  as support, 67–69, 98
  of visuals, 386, 401
Analysis essays
  body paragraphs, 404–406
  concluding paragraphs, 406
  critique form for, 409–10
  introductory paragraph, 404
  sample, 406–408
  structure of, 404–406, 462
Annotate, 33–34, 43
  codes for, 34
  plagiarism and, 358
Antonyms, 632, 667, 672
APA format, 375–81, 383, 405
  electronic sources, 376
  in-text citations, 375–76
  print sources, 376
  References list, 376–80
Apostrophes, 562–68, 581
  contractions and, 562–64
  missing letters or numbers and, 567
  plurals and, 566–67
  possession and, 564–66
Appositives, 542
Argument, 15, 61, 112, 143, 308–34
Argument essays, 309–34
  body paragraphs, 315, 319–20
  complementary modes for, 322–23
  concluding paragraphs, 315, 320–21
  critical thinking and, 309–12
  critique form for, 321–22
  introductory paragraphs, 315, 318–19
  professional, 327–29
  sample, 323–29

  structuring, 315–21
  thesis statements, 317
  topics, 316
  writing, 313–22
Article citations
  magazine, 368, 379
  newspaper, 368, 379
  online periodical, 380
  in reference books, 368–69
  from scholarly journals, 367
Articles, 491–93, 500
  definite, 491, 492
  indefinite, 491, 493
Assumptions, 15–16
Audience
  academic, 114
  assessment of, 113–14
  establishing, 111
  of expository essay, 83
  tone, 650–51
  types of, 114
Author
  assumptions, 354
  bias, 354
  credentials, 354
  point of view, 354
Auxiliary verbs, 470

B

Barszcz, James, 327–29
be verbs, 472–73
Bias, 16
Block quotations, 355–56
Blocks, reading in, 26
Body paragraphs, 83, 88–96, 97–98, 101
  for analysis essays, 404–406
  for argument essays, 315, 319–20
  for cause and effect essays, 269, 271–73
  for classification essays, 203, 206–208
  coherence, 89

for comparison and contrast essays, 293, 295–97
concluding sentences in, 89, 96
for definition essays, 226, 229
development, 89
for example essays, 245, 247–49
for narrative essays, 151, 154–61
for process essays, 179, 182
support, 89
topic sentence, 89
unity, 89
Books citations, 367, 378
Bovée, Courtland L., 189–93
Brackets, 579–80, 581
Brainstorming, 106, 313, 339
"Business School Makes PowerPoint a Prerequisite" (Pope), 13–15

C

"Can You Be Educated from a Distance?" (Barszcz), 327–29
Capitalization, 635–40, 646
Cause and effect essays, 264–86
body paragraphs, 269, 271–73
complementary modes for, 275
concluding paragraphs, 269, 273
critical thinking and, 264–65, 285
critique form for, 274–75
introductory paragraphs, 269, 271
professional, 278–82
questions for, 285
sample, 276–82
structuring, 269–75
thesis statements, 270
topic for, 269
writing, 267–75
Checklists
for building blocks, 101
critical thinking, 10–11, 37–38, 170, 218–19, 238–39, 259–60, 283, 304–305, 330–31
outline, 119
paragraph, 75
paraphrase, 49
peer assessment, 76
revision, 122, 126
spelling, 635
summary, 52
visual detective, 387–88

Classification essays, 198–220
analysis in, 199, 200
body paragraphs, 203, 206–208
complementary modes for, 210
concluding paragraphs, 203, 208–209
critical thinking and, 198–200, 220
critique form, 209–10
introductory paragraphs, 203, 206
professional, 213–17
questions for, 220
sample, 210–17
structuring, 203–10
thesis statements, 205
topics, 204
writing, 201–10
Clauses, 493
combining, 508
dependent, 493, 500
independent, 493, 500
Clichés, 125, 656–59
Clustering, 107
Coherence, 90, 102, 131
in body paragraphs, 89
improving, 95–96
transitions and, 90, 92–94
Colons, 551–56
"The Columbine Syndrome: Boys and the Fear of Violence" (Pollack), 278–82
Commas, 536–47, 557
coordinating conjunctions and, 502, 536–37
in dates, locations, numbers, and titles, 543–44
direct address, 540
interrupters, 541–43
after introductory material, 539–41
items in a series, 537–39
inside quotation marks, 543
quotation marks and, 571
rules, 536–44, 545–46, 557
tag lines and, 540–41
Comma splices, 525–33
Comparison and contrast essays, 288–307
body paragraphs, 293, 295–97
complementary modes for, 299
concluding paragraphs, 293, 297
critical thinking and, 288, 306

critique form for, 298–99
introductory paragraphs, 293, 295
professional, 302–303
purpose, 288
questions for, 306
sample, 300–303
structuring, 293–98
thesis statements, 294
topics, 290, 294
writing, 290–99
Complex sentences, 507, 514
Compound-complex sentences, 507, 514
Compound sentences, 506, 514, 536
Compound subjects, 467
Concluding paragraphs, 83, 96–97, 98, 162, 186, 210, 231–32, 233, 251, 275, 299, 322
Concluding sentences, 60, 75, 76, 77, 80, 101
in body paragraphs, 89, 96
in expository paragraphs, 69–70
Conclusions, 16
of introductory paragraphs, 101
in outlines, 118
Conjunctions, 493–500
coordinating, 493–95, 500, 502, 508, 551
subordinating, 493, 495, 500
Connotations, 386, 653, 654
Context clues, 671–76
Contractions, apostrophes and, 562–64
Coordination, 502, 504, 505, 512–14
Count nouns, 467
noncount *versus*, 468–69
Critical analysis, 45, 56
combining summary and, 53–55, 57
paraphrase *versus*, 45
sample, 54–55
steps for writing, 54
summary *versus*, 45
Critical reading, 415–16, 418–19, 424–25, 429, 437, 443–44, 448–49, 460–61, 462
Critical thinking, 1–57, 481
checklist, 10–11, 37–38, 170, 194–95, 218–19, 238–39, 259–60, 283, 304–305, 330–31
context clues and, 671–75
documented paper and, 347

Critical thinking (*continued*)
  errors and, 603
  essay exams and, 343
  narrowing subjects, 109
  in reading and writing, 2–21
  reading techniques and, 22–43
  sentence variety and, 510
  style and, 650–53
  summary, paraphrase, and critical
    analysis, 46
  thesis statements, 87
  timed essays and, 336
  tone and, 650–53
  tools, 5–10
"Cyberbullying: A Growing Problem"
  (*Science Daily*), 236–37

D

Dangling modifiers, 597–98, 606
Dashes, 576–77, 581
Databases, 351, 382
Daviss, Jackson Jodie, 410–14
Deferred subjects, 469
Definition essays, 222–40
  body paragraphs, 226
  complementary modes for, 233
  concluding paragraphs, 226
  critical thinking and, 240
  critique form, 232–33
  introductory paragraphs, 226
  professional, 236–37
  questions for, 240
  sample, 233–37
  structuring, 227–32
  writing, 224–33
Denotations, 386, 653, 654
Dependent clauses, 493, 500
  combining, 508
  interrupters, 541
  introductory, 539
  word order, 495
Descriptive essays, 146
  body paragraphs, 151, 154–61
  concluding paragraphs in, 151, 161
  critique form for, 162
  introductory paragraphs, 150, 154
  sample, 164–66
  structuring, 151–52
  thesis statements, 151–53
  topics, 151

  writing, 149–63
Details, 156
  concrete, 151
  descriptive, 149
  major supporting, 35
  minor, 35
  sensory, 151
  in T-KED method, 34, 35
Dialect, 125, 655, 656
Dialogue, 150, 159–61, 540–41,
  560, 570
Diction. *See* Word choice
Direct objects, 481–82
"The Discuss Thrower" (Selzer),
  425–28
Documentation formats
  abbreviations, 644
  APA (*See* APA format)
  MLA (*See* MLA format)
Documented paper, 347–49, 382
Douglass, Frederick, 254–58
Dovel, George P., 189–93
Drafting, 103–41,
Dybek, Stuart, 438–42

E

Editing, 121–24, 186
Electronic sources, 365, 369–71
Ellipsis, 578–79, 581
End punctuation, 559–62, 581
  exclamation point, 561–62
  period, 559–60
  question mark, 560–61
English language learners (ELL)
  articles, 492–93
  conjunctions, 495
  count *versus* noncount nouns,
    468–69
  infinitives, 479
  prepositions and prepositional
    phrases, 484
  verbs, 471
Essay exams, 335–44
Essays
  argument, 309–34
  cause and effect, 276–82
  classification, 198–220
  comparison and contrast, 288–307
  definition, 222–40

  example, 242–62
  expository, 78–79, 83
  narrative, 146
  process, 176–96
  timed in-class, 335–44
Evaluation, 16
Evidence, in expository paragraphs, 60
Example essays
  body paragraphs, 245, 247–49
  complementary modes for, 251
  concluding paragraphs, 249
  critical thinking and, 242–43, 261
  critique form, 250–51
  introductory paragraphs, 245, 247
  professional, 254–58
  sample, 251–58
  structuring, 245–51
  thesis statements, 246
  topic for, 245
  writing, 244–51
Exclamation points, 561–62, 581
Expository essays, 83, 102
  body paragraphs, 88–96
  building blocks of, 83–97
  concluding paragraph, 96–97
  introductory paragraph, 84–86
  sample, 98–100
  thesis statement, 86–88
  title, 84
Expository paragraphs, 58–81

F

Fallacy, logical, 309, 310–11
FANBOYS, 502, 514
Faulty parallelism, 595–96, 606
Formal style, 651–52
Formal tone, 651–52
Formatting, 84, 360–61, 366
Fragments, 516–24
  missing subject, 516
  missing verb, 516–17
  subordinate words or phrases, 517
Freewriting, 105–106

G

Gender-specific terms, 659–60
Gerund phrases, 468
"Gotta Dance" (Daviss), 410–14
Grammar, 534–676

H

"Half a Day" (Mahfouz), 169–69
Helping verbs, 470
Henderson, George, 213–17
Homonyms, 667
Homophones, 608, 635
"How to Mark a Book" (Adler), 38–42
Hyphens, 574–76, 581

I

Ice cream sandwich technique, 65–67, 124, 462
Ideas
    generating, 104–15, 108
    organization of, in writing, 116–20
Idioms, 486
Imply, 16
Indefinite articles, 491, 493
Indefinite pronouns, 585, 593–95
Independent clauses, 493, 500
    colons between, 551–52
    periods and, 559
    semicolons connecting, 548
Indirect objects, 481, 482
Infer, 403
Infinitives, 467, 471, 479
Interrupters, commas and, 541–43
In-text citations
    electronic sources, 365
    print sources, 361–64
Introductory paragraphs, 83, 97, 101
Irregular verbs, 474–79

J

Jargon, 651, 655
Journaling, 107

K

Key ideas, in T-KED method, 34, 35

L

"Learning to Read and Write" (Douglass), 254–58
Lee, Chang Rae, 444–47
Logical fallacies, 309, 310–11
Logos, 387

M

Mahfouz, Naguib, 166–69
Main ideas, 56
Mairs, Nancy, 449–59
Major supporting details, 35
"Making the Pitch in Print Advertising" (Bovée, Thill, Dovel, and Wood), 189–93
Mapping, 106
Meier, Daniel R., 421–23
Metaphors, 157, 656
Minor details, 35
Miroff, Nick, 28–33
Misplaced modifiers, 598–600, 606
MLA format, 360–75, 383, 405
    in-text citations, 361–65
    Works Cited list, 365–71
Modern Language Association (MLA) format. *See* MLA format
Modifiers
    dangling, 597–98, 606
    misplaced, 598–600, 606
"Mute in an English Only World" (Lee), 444–47
"The Mystery of Mickey Mouse" (Updike), 430–35

N

Narrative essays, 146
    body paragraphs, 151, 154–61
    complementary modes for, 163–66
    concluding paragraphs in, 151, 161
    critique form for, 162
    introductory paragraphs, 150
    sample, 164–66
    structuring, 151–52
    thesis statements, 151–53
    topics, 151
    writing, 149–63
Noncount (mass) nouns, 467
    count *versus*, 468–69
Noun determiners, 491–93
Nouns, 264, 466–69
Numbers, 640–41, 646
    commas with, 543
    rules for writing, 647

O

Objects, 481–82
    direct, 481
    indirect, 481
"On Being a Cripple" (Mairs), 449–59
"One Man's Kids" (Meier), 421–23
Opinions, 16
Organization, of ideas, in writing, 116–20
Outlines, 117–18, 140, 161
    checklists for, 119
    guidelines for, 117–18
    in prewriting stage, 107–108
    template, 153–54

P

Paragraphs
    body, 83, 88–96, 97–98, 101, 151, 182, 226, 269, 271–73, 315, 319–20, 404–406
    concluding, 83, 101, 151, 161, 162, 186, 226, 231, 233, 269, 273, 315, 320–21, 322, 406
    context clues in, 674–75
    expository, 58–81
    introductory, 83, 97, 101, 150, 182, 226, 269, 271, 315, 318–19, 404
    structures, 70–74
Parallelism, 595–96
Paraphrase, 45–49, 382
    checklist for, 49
    critical analysis *versus*, 45
    summary *versus*, 45
Parentheses, 573–74, 581
Participles, 471–72, 474–79 487–88
Passive voice, 600–602, 606
Past participles, 471
Pathos, 387
Paul, Richard, 3
Peer assessment, 75–78, 81
Periods, 559–60, 581
Photographs, 391–93
Phrases, 482–91
    adjective, 488–89, 489
    adverb, 490–91
    noun, 467, 482–83
    participial, 487–88

Phrases (*continued*)
prepositional, 483–87
verb, 470
verbal, 486
Plagiarism, 56, 358–60
avoiding, 358–60, 383
paraphrase and, 46, 359
summary and, 359
Plurals
apostrophes and, 566–67
spelling rules for, 609
Point-by-point organization pattern, 292–93
Point of view, 105
Point-of-view shifts, 592–95, 601–602, 606
Pollack, William S., 278–82
Pope, Justin, 13–15
Possession
apostrophes and, 564–66
compound nouns and, 565
joint, 566
plural, 565
proper names and, 565–66
singular, 564
Predicates, 465–66, 470–82, 500.
See also Verbs
Prefixes, 667
Prepositional phrases, 483–87
Prepositions, 483–87
Previewing, 24–25
Prewriting, 104–15
Process essays, 175–96
analysis, 176
body paragraphs, 179, 182
complementary modes for, 186, 196
concluding paragraphs, 179, 184
critical thinking and, 176, 183, 196
critique form, 185–86
introductory paragraphs, 179, 182
professional, 189–93
purpose of, 176
questions for, 196
sample, 187–93, 187–95
structure of, 179, 180–85, 196
thesis statements, 180–81
topic, 180
transitions, 182
writing, 178–86

Professional essays
active reading and, 28–33
argument, 327–29
cause and effect, 278–82
classification, 213–17
comparison and contrast, 302–303
critical thinking in, 11–15
definition, 236–37
example, 254–58
narrative, 166–71
process, 189–93
Pronoun-antecedent agreement, 587–89
Pronoun reference, 589–91
Pronouns, 587, 605
indefinite, 585
subject, 469
Pronunciation, 669–71, 676
Proofreading, 124–26, 141
Punctuation, 558–81
apostrophes, 562–68, 581
brackets, 579–80, 581
colons, 551–56
commas, 536–47
dashes, 576–77, 581
ellipsis, 578–79, 581
exclamation points, 561–62, 581
hyphens, 574–76, 581
parentheses, 573–74, 581
periods, 559–60, 581
question marks, 560–61, 581
quotation marks, 568–72, 571–72, 581
semicolons, 547–51
slashes, 577, 581
Purpose
assessment of, 333
establishing, 111–13
writing, 10, 105

Q

Question marks, 560–61, 581
Quotation marks, 568–72, 581
punctuation and, 571–72
Quotations, 382
block, 355–56
ice cream sandwich technique for framing, 405–406
poetry, 356
prose, 355–56

R

"Race in America" (Henderson), 213–17
Reader's logs, 25, 26, 27, 28
Reading
active, 23–28, 43, 387–89
critical thinking in, 1–21
techniques, 22–43
T-KED method, 33–38, 43
Research, for documented paper, 348
Reviewing, in active reading, 27–28
Revising, 78, 121–24, 141
checklist, 122, 126
clarification through, 605
clichés, 658–59, 662
documented paper, 349
essay exams, 337
sample, 131–35
sentences, 514
for sentence variety, 510–11
sexist language, 661–62, 663
summary, 51
topic sentences, 62
Run-on sentences, 525, 528–33

S

Search engines, 351–53
Self-assessment, 75–78, 81
Selzer, Richard, 425–28
Semicolons, 547–51
adding or deleting, 550–551
comma splices and, 526
conjunctive adverbs and, 504, 548
between independent clauses, 548
items in a series and, 549
rules, 557
Sentence-level errors
editing for, 136
proofreading for, 125
Sentence parts, 464–500
Sentences
building blocks of, 465–82
combining, 502–505
complex, 507, 514
compound, 506, 514, 536
compound-complex, 507, 514
concluding, 60, 69–70, 75, 76, 77, 101
declarative, 505, 510, 514

exclamatory, 506, 510, 514
fragments, 516–24
purposes, 505–506
run-on, 525, 528–32
simple, 506, 514
topic, 60, 272, 296, 320
types of, 505–506, 514
Sentence variety, 131, 501–14
critical thinking and, 510
revising for, 510–11
Sexist language, avoiding, 659–63, 664
Shift and construction errors, 582–606
Similes, 157, 656
Slang, 125, 654, 656
Slashes, 577, 581
Sources
databases, 351
evaluation of, 353–54, 382
finding, 350–53, 382
integration of, 355–58, 382
Internet and search engines, 351–53
interviews with experts, 351
libraries for, 350–51
primary, 350, 382
reference, 349, 382
reliability of, 353–54
secondary, 350, 382
types of, 349–50, 382
unbiased, 354
Spell-check, 612–14, 635, 647
Spelling, 608–12, 647
checklist, 635
common letter groupings, 611
commonly confused words, 614–30
dictionary use and, 608
editing for, 135
ei/ie rule, 609–10
homophones, 608
plurals, 609
pronunciation and, 608
proofreading for, 124–25
spell-check, 611–12
suffixes and prefixes, 610–11
Staples, Brent, 416–18
Structure
of analysis essays, 404–406, 462
of argument essays, 315, 333
of cause and effect essays, 269, 285
of classification essays, 203–10, 220
of comparison and contrast essays, 293, 307

of definition essays, 226
essay, 173
of example essays, 245, 261
paragraph, 70–74, 81
of process essay, 179
sentence, 506–509
Style, 664
Subject-by-subject organization pattern, 291
Subjects, 83, 140, 500
compound, 467
deferred, 469
establishing, 111–13
gerund phrase, 468
identification of, 469–70
implied, 468
infinitive as, 467
missing, 516
nouns or noun phrases, 466–69
of sentences, 465–70
simple, 465, 466
types of, 467–68
Subject-verb agreement, 583–87
Subordination, 502–505, 512–13
Suffixes, 667
Summary, 27, 45, 50–55, 382
checklist for, 52
critical analysis *versus*, 45
paraphrase *versus*, 45
plagiarism and, 359
Support
in body paragraphs, 89
concrete, 156–57
ice cream sandwich technique, 65–67
in outlines, 118
for topic sentences, 65, 80
Syllables, 669, 676
Synonyms, 632, 634, 667
Synthesis, 17

T

Tags, 159, 540–41
Tense. *See* Verb tense
"Texting: Blessing or Curse?" (Zellmer), 11–12
Thesaurus
anatomy of entry, 632–33
tips for using, 632–35

Thesis statements, 97, 146
creating, 140, 152–53, 180–81, 205, 227–28, 246, 270, 294, 317
critical thinking questions for, 87
in outlines, 118
writing, 116–17
Thill, John V., 189–93
Thinking and talking, in prewriting, 105
"Thread" (Dybek), 438–42
Timed in-class essays, 335–44
Titles, 101
essay, 84
format, 84
T-KED method, 33–38, 43, 47
Tone, 111, 115, 404
Topics
categories of, 204
generating, 290
narrowing subjects to, 108–10
support for, 121
Topic sentences, 60, 63–64, 97, 118, 203, 320
analytical, 154
in body paragraphs, 89
broad, 62
creating, 89–90
in expository paragraphs, 61–64
highlighting, 33
key ideas as, 35
narrow, 62
revising, 62, 131–32
support for, 65, 80
Transitions, 60, 77, 468
cause and effect, 271
coherence with, 90, 92–94
common, 93–94
comparison and contrast, 207, 296
examples, 249
interrupters, 541
introducing points with, 319
time, 155
unity with, 90

U

Unity, 90–92, 131
in body paragraphs, 89
test for, 91–92
with transitions, 90
Updike, John, 430–35

V

Verbals, 518
Verbs, 264, 470–82
  auxiliary, 470
  base forms of, 472, 473, 474–79
  functions of, 470–72
  helping, 470
  identifying, 479–80
  infinitives, 471
  irregular, 474–79
  missing, 516–17
  past participles, 471
  as predicates, 470–82
Verb tense, 472, 480
  future, 473
  future perfect, 472, 473
  future perfect progressive, 472
  future progressive, 472
  past, 471
  past perfect, 471, 472, 473
  past perfect progressive, 472
  past progressive, 472, 473
  present, 471
  present perfect, 472, 473
  present perfect progressive, 472
  present progressive, 472, 473
  simple future, 472
  simple past, 472
  simple present, 472
Visual analysis, 398–99

Vocabulary, 665–76
  building, 666–69, 676
  context clues, 671–75
  logs, 666–67
  pronunciation, 669–71
Voice
  active, 600
  passive, 600–602, 606

W

"What Adolescents Miss When
    We Let Them Grow Up in
    Cyberspace" (Staples), 416–18
Wood, Marian Burk, 189–93
Word choice, 653–59, 664
  clichés, 656–59
  dialect, 655, 656
  editing for, 135
  foreign words, 655–56
  jargon, 655
  proofreading for, 125
  slang, 654, 656
Writing
  academic, 6
  analysis, 9–10
  assumptions, 8
  bias in, 8
  concluding paragraphs,
    231–32
  conclusions, 9, 249, 297, 321

critical analysis, 54
critical thinking in, 1–21
dialogue, 161
documented paper, 347–49
editing, 121–24
essays about visuals, 384–401
expository paragraphs, 58–81
first draft, 120–21
ideas, 7
organization of ideas, 116–20
peer assessment of, 126
point of view, 9
proofreading, 124–26
purpose, 7
about readings, 402–62
revising, 121–24
self-assessment, 126
stages, 140
summary, 50–51
support, 7
thesis statements, 116–17

Y

Yi-Fu Tuan, 302–303
"Yo Quiero Made in USA" (Miroff),
    28–33

Z

Zellmer, Matthew, 11–12